BREASTED'S ANCIENT TIMES

Second Edition

Please notice these important points:

1. The history of civilization preceding the Greeks and Romans has been completely rewritten to include the rich findings of the last twenty years of investigation and research in the life of early man. See the author's preface, pages iii–v, for a brief summarization of this new material.

2. Many changes have been made throughout the whole book to make it even better adapted to high-school students. Words and phrases that have been found too abstract or difficult have been avoided.

3. The entire book has been reset in larger, more readable type.

4. Many new illustrations touching upon recent discoveries have been added. Selected from the thousands of photographs taken by the expeditions of the Oriental Institute and by other expeditions, and accompanied by legends that are masterpieces of description, they are of the greatest interest and value. See pages 22, 23, 89, 105, 121, 143, 145, 152, 155, 156, 157, 158, 168, 192, 195, 213, 219, 224, 257, 273, 275, 276, 278, 355, 399, 424, 501, 503, 750, 765, 776, 789.

5. Please note also the four very beautiful colored plates—the frontispiece and the pictures facing pages 210, 290, and 506.

6. No effort nor expense has been spared in preparing the map equipment. It includes 23 colored plates as well as many maps in black and white. See List of Maps, pages xii–xiii.

7. Questions for study and discussion and a bibliography for topical studies follow each chapter. See pages 25, 47–48, 94, and so forth.

$2.00, subject to discount

Ginn and Company

1126-1, 35 Printed in U.S.A.

PLATE I. *Portrait Bust of* QUEEN NOFRETETE, *Wife of Ikhnaton*

Found in the studio of a royal sculptor at Amarna, with original colors preserved as shown. (After Borchardt)

ANCIENT TIMES

A · HISTORY · OF · THE · EARLY · WORLD

An Introduction to the Study of Ancient History and the Career of Early Man by

JAMES HENRY BREASTED

Director of the Oriental Institute in The University of Chicago

SECOND EDITION

REVISED AND LARGELY REWRITTEN

GINN AND COMPANY

BOSTON · NEW YORK · CHICAGO · LONDON · ATLANTA · DALLAS · COLUMBUS · SAN FRANCISCO

835.1

The Athenæum Press
GINN AND COMPANY · PROPRIETORS · BOSTON · U.S.A.

PREFACE

It is now eighteen years since the publication of the first edition of this book, and nearly twenty years since it was written. The progress made in the study of the Ancient World during these last twenty years, in spite of the obstacles resulting from the World War since 1918, has probably never been equaled in the history of humanistic research. At The University of Chicago the organization of the Oriental Institute, in the summer of 1919, has contributed substantially to this progress.

One of the most important developments has been the recovery of the evidence disclosing the life of man in the earliest Stone Age in Northeastern Africa by the Oriental Institute's Prehistoric Survey. Similar work in Western Asia, although not covering an extensive territory, has made it possible to sketch Stone Age development in the Near East as a whole, and thus to gain at least an outline of the prehistoric human development entirely around the Mediterranean. It is therefore no longer necessary to begin the Stone Age career of man with a résumé of it exclusively in France and Europe, as was done in the first edition of *Ancient Times*, and then, passing to the Near East for the origins of civilization, to return to Europe again, thus involving a confusing alternation of first Europe, then the Near East, and then Europe again. In the present edition of *Ancient Times* it has been possible to begin the human career with the Early Stone Age entirely surrounding the Mediterranean, including the Near East, and then to continue it in chronological sequence down through the origins of civilization and the subsequent developments of civilized life in the Near East alone, to the point when these influences passed over into Europe.

The range and importance of field research and discovery since 1918 have produced a series of discoveries of epoch-making importance. The Anglo-American Expedition at Ur has revealed a totally new and fundamentally important chapter in the development of earlier civilization in Western Asia. At Ras Shamra, in Ancient Phœnicia, the discoveries of the French expedition under Schaeffer have been of far-reaching importance. The expeditions of the Oriental Institute have likewise disclosed a whole series of new vistas in Assyria, in Babylonia, in Palestine, and also in Persia, where the excavation of the magnificent sculptured stairways at Persepolis has been perhaps the most notable of such disclosures.

While the puzzling Etruscan writing has not yet been deciphered, it is now evident that the Etruscans were a Western Asiatic people who migrated from Anatolia into the Italian peninsula. The resumption of excavation at Troy by Professor Semple of the University of Cincinnati has not yet progressed far enough to reveal all the important results which we may confidently expect from that famous site.

In the investigation of the great problem of the Hittites, substantial progress has been made in the last twenty years. The decipherment of Hittite cuneiform was successfully accomplished by Bedřich Hrozný of Prague during the World War. A good deal of progress has also been made in the decipherment of Hittite hieroglyphic, and it is safe to say that we shall be able to read it in the not distant future. The investigation of these philological problems in the study of the Hittites has been accompanied by extended field researches in the Hittite country of Asia Minor. The excavations of the Oriental Institute at the mound of Alishar, about one hundred and twenty miles east-southeast of Ankara, have for the first time revealed the material evidences of advancing civilization in Anatolia, both before and after the advent of the Hittites, beginning with the Late Stone Age at the bottom of the mound (at a depth of about one hundred feet) and working upward, disclosing stage after stage of human advance, from stone implements, through the discovery of copper, the production of bronze, and the introduction of iron, to a church of the Fifth Century of the Christian Era.

In Egypt the operations of the Harvard-Boston Expedition, under the leadership of Reisner, have given us a totally new revelation of the highly developed culture of the Pyramid Age, especially in the discovery of the tomb of the royal mother of Khufu, or Cheops, the builder of the great Pyramid of Gizeh. The discovery of the tomb of Tutenkhamon by Howard Carter has proved to be an epoch-making disclosure of the beauty and refinement of civilization under the Egyptian Empire, and has perhaps done more to interest a large public in the story of the human past than any other single discovery in the history of archæological research.

In Europe the project for a comprehensive excavation of ancient Athens has made very gratifying progress and has brought forth a large body of inscriptions which will prove invaluable sources of new knowledge still to be fitted into our historical accounts of ancient Greece.

So far as these discoveries have been contributed by the Oriental Institute, even though still unpublished, they have been available for this new edition of *Ancient Times*, and, besides presenting new facts, have contributed especially to the new series of illustrations in this volume. The discoveries of other expeditions, so far as they have been published and rendered accessible, have also been employed both in the revision of the text for the new edition and in the list of illustrations. It is safe to say that there has never before been available such a comprehensive range of illustrative material as this new volume now includes. As a result of all these discoveries the account of the history of civilization preceding the Greeks and the Romans has been entirely rewritten, making this edition practically a new book.

It is a pleasure to express here the author's appreciation of the kindness of his colleagues and friends who have been willing to contribute photographs even before these were available in published form elsewhere. I take this opportunity of thanking the Duke of Alba; Professor Edson S. Bastin; the British Museum; the British Ordnance Survey Office, and O. G. S. Crawford, Esq., the editor of *Antiquity*; the British Royal Air Force Command, Baghdad, Iraq; Professor Edward Capps; Howard Carter, Esq.; M. Franz

Cumont; Sir Arthur Evans; the editor of *Forschungen und Fortschritte*; Professor Ernst E. Herzfeld; Bruce S. Ingram, Esq., editor of the *Illustrated London News*; Professor Franklin P. Johnson; the Metropolitan Museum of Art; Professor Percy E. Newberry; Professor Arno Poebel; Professor George A. Reisner and the Boston Museum of Fine Arts; Mr. John D. Rockefeller, Jr.; Professor Eckhard Unger; the University Museum, University of Philadelphia; Professor Thomas Whittemore and the Byzantine Institute.

Acknowledgment has been made under each cut in cases where monuments or figures have been redrawn from new publications.

To Dr. Edith Williams Ware I am indebted for constant attention to text and proof, for the compilation of index, bibliography, and assigned readings, and especially for a great deal of detailed labor on the extensive illustrative scheme.

In the first edition of *Ancient Times* the comments and suggestions of my old friend James Harvey Robinson were very helpful, and this is equally true of the present revision.

It is a pleasure also to acknowledge here the interest in the new edition evinced by the publishers, especially their constant coöperation in the development of the illustrations.

JAMES HENRY BREASTED

THE ORIENTAL INSTITUTE,
THE UNIVERSITY OF CHICAGO

CONTENTS

PART I. MAN BEFORE CIVILIZATION

PART II. THE ORIGINS AND EARLY HISTORY OF CIVILIZATION IN THE ANCIENT NEAR EAST

LIST OF COLORED PLATES

LIST OF MAPS

ANCIENT TIMES

PART I · MAN BEFORE CIVILIZATION

The Earliest REPRESENTATION *of Domesticated* HORSES *(about* 3000 B.C.)

An example of early picture-writing showing a group of nineteen horses, each represented by the animal's head only. The other signs are numbers, and it is probable that the whole is an inventory of the horses owned by some king or nobleman. The varying positions of the manes as represented on the tablet are significant. The *upraised* manes doubtless indicate stallions, while those that hang down probably indicate mares. The animals without any manes are presumably foals, too young to show any mane. The signs are incised on a clay tablet, discovered by the French at Susa, the ancient capital of Elam. It dates from about 3000 B.C. or possibly a century or two earlier. This evidence would therefore indicate that already at this early date the domesticated horse was found at the east end of the Highland Zone (§ 318), whence he gradually filtered into the Fertile Crescent during the next thousand years, so that he was common in the Age of Hammurapi (§ 212). We now know that around 2000 B.C. the domesticated horse was in use from the Caucasus through Anatolia to the Fertile Crescent, whence he reached Egypt during or after the Eighteenth Century B.C. The discovery, in Scania, in southern Sweden, of a horse's skull dating from about 2400 B.C., having a stone dagger driven deep into the forehead, led some prehistorians to believe that the horse was domesticated in northern Europe. There is now little support for this conclusion, and the evidence from the Orient indicates that the horse was domesticated somewhere in the general region northeast of Persia. There is some uncertainty regarding the date of his arrival in the Fertile Crescent, owing to the discovery of a surprisingly large percentage of the bones of the ancient wild ass (*onager*) in the Babylonian excavations of the Oriental Institute. In Fig. 91 and in our Elamite tablet above, the short ears of the animals represented have been regarded as conclusive evidence that they were horses. But the numerous bones of the wild ass in Babylonia suggest the possibility that all the horse-like animals shown in these representations might be regarded as wild asses, which we know were early used as draft animals in ancient Babylonia. If so, the domesticated horse was introduced among the most civilized peoples as late as 2000 B.C.

Chapter I · *How Mankind began as Food-gatherers*

Section 1. Man's Earliest Ways of Living

How Robinson Crusoe began as a food-gatherer

1. All readers of the story of Robinson Crusoe remember how interested they were in the way in which he managed to supply himself with shelter, tools, furniture, food, clothing, and the other things which he needed for living on the uninhabited island where the terrible storm had cast him ashore. We recall that he had lost nearly everything he had except the clothing he wore. He had no food, but was later able to find young pigeons in nests, as well as turtles along the shore. He also gathered grapes, limes, and lemons. We should notice that he did not *produce* this food; he only *gathered* it as he found it. He was at first, therefore, merely a *food-gatherer*. He had no tools with which to work and at first no weapons with which to defend himself if he met a dangerous wild beast.

How Robinson Crusoe became a food-producer

2. Later, however, when the storm had passed, the waves quieted and Crusoe could see the wreck of the ship not far from shore. Then he swam out to the ship, where he managed to lash together a raft out of pieces of wood and rope. Exploring the ship, he found tools, weapons, seed grain, guns, and many other useful things, which he carried back to the island on the raft. By the use of the tools he was able to build himself a house and make himself clothing, while the seed grain, when planted, brought him plenty of food. In this way he was freed from the need of food-gathering. He had become a *food-producer*. He was thus able to take possession of his island, which became his little world; and as he made it produce the food and other things he needed, he was able thereafter to lead a fairly comfortable life.

3. Now Crusoe was able to do this only because of the things which he found on the ship. If they had not been there, he would have had to find some way of making them. And, indeed, there were certain necessities, like ink, of which the stock he found in the ship's supplies ran out, so that he had to make more. Crusoe, however, had known about these things and had used them in his own country; he could therefore make crude substitutes from memory, such as the spade which he cut out of wood. But the earliest men, who lived thousands on thousands of years ago, were in a much worse situation than Robinson Crusoe. We must think of the world in that long-ago time as if it were mankind's huge island, where the men who wandered about on it were not even so well off as Robinson Crusoe before he visited the ship and built his raft, because even if his wrecked ship had not been there to furnish him with tools, he would have *known* about the tools he had seen from childhood and often used in his own country. But the earliest men had never lived in a country which had tools and implements, for there were no such things anywhere in the world; and because they had never seen or heard of such things and did not even know that they could be made, the earliest men were at first entirely without them.

Earliest man far worse off than Crusoe

4. We all know that our grandfathers never saw an airplane or heard a radio when they were young, because these things had not been invented. In like manner earliest men had never seen or heard of a tool of any kind, because no one in the whole world had even thought of such a thing or knew that such a thing was possible. The first men had nothing but their hands with which to supply their needs. They could not even speak or make a fire. They knew nothing about the many things which make our own lives so easy and convenient and interesting at the present day; all such things had to be invented one after another. Such inventions were made very slowly, and it was many thousands of years before the

Gradual invention of tools and implements; uncivilized life

simplest of such inventions had gradually improved the lives of men. When only a few such improvements had been made, the life of early men was what we should call *uncivilized*.

Things necessary to civilized life

5. After a very long time, however, men made such important discoveries and inventions that their manner of living lost its savagery and greatly improved. We call such men *civilized*. The list of all these discoveries and inventions is much too long to be learned here. Only the most important may be mentioned. First of all came *speech*; then followed a series of inventions. While they were still only *food-gatherers* men learned to make *fire* and produce wooden and stone *tools and weapons* needful in the *gathering* of food. Next they made two discoveries which changed them from *food-gatherers* to *food-producers*. The first of these was *cattle-breeding*, when men found out that they could tame wild cattle and sheep and keep them in pastures and stables; and the second was *agriculture*, when men first learned to plant and cultivate certain of the wild grasses so that these furnished their seed as food and became cultivated grains, or *cereals*, like wheat and barley. After this it needed only the discovery of *metal* and the invention of *writing* to equip men for civilized life and further advance.

Tasmanians, and what they had failed to learn

6. There are still many uncivilized peoples on the earth, but people as completely uncivilized as the earliest men must have been no longer exist. Nevertheless, the lowest savage tribes found by explorers in modern times still led a life very much like that of our earliest ancestors. For example, the Tasmanians, the people whom the Dutch discovered on the island of Tasmania nearly three centuries ago, wore no clothing; they had not yet learned how to build a really roofed hut, but crouched behind a wind screen; they did not know how to make a bow and arrows, or even to fish, except by spearing. They had no goats, sheep, or cows, no horses, not even a dog. They had never heard of sowing seed or raising a crop of any kind. They did not know that clay would harden in the fire, and so they had no pottery jars, jugs, or dishes for food.

Tasmanians, and what they had learned

7. Naked and houseless, the Tasmanians had learned to satisfy only a very few of man's needs; they were still Stone Age men. Yet that which they had learned had carried them a long way beyond the earliest men. They had a simple language, with words for all the customary things they used and did every day. They could kindle a fire, which kept them warm in cold weather, and over it they cooked their meat. They had learned to make very good wooden spears, though without metal tips, for they had never even heard of metal. These spears, tipped with a sharp piece of stone, they could throw with great accuracy and thus bring down the game they needed for food, or drive away their human enemies. They could take a flat piece of sandstone, and by chipping off the edges to thin them they could make a rude knife with which to skin and cut up the game they killed. They were also very deft in weaving cups, vessels, and baskets of bark fiber.

Eastern Mediterranean region; home of earliest civilization

8. For several hundred thousand years earliest men lived a life far less civilized than that of the Tasmanians. This savage life was scattered over wide areas of the Old World. It entirely surrounded the Mediterranean Sea. The savages lived on all its shores and spread far inland: northward to the North Sea and across the British Isles, southward far across Africa in what is now the Sahara Desert, and eastward beyond the Persian Gulf. It was in the region surrounding the *eastern end* of the Mediterranean Sea that civilization arose. We must therefore first turn our attention to the early Mediterranean world.

Early Mediterranean world; its climate and animals

9. The lands of Europe and northern Africa were very different then from what they are today. Lofty forests not only fringed the streams of Europe and clothed its wide plains, but also covered some of the Sahara Plateau, which at that time was a green and well-watered region. Huge hippopotamuses wallowed along the shores of the rivers on both sides of the Mediterranean. Many a fierce rhinoceros, with a horn three

feet in length, charged through the heavy tropical growth; enormous elephants, with shaggy hair two feet long, wandered through the jungles. Myriads of bison grazed on the uplands, and the forests sheltered numerous herds of deer. Especially on the European side wandered vast herds of wild horses. Through Italy and Sicily, as well as at Gibraltar, land-bridges across the Mediterranean connected Europe and Africa. Thus most of these animals could wander *by land* from Africa to Europe or back again. The atmosphere was moist and warm, and echoed to the notes of many tropical birds. This tropical wilderness, filled with its myriads of creatures (fish, fowl, and animals great and small), extended entirely around the Mediterranean Sea.

FIG. 1. FIRE-MAKING WITHOUT MATCHES *by Modern Natives of Australia*

The outfit is very simple, consisting merely of a round, dry stick placed upright, with the lower end in a hole in a dry tree trunk lying on the ground. The native turns the stick rapidly between both hands, and the friction finally generates sufficient heat to produce flame (§ 11)

Life and haunts of earliest men; their wooden weapons

10. With nothing to cover their nakedness, the early savages of this Mediterranean world roamed stealthily through the tropical forests, seeking their daily food of roots, seeds, and wild fruits. They were also hunters, and they listened with keen and eager ear for the sound of small game which they might be able to lay low with their rough wooden clubs. Such weapons were so feeble that these savages often fled in terror as they felt the thunderous tread of the giant animals of the forest or caught dim glimpses of colossal elephants plunging through the deep vistas of the jungle. At night, after cutting up the flesh of their prey with wooden knives and devouring it raw, the hunters slept wherever the hunt had led them. Not knowing how to make a fire to ward off the savage beasts, they lay trembling in the darkness at the roar of the mighty saber-toothed tiger.

FIG. 2. *A Group of North American Indians making* FLINT WEAPONS

The farthest Indian is prying loose a large stone. This is the raw material, which is then taken by the middle Indian, who crashes it down upon a rock and shatters it into fragments. One of these fragments is then taken by the nearest Indian, who holds it in his left hand while he strikes it with a stone in his right hand. These blows flake off pieces of flint, and the Indian is so skillful that he can thus shape a flint hatchet. This process of shaping the flint by blows (that is, by *percussion*) was the earliest and crudest method and produced the roughest stone tools. (After Holmes)

Man learns to kindle fire and use stone

11. At length, however, they learned about fire, perhaps when the lightning kindled a forest tree. They must have learned to fear it, too, as they viewed such terrible volcanoes as Etna and Vesuvius along the Mediterranean. It was a great step forward when at last they learned how to produce it themselves with the whirl-stick (Fig. 1). They could then cook their food, warm their bodies, and harden the tips of their wooden spears with the fire. But their dull wooden knives they could not harden; and so they perhaps learned to make bone knives, or picked up a broken stone and used its ragged edge. When, not less than several hundred thousand years ago, they had learned to *shape* the stone to suit their needs (Fig. 3), and thus to produce a rude tool or weapon, they entered what we now call the Stone Age.

12. The stone weapons and tools which these savages then began to make did not rot and disappear like their bone and wooden ones. We can hold in our hands the very stone tools and implements with which early men maintained themselves in their long struggle to obtain food and to defend themselves from their fierce animal foes, for these earliest men sometimes lost their stone tools and weapons. Later on, such implements were sometimes buried with their owners when they died. In the course of many thousands of years the number of such shaped stones became very large. We are able to find so many of them that they form for us something like a trail which these savage hunters left behind them. By this long trail of stone implements we can follow these early men and see how far they had advanced toward better methods of living. This advance is revealed to us by their increasing skill in shaping stone and by their improvement in some other industries which they gradually learned. In the specimens of their handiwork which still survive we can distinguish three successive ages, which we may call the Early Stone Age, the Middle Stone Age, and the Late Stone Age. Let us now observe man's progress through these three ages, one after another.

Career of early man traceable in the surviving works of his hands

SECTION 2. THE EARLY STONE AGE

13. A stone tool or weapon made by human hands is called an "artifact," a word of Latin origin meaning "made by art" and related to the word "artificial." Stone artifacts, lying on the ground or turned up by the plow, were noticed by our ancestors centuries ago. Since then, for nearly a century, scientific men have been carefully searching for them, especially by systematic digging (called excavation). The study of man's early works is called archæology; hence such digging is called archæological excavation, and we term a man who does such work an archæologist. The search for stone artifacts began

Archæology and study of earliest stone implements

in Europe, especially in France. There the rude stone tools and weapons of the Early Stone Age hunters of Europe and the bones of the huge animals they slew had sometimes been left lying side by side in the sand and gravel far up on the valley slopes where in these prehistoric ages the rivers of France once flowed, before their deep modern beds had been cut out by the water. They have been found in such large numbers in France that great museum collections of stone implements have been established there. Later, similar implements were found to be plentiful in other European countries also. Recent search in North Africa has likewise revealed stone artifacts, in an area stretching from Algiers to the lower Nile valley, and the same is true of Asia along the eastern shores of the Mediterranean. We are thus able to study thousands of stone weapons and implements from all the lands surrounding the Mediterranean. They reveal to us the fascinating story of man's earliest progress, after the Early Stone Age hunters had found that they could chip stones.

Achievements and limitations of Early Stone Age man

14. Although they perished probably in great numbers as their dangerous life went on, these savage hunters continued for thousands of years the uncertain struggle for survival all around the Mediterranean Sea. They finally produced a most useful stone implement, which is commonly called a "fist-hatchet" (Fig. 3), and this they slowly improved. The fist-hatchet was the earliest widely used human device which has survived to our day. The Early Stone Age men learned, probably, to make additional implements of wood; but these have of course rotted and perished, so that we know nothing of them. Single-handed these brave hunters waged war upon all animals. There was not a beast which was not their foe. There was as yet no dog, no sheep, or fowl to which they might stretch out a kindly hand. The ancestor of the modern dog was then the fierce wolf of the forest, leaping upon the hunter unawares; and those beasts which were the ancestors of our modern domestic animals, like the horse, still wandered the forests in a wild state.

15. Then a great change came over the life of these Early Stone Age hunters in Europe and Western Asia. They began to notice that the air of their forest home was losing its tropical warmth. Geologists have not yet found out why, but the climate grew colder; and, as the ages passed, the ice, which all the year round still overlies the region of the north pole and the summits of the Alps, began to descend. This descent of the ice meant that the polar ice-cap grew larger and thus advanced southward on all sides of the pole. It pushed down across Europe, Asia, and North America. In Europe it continued to creep farther and farther southward until it covered England as far down as the Thames, and on the Continent it covered much of Germany. In Asia the ice came down far across Siberia, and it descended from the mountains of Armenia to the upper valley of the Tigris and Euphrates rivers. It was only here that the ice affected the region where civilization later arose. On the continent of North America the southern edge of the ice is marked by lines of bowlders carried and left there by the ice sheet. Such lines of bowlders (called moraines) are found, for example, as far south as Long Island, and westward along the valleys of the Ohio and the Missouri.

Coming of the ice

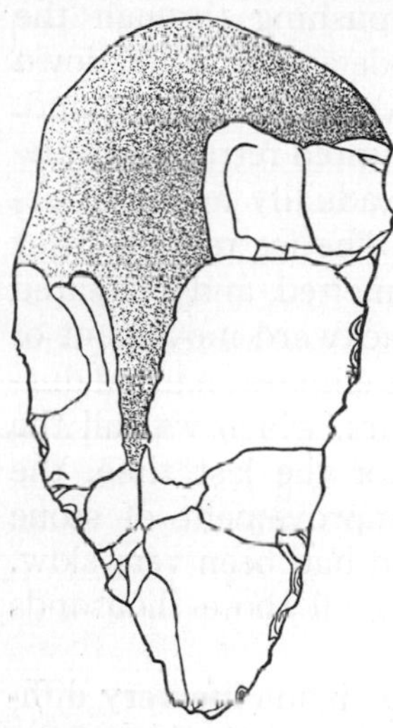

FIG. 3. *A Flint* FIST-HATCHET *of the Early Stone Age found in an Ancient Bed of the Nile*

Rough flint flakes older than the fist-hatchet still survive to show us man's earliest efforts at shaping stone. But the fist-hatchet is the earliest well-finished type of tool produced by man. They have been found all around the Mediterranean, as well as in other parts of the world. The original is about 7½ inches long. The drawing reduces it to about one third. It was usually grasped in the fist by the thicker part, and never had any handle. Handles of wood or horn do not appear until much later (cf. Fig. 19, *4* and *5*). Traces of use and wear are sometimes found on such fist-hatchets. The above specimen was found by the Oriental Institute of The University of Chicago

16. In Europe and the northern part of Western Asia the hunters saw the glittering blue masses of glacier ice, with their crown of snow, pushing through the green of their forest abode and crushing down vast trees in many a sheltered glen or favorite hunting ground. Many of the animals they had so long hunted retreated to the warmer south, and the hunters were gradually forced to accustom themselves to a cold climate. The ice remained for thousands of years; then it slowly melted and retreated northward again. This forward and backward movement of the ice was repeated several times as the climate changed during a period of many thousands of years, which we call the Ice Age. When the ice came down for the last time, the Early Stone Age had ended. The improvement of stone tools and implements during this period had been very slow. It had advanced scarcely at all during all those thousands of years.

Ice Age slows down human progress

17. While the invasion of the ice thus made life very difficult for the Early Stone Age men on the north side of the Mediterranean, we see, by examining the map (p. 13), that the ice never reached the Mediterranean, and that the entire Southern Flatlands in North Africa, the region which we now call the Sahara Plateau, was never visited by the ice. The same atmospheric moisture which in frozen form built up the icy glaciers on the *north* side of the Mediterranean fell as plentiful rain on the *south* side. The Sahara Plateau was therefore well watered and covered with meadows, forests, and jungle growth. Across this fertile region the Early Stone Age hunters

Stone Age men south of the Mediterranean protected from the ice

---

* NOTE ON MAP, PAGE 13. After the Glacial Age, when the ice, which had pushed far south across large portions of Europe and Asia, had retreated for the last time, it was the men of the Great White Race who moved in and occupied these formerly ice-bound regions. So it came about that finally the people of this race inhabited the whole Northwest Quadrant, where eventually was produced the civilization which is ours today. The words "Great White Race" above represent the later spread of the race, but do not mean that they lived on the *ice*! In North Africa these people were dark-skinned, but nevertheless physically they belong to the Great White Race. This map is to be used with frequent consultation of the Racial Diagram of the Great Northwest Quadrant (Fig. 79).

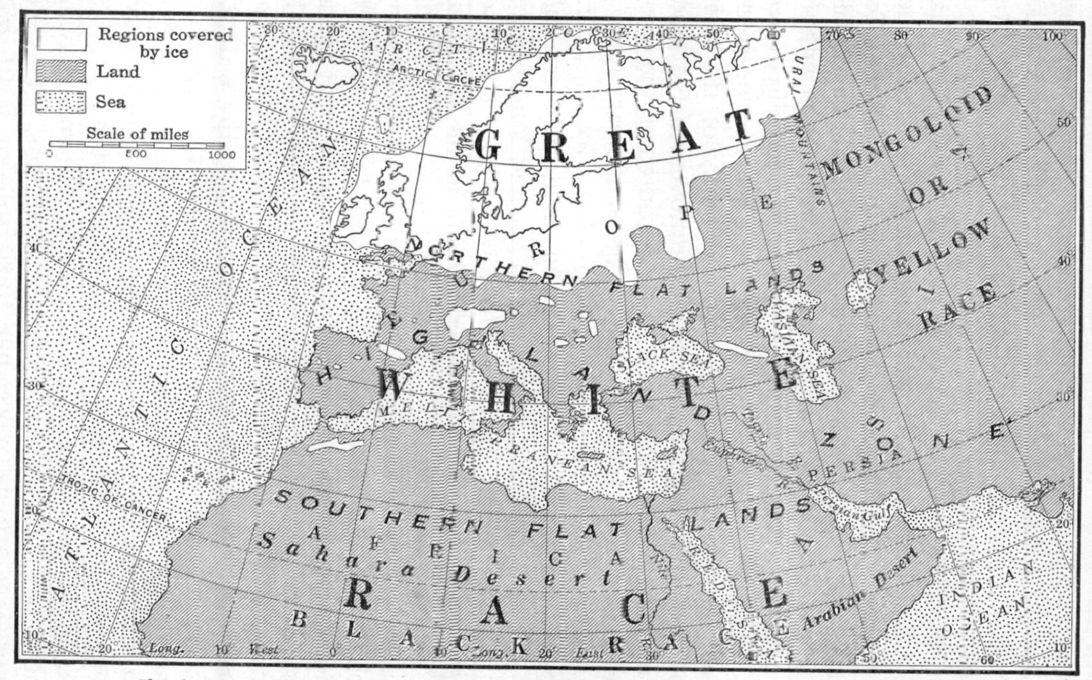

Sketch Map of the NORTHWEST QUADRANT *of the Eastern Hemisphere* IN THE ICE AGE *

pursued the same big game which we saw them hunting on the north side of the Mediterranean. Sometimes they followed the game down into the wide and deep gorge which the Nile had already cut clear across the eastern end of the Sahara (see map, p. 13).

Weapons of the earliest Stone Age hunters found in the Nile gorge

18. The Nile was at that time a much larger river than now. Like the Missouri River it sometimes shifted its bed and then never went back to the old one. One of the now dry beds of this larger early Nile, a stretch over fifty miles long parallel with the present river, has recently been discovered. On digging into its gravels, which are sixty feet deep, the archæologists found that it contained many of the stone weapons of the earliest hunters of the Southern Flatlands, who must have lost them there as they hunted on the banks of the river at least several hundred thousand years ago.

Drying Sahara Plateau slowly becomes uninhabitable

19. At some time before the middle of the Ice Age, when the North African hunters were still in the Early Stone Age, the plentiful rains, which had long watered North Africa, began slowly to fail. The reason for this diminished rainfall is not yet clearly understood. The rainfall in Europe also decreased. As a result of the failing moisture the glacial ice in Europe began to shrink and to retreat toward the north, while the decreasing rainfall in North Africa caused the great Sahara Plateau slowly to dry up. Its parching vegetation gradually disappeared. During a period of many thousands of years the Sahara Plateau was slowly changed into the waterless desert which we know today. Thus, while the hunters on the north side of the Mediterranean were still suffering from the cold and the ice, those on the south side were being slowly driven from their plateau home by lack of water.

20. At this period the Nile valley was of the greatest value to these early hunters of the Southern Flatlands. The valley is a gorge, or canyon, more than thirty miles in width, with steep rock walls varying from a few hundred to a thousand feet in height. With its great river flowing down the gorge

FIG. 4. *The Heights of the* SAHARA PLATEAU *opposite Thebes*

Along the crest of the cliffs, shown in the background, the Early Stone Age hunters had a number of flint workshops. Worked flints are still scattered here so plentifully that one walks on them for hundreds of yards. The tops of these cliffs were the shores of a bay of the larger early Nile (§ 18). And on these shores the hunters sat chipping away at their flint weapons. Many thousands of years later the Nile River had shrunk to its present size, and the Egyptian emperors were having their tombs (§ 146) excavated in the walls of the cliffs which had been formerly cut out by the action of the river. In the center of the photograph may be seen the tomb entrances. The position of the tomb of Tutenkhamon, behind a low hill in the foreground, is indicated by an arrow. The embankment *A–B* is the rubbish from the modern excavation of this tomb

Plateau man finds refuge in the Nile gorge

the valley offered the Early Stone Age hunters a new home with plenty of water. Therefore they shifted their dwellings down into the Nile gorge and made their homes along the banks of the river. Here the bottom of the great Nile trench, although it was as rainless as the desert, was watered by the river, which was plentifully fed from the rainy regions far south of the desert. Protected on both sides by practically rainless desert and unvisited by the ice or the cold of the north side of the Mediterranean, the great valley formed a *sheltered* home. Here the Early Stone Age hunters were soon to advance toward civilization much faster than the men of the same age in Europe, hindered as these prehistoric European hunters were by ice and arctic cold. The stone tools and weapons which reveal this advance to us have been found in great numbers, buried in the rock and gravel terraces formed by the river along its shores.

SECTION 3. THE MIDDLE STONE AGE

Industries of the Middle Stone Age hunters

21. Thus while Europe was struggling with snow and ice the hunters of North Africa had found a warm and genial refuge at the bottom of the great Nile trench. Nevertheless, when the ice came down for the fourth and last time the European hunters of the Early Stone Age had finally improved their stone implements and their manner of living. Then began a new period which we may call the Middle Stone Age. Unable to build themselves shelters from the cold, the hunters of Europe took refuge in limestone caves, where they continued to live for thousands of years. We can imagine such a hunter at the door of his cave, carefully chipping off the edges of his flint tools. By this time he had finally left the rude old fist-hatchet far behind, and he had discovered that by *pressure* with a hard piece of bone he could chip off a line of fine flakes along the edge of his flint tool and thus produce a much finer cutting edge than by chipping with *blows* (or *percussion*), as his ancestors had done.[1] This discovery enabled him to produce a considerable variety of flint tools, — chisels, drills and hammers, polishers and scrapers. The new *pressure*-chipped edges were sharp enough to cut and shape even bone, ivory, and especially reindeer horn. The mammoth furnished the hunters with ivory, and when they needed horn they found great herds of reindeer, driven southward by the ice, grazing before the caverns in which these hunters were living.

22. With their new and keener tools the Middle Stone Age hunters worked out barbed ivory spear-points, which they attached to long wooden shafts, and each carried at his

[1] This new style of flint-chipping may have been brought in by an invasion of another people from the outside.

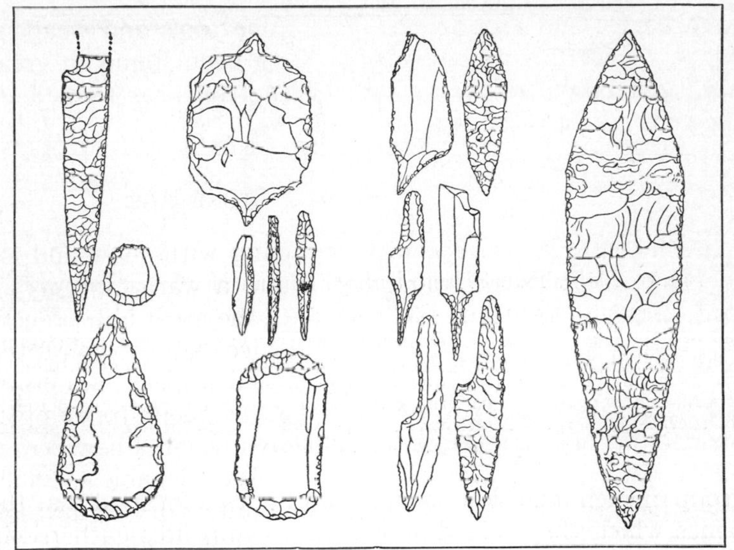

FIG. 5. *Flint* TOOLS *and* WEAPONS *of the Middle Stone Age*

From right to left they include knives, spear-points and arrow-points, scrapers, drills, and various edged tools. They show great skill and precision in flaking (see § 21)

girdle a sharp flint dagger. For straightening their wooden spear-shafts they invented an ingenious shaft-straightener of reindeer horn. Another clever device of horn or ivory was a spear-thrower, by which a hunter could hurl his long spear much farther and with greater force than he could before. Fine ivory needles found by excavation show that these people had learned to protect themselves from the cold and from the brambles of the forest wilderness with clothing made by sewing together the skins of animals.

Middle Stone Age hunters' new weapons and skin clothing

23. Thus equipped, the hunters of the Middle Stone Age were much more dangerous foes of the wild creatures than were the men of the Early Stone Age. In a single cavern in Sicily archæologists have dug out the bones of no less than two thousand hippopotamuses which these Middle Stone Age hunters killed. In France one

Life of Middle Stone Age hunter

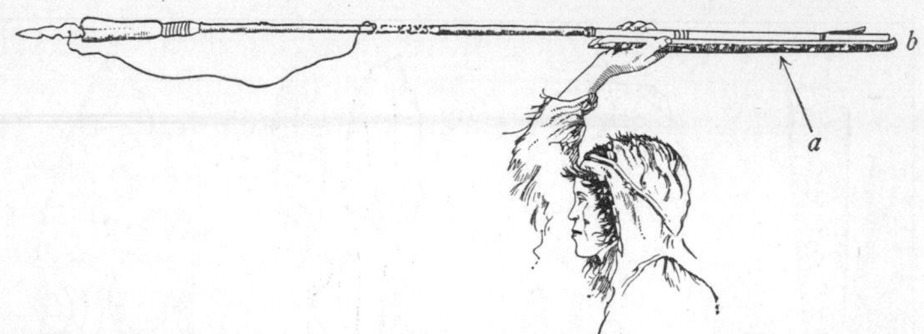

Fig. 6. *Modern Eskimo Hunter hurling a* Spear *with a* Spear-Thrower

The spear lies in a channel in the spear-thrower (*a*), which the hunter grasps at one end. At the outer end (*b*) of the spear-thrower is a hook (cf. Fig. 7, *B*), against which the butt of the spear lies. As the hunter throws forward his arm, retaining the spear-thrower in his hand and allowing the spear to go, the spear-thrower acts like an elongation of his arm, giving great sweep and propelling power as the spear is discharged. Modern schoolboys would not find it hard to make and use such a spear-thrower

group of such men slew so many wild horses for food that the bones which they tossed about their camp fires gathered in heaps, finally forming a layer in some places six feet thick and covering a space about equal to four modern city lots each fifty by two hundred feet. Among such deposits excavators have found even the bone whistle with which a returning hunter was able to announce his coming to his hungry family waiting in the cave. On his arrival there he found his home surrounded by piles of garbage. Amid foul odors of rotting flesh this savage European crept into his cave dwelling at night, little realizing that many feet beneath the cavern floor on which he slept lay the remains of his ancestors in layer upon layer, the accumulations of thousands of years (Fig. 11).

Age of earliest art dawns

24. In spite of the darkness and savagery of their daily life these primitive hunters were standing just at the dawning of the first great light that entered the souls of men. Each of these savage hunters, when he lay down in his cavern at night, could close his eyes and see mind-pictures of the great beasts he had been pursuing all day. He could recall curious trees the shape of which might remind him of an animal, or he might turn as he lay and see a bulging mass of rock in his cavern, which looked like a horse. Thus there might arise in his mind the idea of *resemblance*: the animal and the tree that looked like it, the horse and the rounded rock that looked like the horse. As this thought continued, he began to be aware that resemblance might be produced by his own hands; that is, he could imitate the form of one object by shaping another like it. In this way the possibility of *imitation* awoke in his mind. In that moment art was born, and the soul of man entered a new world, the world of beauty, filled with a light that had never brightened his life before. For ages his *body* had been developing, but in this new realization that he might create beautiful forms out of the storehouse of his memory his *mind* grew and rose to a new and higher level. Sketches on small stones have been found, made by beginners just learning to draw. They are like modern studio exercises, and still show the corrections made by the more skilled hand of the master.

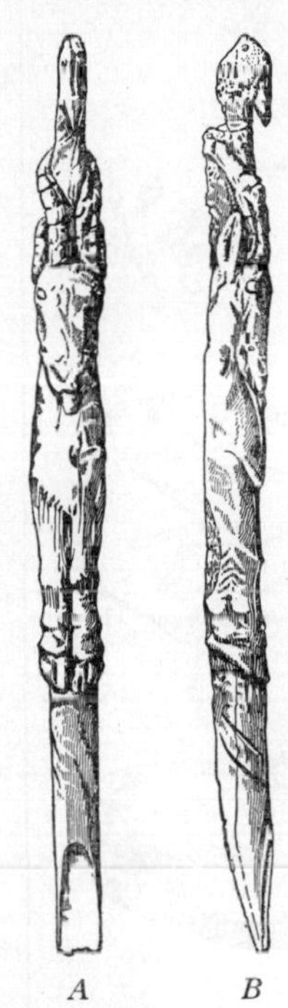

Fig. 7. *Two Views of a* Spear-Thrower *used by a Middle Stone Age Hunter*

(*A*) seen from the front; (*B*) seen from the side. It is carved of reindeer horn to represent the head and forelegs of an ibex. Observe the hook at the top of *B* for holding the butt of the spear-shaft. The spear-thrower and the bow were the earliest devices of man for hurling his weapons with speed

Discovery of Middle Stone Age art

35. This new and *creative* age of man's prehistoric life has been revealed to us in an amazing series of works of art discovered in the Stone Age caverns of Europe. It is not a little surprising to find that these Middle Stone Age hunters of Europe could already carve, draw, and even paint with considerable skill. A Spanish nobleman who had crawled into a cavern on his estate in northern

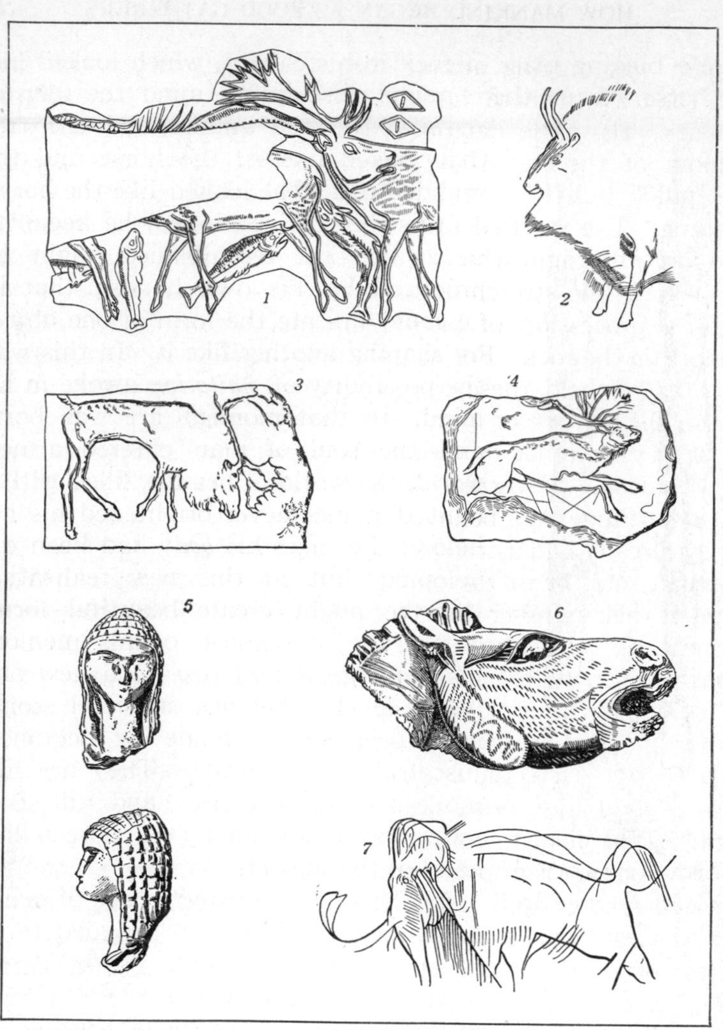

FIG. 8. CARVINGS *made by the Hunters of the Middle Stone Age*

The oldest works of art by man, carved in horn, schist, ivory, and the stone of cavern walls perhaps ten or fifteen thousand years ago. *1*, reindeer and salmon,— hunter's and fisherman's talisman; *2*, bison bull at bay; *3*, grazing reindeer; *4*, running reindeer; *5*, head of woman, front view and profile; *6*, head of wild horse whinnying; *7*, mammoth (an animal long since extinct), showing huge tusks and long hair

Spain was digging among the accumulations on the floor of the cave, where he had found flint and bone implements. His little daughter, who was playing about in the gloom of the cavern, suddenly shouted, "*Toros! toros!*" ("Bulls! bulls!"). At the same time she pointed to the ceiling. The startled father, looking up, beheld a never-to-be-forgotten sight which at once interrupted his flint-digging. In a long line stretching far across the ceiling of the cavern was a procession of bison bulls painted in well-preserved colors on the rock. For at least ten thousand years no human eye had beheld these cave paintings of a vanished race of men, till the eye of a child rediscovered them.

Religion in the Middle Stone Age

26. Other relics of higher life among these early men are few indeed. Nevertheless, even these ancient men of the Middle Stone Age believed in divine beings; they already had a crude idea of the life of the human soul, or of the departed person, after death. When one of their number died, they dressed him in his customary ornaments and supplied him with a few flint implements at least. Then they buried the departed hunter, protected by a rough circle of stones, in the cave beneath the hearth where he had so often shared the results of the hunt with his family. Here the bodies of these early men are found at the present day, lying under the successive layers of refuse which continued to collect over them for ages.

End of the Middle Stone Age

27. As the European hunters of the Middle Stone Age gained greater skill in carving and painting, they filled the caverns of France and northern Spain with pictures of the wild animals they hunted. Similar pictures are numerous in eastern Spain, not in caverns but on the rocks under the open sky; and likewise in North Africa, where they are found from Algiers entirely across the Sahara and eastward to the upper Nile. These widespread cave paintings and rock pictures, with much other evidence, reveal to us the Middle Stone Age hunters on both sides of the Mediterranean. We are now to see how their more favored situation in the Nile valley and their

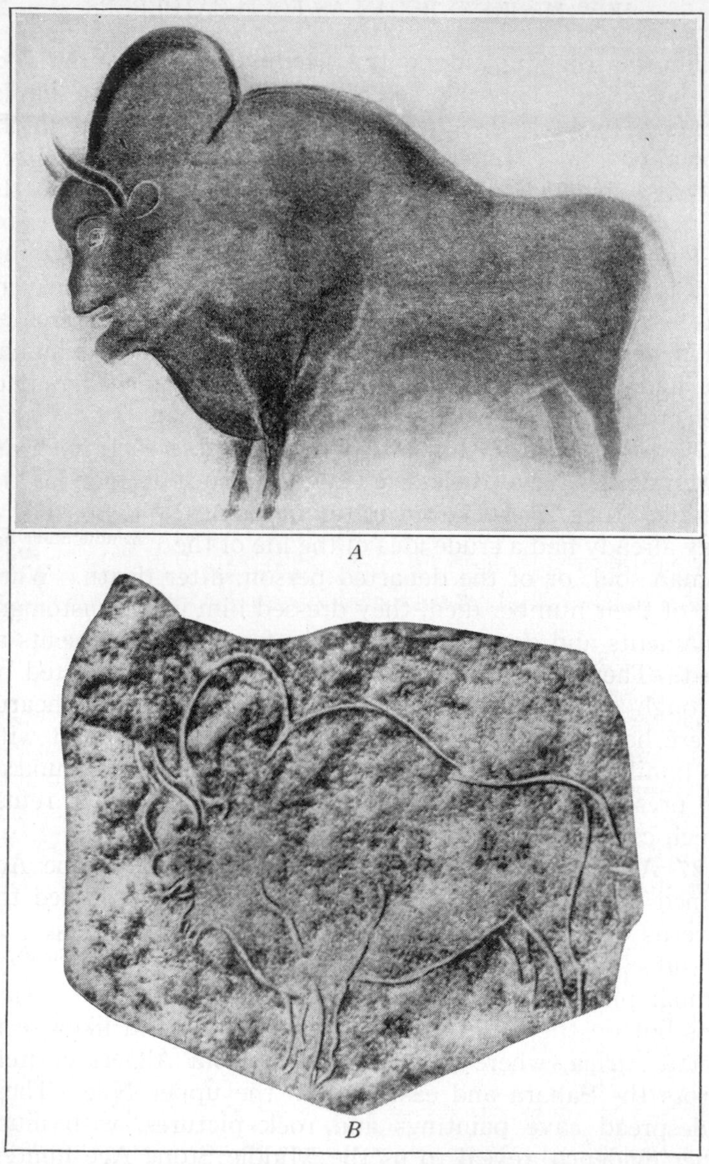

Fig. 9. Cave Painting *of a Bison* (A) *and the Artist's* Preparatory Sketch *on a Small Stone* (B) *

Fig. 10. North African Rock Drawing *of an* Elephant *protecting her Young from the Attack of a Tiger*

The elephant mother throws her trunk around the young one to ward off the tiger, which is preparing to spring. This situation could not have lasted more than a few seconds; but the North African hunter's eye caught the scene, and he probably made a quick sketch then, which he afterward enlarged on a great rock in southern Algiers. The occurrence of such drawings, often in the most inaccessible regions of the desert, is further proof that the Sahara Plateau was, many thousands of years ago, a fertile region enjoying plentiful rains. (After Frobenius and Obermaier)

freedom from the rigors of the European Ice Age enabled the hunters of Egypt to become food-producers and thus to advance far beyond their rivals elsewhere, who long remained as before merely food-gatherers. The hunting life long continued, however; for it is now quite evident that the Nile gorge, with its lofty walls, had become a vast game preserve, where the animals of the Sahara Plateau, as we shall see, took refuge in enormous numbers. The presence of such great herds of wild game must have made the life of the Middle Stone Age hunter much easier.

* This remarkable sketch, scratched on a small stone of the same size as the photograph (*B*), was the ancient cave artist's preparatory study of the splendid bull bison, which he enlarged to nearly fifteen times the size of the sketch (*B*) when he laid out his great painting (*A*) on the cavern wall. He carefully copied on the cavern wall the lines he had scratched on the little stone, and then he finished his noble wall painting in a number of colors. Luckily for us, he threw away his little sketch (*B*), which was finally found by the archæologists some ten thousand years afterward in southern France. (*B* after Gaillard and *A* after Breuil)

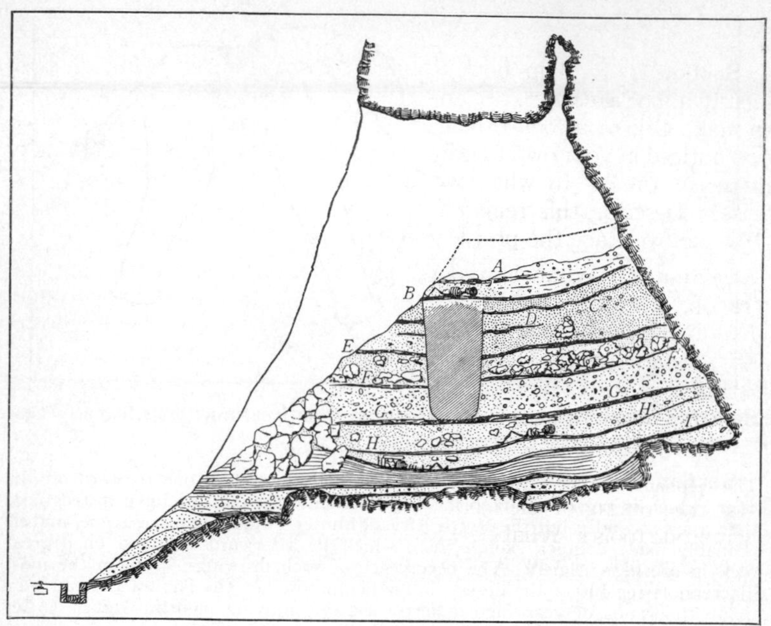

FIG. 11. *A Cross Section showing the* LAYERS OF RUBBISH *and the* HUMAN REMAINS *in a Middle Stone Age Cavern*

This cavern is at Grimaldi, on the Italian coast of the Mediterranean. The entrance is at the left, and the back wall at the right. We see the original rock floor at the bottom, and above it the layers of accumulations, 30 feet deep. The black lines *A* to *I* represent layers of ashes etc., the remains of nine successive hearth-fires, each of which must have been kept going by the natives for many years. The thicker (lightly shaded) layers consisted of bones of animals, rubbish, and rocks which had fallen from the roof of the cavern in the course of ages. The lowermost layers (below *I*) contained bones of the rhinoceros (representing a warm climate), while the uppermost layers contained bones of the reindeer (indicating a cold climate). Two periods, the Early and the Middle Stone Age, are thus represented,— the Early Stone Age below, the Middle Stone Age above. Five burials were found by the excavators in the layers *B*, *C*, *H*, and *I*; layer *C* contained the bodies of two children. The lowermost burial (in *I*) was 25 feet below the surface of the accumulations in the cave. These buried cave-dwellers crossed over from northern Africa and settled on the shores of Europe. Indeed, such prehistoric skulls and bones show that several different races followed one another in Europe during the Stone Age. Since the above drawing was made, excavators digging in front of the cavern have penetrated to a depth of 60 feet below the original surface of the accumulations and have continued to find flint implements and other evidences of human occupation. (After Déchelette)

QUESTIONS

Section 1. Explain how Robinson Crusoe, after being at first merely a food-gatherer, became a food-producer. What things helped to make Crusoe a food-producer? What progress in invention have you noticed in your own lifetime? Describe the life of the Tasmanians in recent times. In what region of the world did civilization first arise? Describe this region and the life of the earliest men there. How can we trace the progress of early man?

Section 2. What is archæology? Describe the earliest stone weapon. Describe the life of the Early Stone Age hunter. What great change came over the life of the Early Stone Age man in Europe and Western Asia? Discuss the climate of North Africa during the Early Stone Age. What proof have we that the Sahara Plateau was habitable in early times? Why did the hunters on the Sahara Plateau retreat into the Nile valley?

Section 3. Where did the Middle Stone Age hunters take refuge after the coming of the ice? What improvements did they make in their stone tools? What new inventions were made? Discuss Middle Stone Age art. Draw a cross section of a cave with contents and describe (Fig. 11).

BIBLIOGRAPHY FOR TOPICAL STUDIES

Evidences of man's prehistory: BURKITT, *Our Forerunners*, pp. 7–35; BUXTON, *Primitive Labour*, chap. viii; COLE, *The Long Road*, chap. i; MARETT, *Anthropology*, pp. 30–59.

Art: BURKITT, *Our Forerunners*, chaps. ix–x; GARDNER, *Art through the Ages*, chap. i; OSBORN, *Man rises to Parnassus*, chap. iii; PEAKE-FLEURE, *Hunters and Artists*, pp. 77–95.

Chapter II · *The Earliest Food-Producers*

Section 4. The Late Stone Age

28. The floor of the Nile gorge was at first lacking in soil, but by the end of the Middle Stone Age the river had already begun to carry down from the highlands of Abyssinia a great deal of black soil. Each season, as the summer rains of the Abyssinian mountains swelled the upper Nile, its waters rose above the banks. As they spread out over the bottom of the Egyptian Nile trench, these muddy waters left a thin layer of black mud. This sediment became at last a deep floor of black soil. It formed a strip wandering from right to left on each side of the winding river. At the present day this floor of black soil, including the strips of it on both sides of the river, is rarely more than ten miles wide. Living in the protected garden land thus formed, the Middle Stone Age men were able to advance to such improvements in manner of life that we must regard them as entering upon a new age which we call the Late Stone Age.

Coming of the black soil; Late Stone Age in Egypt

29. We have already learned that the animals which had so long inhabited the Sahara Plateau also found it necessary to take refuge in the Nile gorge in order to find food and water. The gorge was full of marshes, which offered a welcome home to vast flocks of wild fowl as well as to great herds of wild animals. On the north side of the Mediterranean the hunters had already learned to trap animals, even such large ones as the elephant. Down in the Nile gorge there was not as much room for these animals as they enjoyed in Europe or as they had once found on the plateau. As a result they were thrown into close contact with the human beings. Thus

Animals of the plateau seek refuge in the Nile valley; domestication

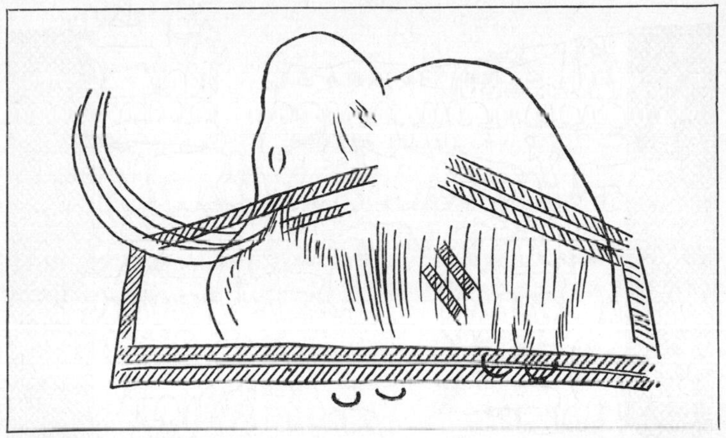

FIG. 12. *Cave Painting of a* MAMMOTH CAUGHT IN A TRAP *of Logs in Southern France*

This painting shows the early stage of man's ability to take wild animals captive. At a later stage this practice led to domestication of animals. (Drawing after Capitan-Breuil-Peyrony)

the Middle Stone Age hunters found it easy to drive whole herds of them into the deep bays in the Nile-valley cliffs and to capture them there. At length it occurred to these hunters to close off such a bay with a stockade having only one entrance, or even to build a stockade of four sides with one gate, into which the game might be driven. Wild game thus fenced in formed a very valuable source of food "on the hoof" and was always ready for use. After a long time these captive animals lost their fear of men and gradually learned to live with them, thus becoming what we call domestic animals, the servants of men.

Discovery of agriculture

30. After a time the Nile-gorge people discovered another new and lasting source of food. Probably for thousands of years the women had been accustomed to gather the seeds of certain wild grasses and had ground them up for food. It was now discovered that such grasses could be planted and watered, so that they would grow better and produce a greater yield of eatable seed.

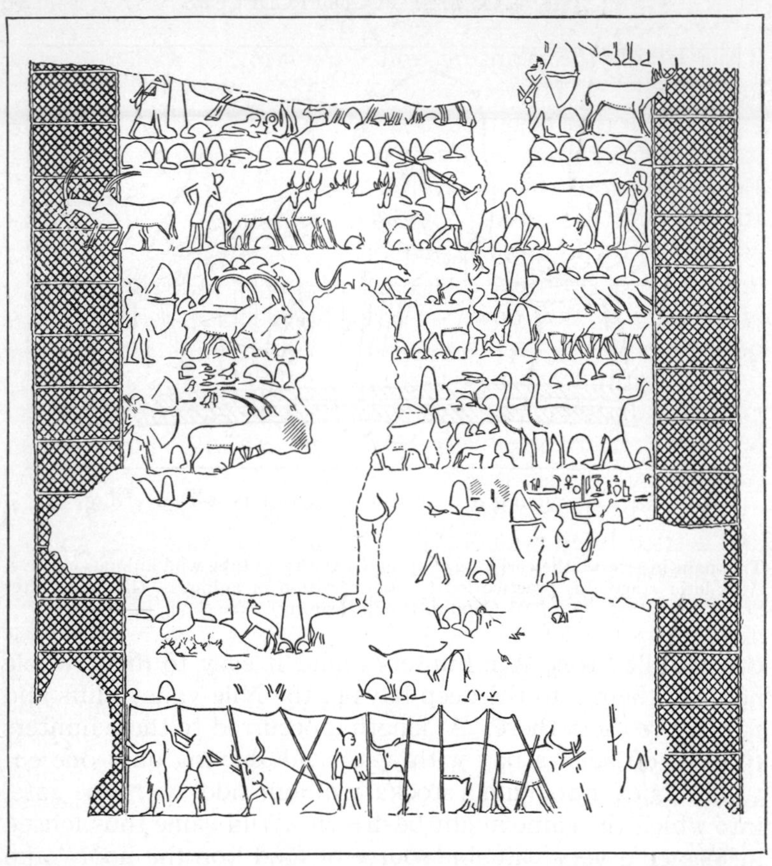

Fig. 13. *Ancient Egyptian Relief showing a* Hunting Inclosure *filled with Animals*

This scene was placed on the wall of a tomb of the Feudal Age. The breaks and gaps are caused by damage to the wall. The wild animals have been driven into an inclosure made of netting. We see the hunters engaged in closing up one end (at bottom edge) by poles connected by lengths of rope, but the far end has been destroyed. Four men, who are armed with bows and arrows, are evidently bent on killing some of the game for immediate use. Other men, in the first and second rows, are using lassos for capturing the animals alive. The inclosure contains a fine catch, consisting of oryxes, gazelles, a leopard, hares, a jackal, ostriches, ibexes, addaxes, four stags, and even a porcupine. In the bottom row the men, who are setting up the final posts in order to close the trap, find it necessary to drive back the wild oxen, which are seeking to escape. (Drawing after Newberry)

Thus began the planting and harvesting of millet, barley, and wheat,[1] which were once only wild grasses.

31. After men began cultivating food in the field and raising it on the hoof, they became for the first time food-*producers*. Being therefore able to produce food *at home*, they found it less necessary to go out as hunters and kill wild animals for food. The wandering life of hunting, therefore, gradually changed. Groups of families settled down to live in one place, where it was possible to look after the tamed animals and to water the fields of grain. Most of the hunters finally became farmers and cattle-raisers, and thus began the age of agriculture and of animal husbandry which we may call the *Age of Food-production.*

Beginning of age of food-production and a settled life

32. We have seen that in this new Age of Food-production and settled life it was possible for men to make fixed homes. Their tools for this purpose were still made of stone, especially flint, but they had learned to use a gritty stone to sharpen the edges. By this method their stone tools were so much improved that we must regard the period as another Stone Age, which we call the Late Stone Age.[2] The homes which they made were at first only woven wattle huts daubed with mud. These were better equipped than formerly, for these

Ground stone tools; improvement of Late Stone Age life

[1] Oats and rye were still unknown and came in much later. The wild ancestors — that is, the wild grasses — from which our cultivated grains came have been discovered in Palestine and in Abyssinia, that is, both in Western Asia and in Eastern Africa.

[2] The Stone Age periods are as follows:

1. Early Stone Age (stone edge made by striking, or *percussion*)
2. Middle Stone Age (chipped stone edge made by *pressure*)

} Called Paleolithic Age by archæologists

3. Late Stone Age (stone edge made by *grinding*) } Called Neolithic Age by archæologists

In Europe, at least, it is probable that these successive improvements were the inventions of invaders of different races, who brought them in, rather than improvements introduced by the same race.

It is helpful to remember that we might also divide the prehistoric age into two periods, thus:

1. The Age of Food gathering, including { *a.* The Early Stone Age; *b.* The Middle Stone Age }
2. The Age of Food-production, beginning with the Late Stone Age

FIG. 14. *Stall-*FEEDING *of Semi-domesticated* ANTELOPES *and* HYENAS *along with Cattle*

The wild creatures, which were taken alive out of the inclosures (Fig. 13), were then stall-fed and partially if not wholly domesticated. Goats (*1*), gazelles (*4*, left end), addaxes (*4*, middle), oryxes (*4*, right end), ibexes (*4*, left), are all shown in the scene above, *eating at their mangers in stables* along with the large cattle (*2*). Many thousands of years before the date of this wall relief these large cattle had been domesticated, and they became the ancestors of our own domesticated cattle. One important detail in the picture indicates that the Egyptians had practiced selective cattle-breeding from a very early date. The hornless breed of cattle (*2*, left end) is secured, or at least perpetuated, by selective breeding. At the bottom (*5*) captive hyenas are being stuffed with food. Among all these animals the Egyptians completed the domestication of the goats and large cattle shown here (*1*, *2*, and *3*); the others (*4*) were but partially domesticated and are now found only in a wild state, especially the hyenas (*5*)

early Nile-dwellers had noticed that clay will harden when heated in the fire. They were therefore able to make many pottery dishes, plates, pots, and jars for the household. At the same time the useful fibers of wild plants such as flax had been discovered, and the women had learned to cultivate these plants, to spin the fibers into thread, and to weave this thread into linen for their clothing.

33. All this happened so long ago that the traces of the little villages of wattle huts erected by the Late Stone Age Egyptians have been covered up under many feet of black soil, brought down since then by the Nile. Nevertheless scanty traces of several of their villages, on ground high enough to be above the reach of the Nile waters, have been discovered. They contained broken wooden sickles with flint edges, for use in harvesting grain, and also small circular pits used for granaries, in which were found small quantities of the grain itself. These are the oldest known evidences of agriculture. With these were bits of linen and pottery vessels, the earliest materials of this kind ever found. The villagers buried their dead along the margin of the black soil on the edge of the desert, at that time above the reach of the Nile waters. These cemeteries of the Late Stone Age men must have contained many graves much like the later one shown in Fig. 26; but unfortunately the cemeteries belonging to the Late Stone Age are now buried deep under the black soil, and nearly all of them are therefore still lost to us.

Villages and cemeteries of Egyptian Late Stone Age

34. In one such cemetery, which has recently been found, the articles buried with the dead in one of the graves included a copper pin (Fig. 16, *11*). It is the oldest implement of metal ever discovered in archæological excavation, for it can hardly be much later than 5000 B.C. It is interesting to follow in imagination the Egyptian who must have first discovered metal as he wandered into the Peninsula of Sinai, where the oldest copper mines are found. It may have been that in this vicinity (see map, p. 66) he happened to bank his camp fire with pieces of copper ore lying about on the ground. The glowing coals of his wood fire would finally roast the fragments of ore piled around to shield the fire, and thus the ore would be "reduced," as the miner says; that is, the copper in metallic form would be released from the lumps of ore. Next morning, as the Egyptian stirred the embers, he would discover in the ashes a few shining beads of metal. We can

Discovery of metal, about 5000 B.C.

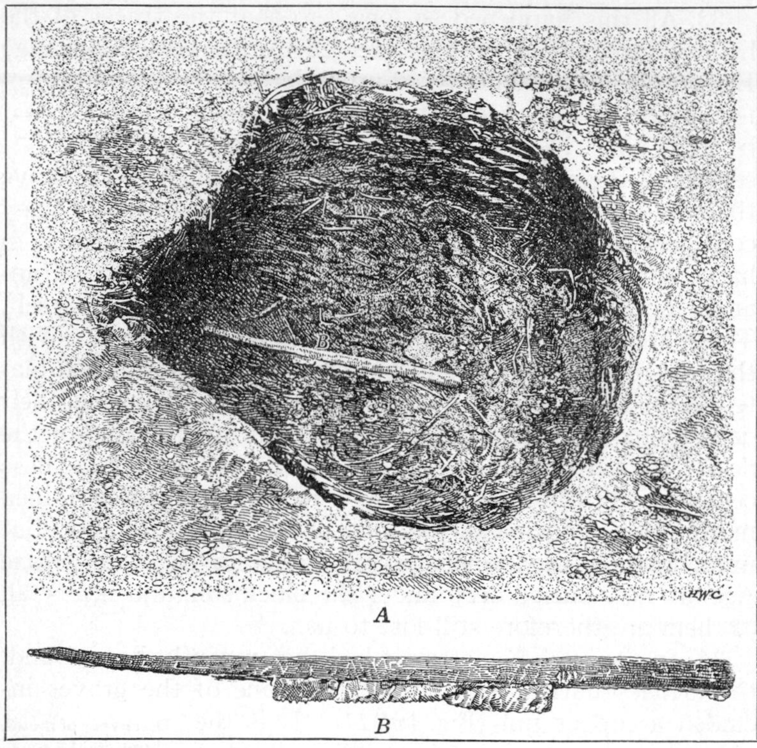

FIG. 15. *Late Stone Age* WOODEN SICKLE (*B*) *with Saw-Tooth Blade of* FLINT, *found in Straw-Lined* GRANARY (*A*)

This prehistoric granary was a shallow pit dug in the earth. Wet mud was smeared on the floor and sides of the pit, and then it was lined with straw. A number of such granaries were found together. Most of them were empty, but some contained quantities of wheat, barley, and other grain. The wooden sickle (*B*) found lying on the bottom of this granary (*A*) is nearly two feet long. A dark, gluelike mass holds the three saw-toothed pieces of flint in place to serve as the cutting edge of the sickle, and they remain fixed as firmly in their groove as they were on that day thousands of years ago when the Stone Age Egyptian dropped the sickle in the pit and perhaps forgot all about it. (After Miss G. Caton-Thompson)

imagine how he may have picked them up and turned them admiringly as they glittered in the sunshine. As the experience was repeated he discovered that these strange, shining beads had come out of the pieces of stone around his fire.

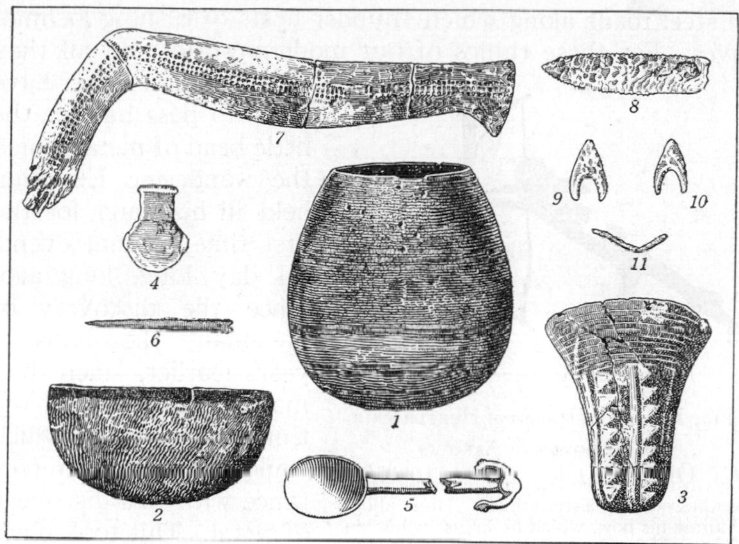

FIG. 16. *Group of* ARTICLES *found in a Late Stone Age Egyptian* CEMETERY

The Late Stone Age Egyptians had learned that clay hardens when baked; they therefore used baked clay for their purely hand-molded household vessels (*1–3*). The thinness and quality of this ware (jar, *1*), the beautifully rippled surfaces (bowl, *2*), were never improved upon by the later Egyptian potters, even after they had invented the wheel to aid them. The Late Stone Age Egyptians employed ivory or bone for cosmetic jars (*4*), spoons (*5*), and needles (*6*), wood and flint for implements (*7–10*). Toward the end of the Late Stone Age they learned to use copper for pins (*11*) or ornaments. Ivory spoons (*5*) were placed in the grave before the face of the dead man and at his hands, so that he might use them for eating his food in the next world. The bone needles (*6*) were used to sew garments of woven material as well as of skin, and were similar to the needles of Middle Stone Age man in Europe. Object *7* was an ancient Egyptian boomerang and probably the ancestor of the Australian boomerang. Saw-edged knives of flint (*8*) and many flint arrowheads (*9* and *10*) are found, but the bows have not been recovered; perhaps they were considered too valuable to be buried. (Drawing after Brunton)

Dawning of the Age of Metal

35. Without knowing it this man stood at the dawning of a new era, the Age of Metal; and if this Egyptian wanderer could have seen it, the little bead of shining copper which he drew from the ashes might have reflected to him a marvelous vision of the future, with metal buildings, great bridges, huge factories roaring with the noise of thousands of machines of metal, and vast stretches of steel roads along which thunder hosts of rushing locomotives. For these things of our modern world, and all they signify, might never have come to pass but for the little bead of metal which the wondering Egyptian held in his hand for the first time on that eventful day long, long ago. Since the discovery of fire many thousands of years earlier, men had made no conquest of the things of the earth which could compare in importance with this discovery of metal. This took place not later than about the year 5000 B.C., that is, at least about seven thousand years ago. But it was to be many centuries before copper tools and weapons came into common use. During this long period, and for some time after, the Late Stone Age life went on just as if metal had not been discovered.

FIG. 17. *Rock Drawing of* HUNTER *with Earliest* BOW AND ARROWS

This Middle Stone Age hunter is pictured on the rocks in eastern Spain. He is about to draw his bow, which he holds in his left hand along with three arrows. These hunters of eastern Spain came from North Africa. (Drawing after Obermaier and Wernert)

36. Meantime the hunters on the north side of the Mediterranean had continued to lead their food-gathering life of the Middle Stone Age, without cattle, grain, pottery, ground stone tools, or linen clothing. The signs left by the ice, as it was drawing back northward for the last time, have led geologists to think that it reached its present latitude nearly nine thousand years ago. At this point, therefore, the men of the Middle Stone Age on the north side of the Mediterranean entered upon weather conditions which gradually became like those of today.

Final retreat of the ice in Europe

37. While the ice was retreating for the last time on the European side of the Mediterranean, and while the North African plateau continued to dry up, influences from North

Africa began to reach the European hunters toward the close of the Middle Stone Age. These influences entered Europe along three routes. There were the two land-bridges at Gibraltar and Sicily (§ 9), which at that time still connected Africa and Europe. The North African hunters seem first to have passed across these land-bridges carrying the bow and arrow, which they had probably invented, and accompanied by the wolflike creatures which they had tamed and which later became stanch friends of man, — the familiar domesticated dogs. The bodies of these hunters, showing clearly their African origin, have been found buried in the cavern of Grimaldi in Italy. It is not impossible that later some of the men of the Nile gorge, with more roving tendencies than the others, wandered across North Africa and passed over these same land-bridges into Europe, and it is highly probable that they took with them their domesticated animals. In this manner, no doubt, there passed over to Europe from Africa also wheat and barley, linen and pottery, together with ground stone tools and implements, of which exactly the same styles and types are found both in Egypt and among the Swiss lake-dwellings (§ 42).

North African influences reach Europe by land-bridges

38. The *third* route by which North Africa was connected with Europe was a water route by way of the large island of Crete (see map, p. 146). Since this island is only about one hundred and eighty miles from the coast of Africa, it served as a midway station and shortened the voyage across the Mediterranean from Africa to Europe. Sir Arthur Evans, in his excavations in Crete, dug down through the remains of palaces of the ancient Cretan kings, and *under* them he found the walls of houses containing *ground* or polished stone axes used by the Late Stone Age men who lived in these houses. In one of the rooms lay a copper ax from Egypt, probably the earliest metal tool ever found in Europe. This copper ax shows very clearly what the Egyptian ships were bringing to Crete and how the earliest metal reached Europe.

North African influences reach Europe by the Cretan route

39. In Europe it was especially beside rivers and water-courses, where there were fertile soil and extensive pastures, that the early communities of food-producers in the Late Stone Age located their settlements. The most important of the European river valleys in this age was that of the Danube. In its lower course the valley expands into what are now the far-spreading and productive plains of Hungary. This region of the lower Danube extends down toward western Asia Minor, through which the Late Stone Age life of Western Asia passed over into eastern Europe, bringing with it cattle-breeding and the cultivation of grain. It is probable that the wide grain fields and extensive pastures of Hungary supported the first large farming communities of Europe as increasing numbers of men abandoned the hunting life and settled down here in fixed dwellings. From the farmers of the Danube the pastoral and agricultural life passed up the great river into the heart of Europe. The remains of the Late Stone Age settlements which at this time spread westward from Hungary disclose great improvements in the manner of living.

Earliest European food-producers on the lower Danube

40. While the earliest of these settlements began with wattle huts, we shall now see that improved, ground-edged tools afterward made possible the construction of wooden houses. If we examine the equipment of the Late Stone Age workmen we find that they had a list of tools almost as complete as that of the modern carpenter. Besides the ax they had chisels, knives, drills, saws, and whetstones, made mostly of flint but sometimes of other hard stones. They had learned also either to attach a wooden handle by lashings around the ax-head or to fit the ax-head into a deer-horn handle, or even to bore a hole in the ax-head and insert a handle. These tools, as found today, often display a polish due to the wear which they have undergone in the hands of the user.

Tools of Late Stone Age man in Europe

41. It is a mistake to suppose that a man could not do good and rapid work with such stone tools. In a recent experiment in Denmark a modern mechanic had his steel ax taken away

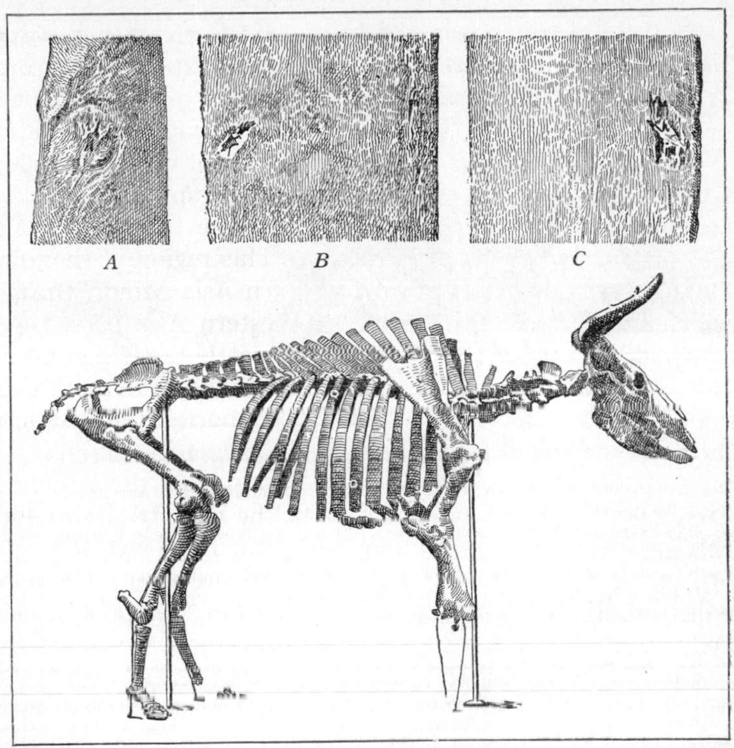

FIG. 18. *Skeleton of a* WILD BULL *bearing the Marks of the Late Stone Age Hunters'* ARROWS *which killed him in the Danish Forests, probably some Nine Thousand Years ago*

A Late Stone Age hunter shot him in the back near the spine (see *upper* white ring on skeleton). The wound healed, leaving a scar on the rib (*A*, above). Later another hunter shot him, and this time several arrows pierced his vitals. One of them, however, struck a rib (see *lower* white ring on skeleton) and broke off. Both sides of this wound, still unhealed, with the broken flint arrowhead still filling it, are shown above in *B* and *C*. While the wounded bull was trying to swim across a neighboring lake he died, and his body sank to the bottom; and the pursuing hunter, on reaching the lake, found no trace of him. In the course of thousands of years the lake slowly filled up, and water 10 feet deep was followed by dry peat, of the same depth, which covered the skeleton of the bull. Here he was found in 1905, and lying with him were found the flint arrowheads that had killed him. His skeleton, still bearing the marks of the flint arrowheads (*A*, *B*, *C*), was removed, and set up in the museum at Copenhagen

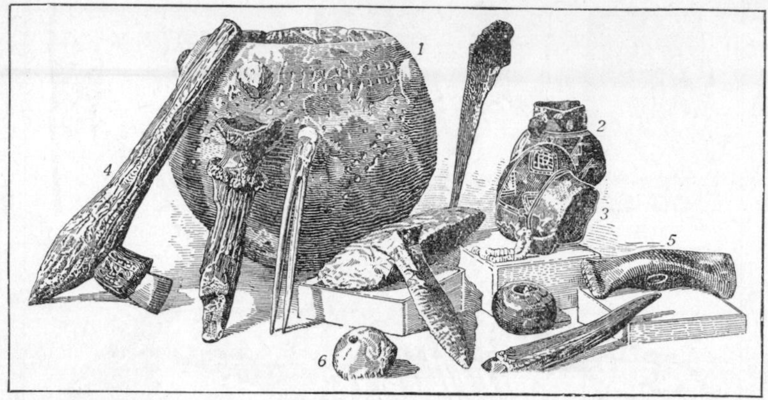

FIG. 19. *Part of the* EQUIPMENT *of a Late Stone Age* LAKE-DWELLER

This group contains the evidence for three important inventions made or received from the Near East by the men of the Late Stone Age: *first,* pottery jars, like *2* and *3,* with rude decorations, — the oldest baked clay in Europe, — and *1,* a large kettle in which the lake-dwellers' food was cooked; *second,* ground-edged tools like *4,* a stone chisel with ground edge, mounted in a deer-horn handle like a hatchet, or *5,* a stone ax with ground edge, and pierced with a hole for the ax-handle; and, *third,* weaving, as shown by *6,* a spinning "whorl" of baked clay, the earliest spinning wheel. When suspended by a rough thread of flax 18 to 20 inches long, it was given a whirl which made it spin in the air like a top, thus rapidly twisting the thread by which it was hanging. The thread, when sufficiently twisted, was wound up, and another length of 18 to 20 inches was drawn out from the unspun flax to be similarly twisted. One of these earliest spinning wheels has been found in the Swiss lakes with a spool of flaxen thread still attached. (From photograph lent by Professor Hoernes)

Effectiveness of stone tools

from him. In its place he was given a stone ax, and although he was not accustomed to the use of stone tools, he was able, in ten working hours, to cut down twenty-six pine trees eight inches in thickness and hew them into logs. Then the *entire work of hewing out the planks and timbers and building a house was done by one mechanic with stone tools in eighty-one days.* It was therefore quite possible for the men of the Late Stone Age to build comfortable dwellings and to attain a degree of civilization far above that of savages.

42. The most plentiful traces of the earliest wooden houses in Europe are to be found in Switzerland. Here groups of families of the Late Stone Age built their villages of wooden

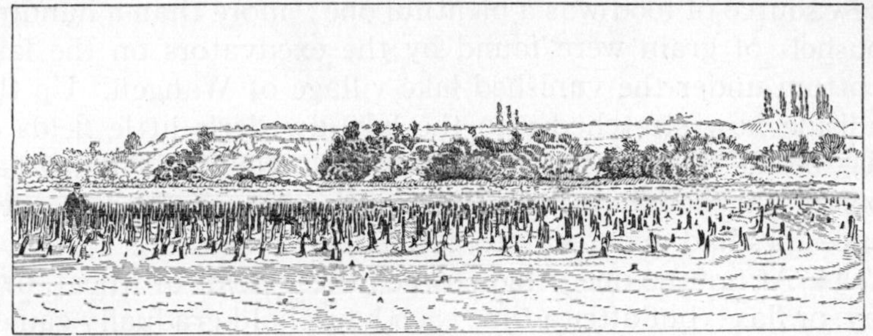

Fig. 20. *Surviving Remains of a Swiss* Lake-Village

After an unusually dry season the Swiss lakes fell to a very low level in 1854, exposing the lake bottom with the remains of the piles which once supported the lake-villages along the shores. Thus was the existence of such villages discovered. It has now been shown that this low level of the water was the *original* level, when the above village was built. It stood, therefore, as we see it here, on the dry land *beside* the lake, and not over the water, as was formerly believed. In the course of thousands of years the water of the Swiss lakes has risen and covered the old shores, including the remains of the pile-villages, and has thus produced the incorrect impression that they were built over the water, and that the piles had been driven into the lake-bottom. Among the projecting piles were found great quantities of tools, household furnishings, and implements like those in Fig. 19; also dugouts and fish nets, wheat, barley, bones of domestic animals, woven flax, etc. There they had been lying some five thousand years. Sometimes the objects were found in two distinct layers, the lower (earlier) containing only *stone* tools, and the upper (later) containing *bronze* tools, which came into the lake-village at a later age and fell down on top of the layer of old stone tools already lying there

houses upon platforms stretching in long lines along the shores of the Swiss lakes. These platforms were supported by piles driven into the ground. Such villages, or groups of *pile-dwellings*, are commonly called *lake-villages*. In a few cases they finally grew to be quite large. At Wangen not less than fifty thousand piles were driven into the ground for the support of the village (see remains of such piles in Fig. 20).

Swiss lake-villages of Late Stone Age

43. The lake-villagers lived a life of peace and prosperity. Their houses were comfortable shelters, and they were supplied with wooden furnishings and pottery hand-formed, that is, without the potter's wheel. The hillsides looking down upon the lake villages were green with fields of barley, wheat, and millet. This

Life of Swiss lake-dwellers

new source of food was a plentiful one; more than a hundred bushels of grain were found by the excavators on the lake bottom under the vanished lake-village of Wangen. Up the hillside now stretched also the lake-dweller's little fields of flax beside the growing grain. Their women sat spinning flax before the doorways, and the rough skin clothing of their ancestors had given way to garments of linen.

Social effects of agriculture

44. At first no one person owned these fields of wheat, barley, or flax; but after a time each household gradually gained the right to cultivate a particular field, and finally they came to set up a claim to it. Thus arose ownership of land. It was to be a frequent cause of trouble in the future life of men, and out of it came the long struggle between the rich and the poor. This system of land ownership established more firmly the settled agricultural life in and around the villages, because it was necessary for the villagers to remain near the little fields where their women had hoed the ground for planting, that they might care for the crop and gather the grain when it ripened.

Flocks and herds; wandering, or nomadic, shepherd life

45. On the other hand, the possession of grass-eating animals feeding on the grasslands created a different class of men, who did not lead a settled life. The pasturage was not everywhere plentiful enough to permit keeping the cattle always in one place. At times the cattle-keepers were obliged to seek pasturage somewhere else; and thus they came to follow a roving life, transporting their wives and children, and driving their flocks about in order to pasture them wherever the grasslands offered food. Such people, made up of herdsmen and shepherds, we call *nomads*, and they still exist today. While the farmers remained settled on their rich farm lands, the nomads took possession of the grasslands which stretched from the Danube eastward along the north side of the Black Sea and thence far over into Asia.

46. Thus grain and cattle created two methods of life side by side, — the settled, agricultural life of grain-raising and the wandering, nomad life of cattle-breeding. It is important to understand these two classes of people, because the grasslands became the home of a numerous *unsettled* population. Such grasslands often became too crowded with the nomad peoples, who then overflowed and overwhelmed the towns and the agricultural settlements. We shall see later Europe invaded over and over again by the hordes of nomads coming in from the eastern grasslands.

Age-long conflict between nomads and townsmen

47. The *settled* communities of the Late Stone Age at last began to leave behind them something more than fragile wooden houses and wattle huts. Toward the close of this age the more powerful chiefs in the large settlements learned to erect tombs, built of large blocks of stone. These tombs are still found fringing the western coast of Europe from the Mediterranean around Spain to the southern Scandinavian shores. There are at the present day no less than thirty-four hundred stone tombs of this age, some of considerable size, on the Danish island of Seeland alone. In France they exist in vast numbers and imposing size, and likewise in England. The enormous blocks in some of these structures were mostly left in the rough; but if cut at all, it was done with stone chisels. Such structures are not of masonry, that is, of smoothly cut stone laid with mortar. They cannot be called works of architecture, — a thing which did not as yet exist in Europe.

Buildings in Late Stone Age Europe

48. When we look at these monuments of the Late Stone Age, still surviving, they prove to us the existence of the earliest towns in Europe; for near every great group of stone tombs there was a town where the people lived who built the tombs. The remains of some of these towns have been discovered. They show us that men were learning to live together in larger numbers and to work together on a large scale. It required power over men and successful management of them to raise the earth walls of such a town, to drive fifty thousand piles supporting the lake-village at Wangen (Switzerland), or to move great blocks of stone for building the chieftain's tomb.

Earliest towns in Europe; the rise of government

Fig. 21. *Air View of the* Great Stone Circle *at Stonehenge, England*

The circle is about one hundred feet across, and a long avenue connecting it with the neighboring Late Stone Age town is still traceable. Stonehenge dates from the beginning of the Copper or Bronze Age (about 2000 B.C.) and marks the end of the Late Stone Age in western Europe, which produced nothing more than this rude architecture in stone until the coming of the Romans. It is thought by some that Stonehenge marks the burial place of certain Stone Age chieftains. (Courtesy of British Ordnance Survey Office and the editor of *Antiquity*)

In these works we see the beginnings of government under the rule of a leader. We may call such a government a state, and many little states, each made up of an earth-walled town with its surrounding fields, and each under a chieftain, grew up in Late Stone Age Europe. Out of such beginnings nations were later to grow.

Festivals and athletic contests of Late Stone Age Europe

49. Furthermore, the stone structures (§ 47) furnish us very interesting glimpses of the life of the Late Stone Age towns. Some of them suggest to us whole communities coming out from the towns on feast days and marching to such places as the huge stone circles at Stonehenge in England (Fig. 21). It has been thought that here they held contests and athletic games in honor of the dead chief buried within the stone circles. Festival processions probably once marched down long avenues marked out by mighty stones. Today,

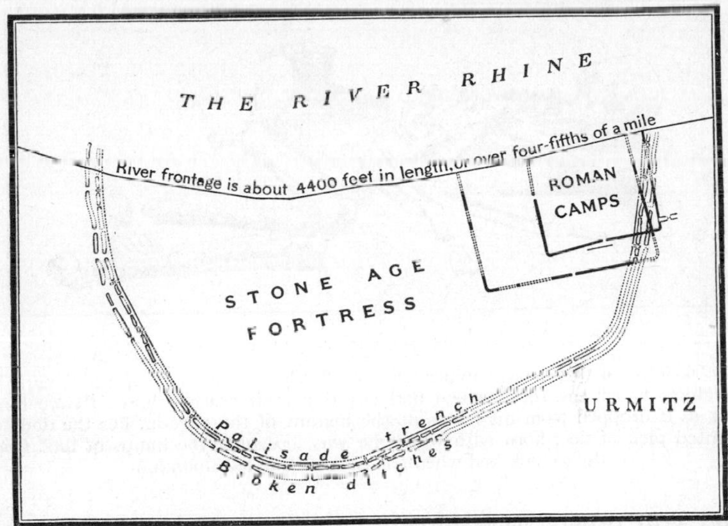

FIG. 22. PLAN *of the* DEFENSES *of a Late Stone Age Town at Urmitz, Germany*

This town was located on a level plain along the river Rhine, just north of the modern city of Coblenz. Excavations show that the defenses consisted of two lines of ditches (now very much broken), which describe a rough semicircle surrounding the city on three sides and extending at both ends of the town to the bank of the Rhine, which formed the defense on the fourth side. Just inside the inner ditch was a wooden palisade, the course of which is marked by the *innermost* line inside the ditches on the plan. Not all of the entrance causeways have been found, but the excavator thinks that there were about twenty-two entrances to the fort, each having a causeway leading across the palisade trench and both ditches. The entrances were probably closed with gates made of irregular wooden beams. It is believed that the entrance causeways enabled the defenders of a settlement to make sudden sallies against a besieging enemy from different points, and all at the same time. Long after the houses and defenses of this Late Stone Age town were in ruins, Roman soldiers built a small and then a larger fortress in one corner. (Drawing after Lehner)

silent and forsaken, they stretch for miles across the fields of the modern farmers, to remind us of forgotten human joys, of ancient customs, and of beliefs long revered by the vanished peoples of Stone Age Europe.

50. While such monuments are relics of the Late Stone Age people at play, other remains show them to us at their work. Men were beginning to adopt trades; for example, some men were probably wood-workers, others were potters,

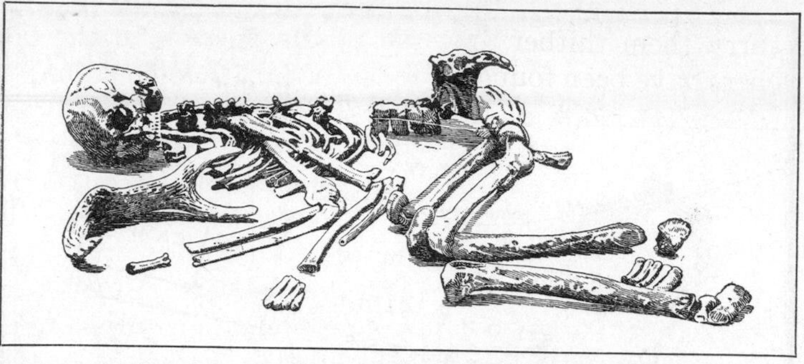

FIG. 23. *Skeleton of a* MINER *of the Late Stone Age*

The skeleton of this ancient miner was found lying on the floor of a flint mine in Belgium, under the rocks which had caved in and crushed him. Before him, just as it dropped from his hands at the instant of the cave-in, lies the double-pointed pick of deer-horn with which he was loosening the lumps of flint from their chalk bed when the rock ceiling fell upon him

and still others were already miners. These early miners burrowed far into the earth in order to reach the finest deposits of flint for their stone tools. In the underground tunnels of the ancient flint mines at Brandon, England, eighty worn picks of deer-horn were found in recent times. At one place the roof had caved in, cutting off a gallery of the mine. Here, behind the fallen rocks, archæologists found two more deer-horn picks bearing a coat of chalk dust in which were still visible the marks of the workmen's fingers, left there as they last laid down these tools thousands of years ago.

Rise of trades at the end of the Late Stone Age; mining

51. Business relations between the villages already existed. Such beginnings of commerce sometimes carried things far and wide. An outstanding example of this was an especially fine variety of French flint, found scattered today in many parts of Europe and recognizable by its color. The amber gathered on the shores of the Baltic was already passing from hand to hand southward to the Mediterranean. Stone implements found on the islands around Europe show that men of this age lived on these islands, and they must have had boats strong enough

Business in Late Stone Age

to carry them thither. Several of the dugouts of the lake-dwellers have been found lying on the lake bottom among the piles, but vessels with *sails* had not yet been invented in Europe. The business of such an age was of course very simple. There were no metals and no money. Buying and selling were only exchange of one kind of wares for another kind. In all Europe there was no writing, nor did the inhabitants of the mainland of Europe *ever* invent a system of writing.

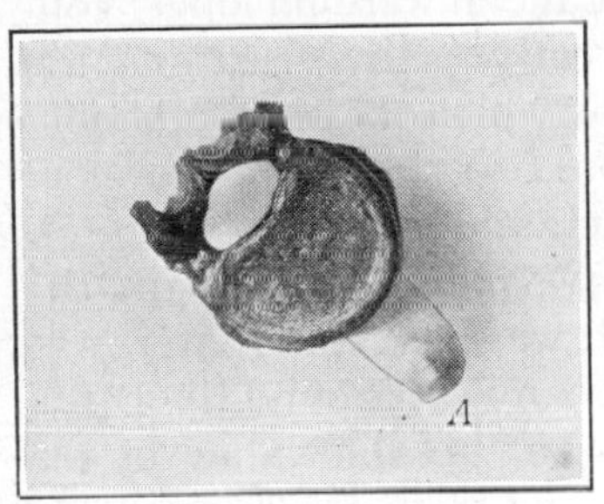

FIG. 24. VERTEBRA *of a Late Stone Age* MAN *with a Flint Arrowhead sticking in it*

The arrowhead (*A*) struck the victim full in the pit of the stomach. It must have been driven by a powerful bow, for it passed clear through to the spinal column, producing peritonitis and death. (Photograph furnished by the great French archæologist Déchelette, who himself fell in battle not long after sending this photograph to the author)

Wars of the Late Stone Age

52. But the intercourse between these earliest villages was not always peaceful. The earthen walls and the wooden stockades with which such towns were protected show us that the chieftain's war-horn must often have summoned these people to repel the enemy. Grim relics of these earliest wars of Europe still survive. A skull taken out of a tomb of this age in Sweden contains a flint arrowhead still sticking in one eye-hole, while in France more than one human bone has been found with a flint arrowhead driven deep into it. A stone coffin found in a Scottish stone heap contained the body of a man of huge size, with one arm almost severed from the shoulder by the stroke of a stone ax. A fragment of stone broken out of the ax blade still remained in the gashed arm bone.

53. Such was the life of Late Stone Age men on the north side of the Mediterranean near the close of this period, about three thousand years before Christ. Long before this, portions of the Gibraltar and Sicilian land-bridges had sunk

beneath the water, and Europe was separated from Africa as it is today. The Late Stone Age villages on the north side of the Mediterranean were no longer connected by land directly with Africa and the Nile valley. Thus the older roads by which they had probably received cattle and grain were closed to them, and no more inventions from Egypt could reach them by those routes. But the sea route by way of Crete was always open, and the civilization of Western Asia, which we shall study later, was also entering Europe across the Ægean Sea, around the Black Sea, and especially, as we have seen, up the valley of the Danube. Nevertheless, after changing from the hunting life to the settled life beside their grain fields and on their pastures, the Stone Age men of Europe made little or no progress. They were still without *writing* for making the records of business and government; they were still without *metals*[1] with which to make tools and to develop industries and manufactures; and they had no *sailing ships* in which to carry on commerce. Without these things they could go no farther. Meanwhile these and many other possessions of civilization were being discovered or invented on the other side of the Mediterranean in Egypt and Western Asia, — in the lands which we now call the Near East.[2]

Late Stone Age Europe at a standstill

54. As we leave Europe to follow the story of the Ancient Near East let us remember that we have been following man's *prehistoric* progress as it went on all around the Mediterranean for several hundred thousand years after he began making stone implements.

Westward movement of civilization

[1] Metal was introduced in *southeastern* Europe about 3000 B.C. and passed like a slow wave, moving gradually westward and northward across Europe. It probably did not reach Britain until about 2000 B.C. Hence we have included the great stone monuments of western Europe (like Stonehenge) in our survey of Stone Age Europe. They were erected long after *southeastern* Europe had received metal but before metal came into common use in *western* Europe.

[2] The term "Far East" is used today to include Japan, China, and India. The term "Near East" became very common during the World War, especially in connection with the relief work called "Near East relief," and is now the most convenient name for the lands grouped about the eastern end of the Mediterranean, although the word "Orient" is still a correct designation of the same region.

In the Near East, beginning before 4000 B.C. and during the thousand years from 4000 to 3000 B.C. (see diagram, Fig. 41), men slowly built up a high civilization, forming the beginning of the *Historic Age*.[1] Civilization thus began in the Near East, where it is between five and six thousand years old. There it long flourished and produced great and powerful nations, while the men of the Late Stone Age in Europe continued to live without metals or writing. As they gradually received these things from the Near East the leadership of civilization both in peace and in war shifted slowly to Europe. As we turn to watch civilization gradually appearing in the Near East, with metals, government, writing, great ships, and many other creations of civilization, let us realize that its later movement will steadily carry us from east to west as we follow it from the Near East to Europe.

QUESTIONS

Section 4. Discuss the conditions in the Nile valley leading to the domestication of animals. Explain what is meant by "the Age of Food-production." Tell something of the life of the earliest Nile men and how we know about them. Describe the probable manner of the discovery of metal. Which metal was it? What great change in Europe ended the Middle Stone Age? How did North African cultural influences reach Europe? Where were the earliest large food-producing communities in Europe? Discuss carpentry with *ground* stone tools. Describe the lake-villages and the life in them. What were the social effects of agriculture? Discuss stone structures and the life they reveal, — industries, traffic, and war. What important things did the Late Stone Age in Europe still lack? Is civilization possible without these things? Where did these things first appear?

[1] We may best describe the Historic Age by saying that it is the age beginning when written documents were first produced by man,— documents which tell us in written words something of man's life and career. All that we know of man in the age previous to the appearance of writing has to be learned from weapons, tools, implements, buildings, and other things (bearing no writing) which he has left behind. These are the things from which we have been learning something of the story of prehistoric man all around the Mediterranean (see Chapter I). The transition from the Prehistoric to the Historic Age was everywhere a slow and gradual one. In the Near East this transition took place in the thousand years between 4000 and 3000 B.C.

BIBLIOGRAPHY FOR TOPICAL STUDIES

Industries of the food-producers: BURKITT, *Our Early Ancestors*, pp. 50–72; BUXTON, *Primitive Labour*, chaps. iii–iv, ix; CHILDE, *Most Ancient East*, chap. iii; CLELAND, *Our Prehistoric Ancestors*, pp. 83–104 and Fig. 53; COLE, *The Long Road*, chap. iii.

Stone implements: British Museum, *Flints*; BURKITT, *Our Early Ancestors*, pp. 102–122; *Our Forerunners*, pp. 65–93; CLELAND, pp. 136–147.

Civilization of the lake-dwellers: CLELAND, pp. 148–168.

NOTE. Below we see the photograph of a group of stone grinders, or mortars, in which early food-producers of North Africa ground the grain which they had learned to plant and harvest. These household flour-mills were found in the remotest regions of the desert on the west of Egypt, hundreds of miles from the Nile. The fact that such mortars were once used in this now dry and desolate portion of the Sahara is further evidence of the existence of a period when the great Sahara Plateau had not yet become desert and early men could still live there and produce their food. The explorer's sun helmet at the right end furnishes a scale for the size of these grinders.

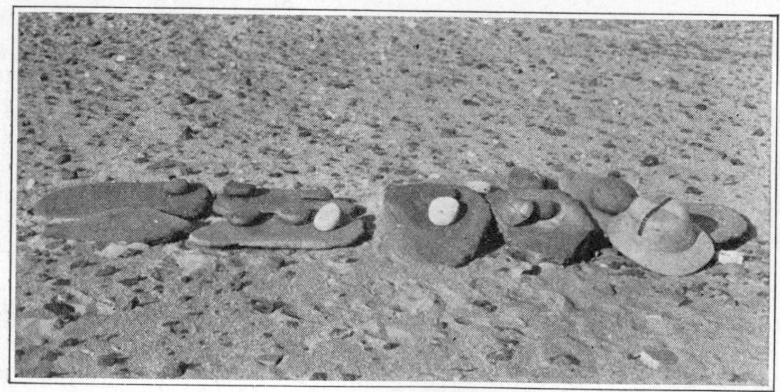

PART II · THE ORIGINS AND EARLY HISTORY OF CIVILIZATION IN THE ANCIENT NEAR EAST

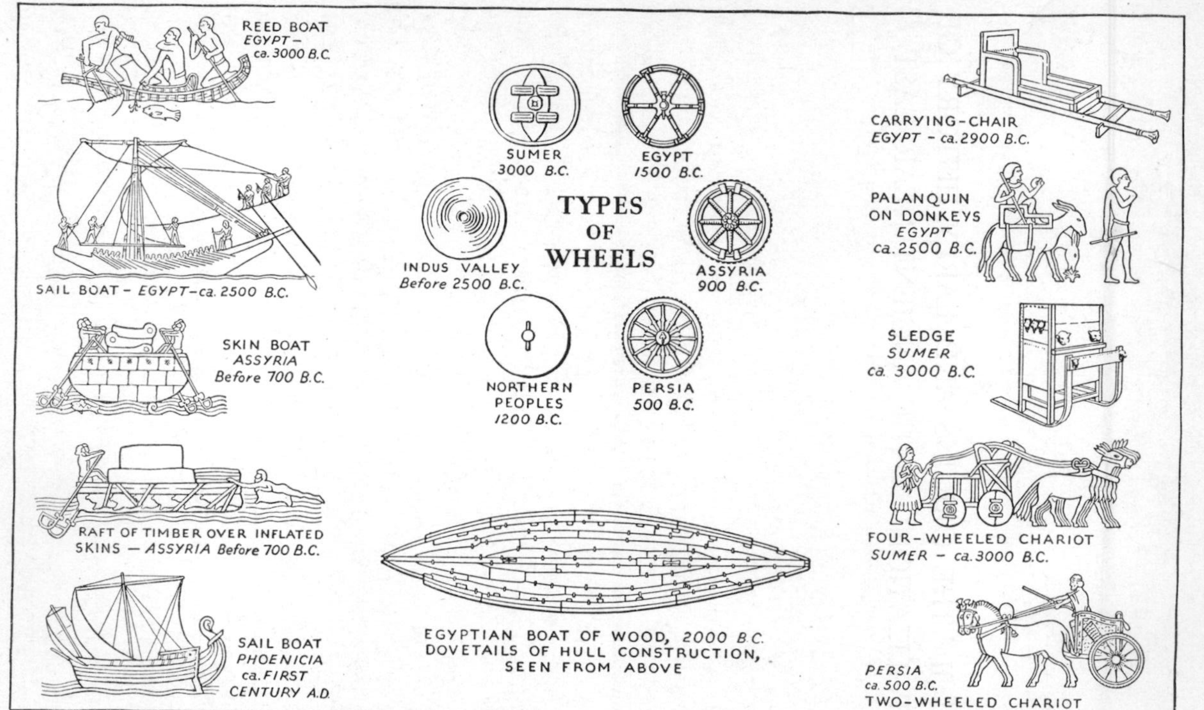
REED BOAT
EGYPT –
ca. 3000 B.C.
SAIL BOAT – EGYPT – ca. 2500 B.C.
SKIN BOAT
ASSYRIA
Before 700 B.C.
RAFT OF TIMBER OVER INFLATED
SKINS – ASSYRIA Before 700 B.C.
SAIL BOAT
PHOENICIA
ca. FIRST
CENTURY A.D.
TYPES
OF
WHEELS
SUMER
3000 B.C.
EGYPT
1500 B.C.
INDUS VALLEY
Before 2500 B.C.
ASSYRIA
900 B.C.
NORTHERN
PEOPLES
1200 B.C.
PERSIA
500 B.C.
EGYPTIAN BOAT OF WOOD, 2000 B.C.
DOVETAILS OF HULL CONSTRUCTION,
SEEN FROM ABOVE
CARRYING-CHAIR
EGYPT – ca. 2900 B.C.
PALANQUIN
ON DONKEYS
EGYPT
ca. 2500 B.C.
SLEDGE
SUMER
ca. 3000 B.C.
FOUR-WHEELED CHARIOT
SUMER – ca. 3000 B.C.
PERSIA
ca. 500 B.C.
TWO-WHEELED CHARIOT

TRANSPORTATION *in the Ancient Near East*

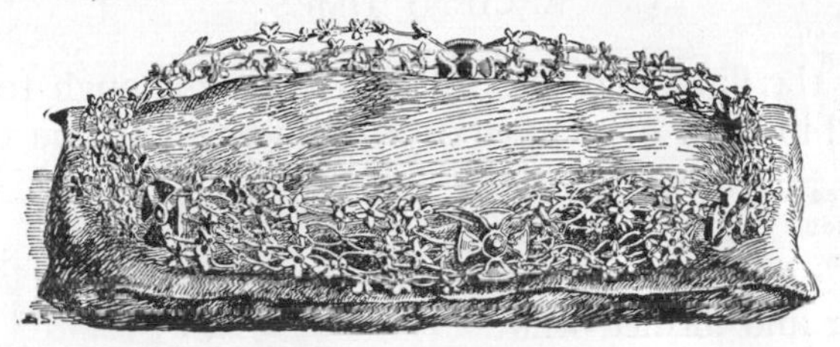

Chapter III · *The Story of Egypt: The Rise of Civilization and the Pyramid Age*

Section 5. The First Union of Egypt and the Rise of Civilization

Agriculture and irrigation

55. As we take up again our study of the early Near East we return to Egypt. We remember how we followed the hunters of North Africa from the drying plateau down to the well-watered floor of the Nile valley, and we recall how these hunters learned to feed herds of once wild cattle in stockades and to plant fields of grain. Grain, of course, cannot grow without water, and these early Egyptians, living in a country without rain, had to make a simple machine for lifting water from the river or from canals filled by the river. In this way the irrigatio[illegible] trenches were kept full of water until the grain ripened. T[illegible] Egyptians of today still continue to use the ancient [illegible] lifting machine (Fig. 25), and our ancestors inherite[illegible] the well sweep once common in New England.

56. The soil of Egypt (§ 28) was enriched each yea[illegible] overflow of the river; for the muddy waters of the Nile co[illegible]tinued to rise above its banks every summer, then to spread

Note. The Tiara, or Diadem, at the top of this page was found resting on the head of an Egyptian princess of the Feudal Age as she lay in her coffin. The diadem had been placed there nearly four thousand years ago. It is in the form of a chaplet, or wreath, of star flowers wrought of gold and set with bright-colored, costly stones, and is one of the best examples of the work of the Egyptian goldsmiths and jewelers. It is shown here lying on a cushion.

far over the flats, and to stand there long enough to deposit a very thin layer of rich earthy sediment. In time this sediment filled a large bay at the mouth of the river and formed what we now call the Nile Delta. At the present day the Delta and the valley above, as far as the First Cataract (see map, p. 66), contain together over twelve thousand square miles of cultivable soil, about the area of Massachusetts and Connecticut. In the Late Stone Age, however, the area which could be cultivated must have been much smaller, for at that time the valley was still largely occupied by extensive marshes, and only here and there between the marshes was [illegible]ossible to plant and [illegible]st a crop. Further- [illegible] the fierce and rapid [illegible] of the river in the [illegible] above the Delta made the shores there less easy to cultivate. But in the Delta, where the river branched out into smaller streams with slower currents, the marshes were easier to reclaim for cultivation.

Soil and area of Egypt, ancient and modern

FIG. 25. *An Egyptian* SHADOOF, *the Oldest of* WELL SWEEPS, *Irrigating the Fields*

The man below stands in the water, holding his leather bucket (*A*). The pole (*B*) of the sweep is above him, with a large ball of dried Nile mud on its lower end (*C*) as a lifting weight, or counterpoise, seen just behind the supporting post (*D*). This man lifts the water into a mud basin (*E*). A second man (in the middle) lifts it from this first basin (*E*) to a second basin (*F*), into which he is just emptying his bucket. A third man (*G*) lifts the water from the middle basin (*F*) to the uppermost basin (*H*) on the top of the bank, where it runs off to the left into trenches spreading over the fields. The low water makes necessary three successive lifts (to *E*, to *F*, to *H*), continued without ceasing, night and day, for one hundred days. The weird and plaintive songs of the shadoof-worker are heard day and night along the Nile

Leadership of the Delta and rise of government

57. Gradually the people of the Delta outstripped the dwellers on the upper river and became more advanced in their manner of living. This advance led to the first regulations of community life, which finally became government. Government is an extensive organization for conducting the affairs of a community or nation. It grew up very slowly as a community felt the need of a leader. The people might first need him to help them defend themselves against their enemies in war, but the leadership of a warrior chieftain did not always result in very good government. Much more useful in the community was a leader to control and guide the men who were appointed to look after the trenches and canals which brought in the water to irrigate the fields. The need of good men to manage this irrigation system, as we call it, would gradually lead to better government.

The overflow of the river (called the inundation) often clogged the canals with mud, so that the men of a whole group of villages would go out together to dig out and clear the canals. They knew that if they did not do so there would be no water for the grain fields, no harvest, and finally no bread. The leader of one of these groups of Delta villages probably became in time a local chieftain who controlled the irrigation trenches and canals of the district. To him the people of the district were obliged to carry every season a share of the grain or flax which they gathered from their fields. These shares of grain or flax were the earliest taxes, and the chieftain's control of the canals and collection of such taxes formed the earliest government.

The Two Kingdoms: Lower Egypt and Upper Egypt

58. Eventually some one of these Delta chieftains, who was probably both a good irrigation engineer and a good fighter, conquered the rival chieftains in the other districts and united all the Delta into a kingdom which we call Lower Egypt, for it was lower on the river. The King of Lower Egypt wore a red crown like this: 𓋔, with a curious spiral in front. There must have been a long line of such Kings of Lower

Egypt, probably lasting for several centuries, but we know the names of only six. They are important, for they are the earliest known royal names in human history. In the same way there also arose another kingdom, extending up the Nile valley from the southern apex of the Delta to the region of the First Cataract. This stretch of over five hundred miles of the valley proper we call Upper Egypt, for it is on the *upper* course of the river, although lower on the map. The King of Upper Egypt wore a tall white crown like this:. Of these Kings of Upper Egypt there must likewise have been a long line, but their names are unknown to us.

The Two Kingdoms: Copper-Stone Age

59. These two kingdoms, Upper Egypt and Lower Egypt, were the earliest known nations. Their rule probably reached back nearly seven thousand years, that is, nearly to the year 5000 B.C., and lasted for some centuries. There was a capital in each kingdom, where the king lived, while the people lived along the river in villages. The royal buildings and the huts of the peasants have all disappeared, but on the edge of the desert behind each village the people buried their dead in shallow pit-graves. The excavation of these graves shows that metal was very little used; for the art of mining was still hardly known, and little metal was to be had. As long as men continued to use metal only for making a few copper pins, or beads for the women, or an occasional tiny chisel, metal played an unimportant part in daily life. Stone tools and weapons still continued in common use.

First union of all Egypt

60. There must have been much traffic between the Two Kingdoms, for they were of course connected by the Nile. Being thus in close contact, they often fell out with each other, and there were many wars between them. Finally, perhaps in the Forty-third Century B.C., although we are not sure about the date, a powerful King of Lower Egypt, whose name we do not know, marched southward out of the Delta and conquered his rival, the King of Upper Egypt. In this manner the Two Kingdoms were united under one king, who became King of

Upper and Lower Egypt. In order to show that he was ruler of both kingdoms he wore a new, double crown like this: 𓋖, made up of the two older crowns of the once separate kingdoms (pp. 53–54). He ruled the earliest known government controlling a population of several millions.

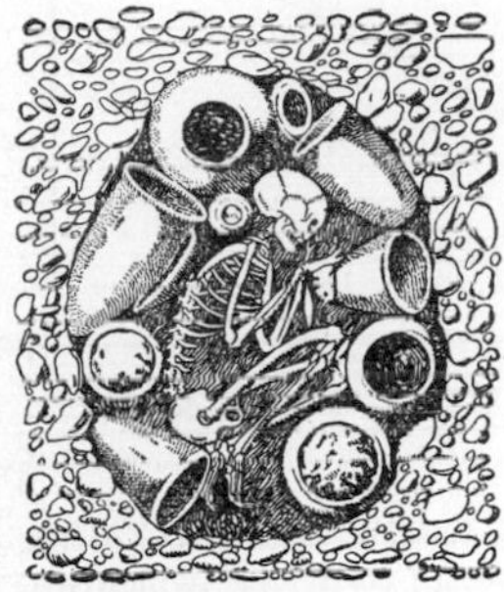

FIG. 26. *Looking down into the* GRAVE *of an Egyptian of the First Union*

An oval pit four or five feet deep. The body is surrounded by pottery jars which once contained food and drink

Place of the First Union in history

61. We shall call this first Kingdom of Upper and Lower Egypt the First Union as a matter of convenience, although this was not its ancient name. It lasted probably over eight hundred years, and had many kings, who lived at Heliopolis (or Sun-City), the first capital of Egypt (see map, p. 66). Situated midway between the Two Kingdoms, Heliopolis always remained the most sacred and influential of Egyptian cities. The history of the First Union is the most important chapter in the entire human story, because civilization arose in the age of the First Union. The people of the two united kingdoms made very important advances resulting in the production or invention of the remainder of those things which modern peoples regard as necessary to civilization (§ 5). Let us now see what those things were.

Beginning of plow culture; introduction of agricultural machinery

62. We have seen that agriculture greatly improved human conditions and made it possible for men to give up the hunting life and to live in villages surrounded by little grain fields. But those grain fields had, up to this time, been cultivated by hand with the hoe, — a slow and laborious method of work. It greatly limited the amount of land which could be cultivated. Only very small fields of grain were possible. Finally it occurred to some clever Egyptian that he might lengthen the handle of his hoe so that it could be fastened to a yoke

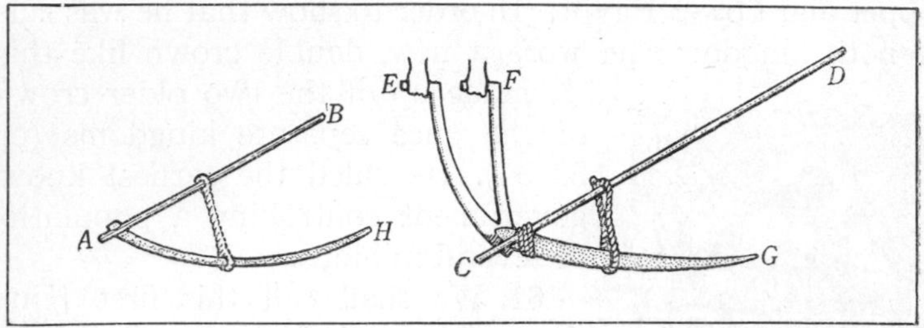

Fig. 27. *An Egyptian Wooden* Hoe *(Left) and the Wooden* Plow *(Right) which grew out of it*

The handle of the hoe (*A–B*) has been lengthened to become the beam of the plow (*C–D*). The upper end (*D*) of the beam was fastened to a yoke which was attached to the horns of the two oxen. To guide the new ox-drawn hoe, handles for the plowman's use (*E* and *F*) were necessary. These were attached at the point where the beam (*C–D*) and plowshare (*C–G*, once the hoe blade *A–H*) met. The first plows had only one handle, affixed to one side of the juncture of beam and share, but the Egyptians soon discovered the advantage of attaching two handles

resting on the horns of two oxen. By affixing handles to the new machine the farmer could then guide it across his fields as the oxen dragged it along before him (Fig. 28). Thus hoe culture was transformed into plow culture.

This invention of the first agricultural machinery marked a new epoch, for it enabled man to begin the use of animal power, that is, power other than the strength of man or woman. In this way much greater power was for the first time applied to the work of cultivating the fields. This meant as much for the increase of food among ancient men as the introduction of improved agricultural machinery has meant in the wealth and progress of the United States. Thus Egypt became the first great agricultural nation. The annual income in grain was not only a source of greatly increased wealth to the people and the government, but also the first *portable* wealth. With it loans could be made, taxes paid, and business debts settled. In an age before there was any money this new and portable form of wealth made an enormous difference and aided in carrying the Egyptians forward toward civilization.

Fig. 28. Plow Culture *as compared with the Older and Much Slower Process of* Hoe Culture

This drawing, based on ancient Egyptian reliefs, shows us the immense advantage in power and speed gained by the man who yoked his oxen to the plow and plowed an acre in a day, while the man who bent all day over the hoe could not possibly do more than scratch the surface of a quarter of an acre. The plow thus multiplied by at least four the amount of acreage that might be put under cultivation. The total harvest of the entire country, therefore, was likewise multiplied by four; the people had four times as much grain as before; the king received four times as much taxes

First national irrigation system

63. The large increase in the extent of the cultivated fields made the central government of the whole nation more important than ever, for the enlarged area of cultivation required an immensely increased amount of water for irrigating the fields. The little local systems of canals were united into one enormous national system, which was controlled from the capital. The irrigation administration thus centralized in the hands of the king was without doubt the first great administrative machine in the history of human government. The king must have been much interested in his Department of Irrigation, for without it he could not expect the farmers to raise large crops or pay taxes into his treasury.

64. The important place occupied by agriculture in the government of the Egyptians may be seen in the names which were adopted for the different seasons of the year. There were three seasons in their first calendar, and they bore the names "Inundation," "Coming Forth" (meaning the coming forth of the fields from the inundation that had covered them), and "Harvest." The people who gave these names to the three seasons must have been irrigating *farmers*, since they named the seasons from the inundation and the condition of the cultivated fields.

Agricultural calendar

65. Each of these three seasons was four months long, and the month was measured by the moon. In like manner the North American Indians used to measure time by moons (that is, the period from one new moon to the next), and they would speak of a journey of sixty days or so as a journey of two moons, meaning two months. Unfortunately the moon-month varies in length from twenty-nine to thirty days, and it does not evenly divide the three hundred and sixty-five days of the year. The Egyptians, however, showed themselves much more practical in removing this inconvenience than did their ancient neighbors in other lands (§ 179).

Moon calendar

66. Probably long before the First Union the people of the Nile valley had discovered the number of days in a year, although they did not at first know that their reckoning of three hundred and sixty-five days overlooked a fraction of about a quarter of a day. Retaining the twelve-month year which was derived from the use of the moon-month, they decided to have a calendar year of twelve months as before, but each of these twelve months under the new calendar was to have thirty days. These twelve thirty-day months thus formed a short year of three hundred and sixty days, to which the new calendar added five feast days, a kind of holiday period five days long at the end of the year. This gave them a calendar year of three hundred and sixty-five days as before. Having the months all of the same length, it was the most practical and convenient calendar ever adopted.

Thirty-day month and first practical calendar

67. By means of astronomy it is possible to compute the date when this calendar year was invented and introduced, and we now know that this great invention was made in 4236 B.C.[1] This is the earliest dated event in human history. It is important to remember also that this early Egyptian calendar, invented in the Forty-third Century B.C., is the very one which has descended to us after more than six thousand years, — unfortunately with inconvenient alterations in the lengths of the months. For these alterations, however, the Egyptians were not responsible, and even the additional quarter of a day, necessitating a leap year of three hundred and sixty-six days every four years, was finally known to the Egyptians.

Earliest fixed date in history

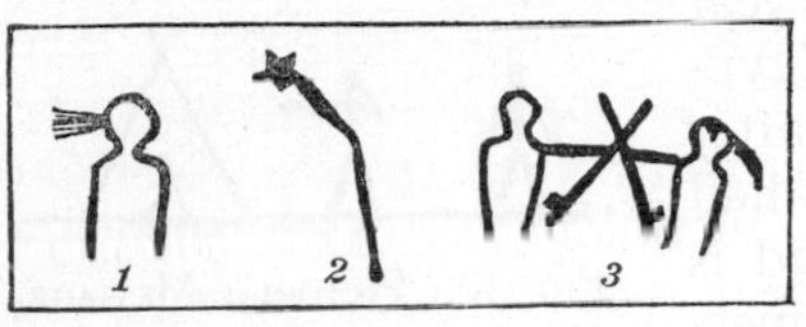

Fig. 29. *Part of a Dakota Chief's List of Seventy-one* Named Years

Lone Dog, a Dakota chief, had a buffalo robe with seventy-one named years recorded on it, beginning in 1800, when he was a child of four. A year when whooping cough was very bad was called the Whooping-Cough Year; its sign shows a human head coughing violently (*1*). Another year, very plentiful in meteors, was called the Meteor Year, and its sign was a rude drawing of a falling meteor (*2*). A third year saw the arrangement of peace between the Dakotas and the Crows; its sign was therefore two Indians, with differing style of hair, indicating the two different tribes, exchanging pipes of peace (*3*). Thus, instead of saying, as we do, that a thing happened in the year 1813, the Indian said it happened in the Whooping-Cough Year, and by examining his table of years he could tell how far back that year was

68. The months in this calendar were numbered, and thus furnished a very practical means of identifying any particular *month*. It did not, however, furnish any way of identifying a particular *year*. If we are dealing only with the *current* year, we may date a business agreement or the time when a payment falls due by simply mentioning the month and the day of the month; but if we are dealing with events in some other year, or if we wish to refer to an occurrence of several years back, the *year* must in some way be identified. Our convenient system of *num-*

Years identified by names

[1] The date, 4241 B.C., formerly calculated for this event, contained a small error in the factors used. After this error is corrected, the calculation gives 4236 B.C. as the correct year.

bering years beginning with some great event, like the birth of Christ, was still unknown. In order to have some means of identifying a particular year when it was long past, the Egyptians gave each year a name after some important event which had happened in it. This method is still in use among the North American Indians and even among ourselves, as people in Chicago say "the year of the great fire," or as English people say "the year of the armistice." We find the earliest written monuments of Egypt dated by means of named years.

FIG. 30. PICTORIAL MESSAGE *Scratched on Wood by Alaskan Indians*

A figure with empty hands hanging down helplessly, palms down, as an Indian gesture for uncertainty, ignorance, emptiness, or nothing, means "no." A figure with one hand on its mouth means "eating" or "food." It points toward the tent, and this means "in the tent." The whole is a message stating, "There is no food in the tent"

Lists of years and kings

69. Lists of year-names then began to be kept. As each year-name usually mentioned some great event, these lists of year-names were thus lists of such events; and when we find one, it is a very instructive record of important happenings. The earliest year-list of this kind in human history now surviving, called the Palermo Stone (because it is preserved in the museum at Palermo, Sicily), began about 3400 B.C. and contained, when complete, the names of some seven hundred years, ending about 2700 B.C. Later the Egyptians found it more convenient to number the years of each king's reign, and then to date events in the first year of King So-and-so or the tenth year of King So-and-so. Finally they had lists of past kings covering many centuries.

Pictorial records

70. Such records were at first only pictures, like those of the Dakota chief's list of years (Fig. 29). As time went on, the *business* of the government and the people made it necessary to have records of transactions. A farmer, for example, might want to know how much he had paid as taxes. He might scratch a rude picture of his basket grain-measure and a number of strokes on the mud wall of his hut, to indicate the number of measures of grain he had paid. The use of these picture signs was the earliest step leading toward writing. Such picture writing survives in use among the still uncivilized North American Indians. The Alaskan natives send messages in picture form, scratched on a piece of wood. Fig. 30 might be read by one man, "No food in the tent," while another might read, "Lack of meat in the tepee" or "No game in the camp." Such pictures thus conveyed ideas only, without representing the *exact words*. Among the American Indians the desire of a chief to record his own brave deeds also led to picture records of them (Fig. 31). It should be noticed again that the *exact words* are not indicated by this record, but the chief's brave action is merely so suggested that it might be put into words in a number of different ways. Such purely picture records had already been made in Egypt under the Two Kingdoms long before the First Union, and they continued to be used occasionally even after the end of the First Union (Figs. 32 and 37).

FIG. 31. PICTORIAL RECORD *of the* VICTORY *of a Dakota Chief named Running Antelope*

This Dakota Indian prepared his autobiography in a series of eleven drawings, of which this is but one. It records how he slew five hostile braves in a single day. The hero, Running Antelope, with rifle in hand, is mounted upon a horse. His shield bears a falcon, the animal emblem of his family, while beneath the horse is a running antelope, which is of course intended to inform you of the hero's name. We see the trail of his horse as he swept around the copse at the left, in which were concealed the five hostile braves whom he slew. Of these, one figure bearing a rifle represents all five, while four other rifles in the act of being discharged indicate the number of braves in the copse

71. But this picture stage, beyond which native American records never passed, was not real writing. Two steps had to be taken before the picture records could become *phonetic writing*, and both of these steps were taken under the kings of the First Union. These two steps were as follows:

First step leading from pictorial to phonetic stage

First, each object drawn had to gain a fixed form, always the same and always recognized as the sign for a *particular word* denoting that object. Thus, it would become a habit that the drawing of a loaf should always be read "loaf," not "bread" or "food"; the sign for a leaf would always be read "leaf," not "foliage."[1]

FIG. 32. *Example of Egyptian* WRITING *in the* PICTORIAL STAGE

Interpretation: Above is the falcon, symbol of a king (cf. the falcon on the shield of Running Antelope in Fig. 31), leading a human head by a cord; behind the head is a thicket of papyrus plants growing out of the ground, to which the head is attached; below is a single-barbed harpoon head and a little rectangle (the sign of a lake). The whole tells the picture story that the falcon king led captive the men of the Harpoon Lake in the Papyrus Land (that is, the Delta)

72. The *second* step then naturally followed; that is, the leaf, for example, might become the sign for the *syllable* "leaf" wherever it might occur. By the same process might become the sign for the syllable "bee" wherever found. Thus, with a means of writing the syllables "bee" and "leaf," the next step was to put them together, , and they would then represent the word "belief." Notice, however, that in the word "belief" the sign has ceased to suggest the idea of an insect. It now represents only the *syllable* "be." That is to say, has become a *phonetic* sign.

Second step leading from pictorial to phonetic stage

73. If the writing of the Egyptians had remained merely a series of pictures, such words as "belief," "hate," "love," "beauty," and the like could never have been written. But when a large number of their pictures had become phonetic signs, each representing

Advantage of phonetic signs

[1] We are of course obliged to use *English* words and syllables here, and consequently the signs also are not Egyptian but are devised for this demonstration.

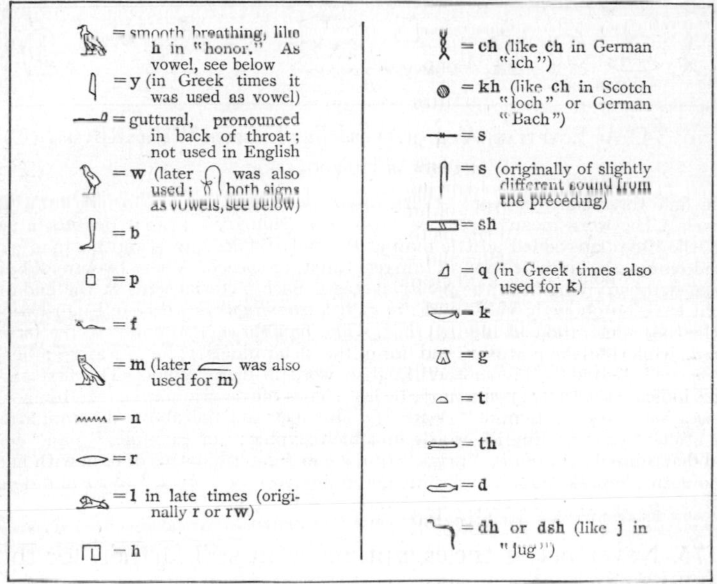

= smooth breathing, like h in "honor." As vowel, see below
= y (in Greek times it was used as vowel)
= guttural, pronounced in back of throat; not used in English
= w (later was also used; both signs as vowels, see below)
= b
= p
= f
= m (later was also used for m)
= n
= r
= l in late times (originally r or rw)
= h
= ch (like ch in German "ich")
= kh (like ch in Scotch "loch" or German "Bach")
= s
= s (originally of slightly different sound from the preceding)
= sh
= q (in Greek times also used for k)
= k
= g
= t
= th
= d
= dh or dsh (like j in "jug")

FIG. 33. *The Egyptian* ALPHABET

Each of these letters represents a consonant. The Egyptians of course *pronounced* their words with vowels as we do, but they did not *write* the vowels. This will be clear from a study of Fig. 34. Just as the consonants *w* and *y* are sometimes used as vowels in English, so three of the Egyptian consonants came to be employed as vowels in Greek times. The first letter (smooth breathing) was thus used as *a* or *e*; the second letter (*y*), as *i*; and the fourth (*w*), as *u* or *o*

a syllable, it was possible for the Egyptians to write any word, whether that word meant a thing of which they could draw a picture or not. This possession of *phonetic* signs was what made real writing for the first time. It arose among these Nile-dwellers earlier than anywhere else in the ancient world.

Syllable signs and sign-groups

74. Egyptian writing contained at last over six hundred signs, many of them representing whole syllables, like . The Egyptian scribes gradually learned many groups of such syllable signs. Each group, like , represented a *word*. Writing thus became for them a large number of sign-groups, each group being a word, and a series of such groups formed a sentence.

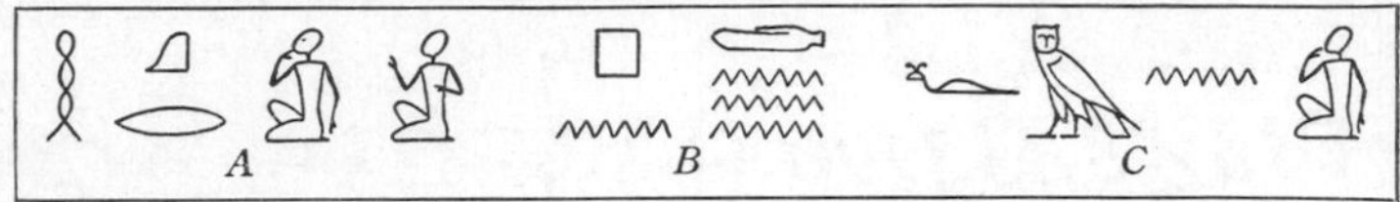

FIG. 34. *An* EGYPTIAN WORD (A) *and Two* ENGLISH WORDS (B) *and* (C) *written in* HIEROGLYPHIC

The first three signs in word *A* are *ch-q-r* (see Fig. 33); we do not know the vowels. The word means "pauper" (literally, "hungry"); as it denotes a person, the Egyptians added a little man at the end. Before him is another man with hand on mouth, an indication of hunger, thirst, or speech. These two are old pictorial signs surviving from the pictorial stage. Such pictorial signs at the end of a word have no phonetic value and are called *determinatives*. *B* is an English word spelled for illustration in hieroglyphic. The first three signs indicate the letters *p-n-d*, while the three wavy lines form the determinative for "water"; hence *p-n-d* spells "pond." *C* is another English word in hieroglyphic. The first three signs indicate the letters *f-m-n*, and the last sign is the determinative for "hunger"; hence *f-m-n* spells "famine." With the alphabet and the above determinatives the student can put English words into hieroglyphic; for example, "man" (*m-n* and determinative of man), "drink" (*d-r-n-k* and determinative of man with hand on mouth), "speak" (*s-p-k* and same determinative), or "brook" (*b-r-k* and determinative for "water," as in "pond")

Alphabetic signs, or letters

75. Nevertheless the Egyptians went still farther, for they finally possessed a series of signs each representing only a *letter*, — that is, *alphabetic* signs, or, as we say, real letters. There were twenty-four letters in this alphabet, which was known in Egypt by the end of the First Union, that is, by the Thirty-fifth Century B.C. It was thus the earliest alphabet known. At that time the Egyptians might have written their language with twenty-four alphabetic letters if the *sign*-group habit had not been too strong for the scribes, just as the *letter*-group habit is strong enough with us today to prevent the introduction of a simplified phonetic system of spelling English. If we smile at the Egyptian's sign-groups, future generations may as justly smile at our often absurd letter-groups.

Invention of writing materials

76. It was probably under the kings of the First Union that the Egyptians invented their *writing materials*. They found out that they could make an excellent paint or ink by thickening water with a little vegetable gum and then mixing in soot from the blackened pots over the fire. Dipping a pointed reed into this mixture,

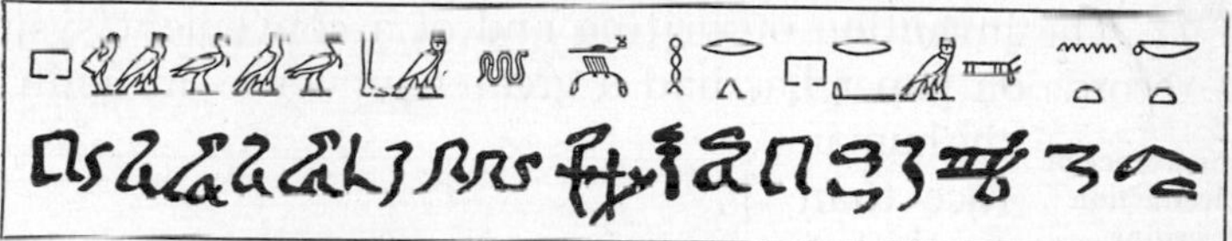

Fig. 35. *An Example of Egyptian* Hieroglyphic *(Upper Line) and its Equivalent in the* Rapid Running Hand *(Lower Line) written with Pen and Ink on Papyrus and called* Hieratic, *the Writing of All Ordinary Business*

The daily business of an Egyptian community of course required much writing and thousands of records. Such writing, after it began to be done with pen and ink on papyrus, soon became very rapid. In course of time, therefore, there arose a rapid, or running, hand in which each hieroglyphic sign was much abbreviated. This running hand is called *hieratic*. It corresponds to our handwriting, while hieroglyphic corresponds to our print. In the above example the signs in the lower row show clearly that they are the result of an effort to make quickly the signs in the hieroglyphic row above (compare sign for sign). We must notice also that the Egyptians wrote from right to left, for this line begins at the right and reads to the left. Vertical lines, that is, downward reading, were also employed (Fig. 58). A third, still more rapid and abbreviated hand, corresponding in some ways to our shorthand, arose later (Eighth Century B.C.). It was called *demotic*, and one of the versions on the Rosetta Stone (Fig. 203) is written in demotic

they found they could write very well. They also learned that they could split a kind of river reed, called papyrus, into thin strips, and that they could write on them much better than on bits of pottery, bone, and wood, which were all they had at first. Desiring a larger sheet, they hit upon the idea of pasting their papyrus strips together with overlapping edges. This gave them a very thin sheet; but by pasting *two* such sheets together, with the grain crossing at right angles, they produced a smooth, tough, nearly white or pale-yellow paper. The Egyptians had thus made the discovery that a thin vegetable membrane offers a most practical surface on which to write, and the world has since discovered nothing better. In this way arose pen, ink, and paper. All three of these inventions descended to us from the Egyptians, and paper still bears its ancient name, *papyros*[1] (Latin, *papyrus*), but slightly changed.

[1] The change from *papyros* to "paper" is really a very slight one, for *os* is merely the Greek grammatical ending, which must be omitted in English. This leaves us *papyr* as the ancestor of our word "paper," from which it differs by only one letter.

77. The invention of writing and of a convenient system of records on paper has had a greater influence in uplifting the human race than any other achievement in the life of man. It was then and is now more important than all the battles ever fought and all the constitutions ever written.

Importance of introduction of writing

FIG. 36. BOAT *carrying the Standard of a Trading Town, painted on a* POTTERY JAR *of the First Union*

These many-oared boats were probably the first vessels to be constructed with wooden hulls. The standard is mounted on the top of a pole set up beside the smaller deck-house. The symbol on the standard is the figure of a bird. A mooring rope is hanging from the bow. The antelopes, ostriches, and plants scattered around in the background represent the scenery through which the boat passed. (Courtesy of the Metropolitan Museum of Art)

78. Writing must have aided greatly in the transaction of business. Under the First Union we find numerous paintings of many-oared Nile boats on the pottery jars found in the graves of the period. These are the earliest boats of which we have any knowledge. They show us that the river towns were carrying on brisk trade with each other; for each boat carries on a pole a standard, the symbol of the town from which it came. The cemeteries of the First Union have thus far yielded about three hundred of these standard-bearing boats, and two hundred and twenty-two of these came from the western Delta. This shows us how the old kingdom of Lower Egypt was leading in commerce. It indicates also that the seaport of Egypt on the Mediterranean was already at the western corner of the Delta, where Alexander the Great later founded Alexandria,

Commerce of the First Union

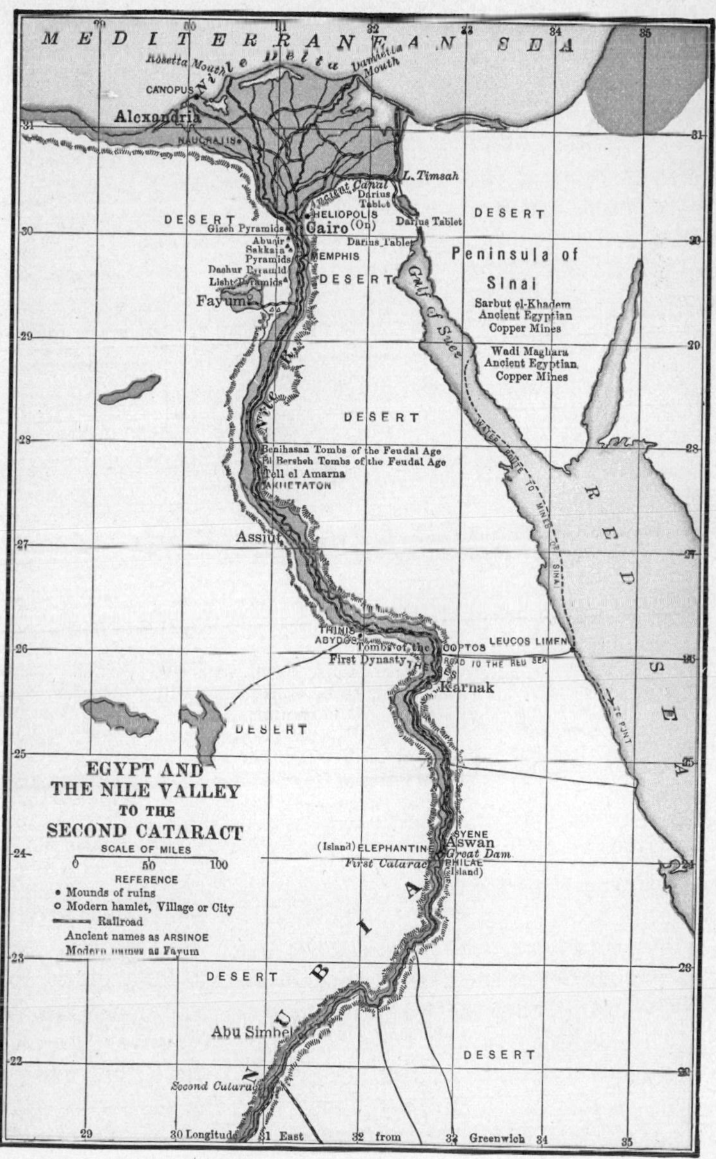
MEDITERRANEAN SEA
Nile Delta
Rosetta Mouth
Damietta Mouth
CANOPUS
Alexandria
NAUCRATIS
L. Timsah
Ancient Canal
Darius Tablet
HELIOPOLIS
Cairo (On)
Darius Tablet
Darius Tablet
DESERT
Gizeh Pyramids
Abusir
Sakkara Pyramids
MEMPHIS
Dashur Pyramid
Lisht Pyramids
Fayum
DESERT
Gulf of Suez
Peninsula of Sinai
Sarbut el-Khadem
Ancient Egyptian
Copper Mines
Wadi Maghara
Ancient Egyptian
Copper Mines
DESERT
Nile R.
DESERT
Benihasan Tombs of the Feudal Age
El Bersheh Tombs of the Feudal Age
Tell el Amarna
AKHETATON
WATER ROUTE TO MINES OF SINAI
RED SEA
Assiut
THINIS
ABYDOS
Tombs of the First Dynasty
THEBES
COPTOS
LEUCOS LIMEN
ROAD TO THE RED SEA
Karnak
TO PUNT
DESERT
EGYPT AND
THE NILE VALLEY
TO THE
SECOND CATARACT
SCALE OF MILES
0 50 100
REFERENCE
• Mounds of ruins
○ Modern hamlet, Village or City
Railroad
Ancient names as ARSINOE
Modern names as Fayum
SYENE
Aswan
Great Dam
(Island) ELEPHANTINE
First Cataract
PHILAE (Island)
NUBIA
DESERT
Abu Simbel
DESERT
Second Cataract
30 Longitude 31 East 32 from 33 Greenwich 34
29
35

the greatest seaport of ancient times. And from there, nearly three thousand years before Alexander, Egyptian trade and civilization were to pass by ship to Crete and thence to Europe.

79. The consolidation of the North and South which we have called the First Union did not endure. In time the two kingdoms fell apart and for a period existed independently side by side. Then there arose a strong leader in Upper Egypt whose name was Menes. First he made himself king of the old kingdom of Upper Egypt. Then he invaded Lower Egypt and conquered it (about 3360 B.C.). This conquest brought about a new union, over which ruled a king of *Upper* Egypt. Menes inherited the civilization of the First Union. Just as the power and prosperity of the First Union was based on plow culture and the production of plentiful grain, so that of the Second Union grew out of the earliest mining on a large scale and the possession of plentiful copper.

Second Union founded by Menes (3360 B.C.)

80. The graves of the cemeteries of the First Union had contained many more tools and implements of copper than those of the Two Kingdoms. Copper axes and chisels were to be had in trade, and a few rare workmen possessed them. The First Union had therefore brought the Age of Metal much nearer. With the Second Union actually began the Age of Metal. The early kings of the Second Union were very proud of their ability to send mining expeditions into the mountains of the neighboring Peninsula of Sinai, and there we still find the long mining tunnels which they drove into the mountains. These are the earliest known copper mines, and the early successors of Menes had their people carve upon the neighboring rocks huge records of their presence there. These scenes are the oldest historical monuments known to us.

Age of Metal; beginning of royal mining expeditions

81. Not only did the early Pharaohs of the Second Union exploit the copper mines of Sinai, but they dispatched expeditions also northward by sea to Byblos, on the coast of

FIG. 37. *Oldest Known Royal* MONUMENT: *Mining Inscription of a King of the* SECOND UNION *Engraved on the Rocks of Sinai*

The king is represented twice wearing the tall white crown of Upper Egypt and once (center) wearing the curious crown of Lower Egypt, thus showing that this particular king ruled both of the old prehistoric divisions of the land. The earliest Egyptians told their story in this way by pictures instead of words. Another part of this picture-story is found in the arrangement of the first two figures at the left. The king, armed with stone mace and dagger (in his belt), grasps a kneeling captive by the hair and raises the mace for a fatal blow. The long-haired, bearded captive is a typical early Asiatic. The pictured story is that this king, by means of the military escort which protected his mining expedition, smote the Asiatics of Sinai and so established his right to mine copper in that region. Placed here as a record of the expedition, these gigantic figures of the Pharaoh, the earliest great historical monument, also served as a warning to any other Asiatics who might be tempted to molest later Egyptian mining expeditions in Sinai. The hieroglyphs in the two little rectangles at right and left give the name of the king. Expeditions, a few centuries later, were writing the whole story in hieroglyphs,— not forgetting even to complain of the heat in Sinai!

Syria. This port was very important because of the forests that lay behind it, and here the timber which Egypt needed was cut and loaded upon the Pharaoh's fleet to be shipped back to the Nile. This commerce across the southeastern corner of the Mediterranean, the earliest known sea-borne trade, was carried in the earliest seagoing ships of which we have any record. The importation of plentiful wood into Egypt resulted in its common use in house-building, boat-building, and all kinds of carpentry and furniture-making.

Egypt obtains wood from Syria

82. For some four hundred years the early kings of the Second Union built their tombs of sun-dried mud brick. A group of these tombs was discovered in Upper Egypt. They are the earliest royal buildings ever found. Then, probably about 3000 B.C., there was built in one of these brick tombs a burial chamber of *limestone blocks*. This was the beginning of architecture in stone, and the direct result of the possession of tools of copper by which the stone building blocks were cut and shaped.

Copper tools and beginning of stone architecture

83. Beginning thus about 3000 B.C., when the Second Union was about four hundred years old, its kings were able to erect stone tombs and stone temples. Such great stone buildings form records of the history of Egypt much fuller than the village cemeteries, with their pit-graves. We remember that these pit-graves are all that survive from the earlier stages of Egypt as a nation down through the Two Kingdoms and the First Union. In sharp contrast to the pit-graves the great stone buildings which began to rise after 3000 B.C. have made the Nile valley seem like a huge historical volume.

Stone buildings as historical records

SECTION 6. THE SECOND UNION OF EGYPT AND THE PYRAMID AGE (THIRTIETH TO TWENTY-FIFTH CENTURY B.C.)

84. In order to read the first chapter of this history in stone we must turn our attention to the royal cemetery at Gizeh. Here we find first the pyramids — the tombs of the kings — and then, clustering about the pyramids, great numbers of much smaller tombs of stone masonry. In these smaller tombs were buried the relatives of the king, and the great men of his court. As we shall see, these men, together with the king about whom they were grouped, formed the government of Egypt. Just as they formed a group around the king's palace in this life, so after death their tombs now cluster around the pyramid. The cemetery is thus a picture of the government of Egypt.

Royal cemetery

Such mighty buildings reveal many things about the men who built them. In the first place, the tombs tell us a great deal in regard to the *religion* of these people. They show us that the Egyptians believed in a life after death, and that to obtain such a life it was necessary to preserve the body from perishing. They built these tombs to shelter and protect the body. From this belief came also the practice of embalming, by which the body was preserved as a mummy (Fig. 71). It was then placed in the great tomb, in a small room deep under the masonry.

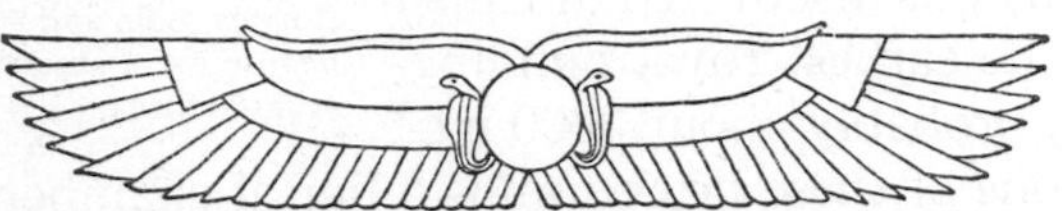

FIG. 38. *Winged* SUN-DISK, *Symbol of the Sun-god*

The sun's disk is in the middle, and two serpents (cobras), one on each side of it, rear their heads. The wings are those of a falcon, for in this form the Sun-god was believed to be a falcon flying across the sky. We shall later see how the other nations of the Near East adopted this Egyptian symbol

Egyptian gods and their symbols

85. The inscriptions in the tombs make known to us the many gods of the Egyptians, but there were two whom they worshiped above all others. The sun, which shines so gloriously in the cloudless Egyptian sky, was their greatest god, and their most splendid temples were erected for his worship. Indeed, the pyramid is a symbol sacred to the Sun-god. (See another symbol in Fig. 38.) They called him Re (pronounced *ray*). The other great power which they revered was the shining Nile. The great river and the fertile soil that he refreshes, and the green life that he brings forth,— all these the Egyptian thought of together as a single god, Osiris, the imperishable life of the earth which revives and fades every year with the change of the seasons. It was a beautiful and comforting thought to the Egyptian that this same life-giving power which furnished him his food in *this* world would care for him also in the *next*, when his body lay out in the cemetery on the edge of the desert. There were many Egyptian gods whose earthly symbols were *animals*, but the animal worship usually attributed to Egypt was a degeneration belonging to the last stage of the dying Egyptian religion. The animals were not gods in this early time, but only *symbols* of the divine beings, just as the winged sun-disk was a symbol of the Sun-god.

86. The great pyramid cemetery of Gizeh tells us about many other things besides the religion of the Egyptians. We have already learned that the Egyptian mechanics now worked with copper tools. The pyramids of Gizeh are a measure of what they could do with those tools. It is difficult to believe that these colossal stone buildings were erected by men whose ancestors, only a few generations earlier, were buried, with their flint knives, in pits scooped out on the margin of the desert. Complete mastery of stone building was a step taken very quickly, but we have seen that it was preceded by a very slow and gradual change from stone tools to those of metal. That Egyptian in Sinai who noticed the first bit of copper must have lived about two thousand years before these pyramids were built, and for almost two thousand years the knowledge of metal had no effect upon building. Only a few generations, indeed less than a century, before the earliest of the great stone pyramids, the Egyptian masons were still building the tombs of their kings out of sun-baked brick. Such a royal tomb was at first merely a chamber in the ground, covered with a flat wooden roof. On this roof was raised a mound of sand and gravel as the king's monument. We recall (§ 82) that the first piece of stone masonry ever put together, so far as we know, was a lining of limestone blocks to form the underground burial chamber of a royal tomb. The structure can hardly be called a building, for, like a cellar wall, it was all below ground.

Advance in building

87. The next step, a real building aboveground, was still of brick. Then, in the Thirtieth Century B.C., the royal architect Imhotep created the first architecture in stone. He built for his king, Zoser, a tomb which is the oldest surviving building of stone masonry in the world. Around this great tomb Imhotep erected a wonderful group of beautiful buildings, of the very

Imhotep, earliest architect in stone building

FIG. 39. *The Oldest Surviving* BUILDING *of Stone Masonry (Thirtieth Century* B.C.)

This terraced building, often called the step pyramid, was the tomb of King Zoser. It is about 200 feet high and in outward form seems to be a series of buildings like No. 6 in Fig. 41, placed one on top of another. It thus formed a tapering building out of which developed the pyramid form

finest limestone masonry, including two more tombs of the royal family. The fronts of these two tombs were adorned with stone supports so gracefully fluted that they look like the slender Greek columns of 2500 years later. And the artist whose mind conceived this beauty deserves far greater fame and respect than do the early kings or conquerors themselves.

Century and a quarter from earliest stone masonry to Great Pyramid

88. The erection of Imhotep's terraced building was an important step toward the construction of a pyramid. A generation later, so rapid was the progress, the king's architects were building the Great Pyramid of Gizeh (2885 B.C.). From the earliest piece of stone masonry to the construction of the Great Pyramid perhaps less than a century and a quarter elapsed. Most of this advance was made during the Thirtieth Century B.C., that is, between 3000 and 2900 B.C.

FIG. 40. *Front of Stone* TOMB-CHAPEL *erected by Imhotep*

Imhotep, the first great architect, was the originator of the pyramid tomb. He made his *stone* buildings with the forms and designs of the *wooden* buildings which were the only architecture of Egypt up to that time. The tall, slender, columnlike supports are not columns in the round, but are attached to ("engaged in") the masonry wall behind them. (After Lauer)

Such rapid progress in man's control of mechanical power can be found in no other period of the world's history until the Nineteenth Century of the Christian Era.

89. This progress becomes very real to us when we know that the Great Pyramid covers thirteen acres. It is a solid mass of masonry containing 2,300,000 blocks of limestone, each weighing on an average two and a half tons; that is, each block is as heavy as a large wagonload of coal. The sides of the pyramid at the base are 756 feet long,[1] and the building was originally nearly 500 feet high. Herodotus tells us that a hundred thousand men were working on this royal tomb for twenty years, and we can well believe it.

Vast size of the Great Pyramid

90. To manage and to feed a hundred thousand workmen around this great building must have required a very skillful ruler and a great number of trained leaders who were in the

[1] It should be remembered that the pyramid is *solid*. Compare the length of the Colosseum (about 600 feet), which is built around a *hollow* inclosure.

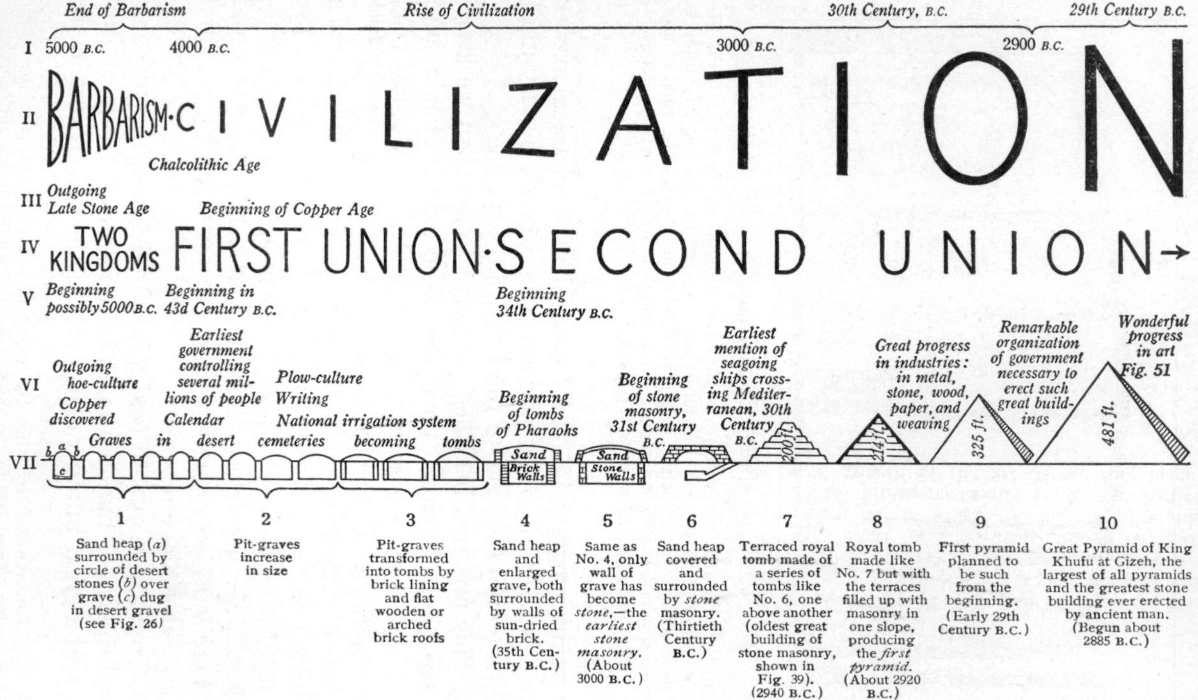

End of Barbarism
Rise of Civilization
30th Century, B.C.
29th Century B.C.
I
5000 B.C.
4000 B.C.
3000 B.C.
2900 B.C.
II
BARBARISM·CIVILIZATION
Chalcolithic Age
III
Outgoing Late Stone Age
Beginning of Copper Age
IV
TWO KINGDOMS
FIRST UNION·SECOND UNION→
V
Beginning possibly 5000 B.C.
Beginning in 43d Century B.C.
Beginning 34th Century B.C.
VI
Outgoing hoe-culture
Copper discovered
Earliest government controlling several millions of people
Calendar
Plow-culture
Writing
National irrigation system
Beginning of tombs of Pharaohs
Beginning of stone masonry, 31st Century B.C.
Earliest mention of seagoing ships crossing Mediterranean, 30th Century B.C.
Great progress in industries: in metal, stone, wood, paper, and weaving
Remarkable organization of government necessary to erect such great buildings
Wonderful progress in art Fig. 51
VII
Graves in desert cemeteries becoming tombs
a
b
b
c
Sand
Brick Walls
Sand
Stone Walls
200 ft.
214 ft.
325 ft.
481 ft.
1
Sand heap (a) surrounded by circle of desert stones (b) over grave (c) dug in desert gravel (see Fig. 26)
2
Pit-graves increase in size
3
Pit-graves transformed into tombs by brick lining and flat wooden or arched brick roofs
4
Sand heap and enlarged grave, both surrounded by walls of sun-dried brick. (35th Century B.C.)
5
Same as No. 4, only wall of grave has become stone,—the earliest stone masonry. (About 3000 B.C.)
6
Sand heap covered and surrounded by stone masonry. (Thirtieth Century B.C.)
7
Terraced royal tomb made of a series of tombs like No. 6, one above another (oldest great building of stone masonry, shown in Fig. 39). (2940 B.C.)
8
Royal tomb made like No. 7 but with the terraces filled up with masonry in one slope, producing the first pyramid. (About 2920 B.C.)
9
First pyramid planned to be such from the beginning. (Early 29th Century B.C.)
10
Great Pyramid of King Khufu at Gizeh, the largest of all pyramids and the greatest stone building ever erected by ancient man. (Begun about 2885 B.C.)
Not more than 125 years (from earliest stone masonry to the Great Pyramid)

FIG. 41. *Diagram of the* PROGRESS OF EGYPT *from Late Stone Age Barbarism to Highly Developed Civilization*

Notice the dates in Row I, beginning possibly 5000 B.C. and extending into the Twenty-ninth Century. In that period of about 2000 years Row II suggests the gradual decline and disappearance of barbarism and the appearance and growth of civilization. Row III indicates this period as the one when stone implements were at first partially and then more largely displaced by copper. The political developments while this was going on are shown in Row IV, beginning with the Two Kingdoms and passing through the First Union to the Second Union. Row VI then lists the most important things which made possible the displacement of barbarism by civilization, and the progress of early civilization. Finally, Row VII shows us how this advance is revealed in ancient cemeteries of Egypt. The body of the Egyptian peasant in Fig. 26 lay at the bottom of a grave above which was a low heap of sand surrounded by a circle of rough desert stones to keep the sand in place. No. *1*, above, shows this grave, cut down through the middle to expose the inside, with the sand-heap above it. In Nos. *2* and *3* we see these pit-graves becoming tombs of sun-dried brick masonry, with superstructures of such masonry appearing for the first time in No. *4*. The series (Nos. *1* to *4*) shows how the circle of stones around the sand-heap became real walls, first of brick (No. *4*) and then of stone masonry (No. *6*), enveloping the whole tomb, with the old sand-heap still in the inside. Tombs like No. *6* were then placed one above the other, producing a tapering terraced building (No. *7*), which was soon improved until it became a pyramid (No. *8*). Thus the sand-heap and its circle of stones were the germ out of which the mighty pyramids grew in the course of fifteen or twenty centuries. Notice how this wonderful growth in the art of building began with the sand-heap in the barbarism of the Late Stone Age, and carried the Egyptians out of barbarism and far into civilization in the thousand years from 4000 to 3000 B.C. It was itself one of the things which marked the early growth of civilization, and architecture passed from the earliest example of stone masonry (No. *5*) to the Great Pyramid in less than a century and a quarter. The Pyramids and their predecessors thus stand like milestones marking the long road by which man passed from barbarism to a highly developed civilization. We learn thus what were the *visible* things that we must understand as making up civilization in the beginning. But there were some necessary things which also reached a high development at the same time and which were *not visible*. These were a belief in right living and kindness to others, and that a good life here was necessary to happiness in the next world. At the close of the Gizeh Period a wise man said, "Established is the man whose standard is righteousness, who walketh according to its way."

king's service. The king who was able to undertake such vast works was the most powerful human being that the world had ever seen. He was so reverenced that the people did not mention him by name, but instead they spoke of the palace in which he lived, that is, Pharaoh, which means, in Egyptian, "Great House." Hence we may call the Second Union the "Age of the Pharaohs."

The Pharaohs

The Pharaoh's government

91. The Pharaoh had two kinds of officials to aid him in carrying on his government. There were the *local* officials who were scattered about through all Egypt, and the *central* officials who lived at the capital near the king. It was the duty of the *local* officials to collect taxes all over Egypt. It was also their business to try the law cases which arose, and every judge had before him the *written law*[1] which bade him judge justly.

The taxes received from the people were not in coined money, which did not yet exist, but in produce, such as live stock, grain, wine, honey, linen, and the like. These were kept in cattle-yards, granaries, and storehouses, — a large group of buildings which formed the treasury and central offices of the king, where hundreds on hundreds of clerks, with their reed pens and their rolls of papyrus, were daily keeping the king's records and accounts. The clerks had lists of the taxpayers' names and how much they owed, and they issued receipts when the taxes were paid, just as at the present day. Such arrangements did not arise in Europe until far down in the Roman Empire.

The royal city

92. Such government buildings made the capital a city of some size, — the largest which the life of man had yet produced. The chief quarter of the royal city was formed by the palace of the Pharaoh and the beautiful gardens which surrounded it. The palace and its grounds, surrounded by the villas of the king's officials, and the offices of the government, especially the great group of treasury buildings, — all these together formed the capital of Egypt, the royal city. It extended far southward from

[1] This Egyptian code of laws has unfortunately been lost.

FIG. 42. *The Great* SPHINX *of Gizeh and the* PYRAMID *of Khafre*

A sphinx was the portrait head of a king attached to the body of a lion. The Great Sphinx was the portrait of King Khafre (Fig. 51), before whose pyramid it lies like a sentinel guarding the mighty cemetery of Gizeh. The body is 187 feet long, and the head is 66 feet high

Gizeh and was later called Memphis. But the city was built of sun-baked brick and wood, and it has therefore vanished.

93. The city of the dead (the pyramids and the tombs clustering around them), being built of stone, has fortunately proved more lasting. It is possible here at Gizeh to follow the history of the royal family and their relatives for about one hundred and ten years. And the other pyramid cemeteries carry us still farther. From the summit of the Great Pyramid there is a grand view southward, down a splendid line of pyramids rising dimly as far as one can see on the southern horizon. We must remember that if each pyramid was a royal tomb, then each tomb of this kind means that a king lived, ruled, and died. One after another for about five hundred years these kings were buried, each in his pyramid, until the pyramid line was over sixty

Length and date of Pyramid Age

FIG. 43. *Relief* SCENE *from the* CHAPEL *of a Nobleman's Tomb in the Pyramid Age*

The tall figure of the nobleman stands at the right. He is inspecting three lines of cattle and a line of fowl brought before him. Note the two scribes who head the two middle rows. Each is writing with pen on a sheet of papyrus, and one carries two pens behind his ear. Such reliefs, after being carved, were colored in bright hues by the painter

miles long and thus marks out for us today some five hundred years of time. This period, from the middle of the Thirtieth to the middle of the Twenty-fifth Century B.C., is the first great age of Egyptian civilization after the land was united under one king.

Tomb-chapels of Pyramid Age; life they reveal

94. The Pyramid Age is the earliest period of human life which is very fully revealed to us in pictures produced at the time. These pictures are preserved in the tombs grouped around the pyramids. A stroll among these tombs is almost like a walk among the busy communities which flourished in this populous valley in the days of the pyramid-builders. Each tomb had its chapel, to which, it was thought, the dead nobleman who was buried beneath the tomb might return every day. Here, therefore, his relatives left food and drink for him. He would also find the stone walls of this room covered from floor to ceiling with carved pictures, beautifully painted, showing the daily life on the great farm or plantation which formed his estate.

FIG. 44. *Peasant* MILKING *in the Pyramid Age*

The cow is restive and the ancient cowherd has tied her hind legs. Behind her another man is holding her calf, which rears and plunges in the effort to reach the milk

Agriculture and cattle-raising; beasts of burden

95. Let us examine some of the pictures carved on the chapel walls. Here we see the tall figure of the nobleman himself as he stands looking out over his fields and inspecting the work going on there. These scenes in the Egyptian tombs of the Pyramid Age are the oldest known pictures showing the work of planting and cultivating a field. Here, too, we see the herds, long lines of sleek, fat cattle, some of them milch cows led up and tied to be milked, others used as beasts of burden, for we notice the oxen drawing the plow. But we find no horses in these tombs of the Pyramid Age, for the horse was still unknown in Egypt. Pictured very often on the walls, however, we see the donkeys with loads of grain on their backs, for it would have been impossible to harvest the fields without them.

Coppersmith and works of metal

96. On the next wall we find again the tall figure of the nobleman overseeing the booths and yards where the craftsmen of his estate are working. Yonder is the coppersmith. He had never heard of his ancestor who picked up the first bead of copper, perhaps two thousand years earlier. Much progress had been made since that day. This man could make excellent copper tools of all sorts, but the tool which demanded the greatest skill was the long, flat ripsaw, which the smith knew how to hammer into shape out of a broad strip of copper five or six feet long. Such a saw may be seen in use in Fig. 46. Besides this he knew how to make one that would saw great blocks of stone for the pyramids. Moreover, this coppersmith was already able to deliver orders of surprising size, such as thirteen hundred feet (about a quarter of a mile) of copper drainpiping for a pyramid temple (Fig. 55).

97. On the same wall we see a craftsman who can cut very hard semiprecious stones. We call him a *lapidary*. He holds up for the nobleman's admiration splendid stone bowls cut from diorite. Although this kind of stone is as hard as steel, the bowl is ground to such thinness that the sunlight glows through its dark-gray sides. Other workmen are cutting and grinding tiny pieces of beautiful blue turquoise. These pieces they set together with wonderful accuracy, so that they form a pattern on the surface of a magnificent golden vase just made ready by the goldsmith. The booth of the goldsmith is filled with workmen and apprentices. They hammer and cast, solder and fit together, richly wrought jewelry which can hardly be improved upon by the work of the best goldsmiths and jewelers of today.

Lapidary, goldsmith, and jeweler

98. In the next space on this wall we find the potter no longer building up his jars and bowls with his fingers alone, as in the Stone Age. He now sits before a small horizontal *wheel*, upon which he deftly shapes the whirling vessel. When the soft clay vessels are ready, they are no longer unevenly burned in an *open* fire, as among the Late Stone Age potters in the Swiss lake-villages, but here in the Egyptian potter's yard are long rows of *closed* furnaces of hard clay as tall as a man. When the pots are packed into these furnaces they are burned evenly, because they are protected from the wind. Here also the craftsmen are making glass in the form of glaze. This art the Egyptians had discovered centuries before. They made brilliant tiles covered with gorgeous glazes for beautifying house and palace walls. Later the Egyptian craftsmen learned how to make glass objects, that is, not merely spread as a glaze on other substances but shaped into many-colored bottles and vases, which were widely exported.

Potter's wheel and furnace; earliest glass

FIG. 45. *Potter's* WHEEL *and* FURNACE

The potter squats before his horizontal wheel, which is like a flat, round plate on which the jar revolves while it is being shaped. He keeps the wheel turning with one hand, and with the other he shapes the soft clay jar as it whirls on the wheel. This wheel is the ancestor of our lathe. The completed pots are stacked in the brick furnace at the left. The furnace is already very hot, for the man tending the fire holds up his hand to shield his face from the heat. The man in the center places the pots in rows. The three men at the right are smoothing off the rough places which the wheel cannot take care of. Perhaps one of them is polishing the outside of the burned pot with a shell,— a custom of the ancient Egyptian as well as of his present-day descendant

Weavers and tapestry-makers

99. The scenes on the wall show us also women weaving linen cloth. The picture, of course, gives no idea of the fineness of the fabric, but fortunately pieces of royal linen, wrapped around the mummy of a king of this age, have survived. This product of the ancient Egyptian *hand* loom is so finely woven that it can scarcely be distinguished from silk, and the best work of the modern *machine* loom is coarse in comparison. With such a hand loom these weavers of Egypt furnished the earliest known specimens of tapestry, to be hung on the walls of the Pharaoh's palace or stretched out to shade the roof garden of the nobleman's villa.

Paper-makers

100. On the next wall we find huge bundles of papyrus reeds, which bare-legged men are gathering along the edge of the Nile marsh. These reeds are split into long, thin strips, which are then laid overlapping and pasted together. The resulting long, narrow sheets are again pasted together "two ply," one on the other, forming tough whitish or pale-yellow paper. Egyptian ships on the Mediterranean (Fig. 56) added bales of this Nile paper to their cargoes and carried it to Syria and Europe. Egypt thus came to be the world's paper mill for 3000 years.

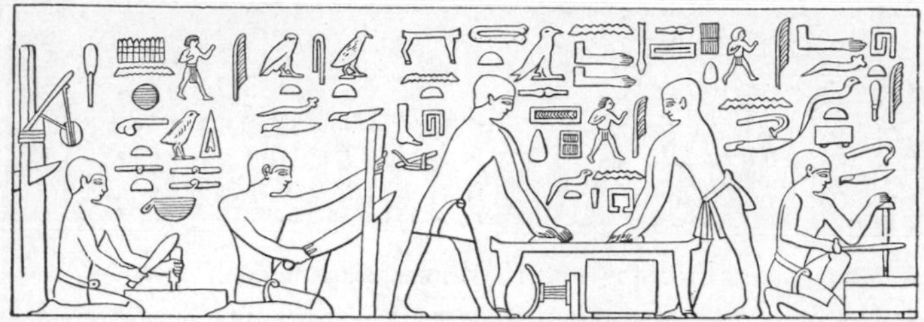

Fig. 46. Cabinetmakers *in the Pyramid Age*

At the left a man is cutting with a chisel which he taps with a mallet; next, a man "rips" a board with a copper saw; next, two men are finishing off a couch, and at the right a man is drilling a hole with a bow-drill. See the carrying-chair of Queen Hetep-heres (Fig. 47) as an example of the Egyptian craftsman's skill

Carpenters, cabinetmakers, and shipbuilders

101. We seem almost to hear the hubbub of hammers and mallets as we approach the next section of wall, where we find the cabinetmakers and shipbuilders at work. Here are the busy cabinetmakers, fashioning luxurious furniture for the nobleman's villa. The finished chairs and couches for the king or the rich are overlaid with gold and silver, inlaid with ebony and ivory, and upholstered with soft leather cushions. Close by the furniture workshops is a long line of curving hulls, with workmen swarming over them like ants, fitting together the earliest seagoing ships as well as river boats.

River commerce; exchange of goods before the existence of money

102. The river shipping which had already begun under the First Union increased now very rapidly as the manufacture of so many different things encouraged exchange among the towns. Indeed, the river must have been fairly alive with boats and barges (often depicted on the tomb walls) bearing goods to be carried either to the treasury of the Pharaoh for taxes or to market. Here on the wall is a picture of the market-place itself. We can watch the shoemaker offering the baker a pair of sandals as payment for a cake, or the carpenter's wife giving the fisherman a little wooden box to pay for a fish, while the potter's wife is willing to give the apothecary two bowls fresh from the potter's furnace in exchange for

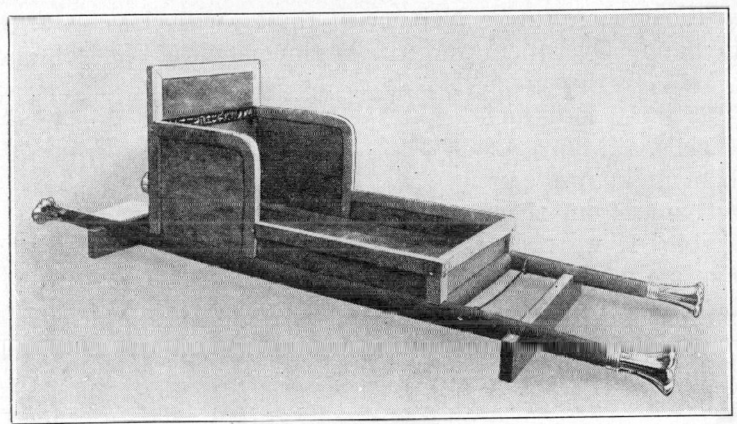

FIG. 47. *The* CARRYING-CHAIR *of Queen Hetep-heres, the Mother of Khufu, Builder of the Great Pyramid of Gizeh (Thirtieth Century* B.C.*)*

After the mother of the great Khufu had been buried, her tomb was entered and partially plundered by tomb-robbers. Thereupon the Pharaoh ordered that her sarcophagus and beautiful furniture be taken from her tomb and placed in a deep shaft just east of the site of the Great Pyramid. Here it was so well hidden that it was never again disturbed. When discovered by the Harvard-Boston expedition, the wooden framework of the furniture had decayed or shrunken almost beyond recognition. But the sheet gold with which the furniture had been overlaid still survived and made it possible to restore each piece by building a new framework of modern wood, which could then be re-covered with the ancient gold overlay. Thus we are today able to see among other things the very chair in which the queen rode when her bearers carried her out to take the air. (Courtesy of the Museum of Fine Arts, Boston)

a jar of fragrant ointment. We see, therefore, that these people had *no coined money* to use, and that in the market-place trade was exchange of actual goods. Such was the business of the common people. If we could see the large dealings in the palace and its offices, we should find there heavy rings of gold of a standard weight, which circulated like money. Rings of copper also served the same purpose. Such rings were the forerunners of coined money.

103. These people in the picture of the market-place on the chapel wall were the common folk of Egypt in the Pyramid Age. Some of them were free men, following their own business or industry; others were slaves, working the fields on the great estates. Neither of these lower classes owned any land. Over them were the landowners, the Pharaoh and

Society in the Pyramid Age

his great lords and officials. Many of them are known to us by name from their tombs. If we could take a walk through the cemetery of Gizeh we could copy a list of them, which would be like a "directory" of the great men of Egypt whose houses formed the wealthy quarter of the royal city when the pyramids of Gizeh were being built nearly five thousand years ago. We might even visit the tomb of the architect who built the Great Pyramid of Gizeh, and we have portrait statues of many other noblemen. Here are also the tombs of the royal family, and excavation has even revealed the magnificent tomb furnishings of King Khufu's mother, Queen Hetep-heres (Figs. 47–49). These gifts to the queen from her husband and her son Khufu furnish us almost our only vision of the royal splendor of the Pyramid Age,[1] revealing to us the art and the life of the royal court fifteen hundred years before the glimpses of royal luxury which we gain from the furniture of Tutenkhamon.

FIG. 48. *The Golden* HIEROGLYPHS *spelling the Name and Titles of Queen Hetep-heres*

Each of these signs is an individual piece, wrought in solid gold by the ancient goldsmith and then applied to the ebony strips which form the back of the carrying-chair (Fig. 47). These human figures, birds, animals, trees, tools, weapons, etc. are among the most exquisite examples of the goldsmith's skill produced by ancient men. They are of about the same date as the marvelous gold work from the early tombs at Ur (p. 155). (Courtesy of the Museum of Fine Arts, Boston)

[1] See Reisner, *Bulletin of the Boston Museum of Fine Arts*, May, 1927, Supplement to Vol. XXV; Vol. XXVI (1928), pp. 76–88; Vol. XXX (1932), pp. 55–60.

104. While the rich furnishings of Queen Hetep-heres reveal to us the luxuries surrounding Egyptian royalty in the Pyramid Age, the tomb walls give us charming pictures from the actual life of the courtiers. There we may see the owner of the tomb seated at ease in his carrying-chair, a kind of wheelless carriage borne upon the shoulders of slaves. After his inspection of his estate where we have been following him, his bearers carry him into the shady garden before his house, where they set down the palanquin and cease their song.[1] His wife advances at once to greet him. Her place is always at his side; she is his sole wife, held in all honor, and enjoys every right which belongs to her husband. This garden is the nobleman's paradise. Here he may recline for an hour of leisure with his family and friends, playing at a game of draughts, listening to the music of the harp played by his wife, or to a three-piece orchestra of harp, pipe, and lute; or watching women entertainers in the slow and stately dances of the time. Meanwhile his children are sporting about among the arbors, splashing in the pool as they chase the fish, playing with ball, doll, and jumping jack, or teasing the tame monkey, which takes refuge under their father's ivory-legged stool. From these pictures we learn for the first time that, after several hundred thousand years of Stone Age savagery and barbarism, family life was beginning to bring a kindly spirit into the lives of men.

Nobleman of the Pyramid Age in his home

Section 7. Art and Architecture in the Pyramid Age

105. The nobleman drops one hand idly upon the head of his favorite hound, and with the other beckons to the chief gardener and gives directions regarding the fresh romaine lettuce which he wishes to try for dinner. The house where this dinner awaits him is large and commodious, built of sun-dried brick and wood. Light and airy, as suits the climate, we find that it has many lat-

The nobleman's house

[1] This song is recorded, with other songs, on the tomb-chapel walls.

ticed windows on all sides. The walls of the living rooms are scarcely more than a frame to support gayly colored hangings which can be let down as a protection against winds and sand storms when necessary. These give the dwelling a very bright and cheerful aspect. The house is a work of art, and we discern in it how naturally the Egyptians demanded beauty in their surroundings. This they secured by making all their *useful* things *beautiful.*

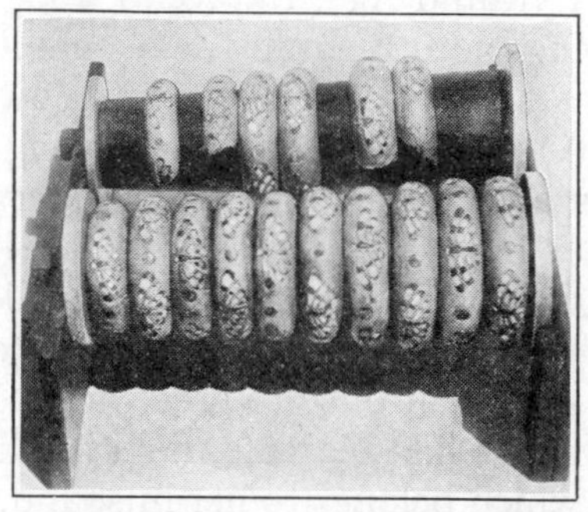

FIG. 49. *The* JEWELS *of Queen Hetep-heres*

These magnificent rings are of silver adorned with dragon flies separated by disks. The designs are recessed, or let into the surface of the silver. The rings are in two sets of eight each, and are graduated in size from small to large as if to fit the swell of the leg above the ankle, or of the arm above the wrist. One of the sets has partially perished; the other is in much better condition. The rings are mounted here upon two cones of wood, restored from a study of the original jewel box in which they were lying when discovered. (Courtesy of the Museum of Fine Arts, Boston)

Art of its furniture and decoration

106. Beauty surrounds us on every hand as we follow the nobleman in to his dinner. The lotus blossoms on the handle of his carved spoon, and his wine sparkles in the deep blue calyx of the same flower, which forms the bowl of his wineglass. The muscular limbs of the lion or the ox, beautifully carved in ivory, support the chair in which he sits or the couch where he reclines. The painted ceiling over his head is a blue and starry heaven resting upon palm-trunk columns (Fig. 55), each crowned with its graceful tuft of drooping foliage carved in wood and colored in the dark green of the living tree; or columns in the form of lotus stalks rise from the floor as if to support the azure ceiling upon their swaying blossoms. Doves and butterflies, exquisitely painted, flit across this indoor sky. Beneath our feet we find the pavement of the dining-hall carpeted in paintings picturing everywhere the deep green of disheveled

FIG. 50. VILLA *of an Egyptian Nobleman*

The garden is inclosed with a high wall. There are pools on either side as one enters, and a long arbor extends down the middle. The house at the rear, embowered in trees, is crowned by a roof garden shaded with awnings of tapestry

marsh grasses, with gleaming water between and fish gliding among the swaying reeds. Around the margin, leaping among the rushes, we see the wild ox tossing his head at the birds twittering on the nodding rush tops, as they vainly strive to frighten away the stealthy weasel creeping up to plunder their nests. Numbers of huge grasshoppers are perched securely on the reed stems, while here and there portly frogs wink demurely from below.

Fig. 51. *Portrait of* King Khafre, *Builder of the Second Pyramid of Gizeh*

Found in his valley temple (Fig. 54). It is carved in excessively hard stone, called diorite. The falcon with protecting wings outstretched is a symbol of the great god Horus (Twenty-ninth Century B.C.)

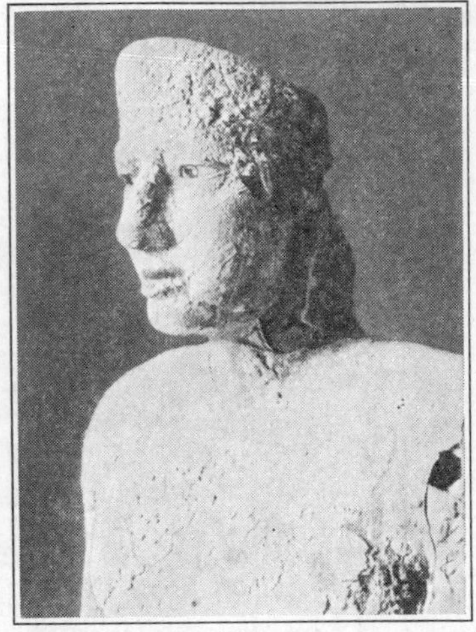

Fig. 52. Head *of a Royal* Statue *of Bronze in the Pyramid Age*

This is a statue of King Pepi I (nearly 2600 B.C.). It was hammered into shape over a wooden form. The metal is incrusted with rust, but owing to the eyes, of inlaid rock crystal, the portrait is very lifelike (cf. Fig. 215)

Painting and relief in tombs and temples

107. It was only because they possessed trained artists that the Egyptians were able to leave the beautifully painted reliefs in their tomb-chapels. Indeed, we can find, in one of the chapels, painted in one corner of the wall, a portrait of the artist himself. Here he has represented himself enjoying a plentiful feast among other people of the estate. His drawings all around us show that he has not been able to overcome all the difficulties of drawing, on a flat surface, objects having thickness and roundness. Animal figures are drawn, however, with great lifelikeness. Perspective is almost entirely unknown to him, and objects in the background or distance are depicted of the same size as those in front. Insects and small animals are carved with attention to detail.

108. The portrait sculptor was the greatest artist of this age. His statues were carved in stone or wood and painted in the colors of real life; the eyes, inlaid with rock crystal, still continue to shine with the gleam of life. The result is that more lifelike portraits have never been produced by any age, although these are the earliest known portraits in the history of art. Such statues of the kings are often superb. They were set up in the Pharaoh's pyramid temple. In size the most extraordinary statue of the Pyramid Age is the Great Sphinx, which stands here in this cemetery of Gizeh. The head is a portrait of King Khafre, the Pharaoh who built the second pyramid of Gizeh, and was sculptured from a promontory of rock which rose high above the royal city. It is the largest portrait ever wrought.

Portrait sculpture

FIG. 53. *Statuette of an Egyptian* POTTER *at Work at his Wheel*

This wizened little potter has in his face a wistful expression and shows individual characterization which suggests that we have here a portrait and not a statue of just any potter. Yet this man was the humble servant of an obscure cemetery official. (From the collection of the Oriental Institute, University of Chicago)

109. We have already mentioned the beauty of the earliest architecture in stone, produced by Imhotep (§ 87), the first architect. A second stage of architecture in stone is revealed to us in the massive granite piers and walls of Khafre's valley temple beside the Sphinx. This splendid hall was lighted by a series of oblique slits, which are really low roof windows. They occupied the difference in level between a higher roof over the

Architecture: earliest clerestory; colonnades

middle aisle of the hall and a lower roof on each side of the middle. Such an arrangement of roof windows, called a clerestory (*clearstory*), passed from Egypt over to Greece and Rome, where the Christian architects finally found it and used it for the roof and windows of the nave in the basilica churches and cathedrals. The weight and massiveness of the piers in Khafre's hall make it a place of grandeur. Less than a century later (Twenty-eighth Century B.C.) it was gracefulness rather than grandeur which the Egyptian architects desired. Instead of these heavy *square* piers or pillars the architects then began to erect slender and graceful *round* columns with beautiful capitals. These shafts, when ranged in rows, formed the earliest known colonnades in the history of architecture (Fig. 55).

FIG. 54. *Restoration of the* CLERESTORY HALL *in the Valley Temple of Khafre*

The roof of this hall was supported on two rows of huge stone piers, each a single block of polished granite weighing 22 tons. This view shows only one row of the piers, the other being out of sight at the right. At the left, above, the light streams in obliquely from the very low clerestory windows. Compare the cross section in Fig. 266. The statues shown here had been thrown by unknown enemies into a well in an adjacent hall, where they were found about eighty years ago. See head of the finest in Fig. 51. (After Hoelscher)

110. The useful and beautiful things which Egypt was now making began to be carried across the Mediterranean to Europe, and by land to Western Asia. These things

FIG. 55. COLONNADES *in the* COURT *of a Pyramid Temple*

Notice the pyramid rising behind the temple. The door in the middle leads to the holy place built against the side of the pyramid. The center of the court is open to the sky; the roof of the porch all around is supported on round columns, the earliest known in the history of architecture. Contrast the square piers, without any capital, which the architect of Khafre put into his temple hall (Fig. 54) two generations earlier than these columns. Each column represents a palm tree, the capital being the crown of foliage. The whole place was colored in the bright hues of nature, including the painting on the walls behind the columns. Among these paintings was the ship in Fig. 56. Thirteen hundred feet of copper piping, the earliest known plumbing, was installed in this building. (After Borchardt)

were a part of the earliest civilization which commerce was thus bringing to Europe and Asia. At the same time, as we shall see, Western Asia also had been making the most surprising advances in civilization. These advances began to exert an influence in Egypt, showing that there was active commerce between Egypt and Asia. This commerce also connected the western Delta and Crete. We have already learned, however, that the Pharaoh had been carrying on some oversea commerce for centuries (§ 81).

Earliest seagoing ships; northward spread of Egyptian civilization

111. Besides continuing the work on their copper mines in Sinai (see map, p. 66) the Pharaohs were also sending caravans of donkeys far up the Nile into the Sudan, to traffic

FIG. 56. *Earliest* REPRESENTATION *of a Seagoing Ship (Twenty-eighth Century* B.C.)

The scene is carved on the wall of a temple (Fig. 55). The people are all bowing to the king whose figure (now lost) stood on shore (at the left), and they salute him with the words written in a line of hieroglyphs above, meaning, "Hail to thee! O Sahure [the king's name], thou god of the living! We behold thy beauty." Some of these men are bearded Phœnician prisoners brought by this Egyptian ship, which, with seven others, had therefore crossed the eastern end of the Mediterranean and returned. The big double mast is unshipped and lies on supports in the stern. The model and ornaments of these earliest known ships spread in later times to ships found in all waters from Italy to India

with the people of the south and to bring back ebony, ivory, ostrich feathers, and fragrant gums. The officials who conducted these caravans were the earliest explorers of inner Africa, and in their tombs at the First Cataract they have left interesting records of their exciting adventures among the wild tribes of the south, — adventures in which some of them lost their lives.[1] The royal fleet was also sent on expeditions to a far-away coastland of the south called Punt, at the southern end of the Red Sea (see map, p. 146), where they found the same products and brought them back by water.

Southern commerce; earliest navigation on the Red Sea

112. We have seen the grandeur and beauty of the civilization gained by the Egyptians of the Pyramid Age. We now realize how many more things the men of the Nile could make than the men of Europe, who were still living in the Stone Age towns at the very time the Egyptian tomb-chapels were built. It was the appearance of all these new things which made the life of Egypt

End of Pyramid Age

[1] The teacher will find it of interest to read these records to the class. See the author's *Ancient Records of Egypt*, Vol. I, §§ 325–336, 350–374.

civilized, especially after 3000 B.C. But the noblemen finally became so powerful that the Pharaohs could no longer control them. Then, in struggles among themselves, they destroyed the Pharaoh's government, soon after 2450 B.C. Thus ended the Pyramid Age, which had lasted some five hundred years,— the age in which men for the first time advanced far into civilization and left barbarism behind (see Fig. 41).

113. We have found that the two things which finally made possible the development of civilization were, first, *agriculture on a large scale* and, second, *plentiful metal.* Now a plentiful supply of metal required extensive mining operations in distant localities. Such enterprises could be carried out only by powerful kings, and these rulers gained the necessary power and wealth from the enlargement of the grain fields made possible by the invention of the plow. This invention went far toward completing the development of *food-production*, but the resulting enlargement of the grain fields would have been impossible without a great *national* system of *irrigation canals.* These canals could never have been dug, or, when dug, could never have been kept in constant operation, without a *government* with a king at its head. Such a government could not carry on its work without *writing* and a *calendar.*

Stages of emerging civilization

114. Back of all these things which we have just listed lies the fact that the Stone Age hunters could not have taken possession of the Nile valley if they had not been able to draw on the wild animals as a source of food. The domestication of the wild animals began the development of *food-production.* The increased control of the wild creatures and final possession of them as domesticated animals were closely connected with the drying of the Sahara, which drove the wild animals into the Nile gorge, where the hunters could much more easily imprison them in stockades. As we continue backward we reach the stage of *food-gathering,* and eventually the Early Stone Age savagery which surrounded the entire Mediterranean until the combination of favorable circumstances

Conditions of shift from savagery to civilization

enabled the inhabitants of the Nile valley to advance far beyond all other peoples of that time. The Age of the Pharaohs was not ended with the fall of the Pyramid-builders. There were two more great ages in the long story of human life on the Nile: the Feudal Age and the Empire. The monuments which these later ages left lie farther up the river, and we must now turn our attention to them.

QUESTIONS

Section 5. Explain the necessity of irrigation in Egypt. What led to the rise of government? Discuss the civilization of the earliest two nations known in human history. Explain the importance of the invention of the plow. Trace the steps by which phonetic writing arose. Where did the first alphabet arise? Discuss the importance of the invention of writing. To what country were the earliest mining expeditions sent, and who sent them? Describe the effect of the use of metal on architecture.

Section 6. What do the tombs of Egypt tell us of the religious beliefs of the people? Study Fig. 41 and tell how the Egyptian tombs reveal the transition from barbarism to civilization. Describe the government of the Pyramid Age. Make a list of the industries revealed in the tomb-chapel pictures. Discuss trade and commerce.

Section 7. Describe the house and garden of a nobleman in the Pyramid Age. Discuss painting and portrait sculpture. Describe the roof windows called clerestory windows (Figs. 54 and 266) and what they finally came to be. Compare the earliest piers (Fig. 54) with the piers (columns) built a hundred years later (Fig. 55). Describe the earliest seagoing ships. Give the date of the Pyramid Age and tell why it was important.

BIBLIOGRAPHY FOR TOPICAL STUDIES

The Pyramid-builders: BREASTED, *Ancient Egyptians*, §§ 94–102; *Bulletin of the Boston Museum of Fine Arts*, April, 1911, pp. 13–20, April, 1915, pp. 29–35, and Supplement to Vol. XXV; QUIBELL, *Egyptian History and Art*, pp. 34–39.

Early explorations: BAIKIE, *Ancient Egypt*, chaps. ix–x; BREASTED, *Ancient Egyptians*, §§ 116–122; QUIBELL, pp. 45–49.

Burial customs: BREASTED, *Religion and Thought*, pp. 62–69; *Bulletin of the Metropolitan Museum of Art*, December, 1920, Part II, pp. 14–32; MASPERO, *Art in Egypt*, pp. 6–21, 28–38, 88–90.

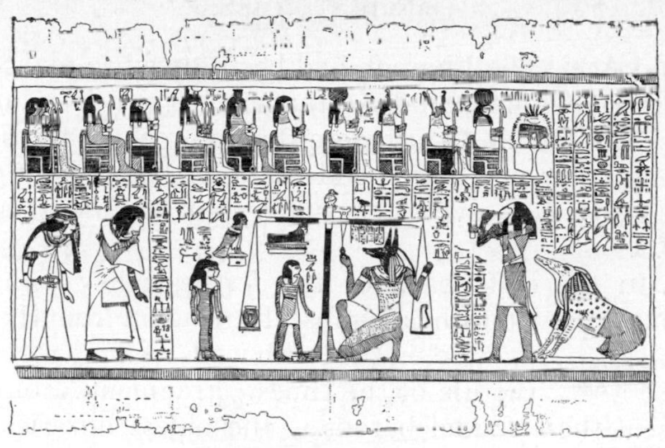

Chapter IV · *The Story of Egypt: The Feudal Age and the Empire*

Section 8. The Feudal Age

115. After the Pyramid Age the leadership of Egypt passed from the north to the south. If we should voyage upriver by steamer from Gizeh we should discover that after a time the great stone pyramids would disappear altogether, but far away in the south we should find other buildings, tombs, and monuments which tell us of two more great ages on the Nile, — the Feudal Age and the Empire. We have seen how the growth in power of the noblemen caused the downfall of the government in the

Meaning of Feudal Age in Egypt

Note. A picture from the Book of the Dead. At the left we see entering, in white robes, the deceased, a man named Ani, and his wife. Before them are the balances of judgment for weighing the human heart, to determine whether it is just or not. A jackal-headed god adjusts the scales, while an ibis-headed god stands behind him, pen in hand, prepared to record the verdict of the balances. Behind him is a monster ready to devour the unjust soul as his heart (looking like a tiny jar) in the left-hand scalepan, is weighed over against right and truth (symbolized by a feather) in the right-hand scalepan. The scene is painted in water colors on papyrus. Such a roll is sometimes as much as 90 feet long and filled from beginning to end with magical charms for the use of the dead in the next world. Hence the modern name for the whole roll, the "Book of the Dead."

Pyramid Age. The Pharaoh had been forced to make grants of lands to these men under arrangements which in later Europe we call feudal. They were thus powerful barons, living like little kings on their broad estates. This Feudal Age of Egypt lasted for several centuries and was flourishing by 2000 B.C.

Tombs and libraries of Feudal Age

116. In the cliffs back of the fertile valley estates the noblemen excavated their tombs. Here again from the scenes painted on the tomb walls we may reconstruct the life of the times. Fragments from the libraries of these feudal barons — the oldest libraries in the world — have also been found, and from these papyrus rolls we actually learn what these people *thought*, as well as how they lived! These oldest of all surviving books are in the form of rolls of papyrus, which were once packed in jars, neatly labeled, and ranged in rows on the nobleman's library shelves. Here are the most ancient story-books in the world, — tales of wanderings and adventures in Asia, tales of shipwreck at the gate of the unknown ocean beyond the Red Sea, the earliest "Sindbad the Sailor," and tales of wonders wrought by ancient wise men and magicians.

Books on kindness and justice

117. Some of the stories tell about the sufferings of the poor and the humble, in the hope of stirring up the rulers of the people to be just and kind in their treatment of the weaker classes. Some describe the wickedness of men and the hopelessness of the future. Others tell of a righteous ruler who was yet to come, a "good shepherd" they called him, meaning a good king. Thus arose the earliest dream of a Messiah. It was believed that he would bring in justice and happiness for all. We notice here a contrast with the Pyramid Age. With the incoming of the Pyramid-builders we saw a tremendous growth in power, in building, and in art; but in the Feudal Age there were men who tried to advance also in still higher things. These things were character and right conduct (see also the explanation under Fig. 57). For the first time, men began to believe that only a good man could hope for a blessed life hereafter.

FIG. 57. CLIFF-TOMB *of an Egyptian Nobleman of the Feudal Age*

This tomb is not a masonry building, like the tombs of the Pyramid Age, but is cut into the face of the cliff and is therefore of solid rock. The chapel entered through this front door contains painted relief pictures, like those of the Pyramid Age, and also many written records. In this chapel the nobleman tells of his kind treatment of his people; he says: "There was no citizen's daughter whom I misused; there was no widow whom I oppressed; there was no peasant whom I evicted; there was no shepherd whom I expelled; . . . there was none wretched in my community, there was none hungry in my time. When years of famine came I plowed all the fields of the Oryx barony [his estate] . . . preserving its people alive and furnishing its food so that there was none hungry therein. I gave to the widow as to her who had a husband; I did not exalt the great above the humble in anything that I gave." All this we can read inscribed in this tomb

118. Probably a number of papyrus rolls were required to contain the drama of Osiris, — a great play in which the life, death, burial, and resurrection of Osiris were pictured. This play was performed at an annual feast in which all the people loved to join. It is our earliest known drama, — a kind of Passion Play; but the rolls on which it was written have perished. Excavation has uncovered fragments of another book roll which sets forth a similar drama in the form of a pageant. In this earliest

Drama and poetry

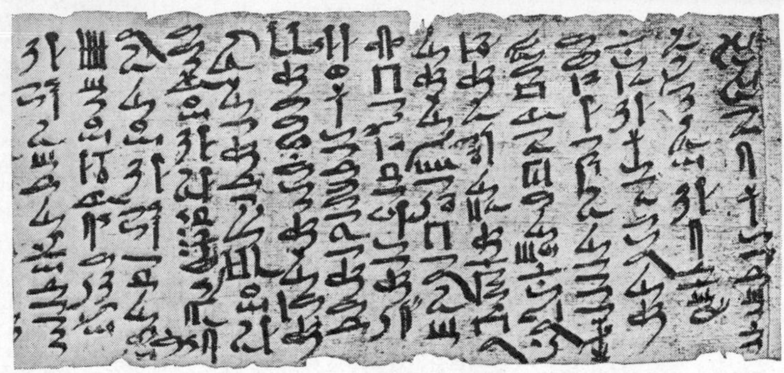

Fig. 58. *A Page from the* Story *of the* Shipwrecked Sailor, *the Earliest "Sindbad," as read by the Boys and Girls of Egypt Four Thousand Years Ago (One Third of Size of Original)*

This page reads: "Those who were on board perished, and not one of them escaped. Then I was cast upon an island by a wave of the great sea. I passed three days alone, with (only) my heart as my companion, sleeping in the midst of a shelter of trees, till daylight enveloped me. Then I crept out for aught to fill my mouth. I found figs and grapes there and all fine vegetables, etc. . . ." The tale then tells of his seizure by an enormous serpent with a long beard, who proves to be the king of this distant island in the Red Sea, at the entrance of the Indian Ocean. He keeps the sailor three months, treats him kindly, and returns him with much treasure to Egypt. The island then seems to have sunk and vanished forever. In form such a book was a single strip of papyrus paper, 5 or 6 to 10 or 12 inches wide, and often 15 to 30 or 40 feet long. When not in use this strip was kept rolled up, and thus the earliest books were rolls, looking, when small, like a high-school diploma or, when large, like a roll of wall paper

preserved play we find parts of the dialogue, with stage directions accompanied by pictures of the action. This papyrus dates from the Eighteenth or Nineteenth Century B.C. and is probably the oldest illustrated book in the world. There were also rolls containing songs and poems, like the beautiful hymn sung by the nobles of the Pharaoh's court as a greeting to the sovereign every morning when he came out of his apartment.

119. It is a surprising fact that even at this early date a number of rolls were needed to deal with the beginnings of science. The most valuable of all contained what had been learned about surgery and the organs of the human body. This earliest known book on surgery is a papyrus roll now preserved in the library of the New York Historical Society. It is the oldest surviving book in which a man tried to discover new facts by careful study of the objects around him, just as Sir Isaac Newton is said to have watched a falling apple and to have received from it a hint of the law of gravitation. This book of surgery is therefore the earliest book of science. Its subject is the human body, and what happens when its parts are injured. It contains the earliest known mention of the human brain, the earliest notice of the fact that the brain controls the limbs and that an injury to it paralyzes them.

Earliest books of science: surgery

120. There are also rolls containing many of the recognized rules of arithmetic, based on the decimal system which we still use; others treat the beginnings of algebra and geometry. In *plane* geometry it is surprising to find that these earliest known mathematicians already had rules for computing correctly the area of a triangle, of a trapezium, and even of a circle, which was figured as the square of eight ninths of the diameter. The value of π which results from this computation is 3.1605, a result surprisingly near the correct value. This led to a rule for the calculation of the area of a hemisphere. It was a method rediscovered by the Greeks 1600 years later. Finally, in dealing with *solid* geometry these mathematical rolls show methods of calculating how many bushels of grain there are in cylinder-shaped granaries of varying depths and diameters. They also explain how to calculate the content of a frustum of a square pyramid, and even the cubical content of a hemisphere could be computed. The formula for solving this problem was not discovered in Europe until 3000 years later. Observations of the heavenly bodies with simple instruments were made; but these records, like those in engineering and geography, have been lost.

Books of science: mathematics

121. Along with this higher progress the Pharaohs of the Feudal Age much improved the government. Every few years they made census lists to be used in taxation, and a few of these, the earliest census sheets in the world, have

FIG. 59. *Restoration of the* FORTIFICATIONS *which* GUARDED THE NILE *at the Southern Entrance to Feudal-Age Egypt*

At either end of the granite barrier obstructing the Nile at the Second Cataract still stand the Feudal Age fortresses erected about four thousand years ago. The two fortresses completely commanded the narrow gap in the barrier, and no boat could descend without the consent of the garrisons. The walls, with towers projecting far beyond them, show full knowledge of the strategics of defense. Cut in the surrounding rocks are records of the greatest yearly height of the Nile during the Feudal Age, when the Pharaohs were much interested in engineering and the control of irrigation. By observing the rise of the river here, word could be sent down the river when plenty of water for irrigation was assured, and thus the king's treasurer knew in advance that he could collect the usual amount of taxes. (After Borchardt)

Administration and irrigation projects in the Feudal Age

survived. These kings erected huge earthen dikes and made large basins for storing up the Nile waters needed for irrigation, thus greatly increasing the yield of the feudal lands and estates. They measured the height of the river from year to year, and their marks of the Nile levels are still to be found cut on the rocks at the Second Cataract. Thus nearly four thousand years ago they were already doing on a large scale what our government has only recently begun to do by its irrigation projects among our own arid lands.

Commerce by sea; a Suez Canal four thousand years ago

122. At the same time these rulers of the Feudal Age tried to reach the wealth of other lands by sea. Their fleets sailed over among the Ægean islands and probably controlled the large island of Crete. They dug a canal from the north end of the Red Sea westward to the nearest branch of the Nile in the eastern Delta, where the river divides into a number of mouths (see map, p. 66). This canal made it possible for the Pharaoh's Mediterranean ships to sail up the easternmost mouth

FIG. 60. *Model of a* TRAVELING BOAT *which belonged to a Nobleman of the Early Feudal Age*

The sail is just being hauled up, showing that the boat is to travel with the wind. As the prevailing wind blows from the north in Egypt, we know that the boat is about to voyage southward. We see the sailors making fast the backstays and hauling on the halyards. The most interesting feature of this boat is the cabin, the interior of which we see in Fig. 61. (Courtesy of Metropolitan Museum of Art)

FIG. 61. FURNITURE *in the Cabin of the Model Traveling Boat* (Fig. 60)

This little cabin is detachable and has here been removed, exposing the furniture. The steward sits watchfully beside the bed under which the trunks of his master have been placed, just as in a modern steamship cabin. (Courtesy of Metropolitan Museum of Art) of the Nile, then to enter the new canal and, passing eastward through it, reach the Red Sea. Thus the Mediterranean Sea and the Red Sea were first connected by a real Suez Canal four thousand years ago. Such a connection was as important to the Egyptians as the Panama Canal is to the United States or the Suez Canal to England. By going through this canal, Nile ships could sail from the eastern Delta directly to the land of Punt and to the straits leading to the Indian Ocean. These waters seemed to the sailors of the Feudal Age the end of the world, and their stories of wonderful adventures in these far-away regions must have delighted many a circle of villagers on the feudal estates.

Military expansion north and south; end of Feudal Age

123. In this age the Pharaoh had organized a small standing army. He could now make his power felt in both north and south, in Palestine and in Nubia. He conquered the territory of Nubia as far south as the Second Cataract (see map, p. 66), and thus added two hundred miles of river to the kingdom of Egypt. Here he erected strong frontier fortresses against the Nubian tribes. The wise rule of the Pharaohs of the Feudal Age did much to prepare the way for Egyptian leadership in the early world. Three of these kings bore the name "Sesostris," which became one of the great and illustrious names in Egyptian history. But not long after 1800 B.C. the power of the Pharaohs of the Feudal Age suddenly declined. Their final fall was due to an invasion of a foreign people called Hyksos, who entered Egypt from Asia.

SECTION 9. THE FOUNDING OF THE EMPIRE

124. The monuments along the river banks have thus far told us the story of two of the three periods[1] into which the career of this great Nile people falls. After the modern Nile traveler has passed the tombs of the Feudal Age and has

[1] These three ages are:

1. The Pyramid Age, about 30th to 25th Century B.C. (Sections 6–7).
2. The Feudal Age, flourishing 2000 B.C. (Section 8).
3. The Empire, about 1580 to 1150 B.C. (Sections 9–11).

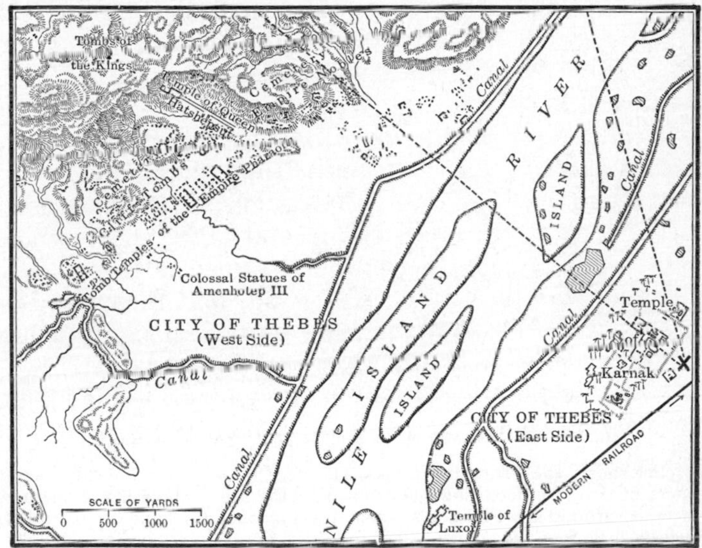

Map of THEBES

This map may be compared with the air view of Karnak (Fig. 60), taken over the point marked X. In the upper left corner are shown the western cliffs, in and along which lie the tombs of the vast cemetery (Fig. 4). In front of these western cliffs, and parallel with them, stretched a long line of temples facing the great temples of Luxor and Karnak on the east side of the river. The houses of the ancient city have passed away

continued his journey over four hundred miles southward from Cairo, he sees mighty masses of stone masonry and lines of tall columns rising among the palms on the east side of the river. They are the ruins of the once great city of Thebes, which tell us the story of the third period, the Empire.

Thebes and the history of the Empire

125. Here we find not only an enormous cemetery but also a series of great temples on both sides of the river (see map, above). The walls of these immense temples are covered with enormous pictures sculptured in relief, depicting the victorious wars of the Egyptians in all directions, but especially in Asia, to which they drove back the Hyksos. In these pictures we

Temple reliefs; arrival of the horse in Egypt

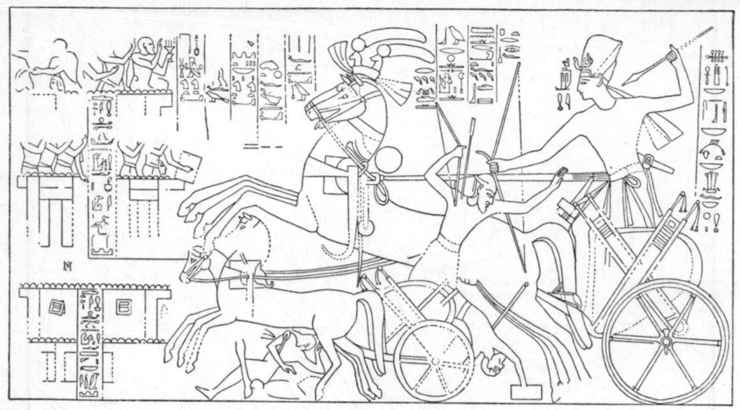

FIG. 62. *A* PHARAOH *of the Empire fighting in his* CHARIOT

This relief shows the Pharaoh (Ramses II) after he has overcome the bearded defenders of two Asiatic strongholds shown at the left. The reins of the horses are fastened around the Pharaoh's waist, leaving both his hands free, and with uplifted spear he is on the point of stabbing the Asiatic chieftain, who is helplessly falling out of the smaller chariot in the foreground. This is one of an enormous series of such scenes, 170 feet long, carved in relief on the outside of the Great Hall of Karnak. Such sculpture was brightly colored and served to enhance the architectural effect of the building, as well as to impress the people with the heroism of the Pharaoh. The color has now disappeared, and the sculpture is battered and weatherworn. (After Wreszinski)

see the giant figure of the Pharaoh as he stands in his war chariot, scattering the enemy before his plunging horses. The Pharaohs of the Pyramid Age had never seen a horse, and this is the first time that we have met horses on the ancient monuments. After the close of the Feudal Age horses began to be imported from Asia, where we shall find them in use at a much earlier time (see § 174). Chariots came with them, and Egypt, having learned warfare on a scale unknown before, became a military empire.

Egypt a military empire

126. The Pharaohs thus became great generals, with a well-organized standing army made up chiefly of archers and heavy masses of chariots. With these forces the Pharaohs conquered an empire which extended from the Euphrates in Asia to the Fourth Cataract of the Nile in Africa (see map I, p. 266). By an empire we

FIG. 63. *An Unfinished* OBELISK *lying in the Granite Quarry at the First Cataract of the Nile*

The top surface of this long shaft of granite was made flat by hammering with ball-shaped "pounders" made of a very hard stone called *dolerite*. The exact shape of the obelisk was then outlined on this flat surface. When hammered with the dolerite pounders along these outlines the granite crumbled and could be removed as dust. As the hammers ground their way downward the workmen thus eventually found themselves hammering at the bottom of long trenches ten to fifteen feet deep. Three faces of the obelisk — that is, the top and two sides — were thus detached from the quarry, but how the fourth side, the bottom, was undercut without cracking the mighty shaft is uncertain. This obelisk is still attached to the quarry along the bottom. After an obelisk was extracted from the quarry, it was dragged along a causeway to the river and then transported by Nile boat to its destination. Our obelisk was left lying here in the quarry because the engineers discovered flaws in the stone. The shaft is 137 feet long and, if extracted, would have weighed over 1100 tons, the largest single block of stone ever quarried by engineers ancient or modern. (Photograph by the Oriental Institute of the University of Chicago)

mean a group of nations subdued and ruled over by the most powerful among them. In much earlier times human government had begun with tiny city-states, which gradually merged together into nations such as Upper and Lower Egypt; but the organization of men had now reached the point where *many nations* were combined into an empire including a large part of the Ancient Near East. This world power of the Pharaohs lasted from the Sixteenth to the Twelfth Century B.C., — a period of somewhat over four hundred years.

Queen Hatshepsut, the first great woman in history

127. The Karnak Temple, which stood in the enormous city of Thebes, now serves as a great historical volume telling us much of the story of the Egyptian Empire. Behind the great hall there towers a huge obelisk, a

Fig. 64. *Part of the* Fleet *of Queen Hatshepsut loading in the Land of Punt*

Only two of Hatshepsut's fleet of five ships are shown. The sails on the long spars are furled, and the vessels are moored. The sailors are carrying the cargo up the gangplanks, and one of them is teasing an ape on the roof of the cabin. The inscriptions above the ships read: "The loading of the ships very heavily with marvels of the country of Punt: all goodly fragrant woods of God's-Land [the East], heaps of myrrh-resin, with fresh myrrh trees, with ebony and pure ivory, with green gold of Emu, with cinnamon wood, *khesyt* wood, with two kinds of incense, eye-cosmetic, with apes, monkeys, dogs, and with skins of the southern panther, with natives and their children. Never was brought the like of this for any king who has been since the beginning." The scene is carved on the wall of the queen's temple at Thebes, in the garden of which she planted the myrrh trees

shaft of granite in a single piece nearly a hundred feet high. It was erected early in the Empire by Queen Hatshepsut, who is regarded as the first great woman in history. There were once two of these enormous monuments, and it was no small task for the queen's engineers to cut out and transport them, and then erect them in this temple. But the queen did not stop with this achievement. She even dispatched an expedition of five ships through the Red Sea to Punt, to bring back the luxuries of tropical Africa for another beautiful terraced temple which she was erecting against the western cliffs at Thebes (map, p. 103). Such deeds reveal quite clearly the ability of this first great woman as a ruler.

128. If we examine the Karnak obelisk of Hatshepsut, we find around the base the remains of stone masonry with which it was once walled in and covered almost up to the top. This was done by the queen's successor, the great soldier Thutmose III, in order to cover up the records which proclaimed

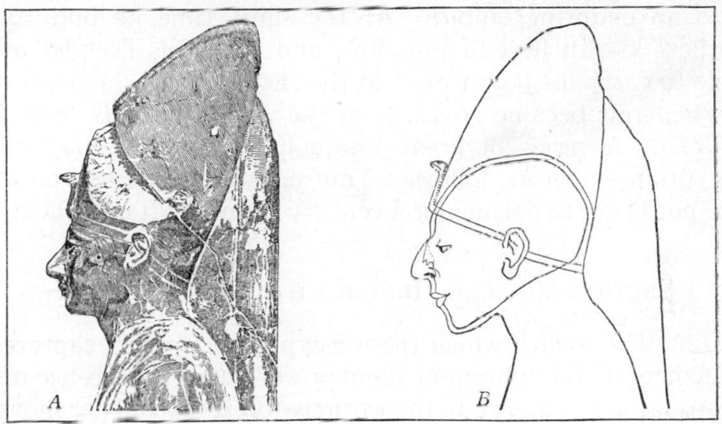

FIG. 65. *Portrait of* THUTMOSE III, *the Napoleon of Ancient Egypt* (A), *compared with his Mummy* (B)

This portrait (*A*), carved in granite, can be compared with the actual face of the great conqueror as we have it in his mummy. Such a comparison is shown in *B*, where the profile of this granite portrait (outside lines) is placed over the profile of Thutmose III's mummy (inside lines). The correspondence is very close, showing great accuracy in the portrait art of this age

to the world the hated rule of a woman. In her great temple he commanded his people to take hammers and smash to pieces over a hundred stone statues of the queen. Everywhere he had the names of Hatshepsut and all the men who aided her cut out and obliterated, including the name of the skillful architect and engineer who had erected the Karnak obelisk and its companion. But the masonry covering the obelisk has since fallen down, thus revealing inscriptions which still proclaim the fame of Hatshepsut.

End of Hatshepsut and triumph of Thutmose III

129. Thutmose III was the first great general in history, the Napoleon of Egypt, the greatest of the Egyptian conquerors. He ruled for over fifty years, beginning about 1500 B.C. On the temple walls at Karnak we can read the story of nearly twenty years of warfare, during which Thutmose crushed the cities and kingdoms of Western Asia and welded them

Campaigns of Thutmose III (1501–1447 B.C.)

into an enduring empire. At the same time he built the earliest known fleet of warships, and with this fleet he was able to carry his power even to the Ægean Sea, where one of his generals became governor of the Ægean islands (map I, p. 266). A series of great Pharaohs, whom we may call Egyptian emperors, followed Thutmose III, and their power did not begin to decline for a century or more after his death.

Section 10. The Higher Life of the Empire

130. The wealth which these Egyptian emperors captured in Asia and Nubia brought them power and magnificence unknown to the world before, especially as shown in their vast and splendid buildings. A new and impressive chapter in the history of art and architecture was begun. The temple of Karnak (§ 127) contains the greatest colonnaded hall ever erected by man (Fig. 67). The vast capital forming the summit of *each* column is large enough to contain a group of a hundred men standing crowded upon it at the same time. The clerestory windows on each side of these giant columns are no longer low, depressed openings, as in the Pyramid Age, but they have now become fine, tall windows, showing us the Egyptian clerestory hall on its way to become the basilica church of much later times (Fig. 266).

Temple architecture

131. Such temples as these at Thebes were seen through the deep green of clustering palms, among towering obelisks and colossal statues of the Pharaohs. The whole was bright with color, and flashing at many a point with bands of sheet gold and silver. Mirrored in the unruffled surface of the

---

* This point of view is behind (east of) the great Karnak Temple at the point marked X in the map (p. 103). We look northwestward across the temple and the river to the western cliffs. From the rear gate below us (lower right-hand corner of view) to the tall front wall nearest the river the temple is nearly a quarter of a mile long and was nearly two thousand years in course of construction. The oldest portions were built by the kings of the Feudal Age, and the latest, the front wall, by the Greek kings (the Ptolemies, Section 63). The standing obelisk of Queen Hatshepsut can be seen rising in the middle of the temple. Beyond it is the vast colonnaded Hall of Karnak, on the outside wall of which are the great war reliefs (Fig. 62). On the left we see the pool, — all that remains of the sacred lake.

FIG. 66. *The Great* TEMPLE OF KARNAK *and the Nile Valley at Thebes seen from an Airplane* *

The area included in this view will be found bounded by two diverging dotted lines on the map of Thebes (p. 103). It will be seen that our view includes only a portion of the ancient city, which extended up and down both sides of the river. (For description of Karnak see note on opposite page)

FIG. 67. *Restoration of the* GREAT HALL OF KARNAK, *Ancient Thebes,— Largest Building of the Egyptian Empire*

It is 338 feet wide and 170 feet deep, furnishing a floor area about equal to that of the cathedral of Notre Dame in Paris, although this is only a single room of the temple. There are one hundred and thirty-four columns in sixteen rows. The nave (three central aisles) is 79 feet high and contains twelve columns in two rows, which the architects have made much higher than the rest in order to insert lofty clerestory windows on each side. Compare the very low windows of the earliest clerestory (Fig. 54). In this higher form the clerestory passed over to Europe

temple lake, it made a picture of such splendor as the ancient world had never seen before. As the visitor entered he found himself in a spacious and sunlit court, surrounded by splendid colonnaded porches. Beyond, all was mystery as he looked into the somber forest of towering columns in the hall behind the court. These temples were connected by long avenues of sphinxes sculptured in stone, forming parkways which united the temples in an impressive group. They thus transformed Thebes into the first great "monumental city" ever built by man, — a city which, as a whole, was itself a vast and imposing monument.[1]

Surroundings of Empire temples at Thebes

132. Much of the grandeur of Egyptian architecture was due to the sculptor and the painter. The colonnades, with flower capitals, were colored to suggest the plants they represented. The enormous battle scenes carved on the temple

[1] City plans which treat a whole city as a symmetrical and harmonious unit are now beginning to be made in America.

Fig. 68. *The Colossal* Columns *of the* Nave *in the* Great Hall of Karnak

These are the columns of the middle two rows in Fig. 67. On the top of the capital of each one of these columns a hundred men can stand at once. These great columns may be seen in the air view (Fig. 66) just at the left of the two obelisks

wall were painted in bright colors. The portrait statues of the Pharaohs, set up before these temples, were often so large that they rose above the towers of the temple front itself (the tallest part of the building), and they could be seen for miles around. The sculptors could cut these colossal figures from a single block, although they were sometimes eighty or ninety feet high and weighed as much as a thousand tons. This is equal to the load drawn by a modern freight train of twenty-five cars, but, unlike the trainload, it was not cut up into small units of weight light enough for convenient handling and loading. Nevertheless the engineers of the Empire moved many such vast figures for hundreds of miles, using the same methods employed in moving obelisks. It was in works of this massive, monumental character that the art of Egypt excelled (Fig. 77).

Painting and sculpture in temples

133. Two enormous portraits of Amenhotep III, the most luxurious and splendid of the Egyptian emperors, still stand on the western plain of Thebes, across the river from Karnak. As we approach them we see rising behind them the majestic western cliffs, in which are cut hundreds of tomb-chapels belonging to the great men of the Empire. Here were buried the able generals who marched with the Pharaohs on their campaigns in Asia and in Nubia. Here lay the gifted artists and architects who built the vast monuments we have just visited. Here in these tomb-chapels we may read their names and often long accounts of their lives. Here is the story of the general who saved Thutmose III's life, during a great elephant hunt in Asia, by rushing in at the critical moment and cutting off the trunk of an enraged elephant which was pursuing the king. Here also was the tomb of the general, Thutiy, who took the city of Joppa in Palestine by concealing his men in panniers loaded on the backs of donkeys, and thus bringing them into the city as merchandise, — an adventure which afterward furnished part of the story of "Ali Baba and the Forty Thieves." The tomb of this general is now covered by rubbish, and we do not even know where it is located; but a

Tombs of great men of the Empire

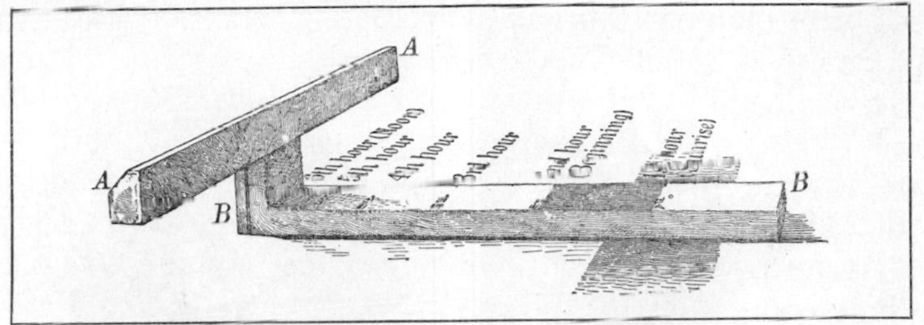

FIG. 69. *The Oldest* CLOCK *in the World,— an Egyptian Shadow Clock*

In sunny Egypt a shadow clock was a very practical instrument. In the morning the crosspiece (*AA*) was turned toward the east, and its shadow fell on the long arm (*BB*), where we see it at the first hour As the sun rose higher the shadow shortened, and its place on the scale showed the hour, which could be read in figures for six hours until noon. At noon the head (*AA*) was turned around to the west and the *lengthening* afternoon shadow on the long arm (*BB*) was measured in the same way. It was from the introduction of such Egyptian clocks that the twelve-hour day reached Europe. This clock bears the name of Thutmose III and is therefore about thirty-four hundred years old. Nearly a thousand years later such clocks were adopted by the Greeks. It is now in the Berlin Museum. The headpiece (*AA*) is restored after Borchardt

golden dish which came out of it is preserved in the Museum of the Louvre in Paris (see Fig. 145).

Furniture and equipment placed in Empire tombs

134. When it has not been plundered by tomb-robbers, such a tomb is a storehouse of ancient household life; for when a wealthy Egyptian died, his family desired to supply him with everything that had made life pleasant in this world, and that they believed might serve to do the same in the life after death (cf. § 94). In the same way the royal family furnished the tomb of a dead Pharaoh with the greatest splendor and gave the departed king a magnificent array of royal furniture and personal ornaments taken from his palace. Such royal tombs, because of the great value of their contents, were plundered and entirely emptied long ago by the ancient Egyptians themselves. The sole exception is the now famous tomb of Tutenkhamon, which was saved by a curious accident. Workmen who were tunneling into the cliff higher up to make the tomb of a later king threw out a great quantity of stone chips, which then slipped down over the face of

FIG. 70. *Portrait* HEAD *thought to be* IKHNATON, *the Earliest Monotheist*

Discovered by Borchardt in the studio of an ancient Egyptian sculptor at Amarna. The head is carved in limestone and conveys a wonderful impression of dreamy beauty. The resemblance to Ikhnaton's son-in-law, Tutenkhamon, is striking, and it may be his portrait

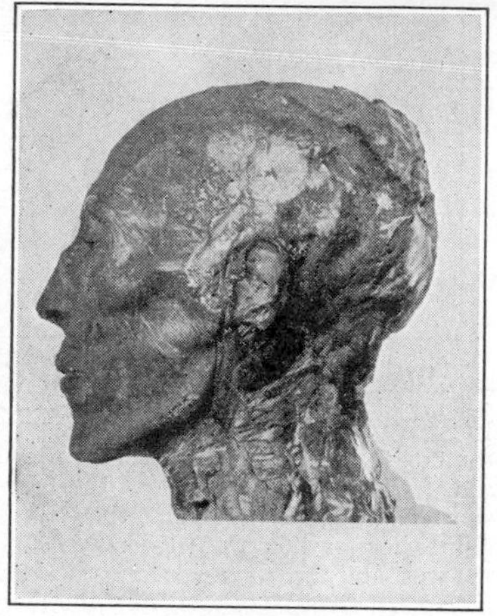

FIG. 71. *Head of the Mummy of* SETI I, *Father of Ramses II*

One of the royal bodies discovered at Thebes (§ 146). The head of Seti is the best-preserved of the entire group, but the royal mummies are all beginning to show evidences of decay. The Egyptian government has accordingly had them removed to a modern tomb at Cairo

Tutenkhamon's tomb and covered it completely. It was so entirely forgotten that, after the fall of the Empire, when the other royal tombs were robbed, no one remembered it.

Religion in the Empire

135. These tombs show us also how much farther the Egyptians had advanced in religion since the days of the pyramids of Gizeh. Each of these great men buried in the Theban cemetery looked forward to a judgment in the next world, where Osiris was the great judge and king. Every good man might rise from the dead as Osiris had done, but in the presence of Osiris he would be obliged to see his soul weighed in the balances over against a feather, the symbol of truth and justice. The dead man's friends put into his coffin a roll of the "Book of the Dead" (headpiece, p. 95), to aid him in the hereafter.

FIG. 72. *King* IKHNATON *sitting at* DINNER *with his Family*

Old Egyptian custom regarded it as unfitting that a Pharaoh should be portrayed as taking part in the everyday affairs of life with his family. On the earlier Egyptian monuments we are given glimpses of only the most formal family groups until we come to study the cliff-tombs of Ikhnaton's followers at Amarna. In violation of all good old custom these noblemen took delight in picturing on the inner walls of their tombs intimate and charming scenes from the life of their beloved young king. In the left center of the above relief he sits at a well-stocked table eating heartily of a huge haunch of meat held in his right hand. The queen, behind him, is demolishing a *whole* roasted fowl and is not in the least ashamed to "eat with her fingers." Seated on smaller chairs beside her, two little princesses follow the example of their parents. The king's mother and her daughter (at right) dine with the royal family. Four serving men, in the center foreground, busy themselves in passing the food, and an orchestra of stringed instruments furnishes the music at the royal dinner

While their ideas about the *next* world were thus growing they were also gaining ideas about *this* world. They had always believed in many gods; but they had thought of the gods (even such an important one as Re, the Sun-god) as ruling only in Egypt, for no one had ever heard of a god who ruled the whole world. The kings of Egypt for two thousand years or more had been ruling only Egypt, and the Egyptians had never thought of any rule that included both Egypt and the larger world outside of it. They had never dreamed of a *whole world* as the kingdom of either a single king or a single god. In the Empire, however, they saw the Pharaoh ruling far beyond the limits of Egypt, and they began to grow accustomed to the idea of a larger rule which included a great part of the world they knew. Thus the question arose in their minds: perhaps the Sun-god ruled more than Egypt, — perhaps he was god of all the world.

Religious revolution of Amenhotep IV (Ikhnaton)

136. When the Empire was some two hundred years old, Amenhotep III's youthful son Amenhotep IV became king, about 1375 B.C. He was convinced that the Sun-god was the god of the whole world, and also that he was the *only* god. There was an old Egyptian word "aton" which meant "sun," and Amenhotep IV took this word as the name for his new god. He commanded that all the people of the Empire should worship only Aton and forget all the old gods. In order that they might do this he closed all the temples and cast out their priests. Everywhere he had the names of the gods erased and cut out, especially on all temple walls. He particularly hated Amon, or Amen, the great Theban god of the Empire to whom was dedicated the great temple at Karnak. His own royal name, Amen-hotep (meaning "Amen is satisfied"), contained this god *Amen's* name, and he therefore changed his name Amenhotep to Ikhnaton, which means "Profitable to Aton."

Ikhnaton's new capital, now called Amarna

137. Ikhnaton, as we must now call him, finally forsook Thebes, the magnificent capital, where there were so many temples of the old gods, and built a new city farther down the river, which he named "Horizon of Aton." It is now called Amarna (see map, p. 66). This city furnishes very valuable information about Ikhnaton and his new religion; for the place was forsaken a few years after Ikhnaton's death, and beneath the rubbish of its ruins today we find the lower portions of the walls of the houses and palaces which the king and his followers built. In the ruins of a sculptor's studio the excavators found many beautiful works, which have greatly increased our knowledge of the wonderful sculpture of the age (Frontispiece). The cliffs behind the city still contain the cliff-tombs of the followers whom the young king was able to convert to the new faith, and in them we find engraved on the walls beautifully sculptured scenes picturing the life of the now forgotten city (Fig. 72).

138. In these Amarna tomb-chapels we may still read on the walls the hymns of praise to the Sun-god, which Ikhnaton himself wrote. They show us the simplicity and beauty of the young king's faith in the sole God. He had gained the belief that one God created not only all the lower creatures but also all races of men, both Egyptians and foreigners. Moreover, the king saw in his God a kindly Father, who maintained all his creatures by his goodness, so that even the birds in the marshes were aware of his kindness and uplifted their wings like arms to praise him, as a beautiful line in one of the hymns tells us. In all the progress of men which we have followed through thousands of years, no one had ever before caught such a vision of the great Father of all. Such a belief in one god is called *monotheism*, which means literally "one-god-ism."

Ikhnaton's hymns to Aton, the sole God

Section 11. The Decline and Fall of the Egyptian Empire

139. A new faith like this could not be understood by the common people in such an early age of the world. The discontented priests of the old gods and the equally dissatisfied soldiers of the neglected army secretly plotted together against the king. Confusion and disturbance arose in Egypt. The consequences in Asia have been revealed to us by a remarkable group of over three hundred letters, found by native diggers in one of Ikhnaton's government offices at Amarna, where

Ikhnaton's troubles at home and abroad

they had lain for over three thousand years. Most of these letters, written on clay tablets in Babylonian writing, proved to be from the kings of Western Asia to the Pharaoh. They form the oldest international correspondence in the world, and show us how these kings were gradually shaking off the rule of the Pharaoh.

Loss of Asiatic empire and death of Ikhnaton

140. The Pharaoh's *northern* territory in Syria (see map I, p. 266) was being taken by the Hittites, who came in from Asia Minor (§ 324), while his *southern* territory in Palestine was being invaded by the Hebrews, who were drifting in from the desert. In the midst of these troubles at home and abroad the young Ikhnaton died, leaving no son behind him. Although a visionary and an idealist, he was the most remarkable religious genius of the early world before the Hebrews; but the faith in one god which he attempted to introduce perished with him.

Feeble reign of Tutenkhamon

141. Ikhnaton lacked a son; but he had gained two sons-in-law by marrying two of his daughters to young nobles of the court. The first son-in-law died, and the second, although he was only ten or eleven years old, was then appointed joint king to rule in company with Ikhnaton. His name was Tutenkhaton (or "Living-Image-of-Aton"). When Ikhnaton died, this lad was possibly twelve years old; nevertheless he became sole king. The revengeful priests of Amon were now in power. They forced the boy-king to leave the new capital at Amarna and to return to Amon's great city of Thebes, where they obliged him to change his name by cutting out the word "Aton" at the end of it and inserting "Amon" in its place. Thus the name "Tutenkhaton" became "Tutenkh*amon*" ("Living-Image-of-Amon"). The worship of Amon and of the other gods of Egypt was restored, and the beautiful Aton faith of Ikhnaton disappeared. After a rule of little more than six years, when not much over eighteen years of age, Tutenkhamon died, having perhaps been put to death by the ambitious priests and soldiers who surrounded him. He

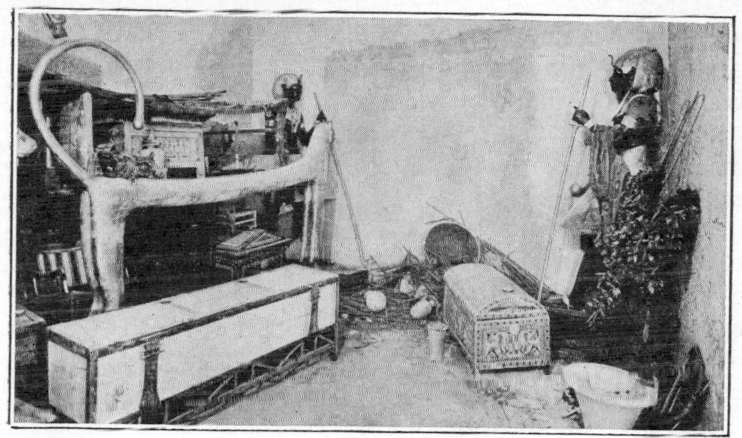

A

B

FIG. 73. *Tomb of* TUTENKHAMON: *North End of Antechamber*

In *A* we see furniture, funeral bouquets, and the sentinel statues of the king standing as if guarding the sealed doorway, the outlines of which may be distinguished by a color darker than the surrounding wall. When the photograph *B* was taken, everything had been removed except the royal statues. The archæologists had also cut out enough of the masonry filling of the sealed door to permit them to enter the burial chamber. The *outer* burial shrine, gold-covered and inlaid with blue glaze, is partially revealed in the background and seen through the doorway. (Courtesy of Howard Carter)

was buried among the emperors, the great ancestors of his wife, Ikhnaton's third daughter. There was no longer a prince of the old Theban family strong enough to maintain its rights. Thus passed away the most powerful family of Pharaohs that Egypt had ever seen. We call them the Eighteenth Dynasty, and they must be remembered as the founders of the first great empire of the early East. They had ruled for some two hundred and thirty years when their line disappeared (about 1350 B.C.).

FIG. 74. *Unbroken* SEAL *on Doorway of Second* SHRINE *in the* TOMB OF TUTENKHAMON *just as it was Found*

Shortly after Tutenkhamon was buried his tomb was entered by robbers, but they were caught in the midst of their plundering. The tomb was then reclosed and resealed, and was not opened again for over 3270 years, that is, until the autumn of 1922 (cf. § 143). The outer doors of the burial shrine had been broken open, but on the inner doors the seal remained intact. The photograph shows it as the author saw it on the day when the burial chamber was reopened by Howard Carter. The seal here shown on the knotted rope fastening the double doors of the burial shrine still retained not only the impression of the king's name but also the thumb-print of the ancient official who put it there. (Courtesy of Howard Carter)

Destruction of monuments of Ikhnaton

142. The reign of Tutenkhamon thus ended before he had reached the years of manhood. It could not be expected that any ruler in his situation could carry on to success such a remarkable effort to transform the religion of Egypt and her empire. As one might tear up the roots

FIG. 75. *Scene at the* ENTRANCE *to the* TOMB OF TUTENKHAMON

The native workmen, under the direction of the excavators, are carrying from the tomb a chest which once contained part of Tutenkhamon's royal clothing. The work of preservative treatment, packing, and transportation of these objects from this tomb was going on from its discovery in 1922 until 1931

FIG. 76. TUTENKHAMON *and his* QUEEN *in their Palace*

The beautiful scene above is from the back of a chair found in the tomb of Tutenkhamon. The workmanship on the piece of furniture here shown is remarkable. The background is of heavy sheet gold, the white garments are of silver, the flesh is of reddish glass, and the ornamental details are incrustations of brightly colored, costly stones. The pleasantly informal picture of the young king and his wife is entirely unknown in earlier Egyptian art, and illustrates the disregard of tradition which was characteristic of Ikhnaton's reign. (Courtesy of Howard Carter)

of a plant, so Ikhnaton's movement attempted to tear out of the hearts of the Egyptian people their long-cherished beliefs, customs, habits, and especially those religious hopes of protection and happiness in the realm of Osiris after death. Very naturally, after Ikhnaton was gone, the people, particularly the priests, made a savage effort to destroy everything that Ikhnaton's artists and craftsmen had produced.

They succeeded so well in this work of destruction that not a great deal has survived to reveal to us the marvelous art and religion of Ikhnaton's revolutionary reign.

Tomb of Tutenkhamon

143. When discovered in 1922, the tomb of Tutenkhamon proved to be of the greatest importance not only because it was a storehouse of works of art and craftsmanship from the age of Ikhnaton but also because it was — as it still remains — the only royal tomb yet found in Egypt practically intact. It was a never-to-be-forgotten experience to enter the antechamber of Tutenkhamon's tomb a short time after its discovery, when nothing had yet been removed from the place. There stood the magnificent furniture of a Pharaoh's palace just as it had been placed in this tomb some three thousand two hundred and seventy years ago. The most splendid piece was a marvelous chair bearing the name of Tutenkhamon on one of its arms. I shall never forget my feelings when I read on the other arm the name "Tutenkh*aton*," the *earlier* form of the young ruler's name. This older form of the name proved that this exquisite chair was the work of *Ikhnaton's* craftsmen, for it had been used in his Amarna palace before Tutenkhamon had been forced to change his name. It thus showed that this wonderful tomb was a treasury of art and life reaching back into the revolution of Ikhnaton, when the human mind had for the first time freed itself from old habits and limitations and had caught a new vision of beauty and of life.

A new line of Pharaohs and beginning of Iron Age

144. When Ikhnaton's revolution thus brought to an end the power of his great family, they were followed by a new line of kings, the greatest of whom were Seti I (Fig. 71) and his son Ramses II (Fig. 77). After desperate efforts these two kings, father and son, were able to restore to some extent the Egyptian Empire. But they were unable to drive the Hittites out of Syria; for these powerful invaders from Asia Minor possessed iron, which they could use for weapons, while the declining Egyptian Empire was the last great power of the Age of Bronze.

FIG. 77. *Colossal* PORTRAIT FIGURE *of* RAMSES II *at Abu Simbel, in Egyptian Nubia*

Four such statues, 75 feet high, adorn the front of this temple, which, like the statues, is hewn from the sandstone cliffs. The faces are better preserved than that of the Great Sphinx (Fig. 42), and we can here see that such vast figures were portraits. The face of Ramses II here closely resembles that of his mummy (Fig. 117). (From a photograph taken from the top of the crown of one of the statues by a University of Chicago expedition)

145. At Thebes the symptoms of the coming fall may be seen even at the present day. If we examine the great war pictures on the Theban temples, we find in the battle scenes of the later Empire numbers of foreigners serving in the Egyptian army. This shows that the Egyptians had finally lost their temporary interest in war and were calling in foreigners to fight their battles. Among these strangers are the peoples of the northern Mediterranean whom we left there in the Late Stone Age. Here on the Egyptian monuments we find them pictured after they had learned from Eastern peoples the art of using metal. With huge bronze swords in their hands we see them serving as hired soldiers (Fig. 152) in the Egyptian army. Their kindred at home and other Mediterranean foreigners finally invaded Egypt in such numbers that the weakened Egyptian Empire fell, in the middle of the Twelfth Century B.C.

Mercenary troops; foreign invaders; fall of the Empire

146. The great emperors were buried at Thebes in a wild and desolate valley in the western desert (Fig. 4). Here, in over forty rock-hewn galleries, some reaching hundreds of feet into the mountain, the bodies of the Empire Pharaohs were laid to rest. But we recall that it was only the tomb of Tutenkhamon (§ 134) which escaped pillage and robbery after the fall of the Empire. Ruling as feeble kings at Thebes, the weak successors of the emperors hurried the royal bodies from one hiding place to another, and finally concealed them in a secret chamber hewn for this purpose in the western cliffs. Here they lay undisturbed until, in 1881, they were discovered and removed to the National Museum at Cairo (Fig. 71). Until recently we were able to look into the very faces of these lords of Egypt and Western Asia who lived and ruled from thirty-five to thirty-one hundred years ago.[1]

Bodies of the emperors

147. Thus ends the story of the Empire at Thebes. The pyramids, tombs, and temples along the Nile have told us

[1] The Egyptian government has now removed these royal bodies to a modern tomb at Cairo.

FIG. 78. RAMSES III *hunting Wild* BULLS *in the Marshes*

The king stands in his swiftly moving chariot, and, leaning far forward with one foot planted outside on the pole of the chariot, thrusts his long spear into the great bulls plunging through the jungle only to sink down mortally wounded at the water's edge. The dashing horses and the vigorous movement of the bodyguard below make this scene probably the most powerful and impressive relief sculpture surviving from ancient Egypt. In its original colors (the water blue, the jungle green), with the pathetic figures of the dying bulls and the gorgeous trappings of the Pharaoh, his chariot, his horses, and his bodyguard, it must have been a scene of rare beauty and brilliance

Significance of Egyptian history and civilization

the history of early Egypt in three epochs: the pyramids of Gizeh and the neighboring cemeteries have disclosed to us the Pyramid Age; the cliff-tombs and the papyrus-roll libraries have revealed the history and civilization of the Feudal Age; and the temples and cliff-tombs of Thebes have given us the story of the Empire. The Nile has thus become for us a great volume of history. Let us remember, however, that, preceding these three great chapters of civilization on the Nile, we also found here the earlier story of how man passed from Stone Age barbarism to a civilization possessed of metal, writing, and government. On the other hand, as we look forward we should remember also that the three great chapters did not end the story; for Egyptian institutions and civilization continued far down into the Christian Age and greatly influenced later history in Europe.

Knowledge of meaning of hieroglyphs lost

148. In this summary of the story of ancient Egypt we have gained our knowledge from the monuments and the written records. However, only a little over a hundred years ago no one knew what these written records meant; for the last men who could read Egyptian hieroglyphs had been dead for over a thousand years, and after their time there was no one who understood the curious writing which travelers found covering the great monuments along the Nile.

Champollion deciphers Egyptian hieroglyphs

149. For a long time scholars puzzled over the strange Nile records, but made little progress in reading them. Then a young Frenchman named Champollion took up the problem, and after years of discouraging failure he began to make progress. He discovered the names of Ptolemy and Cleopatra written both in hieroglyphs and in Greek letters on the same monument. He was thus able to determine the sounds of twelve hieroglyphic signs used in these two names, and he proved them to be alphabetic. Champollion was then able to read several other royal names, and in 1822, in a famous letter to the French Academy, he announced his discovery and explained the steps he had taken. It was not until this point was reached that he was able to make use of the well-known Rosetta Stone (Fig. 203), which enabled him to increase his list of known hieroglyphic signs and to learn the meanings of words. When he died, in 1832, he had written a little grammar and prepared a small dictionary of hieroglyphic. Others took up the work, and thus the monuments of the Nile have gained a voice to tell us the wonderful story of the early advance of men after they had gained civilization.

150. In a similar way the monuments discovered along the Tigris and Euphrates rivers in Asia have been deciphered and have been made to tell their story. They show us that, following the Egyptians, the peoples of Asia emerged from barbarism, developed industries, learned the use of metals, devised a system of writing, and finally rose to the leading position of power in the ancient world. We must now turn, in the next chapter, to the story of the early Near East in Asia, especially the Babylonians.

Transition to Asia

QUESTIONS

Section 8. Describe the civilization of the Feudal Age barons. Discuss the policies of the Pharaohs of the Feudal Age. What great commercial link between two seas was created?

Section 9. How did the Pharaohs who built the Temple of Karnak at Thebes differ from those who built the pyramids? Discuss the first great woman in history. Tell about the reign of the greatest Egyptian general. What was the extent of the Egyptian Empire?

Section 10. What did the Egyptian emperors do with the wealth gained from subject peoples? Describe the great Karnak hall, and tell how the clerestory was improved. Give an account of the Theban cemetery and what it contains. Discuss the earliest belief in one god.

Section 11. What were the consequences of Ikhnaton's movement? Tell about the Amarna letters. Discuss the importance of the discovery of the tomb of Tutenkhamon. What northerners held Syria, and what new weapons did they have? What foreigners invaded Egypt and aided in destroying the Empire? What happened to the bodies of the emperors? Why were our great-grandfathers unable to read hieroglyphic? Discuss its decipherment. Describe the Rosetta Stone and tell how it helped in the reading of Egyptian hieroglyphs (Fig. 203).

BIBLIOGRAPHY FOR TOPICAL STUDIES

Civilization of Feudal Age: BREASTED, *Ancient Egyptians*, §§ 155–166, and *Dawn of Conscience*, pp. 182–206; MASPERO, *Art in Egypt*, pp. 95–122.

Conquests of the emperors: BLACKMAN, *Luxor and its Temples*, pp. 84–110; BREASTED, *Ancient Egyptians*, §§ 214–234, 237–243, 285–310.

Painting and drawing: *Bulletin of the Metropolitan Museum of Art*, July, 1920, Part II, pp. 24–33, and December, 1920, Part II, pp. 33–40; MASPERO, pp. 161–166; PETRIE, *Art and Crafts*, chap. v.

Chapter V · *Western Asia: Babylonia*

Section 12. The Quarter of the Globe where Civilization Grew Up and Developed

Mediterranean world

151. Thus far we have watched the developing life of early men in the regions on both sides of the Mediterranean Sea. In doing so we have found that the lands where these early men lived entirely surrounded the great sea. Together with this fringe of inhabited lands around it, the Mediterranean formed the center of advancing human life, beginning with the earliest appearance of man. While bearing this fact in mind, let us examine as a whole the quarter of the globe in which the Mediterranean Sea occupies such an important part. As we all know, the Mediterranean is surrounded by three continents: Europe on the north, Africa on the south, and Asia on both the east

NOTE. The above scene shows us the SEMITIC NOMADS on the FERTILE CRESCENT along the SEA OF GALILEE. In spring the region is richly overgrown, but the vegetation soon fades. The dark camel's-hair tents of these wandering shepherds are easily carried from place to place as they seek new pasturage. They live on the milk and flesh of the flocks.

and the north. The only early *civilized* life on the African side of the Mediterranean was limited to a narrow strip along the shore (because of the Sahara Desert lying behind) and a narrow line extending southward along the Nile. On the European side of the Mediterranean civilized men moved gradually northward and in time reached the Baltic, the North Sea, and the British Isles. At the Asiatic end of the great sea civilized life developed far inland, and eventually eastward to India and China, although these two countries will concern us very little, as we shall see.

Great Northwest Quadrant

152. Beginning with the Mediterranean, then, we find that its three coast lines, southern, northern, and eastern, together with the lands back of them, formed a great world where the life of early men was developing on three continents,—a narrow belt along the northern end of Africa, the western part of Asia, and a large portion of Europe, only its most northerly parts being omitted. Viewed as one whole, these regions form a great triangle (see diagram, p. 130), including a large part of the northwestern quarter of the Eastern Hemisphere. This triangle, which has been called the Great Northwest Quadrant, has as its base line the southern borders of the desert in Africa and Asia. Its eastern boundary is a north-and-south line roughly coinciding with the Ural Mountains, while on the west and north it extends to the Atlantic and Arctic oceans. In this enormous triangle developed the civilization which Europe and America of today have inherited.

Three geographic zones

153. In the geography of the Great Northwest Quadrant we at once notice two outstanding features: first, the Mediterranean Sea, and, second, the mountain ranges on the north of this sea. The mountain ranges divide the land into three zones, lying likewise in east-and-west lines. There is, first, the long *Highland Zone*, to which the mountains belong, stretching along the northern side of the Mediterranean and then far eastward into the heart of Asia beyond the eastern boundary of our triangle. On the northern side of the Highland Zone there are *Northern*

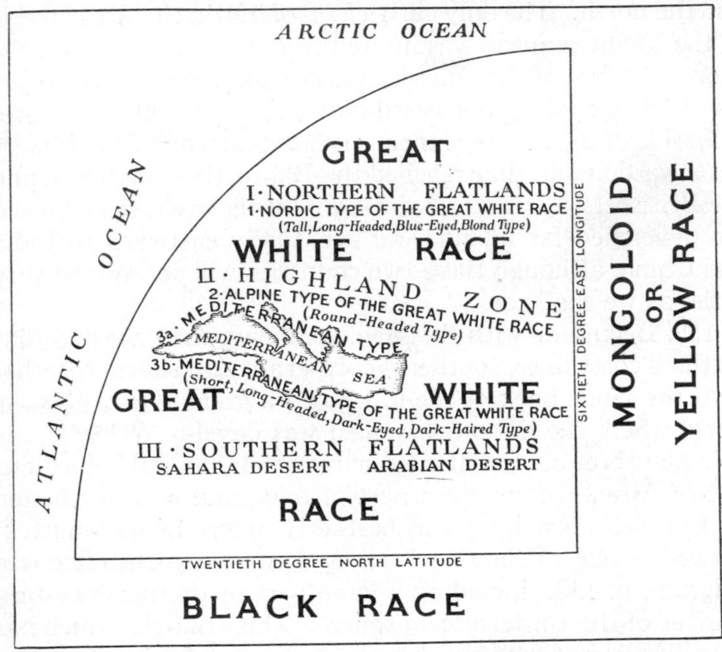

FIG. 79. *Racial Diagram of the Great* NORTHWEST QUADRANT

The diagram is intended to show the three important geographical zones, numbered from north to south, I, II, and III, and to indicate in general the position of the subdivisions of the Great White Race on these three geographical zones (see Fig. 80). At the bottom, below the twentieth degree of north latitude, the general position of the black race is noted; and, similarly, at the right of the sixtieth degree of longitude, it places the Mongoloid, or yellow, race. It should be observed that the above is a rough diagram, not a geographically accurate map. A rough indication of the Mediterranean Sea is inserted to show that it separates the Europeans of the Mediterranean type from those of North Africa. On the south of the Mediterranean the people of the Great White Race are darker-skinned than elsewhere. For more accurate geographical relations the map of the Northwest Quadrant on page 13 should be carefully compared

Flatlands, which likewise stretch far eastward and deep into Asia. On the south side of the Highland Zone there are *Southern Flatlands,* which are largely occupied at the west end by the basin of the Mediterranean. It is important to observe that much of the Southern Flatlands is desert, extending from North Africa eastward across the Red Sea and far into Asia.

154. The peoples of the Great Northwest Quadrant, as far back as we know anything about prehistoric man, have all been members of a race of white men, who have been well called the Great White Race (see Fig. 80). The men of this race created the civilization which we have inherited. If we look outside of the Great Northwest Quadrant, we find in the neighboring territory only two other clearly distinguished races, — the Mongoloids on the east and the Negroes on the south. These peoples occupy an important place in the modern world, but they played no part in the rise of civilization.

Three races

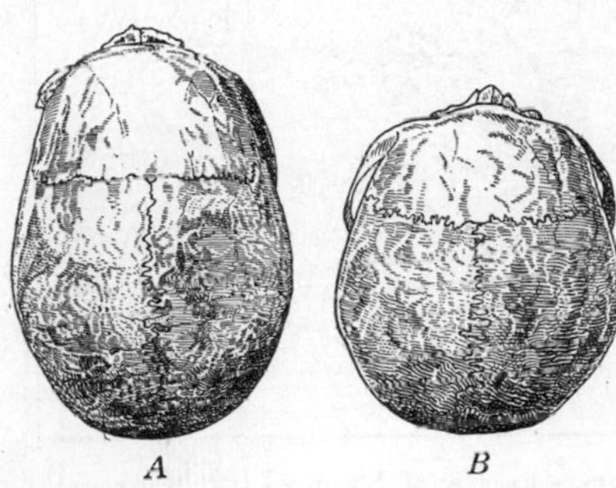

FIG. 80. *Comparison of an Ancient Egyptian* LONG SKULL *(A) and the* SHORT SKULL *(B) of an Ancient Highland Zone Man*

The people of the Great White Race differ markedly in certain physical characteristics. Scientists have found, for instance, that there is a striking variation in the shape of the skull. Based on this difference a rough subdivision of the white race in the Great Northwest Quadrant is sometimes made. On the Northern Flatlands we find fair-haired, *long-headed* people, such as the Scandinavians, who are sometimes called Nordics, and among whom we are familiar with the Swedes and Norwegians. Their neighbors on the south are *round-headed* men dwelling in the Highland Zone, and hence are often called Alpine or Armenoid peoples, such as the Tyrolese, Swiss, and Armenians. On the Southern Flatlands, finally, live dark-haired peoples with *long heads*, now commonly known as the Mediterranean race because they are found on nearly all the shores of the Mediterranean and practically surround it. These three types peopled the whole of the Great Northwest Quadrant, and the ancestors of the population now living there were the creators of the civilization we have inherited. The skull *A* is typical of the Mediterranean race, while *B* illustrates the shortness and greater width of the skull of the Highland Zone man. The scientific term for the long heads is *dolichocephalic*, and for the round heads *brachycephalic*

155. On the *east* of the Northwest Quadrant the isolated plateaus of inner Asia, commonly called High Asia, were early inhabited by the Mongols, or Mongoloids, a race of men with straight, black, wiry hair, round head, almost beardless face, and yellow skin. Among these Mongoloids, civilization did not arise until long after it was far advanced

Mongoloids

FIG. 81. *The Earliest Known* REPRESENTATION *of* NEGRO LIFE (*Thirteenth Century* B.C.)

Under a palm at the left a Negro woman sits stirring an earthen pot over a fire, preparing food. Meanwhile a great commotion has arisen. A large group of defeated soldiers (on the right), fleeing before the wrath of the Egyptian king, have burst into camp. At the left, somewhat in advance of the main group, a wounded soldier is supported by two comrades who lead him to the arms of his wife and two children approaching from the left. In the palm tree beside them a monkey hops up and down and chatters frenziedly at the confusion, and an excited child rushes past to tell the cook of the misfortune which has befallen them. This relief is found in a temple of Ramses II, thus dating to the Thirteenth Century B.C. The gaps in the above picture are due to the breakages in the ancient original relief

in the Northwest Quadrant.[1] The migrations of these yellow men out of High Asia finally carried them in all directions, but they did not reach the Northwest Quadrant until long after civilization there was already highly developed. Groups of Asiatic wanderers related to the Mongoloids finally migrated to the far northeast of Asia, and perhaps about ten thousand years ago they crossed to Alaska. As they wandered farther into America they became the ancestors of the North American Indians, whose bodies, especially their faces, continue to show their Asiatic origin.

[1] Chinese civilization is much later than that of Western Asia and Egypt. The popular impression that it is older is wholly incorrect. No piece of metal as yet found in China can be dated earlier than about 1200 B.C., that is, at least three thousand years later than in Egypt and very much later than in Western Asia. As for writing, there is no surviving document written in Chinese which may be dated any earlier than about the Eleventh, or at the earliest the Twelfth, Century B.C., that is, over two thousand years later than in Egypt and Western Asia.

156. On the *south* of the Northwest Quadrant lay the teeming black world of Africa, as it does today. It was separated from the Great White Race by the broad stretch of the Sahara Desert. The valley of the Nile was the only road leading across the Sahara from south to north. Sometimes the blacks of inner Africa did wander along this road into Egypt, but they came only in small groups. Thus cut off by the desert barrier and living by themselves, they remained uninfluenced by civilization from the north. The Negro peoples of Africa were therefore without any influence on the development of early civilization.

Negroes

SECTION 13. THE LANDS AND RACES OF WESTERN ASIA

157. We have followed the rise and progress of civilization in Egypt on the Southern Flatlands in North Africa, and we must now trace the rise and spread of civilization in Western Asia. In prehistoric times the topography of Western Asia was quite different from what it is at present. At the close of the Ice Age the Persian Gulf extended probably over five hundred miles farther northwest than it does now. Living along the shores of the great gulf, the Stone Age hunters have left their lost flint implements where we now find them still lying. Some of these hunters probably lived also on small islands at that time dotting the great gulf, and at the present day excavation uncovers their stone tools and weapons buried deep in some ruined Babylonian city on a spot which was once an island. For in the Stone Age the Persian Gulf covered all of the area which later became the Plain of Babylonia, and some of Assyria as well. Its northern shores at that time were probably the highlands along the south side of the Highland Zone. In strong contrast with Egypt, therefore, the earliest dwellers along these shores felt the cold of the glaciers on the southern slopes of the Highland Zone. Furthermore, at the end of the glacial period the violent torrents formed by the melting snows and ice in the Highland Zone poured

Post-glacial conditions in Western Asia

FIG. 82. *Typical View of the* MIDDLE EUPHRATES VALLEY

The Euphrates never succeeded in eroding a valley of continuous breadth. It is in some stretches a narrow defile, or cañon; again the valley expands to a width of some miles. Throughout all the desert course of the river, however, its valley never widens so as to create an alluvial floor of sufficient extent to sustain a large population. Although several miles long, the cultivated strip shown here is so narrow that the whole of it would not exceed the area of a good-sized farm in the upper Mississippi valley. (Oriental Institute photograph)

down through this region between the mountains and the Southern Flatlands and cut its cultivable land to pieces, so that it was for a long time unsuited to the settled life that leads to civilization.

Creation of Babylonian Plain

158. The Babylonian Plain did not yet exist, and it was not until long after the Ice Age that it began to be slowly created as the drainage of the Highland Zone carried down the upland soil and spread it in a growing fringe along the northern shores of the Persian Gulf. This soil at last formed a low, level plain, later called Babylonia. This kind of land formation, being dependent on the disappearance of the glaciers, was later than that which took place in Egypt, which never suffered from an invasion of the ice. The Nile brought the soil of Egypt from the tropics, but the soil of the Babylonian Plain was brought by the Two Rivers from the glacial north.

159. The most important early home of men in Western Asia is the borderland between the mountains, or Highland Zone, on the north and the desert of the Southern Flatlands. This borderland between the desert and the mountains is a kind of cultivable fringe of the desert, — a Fertile Crescent[1] having the mountains on one side and the desert on the other (see map, p. 146). It forms roughly a semicircle with the open side toward the south. Its western end is at the southeastern corner of the Mediterranean, the center lies directly north of Arabia, and the eastern end is at the northern end of the Persian Gulf. It lies like a horseshoe opening southward, with one side stretching along the eastern shore of the Mediterranean and the other reaching out to the Persian Gulf, while the center has its back against the northern mountains. The end of the western side is Palestine, Assyria makes up a large part of the center, while the end of the eastern side is Babylonia.

The Fertile Crescent

160. This great semicircle, the Fertile Crescent, may also be likened to the shores of a desert bay, upon which the mountains behind look down, — a bay not of water but of sandy waste, some five hundred miles across, forming a northern extension of the Arabian Desert. This desert bay, a part of the Southern Flatlands, is a limestone plateau of some height, — too high, indeed, to be watered by the Tigris and Euphrates, which have cut cañons obliquely across it. Nevertheless, after the meager winter rains, wide tracts of the northern desert bay are clothed with scanty grass, and spring thus turns the region for a short time into grasslands. The history of Western Asia may be described as an age-long struggle between the mountain peoples of the north and the desert wanderers of these grasslands — a struggle which is still going on — for the possession of the Fertile Crescent, the shores of the desert bay.

The desert bay

[1] There is no name, either geographical or political, which includes all of this great semicircle. Hence in the first edition of this book (1916) the author was obliged to coin a term. It was called, therefore, the Fertile Crescent. The term has since become current and is now widely used.

Arabian Desert and Semitic nomads

161. Arabia is totally lacking in rivers and enjoys but a few weeks of rain in midwinter; hence it is largely desert, very little of which is habitable. Its people are and have been from the remotest ages a branch of the Great White Race called Semites. The Semites have always been divided into many tribes and groups, just as were the American Indians, whom we call Sioux or Seminoles or Iroquois. So we shall find many tribal or group names among the Semites. With two of these peoples we are familiar, — the Arabs, and the Hebrews whose descendants dwell among us. They all spoke and still speak dialects of the same tongue, of which Hebrew was one. For ages they have moved up and down the habitable portions of the Arabian world, seeking pasturage for their flocks and herds. Such wandering shepherds are called nomads, and we remember how their manner of life arose after the domestication of cattle, sheep, and goats (see § 45).

Shift of the nomads from the desert to the Fertile Crescent

162. From the earliest times, when the spring grass of the border wilderness is gone these nomads have been constantly drifting in from the sandy sea upon the shores of the northern desert bay. If they can secure a footing there, they slowly make the transition from the *wandering* life of the desert nomad to the *settled* life of the agricultural peasant. There have been times when this slow shift swelled into a great tidal wave of migration. Then the wild hordes of the wilderness rolled in upon the fertile shores of the desert bay, — a human tide from the desert to the towns, which they gradually overwhelmed. We can see this process going on for thousands of years. Among such movements we are familiar with the passage of the Hebrews from the desert into Palestine, as described in the Bible, and some readers will recall the invasions of the Arab hosts, who, when converted to Mohammedanism, even reached Europe and threatened to girdle the Mediterranean. After they had adopted a settled town life the colonies of the Semites stretched far westward along the Mediterranean, especially in northern Africa, even to southern Spain and the

Atlantic (see Fig. 123, and map, p. 346). But it took many centuries for the long line of their settlements to creep westward until it reached the Atlantic, and we must begin with the Semites in the desert.

Lack of institutions and industries among Semitic nomads

163. Out on the wide reaches of the desert there are no boundaries; the pasturage is free as air to the first comer. No man of the tribe owns land; there are no landholding rich and no landless poor. The men of the desert know no law. The keen-eyed desert marauder looks with envy across the hills dotted with the flocks of the neighboring tribe, which may be his when he has slain the solitary shepherd at the well. But if he does so, he knows that his own family will suffer death or heavy damages, not at the hands of the state but at the hands of the slain shepherd's family. This custom, known as "blood revenge," has a restraining influence like that of law. Under such conditions there is no state or government. Writing and records are unknown, industries are practically nonexistent, and the desert tribesmen lead a life of complete freedom. The governments holding Arabia today are as powerless to control the wandering Arabs of the wilderness as were formerly the American authorities in suppressing the lawlessness of their cowboy herdsmen.

Traffic and caravan

164. The tribesmen drift with their flocks along the margin of the Fertile Crescent till they discern a town among the palm groves. Objects of picturesque interest to the curious eyes of the townsmen, they appear in the market place to traffic for the weapons, utensils, and raiment which the nomads cannot dispense with (headpiece, p. 217). They early learned to carry goods from place to place and thus became not only the common carriers of the settled communities but also traders on their own account, fearlessly leading their caravans across the wastes of the desert bay, lying between Syria-Palestine and Babylonia. They were the greatest merchants of the ancient world, as their Hebrew descendants among us still are at the present day.

Religion of the nomad

165. The wilderness is the nomad's home. Its vast solitudes tinged his soul with solemnity. His imagination peopled the far reaches of the desert with invisible and uncanny beings, and he believed that they inhabited every rock and tree, hilltop and spring. These creatures were his gods, whom he fancied he could control by the utterance of magic charms, — the earliest prayers. He believed that such charms would render these mysterious gods powerless to do him injury and would also compel them to grant him aid.

Tribal god of the nomad

166. The nomad pictured each one of these beings as controlling only a little corner of the great world, perhaps only a well and its surrounding pastures. At the next well, only a day's march away, there was thought to be another god, belonging to the next tribe, for each tribe had a favorite or tribal god, who, as they believed, journeyed with them from pasture to pasture, sharing their food and their feasts and receiving as his due from the tribesmen the firstborn of their flocks and herds.

Nomad's thoughts about his tribal god; his ideas of right

167. The thoughts of the desert wanderer about the character of such a god were crude and barbarous, and his religious customs were often savage, even leading him to sacrifice his children to appease the angry god. On the other hand, the nomad had a dawning sense of justice and of right, and he felt some obligations of kindness to his fellows which he believed were the compelling voice of his god. In Palestine such feelings, much influenced by the moral teachings of the Egyptian wise men, at last became lofty moral vision, which made the Semites the religious teachers of the civilized world.

Semites on the Fertile Crescent

168. As early as 3000 B.C. the Semites were drifting in from the desert and settling in Palestine, on the *western* end of the Fertile Crescent, where we find them in possession of walled towns by 2500 B.C. These earliest Semitic dwellers in Palestine were the predecessors of the Hebrews there. They were a people called Canaanites; farther north settled a powerful tribe known as

Amorites; while along the shores of north Syria some of these one-time desert wanderers, the Phœnicians, had taken to the sea. The earliest city of the Phœnicians was a flourishing harbor town called Byblos. In the mountains behind it were the great cedar forests furnishing valuable timber, which long before 3000 B.C. had led the Pharaohs to take possession of the city and harbor. Here they built a temple to the Lady of Byblos, the goddess of the town. The Phœnician lords of Byblos were subject to the Pharaoh and paid him tribute, — a kind of foreign taxes. They wrote their first inscriptions in Egyptian hieroglyphs, they used Egyptian furniture and utensils, and they wore Egyptian jewelry. Thus all these settled communities of the western Semites gradually learned civilization, drawn at first from Egypt, but later from Babylonia also. Their lands along the eastern end of the Mediterranean were like a corridor forming the highway between these two countries, and they were in constant contact with both (see map, p. 146). We shall take up the story of the Phœnicians later in discussing the history of the Eastern Mediterranean.

Non-Semites of the mountains on the Fertile Crescent

169. While the Semites thus invaded the Fertile Crescent from the *inside* of the semicircle, the peoples on the *outside*, that is, the peoples of the Highland Zone, very early entered the Fertile Crescent and established homes there. These people were not Semites, but seem to have belonged to different groups of the Great White Race. The most important of them were the Hittites, who occupied the western region of the Highland Zone, especially central Asia Minor (Anatolia). For centuries the Hittites and other Highland peoples all along the Fertile Crescent fought with the Semites for its possession.

170. The earliest civilization of Western Asia, and likewise the most important, arose on the eastern end of the Fertile Crescent along the lower courses of the Two Rivers. These two important streams, the Tigris and the Euphrates, rise in the northern mountains, whence they issue to cross the

Fertile Crescent and to cut obliquely southeastward through the northern bay of the desert. Here, on these two great rivers of Western Asia, we can follow through several thousand years the earliest civilization known in Asia. Just as on the Nile, so here on the Two Rivers, we shall find three great chapters in the story.

Two Rivers and three great chapters in their history

171. As on the Nile, so also the earliest of the three chapters of Tigris-Euphrates history will be found in the lower valley near the rivers' mouths. This earliest chapter is the story of Babylonia.[1] As the Two Rivers approached most closely to each other, about one hundred and sixty or seventy miles from the Persian Gulf,[2] they emerged from the desert and entered a low plain of fertile soil, formerly brought down by the rivers. This plain was Babylonia, the eastern end of the Fertile Crescent. But during the first thousand years of the known history of this plain the later city of Babylon had not yet arisen, or was a mere village playing little or no part in the history of the region. The plain was then called Shinar, and "Babylonia" is a name that properly should not be applied to it until the Twenty-first Century B.C. (see § 211).

Earliest chapter of history of the Two Rivers in the Plain of Shinar

172. Rarely more than forty miles wide, the Plain of Shinar contained probably less than eight thousand square miles of cultivable soil, — roughly equal to the state of New Jersey or the area of Wales. It lies in the Mediterranean belt of rainy winter and dry summer, but the rainfall is so scanty (less than seven inches a year)[3] that irrigation of the fields is necessary in order to ripen the grain.

Area and fertility of Plain of Shinar

[1] The other two chapters of the Tigris-Euphrates history are Assyria and the Chaldean Empire (Chapter VI).

[2] This distance applies only to ancient Babylonian and Assyrian days. The rivers have since then filled up the Persian Gulf for from one hundred and fifty to one hundred and sixty miles, and the gulf is that much shorter at the present day (see note under scale on map, p. 146).

[3] Based on British reports for the thirty-seven years from 1887 to 1924. In the United States a rainfall of less than 30 inches per year is considered almost too scanty for successful agriculture.

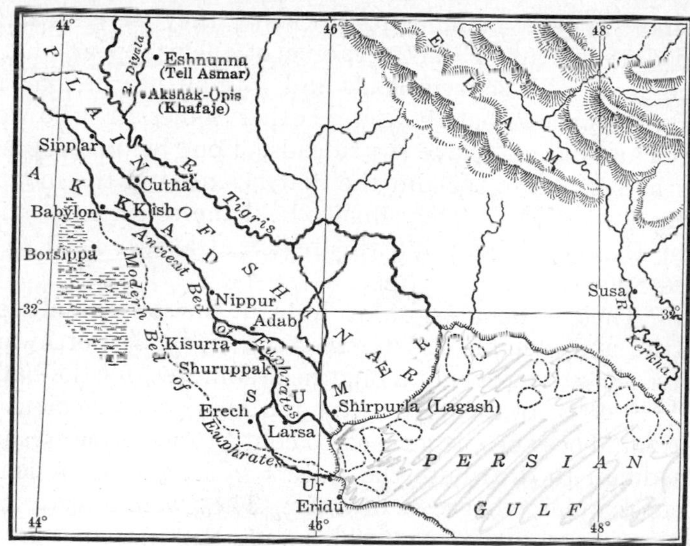

Sketch Map of SUMER *and* AKKAD

When properly irrigated the Plain of Shinar is prodigiously fertile, and the chief source of wealth in ancient Shinar was agriculture. This plain was the scene of the most important and long-continued of those frequent struggles between mountaineer and nomad. We are now to follow the story of the first series of those struggles, lasting well over a thousand years and subsiding after 1900 B.C.

SECTION 14. RISE OF SUMERIAN CIVILIZATION IN THE AGE OF THE CITY-KINGDOMS, AND THE EARLY STRUGGLE OF SUMERIAN AND SEMITE

Unknown race of early Sumerians

173. At a very early period, possibly before 4000 B.C., some of the Highland peoples migrated and settled on the Fertile Crescent. Among them the earliest people clearly revealed to us by the excavations in the Plain of Shinar were called Sumerians. We are still in ignorance of their race. As shown in relief pictures on the most ancient monuments of Shinar they were a round-headed people (cf. Fig. 80). Some of them appear on the monuments with shaven heads and without beards, but the monuments show that there were other Sumerians who wore beards and did not shave their heads. Long before 3500 B.C. they had begun to reclaim the marshes around the mouths of the Two Rivers. They finally held the southern portion of the Plain of Shinar, and this region at length came to be called Sumer.

Material civilization of Sumerians

174. Their settlements of low huts, at first of plaited reeds (wattle) and then of mud brick, crept gradually northward, especially along the Euphrates, for the banks of the Tigris were too high for convenient irrigation. These people learned to control the spring freshets with dikes, to distribute the waters in irrigation trenches, and to reap large harvests of grain. They were already cultivating barley and wheat, which were the two chief grains in Western Asia as they were in Egypt. The Sumerians called the wheat by its Egyptian name. They already possessed cattle, as well as sheep and goats. These animals played such an important part in the life of the Sumerians that one of their important goddesses had the form of a cow, and they believed that she protected the flocks and herds. Recently discovered sculptures in her temple near Ur show us interesting pictures of the dairy industry among the Sumerians of nearly 3000 B.C. Oxen drew the plow, and horses and donkeys pulled *wheeled* carts and chariots. These Sumerian chariots are the earliest known wheeled vehicles, and the wheel as a burden-bearing device appeared here for the first time. Not long after 3000 B.C. horses from the northeastern mountains were already known, although they continued to be rare for nearly a thousand years. At the same time metal had also been introduced, and the smith had learned to fashion utensils of copper, but he had not yet learned to harden the copper into bronze by admixture of tin. Meantime, as in Egypt, stone implements continued to be used for a long time side by side with copper.

FIG. 83. A DAIRY *near Ancient Ur* (*about* 3000 B.C.)

This frieze formed part of the decoration on the front of the little temple of the cow-goddess. It was originally mounted on a plank, edged above and below with a strip of copper. The figures themselves, however, are carved from pieces of shell or limestone and mounted in a thin layer of black bitumen which filled the space between the strips of copper. *Above* is part of a frieze of marching bulls, while *below* is the dairy scene. At the right we see two cows, each with her calf before her. According to Sumerian custom the milking was done from behind, and we see the dairyman, therefore, seated *behind* the cow he is milking. This milking is going on in a cow-yard, of which the gate is seen near the middle, behind the left-hand cow. At this gate two calves are represented with only the fore quarters showing, to indicate that they are coming out of the gate and are only halfway out. At the extreme left four dairymen are at work with the milk. The man at the left plunges his arm deep into a tall pointed jar in order to dip out the last of the milk it contains. Two men in the middle are engaged in pouring the milk through a strainer into a jar on the ground. With his back to the gate the last man sits on a small, square stool while he rolls about on the ground a large jar which serves as a churn and is placed on its side in order that it may more easily be rolled about to produce the agitation of the cream which results in butter. (Courtesy of the University Museum of Philadelphia)

Rise of Sumerian trade

175. Agriculture and cattle-breeding produced most of the wealth which formed the basis of Sumerian life, but there were other important sources of wealth. Besides the metal which we have just mentioned, the wool from the flocks made possible the development of weaving and the production of plentiful woolen cloth. Metal work, woolen goods, and some native products, like dates and grain, developed active trade with other countries of Western Asia. We now know that this trade extended far into Asia, even reaching the mouth of the Indus and the

FIG. 84. *Ancient Babylonian* SEEDER, *or Machine Planter*

The seeder is drawn by a yoke of oxen, with their driver beside them. Behind the seeder follows a man holding it by two handles. It is very pointed and evidently makes a shallow trench in the soil as it moves. Rising from the frame of the seeder is a vertical tube (*a*) on the top of which is a funnel (*b*). A third man walking beside the seeder is shown dropping the grain into this funnel with one hand; with the other he holds what is probably a sack of seed grain suspended from his shoulders. The grain drops down through the tube and falls into the trench made by the seeder. The scene was carved on a small stone seal. (After Clay)

lower valley of that river. At the same time the discovery in Sumer of a seal from the Indus[1] makes the fact of such trade quite certain. There is every indication that this trade passed between the Tigris and the Indus *by land*. It is not yet clear whether the Sumerians had been able to develop sea-going ships for traffic on the Persian Gulf and beyond it. The region of the Two Rivers, of which Sumer formed the southern part, lay between the Eastern Mediterranean world on the west and remoter Asia on the east. Between these two widely separated regions the people of the Two Rivers began very early to carry on extensive commerce, which later spread

[1] Recent excavations in northwestern India, in the lower valley of the Indus River, have uncovered remains of a civilization reaching back to at least 2500 B.C. The discovery by the Oriental Institute of The University of Chicago of the seal shown in Fig. 85 has established this date. In the Indus valley were early towns with houses of burnt brick. The men who built them were already cultivating fields of grain and raising cattle. They had tamed the horse, had learned to harness the bullock to two-wheeled carts, and had taught the elephant to serve as a burden-bearer. Tools of copper and bronze were in use, and craftsmen worked in silver and understood the art of glazing. A form of picture writing had been developed. There are evidences that they had in very early times established trade connections with the Sumerians, from whom, no doubt, they had received their civilization.

FIG. 85. A CYLINDER SEAL *(above) discovered in the Ruins of the Ancient Babylonian City of Eshnunna (cf. Fig. 89) compared with* STAMP SEALS *(below) found in the Lower Indus Valley*

When compared with objects recently excavated in the Indus valley this seal is shown to be of East Indian origin rather than Babylonian. That it was imported is indicated not only by the style of carving but also by the animal subjects chosen for decorating the seal, for the elephant does not appear in the art of the Tigris-Euphrates valley, and the rhinoceros was unknown there. As this seal was found with other objects dating to the Twenty-fifth Century B.C., it is evident that we may date the Indus valley civilization at least as far back as about 2500 B.C.

in a great network of roads and sea routes. These communications not only connected the countries of the Near East with each other but likewise linked the Near East as a whole with the Asiatic world on one side and the Mediterranean world on the other. This commerce from the Two Rivers overlapped with that of Egypt in the Eastern Mediterranean and must have extended to Egypt itself. It was such intercourse between the Two Rivers and Egypt which already in prehistoric times gave these two regions a number of things in common, like the use of the cylinder seal, the pear-shaped war mace, and the use of balanced animal figures in decorative art (see Fig. 94).

176. Trade and government very early led the Sumerians to make records, scratched in rude pictures with the tip of a reed on a flat oval or disk of soft clay. When dried in the sun such a clay record became very hard, and if well baked in an oven it became an almost imperishable pottery tablet. On the earliest surviving specimens of these tablets the writing still employs the old pictures, much as in the beginning. This picture stage was perhaps in use as early as 3500 B.C.

Rise of Sumerian pictorial writing on clay

177. The instrument with which these signs were traced on the clay we call a *stylus*. An example recently discovered by the excavators is made of bone. Others are known to have been made of a strip split from a hard, reedlike bamboo. The end used was triangular in shape (see a scribe holding a stylus in Fig. 105). The writer did not scratch the lines of his picture, but in making a single line he impressed one corner of the tip of the stylus into the soft clay, and then raised it again to impress another line in the same way. Owing to the oblique tilt of the stylus, as well as its shape, each line thus made was wider at one end than at the other, and hence appeared triangular or wedge-shaped, thus ▷— or ⊤. Finally every picture or sign written with such a stylus came to be made up of a group of wedge-shaped lines like [cuneiform sign], which was once a stalk of grain, or [cuneiform sign], once a foot (Fig. 86, *6*, *10*). We therefore call the system *cuneiform* (from Latin *cuneus*, meaning "wedge"), or wedge-form, writing. Pictures made up of these wedge lines became more and more difficult to recognize, especially as speed in writing increased. All resemblance to the earlier pictures finally disappeared.

Sumerian picture signs become cuneiform signs

178. The transition from the picture stage to the phonetic stage was early made. Sumerian writing finally possessed over five hundred and sixty signs, but each of these signs represented a syllable[1] or a word, that is, a *group* of sounds; the Sumerian system never developed an alphabet of the letters which made up the syllables. That is, there were signs for syllables,

Rise of phonetic cuneiform signs; no alphabetic signs

[1] The only exceptions were later the vowels and some surviving pictorial signs which served as graphic hints, like the Egyptian determinatives (Fig. 34).

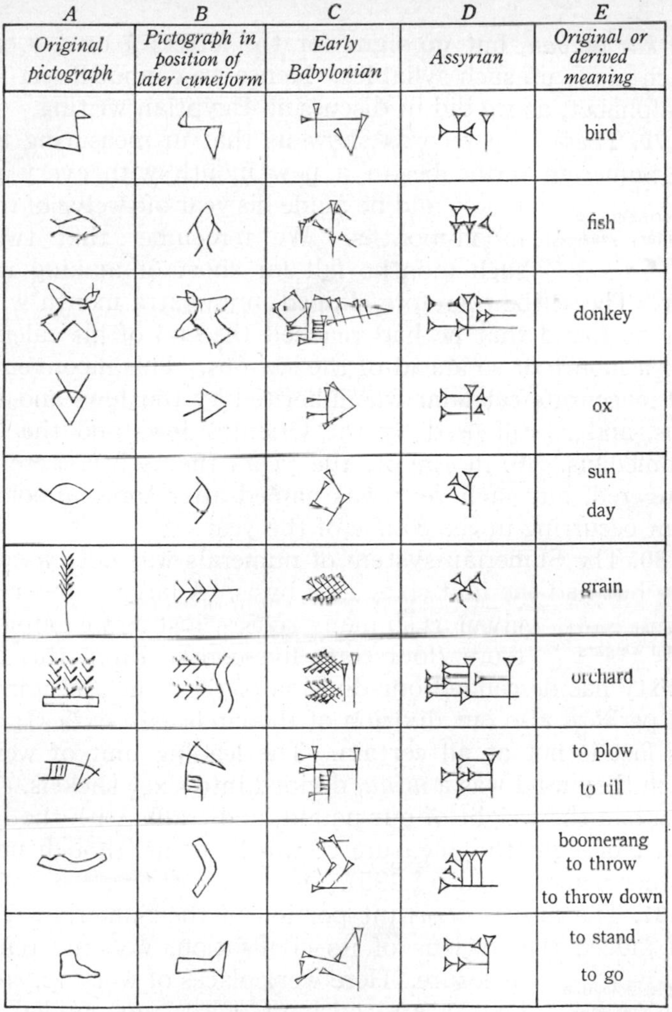

	A	B	C	D	E
	Original pictograph	*Pictograph in position of later cuneiform*	*Early Babylonian*	*Assyrian*	*Original or derived meaning*
1					bird
2					fish
3					donkey
4					ox
5					sun day
6					grain
7					orchard
8					to plow to till
9					boomerang to throw to throw down
10					to stand to go

FIG. 86. *Diagram showing Pictorial Origin of* TEN CUNEIFORM SIGNS

The development of 3 is particularly interesting. In *A* and *B* a short line was inserted in the donkey's right ear to indicate that the open side was turned toward the reader, while the left ear was turned away. In the early cuneiform sign (*C*) this line has survived as a single wedge inside the square which stands for the right ear, and below the square are three horizontal wedges, — all that remains of the left ear. The muzzle is still quite distinct, crossed by two pairs of oblique wedges, once the right eye and nostril. (Compiled and drawn by Professor Arno Poebel)

like *kar* or *ban*, but no signs for the letters *k* or *r*, *b* or *n*, which made up such syllables. Hence we cannot insert here an alphabet, as we did in discussing Egyptian writing.

Sumerian moon calendar; year-names

179. These clay records show us that in measuring time the Sumerian scribe began a new month with every new moon, and he made his year of twelve of these moon-months. We remember that twelve such months fall far short of making up a year. The scribe therefore slipped in an extra month whenever he found that he had reached the end of his calendar year a month or so ahead of the seasons. This inconvenient and inaccurate calendar was inherited by the Jews and Persians, and is still used by the Oriental Jews and the Mohammedans. As in Egypt, the years themselves were not numbered, but each year was named after some important event occurring in the course of the year.

Sumerian numerals and weights

180. The Sumerian system of numerals was not based on tens, but had the unit sixty as a basis. A large number was given as so many sixties, just as we employ a score (fourscore, fivescore). From this unit of sixty has descended our division of the hour and minute, and perhaps also our division of the circle (six sixties); but this last is not at all certain. The leading unit of weight which they used was a *mina*, divided into sixty shekels. The mina had the weight of our pound, and traffic with the East at last brought this measure of weight to us, though under another name (see also § 495).

Temple inclosure and its management

181. The most important portion of the Sumerian town, and indeed the nucleus of its civilization, was the temple inclosure. Here were places of worship, storehouses, and business offices, surrounded and protected by a massive wall. Here ruled a wealthy priesthood. Assisted by scribes, they rented and cared for temple property. The ruler of the town was also the chief priest, and his temple duties kept him about as busy as did the task of ruling the community outside of the temple walls.

FIG. 87. *Early Babylonian* CYLINDER SEAL *(about Twenty-fifth Century* B.C.*)*

Instead of signing his *name* to a clay-tablet document the early Sumerian rolled over the soft clay a little stone roller, or cylinder, engraved with beautiful pictures and sometimes also bearing the owner's name, as here. The impression left by the roller in the soft clay served as a signature. They have been found in great numbers, showing the growth and decline of Babylonian art for some three thousand years, beginning 3000 B.C. This picture shows side view (right) and impression made by rolling (left). The subject of the seal above is the story of Gilgamesh, the Sumerian ancestor of Hercules. He is seen slaying a wild bull (center). His friend Engidu, half man, half bull, wrestles with a lion (at left and right). We can appreciate the excellence of the carving when we realize that this seal is only a little over one inch high

The temples

182. Rising high above the other buildings in the temple inclosure was the tower-temple, which was in general shape almost a cube, though it tapered slightly in a series of steps toward the top. In front were three lofty flights of stairs rising nearly a hundred and fifty feet and converging on a door almost halfway up the front of the building. In the upper part of the tower was a square temple, with a court open to the sky, and a holy place behind it. Probably the first of such tower-temples was built at Nippur as a sanctuary to Enlil, the Sumerian god of the air. Alongside the tower-temple was a low building serving as the temple proper. Here the arrangement was very simple, consisting of a court and the sanctuary. Indeed, it is clear that this lower temple was considered merely as a dwelling of the god, like the dwelling houses of the people in the town.

Sumerian religion and worship

183. To this sanctuary under the shadow of the tower-temple the peasant brought his offering, — a goat and a jar of water containing a few green palm branches intended to symbolize the vegetable life of the land, which the god maintained by the annual rise of the river. The worshiper's jar with the green palm branches in it later became "the tree of life," a symbol often depicted on the monuments of the land. These gifts the worshiper laid before the gods of earth and its green life, of the air, the sky, or the sea, praying that there might be plentiful waters and generous harvests, but praying also for deliverance from the destroying flood which the god had once sent to overwhelm the land. Of this catastrophe the peasant's fathers had told him, and the tradition of this flood finally passed over to the Hebrews.

Sumerian burials and beliefs about the hereafter

184. In one important matter of religion the Sumerians were very different from the Egyptians. The dead were often buried in the town, under the court of a house or the floor of a room, although cemeteries outside a town were not unknown. Of the next world they had only vague and somber impressions, as a gloomy place of darkness and dust beneath the earth, to which all men, both good and bad, descended. However, they shared in a widespread belief that when a man died he would need his household in the next world. Provisions were made, therefore, that the dead man might not be obliged to live without his servants and animals in the life beyond the grave. Very early tombs recently found at Ur have disclosed the dead man's bodyguard, his servants, male and female, his draft oxen still yoked to the chariot, all lying slain at the door of the burial chamber, that they might accompany their master and continue to serve him after death.

Sumerian house and town

185. In the middle of the Sumerian town was usually the temple inclosure, and around it extended the houses of the citizens,— bare rectangular structures of sun-dried brick, each with a court on the north side, and on the south side of the court a main chamber from which the other rooms were entered. At first only a few hundred feet across, the town slowly spread out, although it always remained of very limited extent. Such a town usually stood upon an artificial mound, which it is important for us to examine; for each such mound is a great storehouse of ancient monuments and records.

© The Illustrated London News

FIG. 88. HOUSEHOLD *of a Prince of Ur* AWAITING DEATH *at the Door of his Tomb*

The Anglo-American Expedition under C. L. Woolley, excavating at Ur, discovered the bodies of these men, women, and animals, with their equipment, lying there at the door of the burial chamber. Directed by the archæologists, the modern artist has here raised the dead by depicting them in the positions which they occupied at the last fatal moment before they were slain. This slaughter was made in order that these people might pass on into the next world with their ruler and continue to serve him there

The formation of ancient city mounds

186. The ordinary building material of the entire ancient world was sun-baked brick. The houses of the common people in the Near East even at the present day are still built of these bricks. The walls of such houses in course of time are slowly eaten away by the rains, till after a heavy rain an old house sometimes falls down. When this happens at the present day the rubbish is leveled off and the house is rebuilt on top of it. This practice has been going on for thousands of years. It was the fall of such a house that Jesus had in mind in his parable (Matt. vii, 27). As this process went on for many centuries, it produced a high mound of rubbish, on which the town stood. Many a surviving Oriental town still stands on such an ancient mound; but there are other mounds which

FIG. 89. EXCAVATIONS *at Eshnunna*

These ruins, only fifty miles northeast of Baghdad, mark the site of the ancient city of Eshnunna, now being excavated by the Oriental Institute of The University of Chicago. We see the work of excavation actually going on. The earth is carefully loosened with hand picks, and the loosened débris is taken out in baskets. These baskets are carried away by the laborers to steel dump-cars (see background at right), which run on tracks over ever-growing banks of excavated earth at some distance beyond the limits of the ruins. Down to about 1840 the monuments and records of Babylonia and Assyria preserved in Europe could all be contained in a show case only a few feet square. Since that time, however, such excavations have recovered great quantities of antiquities and records. At Persepolis the Oriental Institute found over 30,000 cuneiform tablets

were long ago abandoned. Mounds so formed are to be found in all the lands of the Ancient Near East (Figs. 89 and 116).

Contents preserved in these ancient mounds

187. The clay tablets containing the household records, letters, bills, receipts, notes, accounts, etc., which were in the houses when they fell, were often covered by the falling walls, and they still lie in the mounds. In the temples and public buildings the documents covered up were frequently important government records, while in the dwelling or offices of the ruler they were often narratives of wars and conquests. Sometimes the ruler placed accounts of his erection of temples or palaces, records of his victories and other great deeds, deep in the foundations of his buildings, in order that later rulers might find them. Besides all these written records many articles of household use or sculptured works of art still lie buried in such mounds.

188. We are thus able to understand how these ruins of the ancient Sumerian cities reveal to us the life which filled the once busy streets, now sleeping under the silent mounds. We see that the most important class of citizens in the town were the free landowners who worked their lands with numerous slaves and carried on trade by caravans and in small boats up and down the river. Over these free middle-class folk were the officials and priests, the aristocrats of the town. Such a community, owning the lands for a few miles round about the town, formed the political unit, or the state, which we call a city-kingdom. The earliest monuments of Babylonia show us that these little city-kingdoms were already in existence throughout a large part of the Plain of Shinar by 3000 B.C. Beginning at about 2900 B.C. the written documents and other monuments enable us to follow the life and the history of these early Sumerian cities for some four centuries. This period forms the first chapter of history in ancient Babylonia. We may call it the Age of the Sumerian City-Kingdoms.

Age of Sumerian city-kingdoms (about 2900–2500 B.C.)

189. In spite of oppressive and dishonest taxation such a community owed much to its ruler, or *patesi* (pronounced *pa-tay'see*). He was useful in a number of matters, but chiefly in two ways: in war and in irrigation. The irrigation canals and dikes required constant repairs. The planting and the harvesting of the fields would have stopped and the whole community would have starved if the ruler had ceased his constant oversight of the dikes and canals and the water supply had been cut off.

Sumerian city-kingdoms and their *patesis*

190. As to war, we can watch more than one of these city rulers marching out at the head of heavily armed troops marshaled in massive phalanx (Fig. 90) or charging the

FIG. 90. *A Sumerian* CITY-KING *leading a* PHALANX *of his Troops*

The king himself, whose face is broken off from the stone, marches at the right, heading his troops, who follow in a compact group. This is the earliest example of grouping men together in a mass, forming a single fighting unit, called a phalanx. This must have required long drill and discipline, after many centuries of loose, irregular, scattered fighting. This was the first chapter in the long history of the art of war, and it took place in Asia. Such discipline was unknown at this time in Egypt. These Sumerian troops have their spears set for the charge, but they carry no bows. Tall shields cover their entire bodies, and they wear close-fitting helmets, probably of leather. They are marching over dead bodies (symbolical of the overthrow of the enemy). The scene is carved in stone and is a good example of the rude Sumerian sculpture in Babylonia in the days of the Gizeh pyramids

enemy in heavy chariots. These war chariots are the earliest known wheeled vehicles; they were mounted on either two or four wheels and drawn by teams of four horses, the oldest known domesticated horses.

Wars among Sumerian city-kingdoms

We found on the Nile the earliest highly developed arts of peace; we find here among the Sumerians the earliest highly developed art of war. When the townspeople heard that a neighboring city-kingdom was trying to take possession of a strip of their land, they were glad to follow the patesi's leadership in order to drive out the invaders. As such occurrences were common, the early history of Sumer was largely made up of the ever-changing fortunes of these city-kingdoms in war.

191. The earliest city to gain the leadership of Sumer was Ur, a city of the extreme south, situated on the Euprhates not far from its mouth, as shown on the map (p. 141) drawn with the coast line in its ancient position. The earliest known king in Western Asia was Mes-anni-padda, who ruled at Ur about 2900 B.C. It was his son who built the little temple to the cow-goddess in a suburb of Ur (see § 174). Four of Mes-anni-padda's descendants ruled in Ur, and this line of five kings is called the First Dynasty (or family) of Ur.

Leadership of Ur

FIG. 91. *Two-Wheeled* CHARIOT *drawn by Earliest Known* DOMESTICATED HORSES

The three fragments forming all but the lower left corner of this plaque were discovered by the Oriental Institute of The University of Chicago in the ruins of Opis (see map, p. 141), fifty miles east of modern Baghdad. An Anglo-American expedition at Ur had earlier found the lower left corner of a similar plaque which completed the chariot and the bodies of the animals (probably wild asses, possibly horses). The complete restoration made from these various fragments is very important, for we have here not only one of the earliest representations of a two-wheeled chariot but also possibly the domesticated horse in Babylonia nearly three thousand years before the Christian Era

192. Recent excavations at the ancient city have resulted in the most surprising discoveries. Far down beneath the accumulated rubbish of fallen buildings were found the tombs of the princes and nobles who were buried there at the time of the First Dynasty. The magnificent equipment of these very early burials rivals that of the tombs of Egypt, and has revealed a new and earlier chapter of Sumerian civilization. The works of the goldsmith disclose remarkable skill and craftsman-

Civilization of Ur: goldsmiths' work; sculpture

ship, as well as refinement of design (Fig. 92), showing how far the life of Western Asia had risen above the Stone Age savagery which had once filled all this region. These kings of the First Dynasty were already able to adorn the little temple of the cow-goddess with impressive works of sculpture in copper. On the platform before the building stood vigorous figures of bulls cast in copper, while the front entrance itself was guarded by a splendid lion-headed eagle with outspread wings hovering over a pair of stags, the whole fashioned of copper. Along the face of the building ran a line of bull figures cut out of heavy sheet copper. Another decorative band crossing the front of the temple was made up of dairy scenes with the figures carved in shell or limestone (Fig. 83).

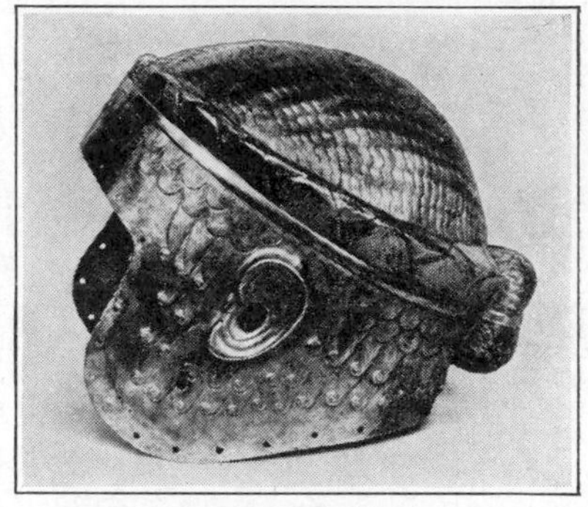

FIG. 92. HELMET OF GOLD *from the Tomb of an Early Noble or Prince of Ur*

The helmet is wrought of heavy sheet gold, on which the goldsmith has engraved the details of the waved and curling hair or wig, and the elaborate headdress. This work is one of the most magnificent examples of the goldsmith's art that have survived from the ancient world. It belonged to a man named Mes-kalam-shar, a prince or noble of Ur. (Courtesy of the University Museum of Philadelphia)

193. The works of the Sumerian sculptors in stone

Sumerian lapidaries

were in the beginning very rough and crude, but the demand for personal seals cut in stone soon developed a beautiful art of engraving tiny figures on a hard

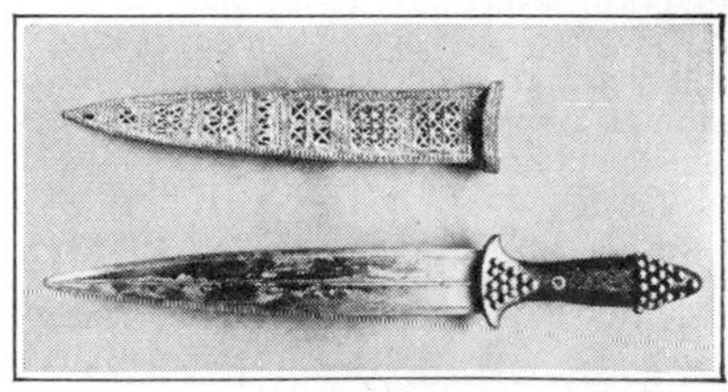

FIG. 93. *Golden* DAGGER *from an Early Tomb at Ur*

The handle is of lapis lazuli mounted in gold, while the sheath has been wrought in openwork of unusually rich and beautiful detail, all likewise done in gold. (Courtesy of the University Museum of Philadelphia)

FIG. 94 SCULPTURE *once adorning the Entrance of the* TEMPLE *of the* COW-GODDESS *near Ur*

In the middle is a lion-headed eagle hovering over the figures of two stags. This balanced arrangement of animal figures is one of the great creations of Sumerian art. The entire monument is seven feet nine inches long. It was probably mounted over the door of the temple, although it had long since fallen down when found by the excavator, Dr. H. R. Hall. It is the largest sculpture in copper of so early a date ever yet found in Western Asia. The eagle is the divine bird which the Sumerians called "Im-dugud," a malicious creature perhaps placed over the door of the temple to frighten away evil powers and protect the place. Such symbols, made up of balanced pairs of animal figures, later passed over into Europe, where they are still used in decorative art and in the heraldic symbols or arms of kings and nations. The eagle still appears in the arms of Austria, Prussia, and other European nations, and finally reached the West as the "American" eagle, — really the Sumerian eagle of five thousand years ago. (Courtesy of the British Museum)

stone surface. We remember that craftsmen who do such work are called lapidaries. The early Sumerian lapidaries soon became the finest craftsmen of the kind in the ancient Oriental world, and their influence has not yet disappeared from our own decorative art.

Ur falls before its rivals

194. Sumerian history really begins with this brilliant chapter of early civilization at Ur, which opened with the reign of Mes-anni-padda. Several rival city-kingdoms of Sumer contended with Ur for the leadership. The rival best known to us was Lagash (see map, p. 141), where excavation has uncovered many important monuments similar to those of Ur. The king of Lagash finally overthrew the king of Ur and captured his city. From this defeat Ur was long unable to recover.

195. While the city-kingdoms of Sumer were thus often fighting among themselves they were also called upon to meet an enemy from the outside. The Semitic nomads of the desert, probably coming from the northwest and moving down the Euphrates, reached the narrow region where the Two Rivers are hardly twenty miles apart. Here they early began to settle north of Sumer, where they first seized the city of Opis, discovered and identified by the Oriental Institute in 1934. At Opis (see map, p. 141) these desert invaders became the earliest Semitic city-kings in ancient Shinar. Other Semitic leaders later did the same at Kish, a city not far from Opis. This region first occupied by the Semites in the northern part of Shinar was finally called Akkad (see map, p. 141), and the leading Semitic settlers there bore the name of Akkadians. Akkad occupied a very strong commercial position on the

The earliest Semitic city-kingdoms

FIG. 95. SEWER MAIN *through the Ancient Babylonian City of* ESHNUNNA *in the Age of Sargon I*

A break in the rear portion of the sewer nearly below the dog shows that the sewer was vaulted at the top. The ancient masons leaned their arch against a thick, heavy wall visible on the right. The top of the arch, leaning against this thick wall, may be seen for some distance beyond the man in the foreground. In the immediate foreground is a branch of the sewer which extends toward the left into a house lying under the rubbish at the left and not yet excavated. There is a long series of such branches connecting the water-closets inside the houses on either side with this sewer and serving to carry away the household sewage. The construction is of burned brick, for sun-dried brick would have collapsed if used for a sewer. This is the oldest such town sewage system ever yet found. Compare Fig. 89

main road from the Two Rivers to the eastern mountains, and its trade always brought it prosperity.

Earliest wars of the Sumerians and the Semites

196. Unlike the Sumerians, these Semitic wanderers of the desert had never learned discipline and drill in war. They depended on their skill as archers, and they therefore gave battle at a distance. Or, if they came to close quarters, they fought single-handed, in open order. Their thin and open line was evidently at first no match for the heavy phalanx of the Sumerians. Thus two hostile races faced each other on the Plain of Shinar: in the north, the half-settled Semitic nomads of Akkad; and in the south, the settled agricultural Sumerians.

SECTION 15. THE FIRST SEMITIC TRIUMPH: THE AGE OF SARGON

Sargon and the first Semitic triumph (ca. 2500–2300 B.C.)

197. Late in the Twenty-sixth Century B.C., that is, about 2500 B.C., there arose in Akkad a Semitic Chieftain named Sargon. So skillful in war was he that he succeeded in scattering the compact Sumerian spearmen and making himself lord of all the Plain of Shinar. The old Sumerian city-kings were defeated, and the Sumerian towns down to the mouths of the Two Rivers submitted to him. He even embarked his troops on the Persian Gulf in his attack on Elam. He led his swift Akkadian archers from the eastern mountains of Elam westward up the Euphrates to the shores of the Mediterranean. From the Mediterranean Sargon seems to have pushed northward into eastern Asia Minor in order to protect the trade which was already active between the silver-bearing regions of southeastern Asia Minor and the merchants of the Two Rivers. Sargon was the first great Semitic leader in history, and he was the first ruler to build up a powerful nation in Western Asia, reaching from Elam on the east to the Mediterranean and far up the Two Rivers toward the west and north (see map, p. 146). His splendid conquests made an impression upon the Tigris-Euphrates world which never faded, in spite of the fact that a serious revolt brought his reign to an end. His conquests were resumed by his grandson Naram-Sin, who even extended them and left his monuments on the upper Tigris.

Semitic Akkadians adopt Sumerian civilization

198. Sargon's conquests forced his nomad tribesmen (the Akkadians) to make a complete change in their manner of life. We may best picture the change if we say that they forsook their tents and built houses of sun-dried brick which could not be picked up every morning and pitched somewhere else at night. At first they did not even know how to write, and they had no industries. Some of them now learned to write their Semitic tongue by using the Sumerian wedge-form signs for the purpose. It was in this age, therefore, that a Semitic language began to be written for the first time. These former nomads had never before attempted to manage the affairs of settled communities,— such business as we call government administration. All this too they were now obliged to learn from the Sumerians. The Semitic Akkadians therefore adopted the Sumerian calendar, weights and measures, system of numerals, and business methods. With the arts of peace the Akkadians gained also those of war. They learned to make helmets of leather and copper weighing over two pounds. These are the earliest-known examples of the use of metal as a protection in war. From such beginnings as these were to come the steel-clad battleships and gun turrets of modern times.

Great Semitic art of Age of Sargon

199. Among other things the Akkadians learned also the art of sculpture, but they soon far surpassed their Sumerian teachers. The relief of Naram-Sin (Fig. 96) belongs among the real triumphs of art in the early world, and is especially interesting as the first great work of art produced by the Semitic race. The beautiful Sumerian art of seal-cutting the Akkadians now carried to a wonderful degree of perfection. The ability of these artists to depict men and animals in violent action marked great progress in art.

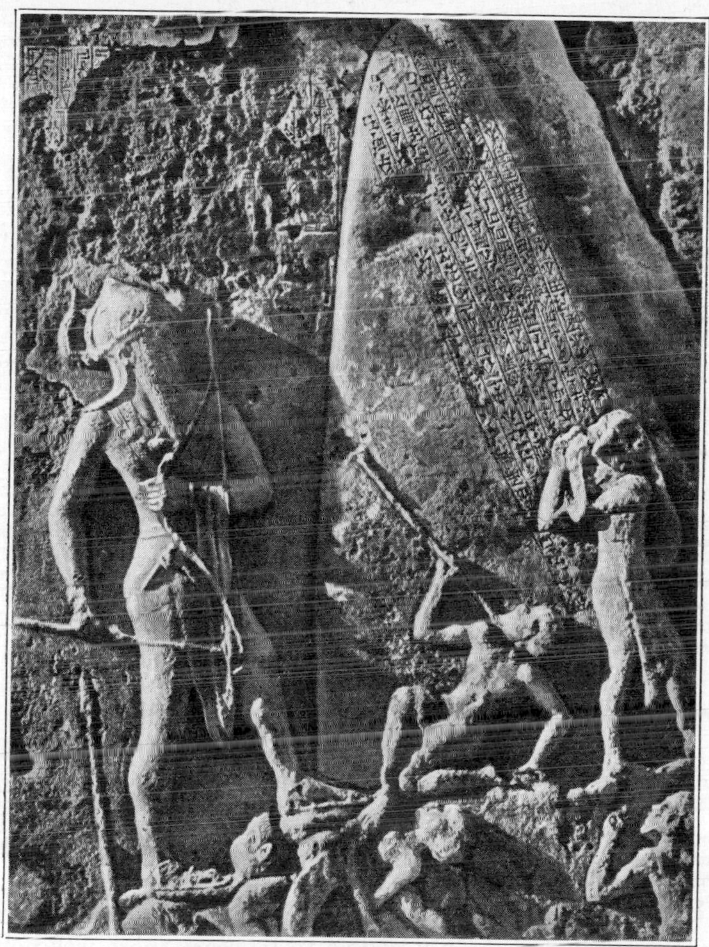

FIG. 96. *A King of Akkad* STORMING A FORTRESS,— *the Earliest Great Semitic Work of Art (Twenty-fifth Century* B.C.)

King Naram-Sin of Akkad (grandson of Sargon) has pursued the enemy into a mountain stronghold in Elam. His heroic figure towers above his enemies, each one of whom has fixed his eyes on the conqueror, awaiting his signal of mercy. The sculptor, with fine insight, has depicted the dramatic instant when the king lowers his weapon as the sign that he grants the conquered their lives. The king's enemies are made much smaller than he, to indicate their inferiority. Compare the superiority of this *Semitic* sculpture of Akkad over the *Sumerian* sculpture of two centuries earlier (Fig. 90)

FIG. 97. *A Semitic* PRINCE *and his Sumerian* SECRETARY

The third figure (wearing a cap) is that of the prince Ubil-Ishtar, who is brother of the king. He is a Semite, as his features show. Three of his four attendants are probably also Semites, with beards and long hair as usual; but one of them (just behind the prince) is beardless and shaven-headed. He is the noble's secretary, for, being a Sumerian, he is skilled in writing. His name, "Kalki," we learn from the inscription in the corner, which reads, "Ubil-Ishtar, brother of the king; Kalki the scribe, thy servant." This inscription is in the Semitic (Akkadian) tongue of the time and illustrates how the Semites have learned the Sumerian signs for writing. The scene is engraved on Kalki's personal seal (cf. Fig. 87), and the above drawing shows the impression left on the soft clay when the seal was rolled over it. It is a fine example of the Babylonian art of seal-cutting in hard stone. The original is in the British Museum

Commingling of Sumerians and Akkadians (Semites)

200. Thus the life of the desert Semites mingled with that of the non-Semitic townsmen on the Babylonian Plain, much as Normans and English mingled in England. On the streets and in the market places of the Euphrates towns, where once the round-headed and often smoothly shaven Sumerian townsmen were the only people to be seen, there was now a plentiful sprinkling of the swarthy, always heavily bearded, long-headed Semites of Akkad. In war the Sumerians continued to serve in the army with shield and spear, along with their Semitic lords carrying only the bow, and in peace the Semitic noblemen could not do without their deft Sumerian clerks.

SECTION 16. UNION OF SUMERIANS AND SEMITES: THE REVIVAL OF UR AND THE KINGS OF SUMER AND AKKAD

Sumerians and Semites unite in kingdom of Sumer and Akkad

201. When at last the Semites of Akkad had been enfeebled by the town life which they had adopted, the line of Sargon declined and fell, having ruled less than two centuries. As a result the Sumerian cities of the south were able to recover control of the country not long after 2300 B.C. Headed by the ancient city of Ur, three of the old Sumerian cities gained the leadership one after another. But the Semites had now been a part of the population of the Babylonian Plain for centuries, and many of them were living in the old Sumerian towns. Henceforth they were therefore recognized as part of the unified nation of the ancient Plain of Shinar, which now for the first time gained a national name. The new nation was called Sumer and Akkad. The kings of this age were both Sumerians and Semites. The period of the kings of Sumer and Akkad (beginning about 2300 B.C.) may be summed up as more than a century of prosperity under the leadership of Ur, followed by two centuries of decline under the successors of Ur. There were conquests northward up the Tigris, including even Assyria, which appears in this connection *for the first time in history*. These conquests also extended eastward into Elam and westward up the Euphrates, where the barbarous western Semites, known as Amorites (see § 168), were dangerous invaders.

Expansion of trade and use of silver as a medium of exchange

202. These conquests brought a large area of Western Asia under a more effective political control than ever before. One of the important results was the greatest development of trade that Western Asia had thus far seen. In the Stone Age we know that men traded in amber and flint and other natural products. With the development of agriculture, measures of barley or wheat served as a convenient scale of values. If A bought from B a river boat worth twenty measures of barley, he might offer in payment an ox worth fifteen measures, and he would then pay in actual grain besides the ox only five more measures of barley. Gradually the increase in the amount of precious metals, however, made them a more convenient medium of exchange. The Babylonians early began to use pieces of silver each weighing a shekel, or the sixtieth part of a pound (mina). When a silver shekel was shaped into a disk, it might be no larger than a dime. It was now possible to give prices and values in weights of silver. The value of silver was about four of silver to one of gold, but as it became more plentiful it decreased greatly in value (§ 224).

Business usages and rise of law

203. This trade has left an enormous body of bookkeeping records in the form of clay tablets found by excavation in the ancient cities of the age. It was at this time that many of the business forms which we still use and which make business transactions a matter of record arose for the first time. Thus grew up business and social customs, especially business credit. These practices gradually came to be regarded as the only ones to be followed, and thus finally became laws controlling the life of the people.

Prosperity, building, and literature

204. Thus able to bring a wide region under orderly laws and enjoying far-reaching trade connections, Ur rapidly gained wealth and power, as revealed to us by its impressive tower-temple and the tombs of three of the greatest kings of Ur, discovered in 1930. Unfortunately these tombs had been plundered by the Elamites and therefore were empty when the modern excavators entered them. The tablets containing the literature of this age have been lost, but some of the schoolbooks and exercise tablets of the boys, who were already studying this literature at school, have survived and are often our only copies of valuable works of literature which have otherwise perished. In such a school there were already clay-tablet treatises on grammar, dictionaries, and lists of signs. The lads could study tablets on arithmetic and geometry, and they might even find on the shelves of the tablet library discussions on medicine and healing. In these the only known cause of disease was evil spirits, which the Babylonians believed could enter the human body. There were also religious hymns, but the greater part of the *real* literature of the age was a series of stories and mythical tales.

Thought and myth. Source of life: the Etana story

205. In simple stories these men of Sumer and Akkad had now begun to answer those natural questions regarding life and death which always rise in the minds of early men. They told of the wonderful adventures of the shepherd Etana when his flocks were stricken with unfruitfulness and no more lambs were born. Etana then mounted on the back of an eagle and rose to the skies in search of the herb in which was the source of life. But as he neared his goal he was hurled to the earth again. This is the earliest tale of flying by man.

Death and eternal life: the Adapa story

206. The dark mystery of death led to the story of the fisherman Adapa. When the south-wind goddess overturned his boat, Adapa flew into a rage and broke her wing. Thereupon he was summoned to the throne of the Sky-god, whose wrath was at length appeased so that he offered to Adapa the bread and water of life. This would have made him immortal and destroyed death, but, suspicious and forewarned of danger, the unhappy Adapa refused the food and thus lost, both for himself and for mankind, the treasure of immortal life.

Immortality: the Gilgamesh story; the deluge story

207. In the same way they told how the gigantic hero Gilgamesh, after many mighty deeds and strange adventures, failed to gain immortal life. Among all these heroes, indeed, there was but one who was granted endless life. Of him there was a strange tale, telling how, together with his wife, he survived the great deluge in a large ship. Then the gods carried them both away to blessedness. But not even the *kings* of Sumer and Akkad were supposed to enter a blessed hereafter, much less the common people. Many of these stories of creation and flood were afterwards known to the Hebrews.

208. Mingled with touches from the life of both Sumerian and Semite, these tales now circulated in both the Semitic and the Sumerian language. Most of them, however, were

FIG. 98. *The* FLIGHT *of Etana to the* SKIES

At the right Etana sits on the back of the flying eagle, with his arm around the bird's neck. Above him is the moon, while, below, two dogs look up after him, barking. At the left approaches a goatherd driving three goats; before them walks a man with hand upraised in wonder. All, including the goats, are looking up in amazement at the flight of Etana. Over the goatherd a potter is making jars, and at the right of his jars a squatting baker is making round loaves. The scene is carved on a cylinder seal, and our drawing shows the impression on the soft clay when the seal is rolled over it

written in Sumerian, and it was this old Sumerian tongue which was regarded as the more sacred. It later continued in use as a kind of sacred language, like Latin in the Roman Catholic church today. The old Sumerian towns were now rapidly declining (Twenty-second Century B.C.), but religious stories were written in Sumerian, centuries after it was no longer spoken.

Decline of Sumerian language; survival as a sacred tongue

209. The period of the kings of Sumer and Akkad represents the highest level of the mixed Sumerian and Akkadian civilization,— that civilization which we now call Babylonian. The power and splendor of Ur in this age were never forgotten, and later, when Hebrew civilization had arisen in Palestine, the Hebrews were very proud to trace back their ancestry to Abraham, believed by them to have been a citizen of Ur toward the close of the great period with which we have been dealing.

Enduring glory of the civilization of Sumer and Akkad

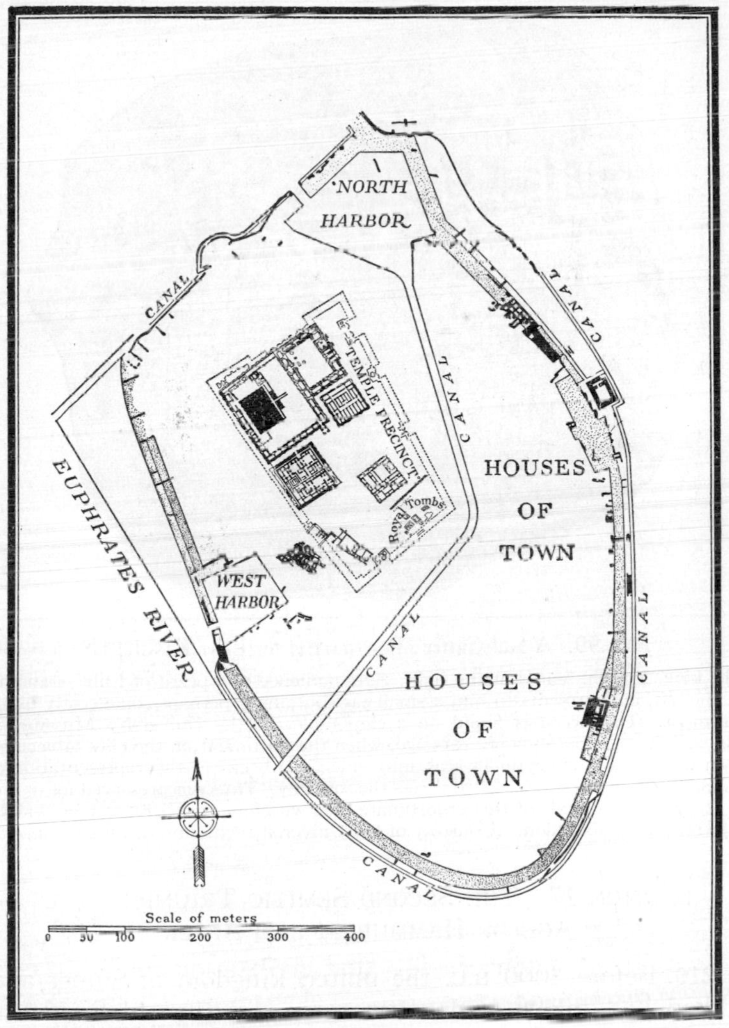

PLAN *of the* CITY OF UR, *according to the Latest Excavations*

Showing that it was a river port lying on the Euphrates, with two harbors and a canal crossing the town. (Drawing after Woolley)

FIG. 99. A *Seal-Cutter's* PORTRAIT *of the* LAST KING *of Ur*

The king, Ibi-Sin, seated at the right, gives audience to a priest of Enlil, standing at the left, and presents to him a small jar containing perhaps some costly oil or ointment. This scene is found on a clay tablet in the University Museum of Philadelphia. Thousands of years ago, when the document on the clay tablet had been written, a stone cylinder seal, into which had been cut this representation of Ibi-Sin and the priest, was rolled across the soft clay. Thus was preserved for us one of the rare memorials of this unfortunate king who fought so valiantly yet vainly to retain his dominion. (Courtesy of the University Museum of Philadelphia)

SECTION 17. THE SECOND SEMITIC TRIUMPH: THE AGE OF HAMMURAPI AND AFTER

End of Sumero-Akkadian power

210. Before 2000 B.C. the united kingdom of Sumer and Akkad had fallen, and never again did the old Sumerian cities hold political leadership. This final fall was due not only to wars among the city-kingdoms themselves but also to foreign invasion, which broke through the frontier defenses in both east and west at the same time. In the east the Elamites seized the Sumerian cities, led captive the last king of Ur, and plundered the royal tombs of the city. In the west a new tribe of Semites, called Amorites, began an invasion of Akkad. Between these two invasions the old Sumero-Akkadian power was slowly but completely crushed.

Amorite seizure of Babylon

211. In the time of the Kings of Sumer and Akkad the Amorites (§ 168) began descending the Euphrates valley, just as the Akkadians had done long before under Sargon. In the middle of the Twenty-first Century B.C. (2050 B.C.) they seized the little town of Babylon, which was at that time still an obscure village on the Euphrates. These Amorite chiefs of Babylon held the place for three hundred years (about 2050 to 1750 B.C.) and made the city finally such an outstanding center of power and civilization that it gave its name to the old Plain of Shinar, which we may thenceforth properly call Babylonia.

Triumph of Hammurapi

212. The earlier Amorite kings of Babylon were not able at once to take possession of all Sumer and Akkad, and the struggle against the Elamites coming in from the east went on for a long time without a decisive victory. Following a century of such warfare, there came to the throne a king named Hammurapi (1948–1905 B.C.). He was the sixth in the Amorite line of kings at Babylon. Hammurapi at once took up the war against the invading Elamites with great vigor. For over thirty years he fought them, before he was able to drive them back into the eastern mountains from which they had come. Then Hammurapi made his city of Babylon for the first time supreme throughout the ancient Babylonian Plain. This long war is an instructive example of the age-long struggle between the mountaineers and the plainsmen for possession of the Fertile Crescent.

Hammurapi the organizer

213. Hammurapi survived his triumph twelve years. While fighting and conquest did not wholly cease, nevertheless these years gave him opportunity to devote himself to peaceful administration, in which he proved himself, as he had done in war, the ablest of his line. He was the second great Semitic ruler, as Sargon had been the first.

Only a few generations earlier his ancestors, like those of Sargon, had been drifting about the desert, without any organization. But he now put forth his powerful hand upon the teeming life of the Babylonian towns, and with a touch he brought in order and system such as Babylonia had never seen before. Two chief sources of information have survived nearly four thousand years to reveal to us the deeds and the character of this great king: these are a large group of his letters and the splendid monument bearing his laws.

Hammurapi's letters: their dictation and preparation

214. Hammurapi's letters afford us for the first time in history a glimpse into the busy life of a powerful Oriental ruler in Asia. They disclose him to us sitting in the executive office of his palace at Babylon, with his secretary at his side. In short, clear sentences the king begins dictating his brief letters, conveying his commands to the local governors of the old Sumerian cities which he now rules. The secretary draws a reed stylus from a leather holder at his girdle and quickly covers the small clay tablet with its lines of wedge-groups. The writer then sprinkles over the soft, wet tablet a handful of dry powdered clay. This is to prevent the clay envelope, which he now deftly wraps about the letter, from adhering to the written surface. On this soft clay envelope he writes the address and sends the letter out to be put into the furnace and baked.

Hammurapi's letters: navigation

215. Messengers constantly hand him similarly inclosed letters. This secretary of Hammurapi is a trusted confidential secretary. He therefore breaks to pieces the hard clay envelopes in the king's presence and reads aloud to him letters from his officials all over the kingdom. The king quickly dictates his replies. The flood has obstructed the Euphrates between Ur and Larsa, delaying a long string of boats which have been tied up and are waiting until the government takes action. The king therefore dictates a letter ordering the governor of Larsa to clear the channel at the earliest moment and make it navigable again.

216. The king is much interested in his vast flocks of sheep, as if the nomad instinct had not altogether vanished from the blood of his line. He orders the officials to appear in Babylon to celebrate the spring sheep-shearing like a great feast. The calendar has slipped forward a whole month in advance of the proper season, and the king sends out a circular letter to all the governors, saying "Since the year hath a deficiency, let the month which is now beginning be registered as a second [month of] Elul."

Hammurapi's letters: feasts and the calendar

217. But he warns the governor that all taxes otherwise falling due within the next month are not to be deferred by this insertion. Delinquent tax-gatherers are firmly reminded of their obligations and called upon to settle without delay. Prompt punishment of an official guilty of bribery is authorized, and we can see the king's face darken as he dictates the order for the arrest of three officials of the palace gate who have fallen under his displeasure. More than once the governor of Larsa is sharply reminded of the king's orders and bidden to see that they are carried out immediately.

Hammurapi's letters: delinquents

218. Many a petitioner who has not been able to secure justice before the board of judges in his home city is led in before the king, confident of just treatment, and none is disappointed. The chief of the temple bakers finds that royal orders to look after a religious feast at Ur will call him away from the capital city just at the time when he has an important lawsuit coming on. He easily obtains an order from the king postponing the lawsuit. The king's interest in the religious feast is here as much concerned as his sense of justice, for many of the letters which he dictates have to do with temple property and temple administration.

Hammurapi's letters: justice and religion

219. With his eye thus upon every corner of the land, alert, vigorous, and full of decision, the great king finally saw how necessary it was to bring into uniformity all the various and sometimes conflicting laws and business customs of the land.

He therefore collected all the older written laws and usages of business and social life, going back to old Sumerian times. These he arranged systematically. He improved them or added new laws where his own judgment deemed wise, and then he combined them into a great code, or body, of laws. It was written, not in Sumerian, as some of the old laws were, but in the Semitic speech of the Akkadians and Amorites. He had it engraved upon a splendid shaft of stone. The new code was set up in the temple of the great god Marduk in Babylon. This shaft has survived to our day, the oldest preserved code of ancient law. Fragments of other copies on clay tablets, the copies used by the local courts, have also been found.

Hammurapi's Code of Laws

Fig. 100. *The* Laws *of* Hammurapi, *the Oldest Surviving Code of Laws*

A diorite shaft nearly 8 feet high, bearing the laws, extending entirely around the shaft and occupying over 3600 lines. Above stands Hammurapi, at the left, receiving the laws from the Sun-god, seated at the right, an impressive work of Semitic art, some 500 years later than Fig. 96

Spirit of Hammurapi's code; position of women

220. Hammurapi's code insists on justice to the widow, the orphan, and the poor; but it also allows many of the old and simple ideas of justice to stand. Especially prominent is the principle that the punishment for an injury should require the infliction of the same injury on the culprit, — the principle of "an eye for an eye, a tooth for a tooth." Injustice often resulted. For example, when a house fell (§ 186) and killed the son of the householder, the guilty builder must also suffer the loss of *his* son, and the innocent son was therefore condemned to die. Marriage was already a relation requiring legal agreements between the man and his wife, and these are carefully regulated in Hammurapi's code. Indeed, the position of woman in this early Babylonian world, as in Egypt, was a high one. Women engaged in business on their own account and even became professional scribes. They must have attended such a school as that described below in Fig. 101.

221. Thus regulated, the busy Babylonian communities prospered as never before. Their products were chiefly agricultural, especially grain and dates, but they had also flocks and herds, from which they obtained wool and leather. The weaving of wool was a great industry, for woolen clothing was commonly worn in Western Asia. Copper had been displaced by bronze, and one document refers to iron, but this metal was still much too rare to play any part in industry. Iron for common use was still nearly a thousand years in the future in Hammurapi's time.

Industries of Hammurapi's time

222. A standing army kept the frontiers safe and quiet, and the slow donkey caravans of the Babylonian merchants, plodding from town to town, were able to penetrate far into the surrounding communities. They were so common on the upper Euphrates that a town there was called Haran (or Kharan), from the Babylonian word *kharanu*, meaning "journey." Many a courtyard was piled high with bales, each bearing a clay seal with the impression of the merchant's name. These clay seals, broken away as the bales were opened, are found today lying in the rubbish of the Babylonian towns, where the modern excavator picks them up, still displaying on one side the merchant's name and on the other the impression of the cord which bound the bale.

Babylonian commerce in Hammurapi's time

223. Such seals and the clay-tablet bills which accompanied the bales had to be read by many a local merchant in the towns of Syria and beyond the passes of the northern mountains. Thus Babylonian cuneiform writing slowly made its way through Western Asia, and the merchants of Syria and the Hittite country in Asia Minor began to write bills and letters of their own on clay tablets. Hammurapi's commercial influence was widely felt in the West. The memory of his name had not wholly died out in Syria-Palestine in Hebrew days a thousand years after his death.

Spread of cuneiform writing through Western Asia

224. While the Babylonian merchants were a powerful class and were even called the rulers in some communities, it was the temples, with their large possessions, which were the center of business life. They dealt in merchandise, controlled extensive lands, and loaned money (silver shekels; see §202) like banks. The rate of interest on loans was high, — twenty per cent a year, payable in monthly installments. Silver had become so plentiful that it had decreased greatly in value. Gold was used sparingly, for it was from twelve to fifteen times as valuable as silver.

Temples the centers of business

225. Commercial interests were therefore the leading influences in Babylonian life, even in religion. The temples, as we have said, had a large place in business life, and religion never proclaimed the rights of the poor and the humble or championed their cause against the rich and powerful. To be sure, the ritual of the temple contained some prayers which indicated a sense of sin and fear of divine displeasure. But the advantages of religion consisted in being able to obtain substantial benefits from the gods and to avoid their displeasure.

Babylonian religion in Age of Hammurapi

226. The people still worshiped the old Sumerian gods, but the political leadership of Babylon had enabled the men of that city to put their Semitic god Marduk at the head of all the gods, and in the old mythical stories they inserted the name "Marduk" where once the ancient Sumerian god Enlil had played the leading part. At the same time the great Asiatic goddess of love, Ishtar, rose to be the leading goddess of Babylon. She was later to

Marduk and Ishtar

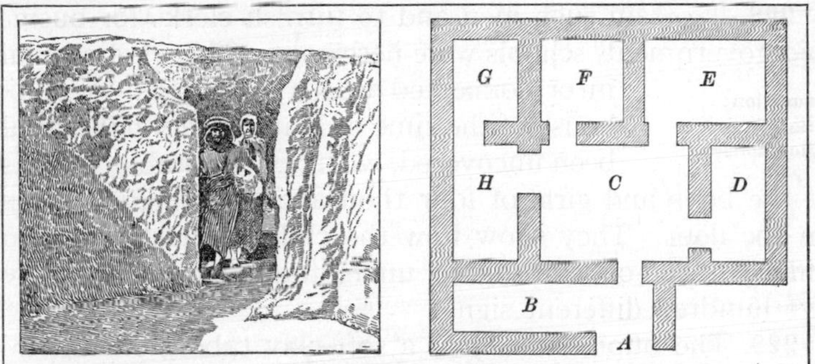

FIG. 101. *An Ancient Babylonian* SCHOOLHOUSE *in the Days of Hammurapi*

On the right is the ground plan of the schoolhouse, which was about 55 feet square. The children went in at the door (*A*), across the end of the long room (*B*), where the doorkeeper sat and perhaps kept a clay-tablet tardy-list of the pupils who came late. Then the children entered a court (*C*), which was open to the sky, and we may suppose that they separated here, the big boys and girls going into their own rooms, while the little ones went into others. Somewhere in the schoolhouse, and probably in the court (*C*), was a pile or box of soft clay, where a boy who had already filled his clay-tablet slate with wedge-marks could quickly make himself a new slate by flattening a ball of soft clay. On the left we look through one of the doors of this oldest schoolhouse in the world as it appeared on the day when it was uncovered by the French in 1894. The native Arab workmen who uncovered it stand in the doorway. The walls of sun-dried brick are still 8 or 9 feet high. (Drawing after Scheil)

pass over to the Mediterranean, there finally to become the Aphrodite of the Greeks and the Venus of the Romans.

Babylonian methods of reading the future, or divination

227. Among the benefits granted by the gods was the ability to foretell the future. This art we call divination, and the priest who practiced it was a diviner. Already under the kings of Sumer and Akkad the skilled diviner could interpret the mysterious signs on the liver of the sheep slain in sacrifice, and his anxious inquirers believed that he could thus reveal the unknown future. He could note the positions of the stars and the planets, and in this manner he could discern the decrees of the gods for the future. These practices later spread westward. Under the Chaldeans star-reading developed into the art of astrology, and then later into the science of astronomy. We shall find the reading of the liver a common practice in Rome.

228. To train such men and to furnish clerks for business and government, schools were necessary. These were usually in or connected with the temple. A schoolhouse of the time of Hammurapi has actually been uncovered, with the clay-tablet exercises of the boys and girls of four thousand years ago still lying on the floor. They show how the child began his long and difficult task of learning to understand and to write over five hundred different signs.

Education: a Babylonian schoolhouse

229. The pupil's slate was a soft-clay tablet, on which he could rub out his exercises at any time by smoothing off the surface with a flat piece of wood or stone. With his reed stylus in his hand he made long rows of single wedges in three positions, horizontal, vertical and oblique. When he could make the single wedges neatly enough, the master set him to work on the wedge-groups forming the signs themselves. Lastly, he was able to undertake words and simple phrases, leading up to sentences and quotations from old documents. One of the tablets found in the schoolhouse contains a proverb which shows how highly the Babylonians valued the art of writing. It reads: "He who shall excel in tablet-writing shall shine like the sun." Doubtless many a Babylonian lad was encouraged, in the long and wearisome task of learning to write, by copying this enthusiastic sentiment.

Education: learning to write

230. Of the higher life of Babylon in this age as expressed in great works of art and architecture very little has survived on the spot. Indeed, the city of Hammurapi has vanished. Not a single building erected by him now stands. Enough remains in other Babylonian mounds to indicate that the arch had by this time assumed a prominent place on the fronts of buildings. The few pieces of sculpture found show little distinction. While the relief scene in which Hammurapi is represented as receiving the law from the Sun-god displays a certain fine dignity and impressiveness, it lacks the freedom and beauty of the Akkadian sculpture (Fig. 96). Even the work of the

Art and architecture in Hammurapi's time

lapidary in seal-cutting falls far short of the beauty which it had attained in the age of Sargon.

Highlanders triumph over Hammurapi's line (about 1750 B.C.)

231. The decline in art was perhaps a prophecy of what was to come, for the Babylonian nation which Hammurapi had so splendidly organized and started on its way hardly survived his death. The Highland peoples, whom Hammurapi had driven out of the Sumerian cities, again descended upon the Babylonian Plain, as the Sumerians had probably done so long before. From the mountains of the east and northeast issued a rude Highland people called Kassites.[1] By gradual migration they filtered into the Fertile Crescent, especially after 1900 B.C., and settled in Babylonia. Hammurapi's successors seem to have been quite unable to keep them out. The Babylonians were now caught between two groups of invaders coming from opposite directions, for the Hittites advanced out of the northwest, and, moving down the Two Rivers, they captured Babylon itself and carried back the plunder of the city to their own country. This Hittite invasion was only a hurried raid, for the Hittites did not remain in Babylonia; but when they withdrew, they had completely overthrown the last of the great family of Hammurapi. Thus, about 1750 B.C., the rough and uncivilized Kassites, who were already settled in Babylonia, had no difficulty in making themselves masters of the country. Their triumph marked the end of old Babylonian progress in civilization. Until its revival under the Chaldeans, over a thousand years later, Babylonia relapsed into stagnation so complete that it was rarely interrupted.

Summary and retrospect

232. As we look back over this first chapter of early human progress along the Two Rivers we see that we have been able to follow it for about a thousand years, beginning probably 2900 B.C. The Sumerians laid the foundations of civilization in Shinar and began a thousand-year struggle with the Semites of the desert.

[1] It was probably these Kassites who brought larger numbers of horses into Babylonia, although they did not appear in Egypt until some 200 years later (§ 125).

In spite of the mingling and union of the two races the Semites triumphed twice under two great leaders,— Sargon (Twenty-fifth Century B.C.) and Hammurapi (Twentieth Century B.C.). The Sumerians then disappeared, and the language of Babylonia became Semitic. The reign of Hammurapi, in spite of some deterioration in art, marks the highest point and the end of the thousand-year development,— the conclusion of the first great chapter of history along the Two Rivers. The scene of the second chapter will carry us up the river valley, just as it did in our study of the Nile.

QUESTIONS

Section 12. Describe the three geographic zones of the Great Northwest Quadrant and their population.

Section 13. Why was the Babylonian Plain long unsuited to settled life? Describe the Fertile Crescent. How can we summarize its history? Describe the life of the desert people. Into what lands did they shift at the west end of the Fertile Crescent? at the east end?

Section 14. Who were the early dwellers in the Plain of Shinar? Describe their writing materials and their writing. Were the Sumerians all united in one nation? List all the objects which an excavator might find in a Sumerian city mound.

Section 15. What outsiders defeated the Sumerians? Who was the first great Semitic king? What did the Akkadians accomplish in art?

Section 16. What nation resulted from the mingling of Sumerians and Akkadians? Discuss the development of trade and the rise of business methods. What became of the Sumerian language?

Section 17. Why may we call Hammurapi a great king? What city first became famous at this time?

BIBLIOGRAPHY FOR TOPICAL STUDIES

Industries and business: DELAPORTE, *Mesopotamia,* chap. iii; JOHNS, *Code,* §§ 4–126; WOOLLEY, *Sumerians,* pp. 112–119.

Royal tombs of Ur: GADD, *History and Monuments of Ur,* pp. 29–40; *Museum Journal of the University of Pennsylvania,* Vol. 19 (1928), pp. 5–34, Vol. 20 (1929), pp. 7–35, Vol. 22 (1931), pp. 248–260; WOOLLEY, *Sumerians,* pp. 35–40; *Ur of the Chaldees,* chap. ii.

Private houses: GADD, pp. 169–172; WOOLLEY, *Sumerians,* pp. 156–162; *Ur of the Chaldees,* pp. 164–171.

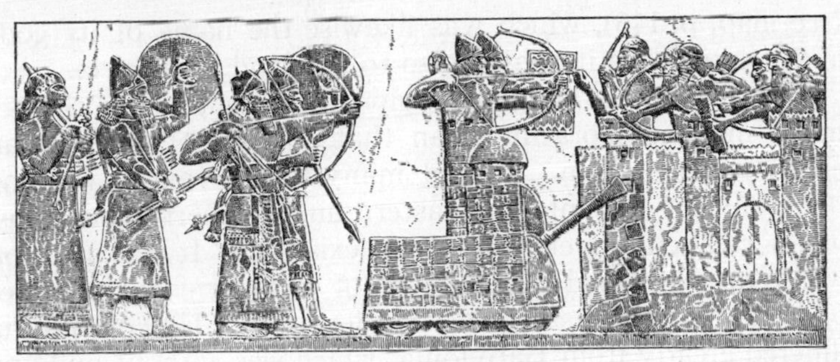

Chapter VI · *Western Asia: The Assyrians and Chaldeans*

Section 18. Early Assyria and her Western Rivals

233. The second chapter of history along the Two Rivers carries us up the river from Babylonia to the northeastern corner of the desert bay. Here was an easily defended elevation possessing a natural strength unknown to the towns in the flat Plain of Shinar. It overlooked the Tigris on the east and the desert on the west and south. The place was known as Assur

Situation of Assur, earliest capital of Assyria

Note. The headpiece shows an Assyrian King attacking a Fortified City (Ninth Century B.C.). A century before the Empire the Assyrians had already developed powerful appliances for destroying a city wall. The city at the right is protected by walls of sun-dried brick like those of Samal (Fig. 103). The defending archers on the wall are trying to drive away a huge Assyrian battering-ram, mounted on wheels, of which only the lower parts are visible, the upper parts being covered by the armor of the battering-ram, which is an ancient "tank" with its front protected by metal armor plate. It carries a fighting tower as high as the city wall, and Assyrians in the top of it direct arrows against the defenders of the wall. Within the tank unseen men work the heavy beam of the ram. It is capped with metal and is shown smashing a hole in the city wall, from which the bricks fall out. An observation tower, with a metal-covered dome and peep-holes, shields the officer in command as he directs operations. In the rear (at the left) is the Assyrian king shooting arrows into the hostile city. He uses a powerful bow, probably invented in Egypt, which will shoot an arrow with great force from 1000 to 1400 feet, and hence he can stand at a safe distance. A scene from the earliest Assyrian palace reliefs which have survived.

(see map, p. 146), which was likewise the name of its god; and it later gave its name also to the land of Assyria.

Climate, soil, and products of Assyria

234. Being in a highland region, Assur enjoyed a climate much more invigorating than that of the hot Babylonian Plain. It had many fertile valleys winding up into the eastern and northern mountains, where rival cities were already in existence. It was a region where an occasional promontory of rock furnished quarries of limestone, alabaster, and harder stone. Herein Assyria differed greatly from Babylonia, which was without building stone and had therefore developed architecture in brick only. These eastern valleys were green with rolling pastures and billowing fields of barley and wheat. Herds of cattle and flocks of sheep and goats dotted the hillsides. Donkeys served as the chief draft animals, and the horse, while not unknown, was not common in the beginning. Here flourished an agricultural population, although the Assyrians finally built up also industries and trade.

Founding of Assur (2900 B.C.) under Sumerian influence

235. This population of the region north of Babylonia was not purely Semitic but contained people of other tongues and probably also of different races and blood. By 2900 B.C. there was already living at Assur a small settlement of Sumerians, whose works of art have been excavated there. At the same time the men whom we call Assyrians were there. It is not wholly certain whence they came or whether they were of pure Semitic race; but they spoke a Semitic language closely related to that which was spoken at Akkad, where we have already seen the western Semites, led by Sargon, forming the first powerful Semitic kingdom in the Twenty-fifth Century B.C. The differences between the language of Akkad and that of Assur were hardly greater than we now find between the dialects of different parts of Germany. The men of Assur at first formed a tiny city-kingdom like those of their Sumerian neighbors in the south. They were in close contact with the Sumerians, whose sculpture and writing they adopted, along with many of the conveniences of Sumerian civilization.

236. While most of the *early* civilization of Assur thus came from the south, the little city-kingdom was equally exposed to influences from the north and west. In Asia Minor there were the hostile Hittite communities, some of which were venturing eastward to the Two Rivers. Assur was perhaps at times ruled by Hittite lords or other outsiders from the west, only to fall back again under the control of the south led by Sargon, the kings of Ur, Hammurapi, or some other ruler of Babylonia. Thus obliged, for over a thousand years after Sargon's reign, to defend their uncertain frontiers against their neighbors on both north and south, the Assyrians were toughened by the strain of unceasing war. The Assyrian state was therefore built up around the army, — at first militia and then a standing army, which became the chief strength of the government. This military state thus developed into a stable and powerful organization, unshaken by the rivalries of city-states such as those which so often weakened and finally overthrew Babylonia. Freed from such internal struggles, Assyria could muster her undivided strength and direct it against her foreign foes. The Assyrian kings early introduced the horse and added chariots to their army, which finally became the strongest military force the early world had yet seen.

Constant defensive warfare develops Assyrian military state

237. At the same time commerce and traffic with surrounding nations brought wealth and power to the young nation. Attracted by the silver mines of southeastern Asia Minor (Cilicia, see map, p. 146), Assyrian merchants were drawn into commerce with the West. Assur thus became an important station on the trade route connecting the peoples in the mountains east of Assyria with those of the west. The Assyrian traders had learned the forms of business which were so highly developed in Ur under its kings of Sumer and Akkad, and settlements of these Assyrian merchants were established at various places in southeastern Asia Minor, in the region later known as Cappadocia. Here excavations have

Assyrian merchants in Asia Minor (beginning in 23d Century B.C.)

uncovered great quantities of the business records of these merchants in the form of cuneiform tablets like those of Assyria. They show us that these foreign merchants from the east continued to carry on business in Cappadocia for at least two hundred years, beginning while the kings of Sumer and Akkad were in power. We shall see later that these settlements from the east had an important part in carrying civilization farther west. Found, as they were, lying in the towns of southeastern Asia Minor, the clay tablets of these Assyrian merchants are for us today like milestones marking the march of civilization from the Two Rivers toward the southeastern part of Europe.

FIG. 102. *List of* LOANS *of Silver made and* SECURITIES *received by an Assyrian Merchant in Asia Minor named Enlil-bani*

Enlil-bani has carefully written out on this tablet a list of nine loans, all of silver, which various people are owing him. He did not make easy terms with these people, and the interest he charged ranged from 24 per cent to 30 per cent. Indeed, one unfortunate debtor was obliged to pay as interest $1\frac{1}{2}$ shekels per month, or 18 shekels per year, on a loan of only 15 shekels, which shows that these Assyrian merchants had learned well the ways of the Babylonian business man

Plentiful silver introduces age of coined money

238. Access to the silver mines of Cilicia now greatly affected business and commerce, for silver rapidly displaced grain as a medium of exchange. Small bars or rods of the metal, and likewise round pieces, were stamped with the weight of the piece and the name of the temple which had issued it. The caravans from the Two Rivers carried these forerunners of coin all over the Near East, and especially into central Asia Minor. Thus gradually began the age of metallic money. With it also arose the idea of credit. Among the tablets of the Assyrian merchants found in the ancient Hittite cities are some which state that each tablet represents so many shekels of silver. They are therefore practically checks or drafts sent in advance as payment for goods which the sender desires shall be forwarded to him. These tablets are the earliest known examples of credit transactions. It was from this region that the convenience of coined money and commercial operations of credit based on money finally passed into Greece and thence spread over Europe.

Western rivals of Assyria: Mitanni and the Phœnicians

239. These connections with the west were of the greatest importance to Assyria. Not only did Assur need access to the metals produced by the west, but as an inland power it could not hope to rule Western Asia without access to the Mediterranean. Two serious obstacles lay between Assur and the western sea. In the bend of the Euphrates, right across the merchant roadways and caravan routes leading from Assyria to the west (see map, p. 146), was located the kingdom of Mitanni. The ruling class here were Indo-Europeans, descendants of those nomads of the northern grasslands who first learned to train horses (§ 316) and drill them for use in battle with the war-chariot. Maintaining themselves on the Euphrates as the earliest known horse-breeding aristocracy, they made Mitanni a dangerous military state. The coming of the domestic horse was the beginning of a new age on the Fertile Crescent. When a squadron of chariots drawn by swift and heavy horses came thundering down upon infantry soldiers, they were scattered like autumn leaves. Driving their terrible chariots, the lords of Mitanni were able to carry their conquests northwestward across the Hittite frontiers. The Assyrians likewise were unable to stand against them. The Mitannians invaded Assyria, captured Nineveh, and for a time even held the Assyrians as a subject people. The second obstacle in the westward path of Assyria was her own kindred, the Semites, along the eastern coast of the Mediterranean. Here the harbor towns of the former Semitic nomads (§ 168)

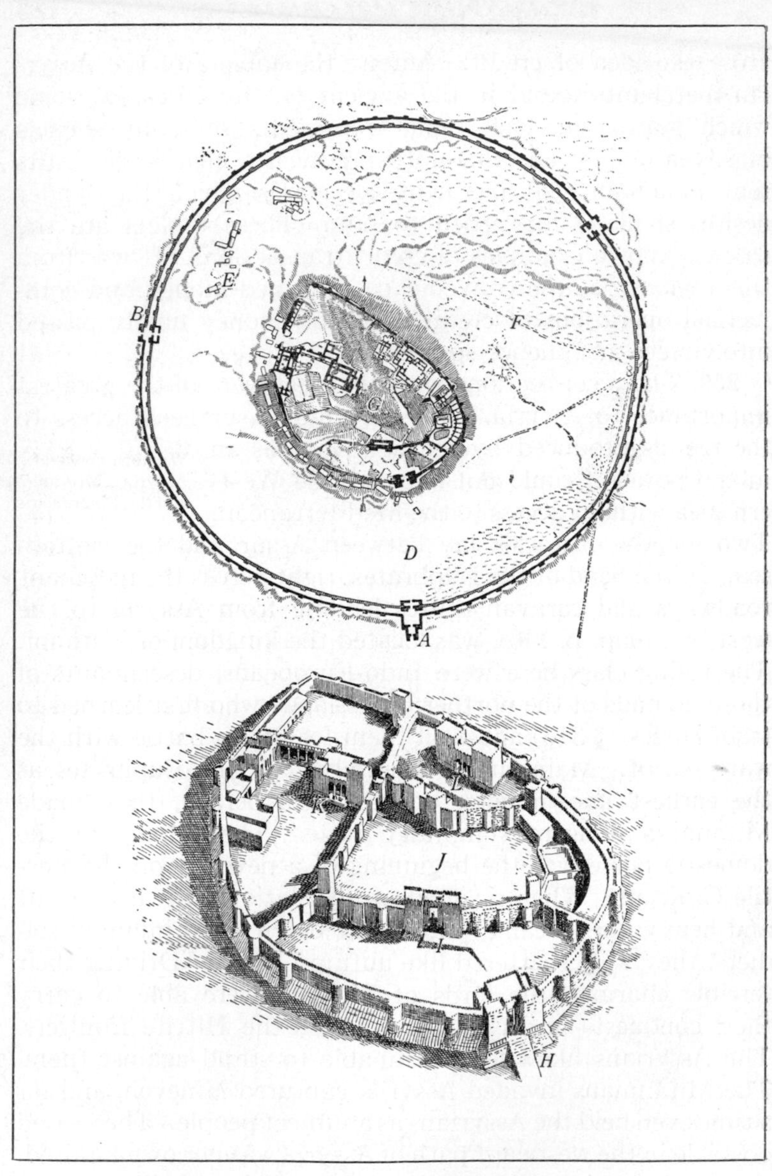

FIG. 103. *The Aramean City of* SAMAL, *One of the Western Rivals of Assyria. (Drawing after Von Luschan)* *

had become a fringe of wealthy Phœnician city-kingdoms. These cities proved obstinate enemies of the Assyrian kings.

New Semitic migration: Hebrews and Arameans

240. Besides the Mitannian horsemen and the Phœnician merchant princes of the west the Assyrians had to face also the dangerous hostility of a new Semitic migration which was both commercial and political. This new wave of Semitic nomads began to roll in upon the Fertile Crescent in the Sixteenth Century B.C. In the Fifteenth Century they were already trying to set up kingdoms on the western shores of the desert bay, that is, Palestine and Syria. These western nomads were the Hebrews in Palestine, and north of them the Arameans,[1] or Syrians, occupying Syria. We recall how the Hebrew nomads under Joshua began the conquest of Palestine, where they eventually gained possession of the whole country (see Chapter VII). They soon held the entire western end of the Fertile Crescent and aided in cutting off Assyria from the sea. After 1200 B.C. the Arameans established a group of flourishing kingdoms in the west. Here, under the influence of Hittite civilization on one side and Egyptian on the other, these Aramean kingdoms of Syria built royal cities and luxurious palaces filled with sumptuous furniture. Among the Aramean kingdoms of Syria the most powerful was Damascus.

[1] The Arameans are often called Syrians, and the region north of Palestine (see map, p. 146) is commonly called Syria. These two names, Syria and Syrians, are not to be confused with Assyria and Assyrians.

---

* PLAN (on opposite page). The city was nearly half a mile across. It was defended by a double wall (*ABC*) of sun dried brick on a heavy stone foundation. The wall was strengthened with towers every 50 feet, entirely around the city, making one hundred towers in all. The castle of the kings of Samal occupied a hill in the middle (*G*), and the houses of the townsmen filled the space between the city walls and the castle (*D, E, F*). These houses, built of sun-dried brick, have disappeared, but the castle can be restored.

RESTORATION OF THE CASTLE (*H, I, J, K, L*). This is the castle, or citadel, marked *G* in the city plan (on opposite page). The walls of sun-dried brick rest on heavy stone foundations widening at the base. Samal in north Syria, midway between the Mediterranean and the Euphrates, received influences both from the Hittites in Asia Minor and from Egypt. The columned porches (*K* and *L*) in front of the palaces were built on a Hittite plan, with columns suggested by Egyptian architecture. Hittite reliefs adorned this porch.

241. The energetic Aramean merchants extended their business far beyond their own kingdoms. They pushed their caravans all along the shores of the desert bay, even as far north as the sources of the Tigris, and they finally controlled the commerce of Western Asia. Their bronze weights, found in the ruins of Nineveh, show us how common were Aramean merchants in the Assyrian market places. Like their kinsmen the Jews in modern civilized states, although not organized as a single nation they were the great commercial leaders of the age.

Peaceful penetration of Aramean commerce

242. The Arameans were a highly civilized race. By 1000 B.C., and probably several centuries earlier, they were using *alphabetic* writing, which they had borrowed from the Canaanites or the Phœnicians. It was the earliest system of writing known which employed *exclusively* alphabetic signs (Fig. 158). Along with the alphabet the Arameans received the Egyptian pen and ink also, conveniences indispensable in the use of the new alphabet. As the Babylonian caravans had in earlier times carried cuneiform tablets throughout Western Asia, so the Aramean caravans, with their bills and receipts, began to carry through the same region the alphabet which was to displace cuneiform signs. Thus the Phœnician-Aramean alphabet spread throughout Western Asia. It passed down the Euphrates to Persia, and, penetrating to the frontiers of India, even furnished the East Indian peoples with their (Sanskrit) alphabet.

Aramean merchants spread first alphabet in Asia

243. The Aramean merchants of course carried their language (called Aramaic) with them, and Aramaic gradually became very common all around the desert bay. Indeed, in the old Assyrian communities the people who spoke Aramaic finally outnumbered the citizens of Assyrian speech. When an Aramean received a cuneiform tablet recording business matters in the Assyrian language, he sometimes took his pen and marked it with memoranda in Aramaic. Assyrian

Assyrian and Aramaic side by side in business and government

tablets bearing such notes in Aramaic have been found in the ruins of Assyrian buildings. Indeed, public business was finally carried on in both languages. Aramean clerks were appointed to government offices, and it was a very common thing for an Aramean official of the Assyrian Empire to keep his records on papyrus, writing with pen and ink on a roll, while his Assyrian associate in office wrote with a stylus on a tablet of clay.

FIG. 104. *An Aramean* KING *of Samal and his* SECRETARY, *who holds an Egyptian Writing Outfit* (*Eighth Century* B.C.)

The king sits at the left on a richly carved throne of ebony, ivory, and gold, with a footstool of the same design. Before him stands his secretary, carrying under his left arm an object which is probably a papyrus roll, drawn in this manner so as to indicate that it is partially unrolled. In his left hand he holds an Egyptian writing case containing pen and ink. The flat relief in which the entire scene is carved had its origin on the Nile. From Syria, in such cities as Samal, it passed to Assyria, where it was immensely improved. (From a photograph by Von Luschan)

244. Aramaic finally became the language of the entire Fertile Crescent. It even displaced its very similar sister tongue, the Hebrew of Palestine, and thus the mercantile tongue of the Arameans, many centuries later, became the language spoken by Jesus and the other Hebrews of his time in Palestine. In the end this widespread commercial civilization of the Arameans left more lasting influences behind than even the powerful military state of the Assyrians. Unfortunately the Aramean city mounds of Syria, with one exception (Fig. 103), still remain unexcavated; hence we have recovered but few monuments to tell us of their builders. Damascus is still the largest city

Complete triumph of Aramaic along the Fertile Crescent

FIG. 105. *Assyrian and Aramean Scribes* RECORDING THE PLUNDER *taken from a Captured Asiatic City (Eighth Century* B.C.)

The captive women and children ride by in ox-carts on their way to slavery in Assyria, and a shepherd drives off the captured flocks. At the left an Assyrian officer reads from a tablet his notes of the spoil taken in the city. Two scribes write as he reads. The first (in front) holds in his left hand a thick *clay tablet,* from which he has just lifted the stylus, grasped in his right hand, as he pauses in his writing. The other scribe holds spread out on his left hand a *roll of papyrus,* on which he is busily writing with a pen held in his right hand. He is an Aramean, writing Aramaic with pen and ink. We see here, then, the two different methods of writing practiced at this time in Western Asia, — the outgoing Asiatic clay tablet and the incoming Egyptian paper, pen, and ink

of Syria, having nearly two hundred thousand inhabitants; but the ruins of all the ancient Aramean buildings must now lie under those of the modern city, and therefore it is unlikely that ancient Damascus will ever be unearthed.

245. We now understand that as the Assyrian armies faced the west they looked out upon an array of hostile nations which might have dismayed any people, however brave. In the foreground were the horsemen of Mitanni; behind them the powerful commercial cities of the Arameans, especially

Damascus; while farther in the rear, along the eastern end of the Mediterranean, was the line of flourishing harbor cities of the Phœnicians. In the far background rose the two mighty world-powers: Egypt on the southwest and the Hittites (Section 27) on the northwest. Undoubtedly the Assyrians remembered that the Hittites had once captured Babylon, and, as we shall later learn, the Hittites had now become a large and powerful empire. By the Fifteenth Century B.C. this Hittite Empire was a worthy rival of Egypt. The Assyrians watched the tremendous struggle between these two great powers for possession of the western end of the Fertile Crescent, which ended in a drawn battle in the Thirteenth Century B.C. They saw both of these powerful western rivals sorely weakened by the struggle until, toward 1200 B.C., as it was further weakened by invasion from behind, the Hittite Empire fell. Half a century later the empire of Egypt also collapsed. Mitanni had at first thrown in her lot with Egypt, but eventually the kingdom of the Mitannian horsemen was also crushed in the far-reaching international struggle. The leading contestants in the Near-Eastern arena had been three — Egypt, Assyria, and the Hittites — struggling in a three-cornered rivalry. By 1150 B.C. the two great western powers had fallen, leaving Assyria to inherit the empire of the East.

Fall of Assyria's greatest rivals: Hittites and Egyptians

246. Confronting Assyria in the west, after the fall of Mitanni, of Egypt, and of the Hittites, there still remained the powerful mercantile civilizations of the western Semites, — the line of harbor towns on the Phœnician coast and the Syrian cities of the Arameans farther inland, especially Damascus. As wealthy commercial rulers the Aramean kings of Damascus were long able to make their city so strong as to block any effort at permanent advance by Assyria toward the Mediterranean. One of the best illustrations of the effect of their power is the fact that for a considerable length of time Damascus sheltered the two little Hebrew kingdoms

Stubborn resistance of Assyria's smaller western rivals

from Assyrian attack (see map, p. 146). The Assyrian armies had marched westward and had crossed the Euphrates by 1300 B.C. They had looked out upon the Mediterranean by 1100 B.C., but for more than three and a half centuries after this the kings of Assur were unable to conquer and hold this western region against the strong group of Aramean, Phœnician, and Hebrew kingdoms. These western kingdoms thus held the Assyrian armies at bay until the Eighth Century B.C. It is important to remember, furthermore, that Assyria had dangerous enemies also in the Highland Zone on her north and east, while on the south was Babylon, likewise often a menace.

Growth of Assyrian civilization before the Empire

247. As Assyrian power after 1000 B.C. thus seemed to pause at the threshold of her coming empire, let us look back for a moment over the long two thousand years of development and see what progress Assur had made in civilization. Until nearly 2000 B.C. the Assyrians, like the Egyptians and Babylonians, used tools of copper. Then the discovery was made, probably by some northern people, that a small amount of tin mixed with copper would produce *bronze*, an alloy much harder and much more easily melted than pure copper. Tools of bronze were very much more effective, and weapons of bronze were far more dangerous, than any which could be made of copper. The Age of Bronze lasted from about 2000 B.C. to about 1000 B.C. Thus the Assyrian armies which marched westward before 1000 B.C. bore weapons of bronze, but after this time iron weapons were obtainable. Iron was already known to man in prehistoric days, but it remained a rarity until the Hittites discovered it in northeastern Asia Minor. From the Thirteenth Century onward the Hittite kings distributed iron throughout the Near East. It was therefore in the first centuries of the Age of Iron[1] that the

[1] The three ages of metal are easily remembered:

The Copper Age, from the Fourth Millennium to about 2000 B.C.
The Bronze Age, from about 2000 to about 1000 B.C.
The Iron Age, from about 1000 B.C. to the modern Age of Steel.

Assyrians were preparing for western conquests, and their success was due, to a large extent, to the use of this metal in warfare.

248. Besides metal the west, particularly the Hittites, brought into Assyrian life other things important to civilization. Under influences from the Hittite art of north Syria the sculptors of Assur learned to tell the story of the king's valiant exploits in elaborate stone pictures cut in flat relief on great slabs of alabaster (Fig. 109 and headpiece, p. 179). These were set up in long rows along the palace walls. As in sculpture, so in architecture, the possession of stone enabled the Assyrians to do what had been impossible in almost stoneless Babylonia. The Assyrian builders could erect heavy foundations of stone under their buildings, as the Hittites and Syrians had long been doing. Above the foundation the Assyrian building itself, however, usually continued to be made of sun-dried brick, as in Babylonia.

Western contributions to Assyrian art and architecture

249. Many of the sacred stories and symbols of the gods which had grown up among the Babylonian communities were taken over by the men of Assur, who copied and studied and revered them; but the Assyrians clung to their old tribal god Assur, from whom came the name of their city and their tribe. In the earlier times, when the Assyrians were still chiefly tillers of the soil, they seem to have thought of Assur as a god of the dying and ever-reviving vegetation, like Osiris in Egypt. However that may be, Assur's oldest symbol was the tree of life, which the Assyrians set up and decorated every spring like a Maypole. Later, when Assyria became a nation of soldiers, they believed that Assur was a fierce god of war, whom they identified with the sun. Religion among the warlike Assyrians, as in Babylonia, had little effect upon the conduct of the worshiper. One reason for this was the fact that the Assyrians had much the same notions of the hereafter as the Babylonians, with no belief in a judgment to come.

Religion of Assur

Fig. 106. *The* Oldest Known Aqueduct : *Constructed by Sennacherib*

The remains of this remarkable feat of engineering skill were excavated in 1933 by the Oriental Institute of the University of Chicago. The aqueduct was a part of Sennacherib's great irrigation project for conveying water from the northern mountains thirty miles away to the fields around Nineveh. Finding that they must carry the water across a small river, the Assyrian engineers constructed a large stone-masonry channel over 900 feet long and almost 80 feet wide, along which the water flowed between parapets 9 feet wide. The water was thus carried not only across the little river, as if on a bridge, but also across the river valley, which was about 1000 feet wide. (Reconstruction and drawing by Seton Lloyd)

SECTION 19. THE ASSYRIAN EMPIRE (ABOUT 750 TO 612 B.C.)

Continued westward expansion of Assyria

250. While the great object of Assyrian expansion was the conquest of the west, in order to gain a foothold on the Mediterranean and to control the trade routes between the east and the west, hostile neighbors in the north, east, and south had often obliged the Assyrian kings to send their armies into these regions. They descended the Tigris with such power that they even captured and ruled for a time their old conqueror Babylon, while it was still under the rule of the half-barbaric Kassites.

After serious reverses Assyria was again pushing her plans of westward expansion by the middle of the Eighth Century B.C. Damascus, combined with the other western kingdoms, made a desperate resistance, only to be slowly crushed. When at last Damascus fell (732 B.C.), the countries of the west were all subdued and made subject kingdoms. Thus the once obscure little city of Assur gained the lordship over Western Asia as head of an empire, a great group of conquered and vassal nations. The story of that empire forms the second great chapter of history along the Two Rivers.

Sargon II of Assyria (722–705 B.C.)

251. In the midst of these great western campaigns of Assyria, while besieging the unhappy Hebrew city of Samaria, the Assyrian king died (722 B.C.,) and the throne then passed to his son. As king this prince took the name of Sargon, the first great Semite of Babylonia, who had reigned eighteen hundred years earlier. The new Sargon, whom we call Sargon II, raised Assyria to the height of her grandeur and power as a military empire. His descendants were the great emperors of Assyria.[1] On the northeast of Nineveh he built a new royal residence on a vaster scale and more magnificent than any Asia had ever seen before. He called it *Dur-Sharrukin* (Sar-

[1] The leading kings of the dynasty of Sargon II are as follows:

Sargon II	722–705 B.C.
Sennacherib	705–681 B.C.
Esarhaddon	681–668 B.C.
Assurbanipal (called Sardanapalus by the Greeks)	668–626 B.C.

Fig. 107. *Restoration of the* Palace *and a Portion of the* City *of Sargonburg, the Royal Residence of Sargon II*

The palace stands partly inside and partly outside of the city wall, on a vast elevated platform of brick masonry containing about 25 acres. Inclined roadways and stairways rise on the *inside* of the city wall. The king could thus drive up in his chariot from the streets of the city below to the palace pavement above. The rooms and halls are clustered about a number of courts open to the sky. The main entrance (with stairs before it leading down to the city) is adorned with massive towers and arched doorways built of richly colored glazed brick and embellished with huge human-headed bulls carved of alabaster. The streets and houses of the city filled the space below the palace within the city walls, which could accommodate some eighty thousand people. The Oriental Institute of The University of Chicago is now engaged in completing the excavation of this city and palace (see Fig. 108). (Drawing after Place)

gonburg). Babylonia in her greatest days had never possessed a seat of power like this. In no uncertain terms it proclaimed Assyria mistress of Western Asia.

Sennacherib (705–681 B.C.)

252. The grandeur of Sargon II was even surpassed by his son Sennacherib, one of the great statesmen of the early Orient. Far up in Asia Minor the name of Sennacherib was known and feared after he plundered Tarsus and the easternmost Ionian Greek strongholds just after 700 B.C. Thence his campaigns swept southward, where he captured the Phœnician harbor towns along

FIG. 108. *A Colossal* WINGED BULL *from the Palace of Sargon*

The entrances to Assyrian palaces were usually guarded by a pair of these huge human-headed bulls. The one shown here is from the palace gateway at Sargonburg (position indicated by arrow in Fig. 107). It now stands in the exhibition halls of the Oriental Institute at The University of Chicago. The figure, carved in calcareous stone similar to alabaster, is sixteen feet high and weighs forty tons. The excavation, transportation to the United States, and preparation for exhibition of this remarkable piece of sculpture therefore formed a very difficult task

the Mediterranean to the very borders of Egypt. To be sure, much of Sennacherib's army was destroyed by a pest from the Delta marshes, which the Hebrews regarded as the angel of the Lord (Yahveh); hence Sennacherib never crossed the Egyptian frontier. But against Babylon, his other ancient rival, he adopted the severest measures. Exasperated by one revolt after another, Sennacherib completely destroyed the venerable city of Hammurapi and even turned the waters of a canal over the desolate ruins.

Egypt conquered by Assyria

253. Thus Babylon was annihilated, but the ancient power on the Nile remained a continual disturber of Assyrian control. A crushing burden of Assyrian tribute had been laid on all subject states, and hence Egypt was constantly able to stir up revolt among the oppressed western peoples, who longed to be freed from the payment of this tribute. Assyria perceived that Egypt's interference must be stopped. Sennacherib's son therefore appeared before the gates of the eastern Delta forts by 674 B.C. Repulsed at first, he returned to the attack; and, although he died before entering the Delta, Egypt at last fell a prey to the Assyrian armies, and Sennacherib's grandson was for a time lord of the lower Nile.

Extent of the Assyrian Empire

254. By 700 B.C. the Assyrian Empire included all of the Fertile Crescent. It thus extended entirely around the great desert bay, but it included furthermore much of the northern mountain country far behind. The conquest of Egypt gave it also the lower Nile valley in the west, though this last was too distant and too detached to be kept long. Built up by irresistible and far-reaching military campaigns which went on for two generations after Sargon II, the Assyrian conquests finally formed the most extensive empire the world had yet seen.

Nineveh becomes Assyrian capital

255. Sennacherib was not satisfied merely to enlarge the old royal residences of his fathers at Assur or at Sargonburg. He devoted himself to the city of Nineveh, north of Assur, and it now became the far-famed capital of Assyria. To secure for the city a sufficient water supply Sennacherib connected it with the streams of the northern mountains by a canal with a magnificent aqueduct (Fig. 106), the oldest aqueduct known. Along the Tigris vast palaces and imposing tower-temples of the Assyrian emperors arose, reign after reign. The lofty and massive walls of Nineveh, which Sennacherib built, stretched two miles and a half along the banks of the Tigris, and it was about eight miles around the inner walls of the city. Here in his gorgeous palace he ruled the Western Asiatic

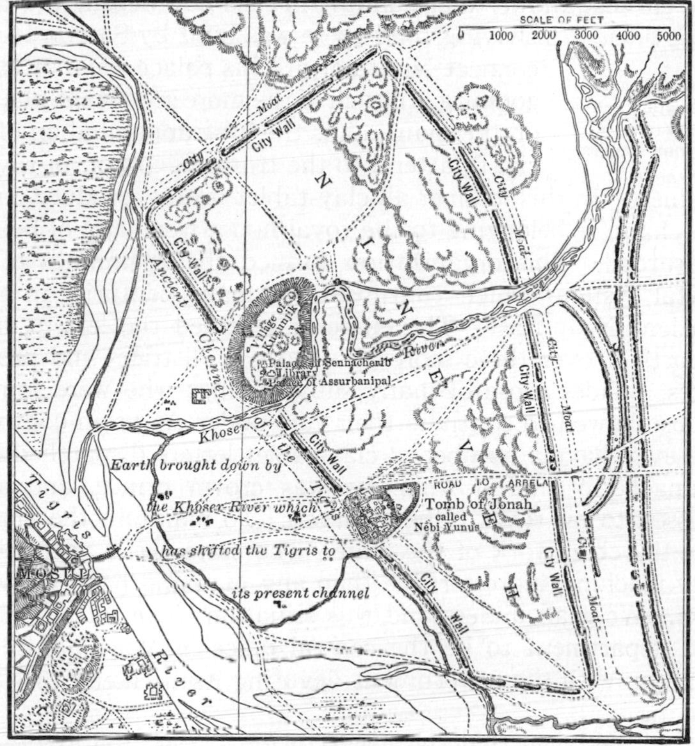

Sketch Map of NINEVEH

Notice the changes in the course of the Tigris, which formerly probably flowed along the west wall of the city. This change has been caused by the Khoser River, which has carried down soil and formed a plain between the wall of the city and the Tigris. In Fig. 199 we have a view from Nebi Yunis, the mound which covers the ruins of the palace of Esarhaddon; and we look along the city wall to the Mound of Kuyunjik. This mound covers the palaces of Sennacherib and Assurbanipal. The remainder of the city was filled with houses and shops of the citizens, and all these less important buildings have disappeared. A destructive overflow of the Khoser River, which flooded the city and broke down a section of the eastern wall, was one of the chief causes of the fall of Nineveh

world with an iron hand, and collected tribute from all the subject peoples, among whom the Hebrews were included.

256. The whole administration centered in the king's business office. He maintained a system of royal messengers.

The earliest known road-building in Asia now began, and the most ancient surviving road there was built by Sargon II to connect Nineveh with his palace-town of Sargonburg. In each of the more important places on the main roads the king appointed an official to attend to the transmission of all royal business. In this manner all clay-tablet letters, produce, and merchandise belonging to the royal house were sure of being forwarded. This organization formed the beginnings of a postal system[1] which continued for many centuries in the Ancient Near East. The emperor received the letters and reports of over three score governors of districts and provinces, besides those of many subject kings who were sometimes allowed to continue their rule under Assyrian control. We even have a number of clay-tablet letters dispatched by Sennacherib himself while he was crown prince, and addressed to his royal father, Sargon. To maintain the army was the chief work of the state. The state was a vast military machine, more terrible than any mankind had ever yet seen. We shall understand this situation if we imagine the war department to be the central office in Washington or London, with the government devoting itself chiefly to supporting it.

Means of communication and organization of Assyrian Empire

257. We recall that the Assyrian forces were the *first large armies completely equipped with weapons of iron.* The bulk of the Assyrian army was composed of archers, supported by heavy-armed spearmen and shield-bearers. Furthermore, Assyria had without doubt learned much from the skillful horsemen of Mitanni (§ 239). The famous horsemen and chariotry of Nineveh became the scourge of the East. For the first time, too, the Assyrians employed the battering-ram and formidable siege machinery. The sun-dried brick walls of the Asiatic cities could thus be battered down or pierced, and no fortified place could long repulse the assaults of the fierce Assyrian infantry.

The weapons of the Assyrians

[1] There are indications that it was already in existence in Asia, under Egyptian rule, as far back as 2000 B.C.

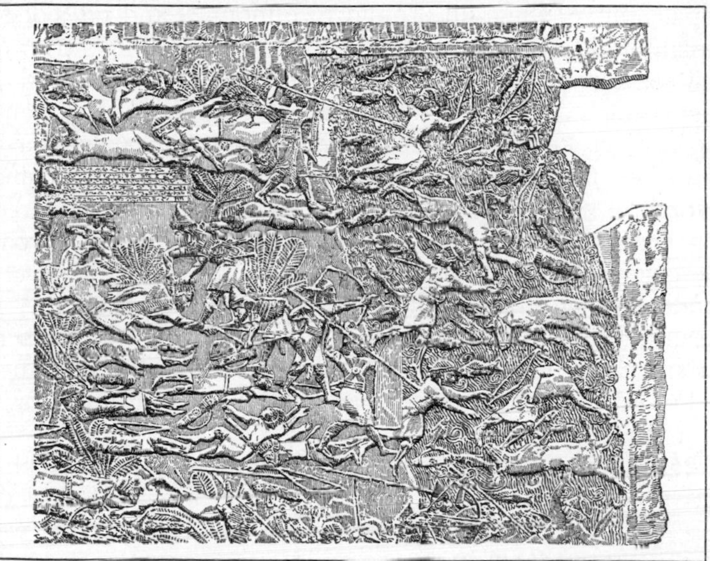

FIG. 109. *Assyrian* SOLDIERS *pursuing the* FLEEING ENEMY *across a Stream*

The stream occupies the right half of the scene. As drawn by the Assyrian artist, it may be recognized by the fish and the curling waves; also by the bows and quivers full of arrows floating downstream, along with the bodies of two dead horses, one on his back with feet up. Two dead men, with arrows sticking in their bodies, are drifting in midstream. Three of the living leap from the bank as their pursuers stab them with spears or shoot them with drawn bow. The Assyrian spearmen carry tall shields, but the archer needs both hands for his bow and carries no shield. The dead are strewn along the shore, occupying the left half of the scene. At the top the vultures are plucking out their eyes; in the middle an Assyrian is cutting off a head; beside him another plants his foot on a dead man's head and steals his weapons. The vegetation along the river is shown among the bodies, with abandoned weapons scattered between

The terrors of the Assyrian army

258. Besides their iron weapons and their war machines the Assyrian soldiers displayed a certain inborn ferocity which held all Western Asia in abject terror before the thundering squadrons of the Ninevites.[1] Wherever the terrible Assyrian armies swept through the land they left a trail of ruin and desolation behind. Around smoking heaps which had once been towns stretched lines of tall stakes, on which were stuck the bodies of rebellious rulers

[1] See Nahum iii, 2–3.

impaled alive, while all around rose mounds and piles of the slaughtered, heaped up to celebrate the great king's triumph and serve as a warning to all revolters. Through clouds of dust rising along all the main roads of the Empire the men of the subject kingdoms beheld great herds of cattle, horses, and asses, flocks of goats and sheep, and long lines of camels loaded with gold and silver (the wealth of the conquered), converging upon the palace at Nineveh. Before them marched the chief men of the plundered kingdoms, with the severed heads of their former princes tied about their necks. As Assurbanipal sat at the banquet table and feasted with his queen in a garden bower, amid birds, fruit, flowers, and music, he looked up at the severed head of the King of Elam hanging on a tree before him.

Civilization of the Assyrian Empire: architecture

259. While the wealth plundered from these defeated kings was necessary for the support of the army, it also served higher purposes. The Assyrian palaces were now imposing buildings, suggesting in architecture the far-reaching power of their builder. In the hands of the Assyrian architects the arch, inherited from Babylonia, for the first time became an imposing monumental feature of architecture. The impressive triple arches of the Assyrian palace entrance, faced with glazed brick in gorgeous colors, were the ancestors of the Roman triumphal arches (Fig. 243). On either side were gigantic human-headed bulls wrought in alabaster (Fig. 108), and above the whole towered lofty castellated walls of baked brick, visible far across the royal city.

Civilization of the Assyrian Empire: sculpture; music

260. Within the palace, as a dado running along the lower portion of the walls, were thousands of feet of relief pictures cut in alabaster. At Nineveh, in a single mound, the excavators cleared seventy-one palace halls and laid bare nearly two miles of such relief scenes, many of which they carried away to the British Museum. These sculptures show much improvement over the work (headpiece, p. 179) of a century before the Empire. They display especially the great deeds of the

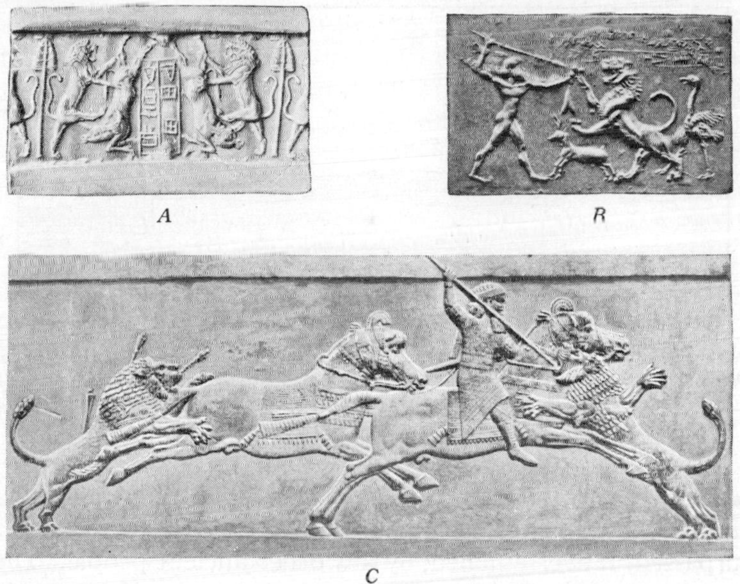

A

B

C

FIG. 110. ANIMAL SCULPTURE *of the Babylonians and Assyrians*

Seal *A* represents the wonderful work of a Babylonian seal-cutter in the time of Sargon of Akkad (§ 199). In balanced heraldic arrangement a lion is twice shown slaying a wild bull. A free and splendidly vigorous treatment of the old subject of combat between man and beast (Fig. 87) is found in Seal *B*. The ostrich adds a humorous touch which indicates that even the somber Assyrian could smile. In the lion hunt (*C*) we have one of the best examples of Assyrian relief sculpture of the reign of Assurbanipal. It clearly shows the influence of the early Babylonian seals on animal sculpture

emperor in campaign and hunting field. The human figures are monotonously alike, hard, cold, and unfeeling; nowhere is there a human form which shows any trace of feeling, either joy or sorrow, pleasure or pain. The Assyrian sculptor's wild beasts, however, are sometimes magnificent in the abandon of animal ferocity which they display. The tiger was in the blood of the Assyrian, and it came out in the work of his chisel. On the other hand, the pathetic expression of suffering exhibited by some of these wonderful animal forms was a triumph of art which the Assyrian sculptor owed to a study of the superb lions and bulls on the exquisite old Babylonian

FIG. 111. *The Egyptian* WELL SWEEP *introduced into Assyria*

With regard to his introduction into Assyria of the Egyptian well sweep (or *shadoof*; cf. Fig. 25) Sennacherib says, "That daily there might be an abundant flow of water of the buckets, I had copper cables and pails made, and instead of pillars I set up great posts and cross-beams over the well-shafts." Then he had reliefs carved on his palace walls, picturing his people using the new device

seals of the age of Sargon of Akkad, nearly two thousand years earlier. Nevertheless the animal sculpture of Assyria was never surpassed, if ever equaled, by any other ancient people. The art of portraiture in statue form never got beyond very crude and unskillful efforts. A tablet recently (1924) discovered in the Berlin Museum contains a poem accompanied by a hitherto unknown system of musical notes intended for musical instruments. This oldest known musical notation shows a scale of five tones and a range of four of these scales. It was played upon a harp of twenty-two strings, an instrument common to the later Mediterranean world, and especially to Egypt. The Assyrians perhaps inherited this musical notation from Babylonia.

Assyrian borrowing from abroad

261. The emperors were obliged to depend much on foreign skill, both in art and in industries. The art of glazing colored brick had been borrowed from Egypt (§ 98). All the patterns of Assyrian decorative art likewise came from Egypt, and their furniture of ebony and ivory, made by Phœnician workmen, often betrays Egyptian origin. Phœnician craftsmen at Nineveh wrought splendidly engraved bronze platters. Sennacherib tells us that he had in his palace "a portico patterned after a Hittite palace," and his predecessors had long before built similar porticos like those they had seen in the Hittite west. It is in this ability to use foreign resources that we must recognize one of the greatest traits of the Assyrian emperors.

262. By means of his new canal and aqueduct Sennacherib was able to irrigate the fine gardens which he laid out along the river above and below Nineveh. Here he planted strange trees and plants from all quarters of his great empire. Among them were cotton trees, of which he says, "The trees that bore wool they clipped and they carded it for garments." These cotton trees came from India. We thus see appearing for the first time in the ancient world the cotton which now furnishes so large a part of our own national wealth.[1] These imports from distant regions show us how far-reaching were the foreign connections of the Assyrian Empire.

Introduction of foreign plants, including the earliest cotton

263. Higher interests were also cultivated among the Assyrians, and literature flourished. Sargon II had already begun collecting a tablet library of old writings, and his successors continued this interest in literature. Assurbanipal, the last great Assyrian emperor and the grandson of Sennacherib, boasts that his father instructed him not only in riding and shooting with bow and arrow but also in writing on clay tablets and in all the wisdom of his time. A great collection of twenty-two thousand clay tablets was discovered in Assurbanipal's fallen library rooms at Nineveh, where they had been lying on the floor for twenty-five hundred years. They are now in the British Museum. In this library the religious, scientific, and literary works of past ages had been systematically collected by the emperor's orders. These collections of tablets, begun under Sargon II, were the earliest libraries known in Asia. The Assyrians were far more advanced in these matters than the Babylonians, and Assyrian civilization was far from being a mere echo of Babylonian culture.

Assurbanipal's library

[1] This cotton tree was doubtless related to the lower-growing cotton plant of our Southern states.

FIG. 112. *Portion of Old Babylonian* STORY OF THE FLOOD *from Assurbanipal's Library at Nineveh*

This large, flat tablet was part of an Assyrian cuneiform book consisting of a series of such tablets. This flood story tells how the hero, Ut-napishtim, built a great ship and thus survived a terrible flood, in which all his countrymen perished. Each of these clay-tablet books, collected in fresh copies by Assurbanipal for his library, bore a mark indicating the king's ownership, just like a bookplate in a modern library. To prevent anyone else from taking the book, or writing his name on it, the Assyrian king's bookplate contained the following warning: "Whosoever shall carry off this tablet, or shall inscribe his name upon it side by side with mine own, may Assur and Belit overthrow him in wrath and anger, and may they destroy his name and posterity in the land"

264. The social and business life of the Assyrians was regulated by a code of laws, which has unfortunately perished. In the ruins of the city of Assur, however, the German excavators found clay tablets forming part of a law book and containing the substance of nearly sixty laws. They reveal the strictest governmental control of marriage and of property rights. For transgressions of the law the punishments decreed are revoltingly cruel, quite commonly including, besides the death penalty, mutilations like the cutting off of fingers, ears, or nose, and even the tearing out of eyes. This over-rigorous control of internal affairs by the Assyrian emperors included a serious mistake in policy. Their wars of conquest led to the destruction of the industrial and wealth-producing population, first within their own territory and then throughout the subject kingdoms. In spite of interest in introducing a new textile like cotton, the Assyrian rulers did not or could not build up industries or commerce like those of Babylonia. The people were chiefly agricultural, and in the old days it had sufficed to call them from their farming for short periods to defend the frontiers. With the expansion of the Empire, however, such temporary bodies of troops were insufficient, and the peasants were *permanently taken from the fields* to fill the ranks of an ever-growing standing army. It is not improbable that the ruling class was buying up the small farms to form great estates. We learn of disused canals and idle fields as we read of Sargon's efforts to restore the old farming communities. Nevertheless, so vast an expansion of the Empire exceeded the power of the standing army to defend it.

Internal decay; economic and agricultural decline

265. As reports of new revolts came in, the harassed ruler at Nineveh forced the subjects of his foreign vassal kingdoms to enter the army. With an army made up, to a dangerous extent, of such foreigners, with industries declining, with fields lying idle, with the commerce of the country in the hands of the Aramean traders, and with Aramean speech more common in the cities of the Empire, even in Nineveh, than that of the Assyrians themselves, — under these conditions the Assyrian nation fast lost its inner strength.

Foreign levies in the army; Arameans controlling trade

266. In addition to such weakness within, there were the most threatening dangers from without. These came, as of old, from both sides of the Fertile Crescent. Drifting in from the desert, the Aramean hordes were constantly occupying the territory of the Empire. Sennacherib in one campaign took more than two hundred thousand captives out of Babylonia, mostly Arameans. At the same time another desert tribe called the Kaldi, whom we know as the Chaldeans, had been for centuries creeping slowly around the head of the Persian Gulf and settling along its shores at the foot of the eastern mountains. They were Semitic nomads, repeating what the Akkadians had done in Akkad and the Amorites in Babylon (§§ 195, 211).

Assaults from without: Chaldeans from the desert

267. On the other hand, in the northern mountains the advancing hordes of Indo-European peoples had been in full view since the incoming of the Mitannian horsemen. Mitanni had long ago disappeared, and the Indo-Europeans were now led by the tribes of the Medes and Persians. These migrations shook the Assyrian state to its foundations. By 616 B.C. the Chaldeans had mastered Babylonia. Nabopolassar, the new Chaldean king at Babylon, who called himself "King of Akkad," marched against the Assyrians and, having twice defeated them, conquered as far north as their earliest capital at Assur, which he failed to capture. The next year (614 B.C.), however, the Medes from the northeastern mountains marched down the Tigris and captured Assur. Nabopolassar arrived too late to share in the assault; but he established an alliance with Cyaxares, the Median king, and together they attacked Nineveh.

Assaults from without: Indo-Europeans from the mountains

268. Weakened by a generation of decline within, the once irresistible armies of Nineveh struggled for two years against this combined assault from without, and then the mighty city of the Assyrian emperors fell (612 B.C.). In the voice of the Hebrew prophet Nahum [1] we hear an echo of the exulting shout which resounded from the Caspian to the Nile as the nations discovered that the terrible scourge of the East had at last been

Fall of Assyria; destruction of Nineveh (612 B.C.)

[1] Nahum ii, 8, 13, and iii entire.

laid low. Its fall was forever; and when two centuries later Xenophon and his ten thousand Greeks marched past the place, the Assyrian nation was but a vague tradition, and Nineveh, its great city, was a vast heap of rubbish as it is today. Even Assyrian speech passed away, and Aramaic became the tongue of the region which had once been Assyria, just as it was also to become the language of Babylonia. The second great chapter of history on the Two Rivers was ended, having lasted but a scant century and a half (about 750 to 612 B.C.).

Progress effected by the Assyrian Empire

269. The fall of Assyria, while dramatically sudden and tragically complete, nevertheless left the nations of Western Asia in a very different situation from that in which the first Assyrian emperors had found them. The rule of a single sovereign had been enforced upon the whole great group of nations around the eastern end of the Mediterranean, bringing these nations together in constant intercourse and thus for the first time creating a Near Eastern world having a common civilization. The methods of governing such an empire had been much improved. It was really in continuance of this organization that the great Persian Empire was built up, sixty years after the fall of Assyria. The Assyrian Empire, especially in its military organization, marked a long step forward in that gradual growth of the idea of all-including world power which culminated at last in the Roman Empire. In spite of its often ferocious harshness the Assyrian rule had furthered civilization. The building of the magnificent palaces in and near Nineveh formed the first chapter in great architecture in Asia. At the same time Nineveh possessed the first libraries as yet known there. Finally, the Assyrian dominion, as we shall see, created the international situation which enabled the Hebrews to gain the loftiest conceptions of their own God, as it obliged them to match him against the great war god of Assyria, — conceptions which have profoundly influenced the entire later history of mankind.

SECTION 20. THE CHALDEAN EMPIRE: THE LAST SEMITIC EMPIRE

Rise of the Chaldean Empire

270. The Chaldeans, the new masters of Babylonia, now founded an empire whose brief career formed the third great chapter of history on the Two Rivers.[1] They were the last Semitic lords of Babylonia. The Chaldeans made their capital at Babylon, rebuilt after its destruction by Sennacherib. They called the land Akkad, although we now know it as Chaldea. While they left the Medes in possession of the northern mountains, the empire of the Chaldeans included the entire Fertile Crescent.

Reign of Nebuchadnezzar (604–561 B.C.)

271. At Babylon, Nebuchadnezzar, the greatest of the Chaldean emperors, now (604 B.C.) began a reign of over forty years, — a reign of such power and magnificence, especially as reflected to us in the Bible, that he has become one of the great figures of Oriental history. Exasperated by the obstinate revolts encouraged by Egypt in the west, Nebuchadnezzar punished the western nations, especially the little Hebrew kingdom of Judah. He finally carried away many Hebrews as captives to Babylonia and destroyed Jerusalem, their capital (586 B.C.).

Magnificent buildings of Chaldean Babylon

272. In spite of long and serious wars the great king found time and wealth to devote to the enlargement and beautification of Babylon. Copying much from Assyria, Nebuchadnezzar was able to surpass his Assyrian predecessors in the splendor of the great buildings which he now erected. In the large temple quarter in the south of the city he rebuilt the temples of the

[1] The three great chapters of history on the Two Rivers are:

1. Early Babylonia, about 2900 to 1750 B.C. (Sargon I, about 2500 B.C.; Hammurapi, about 1948–1905 B.C.). See Sections 14–17.
2. The Assyrian Empire, about 750–612 B.C. See Section 19.
3. The Chaldean Empire, about 612–538 B.C. See Section 20.

With the exception of parts of the first, these three epochs were periods of *Semitic* power. To these we might in later times add a *fourth* period of Semitic supremacy, — the triumph of Islam in the Seventh Century A.D., after the death of Mohammed (§ 1191).

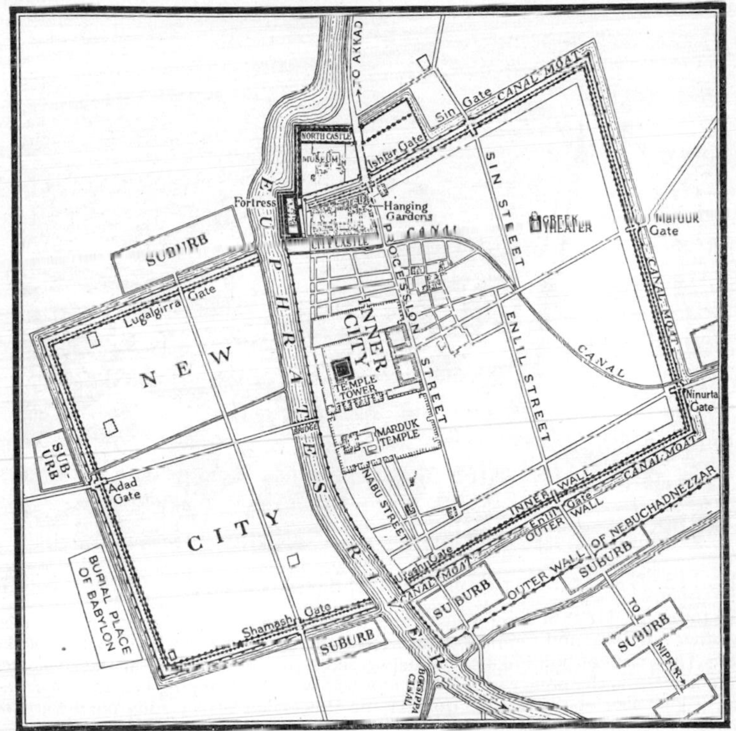

Plan of BABYLON *in the Chaldean Age*

This new plan of Nebuchadnezzar's city is based not only on the remains of buildings and streets as revealed by excavation, but also on ancient clay-tablet maps of Babylon found by the excavators. Such maps are evidence that Babylon, like certain other ancient cities (§ 131), was a "monumental city" built according to a city plan. (After Unger)

long-revered Babylonian divinities. Leading from these to the palace he laid out a festival avenue, or Procession Street, which passed through an imposing gateway called the Ishtar Gate, for it was dedicated to this goddess. Behind it lay the vast imperial palace and the offices of government, while high over all towered the temple-mount, which rose by the Marduk temple as a veritable Tower of Babel. Masses of rich tropical verdure, rising in terrace upon terrace and

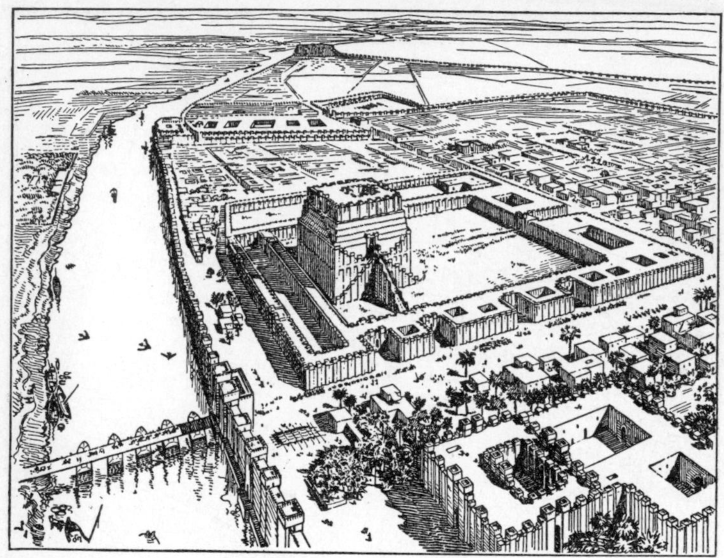

Fig. 113. *The* Restoration *of the City of* Babylon *in the Age of Nebuchadnezzar*

The tower (cf. §182) in the foreground is the great temple of Marduk, surrounded by other buildings and temples of the sacred quarter in the southern section of the city. The group of buildings in the background, by the first bend in the river (see plan, p. 209), is the palace of Nebuchadnezzar, with its Hanging Gardens. On the east (right) side of the temple quarter the Procession Street runs northward to connect with the palace and the Ishtar Gate on the east (right) side of the palace (see Plate II). The Euphrates, flowing along the west (left) side of the city, is crossed by a bridge, the oldest passenger bridge known to us, dating from the Sixth Century B.C. (cf. Fig. 106). Its ruinous piers still stand in the now dry bed of the Euphrates. The enormous fortified walls surrounding the city were the work of Nebuchadnezzar. A campaign of over eighteen years' excavation by the Germans under Koldewey has made this restoration possible. (Drawing after Koldewey).

forming a lofty garden, crowned the roof of the imperial palace. This garden, overlooking the Ishtar Gate, enhanced the brightness of its colored tiles. Here in the cool shade of palms and ferns, inviting to luxurious ease, the great king might enjoy an idle hour with the ladies of his court and look down upon the splendors of his city. These roof gardens of Nebuchadnezzar's palace were the mysterious Hanging Gardens of Babylon, whose fame spread far into the west until they were numbered by the Greeks among the Seven Won-

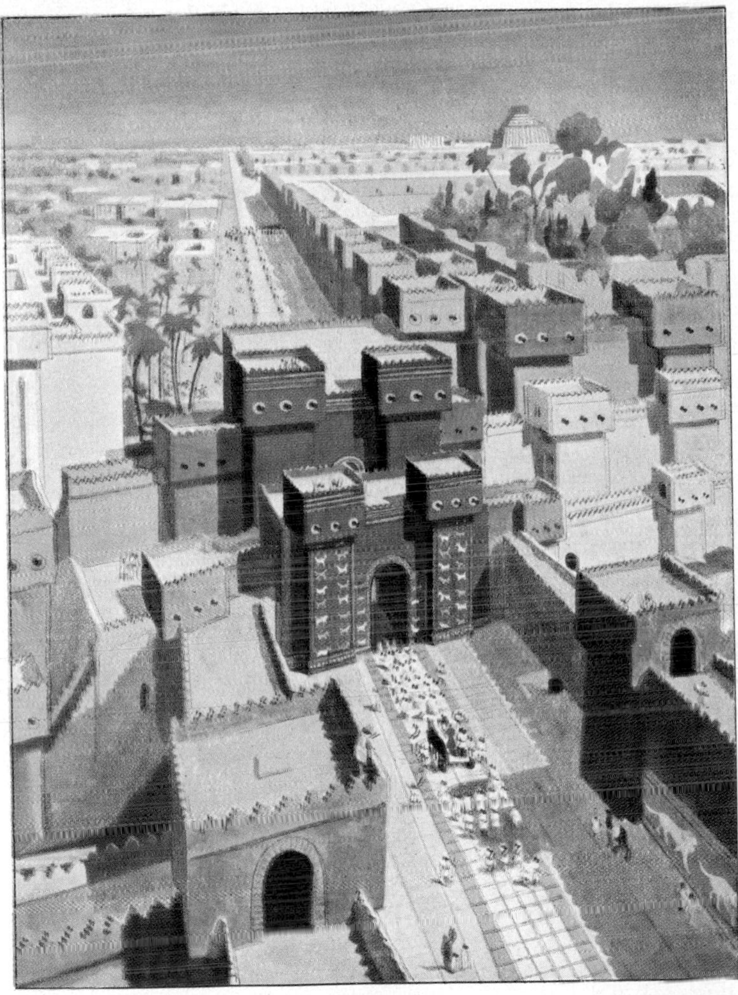

PLATE II. *Restoration of the* BABYLON *of Nebuchadnezzar*

Looking from the palace quarter, past the Ishtar Gate, and along Festival Avenue to the temple quarter and the "Tower of Babel" (in right background). Just at the right of the Ishtar Gate may be seen the palace roof gardens which came to be known as the "Hanging Gardens." (After Unger)

ders of the World. Babylon thus became a monumental city like those of Assyria and Egypt.

273. For the first time Babylonia saw a very large city. It was immensely extended by Nebuchadnezzar, and enormous fortified walls were built to protect it, including one that extended entirely across the plain from the Tigris to the Euphrates above the city. It is this Babylon of Nebuchadnezzar whose marvels over a century later so impressed Herodotus, as is shown in the description of the city which he has left us. This, too, is the Babylon which has become familiar to all Christian peoples as the great city of the Hebrew captivity. Of all the glories which made it world-renowned in its time little now remains. The German excavations here, which continued from 1899 to 1917, revealed for the most part only broken fragments of dingy sun-baked brick walls. With the exception of the Ishtar Gate little is left to suggest the brilliant life which once ebbed and flowed through these streets and public places. The Chaldeans seem to have absorbed the civilization of Babylonia in much the same way as other earlier Semitic invaders of this ancient plain. Commerce and business flourished, the arts and industries were highly developed, religion and literature were cultivated, and their records were put into wedge-writing on clay tablets as of old.

Chaldean Babylon and its civilization

274. Science made surprising progress in one important branch, — astronomy. The Babylonians had continued their ancient practice of trying to discover the future in the heavenly bodies (see § 227). The five planets then known (Mercury, Venus, Mars, Jupiter, and Saturn) were especially regarded as the powers controlling the fortunes of men, and as such the five leading Babylonian divinities were identified with these five heavenly bodies. The names of these Babylonian divinities have descended to us as the names of the planets, but on their way to us through Europe the ancient Babylonian divine names were translated into Roman forms. So the planet of Ishtar, the goddess of love, became Venus, while

Babylonian astrology and names of planets

that of the great god Marduk became Jupiter, and so on. The practice of astrology has survived to our own day; we still unconsciously recall it in such phrases as "his lucky star" or an "ill-starred undertaking."

275. Chaldean astrology has also left an indelible mark on our calendar in the names which we apply to the days of the week. The five planets just mentioned, together with the sun and the moon, make up a group of seven celestial bodies, each of which was an important divinity. As Chaldean temple worship spread into Syria it became customary finally to pronounce the ritual and sing the praise of each god on a certain particular day. Thus the worship of each one of these seven divinities came around every seventh day. The name of the god worshiped on that day was finally transferred to the day itself. In this way the day which was devoted to the Sun-god became Sun-day, the day sacred to the Moon became Mon-day, and so on through the week, until the last day, sacred to Saturn, was called Satur-day. As our language came to us along a northern route, and there are consequently Norse elements in it, the names of several of our week days have reached us in a northern form, like Wednesday (Woden's-day) or Thursday (Thor's-day). Nevertheless they all go back to the old Babylonian gods, who still live on among us in our names of the days of the week.

Celestial origin of names of our days of the week

276. Much more important than these surviving remains of Babylonian astrology were its services in gradually improving the observations of the skies till they became something more than mere fortune-telling. As far back as the Twenty-third Century B.C., in the days of the kings of Sumer and Akkad, the astrologers observed an eclipse of the moon which has now been calculated by a modern astronomer to have occurred in 2283 B.C. But at that remote date such observations were only occasional, and they were also very inaccurate and unsystematic. Gradually it became customary to make more frequent observations, until in 747 B.C., in

Beginning of continuous observations, 747 B.C.; astronomy

FIG. 114. *Both Sides of a Clay* TABLET *forming Part of a Chaldean* ASTRONOMICAL ALMANAC *(Front at Left, Back at Right)*

The observations of the moon are in the left-hand column marked off by the vertical ruling. In the right-hand column are observations of the planets and fixed stars. The following four entries on the back are of great interest:

On the first Mercury rises.
On the third the Equinox.
Night of the 15th, 40 minutes after sunset, an eclipse of the moon begins.
On the 28th occurs an eclipse of the sun.

Kugler has computed the dates of these two eclipses as October 9 and 23 in 425 B.C. This tablet therefore formed part of the great series of Babylonian observations which began in 747 B.C. (Courtesy of the University Museum of Philadelphia)

the reign of the Babylonian king Nabonassar, the series of observations became continuous, and a record of them was carefully kept on file. Unfortunately the complete file has not been preserved. So far as is now known, the oldest tablet from this list was made in the year 568 B.C. It is the oldest surviving carefully made astronomical observation. We now know that these records of the Chaldean astronomers continued for over three hundred and sixty years. They formed the first long series of astronomical observations and the first great body of astronomical knowledge. Indeed, modern astronomers have never yet made such a long-continued and uninterrupted series of observations.[1] It is especially remarkable that such scientific work continued to be carried on even after the Chaldean people had lost their independence and were ruled by Persian sovereigns.

Surveys of celestial motions; Nabu-rimannu; Kidinnu

277. More remarkable than this great body of observations, however, was the use to which the ablest Chaldean astronomers put these records. Not long before 500 B.C., when the files of these continuous observations had been collecting for about two hundred and fifty years, a Chaldean astronomer named *Nabu-rimannu* used them to compile tables of the motions of the sun and moon, in which he recorded his calculations of the time required by these two heavenly bodies to make their revolutions, daily, monthly, yearly, and so forth, exactly dating the eclipses of the sun and the moon, and other important astronomical events. He calculated the length of the year as 365 days, 6 hours, 15 minutes, and 41 seconds. This measurement, made over two thousand years before the telescope was invented, is only 26 minutes, 55 seconds too long. It is the earliest known close approximation to the length of a year. This splendid time-table of the vast celestial clock, put together by Nabu-rimannu, was the earliest great constructive piece of astronomical work. There was a grandeur in it which the mind of man had never achieved before.

A little over a century later another Chaldean astronomer named *Kidinnu* made a similar group of tables of greatly increased accuracy. Indeed, one of his measurements of celestial motions even exceeds in accuracy the figures which have long been in practical use by modern astronomers. This was because he had before him the records of three hundred and sixty years of lunar observations, and no modern astronomer has any such records at his disposal. Kidinnu even proved that there was a difference between the length of the year as measured from equinox to equinox and as measured

[1] The only long-continued modern series of observations that can be compared with those of the Chaldeans are the meridian observations at Greenwich, England, which began in 1750, one hundred and eighty-five years ago.

between two successive arrivals of the earth at its nearest point to the sun.[1]

278. The century-long astronomical observations of the Chaldeans, together with the calculations of Nabu-rimannu and Kidinnu, passed over to the Greeks. They studied the calculations of these two great Chaldean astronomers, whom they called Naburianos and Kidenas; and when the Greek engineer Meton was trying to introduce a scientific calendar at Athens, he took the length of his year from the tables of Nabu-rimannu. Of these two Chaldeans a modern astronomer has said that they "are entitled to a place among the greatest of astronomers." These Chaldean pioneers in astronomy who first revealed to men a *system* of the celestial world, and thus became the founders of astronomical science, should be reverently remembered long after the kings and conquerors of the ancient world have been forgotten.

Chaldeans, the founders of astronomical science

279. While Chaldea thus surpassed in science anything accomplished by Assyria, we see in the new architecture of Chaldean Babylon the influence of Assyrian architecture. The Chaldeans themselves, however, fancied that they were restoring the civilization of the old Babylonia of Hammurapi. The scribes loved to employ an ancient style of writing and out-of-date forms of speech; the kings tunneled deep under the temple foundations and searched for years that they might find the old foundation records buried (like our corner-stone documents) by kings of ancient days.

Oriental revival of the past

280. This dependence upon the past meant decline. After the death of Nebuchadnezzar (561 B.C.), whose reign was the high-water mark of Chaldean civilization, the old civilized lands of the Orient seemed to have lost most of their former power to push forward and make fresh discoveries and new conquests in civilization,

Decline of the old Oriental lands

[1] Students who are taking courses in astronomy will understand that this is practically the discovery of the slow change in the obliquity of the earth's axis,—a change like the wabble of a spinning top, which is often called the precession of the equinoxes.

such as they had been making during three great ages on the Nile and three similar ages on the Two Rivers. Indeed, the leadership of the Semitic peoples in the early world was drawing near its close, and they were about to give way before the advance of the new peoples of the Indo-European race. But before we take up the movements of these new peoples, let us glance briefly at the little Hebrew kingdom, which was destined to influence the history of man more profoundly than any of the great empires of the early world.

QUESTIONS

Section 18. Where does the second chapter of history on the Two Rivers carry us? Describe the region around Assur. Whence did the people of Assur gain the beginnings of civilization? What were some of the results of Assyrian commercial expansion into Asia Minor? Who were the western rivals of Assur? Tell about the Arameans and what they accomplished. What did Assyrian civilization achieve before the Empire?

Section 19. Discuss Damascus and its capture by Assyria. Who was the founder of the leading line of Assyrian emperors? Describe his new city. What was the extent of the Assyrian Empire? How was its government carried on? What can you say about Assyrian warfare? about architecture and sculpture? What can you tell of Assurbanipal? What dangers within and without caused the fall of Assyria? What peoples destroyed Nineveh and when? What progress resulted from the rule of the Assyrian Empire?

Section 20. What empire formed the third chapter of history on the Two Rivers? Write a paragraph describing the achievements of Nebuchadnezzar. What astronomical names have descended to us from the Chaldeans? Explain how the names of our week days originated. Tell of the achievements of the Chaldean astronomers. What race followed the Semitic Chaldeans in Oriental leadership?

BIBLIOGRAPHY FOR TOPICAL STUDIES

Education and literature: DELAPORTE, *Mesopotamia*, pp. 198–223, 339–353; OLMSTEAD, *Sargon*, pp. 173–175; WOOLLEY, *Sumerians*, pp. 108–112.

Cities — Assyrian: BELL, *Architecture in Western Asia*, pp. 137–160; DELAPORTE, pp. 316–326; OLMSTEAD, *Sargon*, pp. 178–192; **Babylonian:** BELL, pp. 175–192; DELAPORTE, pp. 172–177; *History Teacher's Magazine*, Vol. 8, pp. 79–81.

Chapter VII · Western Asia: The Hebrews

Section 21. Palestine and the Predecessors of the Hebrews there

Situation and extent of Palestine, the home of the Hebrews

281. The home of the Hebrews was on the western end of the Fertile Crescent, in a land now called Palestine.[1] It is the region lying along the southeastern corner of the Mediterranean, — a narrow strip between desert and sea; for, while the sea limits it on the west, the wastes of the desert bay sweep northward, forming the eastern boundary of Palestine (see map, p. 146). It was about one hundred and fifty miles long, and less than ten thousand square miles are included within these limits; that is, Palestine was somewhat larger than the state of Vermont.

Geographical character of Palestine

282. Much of this area is unproductive, for the desert intrudes upon southern Palestine and rolls northward in gaunt and arid limestone hills, even surrounding Jerusalem. The valleys of northern Palestine, however, are rich and productive. The entire land is without summer rains and is dependent upon the winter rainy season

Note. The above headpiece shows us a Caravan of Canaanites trading in Egypt about 1900 B.C. as they appeared on the estate of a feudal baron in Egypt. The Egyptian noble had this picture of them painted with others in his tomb, where it still is. Observe the shoes, sandals, and gay woolen clothing, the costume of the Palestinian towns, worn by these Canaanites; observe also the metal weapons which they carry. The manufacture of these things created industries which had begun to flourish among the towns in Syria and Palestine by this time. Notice also the type of face, with the prominent nose, which shows that Anatolian blood was already mixed with the Semitic blood of these early dwellers in Palestine.

[1] On the origin of the name see § 415.

Fig. 115. *Ancient Egyptian Painting of a* Brickyard *with Asiatic Captives engaged in Brickmaking (Fifteenth Century* B.C.)

The Hebrew slaves working in the Egyptian brickyards (see Exod. i, 14, and v, 6–19) must have looked like this when Moses led them forth into Asia. At the left below, the soft clay is being mixed in two piles; one laborer helps load a basket of clay on the shoulder of another, who carries it to the brick-molder, at the right above. Here a laborer empties the clay from his basket, while the molder before him fills with clay an oblong box, which is the mold. He has already finished three bricks. At the left above, a molder spreads out the soft bricks with spaces between for the circulation of air to make them dry quickly in the sun. The overseer, staff in hand, sits in the upper right-hand corner, and below him we see a workman carrying away the dried bricks, hanging from a yoke on his shoulders. Thus were made the bricks used for thousands of years for the buildings forming so large a part of the cities of the ancient world, from the Near East to Athens and Rome

for moisture. There is no opportunity for irrigation, and the harvest is therefore scantier than in lands enjoying summer rains. Only the northern end of the Palestinian coast has any harbors, but these were early seized by the Phœnicians (Sections 36–37). Palestine thus remained cut off from the sea. In natural resources it was too poor ever to develop prosperity or political power like its great civilized neighbors on the Nile and Euphrates or in Syria and Phœnicia.

Palestine, market place of Ancient Near East

283. Here at the western end of the Fertile Crescent, as at the eastern end, the Semitic nomads from the desert bay (reread Section 13) mingled with the dwellers in the northern mountains of the Highland Zone. The northerners, chiefly Early Anatolians (later Hittites) from Asia Minor and Syria, left their mark on the Semites of Palestine. The prominent aquiline

FIG. 116. *Air View of* MOUND *covering* FORTRESS CITY *of Armageddon, or Megiddo*

This city stands at the north end of the pass where the road from Egypt to Babylonia and Assyria crosses the Carmel Range. It is thus a natural fortress guarding the ancient highway between Africa and Asia. For thousands of years, on the Plain of Megiddo, the armies of Asia and Africa have met and fought, — from Thutmose III to Lord Allenby and the Turks in the World War. This great mound was formed by the accumulations of rubbish from fallen buildings (§ 186). An expedition from the Oriental Institute of The University of Chicago is engaged in peeling off stratum after stratum of this "layer cake" of ancient cities, the one at present exposed being the city of Solomon's time (Tenth Century B.C.). All that is preserved of the buildings are the stone foundations, the masonry of which has been found to consist of no more than the "three rows of hewn stone" mentioned in 1 Kings vii, 12. The headquarters of the archæological expedition may be seen in the foreground. (Photograph by Mr. Charles Breasted)

nose, still considered to be the mark of the Semite, especially of the Jew, was really a feature belonging to the non-Semitic Anatolians, who intermarried with the people of Palestine and gave them this Anatolian type of face (see Fig. 126 and § 320). Strange faces from many a foreign clime crowded the market places of Palestine, amid a babel of various languages. Here the rich jewelry, bronze dishes, and ivory furniture of the Nile craftsmen mingled with the pottery of the Ægean Islands and of the Highland civilization, and with the gay woolens of Babylonia. The donkeys which lifted their complaining voices above the hubbub of the market had grazed along the shores of both Nile and Euphrates, and their masters had trafficked beneath the Babylonian tower-temples as well as under the shadow of the Theban obelisks. We recall how traffic with Babylonia had taught these western Semites to write the cuneiform hand. To the caravan coming out of Egypt Palestine was the entrance to the bridge between Africa and Asia, — a middle ground where the civilizations of Egypt and Babylonia, Phœnicia, the Ægean, and the Highland Zone, all represented by their wares, met and commingled as they did nowhere else in the Ancient Near East.

Palestine, battle-ground of Ancient Near East

284. Just as the merchandise of the surrounding nations met in peaceful competition in the markets of Palestine, so the armies of these nations also met there in battle. The situation of Palestine, between its powerful neighbors on the Nile and on the Euphrates, made it the battleground where these great nations fought for many centuries. Over and over again unhappy Palestine went through the experience of little Belgium in the conflict between Germany and France in 1914. For many centuries Egypt held Palestine as a subject country. We recall how Assyria later conquered it and Chaldea enslaved it, and we shall yet find it in the power of Persia. When, therefore, the Hebrews originally took possession of the land, there was little prospect that they would ever long enjoy freedom from foreign oppression.

Section 22. The Settlement of the Hebrews in Palestine and the United Hebrew Kingdom

Hebrew invasion of Palestine (about 1400–1200 B.C.)

285. The Hebrews were all originally men of the Arabian Desert, wandering with their flocks and herds and slowly drifting over into their final home in Palestine. For two centuries (about 1400 to 1200 B.C.) their movement from the desert into Palestine continued. Another group of their tribes had been slaves in Egypt, where they had suffered much hardship under a cruel Pharaoh. They were successfully led out of Egypt by their heroic leader Moses, a great national hero whose achievements his people never forgot. On entering Palestine the Hebrews found the Canaanites already dwelling there in flourishing towns protected by massive walls. The Hebrews were able to capture only the weaker Canaanite towns. As the rough Hebrew shepherds looked across the highlands of northern Palestine they beheld their kindred scattered over far-stretching hilltops, with the frowning walls of many a Canaanite stronghold rising between them. Even Jerusalem in the Judean highlands for centuries defied the assaults of the Hebrew invaders, who had no siege machinery for attacking city walls.

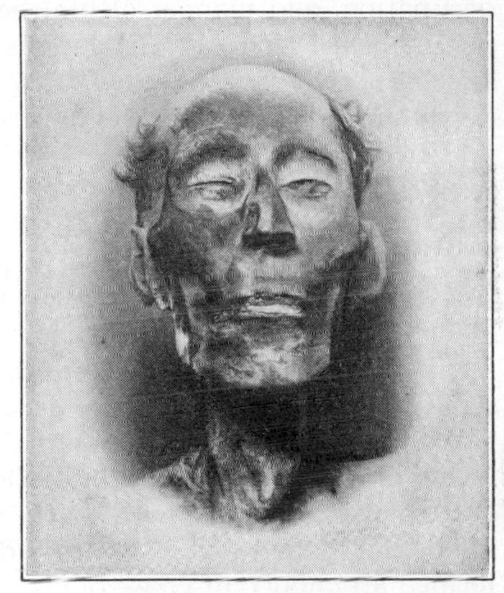

FIG. 117. *Mummy of* RAMSES II, *commonly thought to be the Pharaoh who enslaved the Hebrews*

RAMSES II died about 1225 B.C., that is, over thirty-one hundred years ago. He was about ninety years old

Hebrews adopt Canaanite civilization

286. Let us remember that by that time these unconquered Palestinian towns possessed a civilization fifteen hundred years old, with comfortable houses, government, industries, trade, writing, and religion, — a civilization which the rude Hebrew shepherds were soon adopting; for they could not avoid intercourse with the unsubdued Canaanite towns as trade and business threw them together. This mingling with the Canaanites produced the most profound changes in the life of the Hebrews. Most of them left their tents and began to build houses like those of the Canaanites; they put off the rough sheepskin they had worn in the desert, and they put on fine Canaanite raiment of gayly colored woven wool. After a time, in appearance, occupation, and manner of life the Hebrews were not to be distinguished from the Canaanites among whom they lived. In short, they had adopted Canaanite civilization, just as newly arrived immigrants among *us* soon adopt our clothing and our ways.

Hebrews of South differ in mode of life from those of North

287. These changes did not proceed everywhere at the same rate. In the less fertile South the Hebrews were more attached to the old desert life, so that many would not give up the tent and the old freedom of the desert. The wandering life of the nomad shepherd on the Judean hills could still be seen from the walls of Jerusalem. Here, then, were two differing modes of life among the Hebrews: in the fertile North of Palestine we find the settled life of the town and its outlying fields; in the South, on the other hand, the wandering life of the nomad still went on. For centuries this difference formed an important cause of discord among the Hebrews.

Foundation of Hebrew nation; Saul, the first king

288. Fortunately for the Hebrews, Egypt was in a state of decline by 1100 B.C., and Assyria had not yet conquered the west. But a Mediterranean people called Philistines had at this time migrated from the island of Crete to the sea plain at the southwest corner of Palestine (see map, p. 226). These Philistines formed a highly civilized and warlike nation, or group of city-kingdoms. Hard pressed by the Philistines, the Hebrew local leaders, or judges, as they were called, found it no easy task to unite their people into a nation. About a generation before the year 1000 B.C., however, a popular leader named Saul succeeded in gaining for himself the office of king. The new king was a southerner who still loved the old nomad customs; he was not fond of a fixed abode and preferred to dwell in a tent. In a fierce struggle to thrust back the Philistines, Saul was disastrously defeated, and, seeing the rout of his army, he fell upon his own sword and so died.

289. In a few years the ability of David, one of Saul's daring men-at-arms whom he had unjustly outlawed, won the support of the South. Seeing the importance of possessing a strong castle, the sagacious David selected the ancient fortress on the steep hill of Jerusalem, hitherto held by the Canaanites. The oldest occurrence of the name of the place has recently been found in Egyptian writings over a thousand years older than David's time. He took possession of the venerable city and made it his residence. Here he ruled for a time as king of the South, till his valor as a soldier and his victories on all sides won him also the support of the more prosperous North. The Philistines were now beaten off, and David ruled over an extensive Hebrew kingdom. He enjoyed a long and prosperous reign, and his people never forgot his heroic deeds as a warrior or his skill as a poet and singer.

David (about 1000–960 B.C.)

FIG. 118. LETTER *of the Egyptian Governor of Jerusalem telling of the* INVASION OF PALESTINE *by the Hebrews (Fourteenth Century* B.C.)

The letter is a clay tablet written in Babylonian cuneiform by the terrified Egyptian governor, who begs the Pharaoh (Ikhnaton) for help, saying: "The Khabiru [Hebrews] are taking the cities of the king. No ruler remains to the king, my lord; all are lost." This letter is one of the group of three hundred such cuneiform letters found in a room of Ikhnaton's palace at Tell el-Amarna (or Amarna), and called the Amarna Letters

290. David's son, Solomon, became, like Hammurapi, one of the leading merchants of the East. He trafficked in horses and launched a trading fleet in partnership with Hiram, the Phœnician king of Tyre. His wealth enabled him to marry a daughter of the king of Egypt, and he delighted in Oriental luxury and display. He removed

Solomon and division of his kingdom (about 930 B.C.)

FIG. 119. *Ruins of the* STABLES *of Solomon at Armageddon (Megiddo)*

Many of the square stone piers which supported the roof have disappeared, as has the roof itself, but a number of them remain to show the arrangement of the stables. The horses were tied to these piers, and the tie-holes in the corners of the piers are still preserved. In the middle between the piers we see two solid stone mangers and half of a third manger (*D, D, D*) looking like bathtubs. The horses, standing so that they could eat from these mangers, were ranged in a row of twelve stalls (row *A–A*), facing a second row of twelve (row *B–B*). The passage (*C–C*) between the two rows was intended to enable the grooms to reach and fill the mangers. With five such double rows of horses, these stables accommodated one hundred and twenty animals. (Excavated by the Oriental Institute of The University of Chicago)

the portable tent which the Hebrews had thus far used as a temple, and with the aid of his friend Hiram, who lent him skilled Phœnician workmen, he built a rich temple of stone in Jerusalem. Such splendor demanded a great income, and to secure it he weighed down the Hebrews with heavy taxes. The resulting discontent of his subjects was so great that, under Solomon's son, the Northern tribes withdrew from the nation and set up a king of their own. Thus the Hebrew nation was divided into two kingdoms before it was a century old.

SECTION 23. THE TWO HEBREW KINGDOMS

291. There was much hard feeling between the two Hebrew kingdoms, and sometimes fighting. Israel, as we call the Northern Kingdom, was rich and prosperous; its market places were filled with industry and commerce; its fertile fields produced plentiful crops. Israel displayed the wealth and success of town life. On the other hand, Judah, the Southern Kingdom, was poor; its land was meager; besides Jerusalem it had no large towns; many of the people still wandered with their flocks.

Contrast between the two Hebrew kingdoms

292. These two methods of life came into conflict in many ways, but especially in religion. Every old Canaanite town for centuries had had its local town god, called its *baal*, or "lord." The Hebrew townsmen therefore found it very natural to worship the gods of their neighbors, the Canaanite townsmen. They were thus unfaithful to their old Hebrew God Yahveh (or Jehovah).[1] To some devout Hebrews, therefore, and especially to those in the South, the Canaanite gods seemed to be the protectors of the wealthy class in the towns, with their luxury and injustice to the poor, while Yahveh appeared as the guardian of the simpler shepherd life of the desert, and therefore the protector of the poor and needy.

Effect of this contrast upon religion

293. There was growing reason for such beliefs. Less than a century after the separation of the two kingdoms, Ahab, a king of the North, had had Naboth, one of his subjects, killed in order to seize a vineyard belonging to Naboth, and thus to enlarge his palace gardens. Reports of such wrongs

[1] The Hebrews pronounced the name of their God "Yahveh." The pronunciation "Jehovah" began less than six hundred years ago and was due to a misunderstanding of the pronunciation of the word *Yahveh*.

stirred the anger of Elijah, a Hebrew of old nomad habits, who lived in the desert east of the Jordan. Still wearing his desert sheepskin, he suddenly appeared before Ahab in the ill-gotten vineyard and denounced the king for his seizure of it. Thus this uncouth figure from the desert proclaimed war between Yahveh and the injustice of town life. Elijah's followers finally slew not only the entire Northern royal family but also the priests of the Canaanite gods (or baals). Such violent methods, however, could not accomplish lasting good. They were the methods of Hebrews who thought of Yahveh only as a war god.

Elijah and the violence of the older ideas of Yahveh

294. Besides such violent leaders as these there were also among the Hebrews more peaceable men who likewise chafed under the injustice of town life. These turned fondly back to the grand old days of their shepherd wanderings, out on the broad reaches of the desert, where no man "ground the faces of the poor." This point of view is picturesquely set forth in a simple narrative history of the Hebrew forefathers, — a glorified picture of their shepherd life, as we find it in the immortal tales of the Hebrew patriarchs, of Abraham and Isaac, of Jacob and Joseph. These tales belong among the noblest literature which has survived to us from the past.[1] We should notice also that they are the earliest example of *historical* writing in prose, of finished literary style, which we have inherited from any people.

Earliest historical writing among the Hebrews

295. It is now quite clear that such men were acquainted with the papyrus rolls written by Egyptian social reformers over a thousand years earlier, in defense of the poor and helpless (see § 117). We now know that such Egyptian documents were sometimes translated into Hebrew, for an Egyptian roll has been found containing a collection of wise proverbs, a section of which was included in the Book of Proverbs and later circulated under the name of Solomon. As they read such writings

Egyptian social writings and the Hebrew reformers

[1] See Gen. xxiv, xxvii, xxviii, xxxvii, xxxix–xlvii, 12.

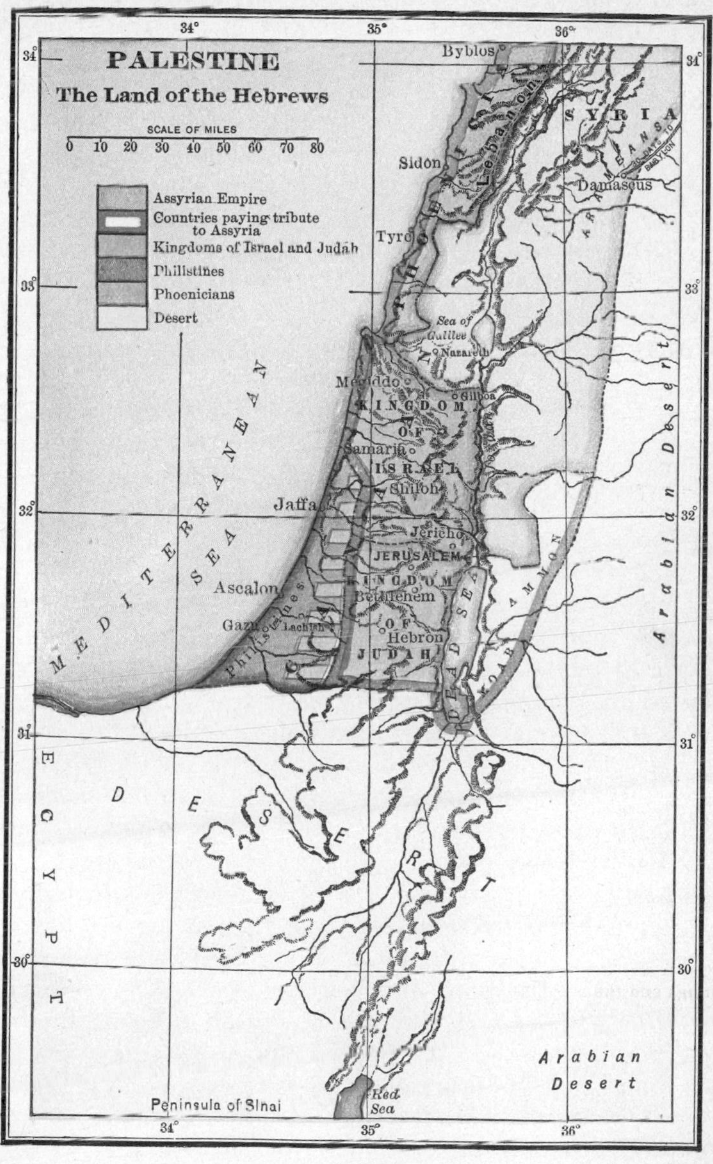
PALESTINE
The Land of the Hebrews
SCALE OF MILES
0 10 20 30 40 50 60 70 80
Assyrian Empire
Countries paying tribute to Assyria
Kingdoms of Israel and Judah
Philistines
Phoenicians
Desert
Byblos
Sidon
Tyre
Damascus
SYRIA
Sea of Galilee
Nazareth
Megiddo
Gilboa
KINGDOM OF ISRAEL
Samaria
Shiloh
Jaffa
Jericho
JERUSALEM
KINGDOM OF JUDAH
Bethlehem
Hebron
Ascalon
Gaza
Lachish
Philistines
MEDITERRANEAN SEA
DEAD SEA
AMMON
MOAB
Arabian Desert
EGYPT
DESERT
Peninsula of Sinai
Red Sea
34°
35°
36°
31°
32°
33°
30°

of the old Egyptian champions of the poor the Hebrew prophets and reformers took courage and gained new ideas.

296. Another century passed, and about 750 B.C. another dingy figure in sheepskin appeared in the streets of Bethel, where the Northern Kingdom had an important temple. It was Amos, a shepherd from the hills of Judah in the South. In the solitudes of his shepherd life Amos had learned to see in Yahveh far more than a war god of the desert. To him Yahveh seemed to be a God of fatherly kindness, not demanding bloody butchery like that practiced by Elijah's followers, but nevertheless a God who rebuked the selfish and oppressive wealthy class of the towns. The simple shepherd could not resist the inner impulse to journey to the Northern Kingdom and proclaim to the luxurious townsmen there the evils of their manner of life.

Amos: peaceful methods of the reformer and prophet

297. We can imagine the surprise of the prosperous Northern Hebrews as they suddenly met this rude shepherd figure, clad in sheepskin, standing at a street corner addressing a crowd of townsmen. He was denouncing their showy clothes, fine houses, beautiful furniture, and, above all, their corrupt lives and hard-heartedness toward the poor among their fellow Hebrews, whose lands they seized for debt and whose labor they gained by enslaving them. These things had been unknown in the desert. By such addresses as these Amos, of course, endangered his life, but he thus became the first social reformer in Asia. We apply the term "prophet" to the great Hebrew leaders who pointed out the way toward unselfish living, brotherly kindness, and a higher type of religion. Thus began in Western Asia the same kind of effort to lead men to show justice and kindness toward all, especially toward the poor, which had long been known in Egypt, and it is probable that Amos had heard of such Egyptian teachings. Fearing that his teachings might be lost if they remained merely spoken words, Amos finally sat down and put his sermons into writing, and thus they have survived to us.

Amos denounces corrupt living of Northern Kingdom

298. While all this had been going on, the Hebrews had been learning to write, as so many of their nomad predecessors on the Fertile Crescent had done before them. They were now abandoning the clay tablet, and wrote on papyrus with the Egyptian pen and ink. They borrowed their alphabet from the Phœnician and Aramean merchants. It is certain that our earliest Hebrew historian's admiration for the *nomad* life did not prevent him from making use of this new and great convenience of *town* life, that is, writing. The rolls containing the beautiful tales of the patriarchs, or bearing the teachings of such men as Amos, were the first books which the Hebrews produced, — their first literature. Such rolls of papyrus were exactly like those which had been in use in Egypt for over two thousand years. The discovery of the household papers of a Hebrew community in Egypt has shown us just how such a page of Hebrew or Aramaic writing looked (Fig. 122). But literature remained the only art the Hebrews possessed. They had no painting, sculpture, or architecture, and if they needed these things they borrowed from their great neighbors, — Egypt, Phœnicia, Damascus, and Assyria.

Hebrews learn to write

Section 24. The Destruction of the Hebrew Kingdoms by Assyria and Chaldea

299. While the Hebrews had been deeply stirred by their own conflicts *at home*, such men as Amos had also perceived and proclaimed the dangers coming from *abroad*, from beyond the borders of Palestine, especially Assyria. Amos, indeed, announced the coming destruction of the Northern Kingdom by Assyria because of the evil lives of the people. As Amos had foreseen, Assyria first swept away Damascus (§§ 240 and 250). The kingdom of Israel, left thus exposed, was the next victim, and Samaria, its capital, was captured by the Assyrians in 722 B.C. (§ 251). Of the unhappy Northern Hebrews 27,290 well-to-do people were carried away as

Destruction of the Northern Kingdom by Assyria (722 B.C.)

FIG. 120. *Hebrews* PAYING TRIBUTE *to the King of Assyria*

The Assyrian king, Shalmaneser III, stands at the left, followed by two attendants. Before him hovers the winged sun-disk. His appearance in the middle of the Ninth Century B.C., campaigning in the west against Damascus, so frightened the Hebrews of the Northern Kingdom that their king (Jehu) sent gifts to the Assyrian king by an envoy, whom we see here bowing down at the king's feet. Behind the Hebrew envoy are two Assyrian officers who are leading up a line of thirteen Hebrews (not included here) bearing gifts of silver, gold, etc. The scene is carved on a black stone shaft set up by the Assyrian king in his palace on the Tigris, where the modern excavators found it. It is now in the British Museum

captives, and the Northern nation, called Israel, was destroyed after having existed for a little over two centuries.

Yahveh, God of Palestine, rival of Assur, god of Assyria

300. The national hopes of the Hebrews were now centered in the helpless little kingdom of Judah, which struggled on for over a century and a quarter more, in the midst of a great world conflict in which Assyria was the unchallenged champion. Thus far thoughtful Hebrews had been accustomed to think of their God as ruling in Palestine only. But now they were learning that Palestine was part of a great political world. Did he have power also over the vast world arena where all the mighty nations were fighting? But if so, was not Assur, the great god of victorious Assyria, stronger than Yahveh, God of the Hebrews? And many a despairing Hebrew, as he looked out over the hills of Palestine, wasted by the armies of Assyria, felt in his heart that Assur, the god of the victorious Assyrians, who ruled nearly all Western Asia, must indeed be stronger than Yahveh, God of the Hebrews.

301. It was in the midst of somber doubts like these, in the years before 700 B.C., that the princely prophet Isaiah, in one great oration after another, addressed the multitudes which filled the streets of Jerusalem. The hosts of Sennacherib were at the gates, and the terrified throngs in the city were expecting at any moment to hear the thunder of the great Assyrian war engines battering down the crumbling walls of their city, as they had crushed the walls of Damascus and Samaria. Then the bold words of the dauntless Isaiah lifted them from despair like the triumphant call of a trumpet. He told them that Yahveh ruled a kingdom far larger than Palestine, — that He controlled the great world arena, where *He*, and not Assur, was the triumphant champion. If the Assyrians had wasted and plundered Palestine, it was because they were but the lash in the

Isaiah and siege of Jerusalem by Sennacherib

FIG. 121. SENNACHERIB, *King of Assyria, receiving* CAPTIVE HEBREWS

The artist, endeavoring to sketch the stony hills of southern Palestine, has made the surface of the ground look like scales. We see the Assyrian king seated on a throne, while advancing up the hill is a group of Assyrian soldiers headed by the grand vizier, who stands before the king, announcing the coming of the Hebrew captives. At the left, behind the soldiers, appear three of the captives kneeling on the ground and lifting up their hands to appeal for mercy. The inscription over the vizier's head reads, "Sennacherib, king of the world, king of Assyria, seated himself upon a throne, while the captives of Lachish passed before him." Lachish was a small town of southern Palestine. Sennacherib captured many such Hebrew towns and carried off over two hundred thousand captives, but even his own records make no claim that he captured Jerusalem. The scene is engraved on a large slab of alabaster, which with many others adorned the palace of Sennacherib at Nineveh as evidence of his power and glory

hands of Yahveh, who was using them as a scourge in his own hands to punish Judah for its wrongdoing.

302. Thus while the people were momentarily expecting the destruction of Jerusalem, Isaiah undauntedly proclaimed a great and glorious future for the Hebrews and speedy disaster for the Assyrians. When at length a pestilence from the marshes of the eastern Nile Delta swept away the army of Sennacherib and saved Jerusalem, it seemed to the Hebrews the destroying angel of Yahveh who had smitten the Assyrian host.[1] Some of the Hebrews then began to see that Yahveh ruled a larger world than Palestine. Their own ideas were stimulated by the great Sun-hymn of Ikhnaton which had long been circulating in Western Asia, as one of the Hebrew Psalms shows. Compare these two passages:

Sennacherib's army destroyed; justification of Isaiah's words

From Ikhnaton's Sun-hymn	*From the 104th Psalm*
How manifold are thy works! They are hidden before men O sole God, beside whom there is no other. Thou didst create the earth according to thy will.	O Lord, how manifold are thy works! In wisdom hast thou made them all: The earth is full of thy riches.

303. Nearly a century after the deliverance from Sennacherib they beheld and rejoiced over the destruction of Nineveh (612 B.C.), and they fondly hoped that the fall of Assyria meant final deliverance from foreign oppression. But they had only exchanged one foreign lord for another, and Chaldea followed Assyria in control of Palestine. Then the unsubmissive Hebrews of Judah met the same fate which their kindred of Israel had suffered. In 586 B.C. Nebuchadnezzar, the Chaldean king, destroyed Jerusalem and carried away the people to exile in Babylonia. The Hebrew nation, both North and South, was thus wiped out after having existed about four and a half centuries.

Destruction of the Southern Kingdom by Chaldea (586 B.C.)

[1] See 2 Kings xix, 32–37.

Section 25. The Hebrews in Exile and their Deliverance by the Persians

Jeremiah and a temple of the Hebrews in Egypt

304. Some of the fugitives fled to Egypt. Among them was the melancholy prophet Jeremiah, who had foreseen the coming destruction of Jerusalem with its temple of Yahveh. He strove to teach his people that each must regard his own heart as a temple of Yahveh, which would endure long after His temple in Jerusalem had crashed into ruin. Recent excavation has restored to us the actual papers of a colony of Hebrews in Egypt at Elephantine (see map, p. 66). These papers (Fig. 122) show that the exiled Hebrews in Egypt had not yet reached Jeremiah's ideal of a temple of Yahveh in every human heart; for they had built a temple of their own, in which they carried on the worship of Yahveh.

Doubts of exiled Hebrews; great prophet of the exile

305. Similarly, the Hebrew exiles in Babylonia were not yet convinced of the truth of the teaching they had heard from their great leaders the prophets. There were at first only grief and unanswered questionings, of which the echo still reaches us:

> By the rivers of Babylon,
> There we sat down, yea, we wept,
> When we remembered Zion [Jerusalem].
> Upon the willows in the midst thereof
> We hanged up our harps.
> . . . .
> How shall we sing Yahveh's song
> In a strange land? (Psalms cxxxvii, 1–4)

Had they not left Yahveh behind in Palestine? And then arose a wonderful teacher[1] among the Hebrew exiles, and out of centuries of affliction gave them the answer. In a series of triumphant speeches this greatest of the earlier Hebrews declared Yahveh to be the creator and sole God of the universe.

[1] A great poet-preacher, a prophet of the exile, whose addresses to his fellow exiles are preserved in sixteen chapters embedded in the Old Testament book of Isaiah (chaps. xl–lv, inclusive).

He explained to his fellow exiles that suffering and affliction were the best possible training and discipline to prepare a people for service. He announced, therefore, that by afflicting them Yahveh was only preparing His suffering people for service to the world, and that He would yet restore them and enable them to fulfill a great mission to all men. He greeted the sudden rise of Cyrus the Persian with joy. All kings, he taught, were but instruments in the hands of Yahveh, who through the Persians would overthrow the Chaldeans and return the Hebrews to their land.

306. Thus had the Hebrew vision of Yahveh slowly grown, from the days of their nomad life, when they had seen him only as a fierce tribal war god, having no power beyond the corner of the desert where they lived, until now, when they had come to see that He was a kindly father and a righteous ruler of all the earth. This was monotheism, a belief which made Yahveh the sole God. They had reached it only through a long development, which brought them suffering and disaster, — a discipline lasting many centuries. Just as the individual today, especially a young person, learns from his mistakes, and develops character as he suffers for his own errors, so the suffering Hebrews had outgrown many imperfect ideas. They thus illustrated the words of the greatest of Hebrew teachers, "First the blade, then the ear, then the full grain in the ear." [1] By this rich and wonderful experience of the Hebrews in religious progress the whole world was yet to profit.

Monotheism reached by Hebrews in exile

307. When the victorious Persian king Cyrus entered Babylon (§ 344), the Hebrew exiles there greeted him as their deliverer. His triumph gave the Hebrews a Persian ruler. With great humanity the Persian kings allowed the exiles to return to their native land. Some had prospered in Babylonia and did not care to return, but at different times enough of them went back to Jerusalem to rebuild the city on a very modest scale and to restore the temple.

Restoration of exiled Hebrews by Persian kings

[1] The words of Jesus; see Mark iv, 28.

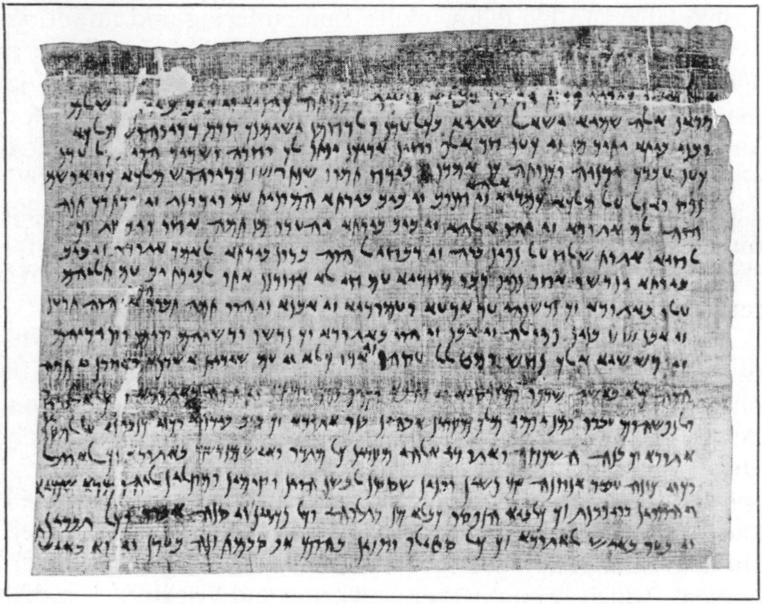

FIG. 122. *Aramaic* LETTER *written by a* HEBREW COMMUNITY IN EGYPT *to the Persian Governor of Palestine in the Fifth Century* B.C.

This remarkable letter was discovered in 1907, with many other similar papers, lying in the ruins of the town of Elephantine in Upper Egypt. Here lived a community of some six or seven hundred Hebrews, some of whom had probably migrated to Egypt before Nebuchadnezzar destroyed Jerusalem. They had built a temple to Yahveh (Jehovah) on the banks of the Nile. This letter tells how the jealous Egyptian priests formed a mob, burned the Hebrew temple, and plundered it of its gold and silver vessels. Thereupon the whole Hebrew community sat down in mourning, and for three years they tried in vain to secure permission to rebuild. Then, in 407 B.C., their leaders wrote this letter to Bagoas, the Persian governor of Palestine, begging him to use his influence with the Persian governor of Egypt to induce him to permit them to rebuild their ruined temple. They refer by name to persons in Palestine who are also mentioned in the Old Testament. The letter is written with pen and ink on papyrus, in the Aramaic language, which was now rapidly displacing Hebrew. This writing used the Phœnician letters long before they were adopted throughout Western Asia. This beautifully written sheet of papyrus, about 10 by 13 inches, bearing the same letters which the Hebrews used (§ 298), shows us exactly how a page of their ancient writings in the Old Testament looked. They read the stories of Abraham, Isaac, Jacob, and Joseph from pages like this.

308. The authority given by the Persian government to the returned Hebrew leaders enabled them to establish and publish the religious laws which have ever since been revered by the Jews. The religion thus organized by the returned Hebrew leaders we now call Judaism, the religion of the Jews. Under it the old Hebrew kingship was not revived. In its place a high priest at Jerusalem became the ruler of the Jews. The Jewish state was thus a *religious* organization, a church with a priest at its head.

Jewish law and Judaism; restored Jewish state a church

309. The leaders of this church devoted themselves to the study of the ancient writings of their race still surviving in their hands. A number of the old writings, some of them mentioned in the Old Testament, had been lost. They arranged and copied the orations and addresses of the prophets, and all the old Hebrew writings they possessed. As time went on, and the service of the restored temple developed, they arranged a remarkable book of a hundred and fifty religious songs, — the hymn book of the second temple, known to us as the Book of Psalms. For a long time — indeed, for centuries — these various Hebrew books, such as the Law, the Prophets, and the Psalms, circulated in separate rolls, and it did not occur to anyone to put them together to form one book.

Editing of Hebrew writings: Prophets and Psalms

310. It was not until Christian times that the Jewish leaders put all these old writings of their fathers together to form one book. Printed in Hebrew, as they were originally written, they form the Bible of the Jews at the present day. These Hebrew writings have also become a sacred book of the Christian nations. In the form of an English translation it is called the Old Testament, and is today the most precious legacy which we have inherited from the Ancient Near East before the coming of Christ. It tells the story of how a rude shepherd folk issued from the wilds of the Arabian Desert to live in Palestine, where they were prepared to understand the

Old Testament and our legacy in Hebrew religion

religious writings of the earlier great nations of the East, especially Egypt, and thus to pass through experiences which made them the religious teachers of the civilized world. And we should further remember that, crowning all their history, there came forth from them in due time the Founder of the Christian religion. One of the most important things that we owe to the Persians, therefore, was their restoration of the Hebrews to Palestine. The Persians thus saved and aided in transmitting to us the great legacy from Hebrew life which we have in the Old Testament and in the life of the Founder of Christianity.

QUESTIONS

Section 21. Describe the situation and character of the land of the Hebrews. Was it likely to offer a tranquil home?

Section 22. Where was the *original* home of the Hebrews? What was the result of their living among the Canaanites? When did they gain their first king and who was he? Who was their leading enemy? Describe the reign of David; of Solomon. What happened to the kingdom after Solomon?

Section 23. Contrast the two kingdoms. How did this contrast affect religion? Compare the methods of Elijah and Amos. What was the work of a prophet? From what people did the Hebrews learn to write and what were the first books of the Hebrews?

Section 24. What danger threatened the Hebrews from abroad? What happened to the Northern Kingdom? What can you say of the work of Isaiah? Tell about Sennacherib's campaign against Jerusalem.

Section 25. What became of the Hebrews of Judah? Discuss the Hebrew conception of Yahveh at the time of the Babylonian exile. What did the returned Hebrews accomplish and by what authority?

BIBLIOGRAPHY FOR TOPICAL STUDIES

Jeremiah and the destruction of Judah: BAILEY and KENT, *Hebrew Commonwealth,* pp. 239–251; CHAMBERLIN, *Hebrew Prophets,* pp. 132–168; KITTEL, *Great Men and Movements,* pp. 334–366; KNOTT, *Student's History of the Hebrews,* pp. 258–264.

Nehemiah: KENT, *History of the Jewish People,* §§ 155–170; KNOTT, *Student's History,* pp. 293–298.

CHAPTER VIII · *Western Asia: The Coming of the Indo-Europeans*

SECTION 26. THE INDO-EUROPEAN PEOPLES AND THEIR DISPERSION[1]

311. We have seen that the Arabian Desert was once a great reservoir of unsettled population, which was continually leaving the grasslands on the margin of the desert and shifting over into the towns to begin a settled life. Corresponding to these grasslands of the *south* there are similar grasslands in the *north.* These northern grasslands stretch from the lower Danube eastward along the north side of the Black Sea through southern Russia

Northern Grasslands

NOTE. The headpiece above shows ANCIENT FIRE ALTARS used by the great Persian kings and located not far from their tombs (Fig. 136).

[1] Section 26 should be carefully worked over by the teacher with the class before the class is permitted to study it alone. The diagram (Fig. 123) should be put on the blackboard and explained in detail by the teacher, and the class should then be prepared to put the diagram on the board from memory. This should be done again when the study of the Greeks is begun (§ 405), and a third time when Italy and the Romans are taken up.

and far into Asia north and east of the Caspian (see map, p. 754). In ancient times they always had a wandering shepherd population, and time after time, for thousands of years, these northern nomads have poured forth over Europe and Western Asia, just as the desert Semites of the south have done over the Fertile Crescent.

Two lines,—Indo-European and Semitic

312. Among these nomads of the north there was in very early times an important branch of the Great White Race which we call *Indo-European*. The early Indo-Europeans were the ancestors of the leading peoples of Europe today. As our forefathers came from Europe, the Indo-European nomads were also our own ancestors. These nomads of the *northern* grasslands began to migrate in very ancient times, moving out along diverging routes. The earliest group of them known to us is the Hittites, who appeared in Asia Minor not later than 2500 B.C., and perhaps earlier. The recent decipherment of Hittite writing has disclosed such words as *vadar*, meaning "water," showing the relation between our own language and that of these ancient Indo-Europeans. The Indo-Europeans as a whole at last extended in an imposing line from the frontiers of India on the east, westward across all Europe to the Atlantic, as they do today; and hence their name, Indo-Europeans. This great northern line was confronted on the south by a similar line of Semitic peoples, extending from Babylonia on the east, through Phœnicia and the Hebrew kingdoms, westward to Carthage and similar Semitic settlements of Phœnicia in the Western Mediterranean (§ 162 and map, p. 346).

Struggle between Indo-European and Semitic lines

313. The history of the ancient world, as we are now to follow it, was largely made up of the struggle between this *southern Semitic* line, which issued from the southern grasslands, and the *northern Indo-European* line, which came forth from the northern grasslands to confront the older civilizations represented in the southern line. Thus as we look at the diagram we see the two great races facing each other across the Medi-

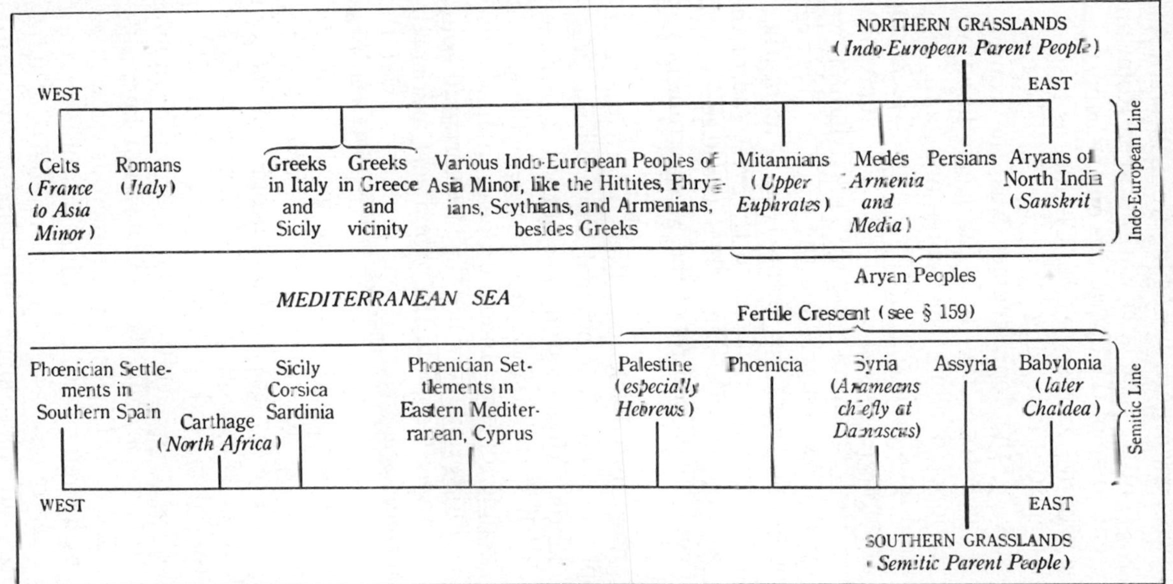

FIG. 123. DIAGRAM suggesting the TWO LINES of *Semitic and Indo-European* DISPERSION

In this explanation and in § 312 the word "line" means much the same as "row." The geographic lines along which these peoples lie are of course not straight. The racial lines sometimes overlie each other, as in Sicily, and are mentioned in both lines. The Egyptians, who physically belong in the southern line, have been omitted because they are not purely Semitic, although physically and in language closely related to the Semites. Notice also that in the West the two races face each other for the most part across the Mediterranean; in the East they confront each other along the Fertile Crescent terranean like two vast armies stretching from Western Asia westward to the Atlantic. The later wars between Rome and Carthage represent some of the operations on the Semitic left wing, while the triumph of Persia over Chaldea is a similar outcome on the Semitic right wing.

Triumph of European end of Indo-European line

314. The result of the long conflict was the complete triumph of our ancestors (the Indo-European line), who conquered along the center and both wings and finally, as represented by the Greeks and Romans, gained unchallenged supremacy throughout the Mediterranean world. This triumph was accompanied by a long struggle for the mastery between the members of the northern line themselves. Among them the victory moved from the east end to the west end of the northern line, as first the Persians, then the Greeks, and finally the Romans gained control of the Mediterranean and Oriental world.

Indo-European parent people and their original home

315. Let us now turn back to a time before the Indo-European people had left their original home on the grasslands. Modern study has not yet determined with certainty the region where the parent people of the Indo-European nomads had their home. The indications now are that this original home was on the great grassy steppe in the region east and northeast of the Caspian Sea. Here, then, probably lived the parent people of all the later Indo-Europeans. At the time when they were still one people they were speaking one and the same tongue. From this tongue have descended all the languages later spoken by the civilized peoples of modern Europe, including, of course, our own English, as we shall see.

Civilization of Indo-European parent people

316. Before they dispersed, the parent people were still in the Stone Age for the most part, though copper was beginning to come in, and the time was not later than 3000 B.C. Divided into numerous tribes, they wandered at will, seeking pasture for their flocks, for they already possessed domestic animals, including cattle and sheep. But chief among their domesticated beasts was the *horse*, which, as we recall, was at first entirely unknown to the civilized Oriental nations. The animal must have been known on the Fertile Crescent not much later than 3000 B.C. The Indo-Europeans employed the horse not only for riding but also for drawing their wheeled carts. The ox already bore the yoke and drew the plow, for some of the tribes had adopted a settled mode of life, and cultivated grain, especially barley. Being without writing, they possessed but little government and organization, but they were the most gifted and the most highly imaginative people of the ancient world.

Dispersion of Indo-European parent people

317. As their tribes wandered farther and farther apart they lost contact with each other. Local peculiarities in speech and customs became more and more marked, finally producing great differences such as always result when peoples speaking the same language are widely separated. We are familiar, for example, with the noticeable differences between the spoken English of England and that of America. While at first the Indo-European groups could doubtless understand one another when they met, these differences in speech gradually became so great that the widely scattered tribes, even if they happened to meet, could no longer make themselves understood, and finally they lost all knowledge of their original kinship. This kinship has been rediscovered in very recent times. The final outcome, in so far as speech was concerned, was the languages of modern civilized Europe; so that, beginning with England in the west and going eastward, we can trace more than one common word from people to people entirely across Europe into northern India. Note the following:

WEST			EAST		
English	**German**	**Latin**	**Greek**	**Old Persian and Avestan**	**East Indian (Sanskrit)**
brother	*bruder*	*frāter*	*phrātēr*	*brātar*	*bhrātar*
mother	*mutter*	*māter*	*mētēr*	*mātar*	*mātar*
father	*vater*	*pater*	*patēr*	*pitar*	*pitar*

In the west the earliest known group of these wanderers from the northern grasslands had entered Asia Minor by 2500 B.C. These were the invaders who founded the Hittite Empire (Section 27). Another Indo-European group pushed southward and westward and easily subdued the population in the great western bend of the Euphrates, where they became the ruling class of a new nation called Mitanni (§ 239). Mitanni, we remember, threatened to block the westward advance of Assyria, but was eventually crushed in the conflict between the Egyptians and the Hittites (§ 245). Farther west the most advanced tribes of the Indo-Europeans had already crossed the Danube and were far down in the Balkan Peninsula by 2000 B.C. Some of them had doubtless entered Italy by this time. These western tribes were, of course, a part of the mixed ancestry of the Greeks and Romans; at least they brought the earliest dialects of Greek and Roman (Latin) speech into Greece and Italy. We shall join them and follow them in their conquest of the Mediterranean. Before doing so, however, we have to watch the advance of the Indo-Europeans in Western Asia and at the eastern end of the Fertile Crescent.

SECTION 27. EARLIEST KNOWN INDO-EUROPEANS AND THE HITTITE EMPIRE

Highland civilization

318. As we look at the Highland Zone in Western Asia we are aware that, hidden within and behind its screen of mountains, important movements of mankind had been going on for a long time in a region we have not yet discussed. Before we do so let us look backward for a moment. In this book we have thus far found that the Stone Age peoples of the Near East rose to a high civilization in two regions: the Nile valley and the Fertile Crescent (especially the valley of the Two Rivers). Recent discoveries are showing us more and more of what was happening in Western Asia farther north. The Highland Zone here includes a broad band of country extending from the Ægean

FIG. 124. *Early* POTTERY *and* SEALS *of the Highland Zone*

The left-hand column (*A*, *B*, and *C*) is a group from Anatolia and represents the craft of the Hittites, who occupied a large western section of the Highland Zone. In the right-hand column we have a similar group (*D*, *E*, and *F*) from Persia. The resemblance between these pairs (*A* and *D*, *B* and *E*, *C* and *F*) suggests the great uniformity of the Highland civilization stretching along the Highland Zone from Persia to Anatolia. It must be remembered that this Highland civilization was older than the Iranian migration which brought the Medes and Persians into the Highland Zone and into its sphere of influence

Sea on the west, eastward along the north side of the Fertile Crescent, and then farther eastward, between the Caspian Sea and the Persian Gulf, to the Iranian Plateau. A glance at the map (p. 146) will show that this region comprises, from west to east, Anatolia (Hittite Asia Minor), Armenia, Media, and Persia. Throughout all this extensive region the Late Stone Age peoples advanced to a Bronze Age civilization, which in many important respects was uniform for this whole Asiatic section of the Highland Zone. Beautiful painted pottery recently found in Persia can sometimes hardly be distinguished from the pottery found in the Hittite country at the other end of the Highland Zone civilization. We cannot yet give this far-reaching early civilization a name; but, naming it geographically, it is convenient to call it the Highland civilization. It is thought to have originated on the Iranian Plateau, and great quantities of its pottery and bronzes have recently been found in western Persia and Media. Connected with it was the earliest civilization in Elam (map, p. 146), which seems to have been very old, — as old, indeed, as the Sumerian civilization. Regarding the race of the Highland peoples who developed this civilization we

FIG. 125. *Remains of a* ROOF SUPPORT (*X*) *from a Wooden House of the Late Stone Age, excavated beneath an Ancient Hittite City of Central Asia Minor*

This support was a tree trunk used to prop the roof timbers of the house. Thousands of years ago the house was covered by the fallen remains of an ancient Hittite city which was built over the spot. When excavated by the Oriental Institute of The University of Chicago the blackened stump of the tree trunk was found, as seen here, still standing on its stone base (*Y*). Very little of the house itself remained, but the stone tools and weapons found in it showed that it was erected by men of the Late Stone Age. The sides of the excavation pit, against which the archæologist is leaning as he makes his notes, are not the walls of the ancient house, but are the accumulated rubbish of later houses which were built on this spot and then fell to ruins. Down through this rubbish, now packed hard, the excavators have dug a pit over 90 feet deep, with vertical walls, which show the marks of the modern pickaxes and shovels

can say very little. Without doubt they were not all of one race, and they seem not to have been Indo-Europeans in the beginning. A very important part in the development of the Highland civilization was played by the peoples who occupied Anatolia, or Hittite Asia Minor, especially because of the metals which they found in their mountains.

Asia Minor (Anatolia), the land of the Hittites

319. Asia Minor, or Anatolia,[1] the greater part of which was for so long occupied by the Hittites, is a vast peninsula from six hundred and fifty to seven hundred miles long and from three to four hundred miles wide, being about as large as the state of Texas. The interior is a lofty table-land, little better than a desert in its central region. Around most of this table-land rise mountain ridges, fringing both the table-land and the sea. On both sides of the mountain fringe are fertile valleys and plains, producing plentiful crops. The seaward slopes of the mountains, especially along the Black Sea, are clad with flourishing forests. The northern shores of Asia Minor, east of the Halys River, rise into ridges containing rich deposits of metal ores, especially iron. The Hittites thus became the earliest distributors of iron when it began to displace bronze in the Mediterranean world and the Near East (§ 247).

Race and prehistoric movements of Early Anatolians

320. In the earliest period before the Indo-European invasions it is convenient to call the inhabitants of the western end of the Highland Zone in Asia *Early Anatolians*. The climate is not favorable to the preservation of ancient bodies, and as yet excavation has recovered the skeletons of very few Early Anatolians. They were without doubt inhabiting this region already in the Late Stone Age, and, like the oldest inhabitants of the Highland Zone elsewhere (Fig. 80), they were a round-

[1] "Anatolia" is a Greek word equivalent to the Latin "Orient"; but usage has given it a much more limited meaning; for it is used to designate only Asia Minor as far east as the upper Euphrates. It has now been discovered that the earliest peoples of this region were not identical with the historic Hittites. Before the incoming of the Hittites we may therefore call the peoples of Asia Minor Anatolians, a term which implies nothing regarding their race or nationality.

headed people. Neither in type of body nor in language were they Indo-Europeans.[1] The Early Anatolians overflowed at both ends of Asia Minor. At the western end some of them migrated to Crete and to the mainland of Greece as early as the Late Stone Age. At the eastern end they poured into Palestine in such multitudes that their unmistakable type of features, with prominent aquiline nose, became the prevailing (Jewish) type in the whole region of Palestine (§ 283). This marked example of the influence of the Early Anatolians in neighboring regions is a striking illustration of their importance in the ancient world.

FIG. 126. *An Ancient* HITTITE *and his Modern Armenian* DESCENDANT

At the left is the head of an ancient Hittite as carved by an Egyptian sculptor on the wall of a temple at Thebes, Egypt, over three thousand years ago. It strikingly resembles the profile of the Armenians still living in the Hittite country, as shown in the modern portrait on the right. The shape of both these heads is that of the typical "round heads" of the Highland Zone. Such a skull is flat behind; its back does not project or overhang (cf. Fig. 80)

Early Anatolians and Indo-European invasion

321. We know very little of these Early Anatolians, and it will require decades of persistent excavation among their earliest settlements before we shall be able to piece together any considerable account of their life and history (Fig. 125). Probably as early as 2500 B.C. the Indo-Europeans of the north and east

[1] Scientifically speaking, there is no Indo-European type of body. It is important to bear in mind that while the vast majority of the Indo-European peoples today are long-heads, there are nevertheless round-headed peoples, like the Swiss and the Armenians, who now speak Indo-European languages. In the same way, there is in the United States a large colored population speaking English, but speaking English — an Indo-European language — does not make Indo-Europeans out of Negroes. Nevertheless, in ancient times the prevailing Indo-European type was long-headed.

began to push in, perhaps through the Caucasus Mountains. Forming the vanguard of Indo-European migration, they were the earliest Indo-Europeans to appear in the arena of history. The latest discoveries have shown that it is these Indo-European invaders of Anatolia whom we should call Hittites. Their invasion was the first of those vast movements of Indo-European migration in Western Asia which, as we shall see later, resulted finally in the conquest of the Fertile Crescent and the whole Near East by the Indo-European Medes and Persians. The Hittites first brought in the horse among the Early Anatolians, as the other Indo-Europeans did also along the Fertile Crescent. The Early Anatolians were not exterminated, but, just as in Mitanni, these horse-breeding invaders seem to have formed the ruling class. In language the result was a mixture of speech. The new, mixed language of course contained some Early Anatolian words, appearing side by side with Indo-European words and grammatical forms. For over a thousand years this mixed speech was an important language of Western Asia, and we shall call it Hittite.

Rise of Hittite civilization

322. When they entered Anatolia the Hittites were barbarians. The rise of the civilization which we may call Hittite was at first due to influence from the Fertile Crescent. In times past, as we remember, Babylonian caravans had traded in Asia Minor, and later Assyrian merchants had settled there. These business communities from the Fertile Crescent made the Hittites acquainted with commercial transactions. In transacting their business the Hittites themselves gradually learned to read clay-tablet bills and invoices written in cuneiform. Excavations have even uncovered fragments of their clay-tablet dictionaries with three columns, the first Sumerian, the second Babylonian or Akkadian, and the third Hittite. Thus they learned to write their own Hittite words in cuneiform. At first they used cuneiform writing only to write Babylonian or Akkadian, the language of Akkad. When they wrote letters to foreigners abroad, they continued to do so in the speech of Babylonia. Eventually, however, they learned to use the cuneiform signs for writing their own mixed speech, which we have called Hittite.[1] Thus the clay tablet became common in the Hittite world, and it was probably through the Hittites that the use of clay tablets passed over into Crete. After the introduction of writing the Hittites made noticeable progress, and by 2000 B.C. they were a highly civilized people. Fully able to compete with the greatest nations of the Ancient Near East, they twice rose, as the rival of Egypt and Assyria. These two great periods we shall call the First Hittite Empire (about 1900 to 1650 B.C.) and the Second Hittite Empire (about 1400 to 1200 B.C.).

First Hittite Empire

323. The earliest Hittite king of whom we have any knowledge is Anitta, who arose in the city of Kussar, in eastern Asia Minor, perhaps about 2000 B.C. The exact location of Kussar is not known. It is quite clear that the Hittites did not then form a single nation, but lived in a number of kingdoms which, like the later Greek kingdoms, were often at war with one another. The leadership was finally gained by the kingdom of Hatti,[2] which lay inside the great bend of the river Halys in central Asia Minor. Its capital was called Hattusas. The kings of Hatti were able to conquer neighboring kingdoms and build up a small empire. Early in the Eighteenth Century B.C. the great king Mursil, the first of that name, arose in Hattusas. In the days when the power of Hammurapi's successors at Babylon was tottering, it was Mursil I who marched down the Euphrates, captured Babylon, and overthrew the last of Hammurapi's line, the First Dynasty of Babylon, about 1750 B.C. (§ 231). Eventually the successors of Mursil I weakened, and before 1600 B.C. the First Hittite Empire fell.

[1] The Hittite tablets contained so many Babylonian word signs that during the World War the Czechoslovakian scholar Bedřich Hrozný succeeded in deciphering the Hittite cuneiform. Since the war our knowledge of Hittite has increased greatly, and the German scholar Emil Forrer has shown that the tablets found at Hattusas contain examples of seven languages besides Hittite.

[2] The name *Khatti* or *Hatti* is of course the origin of our modern name "Hittite." The closeness of the resemblance will be evident when the modern ending *ite* is removed, leaving *Hitt*.

324. The Second Hittite Empire, which arose after 1400 B.C., remained for two centuries the greatest power in Western Asia. Its founder bore the long name Suppilulyuma.[1] He was the ablest soldier Western Asia had seen since the campaigns of Thutmose III, which had begun almost exactly a century before those of the great Hittite king. But now there was no Thutmose III to turn back the powerful Hittite soldier. Weakened by the religious revolution of Ikhnaton, the Egyptians could only helplessly watch the advance of the Hittites as they conquered all Syria and made it Hittite territory. Thereupon Suppilulyuma crossed the Euphrates and crushed the power of Mitanni. Feeble Assyria was at that time the vassal of Mitanni, and the Hittite conqueror of Mitanni was therefore lord over the greater part of Western Asia.

Rise of Second Hittite Empire

325. Among the clay tablets which have been dug up in the Hittite capital of Hattusas there is a remarkable cuneiform letter, written at this time to the great Hittite emperor by a queen of Egypt, possibly the widow of Ikhnaton. She is the queen whose graceful figure we have seen sitting at dinner with her husband and their little daughters, but with no son, in the palace at Amarna (Fig. 72). This letter is striking evidence of the Hittite conqueror's greatness and power, for the Egyptian queen tells him that she has no son to occupy her dead husband's throne, and she begs the Hittite ruler to send one of his sons to become her husband and thus to be the king of Egypt. This marriage, if it had taken place, would have made the Hittite royal family the lords of both the Egyptian and the Hittite Empire. The two together would have formed the greatest empire the world had ever seen. But the Hittite emperor was suspicious of the Egyptian queen's extraordinary proposal, and before sending his son he made an investigation. When, after this delay, he did finally send one of his sons, it was too late. Arriving in Egypt after the

Second Hittite Empire, leader of Western Asia

[1] We do not know much about the pronunciation of Hittite proper names, but this name was probably pronounced "Soop-pee-lool'yu-ma."

powerful enemies of Ikhnaton's family had pushed aside the widowed queen, the young Hittite prince was seized and slain. Thus Suppilulyuma lost the opportunity of gaining control of Egypt without striking a blow. But he had other sons, and these he crowned as the leading kings of Syria, and thus made the northern end of the Egyptian Empire his own. On the south his empire extended down to Palestine, which Egypt continued to hold; on the east beyond the Euphrates his territory included much of Mitanni; and his eastern boundary for a time lay far over toward Assyria. On the north and the west the Second Hittite Empire included the larger part of Asia Minor, and the commercial city of Troy must have felt the pressure of Hittite power, if it was not, indeed, a vassal of the Hittite conqueror. By 1350 B.C. the Hittite Empire was the most powerful state that had ever arisen in Western Asia.

Egypto-Hittite rivalry and treaty of peace

326. The two empires, Egyptian and Hittite, were now rivals for the leadership of the world. It was a rivalry which was fought out for over a quarter of a century between the grandsons of Suppilulyuma and the great Pharaohs Seti I and Ramses II. As the war went on, especially after 1300 B.C., the rise of Assyria gave the Hittite emperors increasing uneasiness. They made treaties with their vassal kings in Syria which pledged them to act as enemies of Assyria. Among the clay tablets dug up at Hattusas is a very interesting letter written by the Hittite emperor, urging the young king of Babylon to attack Assyria from behind. Then, as dissensions arose among the Hittites themselves, Suppilulyuma's grandson, Hattusil, arranged a treaty of peace with Ramses II, who received it from the Hittite king engraved upon a silver tablet. Thus the struggle between these powerful rivals ended. Intimate relations between the two royal families were established. Even the two queens, of Egypt and Hatti, exchanged friendly greetings and letters of congratulation on the new peace pact. These clay-tablet letters, written some time in the 1270's B.C., were found by the modern excavators lying among the royal files and records dug up at the Hittite capital. Later on the Hittite emperor sent his daughter to Egypt to become the wife of Ramses II. On the walls of the Egyptian temples, almost as far south as the Second Cataract in Nubia, the Pharaoh's sculptors carved the scene depicting the arrival of his Hittite bride.

Hittite civilization: the state and its laws

327. The civilization of the Second Hittite Empire attained a high level and had a far-reaching influence. It is important to notice some of its leading achievements. The Hittite state was built up out of a large group of weaker kingdoms conquered by the original kingdom of Hatti. Every year the subject states were obliged to contribute infantry and chariotry to the emperor's army. The emperor's power consisted of this composite army, combined with the soldiers drawn from his own kingdom of Hatti. The government operated under a system of wise laws which even the king himself was bound to obey. The advance of Hittite civilization is disclosed to us in the fact that after the peace with Egypt the Hittite king, perhaps Hattusil, issued a revised code of these laws which was much more humane than formerly. Nearly two hundred paragraphs, forming a large part of this code, have survived on the clay tablets. In this code the king often refers to former, more severe punishments which he is making less severe. For stealing a head of cattle the penalty had formerly been a fine of thirty head, but in the new code this fine was reduced to fifteen. Even for murder capital punishment was not inflicted, and mutilation of the culprit by cutting off ears or nose was not practiced. This Hittite code is therefore far more humane than the savage laws of Assyria, and more so indeed than the codes of Babylonia or Egypt. The respect for law which the Hittite kings display is very remarkable. Indeed, Suppilulyuma admits that his invasion of the Egyptian Empire in Syria was unlawful, and regards an epidemic of plague among his people as a punishment for his offense.

Hittite architecture; sculpture

328. The enlightened attitude of the Hittite kings was doubtless responsible in some degree for the remarkable development among the Hittites along lines other than statecraft. The earliest impressive stone architecture in Asia was the work of the Hittite architects. The powerful walled city of Hattusas which they erected was the first really large city ever built in Asia. It far surpassed the Babylon of that day in size, and the Nineveh of the Assyrian emperors was still some six centuries in the future. The most notable form which the Hittite architects introduced into building was the front of the king's palace, which consisted of a porch in the middle, with its roof supported on two columns, while on either side of the porch was a square tower. The building was called "a house of two towers." It was such a porch which was adopted by the Assyrian emperors in their palaces (§ 261), and it finally reached the Persians.

The Hittite architects understood the value of sculpture as an adornment of architecture. Set up on either side of the central doorway of the king's palace were two splendid sentinel lions carved in stone. This idea of protective animal images was drawn from the similar use of the Egyptian sphinxes, which were likewise taken over by the Hittites. (See also Fig. 108.) Sculpture was further employed in the embellishment of the wall by a dado, consisting of large, flat slabs of stone carved with relief pictures. These were transmitted by the Hittites to Assyria. The Hittites likewise adopted the Egyptian winged sun-disk, which then seems to have passed from them to the Assyrians. At the same time the Hittite sculptors received the early Babylonian symbol of the eagle with outspread wings and a lion's head or sometimes a double head. They passed it on across the Ægean to later Europe, from which it finally came to us in the United States as the American eagle.

329. The clay-tablet cuneiform records of the Hittite emperors are the earliest historical narratives which display a literary prose style. The Hittite scribes were interested in

FIG. 127. *A Hittite Prince* HUNTING DEER

The prince, accompanied by his driver, stands in the moving chariot, shooting with bow and arrow at the fleeing stag. A hound runs beside the horses. Over the scene is an inscription in Hittite hieroglyphs (§ 329). The whole is sculptured in stone and forms a good example of the rather crude Hittite art

literature, and this interest led them to make copies of the old Babylonian writings with evident pleasure. The story of the Babylonian hero Gilgamesh was known throughout the whole of Asia Minor, and he passed from there to Greece under the new name of "Heracles," later "Hercules." Besides historical compositions there were even special treatises, such as an essay on horse-breeding which the Hittites borrowed from Mitanni.

Hittite literature

Unlike the scribes of other great civilizations the Hittite writers were interested in being known as authors, and attached their names to their writings. They were the earliest known self-conscious authors, and they thus show a very modern spirit. As the Hittite emperors began to erect stone buildings they felt the need of a larger monumental style of writing which would make it possible to decorate a building with historical records as the Egyptians did. They therefore devised a system of writing made up of picture signs. With these new hieroglyphic signs they engraved great stone records like those of Egypt. Carved in the face of rocky cliffs or masonry walls, these records still look down upon the traveler throughout a large part of Asia Minor from the Ægean to the Euphrates. Unfortunately this *hieroglyphic* writing of the Hittites has not yet been fully deciphered,[1] and we are still unable to read more than parts of it.

Hittite religion

330. In religion likewise the Hittites were greatly influenced by Babylonian and Egyptian beliefs. This is especially evident in the symbols like the Babylonian eagle and the Egyptian winged sun-disk. The Hittites worshiped two great groups of gods: those of the earth and those of the sky. Side by side with the Earth-Mother, to whom the Hittites were devoted, was their Sun-god, who was evidently taken over from Egypt. He was so prominent that the Hittite emperor even called himself "the Sun."

Permanent influence of Hittite civilization

331. Lying between southeastern Europe and the great civilizations of the Near East, Hittite civilization served as a link connecting the two, and the influences which it passed on to the early Ægean world were of permanent importance. From the Hittite world the Greeks received coinage (§ 495), besides important items in art, architecture, and religion. However, the Hittites are not to be considered as merely carriers of civilization. As we have seen (§§ 328–329), the Hittite Empire made significant original contributions to the cultures of the Ancient Near East. These influences were passed on by Assyria to the Persians, that other great Indo-European people of Western Asia, whom we shall now study.

SECTION 28. THE ARYAN PEOPLES AND THE IRANIAN PROPHET ZOROASTER

332. It is now an established fact that the easternmost tribes of the Indo-European line, having left the parent people, were pasturing their herds in the great steppe on the east of the Caspian by about 2000 B.C. Here they formed

[1] The decipherment, while not yet completed, has made great progress.

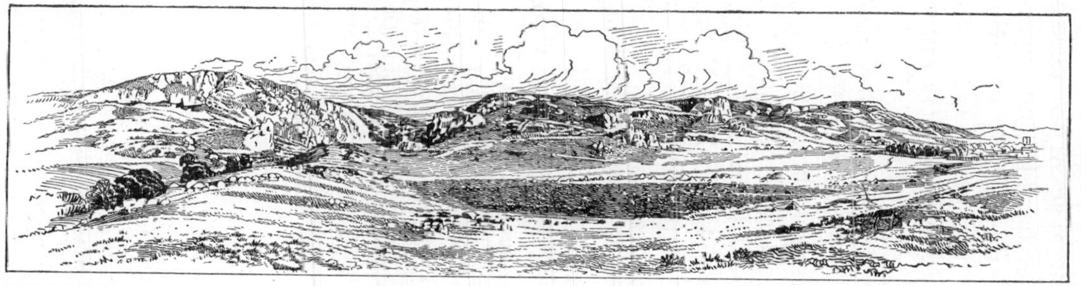

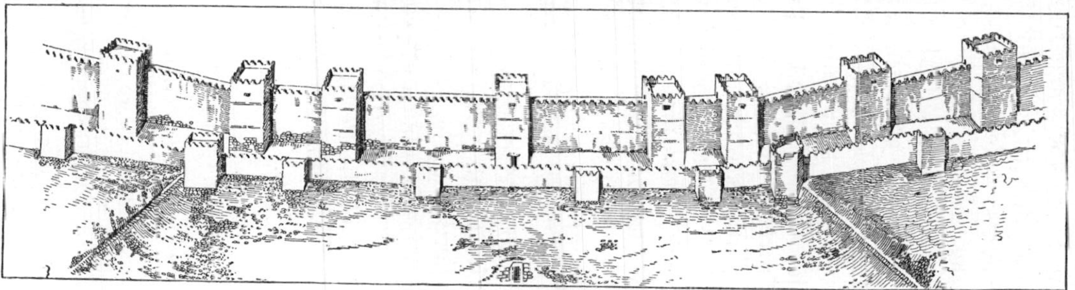

FIG. 128. *The Ancient* CAPITAL *of the Hittites in Central Asia Minor*

The view at the top shows the ruins of the great walled city which covered a group of hills like those of Rome. A modern village close by, called Boghaz-Köi, has given the place its modern name; but the Hittites called the city Hattusas. The view below shows a portion of the masonry walls of the city as they once were, when the Hittite kings lived here in the Thirteenth Century B.C. Excavation by German archæologists at Hattusas revealed also the clay tablets which once filled the state record chambers in the Hittite palace. These records have given us an entirely new conception of the international situation during the Second Hittite Empire. (After Puchstein)

a people properly called the Aryans[1] (see Fig. 123), and here they made their home for some time. The Aryan people had no writing, and they have left no monuments. Nevertheless, the beliefs of their descendants show that the Aryan tribes already possessed a high form of religion, which summed up conduct as "good thoughts, good deeds." Fire occupied an important place in this worship, and they had a group of priests whom they called "fire-kindlers."

Aryans; advance of the eastern wing of the Indo-European line

333. When the Aryans broke up, perhaps about 1800 B.C., they separated into two groups. The eastern tribes wandered southeastward and eventually arrived in India. In their sacred books, which we call the *Vedas*, written in Sanskrit, there are echoes of the days of Aryan unity, and they furnish many a hint of the ancient Aryan home on the east of the Caspian.

Sanskrit-speaking tribes in India

334. The tribes of the other group kept the name "Aryan" in the form "Iran,"[2] so that we call them Iranians. They also left the Aryan home and pushed westward and southwestward into the mountains bordering the Fertile Crescent. The Mitannians were a horse-breeding tribe of this Iranian group. Farther east were two powerful groups of the Iranians called the Medes and the Persians, who were yet to conquer the Fertile Crescent and establish the last great Oriental empire in Western Asia.

Mitannians, Medes, and Persians on the Fertile Crescent

[1] The Indo-European parent people seemingly had no common name for all their tribes as a great group. The term "Aryan" is often popularly applied to the parent people, but this custom is incorrect. "Aryan" (from which "Iran" and "Iranian" are later derivatives) designated a group of tribes, a fragment of the parent people, which detached itself and found a home for some centuries just east of the Caspian Sea. When we hear the term "Aryan" applied to the Indo-European peoples of Europe, or when it is said that we ourselves are descended from the Aryans, we must remember that this use of the word is historically incorrect, though very common. The Aryans, then, were *Eastern* descendants of the Indo-European parent people, as we are *Western* descendants of the parent people. The Aryans are our distant cousins but not our ancestors.

[2] They have given their name to the great Iranian Plateau, which stretches from the Zagros Mountains eastward to the Indus River. This whole region was known in Greek and Roman days as Ariana, which (like "Iran") is of course derived from "Aryan" (see map, p. 498).

FIG. 129. HOUSES *of a* STONE AGE VILLAGE *in Persia, probably about Six Thousand Years Old*

In the background we see the palace terrace of Persepolis (compare Fig. 200), built some 3500 years after this village was forsaken. The walls of the houses throughout the village are still standing up to a height of six or seven feet, with doors and the earliest known windows still preserved. Stone knives and other implements, together with beautifully painted pottery — sometimes containing remnants of food — were found on the floors of these houses in front of the hearths over which the food was cooked. The art displayed in the painted decorations on the pottery is surprisingly advanced. These people lived just at the dawn of the age of metal, as shown by one or two pieces of copper found in the village. At the present day the entire village is about 600 feet long and half as wide. When discovered by Dr. Herzfeld it was covered by a mound rising only ten or twelve feet above the surrounding plain. The village is being excavated by the Oriental Institute of The University of Chicago, and the clearance is still incomplete

Medes receive civilization of Fertile Crescent

335. By the time of the coming of the Iranians the fringe of peoples along the north and east of the Fertile Crescent had adopted much of the more advanced civilization of the Two Rivers. Especially in Elam on the east and in Urartu (Hebrew *Ararat*), in the later Armenian country on the north, the civilization of the Fertile Crescent had been very influential. The Assyrian emperors, especially after 700 B.C., had completely defeated these frontier peoples and broken their power. This was particularly true of the Elamites, whose country was taken over by the Persians. The Indo-European invaders were therefore able to settle in these border states on the east and north of the Fertile Crescent, and there they found cuneiform writing, which had been adopted by the Elamites many centuries earlier and was common in Urartu also. The Medes, who were the leaders of the Indo-European invasion, soon learned cuneiform writing, and the Persians seem to have taken it over from the Medes.

336. After they invaded the Highland Zone, therefore, but before they conquered the Fertile Crescent, the once rude Indo-European shepherds and herdsmen acquired at least a veneer of civilization, although their life and government long remained simple and crude, and in some ways almost barbarous. By 700 B.C. the Medes had established a powerful Iranian empire in the mountains east of the Tigris. It extended finally from the Persian Gulf, where it included the Persians, northwestward in the general line of the mountains, to the Black Sea region. The front of the Indo-European eastern wing was thus roughly parallel with the Tigris at this point, but its advance was not to stop here. As their capital the Medes founded the city of Ecbatana (see map, p. 146) about 700 B.C. It lay directly opposite the pass that led through the Zagros Mountains to the Fertile Crescent and to the city of Babylon itself. A century later Nebuchadnezzar and his successors at Babylon looked, therefore, with anxious eyes at this dangerous Median power, recalling no doubt how in 612 B.C. these same people had so willingly united in the assault against Nineveh.

The Indo-European Medes threaten Semitic Chaldeans

The Chaldeans on the Euphrates represented the leadership of men of Semitic blood from the southern pastures. Their leadership was now to be followed by that of men of Indo-European blood from the northern pastures. As we see the Chaldeans giving way before the Medes and Persians, let us bear in mind that we are watching a great racial change, and remember that these new Iranian masters of the East were our kindred; for both we and they have descended from the same wandering shepherd ancestors, the Indo-European parent people, who once dwelt in the far-off pastures of inner Asia, probably five thousand years ago.

337. All of these Iranians possessed a beautiful religion inherited from old Aryan days before their migration. A generation after the fall of Nineveh, perhaps about 570 B.C.,[1] there was born a Median prophet named Zoroaster. He began to look out upon the life of men in an effort to find a new religion which would supply the needs of man's life. He watched the ceaseless struggle between good and evil which seemed to meet him wherever he turned, and which he found already expressed in the beliefs of his people about the old gods. To him there seemed to be a struggle between a group of good beings, on the one hand, and a group of evil powers, on the other. The Good became to him a divine person, whom he called Mazda, after one of the old gods, or Ahuramazda, which means "Lord of Wisdom," and whom he regarded as God. Ahuramazda was surrounded by a group of helpers much like angels, of whom one of the greatest was the Light, called Mithras. Opposed to Ahuramazda and his helpers, it was finally believed, there was an evil group led by a great Spirit of Evil named Ahriman. It was he who was later inherited by Jews and Christians as Satan.

Religion of Iranians

338. Thus the faith of Zoroaster grew up out of the struggle of life itself and became a great power in life. It was one of the noblest religions ever founded. It called upon every man to stand on one side or the other,— to fill his soul with the Good and the Light or to dwell in the Evil and the Darkness. Whatever course a man pursued, he must expect a judgment hereafter. This was the earliest appearance in Asia of belief in a last judgment. Zoroaster's new faith was an idealization of the old

Judgment hereafter

[1] There has been much difference of opinion about the date of Zoroaster. Several earlier dates formerly seemed possible, but the evidence now seems to favor the Sixth Century B.C.

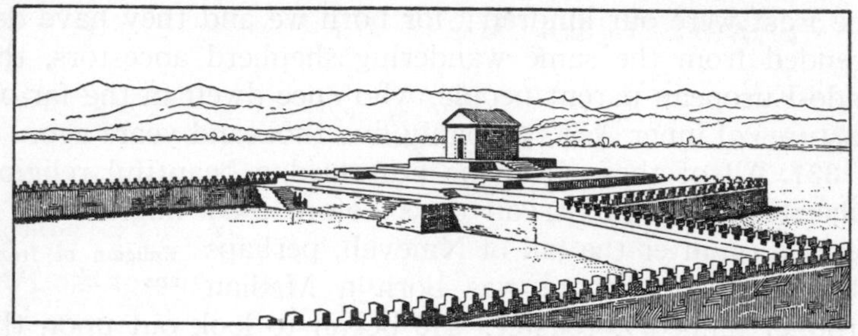

FIG. 130. *Restoration of the Earliest Known Persian* TEMPLE

This temple was recently discovered at Pasargadæ by Herzfeld, who concludes that it was erected by Cyrus himself, near whose palace and tomb it stands. (After Herzfeld)

beliefs and the old gods of his people. Therefore he retained the old Aryan veneration of fire as a visible symbol of the Good and the Light, and he preserved the ancient fire-kindling priests.

Zoroaster establishes his new religion

339. Unable to influence his own people, Zoroaster left the Medes and finally went south to the Persians, preaching his new religion, and perhaps for many years he found but little response to his efforts. We can discern his hopes and fears alike in the little group of hymns he has left, probably the only words of the great prophet which have survived. It is characteristic of the horse-loving Iranians that Zoroaster is said finally to have converted one of their great kings by miraculously healing the king's crippled horse. The new faith had gained a firm footing before the prophet's death, however, and before 500 B.C. it was the leading religion of the Iranians and accepted by the Persian emperors. It is even possible that Darius erected the prophet's tomb. Besides the hymns mentioned above, fragments of his teaching have descended to us in writings put together in the early Christian Era, many centuries after the prophet's death. All together these sacred writings form a book known as the *Avesta*. This we may call the Bible of the Persians.

SECTION 29. THE RISE OF THE PERSIAN EMPIRE

340. No people became more zealous followers of Zoroaster than the group of Iranian tribes known as the Persians. Through them a knowledge of him has descended to us. As we have seen (§ 335), the Persians had settled in Elam at the southeastern end of the Zagros Mountains, just north of the Persian Gulf. Its shores are here little better than desert, but the valleys of the mountainous hinterland are rich and fertile. In these valleys the Persians occupied a district some four hundred miles long. They were still a plain peasant folk, feeding their flocks and herds on the hills and leading a settled agricultural life, with simple institutions, no art, no writing or literature, but with stirring memories of their past.

Emergence of the Persians; their land and traditions

341. They acknowledged themselves vassals of their kinsmen the Medes, who ruled far to the north and northwest of them. One of the Persian tribes, dwelling in the mountains of Elam, was organized as a little kingdom called Anshan. About sixty years after the fall of Nineveh Anshan was ruled over by a Persian named Cyrus, who succeeded in uniting the other tribes of his kindred Persians and forming a nation. Thereupon Cyrus rebelled against the rule of the Medes. He gathered his peasant soldiery, and within three years he defeated the Median king and made himself master of the Median territory (549 B.C.). The extraordinary career of Cyrus was now a spectacle upon which all eyes in the lands of the west were fastened with wonder and alarm.

Cyrus unites Persian tribes and conquers Medes

342. The overflowing energies of the new conqueror and his peasant soldiery proved irresistible. The Persian peasants seem to have been remarkable archers. The mass of the Persian army was made up of bowmen whose storm of arrows at long range overwhelmed the enemy long before the hand-to-hand fighting began. Bodies of the skillful Persian horsemen, hovering on either wing, then rode in and completed the destruction of the foe.

Persian army

These arrangements were taken by the Persians from the Assyrians, the greatest soldiers whom the East had ever seen.

Cyrus conquers the west

343. The great states of Chaldea (Babylonia) and Egypt, Lydia under Crœsus in western Asia Minor, and even Sparta in Greece formed a powerful combination against this sudden menace, which had risen like the flash of a meteor in the eastern sky. Without an instant's delay Cyrus struck at Crœsus of Lydia, the chief author of the hostile combination. One Persian victory followed another. By 546 B.C. Sardes, the Lydian capital, had fallen, and Crœsus, the Lydian king, was a prisoner in the hands of Cyrus. Cyrus at once gained also the southern coasts of Asia Minor. Within five years the power of the little Persian kingdom in the mountains of Elam had swept across Asia Minor to the Mediterranean, as the genius of Cyrus made it the leading nation of the world.

FIG. 131. *Persian* SOLDIERS

Although carrying spears when doing duty as palace guards, these men were chiefly archers, as is shown by the size of the large quivers on their backs. The bow hangs on the left shoulder. The royal bodyguard may also be seen wielding their spears around the Persian king at the battle of Issus (Fig. 198). Notice the splendid robes worn by these palace guards. The figures are done in brightly colored glazed brick,— an art borrowed by the Persians and employed to beautify the palace walls

344. Turning eastward again, Cyrus had no trouble in defeating the Chaldean army led by the young crown prince Belshazzar, whose name in the Book of Daniel (see Dan. v) is a household word throughout the Christian world. In spite of the vast walls erected by Nebuchadnezzar to protect Babylon, the Persians entered the great city in 538 B.C., seemingly without resistance. Thus, only seventy-four years after the fall of Nineveh had opened the conflict between the former dwellers in the northern and the southern grasslands, the Semitic East completely collapsed before the advance of the Indo-European power.

Cyrus conquers Chaldea; collapse of Semitic East

345. Cyrus established his capital and royal residence at Pasargadæ, where the palace of the heroic conqueror has recently been excavated. Very little of it has survived; but on one of the reliefs the lower portion of a royal figure is preserved, and on a fold of the garment, in cuneiform signs, we may still read the words "Cyrus, the great king." Here, also, he built a temple for the faith of Zoroaster, who was probably still living. It is the oldest known Persian temple. Nine years after his capture of Babylon, Cyrus, the first great conqueror of Indo-European blood, fell in battle (529 B.C.) as he was fighting with the nomads in northeastern Iran. His body was reverently laid away in a massive tomb of impressive simplicity at Pasargadæ, and there it was found two hundred years later by Alexander the Great.

Capital and tomb of Cyrus; his death, 529 B.C.

346. All Western Asia was now subject to the Persian king.[1] In 525 B.C., only four years after the death of Cyrus, his son Cambyses conquered Egypt. This conquest of the only remaining ancient Oriental power rounded out the Persian Empire to include the whole civilized East from the Nile Delta, around the entire eastern end of the Mediterranean, to the Ægean, and from this western boundary

Cambyses conquers Egypt; Persia rules the whole civilized East

[1] It will aid the memory to note the three great invasions of the Indo-Europeans in Western Asia. There were, of course, others less important. It will be helpful also to notice that two intervals, of roughly 1000 years each, separate I and II, and II and III.

I. Conquest of Early Anatolian country, about 2500 B.C.
II. Conquest of Mitanni, about 1500 B.C.
III. Conquest of the Fertile Crescent and entire Near East, completed and organized 500 B.C. by the capture of Nineveh (612 B.C.), Sardes (546 B.C.), and Babylon (538 B.C.) and the conquest of Egypt (525 B.C.).

FIG. 132. *The* TOMB *of* CYRUS *at Pasargadæ*

Perhaps built by Cyrus himself alongside his temple and his palace. The columns are a later addition, not belonging to the original monument. The body of Cyrus had lain in this tomb for nearly two hundred years when Alexander the Great (§ 733) found it plundered of its royal ornaments and lying on the floor. He ordered the body restored to its place, and had the tomb chamber closed up. It is now empty. (Photograph by the Oriental Institute of The University of Chicago)

eastward almost to India (see map IV, p. 266). The great task had consumed just twenty-five years (550 to 525 B.C.) since the overthrow of the Medes by Cyrus. It was an achievement for which the Assyrian Empire had prepared the way, and the Persians were now to learn much from the great civilizations which had preceded them.

SECTION 30. THE CIVILIZATION OF THE PERSIAN EMPIRE (530–330 B.C.)

347. The Persians found Babylon a great and splendid city, with the vast fortifications of Nebuchadnezzar stretching from river to river, and his sumptuous buildings visible far across the Babylonian Plain. The city was the center of the commerce of Western Asia, and the greatest market in the early Oriental world. Along the Nile the Persian emperors now ruled the splendid cities whose colossal monuments we have visited. These things and the civilized life which the Persians found along the Nile and the Euphrates soon influenced them greatly, as we shall see.

Persian kings absorb civilization of the East they rule

348. Aramaic, the speech of the Aramean merchants who filled the busy market places of Babylon, had by that time become the language of the whole Fertile Crescent. Business documents were now written in Aramaic, with pen and ink, on papyrus; and clay tablets, bearing cuneiform writing, were slowly disappearing. The Persian officials were therefore obliged to carry on their government business, such as the collection of taxes, in the Aramaic tongue throughout the western half of the Persian Empire, and probably also in much of the eastern half. Even as far as the Nile and western Asia Minor they sent out their government documents in Aramaic, this universal language of business.

Aramaic becomes language of Persian administration in the west

349. The government of the Persian kings, like that of the Assyrian Empire, was thus bilingual, by which we mean that it employed two languages,— Aramaic and the old Persian tongue. Even in writing Persian the Persians often employed Aramaic letters, as we write English with Roman letters. But they already possessed a cuneiform *alphabet*, having probably gained the idea of an alphabet from Aramaic writing. Recent discoveries at Ecbatana, the Median capital, indicate that the Medes devised this new alphabet of thirty-nine *cuneiform* signs, which was now employed for writing Persian on clay tablets. They also used it when they wished to make records on large monuments of stone (Fig. 133).

Persians devise a cuneiform alphabet

350. These cuneiform records of the Persians are very important in that they first enabled us to read the cuneiform inscriptions of Western Asia. When Aramaic had displaced the Babylonian and Assyrian languages, there came a time when no one wrote any more clay tablets or other records in the ancient wedge writing. The latest cuneiform tablet known belongs among the astronomical records of the Chaldeans and was written in the year 7 B.C.[1] Nearly two thousand years ago, therefore, the last man who could read a cuneiform tablet had passed away. The history of Babylonia and Assyria was consequently lost under the city mounds along the Tigris and Euphrates.

Importance of Persian cuneiform documents

351. Now the Persian cuneiform, consisting of only thirty-nine alphabetical signs, was not difficult. In the early Nineteenth Century A.D. Grotefend, a German schoolmaster, identified and read the names of Darius and Xerxes (Fig. 134) and some other Persian words. Various interested European scholars were later able to discover the sounds of nearly all the signs in the Persian cuneiform alphabet. By 1847 Sir Henry Rawlinson, a British army officer, had completed the decipherment of Persian cuneiform, and scholars were then able to read the old Persian inscriptions. But the number of these inscriptions then known was very small. Indeed, the chief value of the ability to read ancient Persian cuneiform records lay in the fact that this Persian writing might form a bridge leading over to an understanding of ancient *Babylonian* cuneiform.

Value of Persian cuneiform in deciphering Babylonian cuneiform

352. Scholars had early discovered that the inscription *C* on the great Behistun monument of King Darius (see Fig. 133) was written with the same cuneiform signs which were also observable on many of the older clay tablets and stone monuments found in Babylonia. It was understood, therefore, that if inscription *C* at Behistun could be deciphered, it would be possible then to read all the ancient documents of Babylonia and Assyria. Within three years Rawlinson, working from the Behistun inscriptions, had deciphered

History of Babylonia and Assyria recovered

[1] The tablet is dated in the year 305 of the Seleucid Era. This era began in 312 B.C. The date of this latest cuneiform document is therefore 7 B.C.

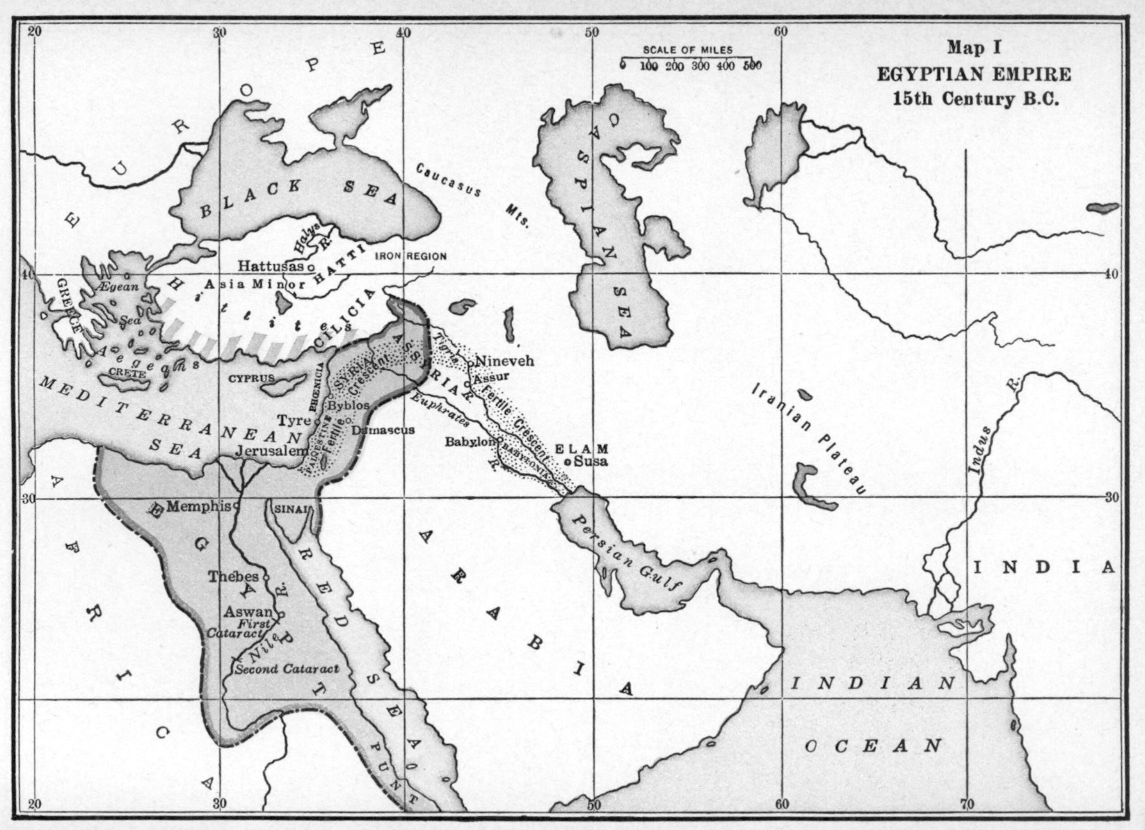

Map I
EGYPTIAN EMPIRE
15th Century B.C.
SCALE OF MILES
0 100 200 300 400 500
EUROPE
BLACK SEA
CASPIAN SEA
Caucasus Mts.
Halys R.
Hattusas
HATTI
IRON REGION
Asia Minor
Hittites
CILICIA
GREECE
Ægean Sea
Aegeans
CRETE
CYPRUS
MEDITERRANEAN SEA
PHŒNICIA
SYRIA
Byblos
Tyre
Damascus
PALESTINE
Fertile Crescent
Jerusalem
ASSYRIA
Tigris R.
Nineveh
Assur
Euphrates R.
Babylon
BABYLONIA
ELAM
Susa
Iranian Plateau
Indus R.
INDIA
Persian Gulf
ARABIA
INDIAN OCEAN
SINAI
RED SEA
PUNT
Memphis
EGYPT
Thebes
Aswan
First Cataract
Nile R.
Second Cataract
AFRICA
20
30
40
50
60
70

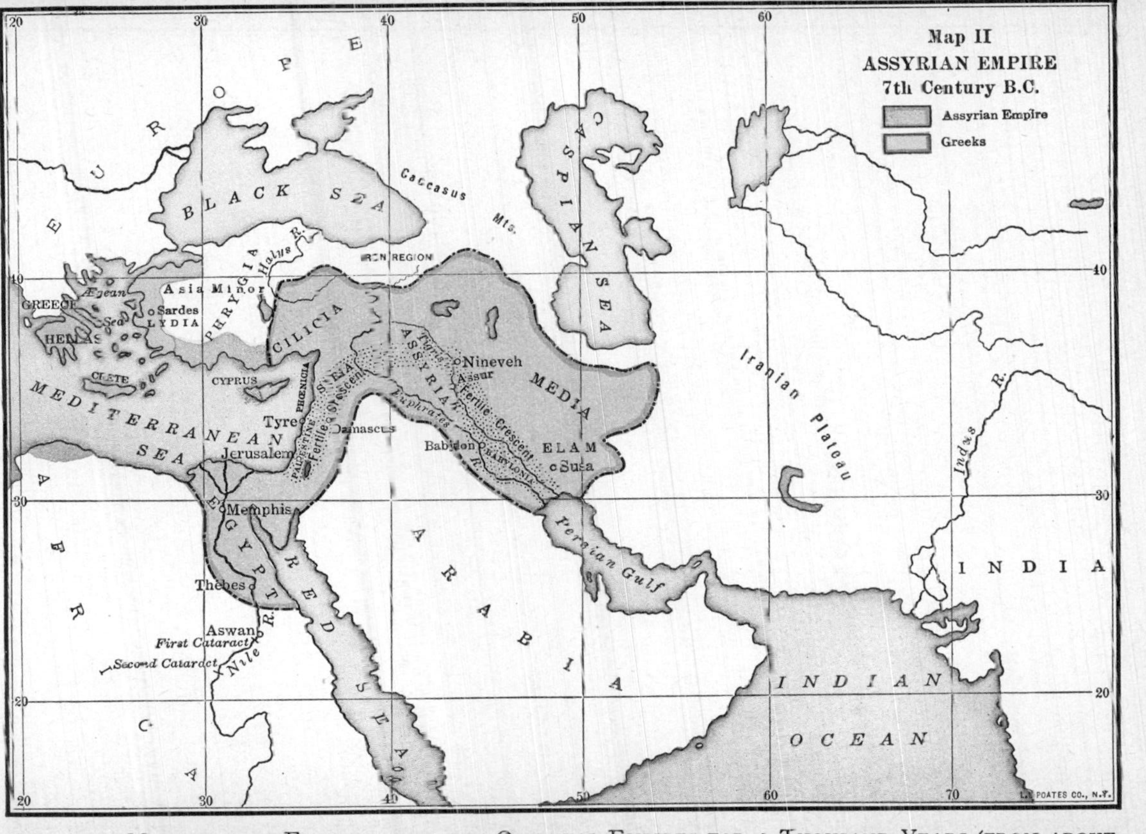

SEQUENCE MAP SHOWING EXPANSION OF THE ORIENTAL EMPIRES FOR A THOUSAND YEARS (FROM ABOUT 1500 TO 500 B.C.). IN FOUR PARTS. (See Map III and Map IV following)

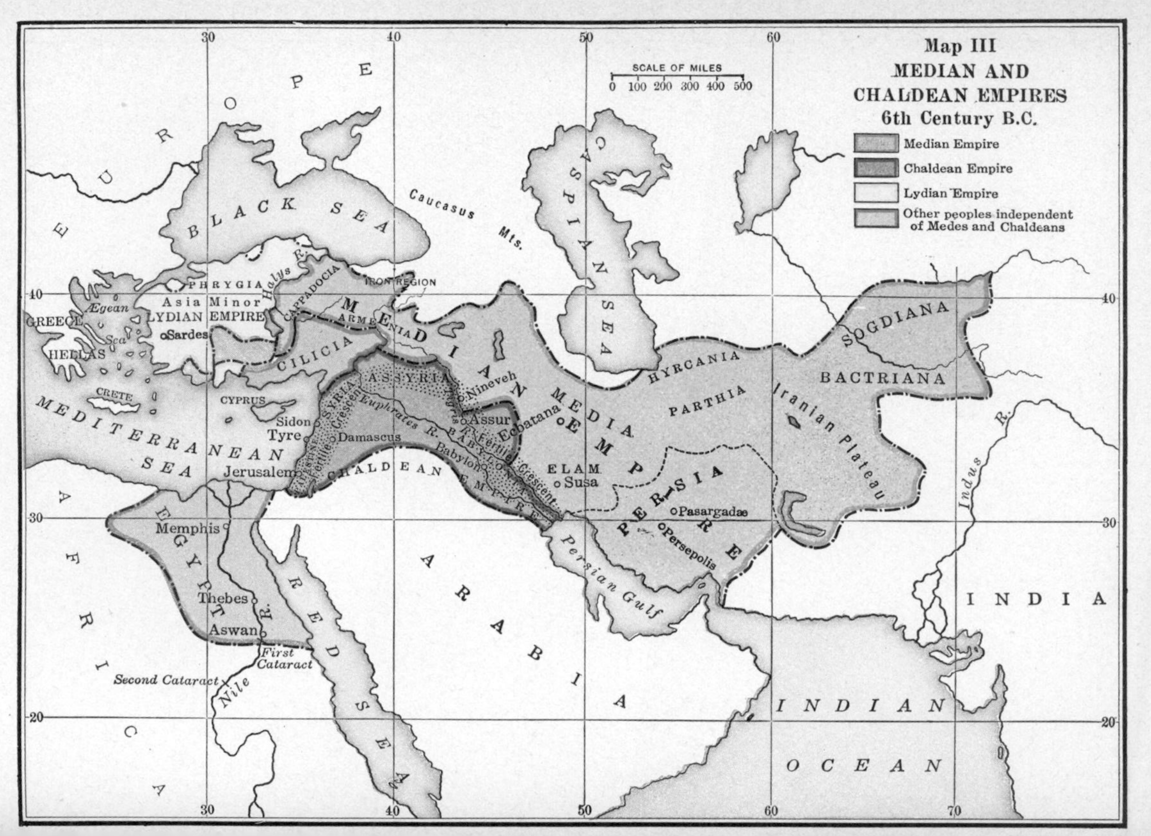
Map III
MEDIAN AND
CHALDEAN EMPIRES
6th Century B.C.
Median Empire
Chaldean Empire
Lydian Empire
Other peoples independent of Medes and Chaldeans
SCALE OF MILES
0 100 200 300 400 500
EUROPE
BLACK SEA
Caucasus Mts.
CASPIAN SEA
PHRYGIA
Halys R.
CAPPADOCIA
IRON REGION
Asia Minor
LYDIAN EMPIRE
Sardes
GREECE
Ægean Sea
HELLAS
CRETE
CILICIA
ARMENIA
MEDIAN EMPIRE
ASSYRIA
Nineveh
Assur
Tigris R.
Ecbatana
MEDIA
HYRCANIA
PARTHIA
SOGDIANA
BACTRIANA
Iranian Plateau
CYPRUS
Sidon
Tyre
SYRIA
Damascus
Euphrates R.
BABYLONIA
Babylon
Fertile Crescent
MEDITERRANEAN SEA
Jerusalem
PALESTINE
CHALDEAN EMPIRE
ELAM
Susa
PERSIA
Pasargadae
Persepolis
Persian Gulf
Indus R.
INDIA
AFRICA
EGYPT
Memphis
Thebes
Aswan
Nile R.
First Cataract
Second Cataract
RED SEA
ARABIA
INDIAN OCEAN
30
40
50
60
70
20

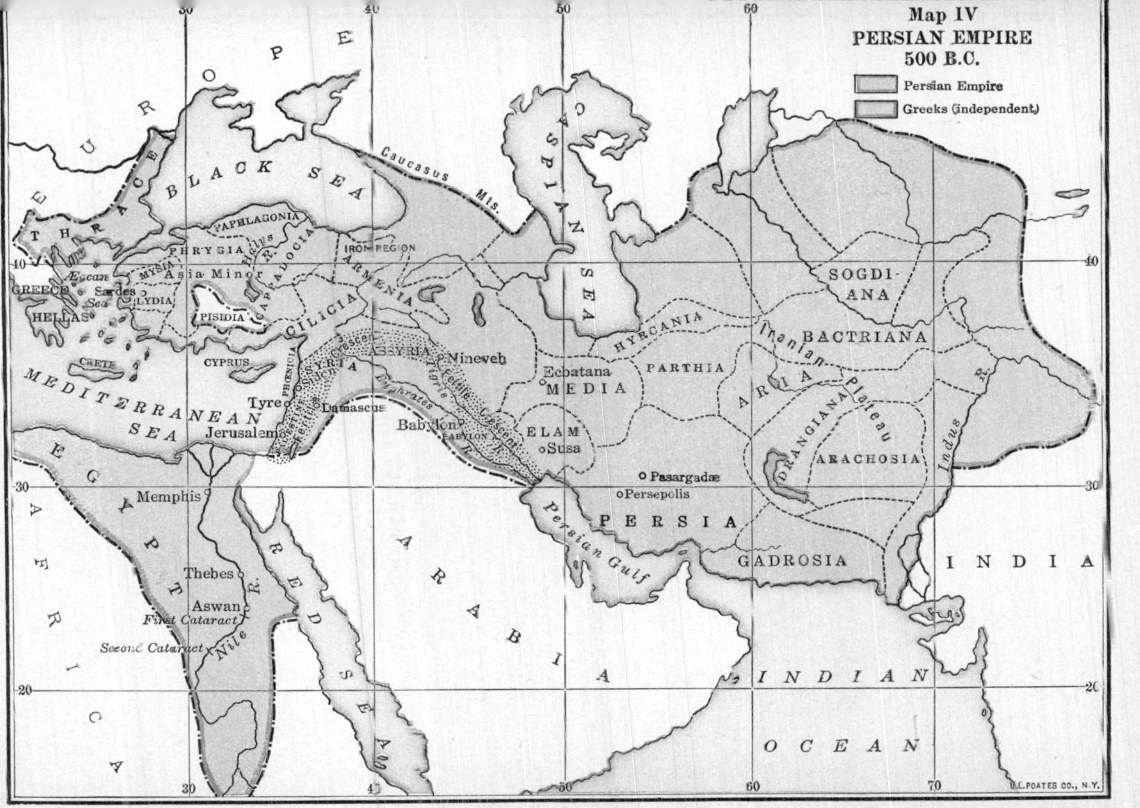

SEQUENCE MAP SHOWING EXPANSION OF THE ORIENTAL EMPIRES FOR A THOUSAND YEARS (FROM ABOUT 1500 TO 500 B.C.). IN FOUR PARTS. (See Map I and Map II preceding)

FIG. 133. *Triumphal Monument of* DARIUS THE GREAT, *the* ROSETTA STONE OF ASIA, *on the Cliff of Behistun*

This impressive monument is the most important historical document surviving in Asia. It is made up of four important parts: the relief sculptures (*A*) and the three inscriptions (*B*, *C*, *D*). *B* is a great inscription in columns some 12 feet high, recording the triumph of Darius over all his enemies in the extensive revolts which followed his coronation. It is in the Persian language, written with the new cuneiform alphabet of thirty-nine letters which the Medes probably devised (§ 340). The other two inscriptions (*C* and *D*) are translations of the Persian (*B*). *C* therefore contains the same record as the Persian (*B*), but it is in the Babylonian language and is written in Babylonian cuneiform, with its several hundred wedge-signs (§ 178). *D*, the third inscription, is also cuneiform, in the language of the region of Elam, and hence is called Elamite. Thus the Great King published his triumph in the three most important languages of this eastern region and placed the record overlooking a main road at Behistun (see map, p. 498), where the men of the caravans passing between Babylon and the Iranian Plateau would look up 300 feet and see the splendid monument 25 feet high and 50 feet wide. To reach it requires a dangerous climb, and it was on this lofty cliff, at the risk of his life, that Sir Henry Rawlinson copied all three of these cuneiform inscriptions (1835–1847). By the use of these copies Rawlinson succeeded in deciphering the ancient Babylonian cuneiform, and this great monument of Darius therefore enabled modern historians to recover the lost language and history of Babylonia and Assyria. It did for Western Asia what the Rosetta Stone did for Egypt. (Drawn from photographs of the British Museum Expedition)

A

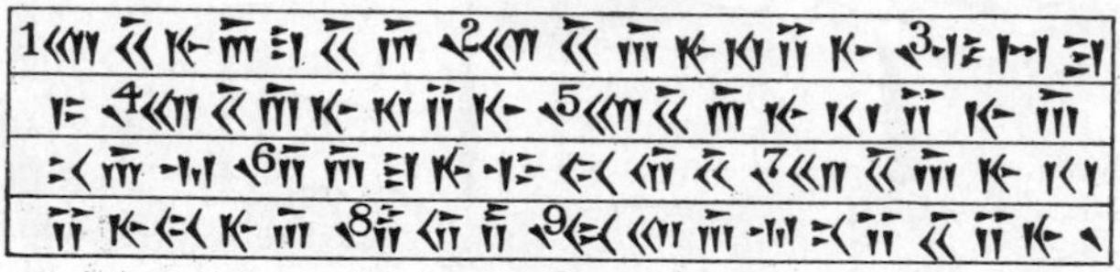

B

Fig. 134. *The Two* Old Persian Inscriptions *which were first Deciphered and Read*

The Persian scribes separated the words in their inscriptions by inserting an oblique wedge between the words. The above Arabic numbers are here added that we may be able to refer to the different words. It will be seen that these numbers (except 1) always stand where the oblique wedge shows a new word begins. Grotefend noticed that the same word is repeated a number of times in each of these inscriptions. In *A* compare Nos. 2, 4, 5, and 6, and they will be recognized as the same word. In *B* it occurs also four times (Nos. 2, 4, 5, and 7). As these inscriptions were found above the figures of Persian kings, Grotefend therefore suspected that this frequent word must be the Persian word for "king." Moreover, as it occurs in both inscriptions as No. 2, the preceding word (No. 1) would probably be the *name* of the king, the two words being arranged thus: "Darius [the] king." Grotefend then found that the words for the titles of the kings of Persia were known in later Persian documents. Guided by the known titles, he attempted the following guess as to the arrangement and meaning of the words:

1	2	3	4
unknown name of a Persian king	[the] king	[the] great	king
5	6	7	8
of kings,	of king	unknown name of a Persian king	the son

etc. (6, 7, and 8 meaning "the son of King So-and-so"). He next experimented with the known names of the kings of Persia, and, judging from their length, he found that the probable name for No. 1 in *A* was "Darius," and for No. 1 in *B* was "Xerxes." The result may be seen in Fig. 135

Babylonian cuneiform also. At once the city mounds of Babylonia and Assyria began to speak and tell us, piece by piece, the three great chapters of history along the Two Rivers, — something over twenty-five hundred years of the story of man in Western Asia, of which the world before had been entirely ignorant. The ability to read the cuneiform records and thus gain this knowledge we owe to the documents left us by the Persian kings.

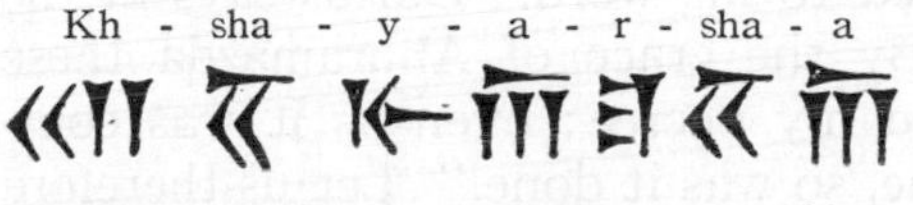

Kh - sha - y - a - r - sha - a

Fig. 135. *The Name of* Xerxes *in Old Persian* Cuneiform

This is the first word in Fig. 134 (*B*), supposed by Grotefend to be "Xerxes." Now, just as our "Charles" is an imperfect form of the ancient name "Carolus," so the name we call "Xerxes" was pronounced by the old Persians *Khshayarsha.* The above seven signs, therefore, should be read Kh-sha-y-a-r-sha-a. Grotefend in this way learned the sounds for which these signs stood. Now some of these signs appear in the word Grotefend thought was "king" in Persian. Hence it was now possible for Grotefend to see if he could find out how to pronounce the ancient Persian word for "king." And the reader can do the same. Let him copy on a slip of paper the first three signs in the word supposedly meaning "king"; for example, use word 2 in Fig. 134. Now take these three signs and compare them with the signs in "Xerxes." The student will find that the three signs he has copied are the same as the first, second, and seventh signs in the word "Xerxes." Let us write down in a row the sounds of these three signs (first, second, and seventh), and we find we have *Kh-sha-a.* The ancient Persian word for "king" must have begun with the sounds *Kh-sha-a.* When we compare this with *shah,* the title of the present king of Persia, it is evident that Grotefend was on the right road to decipher Old Persian cuneiform

Organization of Persian Empire by Darius

353. The organization of the great Persian Empire, stretching from the river Indus to the Ægean Sea (almost as long as the United States from east to west) and from the Indian Ocean to the deserts of the Caspian, was a colossal task. It demanded an effort of organization on a greater scale than any ruler had ever attempted before. It was much too great an undertaking to be completed by Cyrus. Begun by him, it was carried through by Darius the Great (521-485 B.C.), whose organization remains one of the most remarkable achievements in the history of the ancient Orient, if not of the world. The rule of Darius was just, humane, and intelligent, but the subject peoples had of course no voice in government. The Persian sovereign had already come to be called the Great King in the time of Cyrus. All that the Great King decreed was law, and all the peoples bowed to his word. Darius says in the Behistun inscription, "By the grace of Ahuramazda these lands have conformed to my decree; even as it was commanded unto them by me, so was it done." Let us therefore notice an important fact here revealed: this system was not only attempting government on a larger scale than the world had ever seen before, but it was government controlled by *one man*. The ancient world never forgot the example of the vast Persian Empire controlled by one-man power.

Persian provincial system

354. In developing his colossal organization Darius caused himself to be made actual king in Egypt and in Babylonia, but the rest of the Empire he divided into twenty provinces. Each of these provinces was called a satrapy, because it was under a governor called a satrap, who was appointed by the Great King. These arrangements, while similar to those of the Chaldean, Assyrian, and Egyptian empires, were a further development of provincial rule under governors. Indeed, the Persian Empire was the first example of a fully organized group of subject peoples and nations ruled as provinces, — an arrangement which we may call a provincial system. The subject nations, or provinces under Persian rule, enjoyed a good deal of independence in the local matters of their own government as long as they paid regular tribute and furnished recruits for the Great King's army. To discover and prevent local rebellion, such as the revolt of a governor or people against the Persian government, the Great King kept officials residing in each subject state, who were called, after an old Egyptian custom, the King's Ears or the King's Eyes, and whose duty it was to report any evidence of disobedience. All this was an advance upon the rule of the Assyrian Empire.

355. Farm lands were divided into vast domains held by powerful nobles and other great landowners. There were few small land-owning farmers. All paid dues to help make up the tribute collected from every division of the Empire. In the eastern part of the Empire it was paid, as of old, in produce (see Fig. 138). In the western part of the Empire, chiefly Lydia and the Greek settlements in western Asia Minor, the coinage of metal was common by 600 B.C., and there this tribute was paid in coined money. The eastern countries — Egypt, Babylonia, and Persia herself — were not quick to adopt this new convenience. Darius, however, began the coinage of gold and permitted his satraps to coin silver. The rate was about thirteen to one; that is to say, gold was worth about thirteen times as much as silver. Thus the great commercial convenience of coined money issued by the state began to be more common in the Near East during the Persian period.

Lands, tribute, and coinage

356. In general, Darius, like the modern Japanese, showed surprising discernment in selecting the most valuable things in the great civilizations about him for adoption in his own government. He speedily perceived the practical convenience of the Egyptian calendar of twelve thirty-day months, and he introduced it as the calendar of the Persian government. He was likewise impressed with the value of Egyptian medical knowledge. He therefore sent back to Egypt a learned Egyptian high priest, who was a captive in Persia, and gave him instructions to go to Sais, a city of the western Delta, and to restore there an Egyptian medical school which had fallen into decay. Upon a statue of this high priest, now in the Vatican collections at Rome, there is engraved an interesting account of how he carried out the orders of Darius and restored the two buildings of the school. One of these was the school building itself and the other was probably the library. Students from the best families were placed in the school, and it was equipped with all needed "instruments," probably for the practice of surgery. The inscription further states: "His majesty [that is, Darius] did this because he knew the value of this art [the practice of medicine], in order to save the life of every one having sickness." Thus the great Persian established

Darius introduces Egyptian calendar and encourages science

the earliest known medical school as a royal foundation. It was also under Darius that the astronomical studies of the great Chaldean astronomer Nabu-rimannu were carried on at Babylon; and similar researches, continued by Kidinnu, likewise took place under Persian rule (see §§ 276–278).

Darius turns to the sea

357. Nothing shows the wise statesmanship of Darius the Great more clearly than his remarkable efforts to make Persia a great sea power. It was no easy task for an inland nation of shepherds and peasants like the Persians, separated from the water by desert shores, to gain control of the sea. Darius was obliged to employ foreign navigators. He dispatched a skillful Mediterranean sailor named Scylax to explore the course of the great Indus River in India. Then Darius ordered him to sail along the coast of Asia from the mouth of the Indus westward to the Isthmus of Suez. Scylax was the first Western sailor known to have sailed along this south coast of Asia, so little known to Western peoples at that time (about 500 B.C.).

Darius links East and West by a Suez canal

358. At Suez, Darius restored the ancient but long filled-up canal of the Egyptians connecting the Nile with the Red Sea. Along the ancient route of this canal have been found fragments of great stone tablets erected by Darius (see map, p. 66). They bear an account of the restoration of the canal, in which we find the words of Darius: "I commanded to dig this canal, from the stream flowing in Egypt, called the Nile, to the sea [Red Sea] which stretches from Persia. Then this canal was dug as I commanded, and ships sailed from Egypt through this canal to Persia, according to my will." Darius evidently cherished what proved to be a vain hope, that the south coast of Persia might come to share in the now growing commerce between India and the Mediterranean world. As Persia was now lacking in small landowners, so also was she lacking in small and enterprising merchants, who might have become great promoters of commerce.

359. Unlike the Assyrians, Darius treated the Phœnician cities with kindness, and succeeded in organizing a great

FIG. 136. TOMBS OF DARIUS THE GREAT (*Right*) *and* ARTAXERXES I (*Left*) *near Persepolis*

The tomb of Darius the Great is inscribed with his name, besides a long inscription on the front (still unpublished) describing the beautiful Zoroastrian religion. Out of range on the left is the tomb of Darius II, and on the right, also out of range, is the tomb of Xerxes. The remaining three royal tombs belonging to the last three kings of the Achæmenian line (the line of Darius) — Artaxerxes II, Artaxerxes III, and Darius III — are cut in the cliff behind the palaces of Persepolis (Fig. 200). Including the tomb of Cyrus (Fig. 132), we thus have the tombs of all nine of the great kings of Persia, except that of Cambyses, the conqueror of Egypt, which has never been found. The door of the burial chamber in each tomb is in the middle of the colonnaded front. Above this colonnade is a square containing a sculptured picture of the king worshiping Ahuramazda before a fire altar. All these tombs were broken open and robbed in ancient times, like the tomb of Cyrus, and all are now empty except that inside, in niches, still rest the massive stone coffins in which Darius, Xerxes, and the other kings and their families were buried. (Air view by the Oriental Institute)

Phœnician war fleet. We shall find that Darius's son Xerxes could depend upon many hundreds of ships for warfare and transportation in the Eastern Mediterranean when such shipping was needed for the invasion of Europe. Thus the more enlightened Persian kings accomplished what the Assyrian emperors never achieved, and Persia became the first great sea power in Asia.

Persia becomes earliest great sea power in Asia

360. For the first time the ancient world began to develop a wide-spread system of good roads, by which the Persian emperors maintained communication from end to end of the vast Empire. On a smaller scale these roads must have done for the Persian Empire what railroads do for us. Royal messengers maintained a much more complete postal system than that which had already been introduced under the Assyrian Empire. These messengers were surprisingly swift, although merchandise required about as much time to go from Susa or Persepolis to the Ægean Sea as we now need for going around the world. A good example of the effect of these roads was the incoming of the domestic fowl, which we commonly call the chicken. It was originally a wild jungle hen of India which the East Indians tamed, and it was unknown in the Mediterranean until Persian communications brought it from India to the Ægean Sea.

System of roads and communication

361. The ancient Elamite city of Susa, in the Zagros Mountains, was the chief residence and capital. The mild winter air of the Babylonian Plain, however, attracted the sovereign during the colder months, when he went to dwell in the palaces of the vanished Chaldean Empire at Babylon. In spite of its remoteness the earlier kings had made an effort to live in their old Persian home. We have seen that Cyrus built a splendid palace at Pasargadæ, near the battlefield where he had defeated the Medes (see map, p. 498), and Darius also established a magnificent residence at Persepolis, some forty miles south of the palace of Cyrus. It is near the ruins of Persepolis that the tombs of Darius, Xerxes, and the later Persian emperors still stand in their native Persia.

Capital and royal residences

362. The Persian architects had to learn architecture from the old Oriental peoples now subject to Persia. The enormous terraces on which the Persian palaces stood were imitated from Babylonia. The winged bulls at the palace gates, like the magnificent stairways leading up to them, were copied from those of Assyria and the west. The vast colonnades stretching along the front and filling the enormous halls — the earliest colonnades of Asia — had grown up over two thousand years earlier on the

Architecture

FIG. 137. *Excavation of* GRAND STAIRWAY *Leading to* AUDIENCE HALL *of Darius the Great at Persepolis*

Only the nearer half of the stairway is visible from this point, for it is nearly three hundred feet long. It enabled visitors coming from the court below to ascend to the elevated floor of a vast royal audience hall, some of the columns of which are visible on the right (see also Fig. 201). The man at the extreme left is standing on the rubbish which was higher toward the right and had completely covered the stairway from view. At this point the rubbish is made up of the crumbled bricks of a lofty sun-dried brick wall which stood on the right of the stairway and fell down over it, completely concealing it. Most of the workmen engaged in clearing it away are hidden behind the high wall of rubbish at the left. The tripod in the rear is a strong derrick for raising the heavy stones of the sculptures and of the stepped balustrade which were knocked off by the fall of the great sun-dried brick wall and had likewise fallen down into the court. The entire face of the stairway is covered with beautiful relief sculptures, revealing the remarkable art of the Persians in the days of Darius, whose gold and silver tablets bearing his building inscriptions were discovered in the summer of 1933 by the Oriental Institute of The University of Chicago, which is carrying on the Persepolis excavations

Nile. Likewise the gorgeously colored palace walls of enameled brick reached Persia from the Nile by way of Assyria and the west.[1] Thus the great civilizations over which the Persian emperors ruled were merged together in the life of their Empire.

[1] It is very noticeable that the Persian architects did not adopt the arch from Babylonia. On the contrary, each door in the palace of Darius is topped with a *horizontal* block of stone, called a lintel, copied from Egyptian doors.

FIG. 138. *Relief from the* SCULPTURES *on the Face of the* GRAND STAIRWAY *at Persepolis*

The reliefs on the face of the grand stairway shown in the preceding illustration picture the reception of the envoys of twenty-eight Oriental nations, who have come to Persepolis to present their tribute to the Persian emperor. The frieze shown above represents the natives of Cilicia with two magnificent rams forming part of their tribute

Europe and the Persian Empire

363. Such a consolidation of all the civilizations of the Ancient Near East into one vast organization produced a new situation, and one of tremendous importance for the history of Europe. We have seen that Cyrus had carried his victories westward to the shores of the Ægean Sea, and the Greek cities of western Asia Minor fell under Persian sway. Thus the Oriental colossus arose directly alongside southeastern Europe. If we look at the map (map IV, p. 266) and observe how the western advance of the great Empire finally extended, under Darius, to include European territory as far as the Danube, we shall understand that a hostile collision with Greece was unavoidable. This situation was yet to bring about a more complete commingling of the civilizations of the Near East with the life of neighboring Europe than had ever been possible before. These wars between Persia and Europe were not of any great importance to Persia, but they were epoch-making for little European nations like the Greeks, and we must therefore take them up later as a part of the history of Greece.

364. For the Oriental world as a whole, Persian rule meant about two hundred years of peaceful prosperity (ending about 330 B.C.). The Persian kings, however, as time went on, were no longer as strong and skillful as Cyrus and Darius. They loved luxury and ease, and left much of the task of ruling to their governors and officials. This meant corrupt and ineffective government; the result was weakness and decline.

Decline of Persia

365. The later world, especially the Greeks, often represented the Persian rulers as cruel and barbarous Oriental tyrants. This unfavorable opinion is certainly not justified so far as it refers to the earlier Persian rulers. Most of the Persian emperors felt a deep sense of obligation to give just government to the nations of the earth. Darius the Great in the Behistun inscription says: "On this account Ahuramazda brought me help, . . . because I was not wicked, nor was I a liar, nor was I a tyrant, neither I nor any of my line. I have ruled according to righteousness." There can be no doubt that the Persian Empire, the largest the ancient world had thus far seen, enjoyed a government far more just and humane than any that had preceded it in the East.

Character of Persian kings and their rule

366. Many such statements as that of Darius just quoted show that the Persian rulers were devoted followers of Zoroaster's teaching. Their power carried this noble faith throughout Western Asia and especially into Asia Minor. Here Mithras, regarded by Zoroaster as a helper of Ahuramazda, appeared as a hero of light, and finally as a Sun-god, who gradually outshone Ahuramazda himself. From Asia Minor, Mithras passed into Europe, and, as we shall see, the faith in the mighty Persian god spread far and wide through

Spread of Persian religion; competition among Oriental religions

FIG. 139. *Discovery of the* FOUNDATION RECORDS *of Darius the Great's* VAST AUDIENCE HALL *at Persepolis*

We are looking into an excavation under the northeast corner of the great audience hall of Darius. At the bottom of the excavation we see a shallow square box of stone, from which the lid has been removed. The archæologist at the left holds in his hand a large tablet of solid silver, over thirteen inches square, on which is engraved in cuneiform characters a record of Darius the Great. When the archæologist lifted this silver plate out of the box he saw below it another of the same size, but of solid *gold*, bearing the same record as that on the silver plate. After the architects of Darius had deposited the records here they closed the box containing the gold and silver plates with a stone lid and then placed over it the rough stone which is seen here under the left arm of the workman at the right. Since this discovery, excavation at the southeast corner of the same building disclosed another deposit of the same kind containing two more plates of gold and silver bearing records identical with those on the first two plates. These discoveries were made by the Persian Expedition of the Oriental Institute of The University of Chicago, which is excavating at Persepolis

the Roman Empire, to become a dangerous competitor of Christianity; for in matters of religion, as in many other things, the Persian Empire completed the breakdown of national boundaries and marked the beginning of a long period when the leading religions of the East were called upon to compete in a great contest for the mastery among all the nations (§ 1106).

SECTION 31. DECLINE OF ORIENTAL LEADERSHIP: ESTIMATE OF ORIENTAL CIVILIZATION

367. Persia was the last of the great Oriental powers. Before we turn to the rise of civilized Europe let us look back over Oriental civilization for a moment and review what it accomplished in over thirty-five hundred years.

End of leadership of Ancient Near East (after 400 B.C.)

368. First the Ancient Near East domesticated the wild animals, especially cattle, sheep, and goats, which served as food or produced food in the form of dairy products. It domesticated likewise the wild grasses, the seeds of which became our wheat, barley, and other cereal grains, which could be cultivated in large quantities. By these achievements it transformed early men from merely food-gatherers to food-producers. It invented the plow, and by substituting animal power for man power in agriculture it greatly increased the cultivated area, thus putting into the hands of government and society for the first time a large amount of portable wealth. It was these great contributions which made possible the rise of civilized society.

Achievements of Ancient Near East: first food-production

369. While Europe still lay in Stone Age barbarism the peoples of the Ancient Near East gave the world for the first time a whole group of further inventions surpassed in importance only by those of the modern world. Among these were the first highly developed practical arts, such as the use of the potter's wheel, the potter's furnace, the loom and highly elaborate weaving, the earliest metal work (including the difficult art of hollow casting), glass-making, paper-making, and many other similar industries. To distribute the products of these industries among other peoples and carry on commerce the Ancient Near East built the earliest seagoing ships propelled by sails. Its engineers were the first to move great weights and undertake large building enterprises,— large even for us of today.

Achievements of Ancient Near East: inventions

370. The Ancient Near East also gave us the earliest architecture in stone masonry, the clerestory, the colonnade, the arch, and the tower or spire. It produced the earliest refined sculpture, from the wonderful portrait figures and colossal statues of Egypt to the exquisite seals of early Babylonia. It gave us writing and the earliest alphabet. In literature it brought forth the earliest known tales in narrative prose, poems, historical works, social discussions, and even drama. It gave us the calendar we still use. It made a beginning in mathematics and laid the foundations of scientific astronomy. In this work and in the development of surgery it began the practice of a scientific attitude of mind. It first produced government on a large scale, whether of a single great nation or of an empire made up of a group of nations.

Achievements of Ancient Near East: art, writing, etc.

371. Finally, in religion the East developed the earliest belief in a sole God and his fatherly care for all men, and it laid the foundations of a religious life from which came forth the Founder of the leading religion of the civilized world today. For these things — accomplished, most of them, while Europe was still without civilization — our debt to the Ancient Near East is enormous.

Achievements of Ancient Near East: religion

372. Let us see, however, if there are not some important things which the East had not yet gained. The East had always accepted as a matter of course the rule of a king, and believed that his rule should be kindly and just. It had never occurred to anyone there that the *people* should have anything to say about how they should be governed. No one had ever gained the idea of a free citizen, a man feeling what we call patriotism, and under obligations to vote and to share in the government. Liberty as we understand it was unknown, and the rule of the people, which we call democracy, was hardly dreamed of in the Ancient Near East. Hence the life of the individual man lacked the stimulating responsibilities which come with citizenship. Such responsibilities, like that

Lack of citizenship in Ancient Near East

of thinking about public questions and then voting, or of serving as a soldier to defend the nation, quicken the mind and force men to action, and they were among the strongest influences in producing great men in Greece and Rome.

373. Just as the Orientals accepted the rule of *kings* without question, so they believed in the rule of the *gods*. It was a tradition which they and their fathers had always accepted. This limited their ideas of the world about them. They thought that every storm was due to the interference of some god, and that every eclipse must be the act of an angry god or demon. Hence the Orientals made little inquiry into the *natural* causes of such things. In general, then, they suffered from a lack of freedom of the mind, — a kind of intellectual bondage to religion and to old ideas.[1] Under these circumstances natural science could not go very far, and religion was much darkened by superstition, while art and literature lacked some of their greatest sources of stimulus and inspiration.

Lack of freedom of mind in Ancient Near East

374. There were still, therefore, boundless things for mankind to do, — in government, in thought about the natural world, in gaining deeper views of the wonders and beauties of nature, as well as in art, in literature, and in many other lines. This future progress was to be made in Europe, — that Europe which we left at the end of the second chapter in the Late Stone Age. To Europe, therefore, we must now turn, to follow across the Eastern Mediterranean the course of rising civilization as it passed from the Ancient Near East to our European forefathers from four to five thousand years ago.

Future progress to be made in Europe

[1] Some degree of intellectual freedom from tradition was earliest shown by the great unknown surgeon of Egypt (§ 119), and especially by the Egyptian king Ikhnaton, by the Hebrew prophets, and by the Chaldean astronomers; perhaps we could also include Zoroaster. But complete intellectual freedom was first attained by the Greeks.

QUESTIONS

Section 26. Explain in detail what is meant by the term "Indo-Europeans." List the various conflicts between Indo-Europeans and Semites.

Section 27. What is meant by "Highland civilization"? Discuss the first Indo-European invasion of Western Asia. Describe the civilization of the Second Hittite Empire. What influences reached the Hittites from the Fertile Crescent and from Egypt? Why did the Hittites not use their hieroglyphic writing on the clay tablets? What part did the Hittite Empire play in the progress of civilization?

Section 28. What became of the Aryan people when they left their first home? What is the chief difference between the Zoroastrian religion and the other religions which we have previously studied? When did Zoroaster live?

Sections 29–30. What race did Cyrus subdue in the Fertile Crescent? How were the Persian documents used in the decipherment of Babylonian cuneiform? Describe the organization of the Empire by Darius. Discuss his plans for commercial expansion. How did Persian architecture arise?

Section 31. What were the most important things which the Ancient Near East contributed to human life? What other important things had the Ancient Near East not yet produced?

BIBLIOGRAPHY FOR TOPICAL STUDIES

Clay tablets from Hattusas: *Classical Weekly*, Vol. XVIII, No. 22 (April 20, 1925), pp. 171–175.

The spread of Hittite civilization southward: GARSTANG, *Hittite Empire*, pp. 236–278; HOGARTH, *Ancient East*, pp. 50–52; WOOLLEY, *Dead Towns*, pp. 74–95.

The conquests of Cyrus: HOGARTH, pp. 159–167; ROGERS, *History of Ancient Persia*, pp. 35–64.

PART III · THE GREEKS

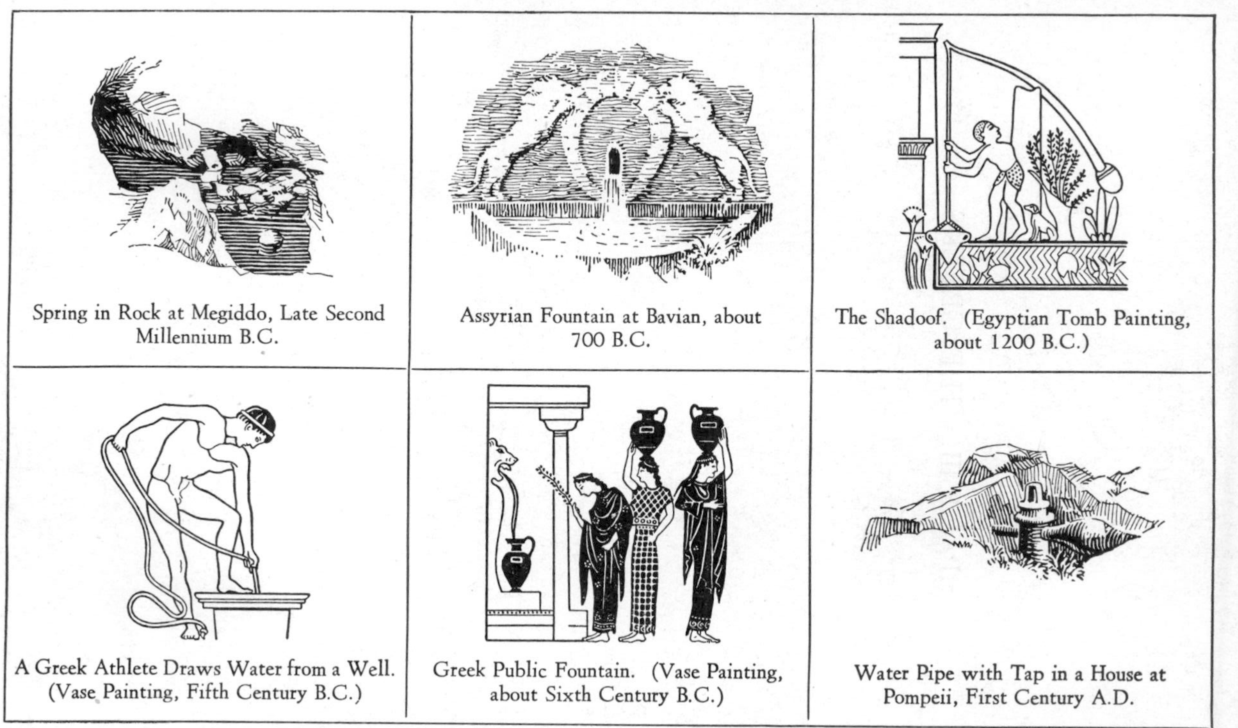

Spring in Rock at Megiddo, Late Second Millennium B.C.

Assyrian Fountain at Bavian, about 700 B.C.

The Shadoof. (Egyptian Tomb Painting, about 1200 B.C.)

A Greek Athlete Draws Water from a Well. (Vase Painting, Fifth Century B.C.)

Greek Public Fountain. (Vase Painting, about Sixth Century B.C.)

Water Pipe with Tap in a House at Pompeii, First Century A.D.

SOURCES *of Community and Household* WATER SUPPLY *in the Ancient World*

CHAPTER IX · *The Eastern Mediterranean World and the Greek Conquest*

SECTION 32. THE ÆGEAN WORLD: THE ISLANDS

375. We have already studied the life of earliest men in Europe, where we followed their progress step by step from the savagery of the earliest Stone Age hunters to the time when they received grain and live stock from the Near East, and as a result were able to shift from the wandering life of the hunter to the settled life of agriculture and cattle-breeding. At that point we were obliged to leave the Europeans and pass over to the Near East, to watch there the first appearance and the gradual growth of civilization, while all Europe remained in the barbarism of the Late Stone Age. Civilization first ap-

Appearance of civilization in southeastern Europe

NOTE. The above drawing shows us the upper part of a STONE VASE carved by a Cretan sculptor. The lower part is lost. The scene depicts a PROCESSION OF CRETAN PEASANTS with wooden pitchforks over their shoulders. Among them is a chorus of youths, or possibly maidens, with wide-open mouths, lustily singing a harvest song, doubtless in honor of the great Earth-Mother, to whom the peasants believed they owed the fertility of the earth. The music is led by a priest with head shaven after the Egyptian manner, and he carries upraised before his face a sistrum, a musical rattle which came from Egypt. The work is so wonderfully carved that we seem to feel the forward motion of the procession.

peared in Europe at its southeastern corner. If we look at a map (p. 146), we find that Europe here thrusts forward its southernmost and easternmost peninsula (Greece), with its island outposts, especially Crete, reaching far out into the Oriental waters so early crossed and recrossed by Egyptian ships. It was thus very natural that the people of this region of Europe should have been the first of all Europeans to learn something of civilization, already so many centuries old in the Near East directly alongside of them.

Ægean Sea and Ægean world

376. The most important center where civilization first appeared in Europe was the Ægean Sea. This sea is like a large lake, almost completely encircled by the surrounding lands (see map, p. 338). Around its western and northern sides stretches the mainland of Europe, on the east is Asia Minor, while the long island of Crete on the south lies like a breakwater shutting off the Mediterranean from the Ægean Sea. From north to south this lakelike sea is at no point more than four hundred miles in length, while its width varies greatly. Its coast is deeply indented with many bays and harbors, and it is so thickly sprinkled with hundreds of islands that it is often possible to sail from one island to another in an hour or two. Indeed, it is almost impossible to cross the Ægean without seeing land all the way, and in a number of directions at the same time. Just as Chicago, Milwaukee, and other towns around Lake Michigan are linked together by modern steamboats, so we shall see incoming civilization connecting the shores of the Ægean by sailing ships. This sea, therefore, with its islands and the fringe of shores around it, formed a region by itself, which we may call the Ægean world.

Climate and products of the Ægean world

377. This region of the Mediterranean enjoys a mild and sunny climate, for it lies in the belt of rainy winters and dry summers. Along the bold and broken but picturesque and beautiful shores, river valleys and small plains descend to the water's edge. These places furnish sufficient soil so that wheat and barley, grapes and olives, may be cultivated without irrigation. Hence bread, wine, and oil were the chief foods, as they are among most Mediterranean peoples to this day. Wine is their tea and coffee, and oil is their butter. So in the Homeric poems (§ 449) bread and wine are spoken of as the food of all, even of the children. In the wet season the uplands are clothed with rich green pastures, where the shepherds may graze the flocks which dot the hillsides far and near. Few regions of the world are better suited to be the home of happy and prosperous communities, grateful to the gods for all their plentiful gifts by land and sea.

The Ægean world a bridge between the Near East and Europe

378. The Ægean world was touched by the civilized life of its Oriental neighbors on the south and on the east. On the distant southern horizon lay the island of Crete, far out in the waters reached by Egyptian ships. On the east was Asia Minor, the land of the Hittites, crossed by highways leading to the Fertile Crescent. We see here, then, that the older Oriental civilizations converged upon the Ægean by two routes: *first* and earliest, by ship across the Mediterranean from Egypt; *second*, by land through Asia Minor from the Euphrates world. Thus the Ægean islands were a bridge connecting the Near East and Europe. Already in the Late Stone Age these islands had unavoidably become outposts of the great Oriental civilizations which we have found so early on the Nile and the Euphrates. It was on the Ægean *islands*, therefore, and not on the *mainland* of Europe, that the earliest high civilization on the north side of the Mediterranean grew up.

People of the Ægean world

379. It is convenient to call the earliest inhabitants of the Ægean world Ægeans, although this term is not racial but purely geographical, meaning the people of the Ægean world before the coming of the Greeks. The Ægeans were inhabiting this region when civilization dawned there (about 3000 B.C.), and they continued to live there for many centuries before the people known to us as the Greeks entered the region. Among the earliest Ægeans were immigrants from Asia Minor, but the majority of these Ægeans, the predecessors of the Greeks in the northern Mediterranean, belonged to the Mediterranean race (Fig. 80). At a time far earlier than any of our written records they not only occupied the mainland of Greece and the islands of the Ægean but had also settled on the neighboring shores of Asia Minor.

From the beginning the leader among the island peoples of the Ægean was Crete. In the Late Stone Age there were already close communications between Crete and Asia Minor. It is known that some of the round-headed people of the Highland Zone migrated from Asia Minor and settled in Crete. They brought with them the Late Stone Age life of the Highland Zone, including the belief in the great Earth-Mother. As a result the religion of Crete always had many beliefs in common with that of the Highland Zone people of Asia Minor. Until as late as about 3000 B.C. the island of Crete, with a population made up of a mixture of the Mediterranean race and a sprinkling of the round-heads from the Highland Zone of Asia Minor, was still living in Late Stone Age barbarism largely drawn from neighboring Western Asia. At Cnossus the wreckage of their Late Stone Age huts was found buried thirty-five feet under the ruins of the palaces later erected there.

Rise of Cretan civilization under Egyptian influence

380. It was a voyage of only one hundred and eighty miles from the northern coast of Africa to the nearest port on the southern coast of Crete, which had therefore long been the link between Egypt on the south and the Ægean Sea on the north (see map, p. 146). A copper ax was found still lying in a Late Stone Age settlement beneath the palaces of Cnossus, showing that Crete probably received copper from the ships of the Nile by 3000 B.C. For a thousand years afterward their progress was slow, but it gained for them some very important things. While the great pyramids of Egypt were being built the Cretan craftsmen learned from their Egyptian neighbors the use of the potter's wheel and the closed oven. They could then shape and bake much finer clay jars and vases.

They learned also to hollow out hard varieties of stone and to make beautifully wrought stone vases, bowls, and jars. These new products of Cretan industries are so much like the work of the Egyptian craftsmen whose workshops we have seen in the pyramid cemeteries that it has been thought there must have been a colony of workmen from the Nile who actually migrated from Egypt to Crete, where they instructed the Cretan craftsmen. The same influence is observable in the growth of Cretan writing. Like the Egyptians and Babylonians, the Cretans employed at first crude picture records. On the tablets so far examined the number of these picture signs, or hieroglyphs, is about one hundred and thirty-five. These picture signs gradually developed into phonetic writing (about 2000 B.C.), — the earliest writing in Europe (if we may regard the islands of the Ægean world as a part of Europe).

381. By 2000 B.C. the Cretans had become a highly civilized people. Near the coast, for convenient access to ships, were the manufacturing towns, with thriving industries in pottery and metal work, which enabled them to trade with other peoples. Farther inland the green valleys of the island must have been filled with prosperous villages cultivating their fields of grain and pasturing their flocks. At Cnossus, not far from the middle of the northern coast (see map, p. 338), there grew up a kingdom which may finally have included a large part of the island. The Late Stone Age town at Cnossus had long since fallen to ruin and been forgotten. Over a deep layer of its rubbish a line of progressive Cretan kings now built a fine palace arranged in the Egyptian manner, with a large number of rooms clustered around a central court. Farther inland toward the south shore arose another palace at Phæstus, perhaps another residence of the same royal family or the capital of a second kingdom.

Rise of sea-kings of Crete (2000 B.C.)

382. These palaces were not fortified castles, for neither they nor the towns connected with them possessed any protecting walls. But the Cretan kings were not without means of defense. They already had their palace armories, where brazen armor and weapons were stored. Hundreds of bronze arrowheads, with the charred shafts of the arrows, along with written lists of weapons and armor and chariots, have been found still lying in the ruins of the armory rooms in the palace at Cnossus. Troops to use these weapons were of course not lacking. Moreover, the Cretan kings early began to build ships both for commerce and for warfare, and it has become a modern habit to call them the "sea-kings of Crete."[1]

Power of sea-kings of Crete

383. Cretan industries henceforth flourished as never before. The potters of Cnossus began to produce exquisite cups as thin and delicate as modern porcelain teacups. These and their pottery jars and vases they painted in bright colors with decorative designs, which made them the most beautiful ware to be had in the East (Fig. 140, *A*). Such ware was in demand in the houses of the rich as far away as the Nile, just as fine French table porcelain is widely sold outside of France at the present day. The new many-colored Cretan vases were so highly prized by the Egyptian nobles of the Feudal Age that they even placed them in their tombs for use in the next world. In these Egyptian tombs modern excavators have recovered them, to tell us the story of the wide popularity of Cretan industrial art in the Nineteenth and Twentieth Centuries B.C. Egyptian ships, common in the Eastern Mediterranean before 3000 B.C., must have been frequent visitors in the Cretan harbors. At the same time the prevailing north wind of summer easily carried the galleys, which the Cretans had learned to build, across to the harbor in the western corner of the Nile Delta, which had flourished there since the days of the First Union. In Egypt the Cretans found a good market for their wares, which they exchanged for many things not found in Crete.

Expansion of Cretan commerce and industry

[1] The sea power of the Cretans has been much exaggerated by recent writers. One of the old Cretan sea-kings, according to later tradition, was named Minos. For this reason early Cretan civilization has been called Minoan, and this is now the most common term applied to it, but in this text we have used the term "Ægean." For the term "Mycenæan" see § 392.

PLATE III. *Restoration of* QUEEN'S APARTMENT *at Cnossus*

The gossiping ladies, the gloves, the pottery jars, metal vase, and other details are restored after relief scenes or objects actually excavated. The rooms themselves are carefully reconstructed in accordance with remains found in the ruins: red gypsum pavement slabs, the carbonized wood of the benches, the fragments of relief panels, friezes, frescoes, and the like. (After Sir Arthur Evans)

FIG. 140. *Two Cretan Vases showing Progress in the Art of Decoration*

The first vase (*A*) is an example of the earlier pottery, painted on a dark background with rich designs in white, orange, crimson, red, and yellow. The potters who made such vases were, together with the seal-cutters, the first really gifted decorative artists to arise in Crete. They flourished from 2000 B.C. onward, in the days of the first palace of Cnossus. We should notice that their designs do not picture carefully anything in nature, like flowers or animals (even though a hint of a lotus flower appears in the angle of the spiral), but the figures are almost purely *imaginative* and drawn from Egyptian art. The second vase (*B*), however, some five hundred years later than the first, shows how the artists of the Grand Age had learned from Egyptian decorative art to take their decorative figures from the *natural* world, for the design consists chiefly of Egyptian lotus flowers. (See § 386.) Such designs were no longer in many colors; on this jar, indeed, they are molded in relief. This jar (*B*) is nearly four feet high, much larger than the first example (*A*). Stone and metal vases of the Grand Age were sometimes superbly decorated with bands of human figures in action

New civilized world of the Eastern Mediterranean

384. About 1700 B.C. the Egyptians and the Cretans both advanced to a new period of power and splendor. This advance created a civilized world of the Eastern Mediterranean, which was to be the source of civilization for Europe and the West. It arose like a great light whose beams penetrated to the gates of the Atlantic at the west end of the Mediterranean and far across the Late Stone Age settlements of Europe, which still lay in the darkness of stagnant barbarism.

385. In this new age the expansion of Cretan business began to require much greater speed and convenience in writing than was possible in using the old picture signs. As a result, just as in Egypt and Babylonia, these picture signs were gradually much abbreviated and reduced to simpler forms, each picture thus becoming only a few strokes. In this more rapid hand, called *linear* writing, the pictures had mostly disappeared, and the number of signs seems to have been less than a hundred. Crete had no papyrus marshes and therefore could not manufacture papyrus paper. Cretan ships, however, had brought back clay-tablet bills of merchandise from the ports of Asia, and thus the Cretans learned to write their new linear hand on clay tablets. In the armory of the new palace, which had arisen on the ruins of the old one at Cnossus, the chests of arms and weapons had each a clay-tablet label hanging in front of it. Great numbers of such clay tablets stored in chests seem to have contained the records, invoices, and bookkeeping lists necessary in conducting the affairs of a large royal household. Masses of these have been found covered by the rubbish and ruins of the fallen palace. In spite of much study, scholars are not yet able to read these precious records, the earliest known writing on the borders of the European world.

The development of Cretan linear writing

386. In the closest contact with Egypt, Cretan civilization now rose to its highest level, and the Cretans entered upon what we may call their Grand Age (1600–1400 B.C.). The older palace of Cnossus had been succeeded by a larger and more splendid building (Fig. 141). In the works of art which filled it we can watch the life of Crete unfolding in all directions. The new palace itself, with its colonnaded hall, its fine stairways, and its impressive open areas, represented the first real architecture in the northern Mediterranean. The palace walls were painted with fresh and beautiful scenes from daily life, all aquiver with movement and action; or, by adopting the Egyptian art of glassmaking, the Cretans adorned them with

The Grand Age in Crete and its art (1600–1400 B.C.)

glazed figures attached to the surface of the wall. The pottery painters had by this time given up the use of many colors. They now employed one dark tone on a light background, or they modeled the design in relief. Thus noble vases were painted in grand designs drawn from plant life or often from the life of the sea, where the Cretans were now more and more at home. On this wonderful pottery we find the most powerful, vigorous, and impressive decorative art of the early Oriental world. Indeed, it belongs among the finest works of decorative art ever produced by any people.

Fig. 141. Restoration *of North* Entrance Passage *in Cretan Palace of the Grand Age at Cnossus*

In the foreground may be seen the inner gateway before which the sentinel stands. On the other side of the gate the passage rises toward the central court (compare Fig. 146). Overlooking the ascending passage on either side are porticos, upon the walls of which were painted scenes of bull-catching and bull-grappling. This restoration was made by Sir Arthur Evans, whose remarkable excavations at Cnossus not only have uncovered the royal palaces but have revealed the whole development of Cretan civilization beginning back with the Stone Age settlement over which the palaces were built. (After Sir Arthur Evans)

Free development of Cretan art under Egyptian influence

387. The method of use and the execution of the work everywhere shows that this art was developing under the influence of Egypt, — for example, walls covered with colored glazed tiles were in use in Egypt nearly two thousand years earlier than in Crete. But the Cretan artist did not follow slavishly the Egyptian model. A growing plant painted on an Egyptian wall seems sometimes so rigid and stiff that it looks as if done with a stencil. The Cretan artist, on the other hand, drew the same plant with such free and splendidly curving lines that we seem to feel the wind swaying the stems, giving us "the soft eye-music of slow-moving boughs." The Cretan sculptor in ivory too, as well as the goldsmith and worker in bronze, wrought masterpieces which remain today among the world's greatest works of art. It is clear that the splendid creations of these free and vigorous artists of Crete had a great influence upon the art of their teachers in Egypt.

City of Cnossus

388. The palace of Cnossus looked out upon a town of plain, sun-dried brick houses. Immediately surrounding the palace was a residential quarter of the larger houses occupied by the nobles and the wealthy Cretans, probably including also the prosperous shipowning merchants. The extent of the dwellings in this aristocratic palace quarter would indicate that it housed about twelve thousand people. Outside of this palace quarter was a broad fringe of smaller and poorer houses which sheltered the traders, potters, metal workers, painters, and other craftsmen, though many of these also lived and worked in the palace itself. This surrounding industrial quarter may have had a population of some seventy thousand souls. Thus the city of Cnossus, with probably over eighty thousand people, was the first large city of Europe. Confident in the strength of their war fleet, the sea-kings of Crete did not surround their city with any protecting wall.

Nobles who lived about the king

389. The lords and ladies of this first city of Europe lived an astonishingly free and modern life. The ladies crowded the palace terraces or grandstands and watched their champions struggling in fierce boxing matches, in which the contestants wore heavy metal helmets; or the assembled court cheered the plucky bull-fighters tossed on the horns of wild bulls, — descendants of those huge creatures which were hunted by the Late Stone Age men of Europe several thousand years before (see Fig. 18). Some of these people lived in comfortable quarters

Fig. 142. *Ivory and Gold* Statuette *of a Cretan Lady of the Grand Age*

The proud little figure stands with shoulders thrown far back and arms extended, each hand grasping a golden serpent, which coils about her arms to the elbow. She wears a high tiara perched daintily on her elaborately curled hair. Her dress consists of a flounced skirt and a tight bodice tapering to her slender waist. The whole forms a costume so surprisingly modern that this little Cretan lady would hardly have created any comment if she had appeared so dressed on one of our crowded city streets in the "gay nineties." The figure is carved in ivory, while the flounces are edged with bands of gold, and the belt about the waist is of the same metal. She represents either the great Cretan mother goddess or possibly only a graceful snake-charmer of the court. In any case, the sculptor has given her the appearance of one of the noble ladies of his time. Even the Greek sculptor never surpassed the vitality and the winsome charm which passed from the fingers of the ancient Cretan artist into this tiny figure. (Courtesy of the Museum of Fine Arts, Boston)

FIG. 143. *Cretan* LORDS AND LADIES *on the* TERRACES *of the Palace of* CNOSSUS

This scene was painted on the walls of the palace as part of the interior wall decoration. It has been somewhat restored as shown above, but it forms a remarkable example of the Cretan artist's ability to produce the impression of an animated multitude of people seen from a distance and blending into a somewhat confused whole. Some of the women have been painted in detail, but the heads of many more have been sketched lightly on the white background. As a whole the men are distinguished by a broad wash of dark background. (Combined and restored after Sir Arthur Evans)

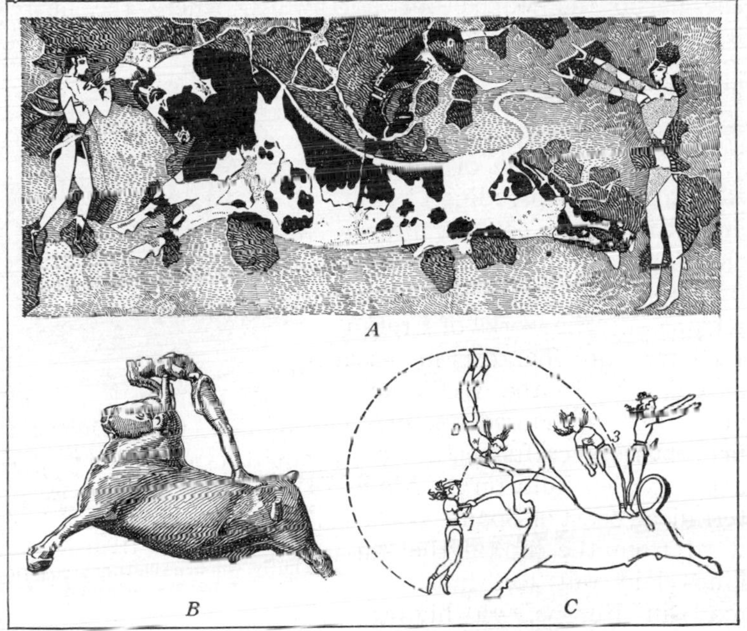

FIG. 144. *Ægean* ACROBATS *in the Bull-Ring*

A is a much-broken wall painting; *B* is a small bronze. In *C* Sir Arthur Evans has suggested in a modern drawing his idea of the successive positions of the bull and the athlete (numbered from 1 to 4) based on a study of *A* and *B* and other ancient sources. As the bull charges, the performer seizes the horns of the animal (*A*, and *C*, 1). Thereupon the bull attempts to toss the acrobat, thus lifting him and enabling him to complete his first backward somersault, so that, letting go the horns of the bull, the acrobat lands on the animal's back. He then either comes down on his hands on the bull's back and shifts to his feet (*A*, and *C*, 3) or he reaches his feet immediately on relinquishing the horns (*B*). Finally, standing on the back of the galloping bull, the athlete takes off in a final leap (*C*, 4). Both boys and girls engaged in this dangerous sport. Modern rodeo experts have reported that these acrobatic feats which seem to be clearly indicated by the ancient sources, are quite impossible, at least to modern cowboys and circus performers. (After Sir Arthur Evans)

in the palace, where they even had bathrooms and sanitary drainage and were surrounded by refined and cultured life.

390. From the palace of Cnossus the Cretan king could issue at the North Gate and, mounting his chariot, ride in half an hour to the harbor, three and a half miles away. At the harbor he looked out northward, where the nearest islands of the Ægean could be clearly seen breaking the northern horizon (see map I, p. 306). Here the trading galleys of the Cretan kings were spreading Cretan art and industries not only among the islands of the Ægean but also far and wide through the Mediterranean. The works of Cretan craftsmen are found as far east as Cyprus. In the West excavation has uncovered the products of Cretan craftsmen in Sicily and very plentifully on the Mediterranean coast of Spain. Southward from the capital the sea-kings laid out the first built road in Europe, — a highway across the island leading to the ports on the southern coast. There were the busy docks piled high with the merchandise en route to and from the already ancient land of the Nile. These Cretan fleets formed the earliest naval power which grew up in the northern Mediterranean, and the student should contrast with them the dugouts of the Late Stone Age. Nevertheless the kings of Crete were not wholly independent. An Egyptian general of Thutmose III (§ 133), in the Fifteenth Century B.C., bore the title of "governor of the islands in the midst of the sea," as the Egyptians called the islands of the Ægean. The sea-kings at Cnossus, therefore, must have come to terms with the Pharaohs as their overlords.

Crete's political and commercial position in the Grand Age

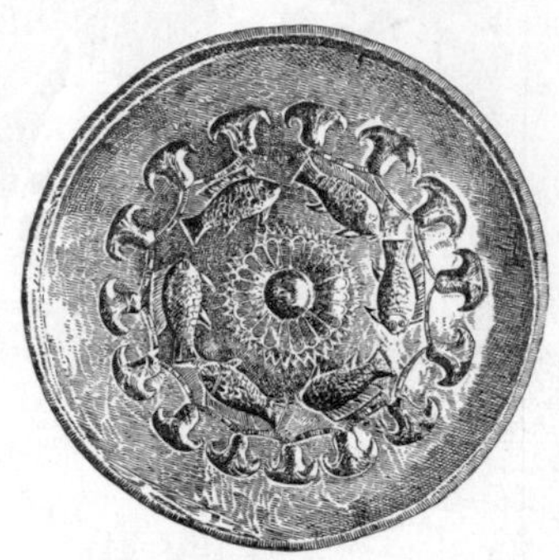

Fig. 145. *Golden* Dish *of the* Egyptian Governor *of the Ægean Islands in the Grand Age*

This golden dish was given by the Pharaoh Thutmose III to his general Thutiy, whom he had made governor of the Ægean Islands

391. Besides the two older centers of civilization on the Nile and the Two Rivers in this age, there thus grew up here in the Eastern Mediterranean, as a *third* great civilization, this splendid world of Crete and the Ægean Sea. It is this third great civilization which forms the chief link between the civilization of the Ancient Near East and the later progress of man in Greece and western Europe. As we have already seen, Asia Minor was also a very important link between the Near East and Europe. To the mainland, therefore, we must now turn, first in Europe and then in Asia Minor.

Crete, the third great civilization in the ancient world

SECTION 33. THE ÆGEAN WORLD: THE MAINLAND

392. The mainland, both in Europe and in Asia Minor, had continued to lag behind the advanced civilization of the islands. Into mainland Greece the Late Stone Age highlanders overflowed from Asia Minor, as we have seen they also overflowed into Crete, and this Late Stone Age barbarism yielded very slowly to the influence of Cretan and Egyptian civilization. As the fleets of Egypt and of Crete pushed their commerce with the mainland of Greece they naturally entered the southern bays, and especially the Gulf of Argos, which looks southward directly toward Crete (see map I, p. 306). Here in the plain of Argos, behind the sheltered harbor, it is not impossible that Cretan nobles, migrating to the mainland, established their settlements. Exposed as they were to barbarian migrations from the north, they dared not live without protecting walls as the sea-kings of Crete were doing. At Tiryns and Mycenæ they built massive strongholds, with foundations and walls of heavy stone masonry (Fig. 146). The Ægean princes who built such strongholds a little after 1500 B.C. imported works of Cretan and Egyptain art in pottery and metal. These triumphs of Cretan art, with fragments of Egyptian glaze and wall decorations, still surviving in the ruins of palaces and tombs, are today the earliest tokens of a life of higher refinement on the continent of Europe. This period (about 1500 to 1200 B.C.) is commonly known as the Mycenæan Age, after Mycenæ, where such civilization was first discovered.

Cretan civilization and the Greek mainland; the Mycenæan Age

393. But the mainland still lagged behind the islands, and civilization remained a narrow fringe along the coast. For a thousand years after the rise of the brilliant Cretan civilization the towns and the villages of the Late Stone Age men behind Thessaly still stretched northward and westward far across Europe. The smoke of their settlements rose through the forests and high over the lakes and valleys of Switzerland. Their roofs dotted the plains and nestled in the inlets of the sea, whence they were thickly strewn far up the winding valleys of the rivers into inner Europe. It was therefore the rivers which furnished the natural routes along which the products of Near Eastern civilization were carried by the traders into the interior of Europe. We have already learned that the most important of these routes was the valley of the Danube, for the lower course of the Danube is nearer to Asia Minor and the Near East than any other great river of Europe. Moving

Europe remains in Late Stone Age barbarism

FIG. 146. RESTORATION *of the* CASTLE *and* PALACE *of Tiryns*

Unlike the Cretan palaces, this dwelling of an Ægean (or perhaps Greek) prince is massively fortified. A rising road (*A*) leads up to the main gate (*B*), where the great walls are double. An assaulting party, bearing their shields on the *left* arm, must here (*C, D*) march with the exposed *right* side toward the castle. By the gate (*E*) the visitor reaches the large court (*F*) on which the palace faces. The main entrance of the palace (*G*) leads to its forecourt (*H*), where the excavators found the place of the household altar of the king. Behind the forecourt (*H*) is the main hall of the palace (*I*). This was the earliest castle in Europe with outer walls of stone. The villages of the common people clustered about the foot of the castle hill. The whole formed the nucleus of a city-state in the plain of Argos. (After Luckenbach)

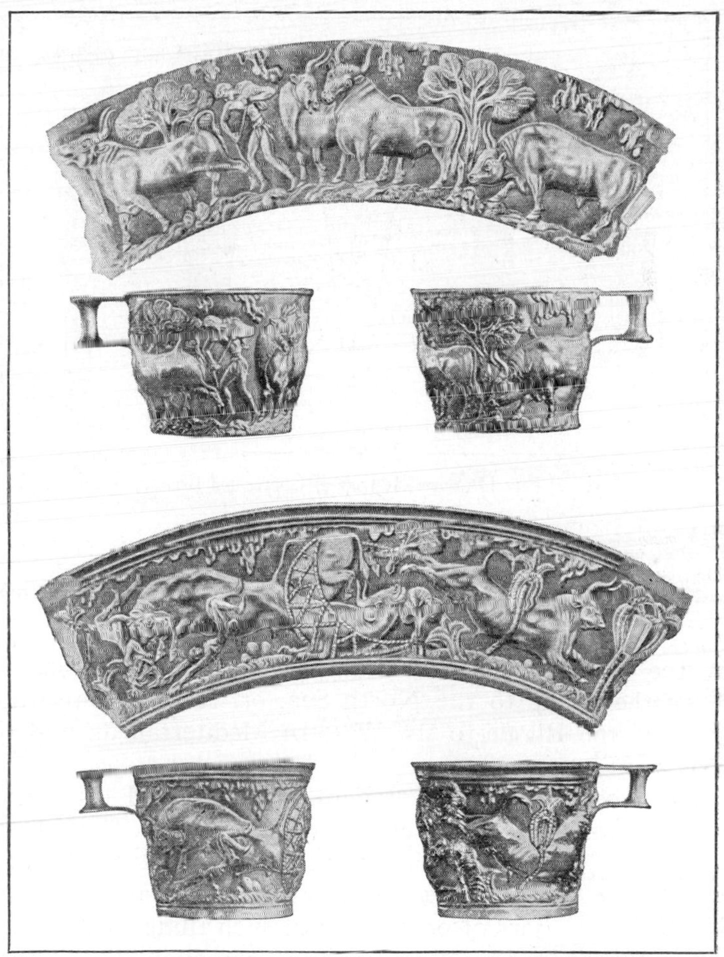

Fig. 147. *Wild-Bull* Hunt *pictured on Two Golden Cups*

These cups were found at Vaphio, near Sparta, whither they were imported from Crete. The goldsmith beat out the marvelous designs with a hammer and punch over a mold, and then put in finer details with a graving tool. His work must be ranked among the greatest works of art ever produced. The scene on the upper cup is concerned with the capture of a half-wild bull by trickery. On the lower cup are shown incidents in bull-grappling and in snaring with the net

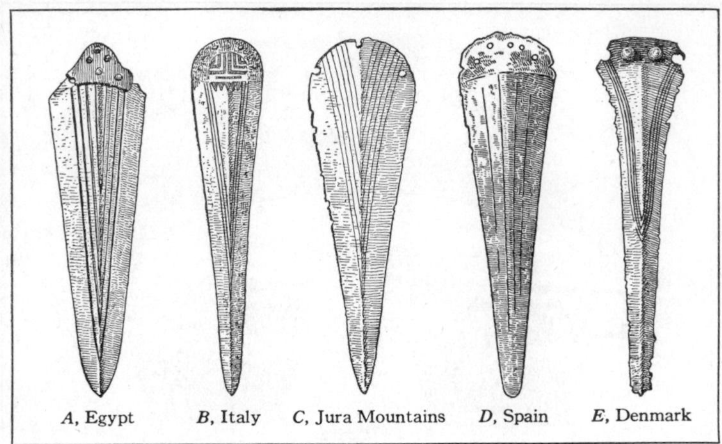

Fig. 148. *Series of Five* Dagger Blades *of Copper and Bronze, showing Influence passing from Egypt to Denmark*

The lost handles were of wood, bone, or ivory, and the rivet holes for fastening them can still be seen. We see in this series how the early Egyptian form (*A*) passed from Egypt through the Mediterranean to Spain (*D*) and across Europe to the Scandinavian countries (*E*)

up the Danube, the trade from the Near East now passed down the Rhine to the North Sea, or, turning southward, followed the Rhone to the Western Mediterranean and the coasts of Spain.

Copper introduced into Late Stone Age Europe

394. The visits of the traders who traversed these river routes from the coast were welcome events. Their wares were eagerly purchased. Some of the Late Stone Age villagers bargained for decorated jars of pottery; but such things were fragile and could not be carried far by land, or in quantities. Others preferred necklaces of glittering blue-glaze beads. Great was the interest when the traders exhibited shining beads or neck-rings of a strange, heavy, gleaming, reddish substance, so beautiful that the villagers trafficked eagerly for them. Most desired of all, however, was the dagger or ax-head made of the same unknown substance. Such ax-heads, although they were much thinner than the stone axes, did

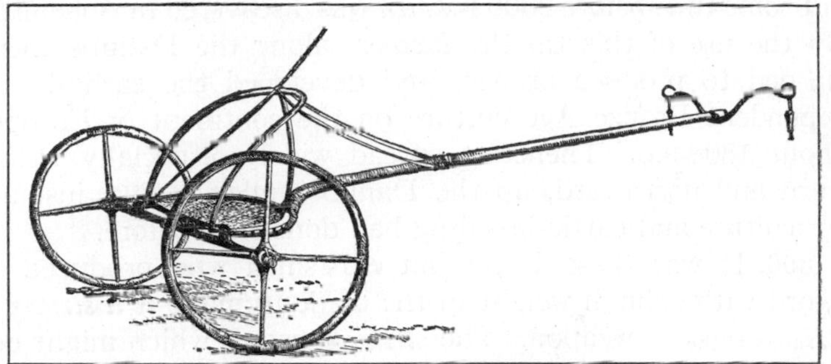

FIG. 149. CHARIOT *made by the Mechanics of Bronze Age Europe*

This chariot is built of elm and ash, with bindings of birch fiber. The birch does not grow south of the Mediterranean, and hence the chariot must have been made on the north side of the Mediterranean. It shows us what good woodwork the Bronze Age craftsmen of Europe could do with bronze tools. It is also an evidence of the far-reaching commerce of the Bronze Age; for it was transported across the Mediterranean to Egypt, where it was placed in a cliff-tomb, to be used by some wealthy Egyptian after death. There it has survived in perfect condition to our day

not break like these, and could be ground to a better edge than the ground-stone ax ever gained. We can imagine with what rapt attention and awestruck faces these Late Stone Age Europeans listened to the traders' tales, telling of huge ships which brought these things to Europe, and which made the rude European dugouts look like tiny chips. Thus, at the dawn of history, barbarian Europe looked across the Mediterranean to the great civilizations of the Nile, the Ægean, and Western Asia, as the North American Indians fixed their wondering eyes on the first Europeans who landed in America, and listened to like strange tales of great and distant peoples.

The discovery of tin and the rise of the Danubian civilization

395. Slowly Europe learned the use of metal. Having reached the islands of southeastern Europe about 3000 B.C., metal passed by slow stages, in the course of a thousand years, into northern and western Europe. It long continued to be used side by side with stone, and it was nearly 2000 B.C. before it gained the leading place as the material for tools and weapons. In the beginning the metal used was copper, but some time before 2000 B.C. *tin* was discovered in Bohemia. By the use of this tin the farmers along the Danube then learned to produce bronze, and developed the earliest independent Bronze Age culture on the continent of Europe about 1800 B.C. Thence it spread widely, especially westward and northward, up the Danube valley (§ 39), just as agriculture and cattle-breeding had done long before.

396. It was these Danubian craftsmen who produced a sword with enough weight in the blade to make it a *striking* weapon. The *striking* sword, which might be brought down upon the foe like the blow of an ax, was far more formidable than the *thrusting* sword, which, as it had been received from Egypt, was only an elongated dagger. The possession of this heavy striking sword gave Europe an enormous military advantage over the Near East and was to alter the course of history.

Invention of the striking sword

397. Notwithstanding the rise of this important Danubian civilization and the development of a more civilized life in general, the Bronze Age peoples of Europe did not advance to a high type of civilization. They still remained everywhere without writing, without architecture in hewn-stone masonry, and without large sailing ships for commerce. The failure to make progress in architecture beyond such rough stone structures as Stonehenge is an illustration of this backwardness of western and northern Europe.

Backwardness of European Bronze Age civilization

398. Along the Asiatic side of the Ægean Sea we find much earlier progress than on the European side, although this was but slightly due to the commerce from Crete, which seems to have had little effect along the shores of Asia Minor. Until after 3000 B.C. all Asia Minor was still without metal, but excavation has not yet found many of the Late Stone Age settlements, which were probably scattered far across the hills and valleys of the Highland Zone (§ 321 and Fig. 125). In the days when Crete was first receiving metal there arose at the northwest corner of Asia Minor a shabby little Late Stone

Late Stone Age on Asiatic mainland (about 3000 B.C.)

FIG. 150. *The* MOUND *containing the* NINE CITIES *of Ancient Troy (Ilium)*

When Schliemann first visited this mound in 1868, it was about 125 feet high, and the Turks were cultivating grain on its summit. In 1870 he excavated a pit like a crater in the top of the hill, passing downward in the course of four years through nine successive cities built each on the ruins of its predecessors. At the bottom of his pit Schliemann found the original once bare hilltop, about 75 feet high, on which the men of the Late Stone Age had established a small settlement of sun-baked brick houses about 3000 B.C. Above the scanty ruins of this Late Stone Age settlement rose, in layer after layer, the ruins of the later cities, with the Roman buildings at the top. The entire depth of 50 feet of ruins represented a period of about thirty-five hundred years from the First (Stone Age) City to the Ninth (or Roman) City. The Second City contained the earliest copper found and a splendid treasure of golden jewelry. This Schliemann believed to be the Troy of Homer's Greek heroes, but we now know that this Second City was built a thousand years before Homer's Troy, which was the Sixth City (see Fig. 151). An American expedition under Professor Semple has resumed excavation here

Age village known to us as Troy. It was probably built by traders attracted by the profitable traffic which was already crossing back and forth between Asia and Europe at this point (see map I, p. 306).

Growth of Troy (2500–1500 B.C.)

399. By 2500 B.C., some centuries after the first metal had been introduced, the rulers of Troy were wealthy commercial kings, and their castle was the earliest fortress in the Ægean world, for it was a thousand years older than the fortresses at Mycenæ and Tiryns. During this thousand years (2500–1500 B.C.) Troy was rebuilt several times, and even when conquered and destroyed, it always regained its prosperity. One cause of this prosperity was probably the importation of tin from the Danube and the development of a profitable industry in bronze. Finally Troy must have controlled a kingdom of considerable extent in northwestern Asia Minor. Thus about 1500 B.C. the splendid and cultivated city of Troy was a powerful stronghold (Sixth City) which had grown up as a northern rival of that sumptuous Cnossus that we have seen in the south. The two rival cities faced each other from opposite ends of the Ægean, but we infer that Cnossus was superior in civilization, for it is still uncertain whether the Trojans of this age could write.

Discovery of Ægean civilization by Schliemann

400. We have been putting together the story of the rise and early history of civilization in the Ægean world and in neighboring Europe and Asia. Only a few years ago this story was entirely unknown. As late as 1870 no one supposed that civilized people had lived in the Ægean world before the Greeks arrived there. Much less did anyone dream that we should ever be able to find the actual handiwork of the predecessors of the Greeks in the Ægean world. The discoverer of the Ægean civilization which we have been studying was Heinrich Schliemann.

Schliemann's excavations: Troy; Tiryns and Mycenæ

401. It was as the fulfillment of a dream of his youth[1] that Schliemann led a body of Turkish laborers to begin excavations in the great mound of Troy in 1870 (see map I, p. 306). In less than four years he uncovered the central portions of nine successive cities. Schliemann believed the Second City to be the Troy of Homer's Greek heroes (but see Fig. 151). He then crossed to the mainland of Greece and began excavating the prehistoric fortress or castle of Mycenæ, where he found a group of tomb chambers containing a magnificent series of vessels and ornaments in gold, including an elaborate golden crown, indicating the royalty of one of the dead. Again Schliemann thought that these things belonged to the Greek heroes of the Trojan wars, but in reality they were older. At the neighboring prehistoric castle of Tiryns Schliemann made similar discoveries. Thus within a

[1] Schliemann was an American citizen of German birth. Before coming to America he had been shipwrecked on the coast of Holland, where he began business, while a mere lad, as a clerk in a little grocery. In the brief intervals of leisure between dealing out smoked herring and rolls of butter he taught himself Greek and began to read Homer. In the infatuated ears of this enthusiastic boy the shouts of the Greek heroes on the plain of Troy mingled with the jingle of small change and the rustle of wrapping paper in the dingy little Dutch grocery. He had not lost this fascinating vision of the early world when, years afterward, he retired from business, after having won a large fortune in Russian petroleum.

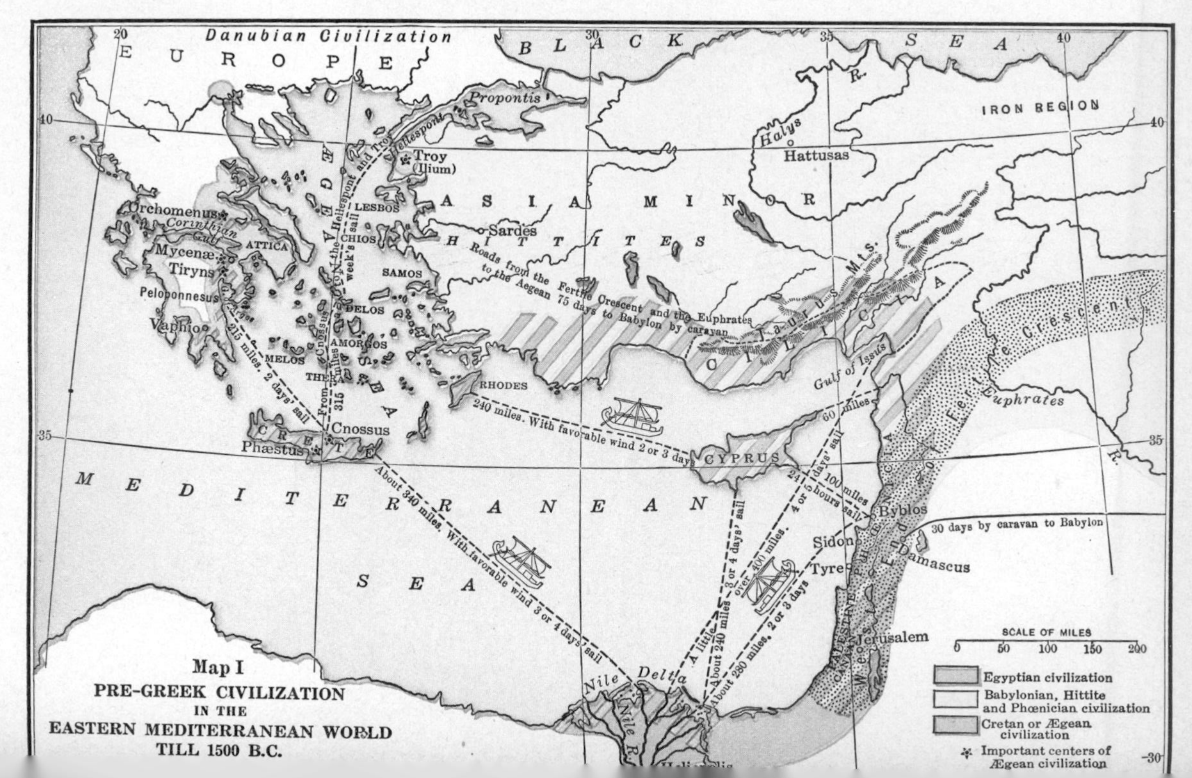

Map I
PRE-GREEK CIVILIZATION
IN THE
EASTERN MEDITERRANEAN WORLD
TILL 1500 B.C.

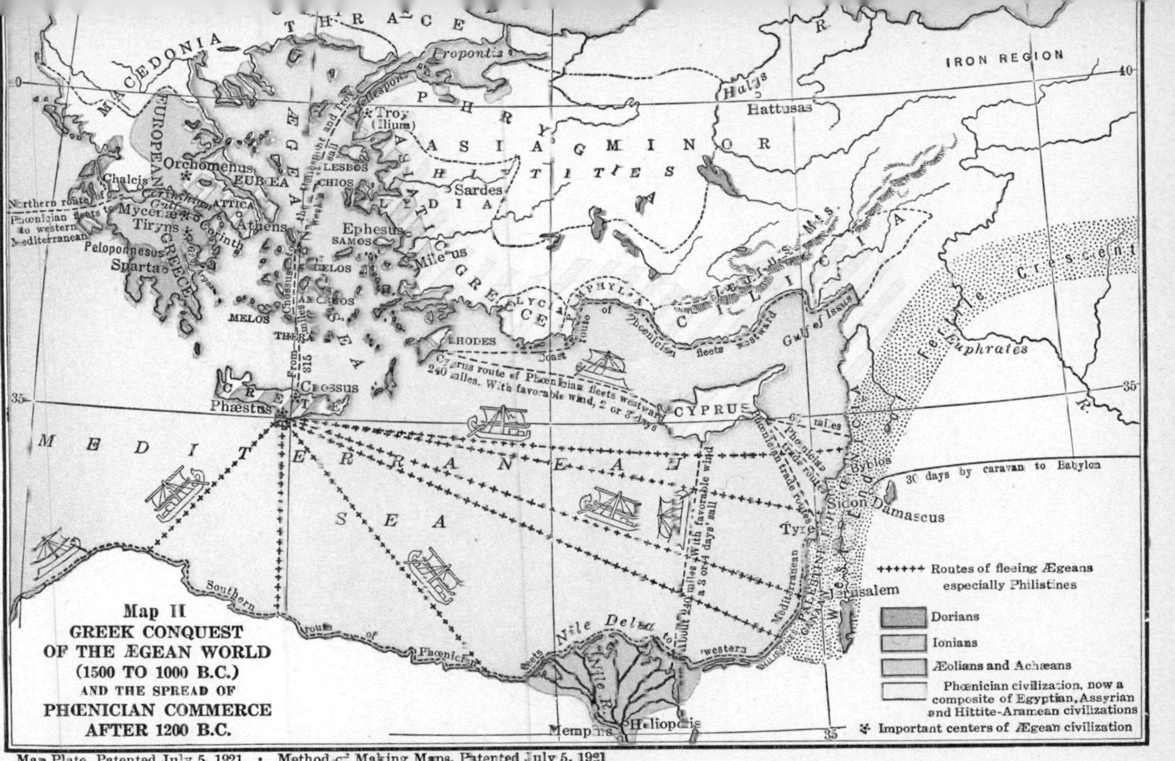

Map Plate, Patented July 5, 1921 • Method of Making Maps, Patented July 5, 1921

SEQUENCE MAP OF THE EASTERN MEDITERRANEAN WORLD FROM THE GRAND AGE OF CRETAN CIVILIZATION (ABOUT 1500 B.C.) TO THE CONQUEST OF THE ÆGEAN BY THE GREEKS

Fig. 151. *The* Walls *of Homeric* Troy (*Built about* 1500 b.c.)

A section of the outer walls of the Sixth City in the mound of Troy. The sloping outer surface of the walls faces toward the right; the inside of the city is on the left. These are the walls built in the days when Mycenæ was flourishing,— walls which protected the inhabitants of the place from the assaults of the Greeks in a remote war which laid it in ruins after 1200 b.c., — a war of which vague traditions and heroic tales have survived in the Homeric poems (§ 449). The walls of the houses of the Seventh City are visible here, resting on those of the Sixth. Schliemann never saw the walls of the Sixth City, because as he dug down in the middle of the mound inside the ancient walls, he covered the walls of the Sixth City with the rubbish he dug out

few years there was disclosed to us a new and entirely unknown world of civilization in the Ægean, which had flourished for centuries before the Greeks appeared there.

Original home of early Ægean civilization

402. The question of the original home of this early Ægean civilization, however, was not settled by Schliemann's work. Since 1900 the excavations in Crete have revealed it as the place where Ægean civilization made its start, and the center from which it passed to the other islands and to the mainland of Greece at Tiryns and Mycenæ. American explorers have had an honorable share in these discoveries, but the credit has been due chiefly to the remarkable excavations of Sir Arthur Evans, the English archæologist, at the city of Cnossus.

403. These discoveries, added to the earlier story of discovery in the Near Eastern lands east and south of the Mediterranean, show us how the civilized peoples all around the eastern end of the Mediterranean, by their industries and commerce, were gradually creating a civilized world of which the Ægean Sea was merely a northern bay. We recall that our first glimpse of this Eastern Mediterranean world was gained from the representations of Egyptian ships which crossed the Eastern Mediterranean nearly three thousand years before the Christian Era (Fig. 56). But now we have studied the peoples on the east and north of the Mediterranean and have seen how, at the close of the Grand Age in Crete, the splendid Ægean civilization had been mingling for centuries with the older Near Eastern civilizations, especially that of the Nile but also with that of Hittite Asia Minor, and through it with the civilization of the Fertile Crescent.

Rise of an Eastern Mediterranean world (3000 to 1200 B.C.)

404. We have seen how the successive Indo-European migrations penetrated the Fertile Crescent and Asia Minor. We are now to see these Indo-European invasions entering likewise the Eastern Mediterranean world. Into this civilized world of the Eastern Mediterranean, with its arts, its industries, and its far-reaching commerce, the uncivilized Indo-Europeans of the north, from behind the Balkan mountains and the Black Sea, were now beginning to intrude. These uncivilized northern Indo-Europeans included, besides others, the earliest Greeks. They were soon to overwhelm the Eastern Mediterranean, and with these northern intruders we must begin not only a new chapter in the history of the Eastern Mediterranean world but an entirely new epoch in the history of man.

Northern intruders

SECTION 34. THE COMING OF THE GREEKS

405. We have watched the invading Indo-European peoples conquering first the Highland Zone, then the Fertile Crescent, and finally even Egypt. Thus in the two thousand years between 2500 and 500 B.C. the Indo-Europeans took possession of practically the entire Near East. We must notice the difference between the invasion of an army, which is not usually lasting, and a permanent migration. In the East the Indo-European immigrants actually settled mainly in the Highland Zone, and to some extent in the Fertile Crescent. These important movements caused great changes not only on the Asiatic and African mainland but likewise in the entire Eastern Mediterranean world. The Indo-European immigrants who had entered Europe were already moving toward the Ægean world as far back as 2000 B.C. They were a large group of tribes whom we now call Greeks. While their eastern kindred were moving southward on the *east* side of the Caspian, as we have seen, the Greeks on the *west* side of the Black Sea were likewise shifting southward from their northern pastures, perhaps along the lower Danube (see map II, p. 306). Some of them possibly crossed the Hellespont and first settled in western Asia Minor, and then afterward crossed the Ægean from Asia into Greece. The others, who remained in Europe, gradually migrated southward on the European side of the Ægean.

Incoming of the Greeks

406. Driving their herds before them, with their families in rough carts drawn by horses, the Greek tribesmen probably looked out upon the fair pastures of Thessaly, the snowy summit of Mount Olympus, and the blue waters of the Ægean not long after 2000 B.C. Unable to write, and possessing only the crudest beginnings of civilization, the Greeks thus entered the highly civilized Eastern Mediterranean world. The wandering shepherds, so often invading the Fertile Crescent to find a settled and civilized town life, furnish us the best possible illustration of the situation of the Greeks as they invaded the Ægean towns and settlements. As the newcomers looked out across the waters they could dimly discern the islands, where flourishing towns were carrying on busy industries, especially in pottery and metal, which a thriving commerce was distributing about the Mediterranean.

Greeks enter the Greek peninsula

Barbarian Greek nomads on borders of Near Eastern world

407. We can imagine the wonder with which these barbarian Greeks must have looked out upon the white sails that flecked the blue surface of the Ægean Sea. It was to be long, however, before these inland shepherds would themselves venture timidly out upon the great waters which they were viewing for the first time. Had the gaze of the Greek nomads been able to penetrate beyond the Ægean isles, they would have seen a vast panorama of great and flourishing Oriental states. Here on the borders of the vast Near Eastern world, and under its influences, the Greeks were now to go forward toward the development of a civilization higher than any the Near East had yet produced, — the highest, indeed, to which ancient man ever attained.

Achæans, then Dorian Greeks, in Peloponnesus (1500 B.C.)

408. Gradually their vanguard pushed southward into the Peloponnesus, and doubtless some of them mingled with the Ægean dwellers in the villages which were grouped under the walls of Tiryns and Mycenæ, just as the Hebrew nomads mingled with the Canaanite townsmen. Some of the Greek leaders very soon captured these Ægean fortresses, just as David took Jerusalem; but our knowledge of the situation in Greece at this time is very meager, because the peoples who settled here could not yet write and therefore have left no written documents to tell the story. These first Greeks who thus entered southern Greece came to be called Achæans.[1] Following the Achæans there seems to have been a second wave of Greek nomads (called the Dorians), who reached the Peloponnesus by 1500 B.C. and probably

[1] The Hittite tablets of Hattusas, however, reveal to us a powerful kingdom on the southern coast of Asia Minor called *Ach-chi-ya-wa* (pronounced Ak-kee-yah'wah), and it is highly probable that we have in this name, written in cuneiform signs, the same name which the Greeks applied to a region of Greece called Achæa. But the people of this earlier, Asiatic Achæa were possibly not Greeks. There are indications that these non-Greek people of the Asiatic Achæa migrated by sea and settled in southern Greece. Mingling there with the incoming Greek immigrants, these Achæans finally gave their name to the earliest Greek settlers, who are usually called Achæans, and in this manner "Achæa" became the name of a part of Greece.

subdued the Achæans as well as the Ægean townsmen, the earlier inhabitants of the region.

409. The Dorians did not stop at the southern limits of Greece, but, learning a little navigation from their Ægean predecessors, they passed over to Crete, where they must have arrived by 1400 B.C. In the days when the conquering Hittite emperors were breaking up the Egyptian Empire in Syria, and the Hebrews were settling in Palestine, the warlike Dorians were crushing Cretan civilization, and the beautiful palaces of the Cretan sea-kings were going up in smoke and flame. For Cnossus, unfortified as it was and without any walled castle, must have fallen an easy prey to the invading Dorians. They took possession of the island and likewise seized the other southern islands of the Ægean. Between 1300 and 1000 B.C. the Greek tribes took possession of the remaining islands, as well as the coast of Asia Minor, — the Dorians in the south, the Ionians in the middle, and the Æolians in the north. Here a memorable Greek expedition in the Twelfth Century B.C., after a long siege, captured and burned the prosperous city of Troy, a feat which the Greeks never forgot (§ 447). During the thousand years between 2000 and 1000 B.C. the Greeks thus took possession not only of the whole Greek peninsula but likewise of the entire Ægean world.

The Greeks take possession of the Ægean world

410. At the invasion of Crete and the fall of Cnossus, about 1400 B.C., the splendid Ægean civilization, which we saw rising so prosperously, was helpless to defend itself against the invaders. Probably few of the common people of the Ægean towns were able to flee. On the other hand, the noble and well-to-do families, forming, all told, considerable numbers, must have taken to the sea and fled. Looking back upon burning towns and villas, they must have witnessed also the destruction of the splendid palace of Cnossus, with all its beautiful treasures of Cretan art. For several generations these Cretan wanderers sought new homes along

Destruction of Ægean civilization and flight of Ægeans

the coasts of the Eastern Mediterranean, and in the Thirteenth Century B.C. a group of them settled on the southern coast of Palestine, where we know them as the Philistines.

411. By 1200 B.C. the displacement of the older populations of the north by the incoming Indo-Europeans was disturbing the entire Eastern Mediterranean world. The whole of Asia Minor had been overrun by another wave of Indo-European migration like that which had once invaded the Highland Zone and conquered the Early Anatolians. These new Indo-Europeans, who came in behind the Greeks, crossed the Hellespont into Asia Minor from Europe. The most important of them were the Phrygians and Armenians. The Hittite Empire, lying directly in their path, was so completely crushed that after 1200 B.C. it entirely disappeared. Many of its communities, following the example of the fleeing Cretans, sought new homes beyond the Mediterranean.

Hittite Empire crushed by new Indo-European invasion

412. The Egyptian monuments of this time reveal these sea-wanderers to us very vividly. Besides the Philistines, whom we have already seen fleeing from Crete, the Egyptian monuments tell us of the sea-roving Achæans who combined with the other displaced peoples to invade Egypt in the last declining days of the Egyptian Empire. This was apparently a second group of Achæans, who had remained in Asia Minor after the invasion of Greece by their earlier kindred. Forced out by the Indo-European invasion, this second group of Achæans did not follow their ancestors to Greece, but joined with other fleeing Asia Minor peoples to seek a new home in Egypt.

Sea-roving Achæans of Asia Minor

413. Among these other fugitives were two important peoples whom we shall meet again: the Sardinians and the Etruscans, both of whom still lived in the Near East and had not yet migrated westward. These two peoples joined the Achæans and other fleeing peoples of the northern Mediterranean. Many of them, probably including their leaders and chief men, took to a sea-roving life in the Eastern Mediterranean.

Sea-roving Sardinians and Etruscans

Fig. 152. *Egyptian* Soldiers Check *the Southward* Flight *of the Northern Peoples*

This migration was caused by intrusion of Indo-Europeans. The Egyptian soldiers, assisted by Sardinian mercenaries (wearing helmets surmounted by ball decorations; see extreme upper left), are driving back with spear and two-edged sword (§ 414) the Philistines (with feathered headdress) and other northern peoples. These wanderers are actually migrating, as shown by the presence of women and children, who are traveling in two-wheeled carts drawn by bullocks in teams of four. The bodies of the invaders in the background confuse the outlines of the picture. Among the shifting peoples of Anatolia who were thus forced to migrate by the invading Indo-Europeans were the Etruscans, who retreated out of Asia Minor and, sailing westward, settled in northern Italy (see §§ 815–817), and later shared in the founding of Rome

Some of the Etruscans settled in the Greek islands, where their inscriptions in the Etruscan language have been found.

Sardinians and Cretan Philistines introduce the sword

414. We have already seen that the elongation of the Egyptian bronze dagger into a heavier weapon probably took place in the north after the discovery of tin in Bohemia. This longer weapon, a dagger long enough to be called a sword, first appears on the Egyptian monuments in the hands of the Cretan Philistines and the Sardinians, who were thus the earliest ancient fighters whom we find armed with the long, two-edged weapon of bronze (Fig. 152). The possession of this longer and heavier weapon made these northerners, especially the Sardinians, probably the most dangerous soldiers in the ancient world of the Thirteenth Century B.C. They were therefore welcomed in Egypt as foreign mercenaries fighting for hire in the Pharaoh's army. While some roving bands of the northerners thus served Egypt, the main body of the "sea-peoples," as the Egyptian monuments call them, kept together for the purpose of invading and conquering Egypt and finding a permanent home there.

Indo-European migration and Eastern Mediterranean world

415. All the great powers of the Ancient Near East were threatened by this vast Indo-European movement, which stretched from the Balkan Peninsula eastward to the upper Euphrates. Its front had set in motion before it a wave of fleeing Ægeans and Asia Minor peoples, who were mostly pre-Indo-European. It was this wave of fleeing northern peoples, and not the Indo-Europeans themselves, that crossed the sea and began to break upon the shores of the eastern and southeastern Mediterranean, from the Nile Delta to the harbors of Phœnicia, in the Thirteenth Century B.C. The onset of these sword-bearing northerners shook the Egyptian Empire to its foundations. Driven back by Ramses III not long after 1200 B.C., and having lost their old northern homes, these unsettled peoples were therefore obliged to seek new homes elsewhere. We recall that a group of the fleeing Cretans called Philistines settled on the coast of Palestine. There they established a nation and gave their name to the country, for our word "Palestine" is simply another form of the word "Philistine." We have already seen that some of the Achæans who had long lived on the southern Asia Minor coast probably migrated to a new home in Greece.

416. Even more important was the effect of the Indo-European invasion on the *Western* Mediterranean. Repulsed by Egypt, the Etruscans took to their ships and sailed far westward around the heel of Italy. On the western coast of the Italian peninsula they found new homes, and here they introduced the first civilization into the Western Mediterranean world. The sword-bearing Sardinians likewise sailed westward and took possession of the island which still bears their name. Other maritime allies of the Etruscans and Sardinians, who appear at this time on the Egyptian monuments, are called the *Sikel* people. It is highly probable that they likewise migrated westward and, settling in the largest of the Western Mediterranean islands, gave it its name of Sicily, probably derived from *Sikeli*.

Indo-European migration and Western Mediterranean world

417. Thus the Indo-European invasion of the Eastern Mediterranean world ushered in a new age in human history; for out of that invasion came the westward migration, which resulted in the first chapter of the history of western Europe. This invasion is likewise the introduction to our own history, for it was the development and expansion of western Europe that made America possible. The Oriental peoples who thus fled from their homes in Eastern Mediterranean lands, driven out by the incoming Indo-Europeans, carried Oriental civilization with them to the Western Mediterranean world. The great westward drift of early Near Eastern civilization, which had finally absorbed the *Eastern* Mediterranean world, had long before been felt in the *Western* Mediterranean, where merchants from the east had for centuries been marketing the products of Near Eastern industries. Now, however, actual colonies of highly civilized peoples from the Eastern

Oriental civilization enters western Europe

Fig. 153. Battle *between a Fleet of Northern Invaders and an Egyptian Fleet*

This scene, sculptured on the wall of an Egyptian temple, is the earliest surviving picture of a naval battle. It represents the defeat of the invading northern Mediterranean peoples by Ramses III not long after 1200 B.C., somewhere along the Syrian coast. Of the nine ships engaged the four with oars and lion's head on prow are Egyptian. The remaining five (goose head on prow) are ships of the invaders. The northerners include Philistines and others. Perhaps this scene explains how the Philistines passed from Crete to Palestine. The invaders carry round shields and spears or two-edged swords, but no bows. The Egyptians, being chiefly archers, were thus able to overwhelm the enemy with their storm of arrows at long range. They then closed in, boarding the enemy ships and taking many prisoners, some of whom may be seen standing bound in the Egyptian ships. For the earliest known grappling iron, shown here, see Fig. 233. The Egyptian throwing it is fourth from the bow of the ship in the upper left corner

Mediterranean were settling in the Western Mediterranean world. This far-westward thrust of ancient Oriental civilization, and with it the beginning of civilization in western Europe, were directly due to the invasion of the Indo-European peoples in the Eastern Mediterranean world. We cannot now follow farther the civilized development of early western Europe, for we have still to return eastward that we may trace the results of the Indo-European invasion of the Eastern Mediterranean world.

Fall of Ægean civilization

418. The Indo-European invaders, including the Greeks, were still in the barbarian stage. Their coming, therefore, broke up the prosperous and civilized communities which we have seen growing up on the north side of the Mediterranean. The collapse of civilization in the Ægean world was complete. It gave way to northern barbarism, little better than the Late Stone Age life which we have already seen in Europe. At least for a time writing disappeared in the Ægean world after the Greek invasion. Enough of Ægean industries survived, however, to form an essential part of the foundation upon which the barbarian Greeks were yet to build up the highest civilization of the ancient world.

Mingling of Ægeans and Greeks

419. Such of the Ægean population as had not fled before the incoming Greeks now began to mingle with their Greek conquerors, just as we have seen the civilized Canaanites of Palestine mingling with the invading Hebrew nomads. Before the coming of the Greeks there were already at least two races living in the Ægean world. There were, first, some of the old prehistoric "round-headed" immigrants from Asia Minor, and their successors the original Asia Minor Achæans, who still survived. Besides these older groups there must have been a second considerable population made up of the "long-headed" Mediterranean race, who had built up the wonderful Cretan civilization. It was this mixed Ægean population of twofold origin which now commingled with the in-coming Greeks. The result was, of course, a mixed race, — the people known to us as the

Greeks of history. How much of the Mediterranean and older Asia Minor blood may have flowed in their veins we are now unable to determine, but the supreme genius of the classical Greeks may well have been due in no small measure to this admixture of the blood of the gifted Cretans, with their open-mindedness toward influences from abroad and their fine artistic instincts.

Triumph of Greek speech

420. This mixture of blood did result in a similar mixture of speech, just as English is made up of French and Anglo-Saxon. Greek, the language of the victorious invaders, gradually became the language of the Ægean world. At the same time, Greek did not blot out every trace of the older language of the region. People continued to call the towns, rivers, and mountains, like Mount Parnassus, by the old names they found in use, just as our fathers found Indian geographical names in America and we have continued to call our greatest river by its old Indian name *Mississippi* ("Father of Waters"). Such names in Greece are today surviving remnants of the prehistoric occupation of the Ægean world by peoples from Asia Minor. It is interesting to notice also that a few probably Ægean words for civilized conveniences, such as the Greek invaders did not possess, likewise survived. So the word "bathtub" in Greek is really an old Ægean word; for of course a race of wandering shepherds, such as the Greeks had been, had no such luxuries, whereas we have recovered the actual bathtubs of the refined Cretans, from whom the Greeks learned the name. Nevertheless the Greek language was already developing as probably the richest and most beautiful instrument of speech man has ever possessed.

Section 35. The Nomad Greeks make the Transition to the Settled Life

421. As the Greeks commingled with the older population they began to make the transition from their former wandering shepherd life to that of the settled agricultural communities among which they found themselves. They had entered a region which favored such a transition. The Greek peninsula contains about twenty-five thousand square miles.[1] It is everywhere cut up by mountains and inlets of the sea into small plains and peninsulas, separated from each other by either the sea or the mountain ridges. No less than five hundred islands are scattered along its deeply indented eastern shores (map, p. 338). For its climate and products see § 377.

Greece and its islands

422. In tranquil summer days one can pass from island to island and cross the entire Ægean Sea from Greece to Asia Minor in a rowboat. This is why a group of shepherd tribes like the Greeks had been able to cross and take possession of the islands of the Ægean and the coast of neighboring Asia Minor. But we must not conclude that at this early stage of their history they had already become a seafaring people. Centuries later we find the Greek peasant-poet Hesiod (700 B.C.) looking with shrinking eye upon the sea. Long after they had taken possession of the Ægean world the Greeks remained a barbarous people of flocks and herds, with little if any commerce by sea.

Early Greeks not a maritime people

423. If we would understand the situation of the Greeks after their conquest of the civilized Ægean world, we must again recall nomad life as we have seen it along the Fertile Crescent in Asia. We remember that the nomads possessed no organized government, for there was no public business which demanded it. Even today among such people no taxes are collected, for no one owns any land which can be taxed. There are no public officials, there are no cases at law, no legal business, and men are controlled by a few customs like the "blood revenge." Such was the condition of the nomad Greeks when they began a settled life in the Ægean world.

Earliest social institutions of the Greeks

[1] About one sixth smaller than South Carolina,— so small that Mount Olympus, on the northern boundary of Greece, is visible over much of the peninsula. From the mountains of Sparta one can see Crete on the one hand and the mountains north of the Corinthian Gulf on the other, separated by a distance of two hundred and twenty-five miles.

Tribes, council, and assembly

424. From their old wandering life on the grasslands they carried with them the loose groups of families known as tribes, and within each tribe an indefinite number of smaller groups of more intimate families called brotherhoods. A council of the old men (elders) occasionally decided matters in dispute or questions of tribal importance, and, probably once a year, or at some important feast, an assembly of all the weapon-bearing men of the tribe might be held, to express its opinion of a proposed war or migration. These are the germs of later European political institutions and even of those in the United States today.[1]

Rise of Greek kings

425. It was perhaps after they had found kings over such Ægean cities as Mycenæ that the Greeks (like the Hebrews) began to want kings themselves. Thus the old-time nomad leaders whom they had once followed in war, religion, and the settlement of disputes became rude shepherd kings of the tribes.

The Greeks begin agriculture

426. Meantime the Greek shepherds slowly began the cultivation of land. This forced them to give up their wandering life and to build houses and live in permanent homes. Nomad instincts and nomad customs were not easily rooted out, however. War and the care of flocks continued to be the occupation of the men, as it had been for centuries on the northern grasslands, while the cultivation of the fields was at first left to the women. Furthermore, flocks and herds continued to make up the chief wealth of the Greeks for centuries after they had taken up agriculture.

427. As each Greek tribe settled down and became a group of villages the surrounding land was divided among the families by lot, though the tribe as a whole long continued to be the only real owner of the land. Nevertheless private ownership of land by families gradually resulted. As a

[1] Compare the House of Lords (= the above council) and the House of Commons (= the above assembly) in England, or, in the United States, the Senate (from the Latin word meaning "old man") and the House of Representatives.

consequence there arose disputes about boundaries, about inheritances in land, and much other legal business, which as it increased required more and more attention by those in authority. The settlement of such business tended to create a government. During the four centuries from 1000 to 600 B.C. we see the Greeks struggling with the problem of learning how to transact the business of settled landholding communities, and how to adjust the ever-growing friction and strife between the rich and the poor, the social classes created by the holding of land and the settled life (cf. § 44).

Rise of land ownership and its consequences

428. We have seen the Semitic nomads struggling with the same problems on the Fertile Crescent, but for them the situation was in one important particular much easier. They found among their settled predecessors a system of writing which they quickly learned; but the old Cretan writing, once used by the Ægean predecessors of the Greeks, had perished. No one had ever yet written a word of the Greek language in this age when the Greeks were adopting the settled agricultural life. This lack of writing greatly increased the difficulties to be met as a government developed and its transactions began. There arose in some communities a "rememberer," whose duty it was to notice carefully the terms of a contract, the amount of a loan, or the conditions of a treaty with a neighboring people, that he might remember these and innumerable other things, which in a more civilized society are recorded in writing.

Lack of writing among early Greeks

429. In course of time the group of villages forming the nucleus of a tribe grew together and merged at last into a city. This was the most important process in Greek political development, for the organized city became the only nation which the Greeks ever knew. Each city-state was a sovereign power; each had its own laws, its own army and gods, and each citizen felt a patriotic duty toward his own city and no other. Overlooking the city from the heights in its midst was the king's castle, which we

Rise of the city-state

call the citadel or acropolis. Eventually the houses and the market below were protected by a wall. The king had now become a revered and powerful ruler of the city and guardian of the worship of the city gods. King and council sat all day in the market and adjusted the business and the disputes between the people. Though crude, corrupt, and often unjust, these continuous sessions for the first time created a state and the first uninterrupted government in Europe.

Rise of Greek civilization in the Age of Kings (1000–750 B.C.)

430. There were hundreds of such city-states throughout the mainland of Greece and the coasts and islands of the Ægean. Indeed, the Ægean world was made up of such tiny nations after the Greeks had made the transition to the settled life there. It was while the Greeks were thus living in these little city-kingdoms under kings that Greek civilization arose. While there were Greek kings long before 1000 B.C., it is especially after that date, during the last two and a half centuries of the rule of the kings (1000–750 B.C.), that we are able to follow the rise of Greek civilization.

QUESTIONS

Section 32. Where did civilization first appear in Europe? Why was this natural? By what two ways was the Ægean world connected with the Near East? What island of the Ægean is nearest to Egypt? Describe the rise of civilization there. Can you mention some evidences of Egyptian influence there? Where did the Cretan sea-kings arise? What survives to tell us of their power? Can you mention some evidence of Cretan commerce? Tell what you know of Cretan writing. Tell something of Cretan decorative art in the Grand Age; of the work of sculptor and goldsmith. Tell something of the life of the people of Crete.

Section 33. Had the European mainland advanced as fast as Crete in civilization? Where do we find evidences of the first civilization on the continent of Europe, and what are they? Date them. What products of Near Eastern civilization reached the Late Stone Age Europeans? How did these things reach Europe? Did the possession of metal raise the Europeans to a high civilization? Explain the importance of the invention of the striking sword. What can you say about the history and civilization of Troy? Who first discovered remains of people who had occupied the Ægean world before the Greeks? Tell something of his life. What did he find at Troy? in Greece? What has excavation in Crete since shown?

Section 34. To what race did the Greeks belong? Whence did they come? Were they accustomed to settled town life? Describe their settlement and spread in the Ægean world. What was the effect upon the predecessors of the Greeks in the Ægean? in Asia Minor? Describe the attempts of the fleeing northerners to find new homes. Name three important groups of these fugitives and tell where they finally settled. What happened to Ægean civilization? to writing? What became of the Ægeans who remained behind? Describe the results as to language.

Section 35. Did the Greeks at once take to the sea? Did they take up town life at once? What social institutions did the Greeks bring with them? What can you say of the social effects of agriculture and landownership? How did the Greeks get along without writing? What became of the villages around each Greek town? Did the Greek towns all unite into one great nation including all the Greeks? Toward what did the Greek feel patriotism? Describe a Greek city-state and its early form of government. Date the period when we are able to trace the rise of Greek civilization.

BIBLIOGRAPHY FOR TOPICAL STUDIES

Cnossos and Cretan civilization: BURY, *History of Greece*, pp. 14–20; GLASGOW, *Minoans*, pp. 30–54; HAWES, *Crete*, pp. 46–75; MILLS, *Ancient Greeks*, pp. 6–19.

Cretan industries and trade: GLOTZ, *Ægean Civilization*, pp. 161–184; HAWES, pp. 37–45.

Mycenæan civilization: BURY, pp. 20–43; JAMES, *Hellenic Heritage*, Vol. I, pp. 117–129; QUENNELL, *Everyday Things in Homeric Greece*, pp. 86–127; TOLMAN-SCOGGIN, *Mycenæan Troy*, pp. 87–111.

Chapter X · *Greek Civilization in the Age of the Kings*

Section 36. The Ægean Inheritance and the Spread of Phœnician Commerce

Beginning of the Iron Age (about 1000 B.C.)

431. In one very important matter the Greek invaders were more fortunate than their Ægean predecessors. The iron which we have seen spreading in the Near East from the Hittite country had at the same time (Thirteenth Century B.C.) also begun to reach the Greeks. It was of course a matter of some centuries before iron tools and weapons entirely displaced those of bronze. Indeed, after iron had been in common use among the Greeks for over five hundred years, the Greek poet Æschylus called it the "stranger from across the sea" or "the Chalybean stranger,"— the Chalybean region being the iron district of Asia Minor (see map, p. 146). By 1000 B.C. iron was common in Greece. The Bronze Age had therefore lasted about a thousand years. We may say that the period

Note. The above headpiece is a Greek Vase-Painting showing a Battle Scene from the Trojan War. In the middle is the Fallen Achilles, for the possession of whose body a desperate combat is going on. Here we see the armor of the early Greek warriors,— a round shield on the left arm, a long spear in the right hand. A heavy two-edged sword was also carried, but the bow was not common. Only one warrior here uses it. The head is protected by a heavy helmet crowned by a tall plume of horsehair, and the body is covered by a bronze corselet, a jacket of metal reaching from the neck to the waist. Below the knees the legs are protected by bronze fronts called greaves. At the extreme left a comrade binds up a wounded warrior, on whose shield is the bird of his family arms (cf. Fig. 31). Behind him the goddess Athena watches the combat. The painting is done in the older style of black figures on a red ground (contrast Fig. 168). The artist has inserted the names of the warriors, some written from left to right and some in the other direction (cf. headpiece, p. 342).

of Ægean civilization coincided with the Copper Age and the Bronze Age together (3000–1000 B.C.), while the civilization of the Greeks arose at the incoming of the Iron Age.

FIG. 154. *Primitive Greek Art as shown in a* PAINTED VASE *of the Age of the Kings*

This very fine specimen, over 3½ feet high, was acquired many years ago by the Metropolitan Museum of New York. It represents Greek art in its beginnings in the Eighth Century B.C. We see that the beautiful flowers, sea plants, and other *natural* objects employed by the Ægeans in their decorative art were abandoned by the early Greek vase-painters in favor of bands of geometrical designs. The scene around the top of the vase is a funeral, with the body lying on a high bier. Below is a procession of warriors with dumb-bell-shaped shields, followed by four-wheeled chariots, each with three horses very rudely drawn. Compare the fine horses painted by the Greeks only a century and a half later (Fig. 162), and the magnificent steeds painted four and a half centuries later (Fig. 198). See also the early Sumerian *two-wheeled* chariot in Fig. 91

Memories of Ægean civilization; dawn of Greek civilization

432. Long after 1000 B.C. the life of the Greeks continued to be rude and even barbarous. Memories of old Ægean splendor lingered in the plain of Argos, and above the Greek village at Mycenæ still towered the massive stone walls of the ancient Ægean princes, who had long before passed away. To these huge walls the Greeks looked up with awe-struck faces, and thought that they had been built by vanished giants called Cyclopes, or with wondering admiration they fingered some surviving piece of rich metal work wrought by the skill of the ancient Ægean craftsmen. The tradition that Crete was the earliest home of their civilization never died out among the Greeks. Without any skill in craftsmanship the Greek shepherds and peasants were slow to take up building, industries, and manufacturing on their own account. Their slowness is also evident in the matter of writing, which, as we have seen, they failed to learn from their Ægean predecessors. For a long time even the dwellings of the Greek kings were usually but simple farmhouses of sun-dried brick, where the swine wandered unhindered into the court or slumbered in the sunshine beside the royal doorway. When they did make a beginning at pottery, the crude paintings with which they decorated this rough ware show that the same methods employed by the Ægean potters in producing their fine ware in Crete a thousand years earlier were still lingering on in a decadent state.

FIG. 155. PHŒNICIAN GARMENT (*Keton*) *adopted by the Greeks*

The garments of women may be seen in Fig. 168

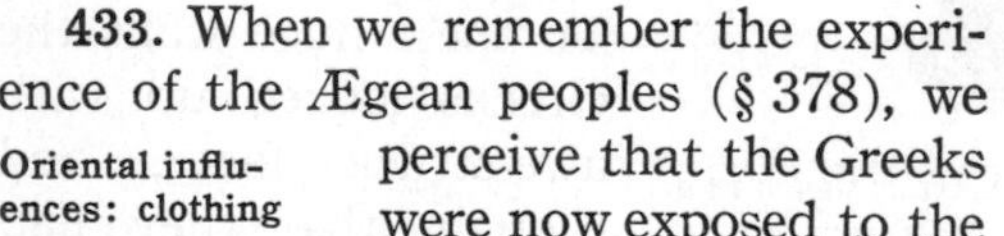

Oriental influences: clothing

433. When we remember the experience of the Ægean peoples (§ 378), we perceive that the Greeks were now exposed to the same Oriental influences which had so strongly affected early Ægean civilization. The Greek townsmen had now put off the shaggy sheepskin of their former nomad life in favor of a shirtlike garment of woven wool (Fig. 155). They had no name for it in Greek, but they heard the foreign merchants of whom they bought it calling it in their language a *keton* (pronounced ke-tōn′; Greek form later [1]Ki-tōn′).

Wares of Phœnician merchants

434. To purchase articles like this, which they did not themselves make, the townsmen often went down to the seashore, where they and their women gathered about a ship drawn up with stern on the beach. Black-bearded Phœnician traders, who overlooked the crowd from the high stern of the ship, tempted the

[1] K = German *ch* as in *ach*.

Greeks with glass or alabaster perfume bottles from Egypt and rich blue porcelain dishes. If the women did not bid for these, they were quite unable to resist certain handsome ivory combs carved with lions in openwork and polished till they shone in the sun. Wealthy Greeks were attracted by furniture elaborately inlaid with ivory carvings, and especially by magnificent large round platters of bronze or even of silver, richly engraved. Splendid purple robes hanging over the stern of the ship enriched the display of golden jewelry with flashes of brilliant color. Here too were the *ketons*, as we should have heard these swarthy strangers from the sea calling them.

Expansion of Phœnician commerce

435. We see, then, that with the fall of the Egyptian Empire (after 1200 B.C.) the ships of Egypt in the Eastern Mediterranean had disappeared. The same fate had at the same time overtaken the fleets of the Ægeans. Thus the Eastern Mediterranean was left unoccupied by merchant fleets, and by 1000 B.C. the Phœnician cities were taking advantage of this opportunity. Once probably dwellers in the desert like the Hebrews, we remember that the Phœnicians had early occupied the towns along the Syrian coast, where they became clever navigators. The Greek craftsmen were as yet quite unable to produce such wares as the Phœnician merchant offered, and hence these Oriental traders did a thriving business wherever they landed.

Phœnicians, earliest explorers of the Western Mediterranean

436. Nor did the Phœnicians stop with the Ægean world. They sought markets also in the West, and they were the discoverers of the westernmost Mediterranean and the Atlantic Ocean. They finally planted settlements as far away as the Atlantic coast of Spain. Their colony of Carthage (map, p. 346) became the most important commercial state in the Western Mediterranean and the most dangerous rival of Rome, as we shall see later. For some three centuries after 1000 B.C. they were the greatest merchants in the Mediterranean, and their far-reaching traffic was beginning the slow creation of a great mercantile Mediterranean world. They had no armies, however, and little political organization. The only Phœnician colony that ever became a strong state was Carthage.

Fig. 156. *Ancient* Phœnician Comb *of Carved Ivory*

Such wares, manufactured at Sidon and Tyre, were distributed by the Phœnician merchants through the Mediterranean as far west as Spain, where combs like this have been found in ancient graves. The lion adorning this comb is of the form that developed in Syria

Growth and character of Phœnician art and industries

437. The Phœnicians learned the methods of manufacturing their goods, in almost all cases, from Egypt. There they learned to make glass and glazed ware, to weave linen and dye it, to cast and hammer and engrave metal. On the other hand, we find that the *designs* employed in their art were international. We remember that it was Phœnician workmen whom the Assyrian kings employed to make furniture and metal work for the royal palace. King Solomon likewise employed Phœnician workmen to build for him the Hebrew temple at Jerusalem (1 Kings, v). After 1000 B.C. the Phœnicians were thus the artistic manufacturers in a great world extending from Nineveh on the east to Italy on the west.

Oriental decorative art reaches Europe

438. On the metal platters and the furniture of carved ivory landed from the Phœnician ships the Greek craftsmen found decorations made up of palm trees, lotus flowers, hunting scenes along the Nile, the Assyrian tree of life, and many other picturesque things, but especially those strange winged creatures of Oriental fancy, the sphinx, the gryphon, the winged horse. As we shall later see, not only the Greeks but also the Etruscans began to imitate these things in their own work. Thus the whole range of Oriental decorative art entered both Eastern and Western Mediterranean civilization, to fill forever after a large place in the decorative art of all civilized peoples of the West, including our own today. At the same time it is highly probable that in the Phœnician workshops in the Ægean islands the Greeks could work side by side with the Phœnician craftsmen and learn how to make hollow bronze casts — an art invented in Egypt — and to manufacture many other things which were bringing such commercial success to the Phœnician merchants in their Ægean colonies. Nevertheless, so little of the refined Ægean art of the Grand Age had survived that there are products of the Greeks in this period that are hardly as good as the work of the artists of the Middle Stone Age.

Fig. 157. *Ancient* Phœnician Platter *of Engraved and Beaten Work*

This silver platter, now in the Berlin Museum, is of beautiful workmanship. A circular stream of water surrounds a rosette in the middle. On the water are four Nile boats (one of them in the form of a swan), outside of which is a circular border of papyrus flowers. Pieces of such metal work have been found as far west as Spain and as far east as Nineveh, whither they were carried by the Phœnician merchants

Section 37. The Phœnicians bring the First Alphabet to Europe

439. But styles of dress, decorative art, and the practical methods of the craftsmen were not the only things which the Phœnician merchants were bringing into Greece. For the Greeks now received from the Phœnicians a priceless gift, far more valuable than all the manufactured wares of the Orient. Indeed, it was the most important foreign contribution that ever reached Europe. This new gift was an alphabet. Between 1800 and 1600 B.C. the western Semites near Egypt had devised an alphabet drawn from Egyptian hieroglyphs. The Phœnicians adopted this system of twenty-two *alphabetic* signs for writing their own language. It contained no signs for syllables, but each sign represented a single consonant. There were no signs for the vowels, which remained unwritten. The western Semites were thus the first to devise a system of writing containing only *alphabetic* signs, that is, true letters. In the Twelfth Century B.C. the Phœnicians were already giving up the inconvenient Babylonian clay tablet and importing great quantities of papyrus paper from Egypt.

Semites devise an alphabet (1800 to 1600 B.C.)

440. The Phœnicians arranged their new letters in a convenient order, so that the whole twenty-two might form a fixed list (Fig. 158, column I), easily learned. Such a list could not be learned without giving to each letter a name. They called the first letter of the alphabet *ox*, because the Phœnician word for ox, that is, *aleph*, began with the first letter. The second letter of the alphabet they called *house*, because *beth*, the Phœnician word for house, began with the second letter, and so on. This was not unlike our old primers, where our great grandfathers learned to say: "*A* is for 'Axe,' *B* is for 'Bed,'" etc. When the children of the Phœnician merchants learned their letters and were called upon to repeat the alphabet, they therefore began: "*Aleph, beth,*" etc., as if our children were to say: "Axe, Bed," etc. instead of "A, B," etc.

Letters of alphabet arranged in fixed order and named

---

* Column I contains the Phœnician alphabet, made up exclusively of consonants. The Phœnicians wrote from right to left, and hence the Greeks at first wrote in the same direction. Several of the names of the warriors in the vase-painting on page 324 are written in this way; hence column II shows letters like *B* "backward," as we say. The Greeks then gradually changed and wrote from left to right, and the next column shows the letters facing as they do in our present alphabet (see *B* in column III). The transition from these later forms of the Greek letters to the Latin forms (column IV) was very easy, and the Latin forms hardly differ from those which we still use (column V).

441. The Phœnicians also had a literature chiefly religious. Their merchants kept all their business records at first on clay tablets but later in their new and convenient alphabet on papyrus. We have seen that the Arameans carried the Phœnician alphabet from the Ægean and the Mediterranean eastward through Asia to India (§ 242). In western Asia Minor and in the Greek islands the Etruscans learned to use the Phœnician alphabet, and later they carried it to Italy when they settled there. In the same way it reached the Greeks, whom we have seen crowding around the Phœnician ships. They often found the Phœnicians handling bits of pale-yellow paper on which were written bills and lists of merchandise in strange black signs. These the Greeks viewed at first with misgivings, as being mysterious and dangerous symbols. One of their songs of this age speaks of them as "baneful signs." Here and there a Greek merchant,

Phœnician alphabet reaches Greeks (about 1000 to 900 B.C.)

I PHŒNICIAN	II EARLY GREEK read from right to left	III LATER GREEK read from left to right	IV LATIN	V ENGLISH
𐤀	A	A	A	A
𐤁	S 8	B	B	B
𐤂	1	Γ	C G	C.G
𐤃	Δ	Δ	D	D
𐤄	∃	E	E	E
𐤅	Y	Ϝ	F V	F.V.U
𐤆	I	I	...	Z
𐤇	B	B	H	E.H
𐤈	⊗	⊗	...	TH.PH
𐤉	ϟ	ϟ	I	I
𐤊	ꓘ	K	...	K.KH
𐤋	V ⊣ 1	L Λ	L	L
𐤌	M	M	M	M
𐤍	И	N	N	N
𐤎	Ξ	Ξ	X	X
𐤏	o	o	O	O
𐤐	1	Γ	P	P
𐤑	M	M	...	S
𐤒	Ϙ	Ϙ	Q	Q
𐤓	ᑫ	P	R	R
𐤔	Ʃ	Σ	S	S
𐤕	T	T	T	T

FIG. 158. *Table showing how the* PHŒNICIAN LETTERS *passed through* GREEK *and* LATIN FORMS *to reach their Present* ENGLISH FORMS*

thumbing the Phœnician tradesman's papyrus bills, finally learned the alphabet in which they were written, and slowly began to note down *Greek* words spelled with Phœnician letters. Thus, possibly as early as 1200 and in all probability not much later than 1000 B.C., the Phœnician alphabet was adopted by the Greeks.

Greeks adopt the Phœnician alphabet and perfect it by adding vowels

442. Here the Greeks early displayed the mental superiority which, as we shall soon discover, they possessed. They noticed that there were no Phœnician letters standing for vowels. They also noticed in the Phœnician alphabet a few letters representing consonants which did not exist in Greek speech. These letters they began to use for the Greek vowels (Fig. 158; compare columns I and II). Thus they took the final step in the process of devising a complete system of alphabetic writing. It slowly spread among the Greek states, beginning in Ionia. For a long time it remained only a convenience in business and administration. For centuries the nobles, unable to read or write, continued to regard writing with misgivings. But even the painters of pottery jars had learned to use it by 700 B.C., when we find it on their decorated vases. Shortly after this it was common among all classes. Neverthless literature long remained an oral matter and was much slower than business to resort to writing.

Phœnician origin of the alphabets of the civilized world

443. The Greek children, in learning to read, used for the letters the same names that had been employed in Phœnicia. The Greeks, not knowing what these strange names meant, altered them somewhat; but the Greek children began to pronounce the foreign names of the letters in the fixed order already settled in Phœnicia, saying "Alpha, beta," etc. (instead of "Aleph, beth," etc.). As a child of today is said to be learning his A B C's, so the Greek child learned his Alpha Beta's, and thus arose our word "alphabet." Therefore the word "alphabet," still containing as it does the names of the first two letters in the Phœnician alphabet, should remind us of the great debt we owe to the Near East, and especially to the Phœnicians, for the priceless gift of alphabetic writing; for the Phœnician alphabet spread from Greece to Italy and at last throughout Europe. Indeed, every alphabet of the civilized world has descended from the Phœnician alphabet.

444. Along with the alphabet the equipment for using it (that is, pen, ink, and paper) for the first time came into Europe. Paper also brought in with it its Oriental names; for the Greeks received from abroad the word *papyros*, designating the Egyptian paper on which they wrote, and we remember that this word, divested of its ancient ending, was easily transformed from *papyr* to our own English form "paper." Much of the papyrus used by the Greeks was delivered to them by Phœnician merchants from Byblos. Just as we apply the word "china" to a kind of table-ware that first came to us from China, so the Greeks often called papyrus *byblos*, after the Phœnician city from which it came. Thus, when they began to write books on rolls of such paper, they called them *biblia*. It is from this term that we received our word "Bible" (literally "book" or "books"). Hence the English word "Bible," once the name of a Phœnician city, is another living evidence that books and the paper of which they are made originated in the Ancient Near East, from which the Greeks received so much.

Oriental origin of the words "paper" and "Bible"

SECTION 38. GREEK WARRIORS AND THE HERO SONGS

445. The Greek nobles of this age loved war and were devoted to fighting and plundering. It was a frequent sight to see the Greek warrior waving farewell to his family before the pillared porch of his home, as he mounted the waiting chariot and rode forth to battle. The vase-painters have often left us pictures of such warriors (headpiece, p. 324). While their protective armor was of bronze, their weapons were at this time commonly of iron, although bronze weapons still lin-

Equipment of the Greek warrior in Age of the Kings

gered on, and in their tales of the great wars of the past the Greeks still told how the heroes of older days fought with bronze weapons.

Battle and the customs of war in the Age of the Kings

446. It was only men of some wealth who possessed a fighting outfit like this. They were the leading warriors. The ordinary troops, lacking armor, were of little consequence in battle, which consisted of a series of single combats, each between two heroes. Their individual skill, experience, and daring won the battle, rather than the discipline of drilled masses. The victor seized his fallen adversary's armor and weapons, and, having fastened the naked body of the vanquished to his chariot, he dragged it triumphantly across the field, only to expose it to be devoured by birds of prey and wild animals. There was thus many a savage struggle to rescue the body of a fallen hero. When a Greek town was captured, its unhappy people were slaughtered or carried away as slaves, and its houses plundered and burned. There was savage joy in such treatment of the vanquished, and such deeds were thought to increase the fame and glory of the victors.

Rise of hero songs

447. Men delighted to sing of valiant achievements on the field of battle and to tell of the stirring deeds of mighty heroes. In the pastures of Thessaly, where the singer looked up at the cloud-veiled summit of Mount Olympus, the home of the gods, there early grew up a group of such songs telling many a story of the feats of gods and heroes,— the earliest literature of the Greeks. Into these songs were woven also vague memories of remote wars which had actually occurred, especially the war in which the Greeks had captured and destroyed the splendid city of Troy. Probably by 1000 B.C. some of these songs had crossed to the coasts and islands of Ionia on the Asiatic side of the Ægean Sea.

448. Here arose a class of professional bards who graced the feasts of king and noble with songs of battle and adventure recited to the music of the harp. Framed in exalted and ancient forms of speech, and rolling on in stately measures,[1] these heroic songs resounded through many a royal hall,—the oldest literature born in Europe. The separate songs were finally woven together by the bards into a connected whole, a great epic cycle clustering especially about the traditions of the Greek expedition against Troy. They were not the work of one man but a growth of several centuries; they were sung by generations of singers, some of whom were still living even after 700 B.C. It was then that these songs were first written down.

Ionian singers

FIG. 159. *An Ideal Portrait of* HOMER

This head, in the Boston Museum of Fine Arts, is a noble example of the later Greek sculptor's ability to create an ideal portrait of a poet whom he had never seen. Such work was unknown in the archaic days of Greece; it was produced in the Hellenistic Age

449. Among these ancient singers there was one of great fame whose name was Homer. His reputation was such that the composition of the whole cycle of songs, then much larger than the remnant which has come down to us, was attributed to him. Then, as the Greeks themselves later discerned the impossibility of Homer's authorship of them *all*, they credited him only with the Iliad,[2] the story of the Greek expedition against Troy, and the Odyssey, the tale of the wanderings of the hero Odysseus on his return from Troy. These are the only two series of songs that have entirely survived, and even the ancient world had its doubts about the Homeric authorship of the Odyssey.

Homer

[1] These were in hexameter, that is, six feet to a line. This Greek verse is the oldest literary form in Europe.

[2] So named after *Ilium*, the Greek name of Troy.

Homeric songs our earliest literary record of the Greeks

450. These ancient bards not only gave the world its greatest epic in the Iliad, but they were, moreover, the earliest Greeks to put into permanent literary form their thoughts regarding the world of gods and men. At that time the Greeks had no other sacred books, and the Homeric songs became the veritable Bible of Greece. They gave to the disunited Greeks a common literature and the inspiring belief that they had once all taken part in a common war against Asia.

Section 39. The Beginnings and Early Development of Greek Religion

Homeric songs and Greek religion

451. Just as devout Hebrews were taught much about their God by the beautiful tales of him in the historical narratives of their forefathers, so the wonderful Homeric songs brought vividly before the Greeks the life of the gods. Homer became the religious teacher of the Greeks. To us too he reveals a great chapter in the story of Greek religion; for, like that of the Hebrews, the religion of the Greeks was a slow growth, passing gradually from a low stage to ever higher and nobler beliefs. There was, therefore, a chapter of Greek religion earlier than the Homeric songs. Let us look for a moment at the religion of Greece *before* the Homeric songs.

Primitive Greek religion before Homeric songs

452. Like all primitive men, every Greek once thought that the trees and springs, the stones and hilltops, the birds and beasts, were creatures possessed of strange and uncanny powers. He thought there was a spirit in the dark recesses of the earth which made the grain sprout and the trees flourish; in the gloomy depths of the waters also he believed there dwelt a like spirit which swayed the great sea; while still another ruled the far sweep of the overhanging sky. As the Greek peasant, terrified by the jagged lightning and the rolling thunder, or grateful for the gently falling rain, looked up into the misty cloudland of the sky, he often saw the solitary eagle soaring across the vast and lonely expanse. To him the lofty, mysterious bird seemed to be the mighty spirit of the sky, who dwelt there and in his wrath smote the great trees with fire, or in kinder moods sent down the refreshing rain. Thus to *some* Greeks the sky spirit seemed to be an eagle.

Rise of worship and its customs

453. Each of these spirits, friendly or hostile, dwelt in a limited region, and it was believed possible to gain its favor or avoid its anger by simple gifts, especially food. The earth spirit might be reached by slaying a sheep and letting the blood flow into the earth, while the sky spirit would be won by burning a thigh of the sheep so that its odor might rise to the sky with the soaring smoke. In time these spirits of the world around the early Greeks became gods and goddesses, and thus arose worship with its sacred customs. There were no temples or houses of worship, and all the simple usages of religion went on out of doors in a grove or in the open air in the court of the house.

Greeks bring Zeus the Sky-god into the Ægean world

454. We remember that the Hebrews never lost their belief in their great God Yahveh, whom they brought with them into the land of Palestine; and so the Greeks likewise brought into Greece various ideas of the great Sky-god whom they had already worshiped in the old days on the grasslands. He had different names: in one valley they called him Raingiver; in another, Thunderbolt. But he was finally known to all as Zeus, which was simply the Greek form of an old word for "sky" in the language of the Indo-European parent people. He became the highest god among all the numerous gods and goddesses revered by the Greeks.

Divinities of Ægean world accepted by Greeks

455. But Greek religion continued to grow after the Greeks had reached the Ægean world. Here they found the Ægeans worshiping the great earth spirit, the Earth-Mother, or the Great Mother, who made the earth bring forth her grain and fruit as the food of man. From the Ægeans the Greeks learned to revere her also. They called her Demeter, and she became one of the great goddesses of Greek religion. The Greeks thus accepted the gods and goddesses whom they found in the Ægean world, just as many of the Hebrews accepted the Canaanite baals which they found already in Palestine.

456. The Homeric songs reveal to us a second chapter in Greek religion. Those nature spirits which had gained a high place as gods and goddesses appeared in the Homeric songs as entirely human in form and in qualities. Of course they possessed more power than mortals, and they enjoyed the gift of immortality. They dwelt in veiled splendor among the clouds on the summit of Mount Olympus. There, in his cloud palace, Zeus the Sky-god, with the lightning in his hand, ruled the other gods like an earthly king. But each of the gods controlled as his own a realm of nature or of the affairs of men.

The gods cf Homer

457. Apollo, the Sun-god, whose beams were golden arrows, was the deadly archer of the gods. But he also shielded the flocks of the shepherds and the fields of the plowman, and he was a wondrous musician. Above all, he knew the future ordained by Zeus, and could, when properly consulted, tell anxious inquirers what the future had in store for them. These qualities gave him a larger place in the hearts of all Greeks than Zeus himself, and in actual worship he became the most beloved god of the Greek world.

Apollo and Athena

Athena, the greatest goddess of the Greeks, seems in the beginning to have ruled the air and swayed the destroying tempests that swept the Greek lands. Such power made her a warrior goddess, and the Greeks loved to think of her with shining weapons, protecting the Greek cities. But she held out her protecting hand over them also in times of peace, as the potters shaped their jars, the smiths wrought their metal, or the women wove their wool. They believed also that she had brought them the olive tree. Of all her divine companions Athena was the wisest in counsel, and an ancient tale told how she had been born in the very brain of her father Zeus, from whose head she sprang forth full-armed. As the

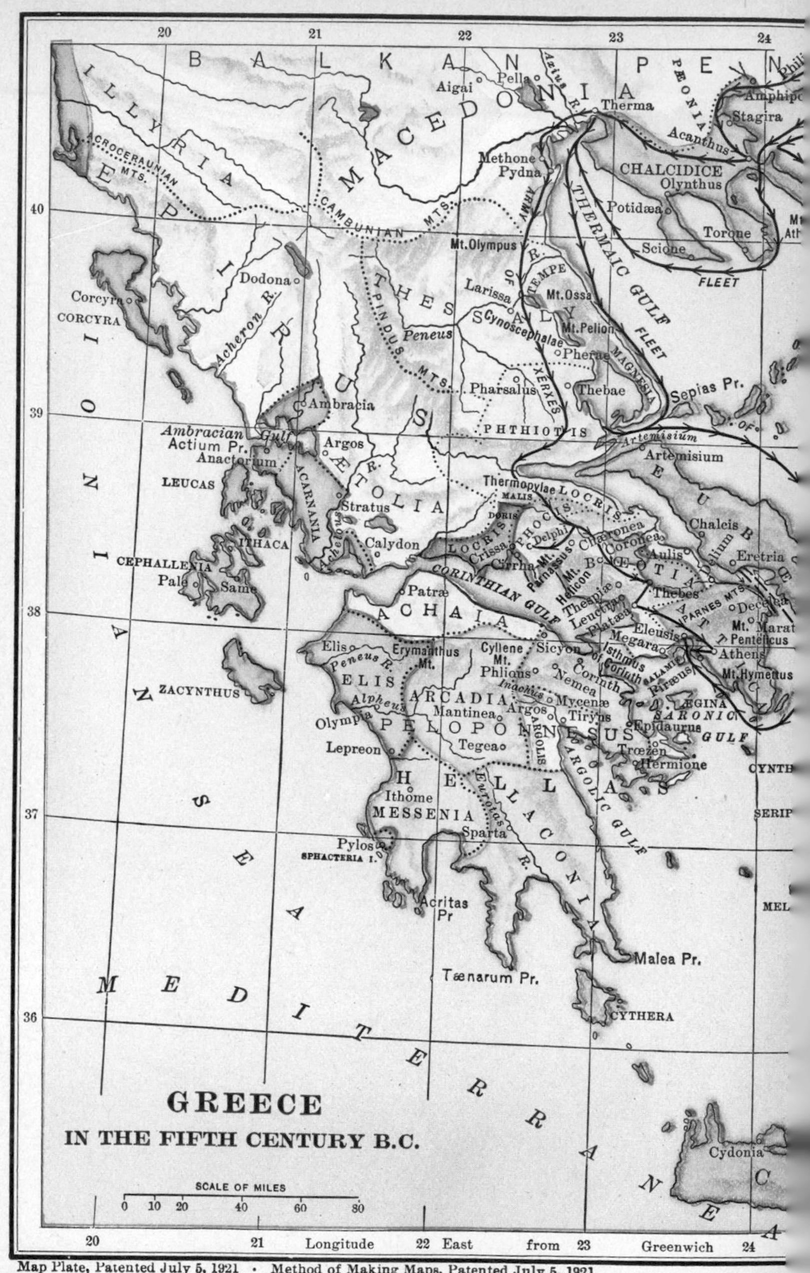

Map Plate, Patented July 5, 1921 · Method of Making Maps, Patented July 5, 1921

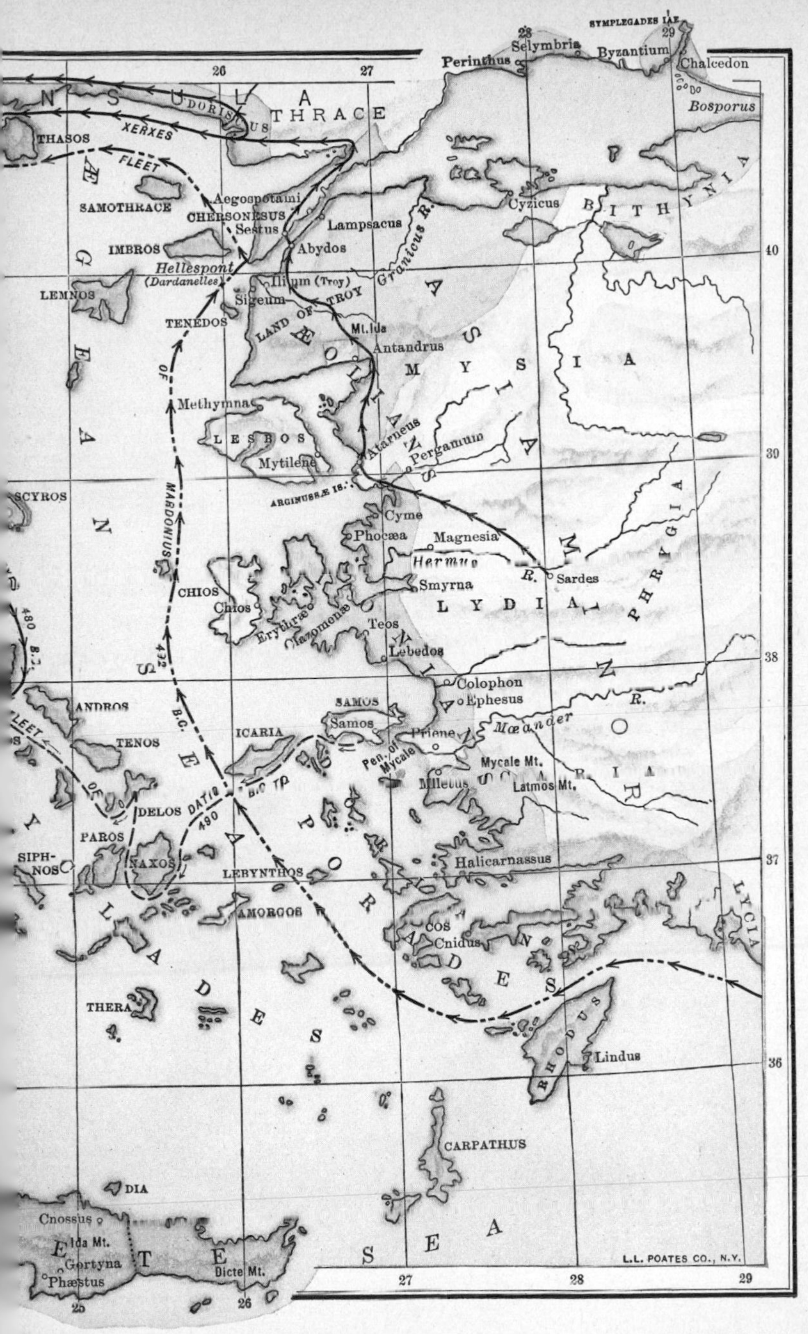
THRACE
Perinthus
Selymbria
Byzantium
Chalcedon
Bosporus
SYMPLEGADES IAE
DORISCUS
XERXES
THASOS
FLEET
SAMOTHRACE
Aegospotami
CHERSONESUS
Sestus
Lampsacus
Abydos
Granicus R.
Cyzicus
BITHYNIA
IMBROS
Hellespont
(Dardanelles)
Ilium (Troy)
Sigeum
LAND OF TROY
LEMNOS
TENEDOS
Mt. Ida
Antandrus
MYSIA
ÆOLIANS
Methymna
LESBOS
Mytilene
Atarneus
Pergamum
ARGINUSSÆ IS.
SCYROS
MARDONIUS
Cyme
Phocæa
Magnesia
Hermus R.
Sardes
MINOR
PHRYGIA
CHIOS
Chios
Erythræ
Clazomenæ
Smyrna
LYDIA
Teos
Lebedos
IONIANS
480 B.C.
492 B.C.
ANDROS
FLEET
TENOS
SAMOS
Samos
Colophon
Ephesus
Mæander R.
ICARIA
Priene
Pen. of Mycale
Mycale Mt.
Miletus
Latmos Mt.
CARIA
DELOS
DATIS
490 B.C.
PAROS
NAXOS
SIPHNOS
LEBYNTHOS
Halicarnassus
AMORGOS
COS
Cnidus
SPORADES
CYCLADES
LYCIA
THERA
RHODUS
Lindus
CARPATHUS
ÆGEAN
DIA
Cnossus
Ida Mt.
Gortyna
Phæstus
Dicte Mt.
CRETE
SEA
L.L. POATES CO., N.Y.
26
27
28
29
40
39
38
37
36
25

divine foster mother of all that was best in Greek life, she was the loveliest of the protecting powers which the quick and sensitive imagination of the Greeks felt everywhere watching over the life and work of men.

458. At the same time a further group of ancient nature spirits had risen to be great gods, each controlling some special realm. In a brazen palace deep under the waters, Poseidon ruled the sea. The Greeks looked to the earth god, Dionysus, for the fruit of the grapevine, and they rejoiced in the wine which he gave them. An old moon spirit had now become Hermes, the messenger of the gods, with winged feet, doing the bidding of the gods, but he was also the patron of the intercourse of men, and hence the god of trade and commerce. Some of the Greeks, however, in the old days, seeing the moon above the forest margin, had believed it to be a goddess, a divine huntress riding through the forests at night. They called her Artemis. Others, however, had fancied the moon to belong in the sky as the wife of Zeus, whom they called Hera, and she became the protectress of marriage. Ishtar, the Semitic goddess of love (§ 226), had now passed over from the Syrian cities by way of Cyprus, to become Aphrodite, the Greek goddess of love.

Other important Greek divinities

459. As all these divinities were pictured in human form, it was but natural that they should be thought of as possessing human traits also. Homer pictures to us the family quarrels between the august Zeus and his wife Hera, just as such things must have occurred in the household life of the Greeks, and certainly in a manner absurdly undignified for exalted divinities. Thus the Greeks thought of the gods as showing decidedly human defects of character. Such gods were not likely to require anything better in the character of men. Religion was therefore not yet an influence leading to good conduct and right living.

Early Greek ideas of conduct; life after death

One reason why the Greeks did not yet think that the gods required good conduct of men was their notion of life after death. They believed that all men passed at death into a gloomy kingdom beneath the earth (Hades), where the fate of good men did not differ from that of the wicked. Here ruled Pluto as king, and his wife, the goddess Persephone. As a special favor of the gods, the heroes, men of mighty and god-like deeds, were endowed with immortality and permitted to enjoy a life of endless bliss in the beautiful Elysian Fields, or the Islands of the Blest, somewhere in the Far West, toward the unexplored ocean. The Greeks seem to have brought with them from their earlier wanderings the custom of burning their dead, but they adopted also the Ægean usage of preserving the body as in Egypt and burying it. The primitive notion that the dead must be furnished with food and drink still survived.

Lack of temples; rise of priests

460. Every household in the little Greek towns felt that the safety of the house was in the hands of Hestia, the goddess of the hearth. But in the Age of the Kings the symbols of the great gods were set up in every house, while in the dwelling of the king there was a special room which served as a kind of shrine for them. There was also an altar in the forecourt, where sacrifices could be offered under the open sky. In so far as the gods had any dwellings at all, we see that they were in the houses of men, and there probably were no temples as yet. Here and there, in some communities, men were to be found who were thought to possess rare knowledge of the desires of the gods. As these men were more and more often consulted by those who felt ignorant of the proper ceremonies of sacrifice and worship, such men gradually became *priests*.

QUESTIONS

Section 36. What metal came in at the rise of Greek civilization? What had happened to the arts and crafts of the Ægeans? Did the Greeks possess any craftsmen? Compare the horses on the Greek vase of the Age of the Kings (Fig. 154) with Middle Stone Age carving. From whom did the Greeks buy manufactured products? What did this commerce teach the Greeks?

Section 37. Tell about the Phœnician alphabet. How did it reach Greece? What is the origin of the word "alphabet"? How far has the Phœnician alphabet spread?

Section 38. Describe early Greek arms and warfare. What was the relation of valiant deeds and song? Around what event did the hero songs cluster? Tell of Homer and the poems attributed to him.

Section 39. How did the Homeric songs affect religion? What can you say of Greek religion before the Homeric songs arose? Name the leading Greek divinities and tell something of each. Discuss Greek beliefs about the dead; customs and places of worship.

BIBLIOGRAPHY FOR TOPICAL STUDIES

Writing and Greek history: AMERICAN COUNCIL OF EDUCATION, *The Story of Writing*; BURY, *Greece*, p. 78; CARY, *Documentary Sources of Greek History*, pp. 1–9 and passim.

Homer and the Iliad: BURY, *Greece*, pp. 69–70; JAMES, *Hellenic Heritage*, Vol. I, pp. 76–103; MURRAY, *Ancient Greek Literature*, chap. i; NORWOOD-DUFF, *Writers of Greece and Rome*, pp. 21–36; *Pageant of Greece*, pp. 15–47 (or HOWE-HARRER, *Greek Literature in Translation*, pp. 1–34).

Greek wearing apparel and the toilet: BRITISH MUSEUM, *Guide to Greek and Roman Life*, pp. 116–132; GULICK, *Modern Traits in Old Greek Life*, pp. 25–32, 49–51; METROPOLITAN MUSEUM OF ART, *Daily Life of the Greeks and Romans*, pp. 47–67.

Archæology and Greek History: CARY, *Documentary Sources*, chap. x; JAMES, *Hellenic Heritage*, Vol. II, pp. 482–503; MAGOFFIN, *The Lure and Lore of Archæology*, pp. 58–68.

NOTE. Below is an archaic Greek plaque showing a potter fashioning a vase on a potter's wheel.

Chapter XI · *The Age of the Nobles and Greek Expansion in the Mediterranean*

Section 40. The Disappearance of the Kings and the Leadership of the Nobles

Geographical influences against union of all Greeks

461. We have seen Greek civilization beginning under Oriental influences. In its *governmental* development, however, the Greek world showed striking differences from what we have seen in the Near East. There we watched the early city-states finally uniting into two large and powerful nations, one on the Nile and another on the Two Rivers. In Greece, however, there

Note. In the Vase-Painting above, the Greek Nobles under the kings are seen taking to the water as Pirates (§ 468), though armed as on land (see headpiece, p. 324). On the ship models, see Fig. 160. The artist who made this painting inserted his name at the extreme right. It reads "Aristonothos made it." This is not only the earliest signed vase but likewise the earliest signed work of art, crude though it may be, in Europe. It shows us that the Greek artist was gaining increasing pride in his work, and it is one of the earliest signs of individuality in Greek history, about 700 B.C.

were influences which tended to prevent such a union of the Greeks into one nation. In the first place, the country was cut up by mountain ridges and deep bays, so that the different communities were quite separated. The cities of Greece were likewise separated from their kindred in the islands and in Asia Minor.

462. Furthermore, no recollection of their former loose unity on the grasslands survived, even in their oldest traditions. They had now lived so long in separated communities that they had developed permanent local habits and local dialects, as different as those of North and South Germany or even more different than those of Louisiana and New England. The various Greek communities thus displayed such intense devotion to their own town and their own local gods that a union of all the Greek city-states into one nation, such as we have seen in the Near East, failed to take place. As a result of these separative influences we find in Greece after 1000 B.C. scores of little city-states such as we have already described. Not only did the islands and the Greek city-states of Asia Minor fail to unite, but on the island of Crete alone there were more than fifty such small city-states.

Other influences operating against political unity

463. Four regions on the mainland of Greece, each forming a pretty clearly outlined geographical whole, like the peninsula of Laconia or that of Attica (see map, p. 338), permitted the union of city-states into a larger nation. The oldest of these four nations seems to have been Argos. The town of Argos subdued the ancient strongholds of Mycenæ and Tiryns and others in the vicinity, forming the nation of Argos and giving its name to the plain. In the same way the kings of Sparta conquered the two peninsulas on the south of them and finally also the land of the Messenians on the west. The two kingdoms of Argos and Sparta thus held a large part of the Peloponnese.

The four unions: Argos and Sparta

464. In the Attic peninsula, likewise, numerous little city-kingdoms were slowly absorbed by Athens, which at last gained control of the entire peninsula. On the northern borders of Attica the region of Bœotia fell under the leadership of Thebes, but the other Bœotian cities were too strong to be wholly subdued. Bœotia, therefore, did not form a nation but a group of city-states in alliance, with Thebes at the head of the alliance. Elsewhere no large and permanent unions were formed. Sparta and Athens, therefore, led the two most important unions among all the Greeks. Let it be borne in mind that such a nation remained a city-state in spite of its increased territory. The nation occupying the Attic peninsula was called Athens, and every peasant in Attica was called an Athenian. The city government of Athens covered the whole Attic peninsula.

The four unions: Athens and Thebes

465. In the process of governing such little city-states the Greeks overthrew many of their kings about 750 B.C., and thus entered upon a new stage of their development, which was again very different from that which we have found in the Near East. However discontented the common people of an Oriental state might become, their discontent never accomplished more than the overthrow of one king and the enthronement of another. The *office* of king was never abolished, nor did any other form of government than that of monarchy ever arise in the ancient East.

Development of the Greek state contrasted with the Near East

466. Among the Greeks too the common people struggled for centuries to better their lot. As we shall see, this long and bitter struggle finally resulted in giving the people in some Greek states so large a share in governing that the form of the government might be called democracy. This is a word of Greek origin meaning "the rule of the people," and the Greeks were the first people of the ancient world to gain it.

Greek state and struggle toward democracy

467. The cause of this struggle was not only the corrupt rule of the kings but also the oppression of the *nobles*. We have watched these men of wealth buying the luxuries of the Phœnician merchants. By fraud, unjust seizure of lands, union of families in marriage, and many other influences the strong men of ability and

Rise of a noble class: eupatrids

cleverness were able to enlarge their lands. Thus there had arisen a class of hereditary nobles, — large landholders and men of wealth called eupatrids.

468. Their fields stretched for some miles around the city and its neighboring villages. In order to be near the king or secure membership in the Council and control the government, these men often left their lands and lived in the city. Such was the power of the eupatrids that the Council finally consisted only of men of this class. Wealthy enough to buy costly weapons, with leisure for continual exercise in the use of arms, these nobles had also become the chief protection of the state in time of war. They were also continual marauders on their own account. As they grew more and more accustomed to the sea they coasted from harbor to harbor, plundering and burning, and returned home laden with rich spoil. Piracy at last became the common calling of the nobles, and a great source of wealth.

Political and military power of eupatrids; piracy

469. Thus grew up a sharp distinction between the city community and the peasants living in the country. The country peasant was obliged to divide the family lands with his brothers. His fields were therefore small, and he was poor. He went about clad in a goatskin, and his labors never ceased. Hence he had no leisure to learn the use of arms, nor any way to meet the expense of purchasing them. He and his neighbors were therefore of small account in war. Indeed, he was fortunate if he could struggle on and maintain himself and his family from his scanty fields. Many of his neighbors sank into debt, lost their lands to the noble class, and became day laborers or, still worse, sold themselves to discharge their debts and thus became slaves. These day laborers and slaves had no political rights and were not permitted to vote in the Assembly.

Misery and weakness of peasants

470. If the peasant desired to exert any influence in government, he was obliged to go up to the city and attend the Assembly of the people there. When he did so, he found but few of his fellows from the countryside gathered there,—a dingy group clad in their rough goatskins. The powerful Council, in beautiful Oriental raiment, was backed by the whole class of wealthy nobles, all trained in war and splendid with their glittering weapons. Intimidated by the powerful nobles, the meager Assembly, which had once been a muster of all the weapon-bearing men of the tribe, became a feeble gathering of a few peasants and lesser townsmen, who could gain no greater recognition of their old-time rights than the poor privilege of voting to concur in the actions already decided upon by the king and the Council. The peasant returned to his little farm and was less and less inclined to attend the Assembly at all.

Weakness of the Assembly

471. It was, however, not alone the people whose rights the nobles were disregarding, for they also began to consider themselves the equals of the king, whose chief support in war they were. The king could not carry on a war without them or control the state without their help. By 750 B.C. the office of the king was in some states nothing more than a name. While the king was in some cases violently overthrown, in most states the nobles established from among themselves certain elective officers to take charge of matters formerly controlled by the king. Thus, in Athens they appointed a noble to be leader in war, while another noble was chosen as *archon*, or ruler, to assist the king in attending to the increasing business of the state. Thus the Athenian king was gradually but peacefully deprived of his powers, until he became nothing more than the leader of the people in religious matters. In Sparta the power of the king was checked by the appointment of a second king, and on this plan Sparta continued to retain her kings. Elsewhere, in the century between 750 and 650 B.C., the kingship quite generally disappeared. The result of the struggle was thus the triumph of the nobles, who had gained control over both the people and the king and were henceforth in power in many states.

Decline and disappearance of kings (800–650 B.C.)

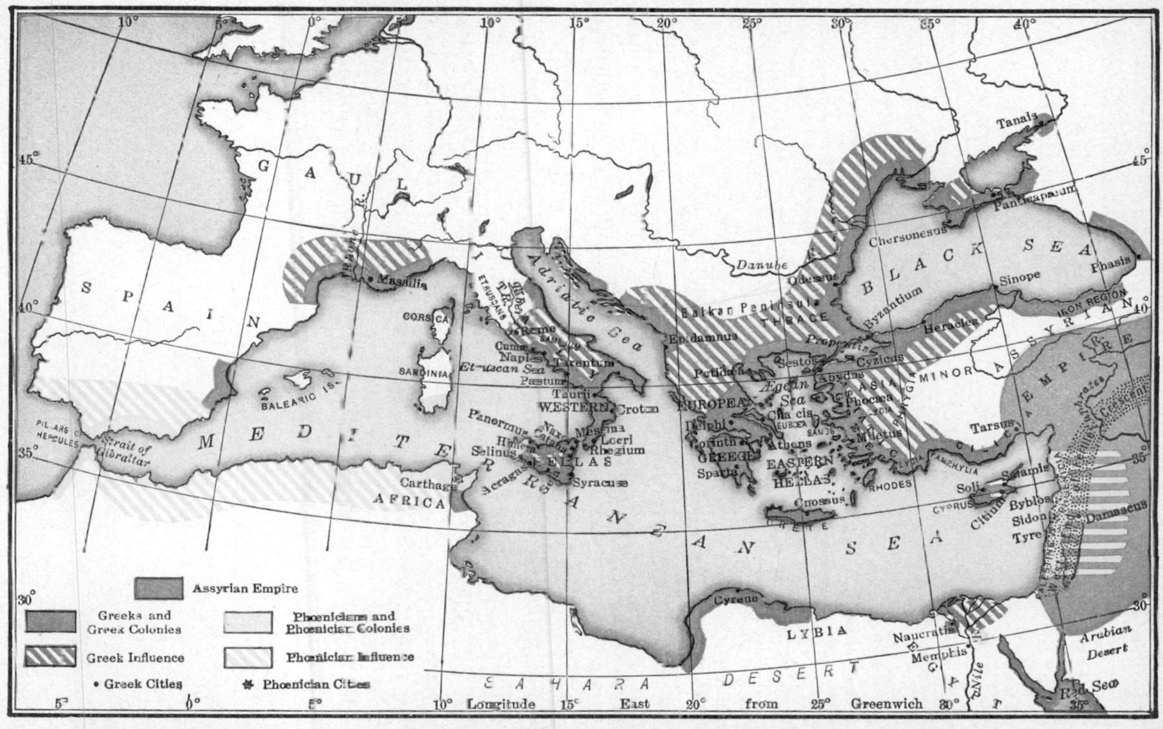

COLONIAL EXPANSION OF THE GREEKS AND PHŒNICIANS DOWN TO THE SIXTH CENTURY B.C.

472. With the disappearance of the king the royal castle was of course vacated. As it fell into decay the shrines and holy places which it contained were still protected and revered as religious buildings, and, as we shall see in discussing architecture, they became temples. In this way the castle of the ancient Attic kings on the citadel mount, called the Acropolis of Athens, was followed by the famous temples there.

Survival of shrines in the old palaces

SECTION 41. GREEK EXPANSION IN THE AGE OF THE NOBLES

473. The Age of the Nobles witnessed another great change in Greek life. Sea-roving and piracy, as we have seen, were common among the nobles. At length, as the Greek merchants gradually took up sea trade, the demand for ships led the Greek mechanics to undertake shipbuilding. They built their new craft on Phœnician models (see Fig. 160), the only ones with which they were acquainted. When the Phœnician merchants entered the Ægean harbors, they now found them more and more occupied by Greek ships. Especially important was the traffic between the Greek cities of the Asiatic coast on the east and Attica and Eubœa on the European side. Among the Asiatic Greeks it was the Ionian cities which led in this commerce.

Beginnings of commerce and shipbuilding among the Greeks

474. The oppressive rule of the nobles and the resulting impoverishment of the peasants was an important influence leading the Greek farmers to seek new homes and new lands beyond the Ægean world. Not only were Greek merchants trafficking with the northern Ægean, but their vessels had penetrated the great northern sea which they called the Pontus, known to us as the Black Sea (see map, p. 346). Their trading stations among the descendants of the Stone Age peoples in these distant regions offered to the discontented farmers of Greece plenty of land with which to begin life over again. Before 600 B.C. they

Greek colonies in the Black Sea

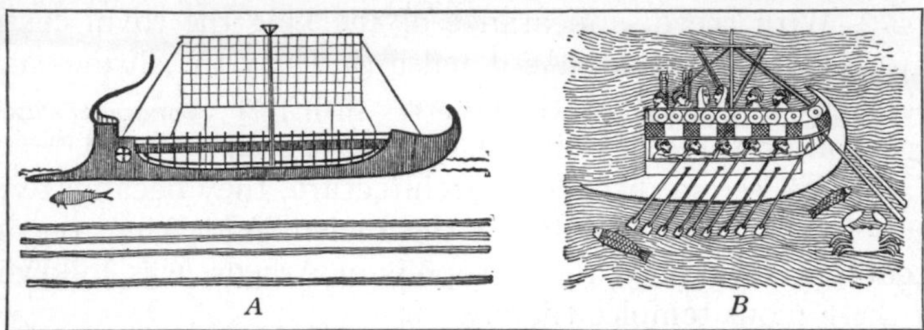

FIG. 160. *An* EARLY GREEK SHIP *and the* PHŒNICIAN SHIP *after which it was modeled*

The earliest ships in the Mediterranean, those of Egypt, were turned up at both ends (Fig. 56), and the early Ægean ships were copies of this Egyptian model (Fig. 153). The Phœnicians, however, introduced a change in the model by giving their ships at the bow a sharp projecting beak below water. Such a Phœnician ship, used by the Assyrian king Sennacherib, is shown here in a drawing from one of his palace reliefs (*B*). The Greeks did not adopt the old Ægean form, turned up at both ends, but took up the Phœnician form with beaked prow, as shown in the vase-paintings, from which the above drawing of an Eighth-Century Greek ship (*A*) has been restored

girdled the Black Sea with their towns and settlements, reaching the broad grain fields along the lower Danube and the iron mines of the old Hittite country on the southeastern coast of the Black Sea. But no such development of Greek genius took place in this harsher climate of the north as we shall find in the Ægean. Not a single great artist or writer ever came from the north. Although the Pontus became the granary of Greece, it never contributed anything to the higher life of the Greeks.

Greek colonies in the east, — southern Asia Minor and Cyprus

475. In the east, along the southern coasts of Asia Minor, Greek expansion was stopped by the Assyrian Sennacherib when he defeated a body of Greeks in Cilicia about 700 B.C., in the earliest collision between the Hellenes and a great power of the Oriental world. The Greek colonies of Cyprus long remained the easternmost outposts of the Greek world. In the south they found a friendly reception in Egypt, and there in the Nile Delta they were permitted to establish a trading city at Naucratis (Mistress of Ships), the predecessor of Alexandria. West of the Delta they eventually founded Cyrene also (map, p. 346).

476. It was the unknown West, however, which became the America of the early Greek colonists. Many a Columbus pushed his ship into this strange region of mysterious dangers on the distant borders of the world, where the heroes were believed to live in the Islands of the Blest. Looking westward from the western coast of Greece, the seamen could discover the shores of the heel of Italy, only fifty miles distant. When they had once crossed to it, they coasted around Sicily and far into the West. Here was a new world. Although the Etruscans and the Phœnicians were already there, its discovery was as momentous for the Greeks as that of America for later Europe (see map, p. 346).

Discovery of the West

477. By 750 B.C. their colonies appeared in this new western world, and within a century they fringed southern Italy from the heel to a point well above the instep north of Naples, where they were stopped by the settlements of the Etruscans. This region of the Greek colonies of southern Italy came to be known as Great Greece (see map, p. 562). Here the Greek colonists looked northward toward the large group of Etruscan cities stretching up to the river Arnus, but they probably gave little heed to the hills in the foreground, crowned by the rude settlements which were destined to become Rome. They did not dream that this insignificant town would yet rule the world, making even the proud cities of their homeland its vassals.

Greek colonies in the West, — southern Italy

478. The Greek colonists likewise crossed over to Sicily and drove out the Phœnician trading posts there, except at the western end of the island, where the Phœnicians held their own. These Greek colonists in the West shared in the higher life of the homeland, and Syracuse, at the southeast corner of the island of Sicily, became at one time the most cultivated as well as the most powerful city of the Greek world. At Massilia (Mar-

Sicily and the Far West

seilles), on the coast of later France, the western Greeks founded a town which controlled the trade up the Rhone valley, and, attracted by the silver mines of Tartessus, they reached over even to the Mediterranean coasts of Spain.

Racial aspects of ancient colonization in the Mediterranean

479. Thus, under the rule of the nobles, the Greeks expanded till they stretched from the Black Sea along the north shore of the Mediterranean almost to the Atlantic. In this imposing movement we recognize a part of the far-outstretched western wing of the Indo-European line (see § 312); but at the same time we remember that in the Phœnician empire of Carthage the Semite had likewise flung out his western wing along the *southern* Mediterranean, facing the Indo-European peoples on the *north* (see map, p. 346).

Question of supremacy in the new Mediterranean world

480. This wide expansion of Greeks and Phœnicians tended at last to produce a great Mediterranean world. Was the leading civilization in that Mediterranean world to be Greek, springing from the Greeks and their colonies, or was it to be Oriental, carried by the Phœnician and Etruscan galleys and spread especially by the far-reaching settlements of the Phœnicians? That was the great question, and its answer was to depend on how Greek civilization succeeded in its growth and development at home in the Ægean, to which we must now turn.

SECTION 42. GREEK CIVILIZATION IN THE AGE OF THE NOBLES

Influences leading toward unity: athletic games

481. We have already noticed the tendencies which kept the Greek states apart and prevented their union as a single nation. There were now, on the other hand, some influences which tended toward unity. Among such influences were the contests in arms and the athletic games, which arose from the early custom of honoring the burial of a hero with such celebrations. In spite of the local rivalries at these contests, a sentiment of unity was greatly encouraged by the celebration and common management of these athletic games. Finally they came to be practiced at stated seasons in honor of the gods. As early as 776 B.C. such contests were celebrated as public festivals at Olympia.[1] Repeated every four years, they finally aroused the interest and participation of all Greece.

482. Religion also became a strong influence toward unity, because there were some gods at whose temples all the Greeks worshiped. The different city-states therefore formed several religious councils, made up of representatives from the various Greek cities concerned. They came together at stated periods, and in this way each city had a voice in such joint management of the temples. These councils were among the nearest approaches to representative government ever devised in the ancient world. The most notable of them were the council for the control of the Olympic games, another for the famous sanctuary of Apollo at Delphi (Fig. 169), and also the council for the great annual feast of Apollo in the island of Delos.

Greek unity favored by religious councils (amphictyonies)

483. These representatives spoke various Greek dialects at their meetings. They could understand each other, however, just as a Scot can make himself understood in southern England, or a citizen from Maine understands another from Louisiana, though they may laugh at each other's oddities of speech. Their common language thus helped to bind together the people of the many different Greek cities. A sentiment of unity also arose under the influence of the Homeric songs, with which every Greek was familiar, — a common inheritance depicting all the Greeks united against the Asiatic city of Troy.

Greek unity furthered by language

484. Thus bound together by ties of custom, religion, language, and common traditions, the Greeks gained a feeling of

[1] Every schoolboy knows that these Olympic games have been revived in modern times as an international project.

race unity which set them apart from other races. They called all men not of Greek blood "barbarians," which was not originally a term of reproach for the non-Greeks. Then the Greek sense of unity found expression in the first all-inclusive term for *themselves*. They gradually came to call themselves Hellenes, and found pleasure in the belief that they had all descended from a common ancestor called Hellen. But it should be clearly understood that this new designation did not represent a Greek *nation* or state, but only the group of Greek-speaking peoples or states, often at war with one another.

Barbarians and Hellenes

485. The lack of political unity evident in such wars was also very noticeable in trade relations. No merchant of one city had any legal rights in another city where he was not a citizen. Even his life was not safe, for no city made any laws protecting the stranger. He could secure protection only by appealing to the old nomad custom of "hospitality," after he had been received by a friendly citizen as a guest. For the reception of any stranger who might have no such friend to be his host a city might appoint a citizen to act as its official host. These primitive arrangements are a revelation of the strong *local* prejudice of each Greek city. The most fatal defect in Greek character was the inability of the various states to forget their local differences and jealousies and to unite into a common federation or great nation including all Greeks.[1]

Greek unity and trade

486. In spite of Oriental luxuries, like gaudy clothing and wavy Oriental wigs, Greek life in the Age of the Nobles was backward. The Greek cities of which we have been talking were groups of dingy sun-dried brick houses, with narrow, wandering streets which we should call alleys. On the height where the palace or castle of the king had once stood was an oblong building of brick, like

Architecture and sculpture

[1] We may recall here how local and sectional differences long prevented the union of Great Britain and also how slow were the thirteen colonies of America to suppress local pride sufficiently to adopt a constitution uniting all thirteen into a nation. It was local differences similar to those among the Greeks which afterward caused the American Civil War.

the houses of the town below. In front it had a porch with a row of wooden posts, and it was covered by a "peaked" roof with a triangular gable at each end. This building was the earliest Greek temple. As for sculpture in this age, the figure of a god consisted merely of a wooden post with a rough-hewn head at the top. When draped with a garment it could be made to serve its purpose.

Rise of written literature; moral progress; patriotism

487. While there were still very few who could read, there was here and there a man who owned and read a written copy of Homer. Men told their children quaint fables, representing animals acting like human creatures, and by means of these tales with a moral made it clear what a man ought or ought not to do. The Greeks were beginning to think about human conduct. The old Greek word for virtue no longer meant merely valor in war, but also kindly and unselfish conduct toward others. Duty toward a man's own country was now beginning to be felt in the sentiment that we call patriotism. Right conduct, as it seemed to some, was even required by the gods, and it was finally no longer respectable for the nobles to practice piracy.

Transference of literary interest to the present

488. Under these circumstances it was natural that a new literature should arise as the Greeks began to discuss *themselves* and *their own* conduct. The old Homeric singers never referred to themselves; they never spoke of their *own* lives. They were absorbed in describing the valiant deeds of their heroes who had died long before. The heroic world of glorious achievement, in which these early singers found their inspiration, had passed away, and eventually their art died also. Meanwhile the problems of the *present* began to press hard upon the minds of men; the peasant farmer's distressing struggle for existence made men conscious of very present needs. Their *own* lives became a great and living theme.

489. The voices that once chanted the hero songs therefore died away, and now men heard the first voice raised in

Europe on behalf of the poor and the humble. Hesiod, an obscure farmer under the shadow of Mount Helicon in Bœotia, sang of the dreary and hopeless life of the peasant, — of his *own* life as he struggled on under a burden too heavy for his shoulders. We even hear how his brother Persis seized the lands left by their father, and then bribed the judges to confirm him in their possession.

Hesiod: earliest cry for social justice in Europe (750–700 B.C.)

This earliest European protest against the tyrannies of wealthy town life was raised at the very moment when, across the corner of the Mediterranean, the once nomad Hebrews were passing through the same experience. The voice of Hesiod raising the cry for social justice in Greece sounds like an echo from Palestine. But we should notice that in Palestine the cry for social justice resulted finally in a *religion* of brotherly kindness, whereas in Greece it resulted in democratic *institutions*, the rule of the people who refused longer to submit to the oppressions of the few and powerful. In the next chapter we shall watch the progress of the struggle by which the rule of the people came about.

QUESTIONS

Section 40. Were the geographical influences in Greece favorable to a political union of all Greeks? Name the important unions and describe the leading two. How did the political development of the Near East differ from that of Greece? What is a democracy? Where did democracies first arise? What was the attitude of the nobles toward democracy? Describe the political power of the nobles; the military power. What was the situation of the peasants? What happened to the Assembly? to the kings?

Section 41. On what models did the Greeks build their first ships? Tell about Greek colonization in the North; in the East; in the South; in the West. What competing race had already colonized in the West?

Section 42. Discuss athletic games as an influence toward unity. Compare the League of Nations and the Greek amphictyonies. How did language favor Greek unity? What names for Greeks and non-Greeks arose? What can you say about the attitude of Greek cities toward Greeks who were not citizens? Were literature and reading now common? What thoughts about conduct were arising? As men began to think about themselves rather than the ancient heroes, what was the effect upon literature? Tell about Hesiod.

BIBLIOGRAPHY FOR TOPICAL STUDIES

The city-state: BOTSFORD, *Source Book*, pp. 97–101; BURY, *Greece*, pp. 163–173; JAMES, Vol. I, *Hellenic Heritage*, pp. 198–203.

The wanderings of Odysseus: BURY, *Greece*, pp. 89–90, 93; JAMES, Vol. I, pp. 142–158; *Pageant of Greece*, pp. 47–70 (or HOWE–HARRER, *Greek Literature*, pp. 34–60); QUENNELL, *Homeric Greece*, pp. 54–70.

Athletic games: BRITISH MUSEUM, *Greek and Roman Life*, pp. 55–60; BURY, pp. 139–144, 157–161; CARY, *Documentary Sources*, pp. 86–87; GULICK, *Modern Traits*, pp. 90–92; JAMES, Vol. I, pp. 210–213.

NOTE. The bronze tablet shown below bears a Greek inscription which certifies to the appointment of the Athenian Dionysios as representative (Greek *proxenos*) for Corcyra (modern Corfu) in Athens. Dionysios was thenceforth supposed to give hospitality and assistance to citizens of Corcyra when they were in Athens. He was expected, furthermore, to receive any ambassadors sent to Athens from Corcyra and to give some attention to the commercial interests of Corcyra in Athens. In return he was granted the right to possess land and house property in Corcyra. The Greek *proxenos* thus corresponded to the *consul* of modern nations.

© British Museum

Chapter XII · *The Industrial Revolution and the Age of the Tyrants*

Section 43. The Industrial and Commercial Revolution

Growth of Greek commerce and industry

490. The remarkable colonial expansion of the Greeks, together with the growth of industries in the home cities, led to profound changes. The new colonies not only had needs of their own, but they also had dealings with the inland, which finally opened up extensive regions of Europe as a market for Greek wares. The home cities at once began to meet this demand

Note. The above headpiece shows us the ruins of the Temple of Hera at Olympia, probably the oldest temple in Greece. The remains of columns which surrounded the outside of the building (cf. Fig. 182) are of different sizes and proportions, for they were inserted at different times to replace the old wooden ones with which the temple was first built. They are of the Doric style (Fig. 165). The walls were of sun-dried brick and have therefore disappeared. In their fall they covered up the magnificent statue of Hermes thought to be by Praxiteles (Fig. 184), which was thus preserved until modern excavators found it.

FIG. 161. *The* ISTHMUS OF CORINTH, *the Link between the Peloponnesus and Northern Greece*

The observer stands on the hills south of ancient Corinth (out of range on the left) and looks northeastward along the isthmus, on both sides of which the sea is visible. On the left (west) we see the tip of the Gulf of Corinth (see map, p. 338), and on the right (east) the Saronic Gulf. The commerce across this isthmus from the Orient to the West made the Gulf of Corinth an important center of traffic westward, and Corinth early became a flourishing commercial city. Through this sole gateway of the Peloponnesus passed back and forth for centuries the leading men of Greece, and especially the armies of Sparta, which lay some 60 miles distant (behind the observer)

for goods of all sorts. The Ionian cities led the way as formerly, but the islands also, and finally the Greek mainland, felt the new impulse. Corinth first, and then Athens, began to share in the increased Greek trade. Ere long the commercial fleets of the Hellenes were threading their way along all the coasts of the northern, western, and southeastern Mediterranean, bearing to distant communities Greek metal work, woven goods, and pottery. They brought back either raw materials and foodstuffs, such as grain, fish, and amber, or finished products like the magnificent utensils in bronze from the cities of the Etruscans in northern Italy. At the yearly feast and market on the island of Delos the Greek householder found the Etruscan bronzes of the West side by side with the gay carpets and rich silver vessels of the Orient.

Greek industry begins to shake off Oriental influence

491. To satisfy the increasing demands of trade, and to meet Phœnician competition, the Greek craftsmen greatly improved their work. During the Seventh Century Greek industries were still unequal to those of the Orient, but after 600 B.C. the Greeks began to surpass their Oriental teachers. In Samos they learned to make *hollow* bronze castings, like those of the Egyptians. They painted pottery with *their own* decorative scenes, taken from the lives of gods and men, and these more and more displaced the rows of Oriental figures, half animal, half human. Thus in industry Greece began to emancipate herself from the Orient.

FIG. 162. *An* ATHENIAN PAINTED VASE *of the Early Sixth Century* B.C.

This magnificent work (over 30 inches high) was found in an Etruscan tomb in Italy, whither it had been exported by the Athenian makers in the days of Solon (§ 505). It is signed by the potter Ergotimos, who gave the vase its beautiful shape, and also by the painter Clitias, whose skillful hand executed the sumptuous painted scenes extending in bands entirely around the vase. These decorations represent the final emancipation of the Greek painter from Oriental influences, and the triumph of his own imagination in depicting scenes from Greek stories of the gods and heroes. Before the end of this century the vase-painters had begun to blacken the whole vase and then to put on their paintings in red on the black background. This method enabled them to add details in black within the figures, and greatly improved their work (see Fig. 168). The Greeks were now the best draftsmen in the world. Note the progress in less than two hundred years (compare Fig. 154)

Greeks introduce industrial slave labor

492. At the same time growing trade obliged every Greek craftsman to enlarge his small shop,— once, perhaps, only large enough to supply the wants of a single estate. Unable to find the necessary workmen, the proprietor who had the means bought slaves, trained them to the work, and thus enlarged his little stall into a factory with a score of hands. Henceforth industrial slave labor became an important part of Greek life.

493. Athens entered the field of industry much later than the Ionian cities, but when she did so she won victories not less decisive than her later triumphs in art, literature, philosophy, and war. The potters early required an extensive quarter of the town to accommodate their workshops (see plan, p. 418). The Athenian factories must have assumed a size quite unprecedented in the Greek world, for of the painted Greek vases (discovered by excavation) which are signed by the artist about half are found to have come from only six factories at Athens. It is not a little impressive at the present day to see the modern excavator opening tombs far toward the interior of Asia Minor and taking out vases bearing the signature of the same Athenian vase-painter whose name you may also read on vases dug out of the Nile Delta in North Africa or taken from tombs in the cemeteries of the Etruscan cities of Italy (Fig. 162). We suddenly gain a picture of the Athenian manufacturers in touch with a vast commercial domain extending far across the ancient world.

Expansion of Athenian commerce

494. Soon the shipbuilder, responding to the growing commerce, began to build craft far larger than the old fifty-oar galleys. The new merchantmen were driven only by sails, an Egyptian invention of ages before. They were so large that they could no longer be drawn up on the strand as before. Hence sheltered harbors were necessary, and for the same reason the anchor was now invented. The protection of such merchant ships demanded more effective warships, and the distinction arose between a man-o'-war, or battleship, and a merchantman. Corinth boasted the production of the first decked warships, a great improvement, giving the warriors above more room and better footing, and protecting the oarsmen below; for warships must be independent of the wind, and

Improvement and enlargement of ships

hence they were still propelled by oars. The oarsmen were arranged in three rows, three men on the same bench, each man wielding an oar, and thus the power of an old "fifty-oar" could be multiplied by three without much increasing the size of the craft. These innovations were all in common use by 500 B.C. With superior equipment on the sea and the marked improvement of their industries the Hellenes were soon beating the Phœnicians in the Mediterranean markets.

Precious metals and coinage in the Near East (700 B.C.)

495. Meantime Greek business life had entered on a new epoch, owing to the introduction of coined money. From the peoples of inner Asia Minor the Ionians had learned to use the precious metals by weight in making business payments after the Oriental manner (§ 202). The basis of weight was the Babylonian *mina*. Sixty such minas (pounds) made a talent, and a talent of silver was worth about $1125. Not long after 700 B.C. the kings of Lydia in Asia Minor (see map, p. 338) began to cut up silver into lumps of a fixed weight, small enough to be of convenient size and value. These they stamped with some symbol of the king or state to show that the state guaranteed their value, and such pieces form the earliest known coins.

Adoption of coinage by Greeks (early Seventh Century B.C.)

496. The Ionian cities soon took over this great convenience, and it quickly passed thence to the islands and the European Greeks. The Athenians divided the mina of silver into a hundred parts. A lump of silver weighing a hundredth part of a mina was worth from eighteen to twenty cents. It became the ordinary small unit of value and still survives as such for large sections of Europe in the French *franc*, Italian *lira*, and Austrian *krone*, all originally worth somewhat less than twenty cents, although they have greatly diminished in value since the World War. The Athenians called this coin a *drachma*, meaning a "handful," because it was equal in value to a handful of small change consisting of little rods of iron or copper used by the common people, like our copper cents. The American dollar was originally five of these drachmas, and

FIG. 163. *Specimens illustrating the* BEGINNING OF COINAGE

These are rough lumps of silver, flattened by the pressure of the stamp Coins *1* and *2* are marked by the bench tool which held the lump while the stamp was struck upon it. This defect was slowly overcome, and the coins became round as the stamp itself was made round instead of square. *1*, both sides of a Lydian coin (about 550 B.C.); *2*, both sides of a coin of the Greek island of Chios (500 B.C.), showing how the Greeks followed the Lydian model (*1*); *3*, both sides of a Carian coin of Cnidus (650–550 B.C.), an example of the square stamp; *4*, both sides of a four-drachma piece of Athens (Sixth Century B.C.), bearing head of goddess Athena and an owl with olive branch. The inscription contains the first three letters of "Athens"

the Athenians themselves issued a four-drachma piece which served as their dollar. The purchasing power of a drachma was in ancient times very much greater than in our day. For example, a sheep cost one drachma, an ox five drachmas, and a landowner with an income of five hundred drachmas ($100) a year was considered a wealthy man.

Rise of a capitalistic class

497. Greek wealth had formerly consisted of lands and flocks, but now men began to accumulate capital in *money*. Loans were made, and the use of interest came in from the Near East. The usual rate was 18 per cent yearly. Men who could never have hoped for wealth as farmers were now growing rich, for the flourishing industries and the commercial ventures on the seas rapidly created fortunes in a class formerly obscure. Thus arose a prosperous industrial and commercial *middle class* who demanded a voice in the government. They soon became a political power of much influence, and the noble class was obliged to consider them. At the beginning of the Sixth Century B.C. even a noble like Solon could say, "Money makes the man."[1]

Greek cities and estates

498. The prosperity we have sketched was still insufficient to produce large cities as we now have them. Athens and Corinth probably had about 25,000 inhabitants each. In spite of commercial prosperity the Greeks were still dependent on agriculture as their greatest source of income. But here again the farms and estates were from our point of view very small. The largest farms contained not over a hundred acres, while a man who had fifty acres was classed among the rich.

Section 44. Rise of the Democracy and the Age of the Tyrants

Decline of the peasantry

499. While the prosperous capitalistic class was thus arising the condition of the peasant on his lands grew steadily worse. His fields were dotted with stones, each the sign of a mortgage, which the Greeks were accustomed to indicate in this way. The wealthy creditors were foreclosing these mortgages and taking the lands, and the unhappy owners were being sold into foreign slavery or were fleeing abroad to escape such bonds. The nobles in control did nothing as a class to improve the situation; on the contrary, they did all in their power to take advantage of the helplessness of the peasants and small farmers.

Industrial class and mass warfare increase the power of the people

500. But new enemies now opposed the noble class. In the first place, the new men of fortune were bitterly hostile to the nobles; in the second place, the improvement in Greek industries had so cheapened all work in metal that it was possible for the ordinary man to purchase weapons and a suit of armor. Moreover, the development of tactics under the leadership of the Spartans had produced close masses of

[1] Though sometimes attributed to Aristodemos.

spearmen, each mass (phalanx) standing like an unbroken wall throughout the battle (compare Fig. 90). The war chariot of the individual hero of ancient times could not penetrate such a battle line. The chariot disappeared and was seen only in chariot races. These changes increased the importance of the ordinary citizen in the army and therefore greatly increased the power of the lower classes in the state.

Disunion among the nobles and rise of the tyrants

501. At the same time the nobles were far from united. Serious feuds between the various noble families often divided them into hostile factions. The leader of a faction among the nobles often placed himself at the head of the dissatisfied people in real or feigned sympathy with their cause. Both the peasants and the new commercial class of citizens often rallied around such a noble leader. Thus supported, he was able to overcome and expel his rivals among the noble class and to gain undisputed control of the state. In this way he became the ruler.

The tyrant and public opinion of his office

502. Such a ruler was in reality a king, but the new king differed from the kings of old in that he had no royal ancestors and had seized the control of the state by violence. The people did not reverence him as of ancient royal lineage, and, while they may have felt gratitude to him, they felt no loyalty. The position of such a ruler always remained insecure. The Greeks called such a man a tyrant, which was not at that time a term of reproach, as it is with us. The word "tyranny" was merely a term for the high office held by this ruler. Nevertheless the instinctive feeling of the Greeks was that they were no longer free under such a prince, and the slayer of a tyrant was regarded as a hero and a savior of the people.

Age of Tyrants (Sixth Century B.C.)

503. By 650 B.C. such rulers had begun to appear, but it was especially the Sixth Century (from 600 to 500 B.C.) which we may call the Age of the Tyrants. They arose chiefly in the Ionian cities of Asia Minor and the islands, and also in Eubœa, Athens, Corinth, and the colonies of Sicily, — that is, in all the progressive Greek city-states where the people had gained power by commercial prosperity. Their rise was a consequence of the growing power of the people, and in spite of public opinion they were the first champions of democracy. Such men as Periander of Corinth and Pisistratus of Athens looked after the rights of the people, curbed the nobles, gave great attention to public works like harbor improvements, state buildings, and temples, and cultivated art, music, and literature.

Earliest written Greek codes of law

504. Hitherto all law, so long ago reduced to writing in the Near East, had been a matter of oral tradition in Greece. It was very easy for a judge to twist oral law to favor the man who gave him the largest present. The people were now demanding that the inherited oral laws be put into writing. After a long struggle the Athenians secured such a written code, arranged by a man named Draco, about 624 B.C. It was an exceedingly severe code; hence our adjective "Draconic," meaning "harsh."

Foreign complications of Athens

505. Meantime the situation in Athens was much complicated by hostilities with neighboring powers. The merchants of Megara had seized the island of Salamis, overlooking the port of Athens. The loss of Salamis and the failure of the nobles to recover it aroused intense indignation among the Athenians. Then a man of the old family to which the ancient kings of Athens had belonged, a noble named Solon, who had gained wealth by many a commercial venture on the seas, roused his countrymen by fiery verses, calling upon the Athenians not to endure the shame of such a loss. Salamis was recovered, and Solon gained great popularity with all classes of Athenians.

Solon elected archon; his financial reforms

506. The result was Solon's election as archon in 594 B.C. He was given full power to improve the evil condition of the peasants. He declared void all mortgages on land and all claims of creditors which endangered the liberty of a citizen. But Solon was a true statesman, and to the demands of the lower classes for a new apportionment of lands held by the nobles he would not yield. He did, however, set a limit to the amount of land which a noble might hold.

FIG. 164. *Ruins of the Ancient* COURTHOUSE OF GORTYNA, *in Crete, and the Early* GREEK CODE OF LAWS *engraved on its Walls*

This hall, dating from the Sixth Century B.C., was a circular building about 140 feet across, which served as a courthouse. If any citizen thought himself unjustly treated, he could appeal to the great code engraved in twelve columns on the inside of the stone wall of the building. It covers the curved surface of the wall for about 30 feet, but extends only as high as would permit it to be read easily. It forms the longest Greek inscription now surviving. This code shows a growing sense of justice toward a debtor and forbids a creditor to seize a debtor's tools or furniture for debt. Compare Solon's policy, § 506

Solon's new code of laws

507. Solon also made a law that anyone who, like Hesiod, had lost a lawsuit could appeal the case to a jury of citizens over thirty years of age, selected by lot. This change and some others greatly improved a citizen's chance of securing justice. Solon's laws were all written, and they formed the first Greek code of laws by which all free men were given equal rights in the courts. Some of these laws have descended to our own time and are still in force.

508. Furthermore, Solon proclaimed a new constitution which gave to all citizens a voice in the control of the state. It made but few changes. It recognized four classes of citizens, graded according to the amount of their income. The wealthy nobles were the only ones who could hold the highest offices, and the peasants were permitted to hold only the lower offices. The government thus remained in the hands of the nobles, but the humblest free citizen could now be assured of the right to vote in the assembly of the people.

Solon's new constitution

509. Solon is the first great Greek statesman of whom we obtain an authentic picture,—chiefly through his surviving poems. The leading trait of his character was moderation, combined with unfailing decision. When all expected that he would make himself tyrant, he laid down his expiring archonship without a moment's hesitation and left Athens for several years, to give his constitution a fair chance to work.

Estimate of Solon

510. Solon saved Attica from a great social catastrophe, and it was largely due to his wise reforms that Athens achieved her industrial and commercial triumphs. But his constitution gave the prosperous commercial class no right to hold the leading offices of government. They continued the struggle for power. Hence Solon's work, though it deferred the humiliation, could not save the Athenian state from subjection to a tyrant.

Solon's work fails to prevent rise of tyrant in Attica

511. Returning from exile, backed by an army of hired soldiers, Pisistratus, a member of one of the powerful noble families, finally held control of the Athenian state. He ruled with great sagacity and success, and many of the Athenians gave him sincere support. Having built a war fleet of probably forty-eight ships, he seized the mouth of the Hellespont (Dardanelles). This control of the gateway to the Black Sea proved of enormous value to Athens in later days. He carried out many public improvements at Athens and transferred to the city the old peasant spring feast of Dionysus, from which were yet to come the theater and the great dramas of Athens. Athenian manufactures and commerce flourished as never

Pisistratus, tyrant of Athens (540–527 B.C.)

before, and when Pisistratus died he had laid a foundation to which much of the later greatness of Athens was due.

512. In spite of their great ability the sons of Pisistratus — Hipparchus and Hippias — were unable to overcome the prejudice of the people against a ruler on whom they had not conferred authority. One of the earliest exhibitions of Greek patriotism is the outburst of enthusiasm at Athens when two youths, Harmodius and Aristogiton (Fig. 167), at the sacrifice of their own lives, struck down one of the tyrants (Hipparchus). Hippias, the other one, was eventually obliged to flee. Thus, shortly before 500 B.C., Athens was freed from her tyrants.

Fall of the sons of Pisistratus

513. The people were now able to gain new power against the nobles by the efforts of Clisthenes, a noble friendly to the lower classes. He broke up the old tribal divisions which had been formed on the basis of blood relationship, and established ten tribes on purely *local* lines of division. He thus cut up the old noble clans and assigned the fragments to different local divisions, where they were in the minority. This prevented the nobles from acting together and broke their power.

Reforms of Clisthenes reduce the power of the nobles

514. In order to avoid the rise of a new tyrant, Clisthenes established a law that once a year the people might by vote declare any prominent citizen dangerous to the state and banish him for ten years. To cast his vote against a man, a citizen had only to pick up one of the pieces of broken pottery lying about the market place, write upon it the name of the citizen to be banished, and deposit it in the voting urn. Such a bit of pottery was called an *ostracon* (Fig. 174). Hence to ostracize a man (literally to potsherd him) meant to interrupt his political career by banishment. Although the nobles were still the only ones to whom the high offices of government were open, the possession of other forms of wealth besides land gave a citizen important political rights, and Athens had thus (about 500 B.C.) gained a form of government which

Ostracism

gave the people a high degree of power. The state was in large measure a democracy.

Expansion of Sparta; foundation of Spartan League

515. Meantime Sparta also had greatly increased in power. The Spartans had pushed their military successes until they held over a third of the Peloponnesian peninsula. The result was that long before 500 B.C. the Spartans had forced the neighboring states into a combination, the Spartan League, which included nearly the whole of the Peloponnese. As the leader of this league Sparta was the most powerful state in Greece. It had no industries, and it therefore did not possess the prosperous commercial class which had elsewhere done so much to overthrow the nobles and bring about the rise of the tyrants. For this and other reasons Sparta had escaped the rule of a tyrant. While it had divided the power of its king by appointing two kings to rule jointly, it was opposed to the rule of the people, and it looked with a jealous eye on the rising democracy of Athens.

SECTION 45. CIVILIZATION OF THE AGE OF THE TYRANTS

Nobles continue to be social leaders; athletic games

516. Although the nobles of Athens had been forced to surrender much of their political power, nevertheless they still held the exclusive right to be elected to the important offices in the government. They continued also to be the leaders in all those matters which we call *social*. The multitudes which thronged to the public games looked down at the best-born youths of Greece contesting for the prizes in the athletic matches, and the wealthier nobles put the swiftest horses into the chariot races. To the laurel wreath which was granted the winner at the Olympic games Athens added a prize of five hundred drachmas when the winner was an Athenian. He was also entitled to take his meals at tables maintained by the state. The greatest poets of the time, especially Pindar, often celebrated the victors in triumphant verses.

517. In the matter of education, noble youths might be found spending the larger part of the day practicing in the public inclosure devoted to athletic exercises. To be sure, writing was now so common that a young man could not afford to be without it, and hence he submitted to some instruction in this art,— a discipline which he was probably very reluctant to exchange for the applause of the idlers gathered around the gymnastic training ground. The women had no share in either the education or the social life of the men, and one of the greatest weaknesses of Greek civilization was the very limited part played by women in the life of the nation.

Education

518. The education of the time was not complete without some instruction also in music. It was in the Age of the Tyrants that the music of Greece rose to the level of a real art. A system of writing musical notes, meaning for music what the alphabet meant for literature, had already existed in Assyria (§ 260), and a similar system now appeared in Greece. The flute had been brought from Egypt to Crete in early times, and from the Cretans the Greeks had received it. Long a favorite instrument, it was now much more cultivated, and one musician even wrote a composition for the flute which was intended to tell the story of Apollo's fight with the dragon of Delphi. The lyre, which formerly had but four strings, was now made with seven, and compositions for the lyre alone were popular. Either of these instruments might be played as the accompaniment of song, or both together, with choruses of boys and girls. Here we have the beginnings of orchestral music as the accompaniment of choruses.

Instrumental music

519. Music had a great influence on the literature of the age, for the poets now began to write verses to be sung with the music of the lyre, and hence such verses are called lyric poetry. From serious discussions like those of Solon (§ 505) the poets passed to songs of momentary moods, longings, dreams, hopes, and fiery storms of passion. Each in his way found a wondrous world within

Lyric poetry: Pindar and Sappho

himself, which he thus pictured in short songs. Probably the greatest of these poets was Pindar of Thebes. Proud of his noble birth, the friend and intimate of tyrants and nobles, but also their fearless admonisher, Pindar gloried both in the pleasures and the responsibilities of wealth and rank. He sang in praise of pomp and splendor with a vividness which makes us see the chariots flashing down the course and hear the shouting of the multitude as the proud victor receives the laurel wreath of triumph. At the same time, his immortal word pictures of the life of the nobles and their triumphs are always suffused with the beauty of unquestioning belief in the gods, especially Apollo, for whom Pindar seemed to speak almost as a prophet. He was the last great spokesman of a dying order of society, — the rule of the nobles, which was to give way to the rule of the people. Another great lyric singer of the age was the poetess Sappho, the earliest woman to gain undying fame in literature.

Festival choruses become drama

520. A favorite form of song was the chorus, with which the country folk loved to celebrate their rustic feasts. The poet Stesichorus, who lived in Sicily, began to write choruses which told the stories of the gods as they were found in the old myths. The singers, as they marched in rustic procession, wore goatskins, and their faces were concealed by masks. Some of the songs were sung responsively by the chorus and their leader. For the diversion of the listening peasants the leader would illustrate with gestures the story told in the song. He thus became to some extent an actor, the forerunner of the actors on our own stage. After Pisistratus introduced the spring feast of Dionysus at Athens, this form of presentation made rapid progress. A second leader was introduced, and dialogue between the two was then possible, though the chorus continued to recite most of the narrative. Thus arose a form of musical play, or *drama*, the action or narrative of which was carried on by the chorus and two actors. The Greeks called such a play a tragedy, which means "goat's play," probably because of the rustic disguise as goats which the chorus had always worn.

521. The grassy circle where the chorus danced and sang was usually on a slope in the hills, from which the spectators had a fine view of the country and the sea beyond. At Athens the people sat on the slope of the Acropolis, and as they watched the play they could look far across the sea to the heights of Argos. Here, under the southern brow of the Acropolis, where Pisistratus laid out the sacred precinct of Dionysus (see plan, p. 418), the theater began to take form and furnished the arrangements which have finally been inherited by us in our theaters.

Origin of the theater

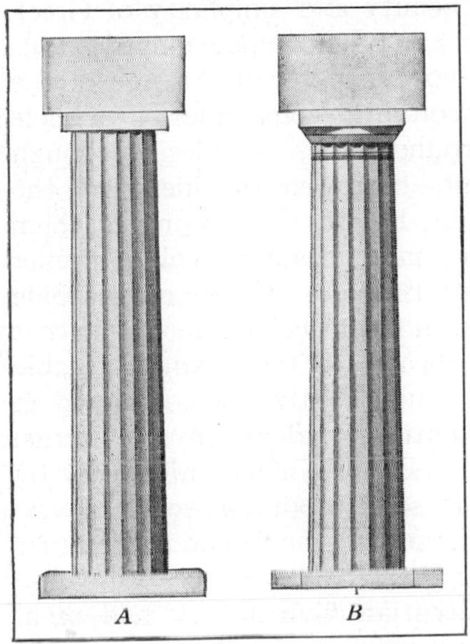

Fig. 165. *An Old* Egyptian Column *and the* Doric Column *derived from it*

The earliest form of column used by the Greeks was a fluted shaft of stone *B* closely resembling the simplest form *A* which we found in Egypt, dating nearly 3000 B.C. Not only the whole idea of a rhythmic row of piers but also the form of each shaft was thus taken by the Greeks from Egypt. The Greeks gave this form completeness and increased beauty by adding a capital and by shaping it with great refinement of line and contour. See also diagram, p. 423

522. The tyrants were so devoted to building that architecture made very important advances. The Greek cities, including the buildings of the government, were still simply groups of sun-dried brick structures. Great stone buildings such as we have seen on the Nile had been unknown in Europe since the time of the Ægeans, but now the rough Greek temples of sun-dried brick were rebuilt in limestone by the tyrants. Indeed, the front of the temple of Apollo at Delphi was even built of marble. At no other time before or since were so many temples erected as in the

Architecture

Greek world in the Age of the Tyrants. In Sicily and southern Italy a number of the noble temples of this age still stand to display to us the beauty and simplicity of Greek architecture even at that early and undeveloped stage (Fig. 214). Instead of the wooden posts of the Age of the Nobles, lines of plain *stone* columns (colonnades) in a style which we call Doric now surrounded these temples. Although the architects of the tyrants borrowed the idea and the *form* of these colonnades from Egypt, they improved them until they made them the most beautiful columns ever designed by early architects. Like the temples on the Nile those of Greece were painted in bright colors.

Sculpture

523. The temples were adorned, in the triangular gable end, with sculptured relief figures of the gods, grouped in scenes representing incidents in the myths. Although at first very much influenced by Oriental reliefs, the sculptors soon produced works of real beauty and independence. In meeting the demand for statues of the victors at the games the Greek sculptors were also much influenced by the Egyptian figures they had seen. Their earliest figures in stone were therefore still stiff and ungraceful (Fig. 166). Moved by patriotic impulses, however, the Athenian sculptors went still farther and attempted a kind of work which never had arisen in the Near East. They wrought a noble memorial of the two youths who endeavored to free Athens from the sons of Pisistratus. It was in the form of a group depicting the two at the moment of their attack on the tyrants, and although it still displayed some of the old stiffness, it also showed remarkable progress in portraying free and vigorous action of the human body. These figures were cast in bronze.

Painting

524. Similar progress was made by the painters of the age. Just as the poets had begun to call upon their own imagination for subject matter, so the vase-painters now began to depict not only scenes from the myths of the gods and heroes but also pictures from the everyday life of the times (see the school, Fig. 177). At the

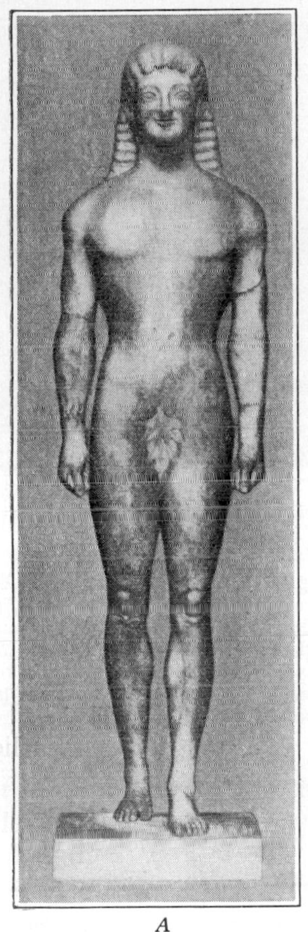

A

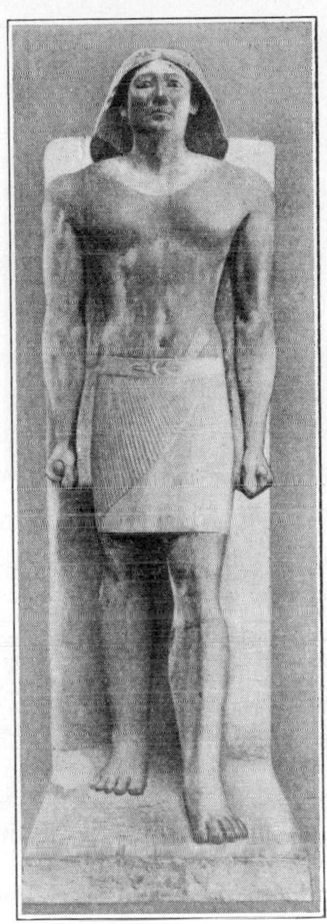

B

FIG. 166. *Early* GREEK STATUE, A, *and* EGYPTIAN PORTRAIT STATUE, B, *by which it was influenced*

The portrait *B* is over two thousand years older than the Greek figure. The Egyptian nobleman (§ 103) stands in the customary posture of such figures in Egyptian art, with the arms hanging down and the left foot thrust forward. The Greek figure *A* stands in the same posture. Both look straight ahead, as was customary in undeveloped art. The Greek figure — as yet far inferior to the older statue — shows clearly the influence of Egyptian sculpture

FIG. 167. *Monument of the* TYRANT-SLAYERS *of Athens,* HARMODIUS *and* ARISTOGITON, *from Two Points of View*

On the slopes of the Areopagus (see plan, p. 418), overlooking the market place, the Athenians set up this piece of sculpture. It was carried off by the Persians after the battle of Salamis, and the Athenians had another made to replace the first one. The original group was afterward recovered in Persia by Alexander or his successors and restored to its old place, where both groups stood, side by side. Our illustration is an ancient copy in marble, probably reproducing the later of the two groups

same time they improved their method greatly. They made drawings of the human figure that were more natural and true than early artists had ever before been able to do. Their skill in depicting limbs shortened by being seen from one end was surprising. These problems, called *foreshortening* and *perspective*, were first solved by the Greek painters. The vases of this age are a wonderful treasury of beautiful scenes from Greek life, reminding us of our glimpses into the life of Egypt two thousand five hundred years earlier, in the tomb-chapel scenes of the Nile.

525. Literature and painting show us that the Greeks of this age were intensely interested in the life of their own time. In the first place, they were thinking more deeply than ever before about conduct, and they were more inclined

FIG. 168. *Greek Vase-Painting, showing the* HOME LIFE OF WOMEN

A maidservant at the right presents to her mistress an Egyptian alabaster perfume bottle. The mistress sits arranging her hair before a hand mirror. At the left a lady is working at an embroidery frame, while a visitor in street costume watches her work. Behind stands a lady with a basket. Notice the grace and beauty of the figures, which at this time were in red (the natural color of the terra cotta), showing through a shining black pigment laid on by the artist

to distinguish between right and wrong. Men could no longer believe that the gods led the evil lives pictured in the Homeric songs. Stesichorus had so high an idea of womanly fidelity that he could not accept the tale of the beautiful Helen's faithlessness, and in his festival songs he told the ancient story in another way. Men now felt that even Zeus and his Olympian divinities must do the right. Mortals too must do the same, for men had now come to believe that in the world of the dead there was punishment for the evildoer. Hades became a place of torment for the wicked, guarded by Cerberus, a monstrous dog, one of those sentinel animals of the Near East of which the Sphinx of Gizeh, also guarding the dead, is the oldest example.

Growing sense of right and wrong; punishment hereafter

526. Likewise it was believed that there must be a place of blessedness in the next world for the good. Accordingly, in the temple at Eleusis scenes from the mysterious earth life of Demeter and Dionysus, to whom men owed the fruits of the earth, were presented by the priests in dramatic form before the initiated, and in some mysterious way those who viewed them received immortal life and might be admitted into the

Blessedness hereafter; mysteries of Eleusis

Islands of the Blessed, where once none but the ancient heroes could be received. Even the poorest slave was permitted to enter this fellowship and be initiated into the mysteries, as they were called.

Oracles

527. More than ever, also, men now turned to the gods for a knowledge of the future in this world. Everywhere it was believed that the oracle voice of Apollo revealed the outcome of every untried venture, and his shrine at Delphi (Fig. 169) became a national religious center, to which the whole Greek world resorted.

Thales and his prediction of an eclipse (585 B.C.)

528. Some thoughtful men, on the other hand, were rejecting the beliefs of older times, especially regarding the world and its control by the gods. The Ionian cities, long the commercial leaders of the Ægean, now likewise led the way in thinking of these new problems. In constant contact with Egypt and the Phœnician cities, they gained the beginnings of mathematics and astronomy as known in the Near East, and one of the Ionian thinkers had indeed set up an Egyptian shadow clock (Fig. 69). At Miletus, the leader of these Ionian cities, there was an able statesman named Thales, who had traveled widely and received from Babylonia a list of observations of the heavenly bodies. From such lists the Babylonians had already learned that eclipses of the sun occurred at periodic intervals. With these lists in his hands Thales could calculate when the next eclipse would occur. He therefore told the people of Miletus that they might expect an eclipse of the sun before the end of a certain year. When the promised eclipse (585 B.C.) actually occurred as he had predicted, the fame of Thales spread far and wide.

529. The prediction of an eclipse, a feat already accomplished by the Babylonians, was not so important as the *consequences* which followed in the mind of Thales. Hitherto men had believed that eclipses and all the other strange things that happened in the skies were caused by the momentary angry whim of some god. Now, however, Thales boldly proclaimed that the movements of the heavenly bodies were in accordance with fixed laws. The gods were thus banished from control of the sky-world where the eagle of Zeus had once ruled. So also when a Greek traveler like Thales visited the vast buildings of the Near East, such as the pyramids of Gizeh, then over two thousand years old, he at once saw that the gods had not been wandering on earth only a few generations before his own time. This fact seemed to banish the gods from the past, and from the beginning of the world likewise.

Natural law versus the gods; Ionian science and philosophy

530. Hence another citizen of Miletus, perhaps a pupil of Thales, explained the origin of animals by assuming a development of higher forms from the lower ones, in a manner which reminds us of the modern theory of evolution. He studied the forms of the seas and the countries, and he made a map of the world. It is the earliest world map known to us, although maps of a limited region were already in use in Egypt and Babylonia. A little later another geographer of Miletus, named Hecatæus, traveled widely, including a journey up the Nile, and he wrote a geography of the world. In this book, as in the map just mentioned, the Mediterranean Sea was the center, and the lands about it for a short distance back from its shores were all those which were known to the author. On page 379 is a map drawn according to Hecatæus' description of the world. Hecatæus also put together a history made up of the mythical stories of early Greece and the tales of the past he had heard in the Near East. After the historian of the Hebrew patriarchs he was the first historical writer of the early world.

Ionian geography and history

531. Another Ionian thinker, who migrated to southern Italy, was Pythagoras. He investigated mathematics and natural science. He or his pupils discovered that the square of the hypotenuse equals the sum of the squares of the other two sides of a right-angled triangle. They also found out that the length of a musical string is in exact mathematical relation to the height of its tone. They likewise discovered that the earth

Ionian mathematics and natural science

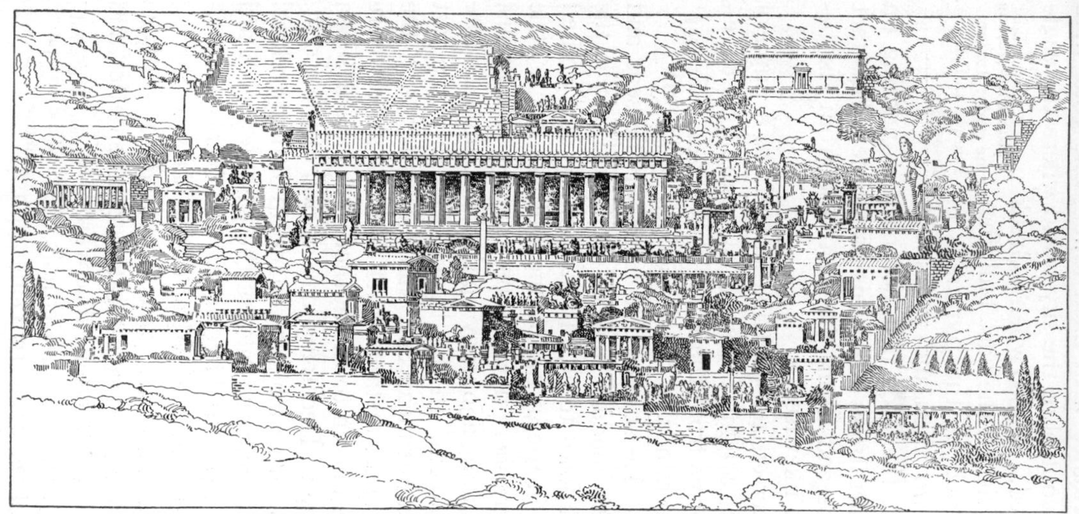

Fig. 169. *The* Buildings of Delphi *restored*

Beginning with the Seventh Century B.C. this place became a national sanctuary of the Greeks, where all Greece and many foreigners came to hear the oracles of the revered Apollo. His temple, many times rebuilt, was a Doric structure which we see rising in the middle of the inclosure. A zigzag way passed up from the lower right-hand corner of this inclosure, and on each side of this way were ranged the treasuries containing the votive offerings of the Greeks to the great god, — the statues and victorious trophies, many of them of gold and silver, presented by states, kings, and individuals. Universal reverence for this famous sanctuary failed to protect it, for it was finally plundered by the Romans (§ 1082). Although the Roman emperor Nero (A.D. 54–68) removed five hundred statues, there were still three thousand left here when Pliny visited the place some years later. Part of a magnificent tripod taken away from here by the Romans to adorn Constantinople may be seen in Fig. 263. Excavated by a French expedition and restored after Homolle-Tournaire

is a sphere which possesses its own motion. Another of these Ionians, in his account of the origin of the earth, called attention to the presence of petrified sea plants and fish in the rocks, to prove that the sea had at one time covered the land.

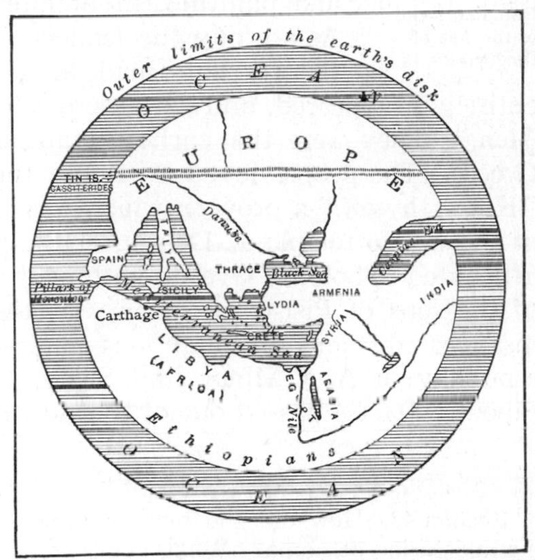

Map of the World *after Hecatæus* (517 B.C.)

532. Thus these Ionian thinkers, having gradually abandoned the old myths, took the natural world out of the hands of the gods. They therefore became the forerunners of natural scientists and philosophers, for they strove to discern what were the *natural* laws which in the beginning had brought the world into existence and still continued to control it. At this point in their thinking they entered upon a new world of thought, which we call *science* and *philosophy*,— a world which had never dawned upon the greatest minds of the early East. This step, taken by Thales and the great men of the Ionian cities, remains and will forever remain the greatest achievement of the human intellect,— an achievement to call forth the reverence and admiration of all time.

Great step taken by Ionian thinkers

533. The Age of the Tyrants was therefore one of the great epochs of the world's history. Under the stimulus of the keen struggle for leadership in business, in government, and in society the minds of the ablest men of the time were wonderfully quickened till they threw off the bondage of habit and entered an entirely new world of science and philosophy.

The inner power of this vigorous new Greek life flowed out in statesmanship, in literature and religion, in sculpture and painting, in architecture and building. As a group the leaders of this age, many of them tyrants, made an impression which never entirely disappeared, and they were called "the Seven Wise Men." They were the earliest statesmen and thinkers of Greece. The people loved to quote their sayings, such as "Know thyself," a proverb which was carved over the door of the Apollo temple at Delphi, or the wise maxim, usually attributed to Solon, "Overdo nothing." After the overthrow of the sons of Pisistratus, however, the tyrants gradually disappeared; and although one survived here and there, especially in Asia Minor and Sicily, Greece at this time (about 500 B.C.) passed out of the Age of the Tyrants.

Summary; end of the Age of the Tyrants

QUESTIONS

Section 43. How did the new colonies of the Greeks influence manufacturing at home? What evidence have we of the extent of Athenian commerce? Discuss the effect upon shipbuilding. What new business convenience came in from the East? How did coinage arise? What leading coins did Athens possess? How did coinage affect business and the accumulation of wealth? From our point of view did the Greeks have any large cities or farms?

Section 44. What was now happening to the Greek farmers? Explain the position and influence of the new industrial class. Were the nobles all united? How did a noble often make himself powerful? How did the Greeks feel toward a tyrant? When may we date the period of the tyrants?

In what form had Greek laws thus far existed? What did the people now demand? What code of laws was made at Athens? Who now aroused Athens to meet her foreign difficulties? What did Solon accomplish after he was elected archon? What can you say of his character? Did his work save Athens from the rule of a tyrant?

What did Pisistratus accomplish? What happened to his sons? How did Clisthenes aid the people? What was ostracism? What was happening meantime in Sparta? How did Sparta feel toward Athens?

Section 45. Describe the social position of the nobles in the Age of the Tyrants. What was lyric poetry? Who was the leading lyric poet? Who was the greatest poetess? How did festal choruses lead to drama?

Had the Greeks any fine buildings before this age? Had there been stone buildings in Europe previous to this time? In what style of architecture were the temples now erected? Where did the form of the Doric column arise? Did the Greeks improve these columns? What other adornment of their temples did the Greek architects employ? Under what influences did Greek sculpture arise? What progress does the monument of the tyrant-slayers show?

Discuss Greek vase-painting in this age. Compare the human figures in Fig. 168 and those in Fig. 154. How was the method of vase-painting improved? What progress was made in ideas of conduct? Discuss the ideas of the hereafter; oracles. What did Thales do? Was he the first to make such a calculation? What conclusions did he make about the gods and their control of the world? How did the modern map-maker get the material for the map on page 379? What new world had the Ionian thinkers entered upon? What can you say of the Age of the Tyrants as a whole?

BIBLIOGRAPHY FOR TOPICAL STUDY

Greek colonies and Greek commerce: BOTSFORD, *Hellenic History*, pp. 59–66; *Source Book*, pp. 106–109; BURY, *Greece*, chap. ii; GULICK, *Modern Traits*, pp. 106–111.

The Greek child and education: BRITISH MUSEUM, *Greek and Roman Life*, pp. 205–208; CARY, *Documentary Sources*, pp. 94–95; DOBSON, *Ancient Education*, pp. 25–44; GULICK, *Modern Traits*, pp. 78–87; METROPOLITAN MUSEUM OF ART, *Daily Life*, pp. 40–46.

Greek literature and science in the Sixth Century B.C.: BOTSFORD, *Hellenic History*, pp. 126–135, 145, 150–157; *Source Book*, pp. 141–150; BURTON, *Discovery of the Ancient World*, pp. 26–29; BURY, *Greece*, pp. 305–308, 319–321; MURRAY, *Greek Literature*, chaps. iii–v; NORWOOD-DUFF, *Writers*, pp. 37–44; *Pageant of Greece*, pp. 79–95 (or HOWE-HARRER, *Greek Literature*, pp. 100–131); POLAND-REISINGER-WAGNER, *Culture of Greece and Rome*, pp. 39–42.

CHAPTER XIII · *The Repulse of Persia*

SECTION 46. THE COMING OF THE PERSIANS

534. The leadership gained by the Ionian cities in the Age of the Tyrants was now seriously checked by their neighbors in Asia Minor. Here still lived the descendants of the Early Anatolians, mingled with the Hittites and other later invaders. The kings of Lydia — the leading Anatolian kingdom — made their capital, Sardes, the strongest city of Asia Minor. From them the practice of coinage had passed to the Greeks. The Lydians had finally conquered all the Greek cities along the Ægean coast of Asia Minor except Miletus, which still resisted capture.

Rise of Lydia in Asia Minor

535. The Lydians had been strong enough to halt the Medes, but we remember that when Cyrus the Persian invaded Asia Minor, he defeated Crœsus and captured Sardes. In the midst of the most remarkable progress in civilization the Ionian cities thus suddenly lost their liberty and became the subjects of Persia, a despotic Oriental power. Moreover, the

Fall of Lydia and advance of Persia to the Ægean

NOTE. The above headpiece represents a scene sculptured in relief on a doorway in the palace of XERXES AT PERSEPOLIS. It shows us XERXES as he was accustomed to appear when enthroned before his nobles, with his attendants and fan-bearers. At Salamis he took his station on the heights of Ægaleos overlooking the bay, and as he sat there viewing the battle below him, he must have been enthroned as we see him here.

sudden advance of Persia to the Ægean made this power at one stroke a close neighbor of the Greek world now arising there.

536. As we have already learned, the Persians represented a high civilization and an enlightened rule; but, on the other hand, the people of the Near East lacked free citizenship, and were, moreover, held in a sort of intellectual bondage to religious tradition. Persian supremacy in Greece would therefore have checked the free development of Greek genius along its own exalted lines. There seemed little prospect that the tiny Greek states, even if they united, could successfully resist the vast Oriental empire, controlling as it did all the countries of the ancient East which we have been studying. Nevertheless the Ionian cities revolted against their Persian lords.

The coming conflict and the revolt of the Ionians

537. During the struggle with Persia which followed this revolt the Athenians sent twenty ships to aid their Ionian kindred. This act brought a Persian army of revenge, under Darius, into Europe. The long march across the Hellespont and through Thrace cost the Asiatic invaders many men, and the fleet which accompanied the Persian land forces was wrecked in trying to round the high promontory of Mount Athos (492 B.C.). This advance into Greece was therefore abandoned for a plan of invasion by water across the Ægean.

First Persian invasion of Europe

538. In the early summer of 490 B.C. a considerable fleet of transports and warships bearing the Persian host put out from the island of Samos, sailed straight across the Ægean, and entered the straits between Eubœa and Attica (see map I, p. 402). The Persians began by burning the little city of Eretria, which had also sent ships to aid the Ionians. They then landed on the shores of Attica, in the Bay of Marathon (see map, p. 418), intending to march on Athens, the greater offender. They were guided by the aged Hippias, son of Pisistratus, once tyrant of Athens, who accompanied them with high hopes of regaining control of his native city.

Second Persian invasion

Fig. 170. *The Plain of* Marathon

This view is taken from the hills at the southern end of the plain, and we look northeastward across a corner of the Bay of Marathon to the mountains in the background, which are on the large island of Eubœa (see map, p. 418). The Persian camp was at the very shore line, where their ships were moored or drawn up. The Greeks held a position in the hills overlooking the plain (just out of range on the left) and commanding the road to Athens, which is 25 miles distant behind us. When the Persians began to move along the shore road toward the right, the Greeks crossed the plain and attacked. The memorial mound (Fig. 171) is too far away to be visible from this point

Consternation in Athens and Greece

539. All was excitement and confusion among the Greek states. The defeat of the revolting Ionian cities, and especially the plundering of Miletus by the Persians, had made a deep impression throughout Greece. An Athenian dramatist had depicted in a play the fate of the unhappy city, and had so incensed the Athenians that they passed weeping from the theater to prosecute and fine the author. Now this Persian foe who had crushed the Ionian cities was camping behind the hills only a few miles northeast of Athens. After dispatching messengers in desperate haste to seek aid in Sparta, the Athenian citizens turned to contemplate the seemingly hopeless situation of their beloved city.

540. Thinking to find the Athenians unprepared, Darius had not sent a large army. The Persian forces probably numbered no more than twenty thousand men, but at the utmost the Athenians could not put more than half this number into the field. Fortunately for them there was among their generals a skilled and experienced commander named Miltiades, a man of resolution and firmness, who, moreover, had lived on the Hellespont and was familiar with Persian methods of fighting. To his judgment the commander-in-chief, Callimachus, yielded at all points. As the citizen-soldiers of Attica flocked to the city at the call to arms Miltiades was able to induce the leaders not to await the assault of the Persians at Athens but to march across the peninsula and block the Persian advance among the hills overlooking the eastern coast and commanding the road to the city. This bold and resolute move roused courage and enthusiasm in the downcast ranks of the Greeks.

The armies and Greek leadership

541. Nevertheless, when they issued between the hills and looked down upon the Persian host encamped upon the Plain of Marathon, flanked by a fleet of hundreds of vessels, misgiving and despair chilled the hearts of the little Attic army, made up as it was of citizen militia without experience in war and pitted against a Persian army of professional soldiers, the victors of many battles. But Miltiades held the leaders firmly in hand, and the arrival of a thousand Greeks from Platæa revived the courage of the Athenians. The Greek position overlooked the main road to Athens, and the Persians could not advance along this road without leaving their line of march exposed on one side to the Athenian attack.

The Greek position

542. Unable to lure the Greeks from their advantageous position after several days' waiting, the Persians at length attempted to march along the road to Athens, at the same time endeavoring to cover their exposed line of march with a sufficient force thrown out in battle array. Miltiades was familiar with the Persian custom of massing troops in the center. He therefore massed his own

Battle of Marathon (490 B.C.)

FIG. 171. *Mound raised as a* MONUMENT *to the* FALLEN GREEKS *on the Plain at Marathon*

The mound is nearly 50 feet high. Excavations undertaken in 1890 disclosed beneath it the bodies of the one hundred and ninety-two Athenian citizens who fell in the battle. Some of their weapons and the funeral vases buried with them were also recovered

troops on both wings, leaving his center weak. It was a battle between bow and spear. The Athenians undauntedly faced the storm of Persian arrows, and then both wings pushed boldly forward to the line of shields behind which the Persian archers were kneeling. In the meantime the Persian center, finding the Greek center weak, had pushed it back, while the two Greek wings closed in and thrust back the Persian wings in confusion. Caught between the two advancing Greek wings, the Asiatic army crumbled into a broken multitude. The Persian bow was useless, and the Greek spear everywhere spread death and terror. As the Persians fled to their ships they left over six thousand dead upon the field, while the Athenians lost less than two hundred men. When the Persian commander, unwilling to acknowledge defeat, sailed around the Attic peninsula and appeared with his fleet before the port of Athens, he found it unwise to attempt a landing, for the victorious Athenian army was already encamped beside the city. The Persians therefore retired, and the Persian emperor's plans for making the Ægean and its harbors a part of his far-reaching naval and commercial expansion were completely blocked. We can imagine with what feelings the Athenian citizens watched the formidable Asiatic fleet of Darius as it finally disappeared.

SECTION 47. THE GREEK REPULSE OF PERSIANS AND PHŒNICIANS

543. Among the men who stood in the Athenian ranks at Marathon was Themistocles, the ablest statesman in Greece, a man who had already occupied the office of archon, the head of the Athenian state. He was convinced of the necessity of building up a strong navy, — a course already encouraged by Pisistratus. As archon Themistocles had therefore striven to show the Athenians that the only way in which Athens could hope to meet the assault of Persia was by making herself undisputed mistress of the sea. He had failed in his effort. But now the Athenians had seen the Persians cross the Ægean with their fleet and land at Marathon. It was evident that a powerful Athenian navy might have stopped them. They began to listen to the counsels of Themistocles to make Athens the great sea power of the Mediterranean.

Rise of Themistocles

544. Darius the Great, whose remarkable reign we have studied, died without obtaining naval leadership in the west and without having avenged the defeat of his army at Marathon. It is clear that his son and successor Xerxes made every effort to carry out his father's naval policy, and he now planned a far-reaching assault on Greek civilization all along the line from Greece to Sicily. This he could do through his control of the Phœnician cities. The naval policy of his father Darius had given the Persians a huge Phœnician war fleet. In so far as the coming attack on Greece was by sea it was

Xerxes continues policy of naval control of Ægean

chiefly a Semitic assault. At the same time Xerxes induced Phœnician Carthage to attack the Greeks in Sicily. Thus the two wings of the great Semitic line, represented by the Phœnicians in both east and west (Carthage), were to attack the Indo-European line, represented in east and west by the Greeks. Xerxes was persuaded by his general Mardonius to adopt the Hellespont route (map I, p. 402).

Themistocles induces Athenians to build a fleet

545. Meantime the Greeks were making ready to meet the coming Persian assault. Soon they saw that Xerxes' commanders were cutting a canal behind the promontory of Athos, to secure a short cut and thus to avoid all risk of such a wreck as had overtaken their former fleet in rounding this dangerous point. When the news of this operation reached Athens, Themistocles was able to induce the Athenian Assembly to build a great fleet of probably a hundred and eighty triremes. The Greeks were then able for the first time to meet the Persian advance by both sea and land (see map I, p. 402).

Third Persian invasion; Themistocles' plan of campaign

546. The masterly plan of action devised by Themistocles corresponded exactly to that of the Persian advance. The Asiatics were coming in combined land and sea array, with army and fleet moving together down the east coast of the Greek mainland. It was as if the Persian forces had two wings, a sea wing and a land wing, moving southward side by side. The design of Themistocles was to meet the Persian sea wing first with full force and fight a decisive naval battle as soon as possible. If victorious, the Greek fleet commanding the Ægean would then be able to sail up the eastern coast of Greece and threaten the communications and supplies of the Persian army in the rear. There must be no attempt of the small Greek army to meet the vast land forces of the Persians, beyond delaying them as long as possible at the narrow northern passes, which could be defended with a few men. An attempt to unite all the Greek states was not successful, but Sparta and Athens combined their forces to meet the common danger. Themistocles was able to induce the Spartans to accept his plan only on condition that Sparta be given command of the allied Greek fleets.

Persians enter Greece

547. In the summer of 480 B.C. the Asiatic army was approaching the pass of Thermopylæ, just opposite the westernmost point of the island of Eubœa (see map, p. 338). Their fleet moved with them. The Asiatic host must have numbered over two hundred thousand men, with probably as many more camp followers, while the enormous fleet contained presumably about a thousand vessels, of which perhaps two thirds were warships. Of these ships the Persians lost several hundred in a storm, leaving probably about five hundred warships available for action. The Spartan king Leonidas led some five thousand men to check the Persians at the pass of Thermopylæ, while the Greek fleet of less than three hundred triremes was endeavoring to hold together and strike the Persian navy at Artemisium, on the northern coast of Eubœa. Thus the land and sea forces of both contestants were face to face.

Battles of Thermopylæ and Artemisium

548. After several days' delay the Persians advanced to attack on both land and sea. The Greek fleet made a skillful and creditable defense against superior numbers, and all day the dauntless Leonidas held the pass of Thermopylæ against the Persian host. Meantime the Persians were executing two flank movements by land and by sea, — one, led by a traitorous Greek, over the mountains to strike Leonidas in the rear, and the other with two hundred ships around Eubœa to take the Greek fleet likewise from behind. A storm destroyed the flanking Persian ships, and a second combat between the two main fleets was indecisive. The flank movement by sea therefore failed, but the flanking of the pass was successful. Taken in front and rear, the heroic Leonidas died fighting at the head of his small force, which the Persian host completely annihilated. The death of Leonidas stirred all Greece. With the defeat of the Greek land forces and the advance of the Persian army the Greek fleet, seriously damaged, was obliged to withdraw to the south. It took up its position in the Bay of Salamis (see map, p. 418), while the main army of the Spartans and their allies was drawn up on the isthmus of Corinth, the only point at which the Greek land forces could hope to make another defensive stand.

Persian advance into Attica and burning of Athens

549. As the Persian army moved southward from Thermopylæ the indomitable Themistocles gathered together the Athenian population and carried them in transports to the little islands of Salamis and Ægina and to the shores of Argolis. Meantime the Greek fleet had been repaired and with reenforcements numbered over three hundred battleships. Nevertheless the courage of many Greeks at Salamis was shaken as they looked northward, where the far-stretching Persian host darkened the coast road, while in the south they could see the Asiatic fleet drawn up off the old port of Athens at Phalerum. High over the Attic hills the flames of the burning Acropolis showed red against the sullen masses of smoke that obscured the eastern horizon and told them that the homes of the Athenians lay in ashes. With masterly skill Themistocles held together the irresolute Greek leaders while he induced Xerxes to attack by the false message that the Greek fleet was about to slip out of the bay.

Battle of Salamis (480 B.C.)

550. On the heights overlooking the Bay of Salamis the Persian king, seated on his throne in the midst of his brilliant Oriental court, took up his station to watch the battle. The Greek position was too cramped for the maneuvers of a large fleet. Crowded and hampered by the narrow sea room, the huge Asiatic fleet soon fell into confusion before the Greek attack. There was no room for retreat. The combat lasted the entire day, and when darkness settled on the Bay of Salamis the Persian fleet had been almost annihilated. The Athenians were masters of the sea, and it was impossible for the army of Xerxes to operate with the same freedom as before. By the creation of its powerful fleet Athens had saved Greece, and Themistocles had shown himself the greatest of Greek statesmen.

Fig. 172. Piræus, *the* Port of Athens, *looking over the Modern City to the Island of Salamis*

The mountains in the background are the heights of the island of Salamis, which is separated from Attica by a narrow channel leading into the Bay of Eleusis (see map, p. 418). This channel is divided in two at its entrance by the low, rocky island of Psyttaleia (its whole length shown here at right). The Persian fleet sailed in from the left (south) and was drawn up in a line facing north between the harbor of Piræus and the island of Salamis. However when the order was given to enter the straits, because of the position of Psyttaleia the Persian ships could not advance in a long front so as to enfold the Greek fleet. Instead the Persians passed on either side of the obstructing island in columns and so were exposed to flank attack from the Greeks, who came into action from the right (northwest of Psyttaleia). Persian troops stationed by Xerxes on Psyttaleia were all slain by the Greeks. (Courtesy of Professor F. P. Johnson)

Retreat of Xerxes in the East; defeat of Carthage in the West

551. Xerxes was now troubled lest he should be cut off from Asia by the victorious Greek fleet. Indeed, Themistocles made every effort to induce Sparta to join with Athens in doing this very thing, but the cautious Spartans could not be prevailed upon to undertake what seemed to them so dangerous an enterprise. If Themistocles' plan of sending the Greek fleet immediately to the Hellespont had been carried out, Greece would have been saved another year of anxious campaigning against the Persian army. With many losses from disease and insufficient supplies, Xerxes retreated to the Hellespont and withdrew into Asia, leaving his able general Mardonius with an army of perhaps fifty thousand men to winter in Thessaly. Meantime the news reached Greece that the army of Carthaginians which had crossed from Africa to Sicily had been completely defeated by the Greeks under the leadership of Gelon, tyrant of Syracuse. Thus the assault of the Asiatics upon the Hellenic world was beaten back in both east and west in the same year (480 B.C.).

Reaction against Themistocles

552. The brilliant statesmanship of Themistocles, so evident to us of today, was not so clear to the Athenians as the winter passed and they realized that the victory at Salamis had not relieved Greece of the presence of a Persian army, and that Mardonius would invade Attica with the coming of spring. Themistocles, whose proposed naval expedition to the Hellespont would have forced the Persian army out of Greece, was removed from command by the factions of his ungrateful city. Nevertheless the most tempting offers from Mardonius could not induce the Athenians to forsake the cause of Greek liberty and join hands with Persia.

Persians again in Attica

553. As Mardonius, at the end of the winter rains, led his army again into Attica, the unhappy Athenians were obliged to flee as before, this time chiefly to Salamis. Sparta, always reluctant and slow when the crisis demanded quick and vigorous action, was finally induced to put her army into the field. When Mardonius in Attica saw the Spartan king Pausanias advancing through the Corinthian isthmus and threatening his rear, he withdrew northward, having for the second time laid waste Attica far and wide. With the united armies of Sparta, Athens, and other allies behind him Pausanias was able to lead some thirty thousand heavy-armed Greeks of the phalanx as he followed Mardonius into Bœotia.

554. In several days of preliminary movements which brought the two armies into contact at Platæa the clever Persian showed his superiority, outmaneuvering Pausanias and even gaining possession of the southern passes behind the

Greeks and capturing a train of their supply wagons. But when Mardonius led his archers forward at double-quick, and the Persians, kneeling behind their line of shields, rained deadly volleys of arrows into the compact Greek lines, the Hellenes never flinched, although their comrades were falling on every hand. With the gaps closed up, the massive Greek phalanx pushed through the line of Persian shields, and, as at Marathon, the spear proved invincible against the bow. In a heroic but hopeless effort to rally his broken lines Mardonius himself fell. The Persian cavalry covered the rear of the flying Asiatic army and saved it from destruction.

Battle of Platæa; final defeat of Persia (479 B.C.)

555. Not only European Greece but Ionia too was saved from Asiatic despotism; for the Greek triremes, having meantime crossed to the peninsula of Mycale on the north of Miletus, drove out or destroyed the remnants of the Persian fleet. The Athenians now also captured and occupied Sestus on the European side of the Hellespont, and thus held the crossing from Asia into Europe closed against further Persian invasion. The final effort of Persia to gain undisputed naval control of the Ægean and all the waters lying between Asia and Europe had been completely defeated. Thus the grandsons of the men who had seen Persia advance to the Ægean had blocked her further progress in the west and thrust her back from Europe. Indeed, no Persian army ever set foot in European Greece again.

Athenian fleet victorious in Ionia and the north

QUESTIONS

Section 46. What was the leading kingdom of Asia Minor beyond the fringe of Greek coast cities? What had happened to these Greek cities in the middle of the Sixth Century B.C.? Who was the last king of Lydia? What happened to him? What great Oriental power thus advanced to the east side of the Ægean? What should you think of the prospects for Greek resistance? What part did Athens take in the revolt of the Ionian cities of Asia? How did the Persians respond? When? Who was their king? Where did they land in Greece? How far is Marathon from Athens? What did the Athenians do? Discuss the numbers of the two armies. Who was the Athenian leader? What position did the Greeks take up, and what advantages were thus gained? Describe the battle of Marathon.

Section 47. Who was Themistocles? What was his policy for the future defense of Athens? Describe the plans of Xerxes for the subjection of Greece. Describe Themistocles' plan of campaign. What was the result of the first two battles? What was the next move of the Persian army? Describe the battle of Salamis. Describe the retreat of Xerxes. Discuss the result of the Greek failure to accept Themistocles' advice in pursuing the Persians. What victory did the Greeks win in Sicily in the same year as the battle of Salamis? What racial conflict does this victory represent? What happened to Themistocles? What did the Persian commander now do? Who was he? Where did the final battle take place? What final results were obtained by the Greeks at sea?

BIBLIOGRAPHY FOR TOPICAL STUDIES

The Ionian Greeks of Asia Minor: BOTSFORD, *Hellenic History*, pp. 158–166; *Source Book*, pp. 152–160; BURY, *Greece*, pp. 229–231, 234–238, 241–247; HERODOTUS, v, 35–36, 99–107, 123–126, vi, 1–20; JAMES, *Hellenic Heritage*, Vol. I, pp. 268–277; MILLS, *Ancient Greeks*, pp. 113–125.

The "presumption of the Persians": BURY, *Greece*, pp. 265–284; CORNFORD, *Religious Thought*, pp. 88–98; JAMES, *Hellenic Heritage*, Vol. I, pp. 387–389; *Pageant of Greece*, pp. 168–170, 179–186, 187–188.

The battle of Platæa: BURY, *Greece*, pp. 289–295; HERODOTUS, ix, 30–72; JAMES, *Hellenic Heritage*, Vol. I, pp. 355–377.

Greek weapons and armor: BRITISH MUSEUM, *Greek and Roman Life*, pp. 70–103 *passim*; METROPOLITAN MUSEUM OF ART, *Daily Life of the Greeks and Romans*, pp. 76–88.

CHAPTER XIV · *The Growing Rivalry between Athens and Sparta, and the Rise of the Athenian Empire*

SECTION 48. THE BEGINNINGS OF THE RIVALRY BETWEEN ATHENS AND SPARTA

Athenian feeling after Salamis

556. As the Athenians returned to look out over the ashes of what was once Athens, amid which rose the smoke-blackened heights of the naked Acropolis (Fig. 179), they began to realize the greatness of their deliverance and the magnitude of their achievement. With the not too ready help of Sparta they had met and crushed the hoary power of Asia. They felt themselves masters of the world. The past seemed narrow and limited. A new and greater Athens dawned upon their vision.

Spartan soldier-citizens

557. Of all this the Spartans, on the other hand, felt very little. The Spartan citizens were all soldiers and devoted themselves exclusively to military training. The state maintained public meals, where each soldier-citizen ate with a group of about fifteen friends, all men, at the same table every day. Each citizen con-

NOTE. The above headpiece is a Greek painting adorning a drinking-cup. It was painted by the artist Nikosthenes, who has signed his name at the right near the lip of the cup: ΝΙΚΟΣΘΕΝΕΣ ΕΠΟΙΕ, which means "Nikosthenes made (it)." The boats are here depicted as skimming along the water, perhaps in a race, and evidently on a smooth summer sea. The painter has brightened the composition with so much buoyancy and liveliness that we are actually made to feel the joy in seafaring eventually developed by the Greeks (cf. § 422).

tributed to the support of these meals, and as long as he paid this contribution he retained his citizenship. His lands were cultivated for him by slaves, and his only occupation was military drill and exercise. The state thus became a military machine.

558. The number of such Spartan soldier-citizens was quite limited, sometimes being all together only a few thousand. As distinguished from the large non-voting population of the other towns in the Laconian peninsula the citizens of Sparta formed a small, superior class. Thus their rule of the larger surrounding population was the tyranny of a limited military class devoted to war and almost without commerce or any interest in the arts and industries. So old-fashioned were they, and so confident in their own military power, that they would not surround their city with a wall. Sparta remained a group of straggling villages, not deserving the name of city and entirely without fine public buildings or great monuments of any kind. Like a large military club or camp it lived off its own slave-worked lands and from the taxes it squeezed out of its subject towns without allowing them any vote. In case of war the two kings were still the military leaders.

Spartan soldier-citizens as a ruling class

559. We can now understand that the stolid Spartans, wearing the fetters of a rigid military organization and gifted with no imagination, looked with misgivings upon the larger world which was opening to Greek life. Although they desired to lead Greece in military power, they shrank from assuming the responsibilities of expansion. They represented the past and the privileges of the few. Athens represented the future and the rights of the many. Greece fell into two camps, as it were: Sparta, the bulwark of tradition and limited privileges; Athens, the champion of progress and the sovereign people. Thus the sentiment of union born in the common struggle for liberty, which might have united the Hellenes into one Greek nation, was followed by an unquenchable rivalry between the two leading states of Hellas, a rivalry so

Conservative Sparta and progressive Athens

FIG. 173. *The* PLAIN *where once* SPARTA *stood*

The olive groves now grow where the Spartans once had their houses. From the mountains (nearly 8000 feet high) behind the plain the visitor can see northeastward far beyond Athens, almost to Eubœa; 100 miles northward, to the mountains on the north of the Corinthian Gulf; and 125 miles southward, to the island of Crete. This view shows also how Greece is cut up by such mountains

persistent that it went on for another century and finally cost the Greeks the supremacy of the ancient world.

560. Themistocles was now the soul of Athens and her policy of progress and expansion. He determined that Athens should no longer follow Sparta. He cleverly hoodwinked the Spartans and in spite of their objections completed the erection of strong walls around a new and larger Athens. At the same time he fortified the Piræus, the Athenian port. When

Themistocles and the fortification of Athens

the Spartans, after the repulse of Persia, relinquished the command of the combined Greek fleets, the powerful Athenian fleet, the creation of Themistocles, was mistress of the Ægean.

Section 49. The Rise of the Athenian Empire and the Triumph of Democracy

Establishment of the Delian League (478–477 B.C.)

561. As the Greek cities of Asia still feared the vengeance of the Persian king, it was easy for the Athenians to form a permanent defensive league with the cities of their Greek kindred in Asia and the Ægean islands. The wealthier of these cities contributed ships, while others paid a sum of money each year into the treasury of the league. Athens was to have command of the combined fleet and collect the money. She placed in charge of the important task of adjusting all contributions of the league and collecting the tribute money a patriotic citizen named Aristides, whose friends called him "the Just" because of his honesty. He had opposed the naval plans of Themistocles and, when defeated, had been ostracized, but he had later distinguished himself at Salamis and Platæa. In spite of his former opposition to Themistocles' plans he now did important service in vigorously aiding to establish the new naval league. The treasure he collected was placed for protection in the temple of Apollo, on the little island of Delos. Hence the federation was known as the Delian League. It was completed within three years after Salamis. The transformation of such a league into an empire, made up of states subject to Athens, could be foreseen as a very easy step. All this was therefore viewed with increasing jealousy and distrust by Sparta.

Rise of Cimon

562. Under the leadership of Cimon, the son of Miltiades the hero of Marathon, the fleet of the league now drove the Persians entirely out of the region of the Hellespont. Cimon did not understand the importance of Athenian supremacy in Greece, and favored a policy of friendship and alliance with Sparta. Hence political

A *B*

Fig. 174. Pottery Sherds *bearing the Names of* Aristides (A) *and* Themistocles (B), *cast as Votes for the Ostracism of these Two Men in the Early Fifth Century* B.C.

The excavation of the Athenian market place (*agora*), carried on by the American School of Classical Studies at Athens since 1930, has turned up quite a number of potsherds having scrawled upon them the names of prominent Athenian citizens who were to be ostracized. The name of Aristides on sherd *A* is spelled *Aristeides* (in Greek ΑΡΙΣΤΕΙΔ[ΕΣ]). The end has been broken off. The name of his father, Lysimachus, is added in a second line. The name of Themistocles on the right-hand sherd *B* is spelled *Themisthokles* (in Greek [ΘΕ]ΜΙΣΘΟΚΛΕΣ). A break has carried away two letters at the beginning of the name. Neokles, the name of his father, is added beneath. These inscribed sherds, called in Greek *ostraka*, are the actual votes cast by two citizens of Athens, — the first (*A*) against Aristides in 483 or 484 B.C., and the second (*B*) against Themistocles in 471 B.C. After these votes had been counted, they were thrown out on some rubbish heap and thus survived to our day as dramatic witnesses to the reckless animosities of Athenian politics which resulted in the banishment of two of the ablest leaders Athens ever produced. (Courtesy of Professor Edward Capps)

conflict arose at Athens over this question. Noble and wealthy and old-fashioned folk favored Cimon and friendship with Sparta, but progressive and modern Athenians followed Themistocles and his anti-Spartan plans.

Fall of Themistocles (472–471 B.C.)

563. Themistocles was unable to win the Assembly; he was ostracized, and at length, on false charges of treason, he was condemned and obliged to flee for his life. The greatest statesman in Athenian history spent the rest of his life in the service of the Persian king, and he never again saw the city he had saved from the Persians and made mistress of an empire.

564. In a final battle Cimon crushed the Persian navy in the west (468 B.C.) and returned to Athens covered with glory. In response to a request from the Spartans for help in quelling a revolt among their own subjects Cimon urged the dispatch of troops to Sparta. Herein Cimon overestimated the good feeling of the Spartans toward Athens, for in spite of the continuance of the revolt the Spartans after a time curtly demanded the withdrawal of the very Athenian troops they had asked for. Stung by this rebuff, to which Cimon's friendly policy toward Sparta had exposed them, the Athenians voted to ostracize Cimon (461 B.C.).

Fall of Cimon

565. The overthrow of Cimon was a victory of the people against the nobles. They followed it up by attacking the Council of Elders, once made up only of nobles. It was called the Areopagus and used to meet on a hill of that name by the market place. The people now passed new laws restricting the power of the Areopagus to the trial of murder cases and the settlement of questions of state religion, thus completely depriving it of all political power. Meantime a more popular council of five hundred members had grown up and gained the power to conduct most of the government business. This it did by dividing itself into ten groups of fifty each, each group serving a little over a month once a year. At the same time the citizen juries introduced by Solon as a court of appeal were enlarged until they contained a body of six thousand jurors divided into smaller juries, usually of five hundred and one each. Such a large, unwieldy jury was really a group or court of temporary judges deciding cases brought before them. Since the poorest citizens could not afford to leave their work to serve on these juries, the people passed laws granting pay for jury service. These citizen courts finally became so powerful that they formed a kind of judicial body which framed and interpreted the laws made by the popular assembly. At last the people were indeed in control.

Areopagus overthrown; leadership of popular council; juries

566. Furthermore, the right to hold office was greatly extended. All citizens were permitted to hold the office of archon except members of the laboring class entirely without property. With one exception there was no longer any *election* of the higher officers, but they were now all *chosen by lot* from the whole body of eligible citizens. The result was that the men holding the once influential positions in the state were now mere chance "nobodies" and hence completely without influence. But at the same time the public services now rendered by so large a number of citizens were a means of education and of very profitable experience. Athens was gaining a more intelligent body of citizens than any other ancient state.

Office of archon open to all except the laboring class

567. There was one kind of officer whom it was impossible to choose by lot, and that was the military commander (*strategus*). This important office remained elective and thus open to men of ability and influence, into whose hands the direction of affairs naturally fell. There were ten of these generals, one for each of the ten tribes established by Clisthenes (§ 513), and they not only led the army in war but also managed the war department of the government and had large control of the government treasury and of the Empire, including foreign affairs. The leader, or president, of this body of generals was the most powerful man in the state, and his office was elective. It thus became more and more possible for a noble with military training to make himself a strong and influential leader and, if he was a man of persuasive eloquence, to lay out a definite series of plans for the nation, and by his oratory to induce the Assembly of the Athenian citizens on the Pnyx to accept them.

Political power still possible to elective strategus

568. After the fall of Cimon there came forward a handsome and brilliant young Athenian named Pericles, a descendant of one of the old noble families of the line of Clisthenes. He desired to build up the splendid Athenian Empire of which Themistocles had dreamed. He put himself at the head of the party of progress

The leadership of Pericles

FIG. 175. *The* PNYX, *the Athenian* PLACE OF ASSEMBLY

The speakers' platform with its three steps is immediately in the foreground. The listening Athenian citizens of the Assembly sat on the ground, now sloping away to the left but at that time probably level. The ground they occupied was inclosed by a semicircular wall, beginning at the farther end of the straight wall seen here on the right, extending then to the left, and returning to the straight wall again behind our present point of view (see semicircle on plan, p. 418). This was an open-air House of Commons, where, however, the citizen did not send a representative but came himself and voted as he was influenced from this platform by great Athenian leaders like Themistocles, Pericles, and Demosthenes. Note the Acropolis and the Parthenon, to which we look eastward from the Pnyx. The Areopagus is just out of range on the left

favoring increased power of the people, although there may be some uncertainty about the sincerity of his belief in democracy; for he secured the passage of a law limiting citizenship exclusively to children of free-born parents on both sides. This reduced the number of citizens. Nevertheless he kept their confidence year after year, and thus secured his continued reëlection as strategus. The result was that he became the actual head of the state in power, or, as we might say, he was the undisputed political "boss" of Athens from about 460 B.C. until his untimely death over thirty years later.

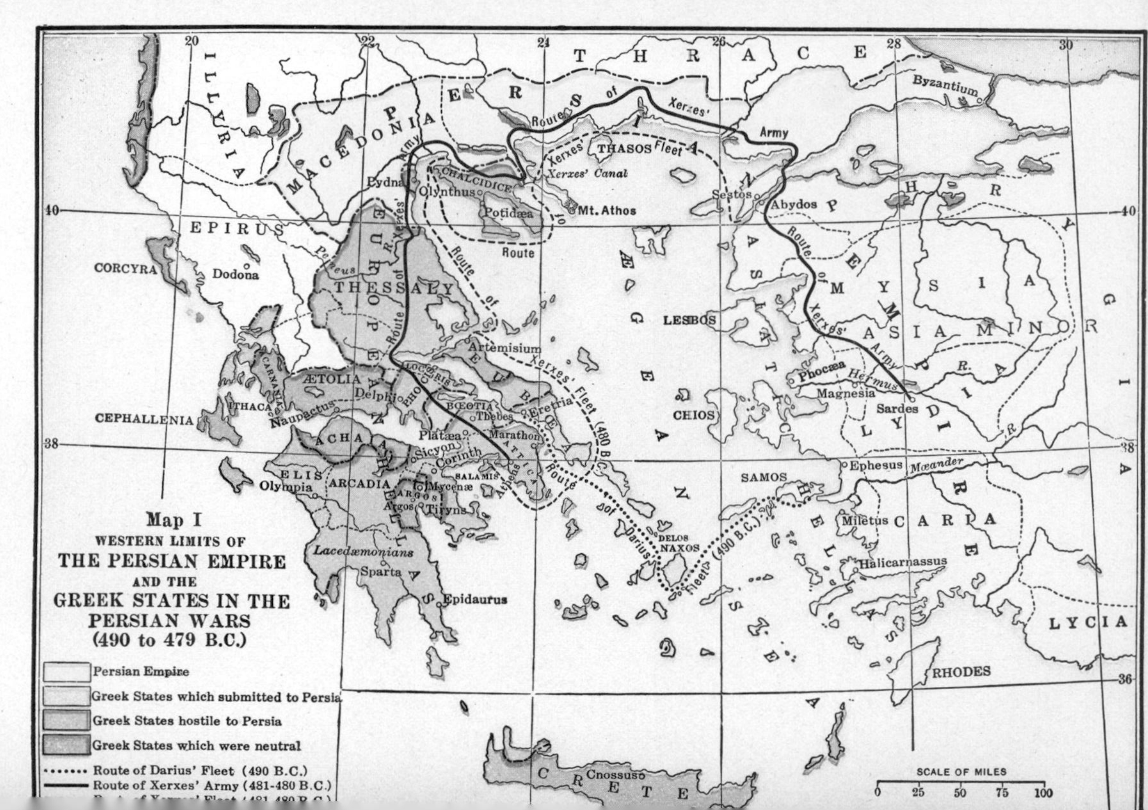
Map I
WESTERN LIMITS OF
THE PERSIAN EMPIRE
AND THE
GREEK STATES IN THE
PERSIAN WARS
(490 to 479 B.C.)
Persian Empire
Greek States which submitted to Persia
Greek States hostile to Persia
Greek States which were neutral
Route of Darius' Fleet (490 B.C.)
Route of Xerxes' Army (481-480 B.C.)
SCALE OF MILES
0 25 50 75 100
THRACE
PERSIA
ILLYRIA
MACEDONIA
EPIRUS
CORCYRA
Dodona
CEPHALLENIA
ITHACA
ACARNANIA
ÆTOLIA
Naupactus
Delphi
THESSALY
EUROPE
Peneus
Pydna
Olynthus
CHALCIDICE
Potidæa
Mt. Athos
Xerxes' Canal
THASOS
Byzantium
Sestos
Abydos
PHRYGIA
MYSIA
ASIA MINOR
LESBOS
CHIOS
SAMOS
Phocæa
Hermus R.
Magnesia
Sardes
LYDIA
Ephesus
Mæander
Miletus
CARIA
Halicarnassus
LYCIA
RHODES
HELLAS
ÆGEAN SEA
DELOS
NAXOS
Route of Darius' Fleet (490 B.C.)
Route of Xerxes' Army
Route of Xerxes' Fleet (480 B.C.)
Artemisium
EUBŒA
Eretria
BŒOTIA
Thebes
Platæa
Marathon
ATTICA
Athens
SALAMIS
Corinth
Sicyon
ACHAIA
ELIS
Olympia
ARCADIA
ARGOS
Mycenæ
Argos
Tiryns
Lacedæmonians
Sparta
Epidaurus
CRETE
Cnossus
20
22
24
26
28
30
40
38
36

Map Plate, Patented July 5, 1921 • Method of Making Maps, Patented July 5, 1921

SEQUENCE MAP SHOWING WESTERN LIMITS OF THE PERSIAN EMPIRE AND THE GREEK STATES FROM THE PERSIAN WARS (BEGINNING 490 B.C.) TO THE BEGINNING OF THE SECOND PELOPONNESIAN WAR (431 B.C.)

Section 50. Commercial Development and the Opening of the Struggle between Athens and Sparta

569. A period of commercial prosperity followed the Persian Wars, which gave the Greeks a leadership in trade like that of the English before the World War. Corinth and the little island of Ægina, at the front door of Attica and visible from Athens, rapidly became the most flourishing trading centers in Greece. They were at once followed, however, by the little harbor town of Piræus, built by the foresight of Themistocles as the port of Athens. Along its busy docks were moored Greek ships from all over the Mediterranean world, for the defeat of the Phœnicians in east and west had broken up their merchant fleets and thrown much of their trade into the hands of the Greeks. Here many a Greek ship from the Black Sea, laden with grain or fish, moored alongside the grain ships of Egypt and the mixed cargoes from Syracuse; for Attica was no longer producing food enough for her own need, and it was necessary to import it. The docks were piled high with goods from the Athenian factories, and long lines of perspiring porters were loading them into ships bound for all the harbors of the Mediterranean. Scores of battleships stretched far along the shores, and the busy shipyards and dry docks, filled with multitudes of workmen, were noisy with the sound of many hammers.

Commercial supremacy of Greeks after Persian Wars; Piræus

570. In spite of much progress in navigation we must not think of these ancient ships of Greece as very large. A merchant vessel carrying from two hundred and fifty to three hundred tons was considered large in Fifth-Century Greece. Ships clung timidly to the shore and rarely ventured to sea in the stormy winter season. They had no compass or charts, there were no lighthouses, and they were often plundered by pirates, so that commerce was still carried on at great risks. Moreover, ships did not last as long as with us, and it was found necessary to keep them under cover in sheds

Limitations of navigation and shipbuilding

when they were not in use; for although the ancient peoples eventually learned to paint the outside of the ships with tar, of course they knew nothing of the copper sheathing which is used for the protection of wooden vessels today.

Profits from commerce and industry

571. On the other hand, the profits gained from sea-borne commerce might be very considerable. A vessel that reached the north shores of the Black Sea or the pirate-infested Adriatic might sell out its cargo so profitably as to bring back to the owner double the first cost of the goods after paying all expenses. Plenty of men were therefore willing to risk their capital in such ventures, and indeed many borrowed the money to do so. Interest was lower than in Solon's day, and money could be borrowed at 10 and 12 per cent. The returns from manufacturing industry were also high, even reaching 30 per cent.

Wealth and wages

572. To measure this increased prosperity of Athens we must not apply the scale of modern business. A fortune of ten thousand dollars was looked upon as considerable, while double that amount was accounted great wealth. The day laborer's wages were from six to ten cents a day, while the skilled craftsman received as much as twenty cents a day. Greek soldiers were ready to furnish their own arms and enter the ranks of any foreign king at five dollars a month. A man of intellect, like an architect, received only from twenty to thirty cents a day, while the tuition for a course in rhetoric lasting several years cost the student from sixty to eighty dollars.

Increase in population of Athens and Attica

573. For nearly thirty years after the Persian Wars it was easy to obtain Athenian citizenship. Some thirty thousand strangers therefore soon settled in Athens to share in its prosperity. Its population rose to above a hundred thousand in the days of Pericles, while the inhabitants of Attica numbered over two hundred thousand. This included probably eighty thousand slaves, still the cheapest form of labor obtainable.

574. As a result of increased business the volume of money in Athens had also greatly increased. The silver tribute and the Attic silver mines furnished metal for additional coinage. In all the markets of the Mediterranean, Athenian silver money was the leading coin, and many Persian darics of gold (worth about five dollars) also came in. Just as with us, as money became more plentiful its value decreased, and a given sum would not buy as much as formerly. That is to say, prices went up. A measure of barley cost twice as much, and a sheep five times as much, as in Solon's day. Nevertheless living would be called very cheap from our point of view. Even the well-to-do citizen did not spend over ten or twelve cents a day in food for his family, and a man of wealth was very extravagant if he owned furniture to the amount of two hundred dollars.

Money and prices

575. Money had now become very necessary in carrying on the government. Formerly service to the state had been without pay. This was quite possible in a nation of peasants and shepherds, but with the incoming of coined money and steady employment in factories it was no longer possible for a private citizen to give his time to the state for nothing. Many a citizen of Athens bought the bread his family needed for the day with the money he had earned the day before. The daily salaries to thousands of jurymen and to the members of the Council of Five Hundred, who were also paid, amounted to not less than a hundred thousand dollars a year. Large sums, even sums that would be large today, were also required for building the sumptuous marble temples now frequently dedicated to the gods, while the offerings, feasts, and celebrations at these temples also consumed great sums.

Cost of government: salaries, temples, religious services

576. Greater than all the other expenses of the state, however, was the cost of war. The cost of arming citizens who could not undertake this expense themselves, and of feeding the army in the field, of course fell upon the state. The war fleet was, however, the heaviest of all such expenses. Besides the first cost of building and equipping the battleships there was always the further expense of maintaining them. A trireme, manned with about

Cost of government: war

two hundred sailors and oarsmen, receiving daily half a drachma (nearly ten cents) per man, cost almost six hundred dollars per month. A fleet of two hundred triremes therefore required nearly a hundred and twenty thousand dollars a month for wages.

577. The problem of securing the funds for maintaining and defending a nation had become a grave one. As for Athens, the Attic silver mines, however helpful, were far from furnishing enough to support the government. The bulk of the state funds had to be raised by taxation. The triumphant democracy disliked periodic taxes, and they assessed taxes only when the treasury was very low, especially in war time. Besides taxes the treasury received a good income from the customs duty on all goods imported or exported through Piræus. The Athenians kept these duties low, assessing only one per cent of the value of the goods until forced by war expenses to raise them. We have already mentioned the contributions (tribute) of the subject states of the Empire (§ 561). The total income of the Athenian state hardly reached three quarters of a million dollars in the days of Pericles.

Income of state: mines, taxes, customs duties

578. Small as this seems to us of modern times, no other Greek state could raise anything like such an annual income. Least of all could Sparta hope to rival such resources. Without the enterprise to enter the new world of commercial competition, Sparta clung to her old ways. She still issued only her ancient iron money and had no silver coins. To be sure, the standing army of Sparta was always ready without expense to the government; but when she led forth the combined armies of the Peloponnesian League, she could not bear the expense longer than a few weeks. The still greater expense of a large war fleet was quite impossible either for Sparta or her league. In so far as war was a matter of money the commercial growth of Athens was giving her a constantly growing superiority over all other Greek states. We can understand, then, with what jealousy and fear Sparta viewed Athenian prosperity.

Sparta financially inferior to Athens

579. Pericles had won favor with the people by his policy of hostility to Sparta. Foreseeing the coming struggle, he greatly strengthened the defenses of Athens by inducing the people to connect the fortifications of the city with those of the Piræus harbor by two Long Walls, thus forming a road completely walled in, which connected Athens and her harbor (plan, p. 418).

New defenses of Athens; Long Walls

580. Not long after Pericles gained the leadership of the people, the inevitable war with Sparta broke out. It lasted nearly fifteen years, with varying fortunes on both sides. The Athenian merchants resented the keen commercial rivalry of Ægina, planted as the flourishing island was at the very front door of Attica. The island was captured after a long siege. Furthermore, Pericles employed the Athenian navy in blockading for years the merchant fleets of the other great rival of Athens and friend of Sparta — Corinth — and thus brought financial ruin on its merchants.

First war between Athens and Sparta (459–446 B.C.)

581. At the same time Athens dispatched a fleet of two hundred ships to assist Egypt, which had revolted against Persia. The Athenians were thus fighting both Sparta and Persia for years. The entire Athenian fleet in Egypt was lost. This loss so weakened the Athenian navy that the treasury of the Delian League was no longer safe, in the little island of Delos, against a possible sea raid by the Persians. Pericles therefore shifted the treasury from Delos to Athens, — an act which made the city more than ever the capital of an Athenian Empire.

War with Persia; the Egyptian expedition

582. When peace was concluded (445 B.C.), all that Athens was able to retain was the island of Ægina, though at the same time she gained control of the large island of Eubœa. It was agreed that the peace should continue for thirty years. Thus ended what is often called the First Peloponnesian War, with the complete exhaustion of Athens as well as of her enemies in the Pelopon-

Peace with Sparta and Persia

nesus. Pericles had not shown himself a great naval or military commander in this war. The Athenians had also arranged a peace with Persia, over forty years after Marathon. But the rivalry between Athens and Sparta for the leadership of the Greeks was still unsettled. The struggle was to be continued in another long and weary Peloponnesian War. Before we proceed with the story of this fatal struggle we must glance briefly at the new and glorious Athens which had been growing up under the leadership of Pericles.

QUESTIONS

Section 48. Describe the Spartan state. What can you say of the reasons for rivalry between Athens and Sparta? What did Themistocles now do?

Section 49. What was the Delian League? To what might it easily lead? Who was Aristides? What policy did Cimon favor? What was Themistocles' attitude toward Cimon's policy? What then happened to Themistocles? to Cimon? What new council arose, and how did it govern? What rights did the people gain? How could a statesman still hold the leadership? Who now became the leader of the people's party?

Section 50. What happened to Greek business after the Persian War? Discuss navigation; business profits. What can you say of the scale of values as compared with today? What happened to the population of Athens? How were prices affected? What were the chief expenses of the Athenian state? its chief sources of income? Could other states raise as much? Sketch the First Peloponnesian War.

BIBLIOGRAPHY FOR TOPICAL STUDIES

Spartan civilization: BOTSFORD, *Hellenic History*, pp. 84–100; *Source Book*, pp. 111–121; BURY, *Greece*, pp. 120–125, 130–136; JAMES, *Hellenic Heritage*, Vol. I, pp. 222–234; MILLS, *Ancient Greeks*, pp. 75–90.

Greek economic life: BOTSFORD, *Hellenic History*, pp. 258–266; BURY, *Greece*, pp. 377–378; CARY, *Documentary Sources*, pp. 48–56, 78–79, 90–93; GULICK, *Modern Traits*, pp. 105–113, 119–139; MILLS, *Ancient Greeks*, pp. 201–203.

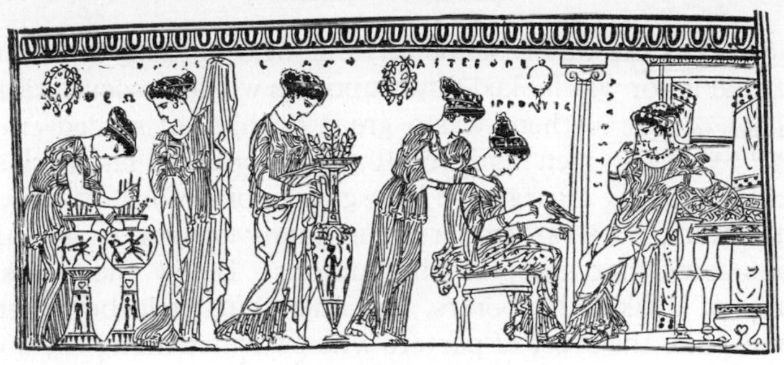

CHAPTER XV · *Athens in the Age of Pericles*

SECTION 51. SOCIETY; THE HOME; EDUCATION AND TRAINING OF YOUNG CITIZENS

583. As we have seen, the population of Attica was made up of citizens, foreigners, and slaves. In a mixed crowd there would usually be among every ten people about four slaves, one or two foreigners, and the rest free Athenians. A large group of wealthy citizens lived in Athens upon the income from their lands. They continued to be the aristocracy of the nation, for land was still the most respectable form of wealth. The wealthy manufacturer hastened to buy land and join the landed aristocracy. The social position of his family might thus become an influential one, but it could not compare with that of a noble.

Athenian society: wealthy classes

NOTE. The above headpiece gives us a glimpse into the HOUSE OF A BRIDE the day after the wedding. At the right, leaning against a couch, is the BRIDE. Before her are TWO YOUNG FRIENDS, one sitting, the other standing, both playing with a tame bird. Another friend approaches carrying a tall and beautiful painted vase as a wedding gift. At the left a visitor arranges flowers in two painted vases, while another lady, adjusting her garment, is looking on The walls are hung with festive wreaths. The furniture of such a house was usually of wood; but if the owner's wealth permitted, it was adorned with ivory, silver, and gold. It consisted chiefly of beds, like the couch above, chairs, footstools (as at foot of couch above), small individual tables, and clothing chests which took the place of closets.

584. On the other hand, anyone who actually performed manual labor was looked down upon as without social station.

Athenian society: poorer classes

Athens was a great beehive of skilled craftsmen and small shopkeepers. These classes were beginning to organize into guilds, or unions, of masons, carpenters, potters, jewelers, and many others, — organizations somewhat like our labor unions. Below them was an army of unskilled laborers, free men but little better than slaves, like the army of porters who swarmed along the docks at Piræus. All these classes contained many citizens. Nevertheless the majority of the Athenian citizens were still the farmers and peasants throughout Attica, although the Persian devastation had seriously reduced the amount of land cultivated.

585. The hasty rebuilding of Athens after the Persians had burned it did not produce any noticeable changes in the houses, nor were there any of great size or splendor. Since the appearance of the first European houses many thousand years had passed, but there were still no beautiful houses anywhere in Europe, such as we found on the Nile. The one-story front of even a wealthy man's house was simply a blank wall, usually of sun-dried brick, rarely of broken-stone masonry. Often without any windows, it showed no other opening than the door, but a house of two stories might have a small window or two in the upper story. The door led into a court open to the sky and surrounded by a porch with columns. Here in the mild climate of Greece the family could spend much of their time as in a sitting room. In the middle stood an altar of the household Zeus, the protector of the family, while around the court opened a number of doors leading to a living room, sleeping rooms, dining room, storerooms, and also a tiny kitchen.

Athenian houses

586. This Greek house lacked all conveniences. There was no chimney, and the smoke from the kitchen fire, though intended to drift up through a hole in the roof, choked the room or floated out of the door. In winter gusty drafts filled the house, for many doorways were without doors, and glass in the form of flat panes for the windows was still unknown. In this mild climate, however, a pan of burning charcoal, called a brazier, furnished enough heat to temper the chilly air of a room. Lacking windows, the ground-floor rooms depended entirely on the doors opening on the court for light. At night the dim light of an olive-oil lamp was all that was available. There was no plumbing or piping of any kind in the house, no drainage, and consequently no sanitary arrangements. The water supply was brought in jars by slaves from the nearest well or flowing spring.

Lack of conveniences in Athenian houses

587. The floors were simply of dirt, with a surface of pebbles tramped and beaten hard. There was no oil paint, and a plain water color wash, such as we call calcimine, might be used on the inside, but if used on the outside would soon wash off, exposing the mud brick. The simplicity and bareness of the house itself were in noticeable contrast with the beautiful furniture which the Greek craftsmen were now producing. There were many metal utensils, among which the ladies' hand mirrors of polished bronze were common, and most numerous of all were lovely painted jars, vases, and dishes, along with less pretentious pottery forming the household crockery; for it will be remembered that Greek pottery was the most beautiful ever produced by ancient man.

Decoration and equipment

588. The view from the Acropolis over the sea of low, flat roofs disclosed not a single chimney, but revealed a much larger city than formerly. Though not laid out in blocks, the city was about ten modern city blocks wide and several more in length. The streets were merely lanes or alleys, narrow and crooked, winding between the bare mud-brick walls of the low houses standing wall to wall. There was no pavement, nor any sidewalk, and a stroll through the town after a rain meant wading through the mud. All household rubbish and garbage were thrown directly into the street, and there was no system of sewage. When a per-

Streets of Athens

son passed a two-story house he might hear a warning cry, and spring out of the way barely in time to escape being deluged with sweepings or filth thrown from a second-story window. The few wells and fountains fed by city water pipes did not furnish enough water to flush the streets, and there was no system of street cleaning. During the hot summers of the south, therefore, Athens was not a healthful place of residence.

FIG. 176. *Statue of the Tragic Poet* SOPHOCLES

The great poet stands in thoughtful repose in an attitude of ease, which incidentally reveals the wonderful beauty of a well-draped Greek costume. The figure is probably our most beautiful Greek portrait, and as a work of art illustrates the sculpture of the Fourth Century B.C., almost a century after Pericles

Costume of men

589. All Athens lived out of doors. Athenian life was beautifully simple and unpretentious, especially since richly embroidered and colored Oriental garments had passed away. Almost all citizens now appeared in the simple white garments which we of modern times have come to associate with the classical Greeks. Gorgeous costume thus disappeared in Greece, as it did among *us* in the days of our great-great-grandfathers. Nevertheless the man of elegant habits gained a practiced hand in draping his costume, and was proud of the gracefulness and the sweeping lines with which he could arrange its folds.

590. The women were less inclined to give up the old finery, for unhappily they had little to think about but clothes and housekeeping; for Greek citizens still kept their wives in the background, and they were more than ever mere housekeepers. They had no share in the intellectual life of the men and could not appear at their social meetings, where serious conversation was carried on; nor were they permitted to witness the athletic games at Olympia. Their position was even worse than in the Age of the Tyrants, and a poetess like Sappho never appeared again among the later Greeks.

Position of women

591. The usual house had no garden, and the children therefore played in the court, running about with toy cart and dog or enjoying a swing at the hands of the nurse. There were no schools for the girls, but when the boy was old enough he was sent to school in charge of an old slave called a pedagogue (*paidagogos*), which really means "leader of a child." He carried the boy's books and outfit. There were no schools maintained by the state and no schoolhouses. School was conducted in his own house by some poor citizen, perhaps by an old soldier or even by a foreigner. In any case the teacher was much looked down upon. He received his pay from the parents, but there was a board of state officials appointed to look after the schools and to see that nothing improper was taught.

Childhood and school

592. Without special education for his work, the teacher merely taught without change the old-time subjects he had learned in his own youth. Proficiency in music was regarded very seriously by the Greeks, not merely for entertainment but also and chiefly as an influence toward good conduct. Besides learning to read and write as of old, the pupil learned by heart many passages from the old poets, and here and there a boy with a good memory could repeat the entire Iliad and Odyssey. On the other hand, the boys still escaped all instruction in mathematics, geography, and natural science. This was doubtless a welcome exemption, for the masters were severe and the Greek boy hated both school and schoolmaster.

Subjects taught at school

593. When the Athenian lad reached the age of eighteen years and left school, he was received as a citizen, provided that both his parents were of Athenian citizenship. The

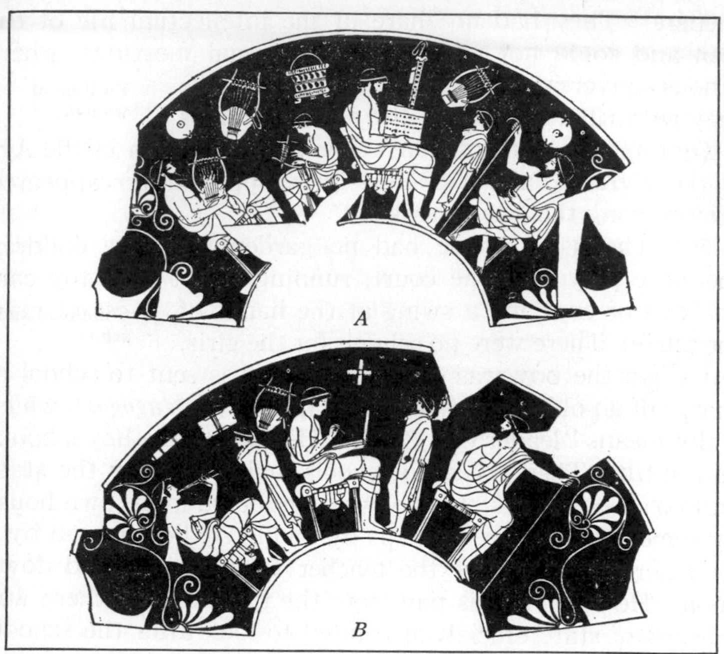

FIG. 177. *An* ATHENIAN SCHOOL *in the* AGE OF PERICLES

These scenes are painted around the center of a shallow bowl; hence their peculiar shape. In *A* we see at the left a music teacher seated at his lyre, giving a lesson to the lad seated before him. In the middle sits a teacher of reading and literature, holding an open roll from which the boy standing before him is learning a poem. Behind the boy sits the pedagogue (§ 591). In *B* we have at the left a singing lesson, aided by the flute to fix the tones. In the middle the master sits correcting an exercise handed him by the boy standing before him, while behind the boy sits the pedagogue as before

oath which he took was a solemn reminder of the obligations he now assumed. It had been composed by Solon, and it called upon the youth "never to disgrace his sacred arms; never to forsake his comrade in the ranks, but to fight for the sacred temples and the common welfare, whether alone or with others; to leave his country not in a worse but in a better state than he found it; to obey the magistrates and the laws and to defend them against attack; finally, to hold in honor the religion of his country."

Attainment of citizenship

594. The youth then spent a year in garrison duty at the harbor of Piræus, where he was put through military drill. Then at nineteen the young recruits received spear and shield, given to each by the state. Thereupon they marched to the theater and entered the orchestra circle, where they were presented to the citizens of Athens assembled in the theater before the play. Another year of garrison service on the frontier of Attica usually completed the young man's military service, although some of the recruits, whose means permitted, joined the small body of select Athenian cavalry.

Incoming citizens' military service

595. On completion of his military service, if the wealth and station of his family permitted, the Athenian youth was more than ever devoted to the new athletic fields in the beautiful open country outside the city walls. On the north of Athens, outside the Dipylon Gate, was the field known as the Academy. It had been adorned by Cimon, who gave great attention to the olive groves, and, with its shady walks and seats for loungers, it became a place where the Athenians loved to spend their idle hours. On the east of the city there was another similar athletic ground known as the Lyceum. The later custom of holding courses of instructive lectures in these places finally resulted in giving to the words "academy" and "lyceum" the associations which they now possess for us.

Athletic grounds: Academy and Lyceum

596. The chief events were boxing, wrestling, running, jumping, casting the javelin, and throwing the disk. Omitting the boxing, the remaining events formed a fivefold match called the *pentathlon*, which it was a great honor to win at Olympia. The earliest contest established at Olympia seems to have been a two-hundred-yard dash, which the Greeks called a *stadion*, that is, six hundred Greek feet. Many other contests were added to this, and in the age of Pericles boxing, or boxing and wrestling combined, the pentathlon, chariot racing, and horseback races made up a program in which all Greek youths were anxious to gain distinction. A generation later some of the philosophers

Athletic events of the Greeks

severely criticized the Greeks for giving far too much of their time and attention to athletic pursuits.

Social and other diversions

597. But other pastimes less worthy were common. An hour or two of gossip with his friends in the market place often preceded the Greek youth's daily visit to the athletic grounds. The afternoon might be passed in dawdling about in the barber shop or dropping in at some drinking resort to shake dice or venture a few drachmas in other games of chance. As the shadows lengthened in the market place the youth frequently joined a company of young men at dinner at the house of a friend. Often followed by heavy drinking of wine and much singing with the lyre, such a dinner might break up in a drunken carouse leading to harum-scarum escapades upon the streets, that in our time would cause the arrest of the company for disorderly conduct.

Section 52. Higher Education, Science, and the Training gained by State Service

Coming of the Sophists

598. On the other hand, there were serious-minded men to whom such dinners meant delightful conversation with their companions on art, literature, music, or personal conduct. Such life among the Athenians had now been quickened by the appearance of more modern private teachers called Sophists, a class of new and clever-witted lecturers who wandered from city to city. Many a bright youth who had finished his music, reading, and writing at the old-fashioned private school annoyed his father by insisting that such schooling was not enough and by demanding money to pay for a course of lectures delivered by one of these new teachers.

599. For the first time a higher education was thus open to young men who had hitherto thought of little more than a victory in the Olympic games or a fine appearance when parading with the crack cavalry of Athens. The appearance of these new teachers therefore marked a new age in the history of the Greeks, but especially in that of Athens. In the first place, the Sophists recognized the importance of effective public speaking in addressing the large citizen juries or in speaking before the assembly of the people. They therefore taught rhetoric and oratory with great success, and many a father who had no gift of speech had the pleasure of seeing his son a practiced public speaker. It was through the teaching of the Sophists also that the first successful writing of Greek prose began. At the same time they really founded the study of language, which was yet to become grammar. They also taught mathematics and astronomy, and the young men of Athens for the first time began to learn a little natural science. Thus the truths which Greek philosophers had begun to observe in the days of Thales were, after a century and a half, beginning to spread among the people.

Higher education offered by Sophists

600. In these new ideas the fathers were unable to follow their sons. When a father of that day found in the hands of his son a book by one of the great Sophists, which began with a statement doubting the existence of the gods, the new teachings seemed impious. The old-fashioned citizen could at least vote for the banishment of such impious teachers and the burning of their books, although he heard that they were read aloud in the houses of the greatest men of Athens. Indeed, some of the leading Sophists were friends of Pericles, who stepped in and tried to help them when they were prosecuted for their teachings. The revolution which had taken place in the mind of Thales was now taking place in the minds of ever-increasing numbers of Greeks, and the situation was yet to grow decidedly worse in the opinion of old-fashioned folk.

Intellectual revolution; chasm between young and old

601. In spite of the spread of knowledge due to the Sophists the average Athenian's acquaintance with science was still very limited. This gave him great trouble in the measurement of time. He still called the middle of the forenoon the "time of full market," and the Egyptian shadow clock in the market place had not yet led him to speak of an hour of the day by *number*, as the Egyptians had been doing for a thousand years. When it was necessary to limit the length of a citizen's speech before the law court, it was done by allowing him to speak as long as it took a given measure of water to run out of a jar with a small hole in it. The Greeks still used the moon-months, and they were accustomed to insert an extra month every third, fifth, and eighth year. To be sure, they had often seen on the Pnyx, where the Assembly met, a strange-looking tablet bearing a new calendar, set up by a builder and engineer named Meton. From the work of the Chaldean astronomers (§ 278) this man had learned the length of the year with only a small error. He had then devised his new calendar with a year still made up of moon-months, but so cleverly arranged that the last day of the last moon-month in every nineteenth year would also be the last day of the year as measured by the sun. But all this was quite beyond the average citizen's puzzled mind. The archons too shook their heads at it and would have nothing to do with it. The old, inconvenient, inaccurate moon-month calendar, with three thirteen-month years in every eight years, was quite good enough for them and continued in use.

Limited knowledge of science shown in time measurement

602. Individual scientists continued to make important discoveries. One of them now taught that the sun was a glowing mass of stone "larger than the Peloponnesus." He maintained also that the moon received its light from the sun, that it had mountains and valleys like the earth, and that it was inhabited by living creatures. Travel was difficult, for there were no passenger ships. Except rough carts or wagons, there were no conveyances by land. The roads were bad, and the traveler went on foot or rode a horse. Nevertheless, Greeks with means were now beginning to travel more frequently. This, however, was for information; travel for pleasure was still a century and a half in the future. From long journeys in

Progress of astronomy and geography

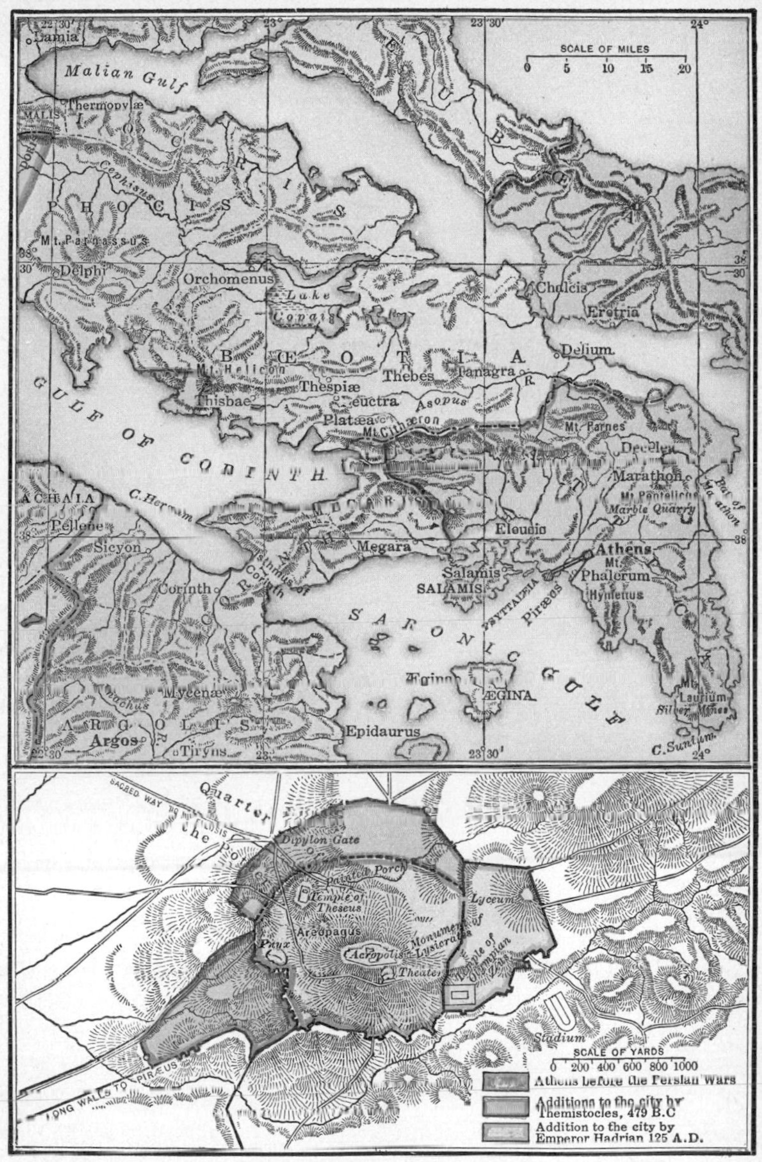

CENTRAL GREECE AND ATHENS

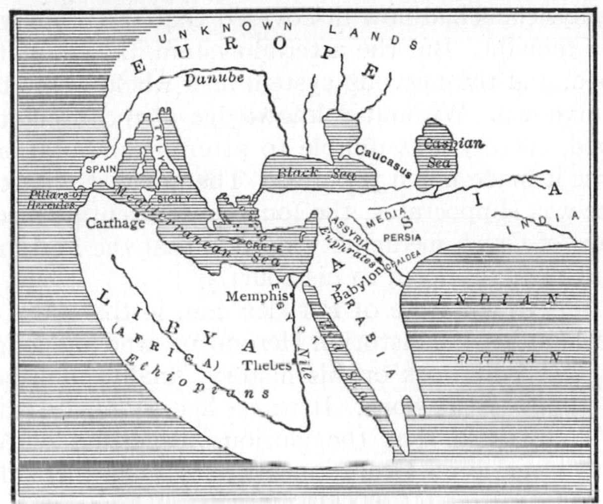

Map of the WORLD *according to* HERODOTUS

Egypt and other Eastern countries Herodotus returned with much information regarding these lands. His map showed that the Red Sea connected with the Indian Ocean, a fact unknown to his predecessor Hecatæus (see map, p. 379). The scientists were still much puzzled by the cold of the north and the warmth of the south, a curious difference which they could not yet explain.

Progress in medicine

603. Herodotus must have seen in Egypt the earliest known government medical school, which had been restored and endowed by Darius only a generation earlier. Although without the microscope or the assistance of chemistry, medicine nevertheless had made progress. In the first place, the Greek physicians rejected the older belief that disease was caused by evil demons, and, like the great unknown Egyptian surgeon, they tried to find the *natural causes* of the ailment. To do this they sought to understand the organs of the body. Following the Egyptian surgeon's discovery that the brain was the source both of the nervous control and also of the paralysis of the limbs, the

Greek physicians had now discovered that the brain was the organ of thought. But the arterial system, the circulation of the blood, and the nervous system as a whole were still entirely unknown. Without a knowledge of the circulation of the blood, surgery was unable to attempt amputation, but otherwise it made much progress. The greatest physician of the time was Hippocrates, the founder of scientific medicine. The fame of Greek medicine was such that the Persian king called a Greek physician to his court.

Progress in the writing of history; Herodotus

604. Just at the close of Pericles' life, in the midst of national calamities, the historian Herodotus, who had long been at work on his history, finally published his great work. It was a history of the world so told that the glorious leadership of Athens would be clear to all Greeks and would show them that to her the Hellenes owed their deliverance from Persia. Throughout Greece it created a deep impression, and so tremendous was its effect in Athens that in spite of the financial drain of war the Athenians voted Herodotus a reward of ten talents, some twelve thousand dollars. In this earliest history of the world which has come down to us Herodotus traced the course of events as he believed them to be directed by the will of the gods and as prophesied in their divine oracles. There was little or no effort to explain historical events as the result of natural processes.

Education and discipline gained from state service

605. Besides the instruction received from the Sophists by many young men their constant share in public affairs was giving them an experience which greatly assisted in producing an intelligent body of citizens. In the Council of Five Hundred, citizens learned to carry on the daily business of the government. On some days also as many as six thousand citizens might be serving as jurors. This service alone meant that one citizen in five was engaged in duties which sharpened his wits and gave him some training in legal and business affairs. At the same time such duties kept constantly in the citizen's mind his obligations toward the state and community.

606. This led many citizens to surprisingly generous contributions. It was not uncommon for a citizen to undertake the entire equipment of a warship except the hull and spars, though this service may have been compulsory. At national festivals a wealthy man would sometimes furnish a costly dinner for all the members of his "tribe." The choruses for public performances, especially at the theater, were organized by private citizens, who paid large sums for their training and for their costumes. We know of one citizen who spent in the voluntary support of feasts and choruses in nine years no less than fourteen thousand dollars, a considerable fortune in those days.

Voluntary contributions by citizens

607. Public festivals maintained by the state also played an important part in the lives of all Athenians. Every spring at the ancient Feast of Dionysus (§ 520) the greatest play-writers each submitted three tragedies and a satyric drama to be played in the theater for a prize given by the state. All Athens streamed to the theater to see them. Many other state festivals, celebrated with music and gayety, filled the year with holidays so numerous that one fell every six or seven days. The great state feast, called the *Panathenæa*, occurred every four years. A brilliant procession, made up of the smart young Athenian cavalry, groups of dignified government officials, priests, and sacrificial animals, marched with music and rejoicing across the market place, carrying a beautiful new robe embroidered by the women of Athens for the goddess Athena. The procession marched to the Acropolis, where the robe was delivered to the goddess amid splendid sacrifices and impressive ceremonies. Contests in music and in athletic games, war dances, and a regatta in the channel off Salamis served to furnish entertainment for the multitude which flocked to Athens for the great feast.

State feasts

SECTION 53. ART AND LITERATURE

608. Although the first fifteen years of the leadership of Pericles were burdened with the Spartan and Persian Wars, the higher life of Athens continued to unfold. Under influences like those we have been discussing, a new vision of the glory of the state, discerned nowhere else in the world before this age, caught the imagination of poet and painter, of sculptor and architect; and not of these alone but also of the humblest artisan and tradesman, as all classes alike took part in the common life of the community. Music, the drama, art, and architecture were profoundly inspired by this new and exalted vision of the state, and the citizen found great works of art so inspired thrust into the foreground of his life.

Higher life of imperial Athens; the glorified state

609. It will aid us in our effort to understand the Athens of this age if in imagination we follow an Athenian citizen and note a few of the noble monuments that met his eye as he went about the new Athens which Pericles was creating. When he wandered into the market place and stood chatting with his friends under the shade of the plane trees, he found at several points colonnaded porches looking out upon the market. One of these, which had been presented to the city by Cimon's family, was called the Painted Porch; for the wall behind the columns bore paintings by Polygnotus (an artist from one of the island possessions of Athens), a gift of the painter to the Athenians, depicting their glorious victory at Marathon. Here in splendid panorama was a vision of the heroic devotion of the fathers. In the thick of the fray the citizen might pick out the figure of Themistocles, of Miltiades, of Callimachus (who fell in the battle), of Æschylus the great tragic poet. He could see the host of the fleeing Persians and perhaps hear some old man tell how the brother of Æschylus seized and tried to stop one of the Persian boats drawn up on the beach, and how a desperate Persian raised his ax and slashed off the hand of the brave Greek. Perhaps among the group of eager listeners he

Painting

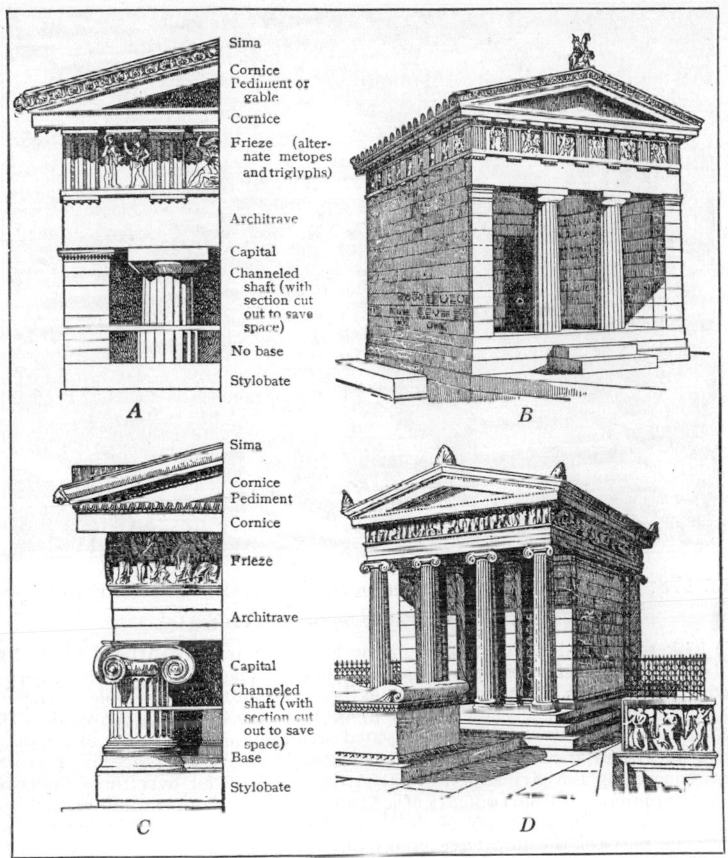

Comparative Diagram of the Two Leading GREEK STYLES OF ARCHITECTURE, *the* DORIC (*A and* B) *and the* IONIC (*C and D*)

The little Doric building *B* is the treasury of the Athenians at Delphi (Fig. 169), containing their offerings of gratitude to Apollo. On the low base at the left side of the building were placed the trophies from the battle of Marathon. Over them on the walls are carved hymns to Apollo, with musical notes attached, one of the oldest Greek musical notations surviving. The beautiful Ionic building *D* is a restoration of the Temple of Victory on the Athenian Acropolis (Fig. 180, *D*, and headpiece, p. 441). Contrast its slender columns with the sturdier shafts of the Doric order, and it will be seen that the Ionic is a more delicate and graceful style. *A* and *C* show details of both styles. (After Luckenbach)

FIG. 178. *Excavations being carried on in the* ATHENIAN MARKET PLACE (*Agora*) *by the* AMERICAN SCHOOL AT ATHENS

We look southward directly through the houses of modern Athens which had to be bought up before the clearance could begin. The excavated area was covered by such houses. Just out of range on the right (west) is the temple of Theseus (Fig. 179), while far back and entirely invisible on the left is the Acropolis. The ruined walls which we see in the excavated area are almost all parts of buildings much later than ancient Athens, although this extensive clearance has revealed facts concerning the civilization of the Attic peninsula for over three thousand years, beginning with the contents of a Mycenæan burial and concluding with the frescoes of a Byzantine chapel of the Seventeenth Century A.D. The foundations of certain parts of the stoa have been cleared, and there have been found fragments of architecture and sculpture which probably belonged to this building. Many important works of art, including interesting examples of Roman portrait-heads, have been uncovered, and over a thousand new inscriptions have been found. Some of the latter are of great historical importance, chief among them being the auction list of the property of Alcibiades sold after his conviction on the charge of impiety in 415 B.C. (see § 639) during the Sicilian expedition. See also the two ostraka in Fig. 174. (Courtesy of Professor Edward Capps)

noticed one questioning the veteran carefully and making full notes of all that he could learn from the graybeard. The questioner was Herodotus, collecting from survivors the tale of the Persian Wars for his great history, which was yet to move all Greece with its inspiring story of Athenian greatness.

610. Behind the citizen rose a low hill, known as Market Hill, around which were grouped plain, bare government buildings. Here were the assembly rooms of the Areopagus and the Council of Five Hundred. The Council's Committee of Fifty, carrying on the current business of the government, also had its offices here. The citizen recalled how, as a member of this Council, he had lived here for over a month while serving on that committee and had taken his meals in the building before him, at the expense of the state, along with the Athenian victors in the Olympic games and other deserving citizens who were thus pensioned by the government. In spite of the growing sentiment for the glory of the state these plain buildings, like the Athenian houses, were all built of sun-dried mud brick or, at most, of rough rubble. The idea of great and beautiful buildings for the offices of the government was still unknown in the Mediterranean world, and no such building yet existed in Europe.

Lack of fine buildings for government offices

611. The sentiment toward the state was so mingled with reverence for the gods who protected the state that patriotism was itself a deeply religious feeling. Hence the great public buildings of Greece were temples and not quarters for the offices of the government. As the citizen turned from the Painted Porch, therefore, he might observe, crossing the market, many a creaking wagon heavily loaded with white blocks of marble for a new and still unfinished temple of Theseus, the hero-god, who, as the Athenians thought, had once united Attica into a single nation.

Great public buildings are temples

612. Above him towers the height of the Acropolis, about one thousand feet in length, — two of our city blocks. There, on its summit, had always been the dwelling place of Athena, whose arm was ever stretched out in protection over her beloved Athens. But for long years after the repulse of the Persians the Acropolis rose smoke-blackened over the rebuilt houses of the city, and no temple of Athena appeared to replace the old building of Pisistratus, which the Persians had burned. Now at last

Plans of Pericles for the restoration of the Acropolis

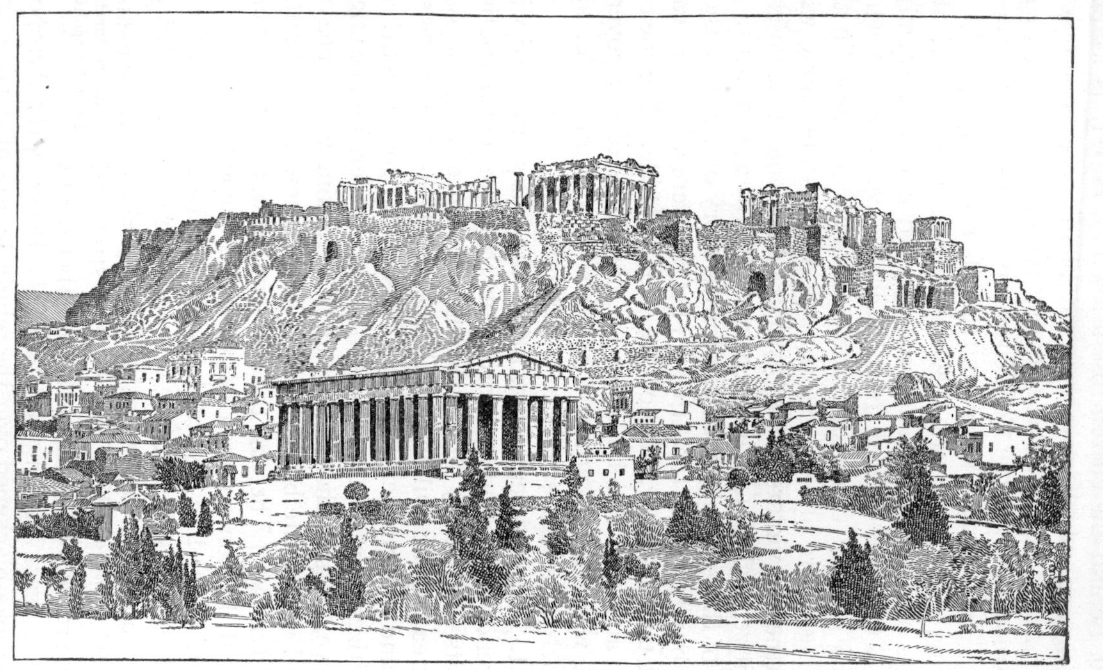

FIG. 179. *The So-called* TEMPLE OF THESEUS *and the* ACROPOLIS OF ATHENS *

Pericles has undertaken the restoration of the ancient shrines on a scale of magnificence and beauty before unknown anywhere in the Greek world. His sumptuous plans have demanded an expense of about two and a quarter millions of dollars, — a sum far exceeding any such public outlay ever heard of among the Greeks. As he passes the Market Hill, where the Areopagus meets, the citizen remembers the discontented mutterings of the old men in this ancient Council as they heard of these vast expenses, and he smiles in satisfaction as he reflects that this unprogressive old body, once so powerful in Athenian affairs, has been deprived of all power to obstruct the will of the people. From here he also catches a glimpse of the Pnyx, where he has heard Pericles make one eloquent speech after another before the assembly of the people in support of his new building plans, and he recalls with what enthusiasm the citizens voted to adopt them.

Entrance to the Acropolis; the Parthenon

613. As he looks up at the gleaming marble shafts he feels that the architectural splendor now crowning the Acropolis is the work of the Athenian *people*, a world of new beauty in the creation of which every Athenian citizen has had a voice. Here before him rise the imposing marble colonnades of the magnificent monumental entrance to the Acropolis. It is still unfinished, and the architect Mnesicles, with a roll of plans under his arm, is perhaps at the moment directing a group of workmen to their task. He is beginning to employ a new style of column, called the Ionic; it is lighter and more ornate than the stately Doric. From the height above, the tinkle of many distant hammers tells where the stonecutters are shaping the

---

* In this view we stand inside the wall of Themistocles, near the Dipylon Gate in the Potters' Quarter (see plan, p. 418). In the foreground is the temple of Theseus, built of Pentelic marble. It was finished a few years after the death of Pericles, but now, after twenty-three hundred years or more, it is still the best preserved of all ancient Greek buildings. The buildings we see on the Acropolis are all ruins of the structures erected after the place had been laid waste by the Persians. The Parthenon, in the middle of the hill (see Fig. 180), shows the gaping hole caused by the explosion of a Turkish powder magazine ignited by a Venetian shell in 1687, when the entire central portion of the building was blown out. The space between the temple of Theseus, the Areopagus, and the Acropolis (see plan, p. 418) was largely occupied by the market place of Athens.

FIG. 180. *Restoration of the* ATHENIAN ACROPOLIS

The lower entrance *A* is of Roman date. Beyond it we have on the right the graceful little Temple of Victory *B* (see headpiece, p. 441), while before us rises the colonnaded entrance building *C* designed by Mnesicles. As we pass through it we stand beside the colossal bronze statue of Athena *D* by Phidias, beyond which at the left is the ancient sanctuary of the Erechtheum *F* (§ 677). To the right, along the southern edge of the hill, is the wonderful temple of the Parthenon *E*. It looks down upon the theater *H*. The other theater-like building *I*, in the foreground, is a concert hall built by Herodes Atticus, a wealthy citizen, in Roman times (Second Century A.D.). *G* is the foundation of an ancient temple (now destroyed) older than the present Parthenon

marble blocks for the still unfinished Parthenon, a noble temple dedicated to Athena (Fig. 182); and there, too, the people often see Pericles intently inspecting the building, as Phidias the sculptor and Ictinus the architect of the building pace up and down the inclosure, explaining to him the progress of the work. It was in these wondrous Greek buildings that the architect and the sculptor working hand in hand produced a marvelously harmonious result.

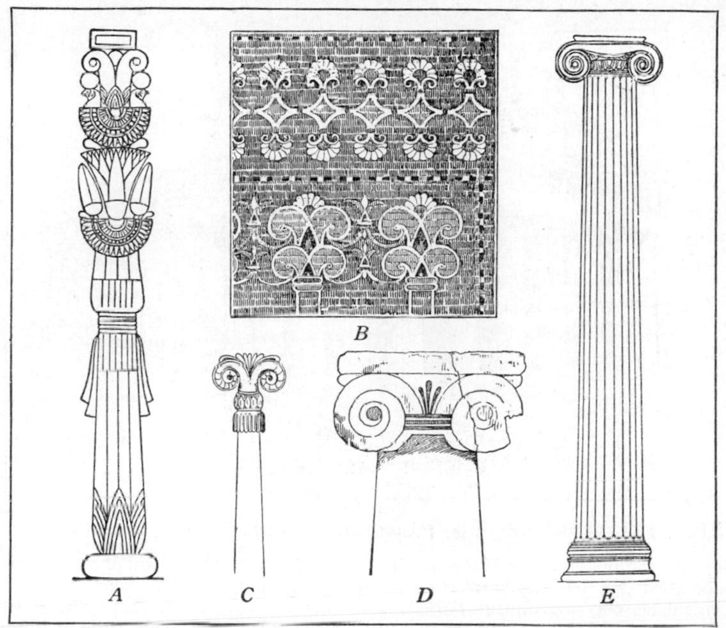

FIG. 181. *The* IONIC COLUMN *and its* ORIENTAL PREDECESSORS

A is a column of wood as used in houses and shrines in Egypt (Fifteenth Century B.C.); notice at the top of *A* the lily with the ends of the petals rolled over in spirals called *volutes*. *B* is part of a wall from the throne room of Nebuchadnezzar at Babylon, with beautifully decorative designs in colored glazed brick containing the same lily design. *C* shows us a capital used in the beginnings of Greek architecture in Asia Minor, with the lily petals forming the volutes rolled farther over but still showing its relationship with *A*. This process is carried so far in *D*, a capital dug up on the Acropolis of Athens, that we lose sight of the lily. *E* finally shows us the fully developed Ionic column, in which the volutes hardly resemble any longer the lily from which they came. This column *E* is taken from the colonnade of the Temple of Victory on the Acropolis of Athens. Examples of this style of column are now common in our own public buildings. (After Puchstein)

Phidias and the sculptures of the Parthenon

614. Phidias is the greatest of the sculptors at Athens. In a long band of carved marble extending entirely around the four sides of the Parthenon, at the top inside the colonnades, Phidias and his pupils have portrayed, as in a glorified vision, the sovereign people of Athens moving in the stately procession (Fig. 183) of the Panathenaic festival. To be sure, these are

FIG. 182. *Restoration of the* PARTHENON *as it was in the Fifth Century* B.C.

The restoration shows us the wonderful beauty of the Doric colonnades as they were when they left the hands of the builders. The gable ends each contained a triangular group of sculpture depicting the birth of Athena and her struggle with Poseidon, god of the sea, for possession of Attica. The wonderful frieze of Phidias extended around the building, at the top of the wall, inside the colonnades. (After Thiersch and Michaelis)

not individual portraits of actual Athenian folk, but only types which lived in the exalted vision of the sculptor, and not on the streets of Athens. But such sculpture had never been seen before. How different is the supreme beauty of these perfect human forms from the cruder figures which adorned the temple burned by the Persians. The citizen has seen the shattered fragments of these older works cleared away and covered with rubbish when the architects leveled off the summit of the Acropolis.[1] Inside the new temple gleams the colossal figure of Athena, wrought by the cunning hand of Phidias in gold and ivory. Even from the city below the citizen can discern, touched with bright colors, the heroic

[1] Until modern times they lay buried under the rubbish on the slope. The excavations of the Greek government have recovered them, and they are now in the Acropolis Museum at Athens.

FIG. 183. *Part of the* PARTHENON FRIEZE OF PHIDIAS, *showing* ATHENIAN YOUTHS *riding in the* PANATHENAIC FESTIVAL

Notice the wonderful movement of the horses, and compare them with the horses of the barbarous Greek vase-painters three centuries earlier (Fig. 154). The reins and trappings of the steeds shown here were of metal and have disappeared

figures of the gods with which Phidias has filled the triangular gable ends of the building. Out in the open area behind the colonnaded entrance rises another great work of Phidias, a colossal bronze statue of Athena, seventy feet high as it stands on its tall base. With shield and spear the goddess stands, the gracious protectress of Athens, and the glittering point of her gilded spear can be seen shining like a beacon far across the land, even by the sailors as they round the promontory of Mount Hymettus (see map, p. 418) and sail homeward.

The drama: Æschylus

615. In spite of the Sophists these are the gods to whom the faith of the Athenian people still reverently looks up. Have not Athena and these gods raised the power of Athens to the imperial position which she now occupies? Do not all the citizens recall Æschylus' drama "The Persians"? It told the story of the glorious victory of Salamis, and in it the memories of the great deliverance from Persian conquest were enshrined. How that tremendous day of Salamis was made to live again in the imposing picture which the poet's genius brought before them, disclosing the mighty purpose of the gods to save Hellas!

Theater and people

616. As he skirts the sheer precipice of the Acropolis the citizen reaches the theater, where he finds the people are already entering, for the feast of Dionysus has arrived. Only yesterday he and his neighbors received from the state treasury the money for their admission. It is natural that they should feel that the theater and all that is done there belong to the people, and not the less as the citizen looks down upon the orchestra circle and recognizes his friends and neighbors and their sons in the chorus for that day's performance. The seats are of wood, and they occupy the slope at the foot of the Acropolis. Hence they are not elevated on timbers, and there is no danger of their falling and killing the spectators, as they once did when the theater was a temporary structure in the market place, in the days of the citizen's grandfather. All the citizens have

FIG. 184. *Praxiteles' Figure of* HERMES *playing with the* CHILD DIONYSUS

This wonderful statue was discovered in the ruins of the Hera temple at Olympia (headpiece, p. 356) and is one of the few original works of the great Greek sculptors found in Greece. Nearly all such Greek originals have perished, and we know them only in Roman copies (§ 1092). In his uplifted right hand (now broken off) the god probably held a bunch of grapes, with which he was amusing the child (§ 681). Some archæologists have recently expressed doubt that this is a work of Praxiteles turned out, including some less worthy and intelligent, who do not hesitate to indulge in cat-calls or pelt the actors with food if the play displeases them. The play would seem strange enough to us, for there is little or no scenery, and the actors, who are always men, wear grotesque masks, a survival of old days. The narrative is largely carried on in song by the chorus, but this is varied by the dialogue of the actors, and the whole is not unlike an opera.

617. A play of Sophocles is on, and the citizen's neighbor in the next seat leans over to tell him how as a lad many years ago he stood on the shore of Salamis, whither his family had fled, and as they looked down upon the destruction of the Persian fleet this same Sophocles, a boy of sixteen, was in the crowd looking on with the rest. How deeply must the events of that tragic day have sunk into the poet's soul! For does he not see the will of the gods in all that happens to men? Does he not celebrate the stern decree of Zeus everywhere hanging over human life, at the same time that he uplifts his audience to adore the splendor of Zeus, however dark the destiny he lays upon men? For Sophocles still believes in the gods, and is no friend of the Sophists. Hence the citizen feels that Sophocles is a veritable voice of the people, exalting the old gods in the new time. Moreover, in place of the former *two*, Sophocles has *three* actors in his plays, a change which makes them more interesting and full of action. Even old Æschylus yielded to this innovation once before he died. Yet too much innovation is also unwelcome to the citizen.

Sophocles

618. The citizen feels this especially if it is one of the new sensational plays of Euripides which is presented. Euripides is the son of a farmer who lives over on the island of Salamis. He has for some time been presenting plays at the spring competition. He is a friend and companion of the Sophists, and in matters of religion his mind is shadowed with doubts. His new plays are all inwrought with problems and mental struggle regarding the gods, and they have raised a great many questions and

Euripides

doubts which the citizen has never been able to banish from his own mind since he heard them. The citizen determines that he will use all the influence he has to prevent the plays of Euripides from winning the prize. Indeed, Sophocles suits all the old-fashioned folk, and it is very rarely that Euripides has been able to carry off the prize, in spite of his great ability. The citizen feels some anxiety as he realizes that his own son and most of the other young men of his set are enthusiastic admirers of Euripides. They constantly read his plays and talk them over with the Sophists.

Fig. 185. Euripides

The name of the poet is engraved in Greek letters along the lower edge of the bust

Comedies

619. The great tragedies were given in the morning, and in the afternoon the people were ready for less serious entertainment, such as the comedy offered. Out of the old-time masques and burlesque frolics of the village communities at country feasts the comedy had developed into a stage performance, with all the uproarious antics of the unbridled comedian. The playwriter did not hesitate to introduce the greatest dignitaries of the state. Even Pericles was not spared, and great philosophers and thinkers like Socrates, or a serious-minded tragic poet like Euripides, were shown in absurd caricatures and made irresistibly ridiculous on the stage, while the multitudes of Athens vented their delight in roars of laughter mingled with shouts and cheers. Parodies on great passages of literature, too, were sure of a quick response, so keen was the wit of the Athenians and so widespread the acquaintance of the people with the literature which they had inherited.

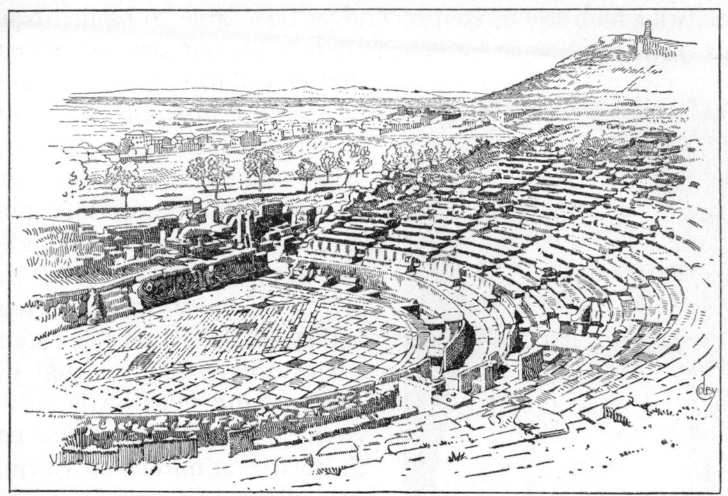

FIG. 186. *The* THEATER OF ATHENS

This theater was the center of the growth and development of Greek drama, which began as a part of the celebration of the spring feast of Dionysus, god of the vine and the fruitfulness of the earth. The temple of the god stood here, just at the left. Long before anyone knew of such a thing as a theater, the people gathered to watch the celebration of the god's spring feast at this place, where they formed a circle about the chorus, which narrated in song the stories of the gods (§ 520). This circle (called the orchestra) was finally marked out permanently, seats of wood for the spectators were erected in a semicircle on one side, but the singing and action all took place in the circle on the level of the ground. On the side opposite the public was a booth, or tent (Greek, *skēnē*, "scene"), for the actors, and out of this finally developed the stage. Here we see the circle, or orchestra, with the stage cutting off the back part of the circle. The seats are of stone and accommodated possibly seventeen thousand people. The fine marble seats in the front row were reserved for the leading men of Athens. The old wooden seats were still in use in the days when Æschylus, Sophocles, and Euripides presented their dramas here (§§ 615–618). From the seats the citizens had a grand view of the sea, with the island of Ægina, their old-time rival (§ 580), and even the heights of Argolis, 40 miles away, were visible, for orchestra and seats continued roofless, and a Greek theater was always open to the sky. In Roman times a colonnaded porch across the back of the stage was introduced. For the best-preserved early Greek theater see tailpiece, p. 440

620. When all was over they must wait until the next spring feast of Dionysus before they were privileged to see any more plays. But meantime they were greatly interested in the decision of the jury of citizens awarding prizes for tragedy and for comedy, and a bronze tripod to the citizen who had equipped and trained the best chorus. Moreover, the interest in drama and the theater continued, for the next competition soon demanded that probably two thousand men and boys of Athens should put all their leisure time into learning the parts written out for them on sheets of papyrus, and into training and rehearsals for the various choruses. Thousands of citizens, too, were reading the old plays that had already been presented.

Continued and widespread interest in drama and literature

621. For now at length books too had come to take an important place in the life of Athens. Rows of baskets of cylindrical shape held the books which filled the shelves in our Athenian citizen's library. Homer and the works of the old classic poets were now written on long rolls of papyrus, as much as a hundred and fifty or sixty feet in length. To one of these rolls the educated Greek sat down as the Egyptian had so long before been accustomed to do (Fig. 196). For lack of good artificial light, reading was necessarily done mostly by day, but studious Greeks also ventured to try their eyes in reading by the dim olive-oil lamp. Besides literary works all sorts of books of instruction began to appear. The sculptors wrote of their art, and Ictinus produced a book on his design of the Parthenon (§ 613). There was a large group of books on medicine, bearing the name of Hippocrates. Textbooks on mathematics and rhetoric circulated, and the Athenian housekeeper could even find a cookbook at the bookshop.

Books and reading

622. In our study of the Egyptian Empire we found that a thousand years before the days of Pericles there was a group of gifted men who created at Thebes a grand and imperial city of noble architecture. But that group of great Egyptians was not made up of *citizens*, nor had the multitudes of Thebes any share in government or in the creation of the magnificent city. It was very different in the Athens of Pericles. Here had grown up a whole community of intelligent men, who were the product of the most active interest in the life

Contrast between Athens and Egyptian Thebes

and government of the community, constantly sharing in its tasks and problems, in daily contact with the greatest works of art in literature, drama, painting, architecture, and sculpture, — such a wonderful community, indeed, as the ancient world, Greek or Oriental, had never seen before.

The old Athens and the new

623. Not only was it totally different from any that we have found in the Ancient Near East, but we see also how very different from the Athens of the old days before the Persian Wars was this imperial Athens of Pericles, — throbbing with new life and astir with a thousand questions eagerly discussed at every corner. Keenly awake to the demands of the greater state and the sovereign people, the men of the new Athens were deeply pondering also the duties and privileges of the individual, who felt new and larger visions of himself conflicting with the exactions of the state and the old faith. Troubled by serious doubts, they were nevertheless clinging with wistful apprehension to the old gods and the old truths. Under Pericles, Athens was becoming, as he desired it should, the teacher of the Greek world. It now remained to be seen whether the *people*, in sovereign control of the state, could guide her wisely and maintain her new power. As we watch the citizens of Athens endeavoring to furnish her with wise and successful guidance we shall find another and a sadly different side of the life of this wonderful community.

QUESTIONS

Section 51. What can you say of the population of Attica as to social classes? Discuss the rich and the poor. Were there any beautiful houses in Europe in Pericles' time? Describe an Athenian house of this age,— its conveniences; its equipment; its decoration. What were the streets of Athens like? Describe Greek costume in this age. What was now the position of women? Describe the usual school and its teacher. What oath of citizenship did a boy take? Tell about his military service; his athletic training. What was the Academy? the Lyceum? What were the chief events in athletics?

Section 52. What new private teachers now began to appear? What did these men teach? Did a boy learn from them anything which his father had not been taught? What did the fathers think about the teaching of the Sophists? Was there any general knowledge of science? How was the time of day designated? How was time measured within the day? within the year? What discoveries were made in astronomy? in geography? How much more information about the world had Herodotus than had Hecatæus? (Cf. maps, pp. 379 and 419.) What progress was made in medicine? in history-writing? How did government business train the citizens of Athens? Tell about voluntary contributions by the citizens. What can you say about official state feasts at Athens?

Section 53. How did warmth of patriotic feeling affect music, the drama, art, and architecture? Discuss the painting of Marathon in the Athenian market place. Were there any fine government office buildings in Athens under Pericles? What was the material of such buildings? Sketch the capital of a Doric and the capital of an Ionic column. Compare these two styles of architecture. What were the beautiful public buildings of Greece at this time? How did the Athenian Acropolis look after the Persian Wars? What did Pericles do about it? Who opposed him? How did he put his plan through? Who assisted Pericles in carrying out the actual work on the Acropolis? What buildings did they erect? Describe the sculpture of Phidias.

What play did Æschylus write about the war with Persia? Describe the theater where such plays were presented at Athens. Did a citizen pay for his own ticket? Describe a play in such a theater. Who was Sophocles? What did he think about the gods and the Sophists? How many actors did he have? What did Euripides think about the gods? Was it to Sophocles or to Euripides that the Athenians voted the most prizes? Why? What did an old-fashioned citizen think about having his son read the plays of Euripides? Tell about the comedies played at Athens. How did the Athenians take part in drama and music? What did a book look like in this age? What books could a citizen find at the bookshop? Contrast Athens and Egyptian Thebes. In what ways was the Athens of Pericles different from that of Solon?

BIBLIOGRAPHY FOR TOPICAL STUDIES

Social customs of the Greeks: BRITISH MUSEUM, *Greek and Roman Life*, pp. 196–202, 216–219; GULICK, *Modern Traits*, pp. 14–25, 32–56; METROPOLITAN MUSEUM OF ART, *Daily Life of Greeks and Romans*, pp. 32–39, 68–75; MILLS, *Ancient Greeks*, pp. 207–220; POLAND-REISINGER-WAGNER, *Culture of Greece and Rome*, pp. 232–235, 240–242.

The theater and Greek drama: BOTSFORD, *Hellenic History*, pp. 295, 297, 330; GULICK, *Modern Traits*, pp. 147–151; JAMES, *Hellenic Heritage*, Vol. II, pp. 378–383, 414–439; METROPOLITAN MUSEUM OF ART, *Daily Life*, pp. 13–18; *Pageant of Greece*, pp. 96–128 (or HOWE-HARRER, *Greek Literature*, pp. 224–334); POLAND-REISINGER-WAGNER, *Culture*, pp. 42–55.

Aristophanes: JAMES, *Hellenic Heritage*, Vol. II, pp. 172–173, 404–413; MURRAY, *Aristophanes and the War Party* (48 pages); NORWOOD-DUFF, *Writers*, pp. 76–85; *Pageant of Greece*, pp. 129–157 (or HOWE-HARRER, *Greek Literature*, pp. 334–387).

NOTE. The tailpiece below shows us the theater of Epidaurus, which is unusually instructive because it is the best-preserved of the Greek theaters. Although it was built late in the Fourth Century B.C., we see that the orchestra circle is still complete and has not been cut into by later stage arrangements behind it as at Athens (Fig. 186).

Chapter XVI · The Struggle between Athens and Sparta, and the Fall of the Athenian Empire

Section 54. The Tyranny of Athens and the Second Peloponnesian War

States of Athenian Empire become helpless subjects

624. While Athens under the guiding hand of Pericles had thus made herself the chief center of refined and civilized life in the Greek world, her political situation was in a number of ways becoming a serious one both within and without her Empire. When the danger from Persia had long passed and some of the island states of the Empire wished to withdraw, Athens

NOTE. The above headpiece shows us the lovely little TEMPLE OF VICTORY, still standing on the Acropolis (*B* in Fig. 180). It was demolished by the Turks, who built a battery out of its blocks. When the Turkish works were cleared away in 1835, the fragments of the temple were discovered and it was put together again. The roof, however, is still lacking (but see *D* in restoration, p. 423). It was probably built, or at least begun, in the latter part of the leadership of Pericles. The columns display the incoming Ionic form (Fig. 181) and are among the most beautiful examples of this style, or, as it is commonly called, "order."

would not permit them to do so. She sent out her war fleet, conquered them, and forced them to pay money tribute instead of contributing ships. Often many of their citizens were driven out, and their lands were divided among the Athenian settlers. A section of the Athenian fleet was on constant duty sailing about in the Ægean and collecting the tribute money by force. These funds were used by Athens as she pleased, and the magnificent buildings of Pericles were paid for out of this tribute.

Change in policy of Athens regarding citizenship

625. Moreover, the democracy of Athens was most undemocratic in its treatment of these outsiders in the other cities of the Empire. For, about the middle of the century, the Athenians, led by Pericles, abolished the former liberal policy of granting citizenship to outsiders and passed a very strict law limiting Athenian citizenship to those whose parents were themselves citizens of Athens. This law kept the people of the Empire really foreigners and deprived Athens of the large body of loyal citizens which she might have gained from among the subject cities.

Tyranny of Athens; discontent in her Empire

626. At the same time Athens forced the people of the Empire to come there to settle their legal differences before her citizen juries. For this purpose the people of distant island states were often obliged to make the expensive and inconvenient journey to Athens. There was no feeling of unity within the Empire, for the council of representatives from the states of the Empire, which once guided its affairs, no longer held any meetings. Athens was in complete control and governed them as she liked. They saw how much easier were the conditions under which the members of the Spartan League lived, and more than one of them sent secret messages to Sparta, with the purpose of gaining its aid in throwing off Athenian control.

627. While such was the state of affairs within the Athenian Empire, conditions outside were even more serious. The outward splendor of Athens, her commercial prosperity, the visible growth of her power, her not very conciliatory attitude toward her rivals, and the example she offered of the seeming success of triumphant democracy, — all these were causes of jealousy to a backward and conservative military state like Sparta, where most of the citizens were still unable to read, iron money continued in use, and the town remained an open settlement without walls or defenses. Moreover, this feeling of unfriendliness toward Athens was not confined to Sparta but was quite general throughout Greece. The merchants of Corinth found Athenian competition a continuous vexation, and when Athenian possessions in the north Ægean revolted and received support from Corinth and Sparta, the fact that hardly half of the thirty years' term of peace had expired did not prevent the outbreak of another war, which we call the Second Peloponnesian War.

Hostility of the rivals of Athens

628. It seemed as though all European Greece not included in the Athenian Empire had united against Athens; for Sparta controlled the entire Peloponnesus except Argos, and, north of Attica, Bœotia (led by Thebes) and its neighbors on the west were hostile to Athens. The support of Athens consisted of the Ægean cities which made up her Empire and a few outlying allies of little power. She began the struggle with a large war treasury and a fleet which made her undisputed mistress of the sea. But she could not cope with the land forces of the enemy, which, some thirty thousand strong, had planned to meet in the isthmus in the spring of 431 B.C. Accordingly Pericles' plan for the war was to throw all the resources of Athens into naval enterprises and make no effort to defend Attica by land. When the Peloponnesian army entered Attica, the country communities were directed by Pericles to leave their homes and take refuge in the open markets and squares of Athens, in the sanctuaries, and especially between the Long Walls leading to the Piræus. Here they were safe behind the strong defenses of Athens and her port. To offset the devastation of Attica by the Spartan army all that Athens could do was to organize destructive

Second Peloponnesian War (431 B.C.); strategy of Pericles

sea raids and inflict as much damage as possible along the coasts of the Peloponnesus or blockade and destroy Corinthian commerce as of old.

The plague in Athens

629. The masses of people crowded within the walls of Athens under the unsanitary conditions we have already described exposed the city to disease; a plague, brought in from the Orient, raged with intermissions for several seasons. It carried off probably a third of the population, and from this unforeseen disaster Athens never recovered. Constantly under arms for the defense of the walls, deprived of any opportunity to strike the enemy, forced to sit still and see their land ravaged, the citizens at last broke out in discontent.

Decline and fall of Pericles

630. Even before the beginning of the war there had been signs that the power of Pericles was waning. He was a thoroughly modern man, associated openly with the Sophists, and very evidently held their views. We can understand what this meant to the people if we imagine one of our own political leaders of today declaring himself an infidel. One of Pericles' particular friends among the Sophists had been prosecuted by the people for irreligious views. He was legally condemned for his infidelity and, in spite of all that Pericles could do, was obliged to flee from Athens. At the same time a popular attack on the honesty of Pericles' friend Phidias, the great sculptor, resulted in his being thrown into prison, where he died. Finally Pericles himself lost control; he was tried for misappropriation of funds, and was found guilty and fined.

Restoration and death of Pericles (429 B.C.)

631. The absence of his steadying hand and powerful leadership was at once felt by the people, for there was no one to take his place, although a swarm of small politicians were contending for control of the Assembly. Realizing their helplessness, the people soon turned to Pericles again and elected him strategus. But the great days of his leadership were over. His two sons died of the plague. Then he was himself stricken with it and died soon after his return to power (429 B.C.). Great statesman as he was, he had left Athens with a system of government which did not provide for the continuation of such leadership as he had furnished, and without such leadership the Athenian Empire was doomed.

Lack of leaders after the death of Pericles

632. Men of the prosperous manufacturing class now came to the fore. They possessed neither the high station in life, the ability as statesmen, nor the qualities of leadership to win the confidence and respect of the people. Moreover, these new leaders were not soldiers and could not command the fleet or the army as Pericles had done. The most notable exception was Alcibiades, a brilliant young man, who was a relative and ward of Pericles, and who might have become the savior of Athens and of Greece. As it happened, however, this young leader was more largely responsible than anyone else for the destruction of the Athenian Empire and the downfall of Greece. Lacking the steadying hand of a statesman whose well-formed plans and continuous policy might furnish a firm and guiding influence, the management of Athenian affairs fell into confusion. The youthful Aristophanes pictured the rudderless condition of the ship of state in one clever comedy after another, in which he ridiculed in irresistible satire the pretense to statesmanship of such "men of the people" as Cleon the tanner.

Incident of Mitylene

633. A typical example of the ill-considered actions of the Assembly was their treatment of the revolting citizens of Mitylene. When the people of Mitylene were finally subdued, the Assembly on the Pnyx voted that they should all be put to death, and a ship departed with these orders. It was with great difficulty that a more moderate group in the Assembly secured a rehearing of the question and succeeded in inducing the Athenian people to modify their barbarous action so that the condemnation and execution which they had voted should apply to the ringleaders only. A second ship then overtook the first barely in time to save from death the entire body of the citizens of Mitylene.

634. In spite of such revolts Athenian naval supremacy continued; but as the war dragged on, the payment of army and fleet reduced Athenian funds to a very low state. Cleon the tanner was a man of great energy and a good deal of financial ability. He succeeded in having an income tax introduced, and later on the tribute of the Ægean cities was raised. But, having always been a manufacturer, he lacked military experience. For years the operations on both sides were in most cases utterly insignificant.

Cleon the tanner

635. The attack of the allies on Athens did not succeed in breaking up her Empire and overthrowing her leadership of the Ægean cities. It was the devastation wrought by the plague which had seriously affected her. Athens and the whole Greek world were demoralized and weakened. The contest had in it no longer the inspiration of a noble struggle such as the Greeks had maintained against Persia. Unprecedented brutality, like that at first adopted toward Mitylene, gave the struggle a savagery and a lack of respect for the enemy which completely obscured all finer issues, if there were any such involved in the war. When Cleon died, Athenian leadership fell into the hands of a wealthy and noble citizen named Nicias, a man of no ability. When ten years of indecisive warfare had passed, Nicias arranged a peace to be kept for fifty years. Each contestant agreed to give up all new conquests and to retain only old possessions or subject cities (see map II, p. 402).

First ten years of war; the Peace of Nicias (421 B.C.)

Section 55. Third Peloponnesian War and Destruction of the Athenian Empire

636. Meantime serious difficulties arose in carrying out the conditions of the peace. One of the northern subject cities of Athens which had gone over to Sparta refused to return to Athenian allegiance. Athens took the questionable ground that Sparta should force the unwilling city to obey the terms of peace. It was at this juncture that Athens especially needed such guidance

Difficulties in maintaining the new peace

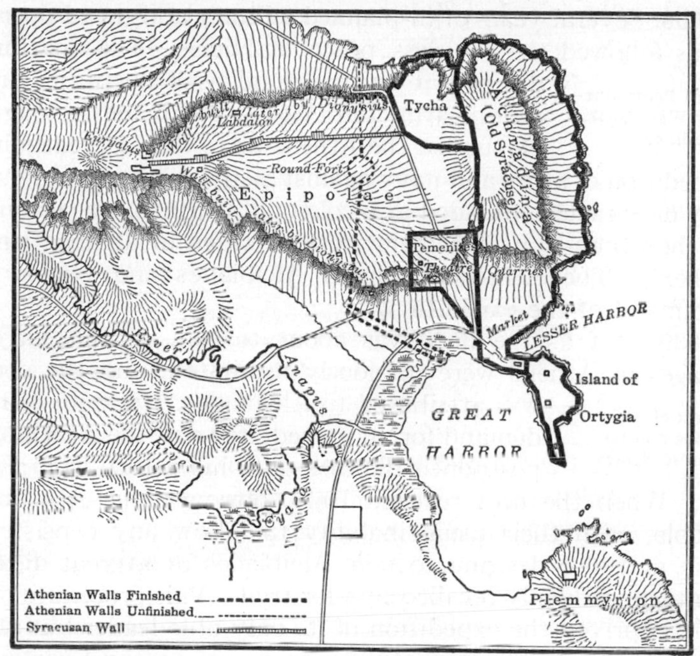

Plan of the SIEGE OF SYRACUSE

as a statesman like Pericles could have furnished. She was obliged to depend upon the feeble leadership of Nicias and the energetic but unprincipled Alcibiades.

637. Nicias continued to urge a conciliatory attitude toward Sparta, but he failed of election as strategus. On the other hand, the gifted and reckless Alcibiades, seeing a great opportunity for a brilliant career, did all that he could to excite the war party in Athens. He was elected strategus, and, in spite of the fact that troubles at home had forced Sparta into a treaty of alliance with Athens, Alcibiades was able to carry the Assembly with him. He then involved Athens in an alliance with Argos against Sparta. In this way Attica, exhausted with plague and ten years of warfare, was enticed into a life-and-death struggle which was to prove final.

Alcibiades brings on war again

Third Peloponnesian War; Sicilian expedition

638. Several years of ill-planned military and naval operations followed the fruitless peace of Nicias. The Spartans did not at once respond with hostilities and sent no army into Attica. Alcibiades at length persuaded the Athenians to plan a great joint expedition of army and navy against Sicily, where the mighty city of Syracuse, founded as a colony of Corinth, was leading in the oppression of certain western cities in alliance with Athens. The Athenians placed Alcibiades and Nicias in command of the expedition.

Arrest of Alcibiades and his flight to Sparta

639. Just as the fleet was about to sail, certain sacred images in Athens were impiously mutilated, and the deed was attributed to Alcibiades. In spite of his demand for an immediate trial, the Athenians postponed the case until his return from Sicily. When the fleet reached Italy, however, the Athenian people, with their usual inability to follow any consistent plan and also desiring to take Alcibiades at a great disadvantage, suddenly recalled him for trial. This procedure not only deprived the expedition of its only able leader but also gave Alcibiades an opportunity to desert to the Spartans, which he promptly did. His advice to the Spartans now proved fatal to the Athenians.

Incompetence of Nicias

640. The appearance of the huge Athenian fleet off their coast struck dismay into the hearts of the Syracusans, but Nicias entirely failed to see the importance of immediate attack before the Syracusans could recover and make preparations for the defense of their city. He wasted the early days of the campaign in ill-planned maneuvers, only winning a barren victory over the Syracusan land forces. When Nicias was finally induced by the second general in command to begin the siege of the city, courage had returned to the Syracusans, and their defense was well organized.

641. The Athenians now built a siege wall behind Syracuse nearly across the point of land on which the city was situated, in order to cut it entirely off from the outside world. The spirit of the Syracusans was much depressed, and surrender seemed not far off. Just at this point Gylippus, a Spartan leader, and his troops, sent by the advice of Alcibiades, succeeded in passing the Athenian lines and gained entrance to the city. The courage of the Syracusans was at once restored. The Athenians were thrown upon the defensive. Meantime the Syracusans had also organized a fleet. The Athenian fleet had entered the harbor, and in these narrow quarters they were unable to maneuver or to take advantage of their superior seamanship. After some Athenian success at first, the fleet of Syracuse was victorious.

Athenian siege unsuccessful

642. There was now no prospect of the capture of the city, and Nicias would have withdrawn, but the leaders at home would not allow it. In spite of renewed Spartan invasion the blinded democratic leaders sent out another fleet and more land forces to reënforce Nicias. No Greek state had ever mustered such power and sent it far across the waters. All Greece watched the spectacle with amazement. A night assault by the reënforced Athenians failed with large losses, and the position of the whole expedition at once became a dangerous one.

Reënforced Athenians repulsed

643. With disaster staring them in the face there was nothing for the Athenians to do but withdraw. But just at this point an eclipse of the moon occurred, and the superstitious Nicias insisted on waiting for a favorable moon. This month's delay was fatal. The Syracusans blockaded the channel to the sea and completely shut up the Athenian fleet within the harbor. An attempt to break through and escape failed disastrously. The desperate Athenian army, abandoning sick and wounded, endeavored to escape into the interior, but was overtaken and forced to surrender. The Syracusans treated the captured Athenians with savage barbarity. Thus the Athenian expedition was completely destroyed (413 B.C.). This disaster, together with the earlier ravages of the plague, brought Athens near the end of her resources.

Capture of the Athenian fleet and army at Syracuse (413 B.C.)

Fig. 187. Stone Quarries of Syracuse *in which the Athenians are said to have been Imprisoned*

We look across the deep quarry and the Lesser Harbor to the ancient island of Ortygia (see map, p. 447). It is now a cape, occupied by the modern city, of which we can see the buildings. The quarries are overgrown with ivy and masked with beautiful green foliage. Here the seven thousand Athenians captured by the Syracusans are thought to have been imprisoned without sufficient water and provisions, so that most of them died

Spartan garrison in Attica

644. Heretofore Sparta had stood more or less aloof, seemingly unwilling to break the peace of Nicias, and had not invaded Attica. But now, seeing the unprotected condition of Athens after the dispatch of the Sicilian expedition, Sparta again invaded Attica and, on the advice of Alcibiades, occupied the town of Decelea,[1] almost within sight of Athens. Here the Spartans established a permanent fort held by a strong garrison, and thus placed Athens in a state of perpetual siege. All agriculture ceased, and the Athenians lived on imported grain. The people now understood the folly of having sent away on a distant expedition the ships and the men that should have been kept at home to repel the attacks of a powerful and still uncrippled foe.

[1] On this account the war with Sparta which now followed, lasting nine years (from 413 to 404 B.C.), is often called the Decelean War.

645. After these disasters the Athenian Empire began to show signs of breaking up. The failure of the democracy in the management of the war enabled the nobles to denounce popular rule as unsuccessful. The nobles regained power for a time; violence and bloodshed within were added to the dangerous assaults of the enemy from without. The finances were in a desperate condition. The tribute, already raised to the breaking point, was abolished, and a customs duty of five per cent was levied on all goods exported or imported. The plan was a success and brought in a larger income than the tribute, but the measure did not unite or quiet the discontented communities of which the Empire was made up. One after another they fell away. Spartan warships sailed about in the Ægean, aiding the rebels, who had of course dared to revolt only on promise of such assistance from Sparta.

Internal troubles of the Athenian Empire

646. To add to the Athenian distress the powerful Persian satrap in western Asia Minor was supporting the Spartan fleet with money. Indeed, both Athens and Sparta had long been negotiating with Persia for aid, and Sparta had recognized Persian rule over the Greek cities of Asia. The Greek islands and the cities of Asia Minor which had once united in the Delian League with Athens to throw off Persian rule were now combining with Sparta and Persia against Athens. Thus the former union of the Greeks in a heroic struggle against the Asiatic enemy had given way to a disgraceful scramble for Persian support and favor.

Persia aids Peloponnesians against Athens

647. Meantime the traitorous Alcibiades, under the protection of the Persian satrap, had himself encouraged the revolters against Athens, hoping that her distress would finally oblige her to recall him and seek his aid. He was not disappointed. The small fleet which the Athenians were still able to put into the fight called upon Alcibiades for help, and finally put itself under his command, without any authorization from Athens. In several conflicts, chiefly through

Alcibiades recovers command of the Athenian fleet (411 B.C.)

the skill of Alcibiades, the Peloponnesian fleet was completely destroyed, and Athens regained the command of the sea.

Restoration of Alcibiades (407 B.C.)

648. Sparta now made offers of peace; but Alcibiades skillfully used the war sentiment in the fleet against their acceptance, and the democratic leaders in power at Athens also refused to make peace. Alcibiades was then (407 B.C.) elected strategus and legally gained command of the fleet which he had already been leading for four years. At the head of a triumphant procession he entered Athens again for the first time since he had left it for Sicily eight years before. He was solemnly purified from the religious curse which rested upon him, and his fortune, which had been confiscated, was returned to him.

Fall of Alcibiades

649. It now needed only the abilities of such a leader as Alcibiades to accomplish the union of the distracted Greek states and the foundation of a great Greek nation. At this supreme moment, however, Alcibiades lacked the courage to seize the government, and the opportunity never returned again. When he put to sea again, a slight defeat, inflicted on a part of his fleet when he was not present, cost him the favor of the fickle Athenians. When they failed to reëlect him strategus, he retired to a castle which he had kept in readiness on the Hellespont. He never saw his native land again, but died some years later in exile, the victim of a Persian dagger.

Athenian victory of Arginusæ; commanders executed (406 B.C.)

650. The Athenians had now lost their ablest leader again, but they continued the war on the sea as best they could. They won another important victory over a new Peloponnesian fleet on the coast of Asia Minor, by the little islands of Arginusæ. As the battle ended, a storm arose which prevented the commanders from saving the Athenian survivors clinging to the wreckage. For this accident the Athenian commanders were accused, before the Assembly, of criminal neglect and condemned to death. In spite of all that could be done, six of the eight naval commanders were executed. The other two commanders had been wise enough to flee from such justice as they might expect at the hands of the Athenian democracy.

651. Athens now suffered worse than ever before for lack of competent commanders. The fleet, numbering about one hundred and eighty triremes, was placed in the command of a group of officers, each of whom was to lead for a day at a time. The democratic leaders who had made this absurd arrangement watched the fleet sail out to continue a war which they themselves were prolonging by again refusing Spartan proffers of peace. For several days in succession the Athenians sailed out from their station near the river called Ægospotami, on the Hellespont, and offered battle to the Peloponnesian fleet lying in a neighboring harbor. But the Peloponnesians refused battle. On their return from these maneuvers each day, the Athenians left their ships along the beach and themselves went ashore. Alcibiades, from the neighboring castle where he lived during his exile, came down and pointed out to the Athenian commanders the great danger they ran in leaving the fleet in this condition so near the enemy. His advice received no attention. The able Spartan Lysander, the commander of the Peloponnesian fleet, seeing this daily procedure, waited until the Athenians had gone ashore and left their ships as usual. Then, sailing over, he surprised and captured practically the whole Athenian fleet.

Capture of Athenian fleet at Ægospotami (405 B.C.)

652. At last, twenty-seven years after Pericles had provoked the war with Sparta, the resources of Athens were exhausted. Not a man slept on the night when the terrible news of final ruin reached Athens. It was soon confirmed by the appearance of Lysander's fleet blockading the Piræus. The grain ships from the Black Sea could no longer reach the port of Athens. The Spartan king pitched his camp in the grove of the Academy and called on the city to surrender. For some months the stubborn democratic leaders refused to accept terms of peace which meant the complete destruction of Athenian power; but the pinch of hunger

Surrender of Athens and fall of Athenian Empire (404 B.C.)

finally convinced the Assembly, and the city surrendered. The Long Walls and the fortifications of the Piræus were torn down, the remnant of the fleet was handed over to Sparta, all foreign possessions were given up, and Athens was forced to enter the Spartan League. These hard conditions saved the city from the complete destruction demanded by Corinth. Thus the century which had begun so gloriously for Athens with the repulse of Persia — the century which under the leadership of such men as Themistocles and Pericles had seen her rise to supremacy in all that was best and noblest in Greek life — closed with the annihilation of the Athenian Empire (404 B.C.).

QUESTIONS

Section 54. How did Athens treat the subject states of her Empire? What was now her policy regarding citizenship? What was the attitude of the Greek states toward the Athenian Empire? Who were the enemies of Athens in the Second Peloponnesian War? What was Pericles' plan of campaign? What disaster overtook Athens? What was the attitude of the Athenians toward Pericles? What kind of leadership did the Assembly furnish? What business man tried to lead the nation? How did he succeed? What was the result of ten years of war?

Section 55. Who was chiefly responsible for the reopening of the war? What great expedition did the Athenians plan? Tell the story of the expedition and its end. What was now the condition of the Athenian Empire? What part did Persia play in the war? How did the Athenians treat their naval commanders? What was the situation of Athens after the loss of her fleet? What conditions did Sparta make? Contrast the beginning and the end of the Fifth Century in Athenian history.

BIBLIOGRAPHY FOR TOPICAL STUDIES

Athens captures Pylos and Sphacteria: BURY, *Greece*, pp. 429–438; JAMES, *Hellenic Heritage*, Vol. II, pp. 153–165; THUCYDIDES, IV, iii ff.

Alcibiades: BOTSFORD, *Source Book*, pp. 223–227; BURY, *Greece*, pp. 466–471; JAMES, *Hellenic Heritage*, Vol. II, pp. 178–189 *passim*, 238–243.

Chapter XVII · *The Final Conflicts among the Greek States*

Section 56. Spartan Leadership and the Decline of Democracy

653. The long struggle of Athens for the political leadership of the Greek world had ignominiously failed. It now remained to be seen whether her victorious rival, Sparta, was any better suited to undertake such leadership. No nation which devotes itself exclusively to the development of military power, as Sparta had done, is fitted to control successfully the affairs of its neighbors. Military garrisons commanded by Spartan officers were now placed in many of the Greek cities, and Spartan control was maintained in a much more offensive form than was the old tyranny of Athens.

Unfitness of Sparta for the leadership of the Greeks

NOTE. The above headpiece shows us the lovely PORCH OF THE MAIDENS, built to adorn the temple on the Acropolis known as the Erechtheum (*F* in Fig. 180). This was a very ancient sanctuary of Athena, supposed to have gained its name because it was originally a shrine in the castle of the prehistoric king Erechtheus on the Acropolis. It was believed to stand on the spot where Athena overcame Poseidon in her battle with him for the possession of Attica, and here was the mark of the Sea-god's trident which he struck into the earth. Here also grew the original olive tree which Athena summoned from the earth as a gift to the Athenians.

Fig. 188. Tomb of Spartans *who assisted the Athenian State in Civil War*

Recent excavation in the cemetery outside the Dipylon Gate at Athens has revealed the burial place of those Spartans who died in action while helping the Athenian oligarchs (§ 654) to put down the uprising of the people in 403 B.C. Xenophon in his book *Hellenica* wrote in detail of this struggle. He gave the names of the more important Spartans who were killed in the final conflict, and stated that the Athenians had accorded them burial in the street of tombs (headpiece, p. 489) on the sacred road which passes through the outer Ceramicus. In this street were entombed all persons honored with a public funeral. It must have been a very impressive moment, therefore, when the excavator's spade uncovered the stones which marked this burial, and modern archæologists found carved upon them the names of the very men recorded by Xenophon over two thousand years ago. (Courtesy of *Forschungen und Fortschritte*)

Struggle between the oligarchy and the democracy

654. By such violent means Sparta was able to repress the democracies which had everywhere been hostile to her. In each city the Spartans established and supported by military force the rule of a small group of men from the noble, or upper, class. This group was called an *oligarchy*, from a Greek term meaning "rule of a few." The oligarchs were guilty of the worst excesses, murdering or banishing their political opponents and confiscating their fortunes. When the people regained power, they retaliated in the same way and drove the oligarchs from the city. As this kind of conflict went on in Athens, both parties banished so many that there was always a large number of the leading Athenian citizens living in exile. From their foreign homes they plotted against their banishers and formed a constant danger from abroad.

655. In spite of the failure of oligarchy, thoughtful men everywhere regarded popular rule also as an open failure. The splendid achievements of citizenship under Pericles must not blind us to the weaknesses of Athenian democracy. Some of these we have already seen in following the course of the Peloponnesian Wars, but the same weaknesses were evident in the people's control of the internal affairs of Athens. Let us examine some of the leading matters in which popular control had failed and continued to fail.

Disrepute and weaknesses of democracy

656. Nowhere were the mistakes of democracy more evident than in the Athenian law courts. The payment of the large citizen juries often exhausted the treasury. When there was no money in the treasury with which to pay the juries, the jurymen, who preferred such service to hard work, found it very easy to fill the treasury again by fining any accused citizen brought before them, whether he was guilty or innocent. More than one lawyer of the time urged the court to confiscate the fortune of an accused citizen in order that the jurymen to whom the lawyer was talking might thus receive their pay. It became a profitable trade to bring accusations and suits against wealthy men on all sorts of trumped-up charges. A man thus threatened usually preferred to buy off his accusers, in order to avoid going before five hundred poor and ignorant jurors.

Corruption and class prejudice of Athenian citizen juries

657. In the days of Solon we remember that the rule of the *upper* classes over the lower was so oppressive that it almost resulted in the destruction of the state (§ 510). In the course of less than two hundred years the *lower* classes had gained complete control, and their rule, as we have just seen, became so corruptly oppressive toward

Evils of one-sided class rule

the upper classes that the final situation was again one-sided class rule, as bad as any that Athens had ever seen. To Athenian misfortunes in foreign wars was thus added the constant violence of weakening inner struggles between classes.

Unwise financial policy of the democracy

658. Another weakness of popular rule was its unwise financial policy, which continually exhausted the treasury of Athens. Her empty treasury was due to a number of causes, chiefly three: first, the payment of large numbers of citizens for services to the state, especially the thousands of citizen-jurors; second, the payment to all citizens of "show money" (§ 616), a heavy drain on the treasury; and, third, the long-continued expenses and losses of war (§ 576).

Expensive means of collecting taxes

659. To these we might add the expensive means of collecting taxes employed by both parties. Unlike the great Oriental governments we have studied (§ 91), no Greek state possessed any officials who could undertake the task of collecting taxes. It therefore sold its tax claims to the highest bidder, who then had the right to collect the taxes. In order to secure the large sums necessary for making such bids, a number of wealthy men would form themselves into a company. These companies, by secretly combining, gained a monopoly in the business of tax collecting. Their bid was always far less than the amount of the tax claims to be collected. Thus the people paid far more taxes than the state received from the collectors, into whose pockets the difference went. Consequently the rate of taxation at Athens was now high, being at least from one to two per cent of a man's fortune and sometimes much higher.

Exhaustion of temple treasures; bankruptcy of Greek states

660. The Athenians had early begun to use the treasure which had accumulated in the temple of Athena. The obligation to pay back this borrowed treasure was engraved upon a stone tablet set up on the Acropolis. To this day the surviving fragments of this broken stone bear witness to the unpaid debt to Athena and the bankruptcy of Athens. After the long struggle between Athens and Sparta was over, all the Greek states were practically bankrupt. An admiral or a general of this time often found himself facing the enemy without the money to pay his forces or to feed them. At the same time, if he failed in his campaign, he would be punished for his failure by the democracy at home. There were times when the Athenian courts ceased to hold any sessions, for lack of funds to pay the citizen juries, and a man with an important lawsuit on his hands could not get it tried.

661. Under these circumstances the Mediterranean states for the first time began to study the methods and theory of raising money for government expenses. A beginning was thus made in the science of national finance and political economy. Nevertheless the method of collection of the taxes continued to be that of "farming" out the undertaking to the highest bidder. In this matter the Near East still remained far in advance of the northern Mediterranean states. From now on, the finances of a nation became more and more a matter of special training, and it became more difficult for the average citizen without experience to manage the financial offices of the government.

Beginnings of financial theory and political economy

662. Notwithstanding the great losses in property and in men during the long Peloponnesian Wars, Athens at length began to recover herself. The farms of Attica had been laid waste so often by the Spartan armies that agriculture never wholly recovered its former prosperity. There was a tendency among farmers to sell their land and to undertake some form of manufacturing in the city. This was a natural thing to do, for the industries of Athens offered attractive opportunities to make a fortune. At the same time, men who had already gained wealth in manufactures bought one farm after another. This was a process which would finally concentrate the lands of Attica in the hands of a few large city landlords who were not farmers but worked their great estates (each made up of many farms) with slaves under superintendents. The land-owing farmers who worked their

Beginning of the decline of farming, large landowners appear

own lands and lived on them tended to disappear. In their place the great estates common in neighboring Asia Minor under the Persians were also appearing among the Greeks.

Growth of manufacturing and rise of banks

663. Athens was still the leading business center and the greatest city in the Mediterranean world. While manufacturing business was not often conducted by companies, groups of wealthy men, as we have seen, united to furnish the large sums necessary to bid for the contract to collect the taxes. Such combinations formed one of the evils of Athenian business life, as they have sometimes done in our own time. Other men combined their capital to form the first banks in Greece, about 400 B.C. The Greeks no longer left their accumulated money in a temple treasury for safe-keeping, but gave it to some bank that it might be loaned out, used in business, and earn interest. Athens thus became the financial center of the world, as New York and London are today, and her bankers became the proverbially wealthy men of the time. The most successful among them was Pasion, a former slave, who had been able to purchase his liberty because of his great business ability.

Rise of prices; growing luxury

664. As the banking system resulted in keeping more money in circulation, the old increase in prices went on, and the expenses for government were consequently higher; but the democracy continued to pay itself vast sums for jury service and show money. There was a freer use of money in private life among the well-to-do classes. The houses of these people began to display rooms with painted wall decorations and adorned with rugs and hangings. An orator of the time condemns such luxurious houses, which he says were unknown in the days of Miltiades and the Persian War, just as some criticize our own fine modern houses and contrast them with the simplicity of George Washington and Revolutionary days.

665. Men were now becoming more and more interested in their own careers, and they were no longer so devoted to the state as formerly. This was especially true in the matter of military service. Except in Sparta a Greek had heretofore left his occupation for a brief space to bear arms for a single short campaign, and then returned to his occupation. Such men made up a citizen militia, no more devoted to arms than our own modern militia. But the long Peloponnesian Wars had kept large numbers of Greeks so long under arms that many of them permanently adopted military life and became professional soldiers, serving for pay wherever they could find opportunity. Such soldiers serving a foreign state for pay are called mercenaries. There were few unoccupied lands to which a young Greek could migrate as in the colonizing age, and Persia blocked all such enterprises in the East. The Greek youths who could find no opportunities at home were therefore enlisting as soldiers in Egypt, in Asia Minor, and in Persia, and the best young blood of Greece was being spent to strengthen foreign states instead of building up the power of the Greeks.

Rise of the professional soldier as a result of the Peloponnesian Wars

666. During the Peloponnesian Wars military *leadership* had also become a profession. It was no longer possible for a citizen to leave private life and casually assume command of an army or a fleet. Athens produced a whole group of professional military leaders whose romantic exploits made them famous throughout the ancient world. Among these commanders the most famous was Xenophon. About the year 400 B.C. he took service in Asia Minor with Cyrus, a young Persian prince, who was planning to overthrow his brother, the Persian king. With ten thousand Greek mercenaries Cyrus marched entirely across Asia Minor to the Euphrates, and down the river almost to Babylon. Here the Greeks defeated the army of the Persian king; but Cyrus was killed, and the Greeks were therefore obliged to retreat. Xenophon led them up the Tigris past the ruins of Nineveh; and after months of fighting in dangerous mountain passes, suffering from cold and hunger, the survivors struggled on until they reached the Black Sea and finally gained Byzantium in safety.

Rise of professional military leaders; Xenophon

667. Of this extraordinary raid into the Persian Empire Xenophon has left a picturesque account called the *Anabasis* ("up-going"), one of the great books which have descended to us from ancient times. As he explained the military operations involved, the book became one of the treatises on military science which began to appear at this time. Military leaders were discussing the theory of operations in the field, methods of strategy, and the best kinds of weapons. In Pericles' day the Spartans made no attempt to attack the walls of Athens, because the Greeks then knew nothing about methods of attacking fortifications. The Phœnician Carthaginians, however, had carried the Assyrian siege devices to the west, where the western Greeks had now learned to use them in Sicily. From Sicily the use of battering-rams, movable towers, and the like was carried to Greece itself, and against attack with such equipment Athens would no longer have been safe. The Mediterranean, which had so long ago received the arts of peace from the Near East, was now also learning to use war machinery from the same source. At the same time larger warships were constructed, some having as many as five banks of oars, and the old triremes with three banks could no longer stand against such powerful ships. All such equipment made war more expensive than before.

Rise of military science; siege machinery; warships

668. The remarkable feat of Xenophon's Ten Thousand finally stirred Spartan ambition to undertake conquest in Persian territory in Asia Minor. The Spartans therefore abandoned the policy of accepting Persian gold which had enabled Lysander to build the fleet that had crushed Athens at the end of the Peloponnesian Wars. Taking up a new line of action, the Spartans hired the surviving two thirds of the Ten Thousand, but the rule of Sparta had caused such dissatisfaction that her victories in Asia Minor were offset by revolts in Greece. In one of these Lysander was killed. The outcome of these rebellions was a league of Athens and Thebes against Sparta. Even Corinth, the old-time enemy

Sparta's war against Persia; Corinthian War (395–387 B.C.)

of Athens, joined this league, and Argos also came in. Behind this combination was Persia, whose agents had brought it about in order to weaken Sparta. It was one of the ironies of the whole deplorable situation that a fleet of Athens made common cause with the Persians and helped to fasten Persian despotism on the Greek cities of Asia. The Greeks had learned nothing by their long and unhappy experience of fruitless fighting, and thus began an eight years' struggle called the Corinthian War. The Athenians had been able to rebuild a fleet, with which they now destroyed the fleet of Sparta. They were then in a position to erect the Long Walls again.

669. At length the Persians began to fear lest Athens should again be strong enough to endanger Persian control in Asia Minor. The Spartans therefore found it easy to arrange a peace with Persia. The Greek states fighting Sparta were equally willing to come to terms; and when peace was at last established in Greece, it was under the humiliating terms of a treaty accepted by Hellas at the hands of the Persian king. It is known as the King's Peace (387 B.C.). It did not end the leadership of Sparta over the Greek states, and the Greek cities of Asia Minor were shamefully abandoned to Persia. The period following the King's Peace brought only added discontent with Sparta's illegal and tyrannical control, and no solution of the problem of how the Greek states were to establish satisfactory national relations among themselves.

The King's Peace (387 B.C.)

Section 57. The Fall of Sparta and the Leadership of Thebes

670. For twenty-five years since the last Peloponnesian War the Spartans had been endeavoring to maintain control of the Greek world, but in the end the Spartans were more hated than Athens had ever been. Then a group of fearless and patriotic citizens at Thebes succeeded in slaying the oligarchs, the Spartan garrison surrendered, and a democracy was set up, which gained the leadership of all Bœotia. At the same time Athens, which on the whole had been greatly strengthened by the terms of the King's Peace, was able to begin the formation of a second naval alliance like the original league from which the Athenian Empire had sprung. The Spartans met disaster on land; and when this was followed by the defeat of their fleet by Athens, they were ready for peace.

Thebes and a new Athenian league against Sparta (378 B.C.)

671. To arrange this peace all the Greek states met at Sparta. As such meetings gave them experience in the united management of their common affairs for the welfare of all Hellas, Spartan leadership might have held the Greek states together, and, by giving them all a voice in the control of Hellas, Sparta might still have finally united the Greeks into a great nation. But when the conditions of peace were all agreed upon, the Spartans refused to allow Thebes to speak for the whole of Bœotia. The Thebans would not enter the compact on any other terms, and the peace was concluded without them. This left Sparta and Thebes still in a state of war.

Peace congress of the Greek states at Sparta

672. All Greece now expected to see the Thebans crushed by the heavy Spartan phalanx, which had so long proved irresistible. The Spartan plan of battle hitherto followed by all commanders consisted in making the phalanx of the right wing very heavy and massive, by arraying it many warriors deep. The effect was that of a heavy mass play in American football, only we must picture the phalanx as carrying out the operation on a large scale. Having broken through at the first onset, the victorious phalanx could then cut down singly the scattered soldiers who had given way before them. The Theban commander Epaminondas knew in advance the only "play" which the Spartans had ever used. He therefore devised an altogether novel arrangement of his troops by drawing up his line so that it was not parallel with that of the Spartans, his right wing being much farther from the Spartan line than his left. At the same time he

Spartan military tactics versus tactics of Epaminondas

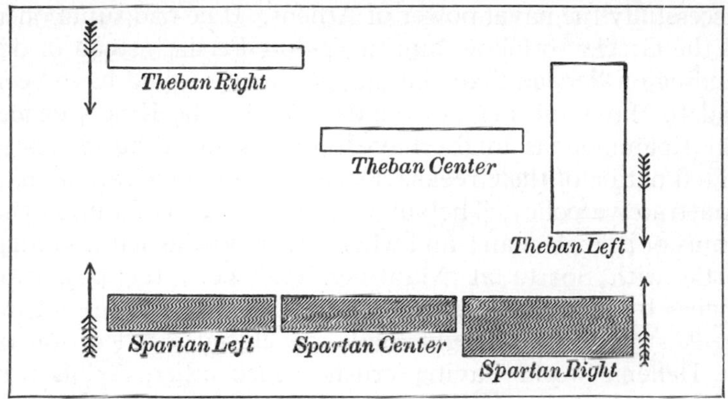

Plan of the BATTLE OF LEUCTRA (371 B.C.)

The Theban battle line really presents an *oblique front*, an extraordinary military invention, which was adopted by Philip of Macedon and then employed by Alexander the Great in his three greatest victories over the Persians

massed his troops on his left wing, which he made fifty shields deep, to meet the shock of the heavy Spartan right wing.

673. The battle took place at Leuctra in southern Bœotia. As the lines moved into battle the massive Theban left wing, being farthest advanced, met the Spartan line first and was at first engaged alone. Its onset proved so heavy that the Spartan right opposing it was soon crushed, and the rest of the Spartan line also gave way as the Theban center and right came into action. Over half of the Spartans engaged were slain and with them their king. The long-invincible Spartan army was at last defeated, and the charm of Spartan prestige was finally broken. After more than thirty years of leadership (since 404 B.C.) Spartan power was ended.

Battle of Leuctra and fall of Sparta (371 B.C.)

674. A third Greek state was now victorious on land, and it remained to be seen whether Thebes could accomplish what Athens and Sparta had failed in doing. Epaminondas at once made a fatal mistake in policy. He followed the example of Sparta, and by accepting Persian gold he was able to build a fleet and thus oppose

Fall of Thebes; Greece helpless

successfully the naval power of Athens. If he had summoned all the Greeks to follow him in *fighting* Persia instead of depending on Persian financial aid, all Greece would have been glad to throw off Persian bondage under the King's Peace, and Epaminondas might have founded an enthusiastically united nation of the Greeks. Depending on force rather than an attractive policy, Theban supremacy was based upon the genius of a single man; and when Epaminondas fell in a final battle with Sparta at Mantinea (362 B.C.), the power of Thebes by land and sea collapsed. Thus, the only powerful Greek states which might have developed a federation of the Hellenic world having crushed each other, Hellas was ready to fall before any conqueror from the outside. The Greek world, whose civilization was everywhere supreme, was politically prostrate and helpless.

Progress of Greeks in higher life

675. It was less than two generations since the death of Pericles, and there were still old men living who had seen him in their childhood days. We have been following the *political* fortunes of Athens, Sparta, and Thebes during these two generations, but our narrative has been very far from telling the whole story; for in spite of their political decline during the two generations since Pericles, the Greeks, and especially the Athenians, had been achieving things in their higher life — in art, architecture, literature, and thought — which made this period perhaps the greatest in the history of man. To these achievements since the death of Pericles we must now turn back.

QUESTIONS

Section 56. Why was Sparta unfitted to control the Greek states? What is an oligarchy? How did it succeed? Had democracy succeeded any better? Describe the abuses practiced by the citizen-juries. Was class rule by the poor any better than class rule by the rich? What practices kept the Athenian treasury empty? What was the Athenian method of collecting taxes? Why was it unprofitable for the state? Describe the effects of lack of money on the work of government. What did the Greeks do in order to understand the national finances?

What was happening to small farm-owners? Discuss business and finance at this time. How had the long Peloponnesian Wars affected the citizen soldiers of Greece? Tell the story of Xenophon and the Ten Thousand. How has this story come down to us? What science was now arising? Where did the Greeks learn the use of siege machinery? What did the raid of the Ten Thousand lead Sparta to do? Sketch the Corinthian War. What was the result?

Section 57. What combination was formed to overthrow the leadership of Sparta? What happened at the peace conference of Greek states? Describe Spartan military tactics. How did Epaminondas plan to meet the Spartan tactics? Where and when did the armies meet? What was the result? Did Thebes succeed in leading the Greek states? What mistake did Epaminondas make? In what condition politically was the whole Greek world?

BIBLIOGRAPHY FOR TOPICAL STUDIES

Banks and money: BOTSFORD-SIHLER, *Hellenic Civilization*, pp. 515–522; BRITISH MUSEUM, *Greek and Roman Life*, pp. 15–19; BURY, *Greece*, p. 586; CARY, *Documentary Sources*, pp. 97–110; GULICK, *Modern Traits*, pp. 113–119; METROPOLITAN MUSEUM OF ART, *Daily Life*, pp. 116–118.

The writings of Xenophon: BOTSFORD, *Source Book*, pp. 247–256, 283–288; BOTSFORD-SIHLER, pp. 430–447, 488–508; BURY, *Greece*, pp. 517–530, 826; CORNFORD, *Religious Thought*, pp. 175–179, 238–244; JAMES, *Hellenic Heritage*, Vol. II, pp. 339–350; MCCARTNEY, *Warfare by Land and Sea*, pp. 64–68; *Pageant of Greece*, pp. 242–250; XENOPHON, *Anabasis*.

Epaminondas: BOTSFORD, *Source Book*, pp. 258–264; BOTSFORD-SIHLER, pp. 537–541; BURY, *Greece*, pp. 566–567, 572–574, 591–595, 603–612 *passim*, 617, 622–626; MCCARTNEY, *Warfare*, pp. 68–70; MILLS, *Ancient Greeks*, pp. 322–328.

Chapter XVIII · *The Higher Life of the Greeks from the Death of Pericles to the Fall of the Greek States*

Section 58. Architecture, Sculpture, and Painting

Decline of state support of art and architecture

676. The long wars and the demands of the democracy had swallowed up the wealth of Athens; the great and splendid works of the Age of Pericles were therefore no longer possible. At the same time Athens was obliged to rebuild her fortifications, erect war arsenals, and build sheds for her battleships. The old temporary wooden seats of the theater were replaced by a permanent structure of stone. Here and there other Greek cities also were building durable stone theaters like that at Athens.

NOTE. The above headpiece is a restoration by Adler of the famous TOMB OF KING MAUSOLUS OF CARIA, called after him the Mausoleum. We now call any splendid tomb a mausoleum, thus preserving the old Hittite name of this king. It was, when first built (in the middle of the Fourth Century B.C.), the most magnificent tomb on the north side of the Mediterranean, and it was because of its widespread fame that its name was preserved. Upon a high rectangular base a fine Ionic colonnade supported a step pyramid, upon which, crowning the whole monument, rose a splendid four-horse chariot bearing the king and queen. The work was designed and built by the architect and sculptor Pythius, and adorned with sculpture by Scopas and other Athenian sculptors whom the queen called to Caria for the purpose.

Permanent stadiums for races were likewise erected by some communities. The maintenance of art and architecture in this age was, however, largely in the hands of individual artists, who were not supported by the state but were producing works of art for private buyers.

FIG. 189. A CORINTHIAN CAPITAL

The shaft of this column has been cut out in the drawing between the base and the capital to save space. The leaves of the acanthus alternate in two rows around the capital and are crowned by volutes rising to the four corners of a flat block upon which the supported stone above rests

677. Nevertheless the Erechtheum, one of the most beautiful buildings ever erected, a temple which had been begun before Pericles' death, was continued and for the most part completed during the unhappy days of the last Peloponnesian War. It was built in the Ionic style, adorned with colonnades of wonderful refinement and beauty, and at one corner was an exquisite porch, with its roof supported by lovely marble figures of Athenian maidens (headpiece, p. 455).

Erechtheum on the Athenian Acropolis

678. Egyptian artists, as we remember, had long before crowned their columns with a capital representing growing flowers or palm-tree tops. The Greek architects now profited by this hint. Perceiving the great beauty of their own acanthus plant, they designed a capital adorned with a double row of acanthus leaves. This new capital was richer and more sumptuous than the simpler Doric and Ionic forms. Columns with these capitals are now called Corinthian, although one of the earliest examples of such columns still survives at Athens.

Rise of the Corinthian style of architecture

679. While Athens no longer possessed the means to erect great state temples, other Greek states were not all so financially exhausted. In Asia Minor the widowed queen of Mausolus,[1] the wealthy king of the Carians, so revered the memory of her royal husband that she devoted vast riches to the erection of a magnificent marble tomb for him. It was so splendid that it became one of the most famous monuments of the ancient world (headpiece, p. 468). While imposing as a monument of architecture, the Mausoleum was most impressive because of the rich and remarkable sculpture with which it was adorned by the greatest sculptors of the Greeks.

Mausoleum in Asia Minor

680. Sculpture had made great progress since the days of Pericles. Phidias and his pupils depicted the gods, whom they wrought in marble, as lofty, majestic, unapproachable beings, lifted high above human weaknesses and human feeling. We remember that even the *human* figures of Phidias were not the everyday men and women, youths and maidens, whom we might have met on the streets of Athens. When Phidias and his pupils had passed away, the sculptors who followed them began to put more of the feeling and experience of daily human life into their work, and thus brought their subjects nearer to us. Among them we must give a high place, perhaps the highest place, to the great Athenian sculptor Praxiteles.

Contrast between the sculpture of the Periclean Age and later work

681. His native city being without the money for great monumental works, Praxiteles wrought individual figures of life size, and most of these for foreign states. Unlike the majestic and exalted figures of Phidias, the gods of Praxiteles seem near to us. They at once appeal to us as being human like ourselves, interested in a life like ours, and doing things which we should like to do ourselves. As they stand at ease in attitudes of repose the grace and balance of the flowing lines give them a splendor of beauty unattained by any earlier sculpture of the Greeks. In great contrast to the work of Praxiteles was that of

Sculpture of Praxiteles and Scopas

[1] The royal name "Mausolus" is probably a later form of the old Hittite royal name "Mursil."

FIG. 190. TWO GREEK GODS *as Sculptured by Praxiteles*

Notice the wonderful ease and grace with which these figures in repose are poised. In a country where lizards were darting along every sunny wall, a lad with a stone ready to throw was a frequent sight. This common human action is the one which Praxiteles chose for his Apollo (*B*), and he has depicted the satyr (*A*) in an equally natural posture, with drinking horn and a bunch of grapes. These very human gods are quite different from those of Phidias (§ 680)

Scopas, who did much of the sculpture of the Mausoleum. He loved to fashion figures not in tranquil moods but in violent action, in moments of passionate excitement, like that of warriors in battle. The *faces* sculptured by Praxiteles and Scopas were no longer expressionless, as in earlier sculpture, but the artists began to put into them some of their own inner feeling. The artist's own individual life thus began to find expression in his work. In many ways the sculpture of this age was much influenced by the work of the painters, who really led the way.

FIG. 191. BATTLE SCENE *from the Sculptures of the* MAUSOLEUM *in the Manner of Scopas*

The superb vigor and violent action of these ancient warriors are in sharp contrast to the tranquillity and repose of Praxiteles' figures. Unfortunately not a single one of the very numerous works of Scopas has survived. A number of fragments are supposed to be his work, and some of the frieze scenes surviving from the Mausoleum may be the work of his hands. The above scene is not ascribed to him, but shows his influence and is a fine example of the sculpture of violent action

Rise of paintings on wood

682. The introduction of portable paintings on wooden tablets made it easier for the painters to follow their own individual feelings, for they were thus freed from the necessity of painting large scenes on the walls of state buildings (§ 609). As we have already learned, no oil colors were known in the ancient world, but the Greek painters now adopted the Egyptian method of mixing their colors in melted wax and then applying the fluid wax, with a brush and palette knife, to a wooden tablet. The painter could then work in his own studio to please his own fancy, and could sell his paintings to any private purchaser who wished to buy. It thus became customary for people of wealth to set up paintings in their own houses, and in this way the private support of art increased and painting was greatly stimulated.

683. An Athenian painter named Apollodorus now began to notice that the light usually fell on an object from *one side*, leaving the unlighted side so dark that but little color

FIG. 192. *A Wall-Painting at* POMPEII *showing the* SACRIFICE OF IPHIGENIA

The works of the great Fourth Century artists have all perished, but it is supposed that the later house decorators and wall-painters of Italy copied the old masterpieces. Hence the scene here shown probably conveys some impression of old Greek painting. The scene shows us the maid Iphigenia as she is carried away to be slain as a sacrifice. The figure at the left, standing with veiled face, suggests, as often in modern art, the dreadfulness of a coming catastrophe, which human eyes are unwilling to behold. Note the skill with which human limbs are made to show thickness and roundness

showed on that side, while on the lighted side the colors came out very brightly. When he painted a woman's arm in this way, lo, it looked round and seemed to stand out from the surface of the painting; whereas up in the Painted Porch all the human limbs in the old painting of Marathon

Fig. 193. Greek Boy *pulling out a Thorn* (A) *and a Later* Caricature *of the Thorn-Puller* (B)

The graceful figure of the boy so seriously striving to remove the thorn was probably wrought not long after the Persian Wars. It was very popular in antiquity, as it has also been in modern times. The comical caricature (*B*) in clay (terra cotta), though it has lost one foot, is a delightful example of Greek humor expressed in parody

looked perfectly flat. By representing figures in the background of his paintings as smaller than those in front, Apollodorus also introduced what we now call perspective. As a result his paintings had an appearance of depth; and when he painted the interior of a house, one seemed to be looking into the very room itself. He was called by the Athenians the "shadow painter," and the good old-fashioned folk shook their heads at his work, preferring the old style. Even the great philosopher Plato condemned this new method of painting as employing devices and creating illusions of depth which were really deception.

Discovery of how to paint light, shadow, and perspective

684. Nevertheless the new method triumphed, and the younger painters who adopted it produced work which was the talk of the town. People gossiped about it and told how a painter named Zeuxis, in order to outdo his rival Parrhasius, had painted some grapes so naturally that birds flew up to the painting and pecked at them. Thereupon Parrhasius invited Zeuxis over to his studio to inspect a painting of his. Zeuxis found it covered with a curtain, which he attempted to draw aside; but his hand fell on a painted surface, and he discovered to his confusion that the curtain was no more real than his own painted grapes had been. Unfortunately all such Greek paintings have perished, and we have only later copies at Pompeii.

Triumph of new method of painting

FIG. 194. ATHENIAN GRAVESTONE *showing a Daughter saying Farewell to her Parents*

This tombstone of a young girl shows us the fine feeling of which even a Greek graveyard stonecutter was capable. He has depicted the last farewell of the parents as their daughter is carried away by death. The mother, seated at the left, grasps the young girl's hand, while the father stands with his fingers in his beard in somber and meditative resignation

685. The vase-painters of the time likewise often copied the famous works of the leading sculptors and painters; but after a wonderful revival in the last Peloponnesian War the art of vase-painting passed into a melancholy decline from which it never recovered. At the same time, in order to meet the rising desire for objects of art among the people, small artists began to furnish delightful miniature copies of famous classic works,

The vase-painters and other artist-craftsmen

or, again, they made amusing caricatures of such well-known classics (Fig. 193, *B*). At the same time even stonecutters wrought tombstones bearing reliefs done with a soft and melancholy beauty, breathing the wistful uncertainty with which the Greeks of this age were beginning to look out into the shadow world beyond the grave.

Section 59. Religion, Literature, and Thought

Age of conflict after the death of Pericles

686. Any young Athenian born at about the time of Pericles' death found himself in an age of conflict wherever he went, — an age of conflict *abroad* on the field of battle as he stood with spear and shield in the Athenian ranks in the long years of warfare between Athens, Sparta, and Thebes; an age of conflict *at home* in Athens amid the excited shouting and applause of the turbulent Assembly or the tumult and even bloodshed of the streets and markets of the city as the common people, the democracy, struggled with the nobles for the leadership of the state; and, finally, an age of conflict *in himself* as he felt his once confident faith in old things struggling to maintain itself against new views.

Athenian citizen's religion and early life

687. He recalled the childhood tales of the gods, which he had heard at his nurse's knee. When he had asked her how Athena and the gods looked, she had pointed to a beautiful vase in his father's house, bearing graceful paintings of Athena presenting the olive tree to the Athenians, and of the angry Sea-god striking his trident into the ground and leaving a mark which the lad's nurse had shown him at the Erechtheum on the Acropolis. There were the gods on the vase in *human* form, and so he had long thought of them as people like those of Athens. He had learned, too, that they were close by, for he had seen his father present gifts to them at household feasts. Later, when he went to school and memorized long passages of the Homeric poems, he had learned more about their adventures on earth. Then he had stood on the edge of the crowd with his parents watching the magnificent state feasts, like the Panathenæa (§ 607), supported at great expense, in order to honor the gods and keep them favorable to Athens. Hence everyone seemed to him to believe that the gods had all power over Athens. On such occasions he vaguely felt the majesty and grandeur of the great gods; but when he looked upon figures of them sculptured by such artists as Praxiteles, the gods again appeared very much like earthly folk, as he had seen them on the vase in his childhood.

688. He had never had any religious instruction, for there was nothing like a church, a clergy, or any religious teachers. There was no sacred book revered by all, like our Bible. He had not been taught that the gods had any interest in him or his conduct, or that they required him to be either good or bad. As long as he did not neglect any of the ceremonies desired by the gods, he knew he need have no fear of them. At the same time he realized that if he lived an evil life, he might be condemned to enter at death a dark and gruesome dwelling place beneath the earth. On the other hand, a good life might bring him at last to the beautiful Elysian Fields.

Religion and conduct

689. One of the ways of reaching this place of blessedness was by initiation into the mysteries of Eleusis. Another way was to follow the teachings of the beggar-priests and soothsayers of Orpheus. These wandering teachers, like traveling revival preachers of today, went about in all Greece, followed by hordes of the poor and ignorant, who eagerly accepted their mysterious teachings and were promised every blessing. The more mysterious it all was, the better the multitude liked it. These teachings were recorded in the wonderful book of Orpheus, which finally gained wide circulation among the common people. It came nearer to being the sacred book of the Greeks than any other that ever arose among them. All the lower classes believed in magic and were deeply impressed by the mysterious "stunts" of the magicians and soothsayers, whom they consulted on all the ordinary acts of life.

Religion of the multitude

690. Down at the Piræus the Athenian citizen found the busy streets crowded with foreign merchants from Egypt, Phœnicia, and Asia Minor. They too had their assurances of divine help and blessedness, and they brought with them their strange gods, — the Great Mother from Asia Minor, Isis from her lovely temple at Philæ, above the First Cataract of the Nile (Fig. 202), and Egyptian Amon from his mysterious shrine far away in the Sahara, behind the Greek city of Cyrene. The famous Greek poet Pindar had written a poem in his honor and had erected a statue of the great Egyptian god. As a deliverer of oracles revealing the future, Amon had now become as great a favorite among the Greeks themselves as Apollo of Delphi. There was an Athenian ship which regularly plied between the Piræus and Cyrene, carrying the Greeks to Amon's distant Sahara shrine. Egyptian symbols too were common on Greek tombstones.

Foreign gods from the Near East

691. Some of these foreign beliefs had once greatly impressed our citizen in his younger days. Then, when he left his boyhood teacher behind and went to hear the lectures of a noted Sophist, he found that no one knew with any certainty whether the gods even existed; much less did anyone know what they were like. He now looked with some pity at the crowds of pilgrims who filled the sacred road leading to the hall of the mysteries at Eleusis. He had only contempt for the mob which filled the processions of the strange Oriental gods and almost every day marched with tumult and flute-playing through the streets of Athens. While he could not follow such superstitions of the ignorant poor, he found, nevertheless, that he was not yet quite ready to throw away the gods and reject them altogether, as some of his educated neighbors were doing.

Athenian citizen's later uncertainties

692. He recalled the days of his youth, when he had detested these very doubts which he had now taken up. With great enjoyment he had once beheld the caricatures of Aristophanes, the greatest of the comedy writers. Our citizen had shouted with delight at Aristophanes' mockery of the

doubts and mental struggles of Euripides (§ 618) or at the ridicule which the clever comedy heaped upon the Sophists.

Fig. 195. Socrates

This is not the best of the numerous surviving portraits of Socrates, but it is especially interesting because it bears under the philosopher's name nine inscribed lines containing a portion of a conversation of Socrates with one of his friends as reported by Plato in his *Crito*

Victory of doubt, and triumph of Euripides

Since then, however, had come the new light which he himself had gained from the Sophists. Whatever the gods might be like, he was sure that they were not such beings as he found pictured among his heroic forefathers in the Homeric poems. Now he had long since cast aside his Homer. In spite of Aristophanes he and his educated friends were all reading the splendid tragedies of Euripides, with their uncertainties, struggles, and doubts about life and the gods. Euripides, the victim of Aristophanes' ridicule, to whom the Athenians had rarely voted a victory during his lifetime, had now triumphed; but his triumph meant the defeat of the old, the victory of doubt, the overthrow of the gods, and the incoming of a new age in thought and belief. But the old died hard, and the struggle was a tragic one.

Aristophanes and Socrates

693. The citizen remembered well another comedy of Aristophanes, which had likewise found a ready response from the Athenian audience. It had placed upon the stage the rude and comical figure of a poor Athenian named Socrates, whom Aristophanes had represented as a dangerous man, to be shunned or even chastised by good Athenians. He was the son of a stonecutter, or small sculptor. The ill-clothed figure and ugly face of Socrates had become familiar in the streets to all the folk of Athens since the outbreak of the second war with Sparta. He was accustomed to stand about the market place all day long, engaging in conversation anyone he met and asking a great many questions. Our citizen recalled that Socrates' questions left him in a very confused state of mind, for he seemed to call in question everything which the citizen had once regarded as settled.

694. Yet this familiar and homely figure of the stonecutter's son was the personification of the best and highest in Greek genius. Without desire for office or a political career, Socrates' supreme interest nevertheless was the state. He believed that the state, made up as it was of citizens, could be purified and saved only by improving the individual citizen through the education of his mind to recognize virtue and right.

The state the chief interest of Socrates

695. Herein lies the supreme achievement of Socrates: namely, his unshakable conviction that the human mind is able to recognize and determine what are virtue and right, truth and honesty, beauty, and all the other great ideas which mean so much to human life. To him these ideas had *reality*. He taught that by keen questioning and *discussion* it is possible to reject error and discern these realities. Inspired by this impregnable belief, Socrates went about in Athens engaging all his fellow citizens in such discussion, convinced that he might thus lead each citizen in turn to a knowledge of the leading and compelling virtues. Furthermore, he firmly believed that the citizen who had once recognized these virtues would shape every action and all his life by them. Socrates thus revealed the power of virtue and of similar ideas by argument and logic, but he made no appeal to religion as an influence toward good conduct. Nevertheless, he showed himself a deeply religious man, believing with devout heart in the gods, although they were not exactly those of the fathers, and even feeling, like the Hebrew prophets, that there was a divine voice within him, calling him to his high mission.

Belief in man's power to discern and follow the great truths

Public opinion of Socrates

696. The simple but powerful personality of this greatest of Greek teachers often opened to him the houses of the rich and noble. His fame spread far and wide; and when the Delphian oracle was asked who was the wisest of the living, it responded with the name of Socrates. A group of pupils gathered about him, among whom the most famous was Plato. But his aims and his noble efforts on behalf of the Athenian state were misunderstood. His keen questions seemed to throw doubt upon all the old beliefs. The Athenians had already vented their displeasure on more than one leading Sophist who had rejected the old faith and teaching.

Trial and death of Socrates (399 B.C.)

697. So the Athenians summoned Socrates to trial for corrupting the youth with all sorts of doubts and impious teachings. Such examples as Alcibiades, who had been his pupil, seemed convincing illustrations of the viciousness of his teaching; many had read and still more had seen with growing resentment the comedy of Aristophanes in which the great teacher was held up to contempt and execration. Socrates might easily have left Athens when the complaint was lodged against him. Nevertheless he appeared for trial, made a powerful and dignified defense, and, when the court voted the death penalty, passed his last days in tranquil conversation with his friends and pupils, in whose presence he then quietly drank the fatal hemlock (399 B.C.). Thus the Athenian democracy, which had so fatally mismanaged the affairs of the nation in war, brought upon itself much greater reproach in condemning to death, even though in accordance with law, the greatest and purest soul among its citizens.

Influence of Socrates after his death

698. The undisturbed serenity of Socrates in his last hours, as pictured to us in Plato's idealized version of the scene, profoundly affected the whole Greek world and still forms one of the most precious possessions of humanity. He was the greatest Greek, and in him Greek civilization reached its highest level. But the glorified figure of Socrates as he appears in the writings of his pupils was to prove more powerful even than the living teacher.

699. Meantime there had been growing up a body of scientific knowledge about the visible world which men had never possessed before. Moreover, this new scientific knowledge was no longer confined to the few philosophers who were its discoverers, as formerly had been the case. Our doubting citizen had at home a whole shelf of books on natural science. It included a treatise on mathematics, an astronomy in which the year was at last stated to contain $365\frac{1}{4}$ days, a zoölogy, and a botany. There was also a mineralogy, a pamphlet on foretelling the weather, and a treatise on the calendar, besides several geographies with maps of the world then known. There were, in addition, practical books

Spread of scientific knowledge among the people

FIG. 196. *Greek* PHYSICIAN *reading from a Roll*

It will be seen that the physician holds the roll so that he rolls up a portion of it with one hand as he unrolls another portion with the other. He soon has a roll in each hand, while he holds, smoothly stretched out between the two rolls, the exposed portion, from which he reads a column of writing like that which we see photographed from the oldest preserved Greek book-roll, in Fig. 218. Such a column formed for him a page; but when it was read, instead of turning a page as we do, he rolled it away to the left side and brought into view a new column from the other roll on the right side. The physician has taken the roll from a cabinet, the upper shelf of which still holds eight other rolls arranged in a pyramid-like pile. From the cases of surgical instruments standing open on the top of the cabinet we may assume that these rolls contained informative medical material, perhaps discussions of the parts and operations of the human body and suggestions for treatments of injuries such as may be found in the roll of the unknown Egyptian surgeon (§ 119). (After Birt) of guidance and instruction on drawing, war, farming, raising horses, and even cooking, although the last was not new.

700. There was also, in our citizen's library, a remarkable history treating the fortunes of nations in the same way in which natural science was treated. Its author was Thucydides, the first scientific writer of history. A generation earlier Herodotus' history had ascribed the fortunes of nations to the will of the gods; but Thucydides, with an insight like that of modern historians, traced historical events to their *earthly* causes in the world of men where they occur. There stood the two books, Herodotus and Thucydides, side by side in the citizen's library. There was only thirty years or so between them, but how different the beliefs of the two historians, the old and the new! Thucydides was one of the greatest writers of impressive prose that ever lived, although he sometimes disfigured his pages with obscure and crabbed paragraphs. His book, which told the story of the long wars resulting in the fall of the Athenian Empire, was received by the Greeks with enthusiastic approval. It has been one of the world's great classics ever since.

Scientific writing of history

701. The success of Thucydides' work in prose shows that the interest of the Athenians was no longer in poetry but in the new and more youthful art of prose. Poetry, including play-writing, noticeably declined. A successful public speech was now written down beforehand, and the demand for such addresses in the Assembly, and especially before the citizen-juries, was a constant motive for the cultivation of skillful prose writing and public speaking.

Decline of poetry and triumph of prose

702. The teachers of rhetoric at Athens, the successors of the old Sophists, became world-renowned, and they made the city the center of education for the whole Greek world. The leader among them was Isocrates, the son of a well-to-do flute manufacturer. Having lost his father's fortune in the Peloponnesian Wars, he turned for a living to the teaching of rhetoric,

Athens the center of education; Isocrates

in which he soon showed great ability. He chose as his theme the great political questions of his time. He was not a good speaker, and he therefore devoted himself especially to the *writing* of his speeches, which he then published as political essays. Throughout Greece these remarkable essays were read, and Isocrates finally became the political spokesman of Athens, if not of all Greece. His written speeches had a great influence also outside of Greece, especially on Philip, the Macedonian king.

Rise of science of government

703. Notwithstanding the new interest in natural science the affairs of *men* rather than of *nature* were the burning questions at Athens. How should the governmental affairs of a community of men be conducted? What should be the proper form of a free state? These were the problems which Athenian experience and the efforts of Socrates toward an enlightened citizenship had thrust into the foreground. What should be the form of the ideal state? The Near East had already had its social idealism. In the Near East, however, it had never occurred to the social dreamers to discuss the *form of government* of the ideal state. They accepted as a matter of course the monarchy under which they lived as the obvious form for the state. But in Greece the question of the form of government, whether a kingdom, a republic, or an aristocracy, was now earnestly discussed. Thus there arose a new science, the *science of government*.

Plato

704. Plato, the most gifted pupil of Socrates, published much of his beloved master's teaching in the form of dialogues which supposedly reproduced the discussions of the great teacher himself. It is to these writings that we owe our knowledge of the philosophy of Socrates. Then, after extensive travels in Egypt and the West, Plato returned to Athens, where he set up his school in the grove of the Academy (§ 595). Convinced of the hopelessness of democracy in Athens, he reluctantly gave up all thought of a career as a statesman, to which he had been strongly drawn, and settled down at Athens to devote himself to teaching.

705. Plato was both philosopher and poet. The *ideas* which Socrates maintained the human mind could discern became for Plato eternal realities, having an existence independent of man and his mind. The human soul, he taught, had always existed, and in an earlier state had beheld the great ideas of goodness, beauty, evil, and the like, and had gained an intuitive vision of them which in this earthly life the soul now recalled and recognized. The elect souls, gifted with such vision, were the ones to control the ideal state, for they would necessarily act in accordance with the ideas of virtue and justice which they had discerned. It was possible by education, thought Plato, to lead the souls of men to a clear vision of these ideas.

Plato's development of Socratic ideas

706. In a noble essay entitled *The Republic* Plato presented a lofty vision of his ideal state. Here live the enlightened souls, governing society in righteousness and justice. They do no work, but depend on craftsmen and slaves for all menial labor. And yet the comforts and leisure which they enjoy are the product of that very world of industry and commerce in a Greek city which Plato so thoroughly despises. The plan places far too much dependence on education and takes no account of the dignity and importance of labor in human society. Moreover, Plato's ideal state is the self-contained, self-controlling city-state as it had in times past supposedly existed in Greece. He failed to perceive that the vital question for Greece was now *the relation of these city-states to each other.* He did not discern that the life of a cultivated state unavoidably expands beyond its borders, and by its needs and its contributions affects the life of surrounding states. It cannot be confined within its *political* borders, for its *commercial* borders lie as far distant as its galleys can carry its produce.

Plato's ideal state

707. Thus boundary lines cannot separate nations; their life overlaps and interfuses with the life round about them. It was so within Greece, and it was so far beyond the borders of Greek territory. There had grown up a *civilized* *world* which was reading Greek books, using Greek utensils, fitting up its houses with Greek furniture, decorating its house interiors with Greek paintings, building Greek theaters, learning Greek tactics in war, — a great Mediterranean and Oriental world bound together by lines of commerce, travel, and common economic interests. For this world, as a coming *political* unity, the lofty idealist Plato, in spite of his travels, had no eyes. To this world, once dominated by Oriental culture, the Greeks had given the noblest and sanest ideas yet attained by the mind of civilized man, and to this world likewise the Greeks should have given political leadership.

Growth of a Hellenized world

708. But while the Greeks were continually enfeebled by their own petty wars, the real political leadership of them all was held by the Persian king by the simple means of extending financial support first to Sparta, for the maintenance of the fleet that defeated Athens, and later to other Greek states. Men of practical views, like Isocrates, clearly understood the situation at this time. Isocrates urged the Greeks to bury their petty differences and expand their purely *sectional* patriotism into loyalty toward a union of the whole Greek world. Isocrates does not seem to have thought of this union as one like that of the United States, but rather as a military alliance under united leadership. He told his countrymen that, so united, they could easily overthrow the decaying Persian Empire and make themselves lords of the world, whereas now, while they continued to fight among themselves, the king of Persia could do as he pleased with them. In an inspiring address distributed to the Greeks at the Olympic games Isocrates said, "Anyone coming from abroad and observing the present situation of Greece would regard us as great fools struggling among ourselves about trifles and destroying our own land, when without danger we might conquer Asia." To all Greeks who had read Xenophon's story of the march of his Ten Thousand the weakness of the Persian Empire was obvious. Every motive toward unity was present.

Motives toward unity: Isocrates and Xenophon

709. Nevertheless no Greek city was willing to submit to the leadership of another. *Local* patriotism, like the sectionalism which brought on the American Civil War, prevailed, and unalterable disunion was the end of Greek political development. As a result the Greeks were now to be subjected to an outside power which had never had any share in advancing Greek culture. Thus the fine theories of the ideal form of the state so warmly discussed at Athens were now to be met by the hard fact of irresistible power in the hands of a single ruler, — the form of power which the Greek republics had in vain striven to destroy.

Unalterable disunion the end of Greek political development

710. But in spite of this final and melancholy collapse of Greek political power, which even the wealth and splendor of the western Greek cities in Italy and Sicily, like Syracuse, had not been able to prevent, what an incomparably glorious age of Greek civilization was this which we have been sketching! The rivalries which proved so fatal to the political leadership of the Greeks had been a constant incentive spurring them all on, as each city strove to surpass its rivals in art and literature and all the finest things in civilization. Great as the age of Pericles had been, the age that followed was still greater. The tiny Athenian state, with a population not larger than that of Plymouth (England) or Omaha (Nebraska), and having at most twenty-five or thirty thousand citizens, had furnished in this period a group of great names in all lines of human achievement such as never in all the history of the world arose elsewhere in an area and a population so limited. In a book like this we have been able to offer only a few hints of all that these men of Athens accomplished. Their names today are among the most illustrious in human history, and the achievements which we link with them form the greatest chapter in the higher life of man. Furthermore, Greek genius was to go on to many another future triumph, in spite of the loss of that political leadership which we are now to see passing into other hands.

Supremacy of Greek genius in spite of political collapse

QUESTIONS

Section 58. What was the effect of the long wars upon art in Athens? What new style of architecture was coming in? Describe the Mausoleum. How did the sculpture of Praxiteles differ from that of Phidias? What kind of figures did Scopas love to carve? What new process of producing portable paintings came in? What new method of painting did Apollodorus introduce? Have any of these paintings survived? How do we know how they looked? What kind of small works did the lesser artists produce?

Section 59. In what respects was the age following Pericles one of conflict? What did an Athenian child of this time learn about the gods? What did he believe about his own conduct and the relation of the gods to it? What did the common people believe? What teachers did they follow? From whom did the educated citizen learn to doubt the gods? Whose tragedies were he and his friends reading? Did this mean the suppression or the triumph of doubt?

How did Socrates spend most of his time? What was his purpose in doing this? Can you sum up his teachings? What was the general opinion about his wisdom and character? What did the Athenians finally do in order to silence Socrates?

What was the condition of scientific knowledge at Athens? How did the history of Thucydides differ from that of Herodotus? Who was the leading teacher of rhetoric and prose writing at Athens? What can you say of the life of Plato? What did he teach about government? What great question did he fail to perceive? Why had not the Greeks given the world of Greek culture also political unity? How did practical men like Isocrates feel about this problem? Did the Greeks follow his advice? What was to be the result?

BIBLIOGRAPHY FOR TOPICAL STUDIES

Greek industrial art: BRITISH MUSEUM, *Greek and Roman Life*, pp. 172–178; GARDNER, *Art through the Ages*, pp. 88–98; MILLS, *Ancient Greeks*, pp. 203–206; POLAND-REISINGER-WAGNER, *Culture of Greece and Rome*, pp. 210–215; RICHTER, *The Craft of Athenian Pottery* (108 pp.).

Trial and death of Socrates: MILLS, *Ancient Greeks*, pp. 367–378; MURRAY, *Ancient Greek Literature*, pp. 174–177, 297–299; *Pageant of Greece*, pp. 271–282.

Chapter XIX · *Alexander the Great*

Section 60. The Rise of Macedonia

711. On the northern frontiers, in the mountains of the Balkan Peninsula, Greek civilization gradually faded and disappeared, merging into the barbarism which had descended from Stone Age Europe. These backward northerners, such as the Thracians, spoke Indo-European tongues akin to Greek, but their Greek kindred of the south could not understand them. A veneer of Greek civilization began here and there to mask somewhat

Uncultivated states of Balkan Peninsula and the north

Note. The above headpiece shows us one of the streets where it was the custom of both the Greeks and the Romans to bury their dead. It was outside the Dipylon Gate (plan, p. 418), on the Sacred Way, leading to Eleusis, both sides of which were lined for some distance with marble tombstones, of which Fig. 194 is an example. The Roman Sulla (§ 984), in his Eastern war, while besieging Athens, piled up earth as a causeway leading to the top of the wall of Athens at this point. The part of the cemetery which he covered with earth was thus preserved, to be dug out in modern times. The most recent excavations in this street are shown in Fig. 188. In this cemetery the Athenians of Socrates' day were buried. The monument at the left shows a brave Athenian youth on horseback, charging the fallen enemy. He was slain in the Corinthian War (§ 668) and buried here a few years after the death of Socrates.

the rough and uncultivated life of the peasant population of Macedonia. The Macedonian kings began to cultivate Greek literature and art. The mother of Philip of Macedon was grateful that she had been able to learn to read and write Greek in her old age.

Philip of Macedon and his policy of expansion

712. Philip himself had enjoyed a Greek education. He could read the published speeches of Isocrates, and we shall see that he heeded their advice. When he gained the power over Macedonia, in 360 B.C., he therefore understood perfectly the situation of the disunited Greek world. He planned to make himself its master, and he began his task with the ability both of a skilled statesman and of an able soldier. With clear recognition of the necessary means he first created the indispensable military power. As a hostage at Thebes he had learned the value of the oblique battle front under the eye of Epaminondas himself, the conqueror of the Spartans. But Philip surpassed his teacher.

Philip creates Macedonian infantry

713. From the peasant population of his kingdom Philip drew off a number large enough to form a permanent, or standing, army of professional soldiers who never expected again to return to the flocks and fields. These men he armed as heavy infantry of the phalanx as he had seen it in Greece, only he made the phalanx deeper and more massive and gave his men longer spears. They soon became famous as the "Macedonian phalanx."

Philip's tactics; cavalry and infantry in unified operations

714. Heretofore horsemen had played but a small part in war in Europe. The Persians had begun to show that groups of *horsemen* were far more speedy, flexible, and powerful than the cumbrous chariots of the old Oriental armies. Horses were plentiful in Philip's kingdom, and the nobles forming a warrior class had always been accustomed to fight on horseback in a loose way, each for himself. Philip now drilled these riders to move about and to attack in a single mass. The charge of such a mass of horsemen was so terrible that it might of itself decide a battle. Philip thus gave to cavalry a place in warfare which it held for two thousand years. He then further improved the art of war by a final step, the most important of all. He so combined his heavy phalanx in the *center* with the disciplined masses of horsemen on each *wing* that the whole combined force, infantry and cavalry, moved and operated as one great unit. Advancing with an oblique battle front Philip's army was an irresistible machine in which every part worked together with all the others.

Advantages of one-man control; Philip's northern conquests

715. This new chapter in the art of warfare was possible only because a single mind was in unhampered control of the situation. The Greeks were now to witness the practical effectiveness of one-man control as exercised by a skillful leader for many years. With statesmanlike insight Philip first began his conquests in the region where he might expect the least resistance. He steadily extended the territory of his kingdom eastward and northward until it reached the Danube and the Hellespont.

Two parties at Athens: Isocrates

716. His progress on the north of the Ægean soon brought him into conflict with the interests of the Greek states which owned cities in this northern region. Philip's conquests were viewed with mixed feelings at Athens, toward which the Macedonian king himself felt very friendly, for he had the greatest admiration for the Greeks. Two policies therefore arose at Athens. One of them proposed to accept Philip's proffered friendship, and recognized in him the uniter and savior of the Greek world. The leading advocate of this policy was Isocrates, now an aged man. The other policy, on the contrary, denounced Philip as a barbarous tyrant who was endeavoring to enslave the free Greek cities.

Demosthenes

717. The leader of this anti-Macedonian policy was Demosthenes, an Athenian lawyer and politician who had made himself a powerful orator. In one passionate appeal after another he addressed the Athenian people as he strove to arouse them to the growing danger threatening the Greek states with every added triumph of Philip's formidable army. By the whirlwind of his marvelous eloquence he carried the Athenian Assembly with him. His *Philippics,* as his denunciations of King Philip are called, are among the greatest specimens of Greek eloquence and have become traditional among us as noble examples of oratorical power inspired by high and patriotic motives. But they were very immoderate in their abuse and denunciation of his opponents in Athens, nor can it be said that they display a statesmanlike understanding of the hopelessly disunited condition of the ever-warring Greek states and the necessity of immediate union.

Fig. 197. Demosthenes

Influence of Isocrates on the policy of Philip

718. On the other hand, the policy proposed by Isocrates was one of such practical wisdom that it appealed even to Philip of Macedon. Indeed, when the king read the statesmanlike speeches of Isocrates, he was greatly influenced by them. The proposal which he found in them, that he should make himself the leader of the federated Greeks in a war against the Persians, was the most important measure in the policy of Isocrates, and Philip adopted it completely without any reservations. His motives in doing so, however, were of course very different from those which Isocrates imagined, for Philip was thinking only of the advancement of Macedonian power. Philip's ideas of a federation of the Greeks were also his own and very different from those of Isocrates.

719. The outcome of the struggle which unavoidably came on between Philip and the Greek states showed that the views of Isocrates, while less ideally attractive, were far more sagacious and statesmanlike than those of Demosthenes. After a long series of hostilities Philip defeated the Greek forces in a final battle at Chæronea (338 B.C.) and firmly established his position as head of a league of all the Greek states except Sparta, which still held out against him. He had begun operations in Asia Minor for the freedom of the Greek cities there, when, two years after the battle of Chæronea, he was stabbed by a resentful noble during the revelries at the wedding of his daughter (336 B.C.).

Philip gains the leadership of the Greeks (338 B.C.)

720. The power passed into the hands of his son Alexander, a youth of only twenty years. Fortunately Philip also left behind him in the Macedonians of his court a group of men of remarkable ability. These great men were to become the leaders of the vast Oriental world ruled by Persia. They were devoted to the royal house, and Alexander's early successes were in no small measure due to them; but their very devotion and ability, as we shall see, later brought the young king into a personal conflict which contained all the elements of a tremendous tragedy.

Successors of Philip of Macedon

721. When Alexander was thirteen years of age his father had summoned to the Macedonian court the great philosopher Aristotle (§ 794), a former pupil of Plato, to be the teacher of the young prince. Under his instruction the lad learned to understand the value of science and to know and love the masterpieces of Greek literature, especially the Homeric songs. The deeds of the ancient heroes touched and kindled his youthful imagination and lent a heroic tinge to his whole character. Philip had had the figure of Heracles (Hercules) as his ancestor stamped on his coins; Alexander believed that through his father he was descended from Heracles, and that his ancestry could be traced back through his mother to Achilles. As he grew older and his mind ripened, his whole personality was imbued with the splendor of Greek genius and Hellenic culture. Such ideas were fitted to develop into universalism, the dream of a united world, which had been first discerned by Ikhnaton of Egypt a thousand years earlier.

Education and character of Alexander the Great

Section 61. Campaigns of Alexander the Great

722. The Greek states were still unwilling to submit to Macedonian leadership, and they fancied they could overthrow so youthful a ruler as Alexander. They were soon to learn how old a head there was on his young shoulders. When Thebes revolted against Macedonia for the second time after Philip's death, Alexander, knowing that he must take up the struggle with Persia, realized that it would not be safe for him to march into Asia without giving the Greek states a lesson which they would not soon forget. He therefore captured and completely destroyed the ancient city of Thebes, sparing only the house of the great poet Pindar. All Greece was thus taught to fear and respect his power, but learned at the same time to recognize his reverence for Greek genius. After Athens had legally acknowledged the leadership of Alexander, Demosthenes had personally accepted 300 talents from the Persians for use against Macedonia; but Alexander, having forgiven Athens, even pardoned the blundering Demosthenes, and thereupon the Greek states, with the exception of Sparta, reaffirmed their acceptance of Philip's league and elected Alexander as its leader and general. As a result they all sent troops to increase his army.

Alexander subjugates the Greek states and heads a Greek league

723. The Asiatic campaign which Alexander now planned was to vindicate his position as the champion of Hellas against Asia. He thought to lead the united Greeks against the Persian lord of Asia, as the Hellenes had once made common cause against Asiatic Troy. Leading his army of Macedonians and allied Greeks into Asia Minor, he therefore stopped at Troy and camped upon the plain where the Greek heroes of the Homeric songs had once fought. Here he worshiped in the temple of Athena, and prayed for the success of his cause against Persia. He thus contrived to throw around himself the heroic atmosphere of the Trojan War, till all Hellas beheld the dauntless figure of the Macedonian youth, as it were

Alexander, champion of Hellas against Asia

a new Achilles, against the background of that glorious age which in their belief had so long ago united Greek arms against Asia (§ 450).

724. Meantime the Persian king had hired thousands of Greek heavy-armed infantry, and they were now to do battle against their own Greek countrymen. At the river Granicus, in his first critical battle, employing the oblique battle front which his father had learned from Epaminondas, Alexander had no difficulty in scattering the forces of the western Persian satraps. Following the Macedonian custom, the young king, then but twenty-two years of age, led his troops of the advanced wing into the thick of the fray and exposed his royal person without hesitation. But for the timely support of Clitus, the brother of his childhood nurse, who bravely pushed in before him at a critical moment, the impetuous young king would have lost his life here. Marching southward, he took the Greek cities one by one and freed all western Asia Minor forever from the Persian yoke.

Battle of the Granicus (334 B.C.) and conquest of Asia Minor

725. But a huge Persian fleet was still master of the Mediterranean. It was at this juncture that the young Macedonian, little more than a boy in years, began to display his mastery of a military situation which demanded the completest understanding of the art of war. He had left a strong force at home, and he believed that the lesson of his destruction of Thebes would prevent the Persian fleet in the Ægean from arousing Hellas to rebellion against him during his absence. He therefore pushed boldly eastward. Following the route of the Ten Thousand, Alexander led his army safely through the difficult pass called the Cilician Gates (see map, p. 498) and rounded the northeast corner of the Mediterranean. Here, as he looked out upon the Fertile Crescent, there was spread out before him the vast Asiatic world of forty million souls, where the family of the Great King had been supreme for two hundred years. In this great arena he was to be the champion for the next ten years (333–323 B.C.).

Alexander's march through Asia Minor

Defeat of Darius III at the battle of Issus (333 B.C.)

726. At this important point, by the Gulf of Issus, Alexander met the main army of Persia, under the personal command of the Great King, Darius III, the last of the Persian line. The tactics of his father Philip and of Epaminondas, always to be the attacking party, were continued by Alexander in spite of the enemy's strong defensive position behind a stream. His attack was on the old plan of the oblique battle line (§ 672), with the cavalry forming the right wing nearest the enemy. Heading this cavalry charge himself, Alexander led his Macedonian horsemen across the stream in such a fierce assault that the opposing Persian wing gave way. Along the center and the other wing the battle was still being hotly fought and was indecisive; but as Alexander's victorious horsemen of the right wing turned toward the left and attacked the exposed Persian center in the flank, the Macedonians swept the Asiatics from the field. Leaving his right wing still bravely fighting, Darius fled and his disorderly retreat never stopped until it had crossed the Euphrates. The Great King then sent a letter to Alexander desiring terms of peace and offering to accept the Euphrates as a boundary between them, all Asia west of that river to be handed over to the Macedonians.

---

* The artist who designed this great work has selected the supreme moment when the PERSIANS (at the right) are endeavoring to rescue their king from the onset of the MACEDONIANS (at the left). ALEXANDER, the bareheaded figure on horseback at the left, charges furiously against the PERSIAN KING (DARIUS III), who stands in his chariot (at the right). The Macedonian attack is so impetuous that the Persian king's life is endangered. A PERSIAN NOBLE dismounts and offers his riderless horse, that the king may quickly mount and escape. Devoted PERSIAN NOBLES heroically ride in between their king and the Macedonian onset, to give Darius an opportunity to mount. But Alexander's spear has passed entirely through the body of one of these Persian nobles, who has thus given his life for his king. Darius throws out his hand in grief and horror at the awful death of his noble friend. The driver of the royal chariot (behind the king) lashes his three horses, endeavoring to carry Darius from the field in flight. This magnificent battle scene is put together from bits of colored glass (mosaic) forming a floor pavement, discovered in 1831 at the Roman town of Pompeii. It has been injured in places, especially at the left, where parts of the figures of Alexander and his horse have disappeared. It was originally laid at Alexandria and suffered this damage in being moved to Italy. It is a copy of an older Hellenistic work, a painting done at Alexandria (§ 773). It is one of the greatest scenes of heroism in battle ever painted, and illustrates the splendor of Hellenistic art.

FIG. 198. ALEXANDER THE GREAT *charging the Bodyguard and Officers of the Persian King at the* BATTLE *of* ISSUS*

727. It was a dramatic picture, the figure of the young king, standing with this letter in his hand. As he pondered it he was surrounded by a group of the ablest Macedonian youth, who had grown up around him as his closest friends, but likewise by old and trusted counselors upon whom his father before him had leaned. The hazards of battle and of march, and the daily associations of camp and bivouac, had wrought the closest bonds of love and friendship and intimate influence between these loyal Macedonians and their ardent young king.

Situation after Issus, and Alexander's friends

728. As he considered the letter of Darius, therefore, his father's old general Parmenio, who had commanded the Macedonian left wing in the battle just won, proffered him serious counsel. We can almost see the old man leaning familiarly over the shoulder of this imperious boy of twenty-three and pointing out across the Mediterranean as he bade Alexander remember the Persian fleet operating there in his rear and likely to stir up revolt against him in Greece. He said too that with Darius behind the Euphrates, as proposed in the letter, Persia would be at a safe distance from Europe and the Greek world. The campaign against the Great King, he urged, had secured all that could reasonably be expected. Undoubtedly he added that Philip himself, the young king's father, had at the utmost no further plans against Persia than those already successfully carried out. There was nothing to do, said Parmenio, but to accept the terms offered by the Great King.

Advice of Parmenio after Issus

729. In this critical decision lay the parting of the ways. Before the kindling eyes of the young Alexander there rose a vision of world empire dominated by Greek civilization, — a vision to which the duller eyes about him were entirely closed. He waved aside his father's old counselors and decided to advance to the conquest of the whole Persian Empire. In this far-reaching decision he disclosed at once the powerful personality which represented a new age. Thus arose the conflict which never ends, — the conflict between

Alexander's decision after Issus; friction with his friends

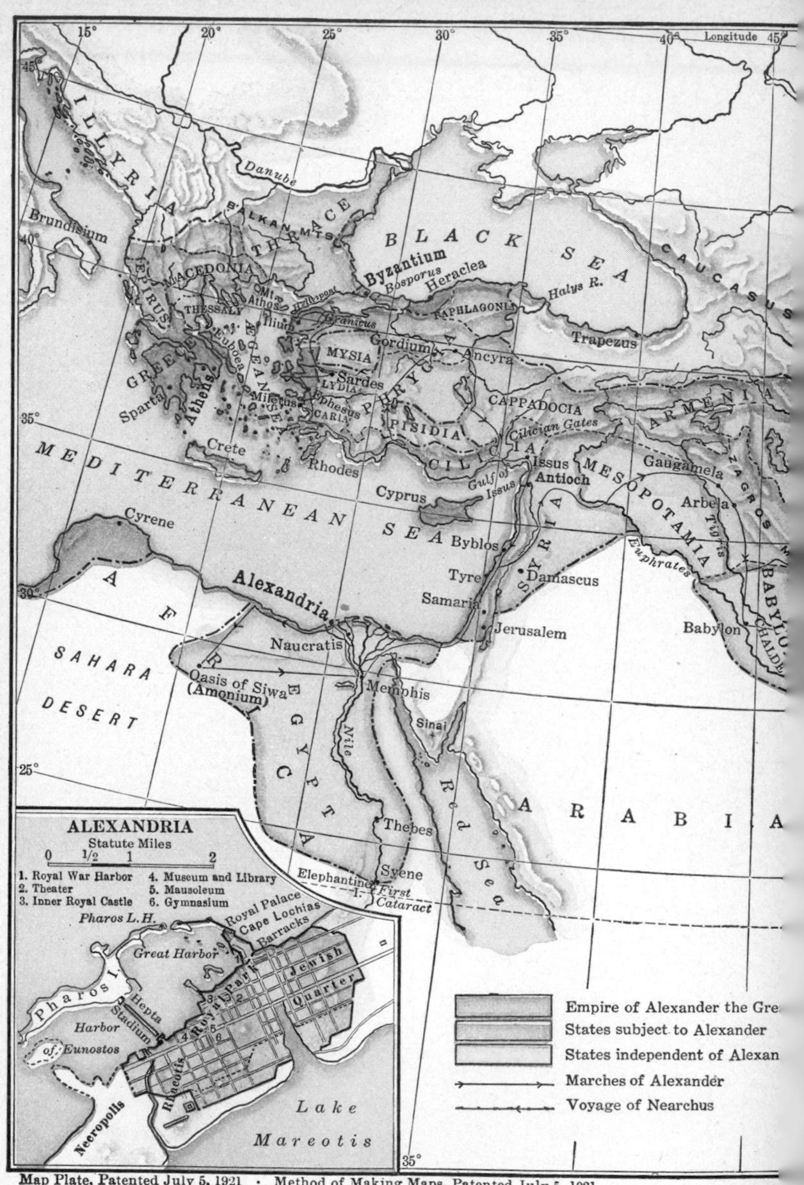

ILLYRIA
Danube
BALKAN MTS.
THRACE
MACEDONIA
EPIRUS
THESSALY
GREECE
Brundisium
Athens
Sparta
Byzantium
Bosporus
Heraclea
BLACK SEA
Halys R.
CAUCASUS
PAPHLAGONIA
Trapezus
Gordium
Ancyra
MYSIA
Sardes
LYDIA
Ephesus
Miletus
CARIA
PHRYGIA
PISIDIA
CAPPADOCIA
ARMENIA
Cilician Gates
CILICIA
Issus
Antioch
Gulf of Issus
MESOPOTAMIA
Gaugamela
Arbela
ZAGROS
Tigris
Euphrates
BABYLONIA
CHALDEA
Babylon
Crete
Rhodes
MEDITERRANEAN SEA
Cyprus
Cyrene
Byblos
SYRIA
Tyre
Damascus
Samaria
Jerusalem
Alexandria
AFRICA
Naucratis
SAHARA DESERT
Oasis of Siwa (Amonium)
Memphis
EGYPT
Nile
Sinai
Red Sea
ARABIA
Thebes
Syene
Elephantine
First Cataract
Longitude
ALEXANDRIA
Statute Miles
1. Royal War Harbor
2. Theater
3. Inner Royal Castle
4. Museum and Library
5. Mausoleum
6. Gymnasium
Pharos L.H.
Royal Palace
Cape Lochias
Barracks
Great Harbor
Pharos I.
Heptastadium
Harbor of Eunostos
Royal Park
Jewish Quarter
Rhacotis
Necropolis
Lake Mareotis
Empire of Alexander the Gre
States subject to Alexander
States independent of Alexan
Marches of Alexander
Voyage of Nearchus

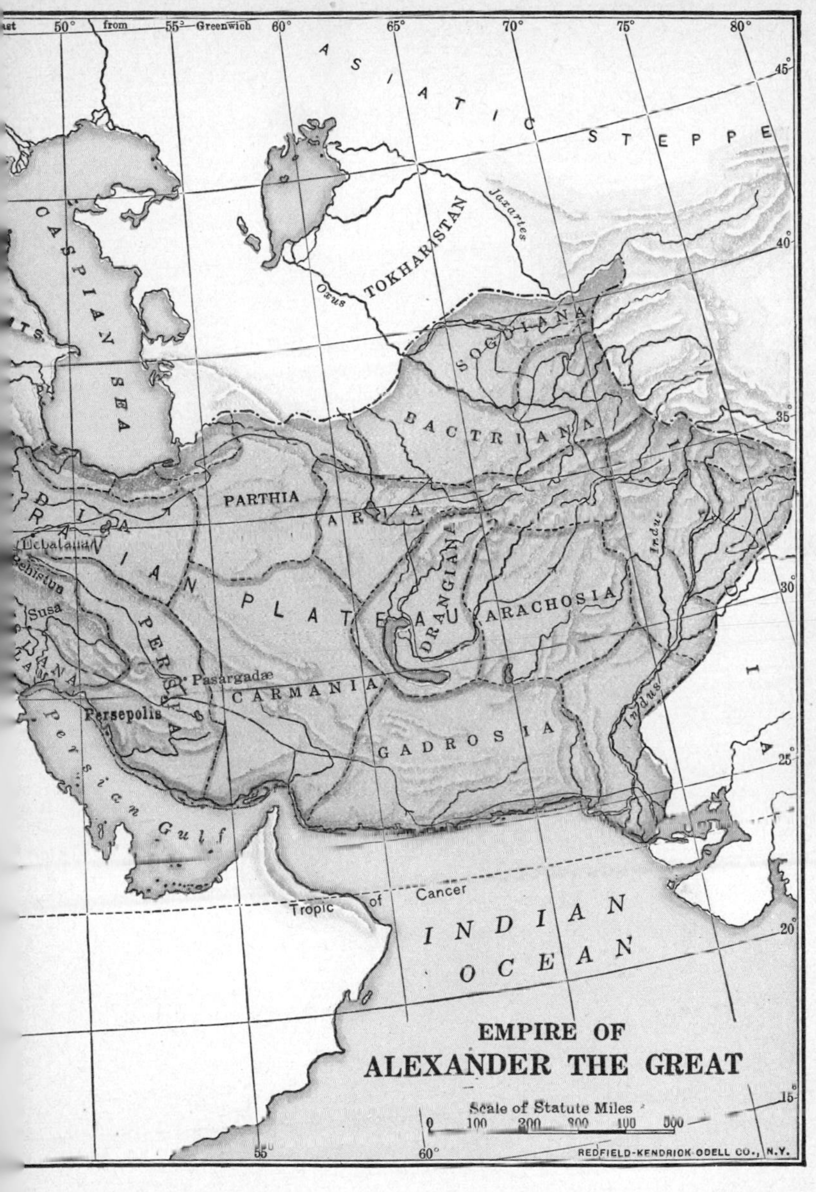

ASIATIC STEPPE
CASPIAN SEA
TOKHARISTAN
Jaxartes
Oxus
SOGDIANA
BACTRIANA
PARTHIA
ARIA
DRANGIANA
ARACHOSIA
IRANIAN PLATEAU
Ecbatana
Behistun
Susa
SUSIANA
PERSIA
Pasargadæ
Persepolis
CARMANIA
GADROSIA
Indus
INDIA
Persian Gulf
Tropic of Cancer
INDIAN OCEAN
from Greenwich
EMPIRE OF
ALEXANDER THE GREAT
Scale of Statute Miles
0 100 200 300 400 500
REDFIELD-KENDRICK-ODELL CO., N.Y.

the new age and the old, just as we have seen it at Athens. Never has it been more dramatically staged than here in the daily growing friction between Alexander and that group of devoted, if less gifted, Macedonians who were now drawn by him into the labors of Heracles,— the conquest of the world.

730. The danger from the Persian fleet was now carefully and deliberately met by a march southward along the eastern end of the Mediterranean. All the Phœnician seaports on the way were captured. Here Alexander's whole campaign would have collapsed but for the siege machinery, the use of which his father had learned from the western Greeks. Against the walls of Tyre Alexander employed machines which had been devised in the Near East and which he was now bringing back thither with Greek improvements. He captured the strong city after a terrible seven months' siege. Feeble Egypt, so long a Persian province, then fell an easy prey to the Macedonian arms. The Persian fleet, thus deprived of all its home harbors and cut off from its home government, soon scattered and disappeared.

Conquest of Phœnicia and Egypt; dispersion of Persian fleet

731. Having thus cut off the enemy in his rear, Alexander returned from Egypt to Asia, and, marching along the Fertile Crescent, he crossed the Tigris close by the mounds which had long covered the ruins of Nineveh (Fig. 199). Here, near Arbela, the Great King had gathered a vast army for a last stand. The Persians had not studied the progress in the art of war made by the Greeks and the Macedonians, and they were as hopelessly behind the times as China was in her war with Japan in 1894–1895. They had prepared one new device, a body of chariots with scythes fastened to the axles and projecting on each side. But this device failed to save the Persian army. Although greatly outnumbered, the oblique battle front of the Macedonians again crushed the Asiatic army and forced the Great King into ignominious flight. In a few days Alexander was established in the winter palace of Persia in Babylon (§ 361).

Alexander's march to Persia: battle of Arbela (331 B.C.)

Fig. 199. *View across the Ruins of* Nineveh *near where Alexander the Great overthrew the Last Army of the Persian Empire*

We are supposed to be standing in a modern cemetery on the mound which covers the ruins of the palace of the Assyrian emperor Esarhaddon. We look along the city wall *A* to the Mound of Kuyunjik (extending to *B*), which contains the ruins of the palaces of Sennacherib and Assurbanipal. Past this mound (compare plan, p. 197) runs the road from Mosul to Arbela, about 30 miles east. These ruins must have been much like this when Alexander marched past them less than three hundred years after the city was destroyed. Although no systematic clearance of all the chief buildings has ever been done here, a great many important monuments have been dug out, like the library of Assurbanipal. The tents in the photographs are those of British East Indian troops stationed here after the World War

Darius III killed (330 B.C.); Alexander lord of ancient East

732. As Darius fled into the eastern mountains he was stabbed by his own treacherous attendants (330 B.C.). Alexander rode up with a few of his officers in time to look upon the body of the last of the Persian emperors, the lord of Asia, whose vast realm had now passed into his hands. He punished the murderers and sent the body with all respect to the fallen ruler's mother and sister, to whom he had extended protection and hospitality. Thus at last both the valley of the Nile and the Fertile Crescent, the homes of the two earliest civilizations, whose long and productive careers we have already sketched, were now in the hands of a European power and under the control of a newer and higher civilization. Less than five years had passed since the young Macedonian had marched into Asia.

Fig. 200. *Air View of the Ruins of the* Great Palaces *at Persepolis burned by Alexander the Great*

Darius began these buildings some two hundred years before they were destroyed by Alexander. The thirteen tall columns still standing at the left belong to a *public* building, the great audience hall of Darius, of which the grand stairway is seen in Fig. 137. The *private* palaces, which were the *dwellings* of the Persian emperors, occupy the corner nearest to the observer. One of these, the harem palace of Darius and Xerxes has been restored by the expedition of the Oriental Institute now excavating the place, and is being used as living quarters for the expedition staff. In preparing this building place Darius first raised a vast platform or terrace, 1000 by 1600 feet in size, and faced it with a massive stone wall fifty feet high, built of gigantic blocks. On this spacious terrace he laid out the palaces and public buildings. Since then the drainage of over two thousand years has carried down from the mountains above a great mass of crumbled rock. All these accumulations, together with the rubbish of fallen walls, covered all but the higher portions of the buildings. In clearing away these accumulations the excavators have found large quantities of the ashes of the great fire, supposedly that of Alexander the Great, which destroyed the place and left it much as it now appears

Alexander captures Persian royal cities

733. Although the Macedonians had nothing more to fear from the Persian arms, there still remained much for Alexander to do in order to establish his empire in Asia. On he marched through the original little kingdom of the Persian kings, whence Cyrus, the founder of the Persian Empire, had victoriously issued over two hundred years before. He stopped at Susa, the capital of Persia, to which so many rival Greek embassies had come to seek Persian support against their own Greek neighbors, and to carry away Persian gold to build a Spartan fleet or keep a pro-Persian politician like Demosthenes talking. To all this Alexander had now put an end. From Susa he then passed on to Pasargadæ to visit the tomb of Cyrus. At Persepolis he gave a dramatic evidence of his supremacy in Asia by setting fire to the Persian palaces with his own hand, as the Persians had once done to Miletus and to the temples on the Athenian Acropolis. By some historians this deed is regarded as merely a symbolical act of revenge; others accept the later gossip that, carried away by the excesses of a drunken revel, Alexander hurled the torch which destroyed the most magnificent buildings the East had ever produced. Certain it is that he afterward expressed his regret.

Alexander's campaigns in Far East (330–324 B.C.)

734. After touching Ecbatana in the north, and leaving behind the trusted Parmenio in charge of the enormous treasure of gold and silver, accumulated for generations by the Persian kings, Alexander again moved eastward. In the course of the next six years, while the Greek world waited in wonder, the young Macedonian seemed to disappear in the mists on the far-off fringes of the known world. He marched his army in one vast loop after another through the heart of the Iranian Plateau (see map, p. 498), northward across the Oxus and Jaxartes rivers, southward across the Indus and the frontiers of India, where at last the murmurs of his intrepid army forced him to turn back.

735. With a fleet of 800 craft he descended the Indus and even sailed the waters of the Indian Ocean, where he and

PLATE IV. GREEKS *and* PERSIANS HUNTING LIONS *with Alexander the Great*

Alexander is out of range at the left. A Greek on horseback endeavors to pierce the wounded lion with his spear. A Persian on foot wields an ax. The scene is carved in relief on a marble sarcophagus, found at Sidon in 1881; the colors are exactly those of the original, now in the museum at Istanbul (Constantinople). It was made not long after Alexander's death, and is one of the greatest works of Hellenistic art. (After Winter, *Alexandermosaik*)

742. Four years later the young king found that this divinity which he began to claim lacked outward and visible manifestations. As an outward observance vividly suggesting his character as a god he adopted the Oriental requirement that all who approached him on official occasions should bow down to the earth and kiss his feet. He also sent formal notification to all the Greek cities that the league of which he had been head was dissolved, that he was henceforth to be officially numbered among the gods of each city, and that as such he was to receive the state offerings which each city presented.

Alexander demands formal deification by cities of dissolved league

743. Thus were introduced into Europe absolute monarchy and the divine right of kings. Indeed, through Alexander there was transferred to Europe much of the spirit of that Orient which had for a short time been repulsed at Marathon and Salamis, but which Greek dealings with Persia had done much to introduce. But these measures of Alexander were not the efforts of a weak mind to gratify a vanity so drunk with power that it could be satisfied only with superhuman honors. They were carefully devised political measures, dictated by state policy and systematically developed step by step for years.

Absolute monarchy and divine right of kings

744. This superhuman station of the world-king Alexander was gained at tragic cost to Alexander the Macedonian youth and to the group of friends and followers about him. Beneath the Persian robes of the state-god Alexander beat the warm heart of a young Macedonian. He had lifted himself to an exalted and lonely eminence whither those devoted friends who had followed him to the ends of the earth could follow him no longer. Neither could they comprehend the necessity for measures which thus strained or snapped entirely those bonds of friendship which linked together comrades in arms. And then there were the Persian intruders treated like the equals of his personal friends (Plate IV) or even placed over them! The tragic consequences of such a situation were inevitable.

Macedonians alienated by deification and internationalism

745. Early in those tremendous marches eastward, after Darius's death, Philotas, son of Parmenio, had learned of a conspiracy against Alexander's life, but his bitterness and estrangement were such that he failed to report his guilty knowledge to the king, who nevertheless learned of the conspiracy. The conspirators were all given a fair and legal trial, and Alexander himself suffered the bitterness of seeing a whole group of his former friends and companions, including Philotas, condemned and executed in the presence of the army. The trusted Parmenio, father of Philotas, still guarding the Persian treasure at Ecbatana, was also implicated, and a messenger was sent back with orders for the old general's immediate execution. This was but the beginning of the ordeal through which the man Alexander was to pass in order that the world-king Alexander might mount the throne of a god.

Execution of Philotas, Parmenio, and their friends

746. Clitus also, who had saved his life at the Granicus, was filled with grief and indignation at Alexander's political course. At a royal feast, where these matters came up in conversation, Clitus was guilty of unguarded criticisms of his lord, and then, entirely losing his self-mastery, he finally heaped such unbridled reproaches upon the king that Alexander, rising in uncontrollable rage, seized a spear from a guard and thrust it through the bosom of the man to whom he owed his life. As we see the young king thereupon sitting for three days in his tent, speechless with grief and remorse, refusing all food, and prevented only by his officers from taking his own life, we gather some slight impression of the terrible personal cost of Alexander's state policy.

Alexander slays his friend Clitus

747. Similarly, the demand that all should prostrate themselves and kiss his feet on entering his presence cost him the friendship of the historian Callisthenes. Although Alexander soon abandoned this requirement, nevertheless, not long afterward, Callisthenes was likewise found criminally guilty toward the king in connection

Execution of Callisthenes

with a conspiracy of the noble Macedonian pages who served Alexander, and he was put to death. He was a nephew of the king's old teacher, Aristotle, and although the friendship between master and royal pupil did not end, the old relationship could never be restored.

748. On his return to Babylon Alexander was overcome with grief at the loss of his dearest friend Hephæstion, who had just died. He arranged for his dead friend one of the most magnificent funerals ever celebrated. Then, as he was preparing for an expedition to circumnavigate and subjugate the Arabian peninsula and thus be free to carry out his great plans for the conquest of the Western Mediterranean, Alexander himself fell sick, probably of a malarial fever which after a few days caused his death (June, 323 B.C.). He was thirty-three years of age and had reigned thirteen years. Although so short his was without doubt the most influential and impressive individual life that the world had ever seen. In many ways his influence was felt throughout the entire world of that day from Rome to China, especially in science, art, commerce, and statesmanship. Alexander's support of science and his persistent interest in it have led many governments ever since to realize that an enlightened government must support science. His campaigns and the cities he founded carried Greek civilization far into Asia and spread Greek art throughout India and China, transforming the art of those countries. World commerce was enormously increased by the removal of all national barriers. In statesmanship Alexander's shadow, like that of some giant tree, fell far across Europe; and it is still there. He showed Europe that their little local powers and city republics must finally fall under one government, which his experience in the East had shown was to be an Oriental despotism. When we reach the story of Rome we shall find that Julius Cæsar and Mark Antony were planning just such an Oriental monarchy as that of Alexander's vast empire. The efforts of Augustus to preserve the forms of the old Roman Republic could not prevent it from becoming

Death of Alexander (323 B.C.)

another Oriental despotism like that of Alexander. In a word, the brief life of Alexander the Great completely transformed the world.

QUESTIONS

Section 60. What was the policy of Philip of Macedon? What new developments in the art of warfare did he introduce? What did the Athenians think about his plans? What was the outcome of Philip's struggle with the Greeks? How was Philip's successor educated?

Section 61. Discuss Alexander's relations with the Greeks. As whose champion did he contrive to make himself appear? Describe his conquest of Asia Minor. Where and when did he first defeat the main Persian army? What proposal did the Persian king make? What did Alexander do? What conflict arose? How did he dispose of the Phœnician fleet? Where did Alexander go after conquering Egypt? Describe his next encounter with the Persians. Trace on the map the marches and campaigns of Alexander after the Battle of Arbela and tell what he accomplished.

Section 62. What scientific enterprises did Alexander undertake? Discuss his plans for merging Greek and Asiatic civilization. What further great plans of conquest did he have? What was to be his own position in the new empire? How had he prepared for this position while he was in Egypt? What effect had all this upon his friends? Where, when, and how did Alexander die?

BIBLIOGRAPHY FOR TOPICAL STUDIES

Demosthenes, citizen of Athens: BOTSFORD, *Source Book*, pp. 266–269; BOTSFORD-SIHLER, *Hellenic Civilization*, pp. 401–407, 510–514, 530–537; BURY, *Greece*, pp. 704–708, 716–719, 736–737, 829–832; MILLS, *Ancient Greeks*, pp. 335–342; MURRAY, *Ancient Greek Literature*, pp. 353–369; *Pageant of Greece*, pp. 358–366.

Isocrates, citizen of Hellenistic world: BURY, *Greece*, pp. 583–585, 714–715; DOBSON, *Ancient Education*, pp. 81–86; MURRAY, *Ancient Greek Literature*, pp. 341–352.

PART IV · THE MEDITERRANEAN WORLD IN THE HELLENISTIC AGE AND THE ROMAN REPUBLIC

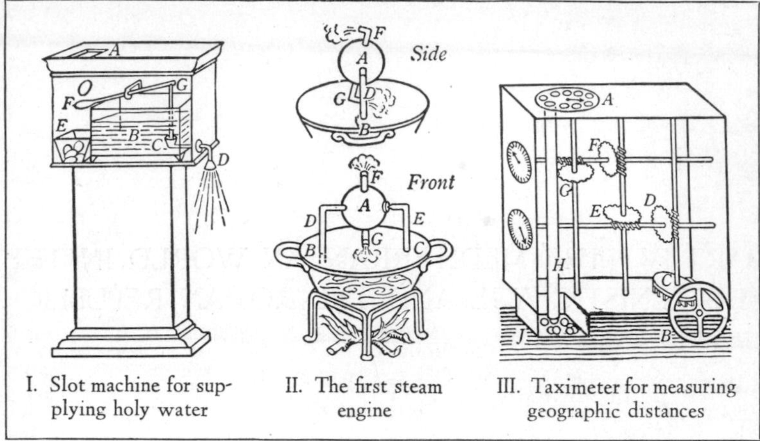

I. Slot machine for supplying holy water

II. The first steam engine

III. Taximeter for measuring geographic distances

Mechanical Devices and INVENTIONS *of the Hellenistic Age*

The above machines, invented in the Hellenistic Age, are found described in books written somewhere around the First Century A.D. by Hero of Alexandria and the Roman Vitruvius. **I** illustrates the principle of the lever. An inner vessel *B* contains holy water, which flows out through the vent *C* and the outside tube *D*. The vent *C* is kept closed by the lower end of a vertical rod *CG*. This rod is raised and lowered by a lever *FG*, flattened into a small disk at *F*. The rod *CG* is heavy enough by its own weight to keep the vent *C* closed; but when a coin is dropped through the slot *A* it falls upon *F*, where it rests long enough to depress the lever at *F*, thus raising the other end at *G* and lifting the rod *CG*. This opens the vent through which the holy water flows into the worshiper's hand at *D* until the coin falls off at *F* and drops into the money box *E*. Such boxes at the doors of the Hellenistic temples enabled the priesthood to sell holy water without an attendant. **II** shows how heat energy may be changed into mechanical energy and motion. A cauldron *B–C* of boiling water has a steam-tight cover. Above it a hollow ball *A* is supported by the tube *D* and the rod *E*, which does not penetrate either the ball or the top of the cauldron. The ball *A* is pivoted on the rod *E*. The tube *D* enters both the ball and the top of the cauldron, and therefore conducts the accumulating steam from the cauldron into the hollow ball, where it escapes with a roar through the small bent pipes *F* and *G*. The recoil of this escaping steam causes the ball to rotate. **III** illustrates two principles of the *toothed*, or *cog*, wheel: (1) when the teeth of two such wheels catch in each other, the wheels always rotate in opposite directions; (2) by making one wheel large and one small, power may be multiplied. The wheel *B*, which rolls on the surface of the road, has attached to its axle a peg fitting into the cogs of the wheel *C*, which is thus rotated. Its rotation is transmitted upward through the gears *D*, *E*, *F*, and *G*. On the top of the vertical shaft *G* is attached a flat disk *A*, which is perforated with a circular line of holes. Pebbles are placed in these holes, where they rest on the top of the box. As the disk *A* revolves it drags the pebbles along; and when a pebble comes over the top of the tube *H*, it falls down through the tube into the box *J*. The machine is so geared that for every mile that is traveled one pebble falls into the box *J*, where the number of pebbles indicates the distance traveled

CHAPTER XX · *The Heirs of Alexander*

SECTION 63. THE HEIRS OF ALEXANDER'S EMPIRE

749. Alexander has been well termed "the Great." Few men of genius — certainly in so brief a career — have left so indelible a mark upon the course of human affairs. By his remarkable conquests he gained for the Greeks that supremacy in *government* which, as we have seen, they had long before attained in their *civilization*. His death in the midst of his colossal designs was a fearful calamity, for it made impossible forever the unification of Hellas and of the ancient world by the power of that gifted race which was now civilizing the world. Of his line there remained in Macedonia an epileptic half brother and, ere long, Alexander II, the son of Roxana, born

Consequences of Alexander's death

NOTE. The headpiece above shows a view of modern ANTIOCH IN SYRIA. The great decisive battle among the generals of Alexander the Great at Ipsus in Phrygia in central Asia Minor (301 B.C.) made Seleucus lord of Asia (§ 753). He then founded this city of Antioch, named after his father, Antiochus. It finally became a great commercial center, a magnificent city of several hundred thousand inhabitants. Many appalling earthquakes have destroyed the ancient city, and the modern town shown above has less than thirty thousand inhabitants.

in Asia after Alexander the Great's death. Conflicts among the leaders at home swept away all these members of Alexander's family, even including his mother.

Alexander's successors; their kingdoms in Europe, Asia, and Africa

750. His generals in Babylonia found the plans for his vast Western campaign lying among his papers, but no man possessed the genius to carry them out. These able Macedonian commanders were soon involved among themselves in a long and tremendous struggle, which slumbered only to break out anew. The ablest of them was Alexander's general Antigonus, who determined to gain control of all the great Macedonian's vast empire. Then followed a generation of exhausting wars by land and sea, involving the greatest battles thus far fought by European armies. Antigonus was killed, and Alexander's empire fell into three main parts, in Europe, Asia, and Africa, with one of his generals or one of their successors at the head of each. In Europe, Macedonia was in the hands of Antigonus, grandson of Alexander's illustrious commander of the same name, who sought to maintain control of Greece; in Asia, most of the territory of the former Persian Empire was under the rule of Alexander's general Seleucus; while in Africa, Egypt was held by Ptolemy, one of the cleverest of Alexander's Macedonian leaders (see map I, p. 514).

Egyptian empire of the Ptolemies

751. In Egypt, Ptolemy gradually made himself king and became the founder of a dynasty, or family, of successive kings, whom we call the Ptolemies. Ptolemy at once saw that he would be constantly obliged to draw Greek mercenary troops from Greece. With statesmanlike judgment he therefore built up a fleet which gave him the mastery of the Mediterranean. He took up his residence at the great harbor city of Alexandria, the city which Alexander had founded in the western Nile Delta. As a result it became the foremost commercial port on the Mediterranean and the most magnificent city of the ancient world. Indeed, for nearly a century (roughly, the Third Century B.C.) the Eastern Mediterranean from Greece to Syria and from the

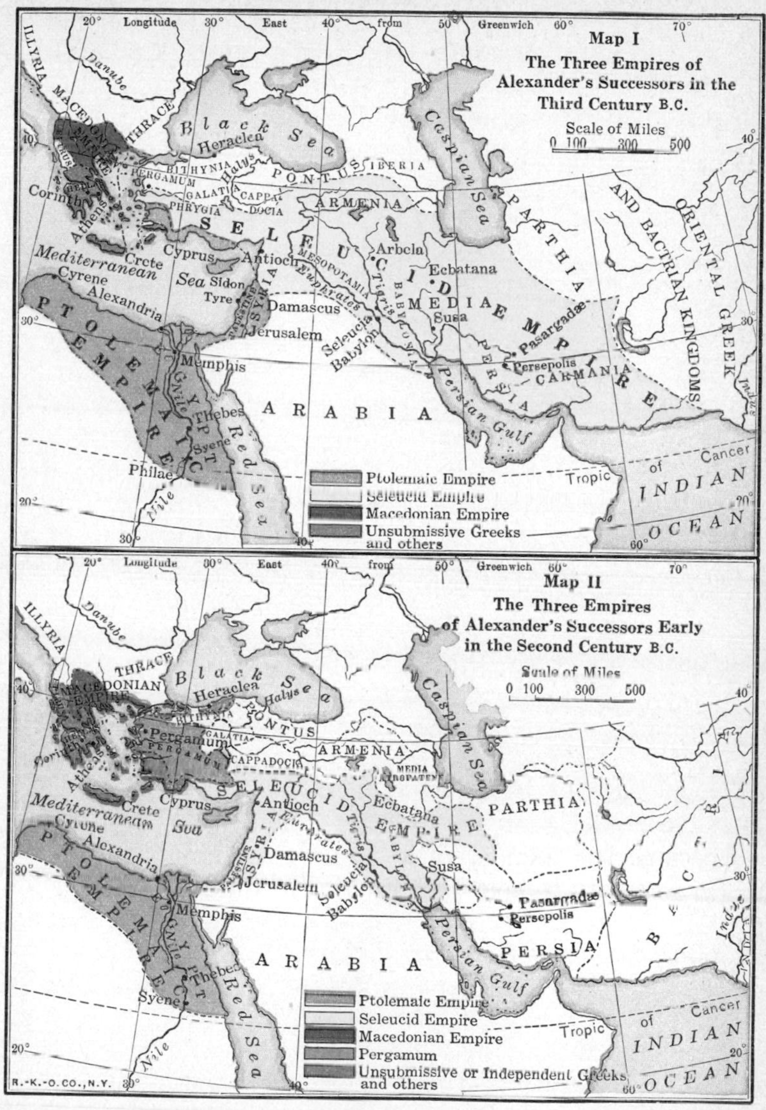

SEQUENCE MAP SHOWING THE THREE EMPIRES OF ALEXANDER'S SUCCESSORS FROM THE THIRD CENTURY B.C. TO THEIR DECLINE AT THE COMING OF THE ROMANS AFTER 200 B.C.

FIG. 202. *Airplane View of the* ISLAND *and* TEMPLES *of* PHILÆ

Much of the architecture on the island of Philæ (map, p. 66) was the work of the Ptolemies and well illustrates the prosperity of Egypt under its Macedonian kings. Until a few years ago the palm-shaded temples made the island the most beautiful spot in Egypt and one of the most beautiful in the world. Since the erection of a colossal irrigation dam below Philæ the buildings have been covered with water during a large part of each year, and as a result they are doomed to perish. (Courtesy of British Ordnance Survey Office and the editor of *Antiquity*)

Ægean to the Nile Delta was an Egyptian sea. As a barrier against their Asiatic rivals the Ptolemies also took possession of Palestine and southern Syria. Thus arose in the Eastern Mediterranean an Egyptian empire like that which we found nearly a thousand years earlier in our voyage up the Nile as we visited the great buildings of Thebes. Following the example of the Pharaohs, the Ptolemies reached out also into the Red Sea with their fleets, and from the Indian Ocean to the Hellespont, from Sicily to Syria, the Egyptian fleets dotted the seas, bringing great wealth into the treasury of the ruler (map I, p. 514).

Ancient Oriental monarchy of the Ptolemies

752. Although these new Hellenistic rulers of Egypt were Europeans, they did not set up a Greek or European form of state. They regarded themselves as the successors of the ancient Pharaohs, and like them they ruled over the kingdom of the Nile in absolute and unlimited power. To three Greek cities on the Nile, one of which was Alexandria, they granted the right to manage their own local affairs, like a city of Greece. Otherwise there were no voting *citizens* among the people of Egypt, and, just as in ancient Oriental days, they had nothing whatever to say about the government or the acts of the ruler. The chief purpose of the ruler's government was to secure from the country as large receipts for his treasury as possible, in order that he might meet the expenses of his large war fleet and his army of Greek mercenaries. Persian coins had been common in Egypt under the Persian satraps, but Egypt had never issued any coinage of her own. The first Ptolemy issued the first state coinage in Egypt, and taxes were collected both in *money* and in produce. All banks were owned by the government, and thus banking and also the sale of many staple supplies were made government monopolies. These innovations did not greatly alter the vast organization of local officials, trained to carry on the business of assessing and collecting taxes, which Egypt had been operating for thousands of years. The Greek states possessed no such organization, and the Ptolemies found it too useful to be interfered with. The tiniest group of mud huts along the river was ruled and controlled by such officials. Thus the Macedonians ruling on the Nile were continuing an ancient Oriental absolute monarchy. The example of this ancient form of state, thus preserved, was of far-reaching influence throughout the Mediterranean world and finally displaced the democracies of the Greeks and Romans.

Asiatic empire of the Seleucids

753. Although they were not as powerful as the Ptolemies, the Seleucids, as we call Seleucus and his descendants, were the chief heirs of Alexander, for they held the larger part of his empire, extending from the Ægean to the frontiers of India. Its boundaries were not fixed, and its enormous extent made it very difficult to govern and maintain. The fleet of the Ptolemies hampered the commercial development and prosperity of the Seleucids, who therefore found it difficult to reach Greece for trade, troops, or colonists. They gave special attention to the region around the northeast corner of the Mediterranean extending to the

Euphrates, and here the Seleucids endeavored to develop another Macedonia. Their empire is often called *Syria,* after this region, where Antioch, on the lower Orontes, became the commercial rival of Alexandria and the greatest seat of commerce in the northern Mediterranean.

754. In government the Seleucids adopted a very different plan from that of the Ptolemies. Seleucus was in hearty sympathy with Alexander's plan of transplanting Greeks to Asia and thus of mingling Greeks and Asiatics. He and his son Antiochus I founded scores of new Greek cities through Asia Minor, Syria, down the Two Rivers, in Persia, and far over on the borders of India. These cities were given self-government on the old Greek plan; that is, each city formed a little republic, with its local affairs controlled by its own citizens. The great Seleucid empire was thickly dotted with these little free communities.

Government of Seleucids: free cities

755. To be sure, they were under the king, and each of them paid him tribute or taxes. The form which the royal authority took was the one, so ancient in the Orient, which Alexander had already adopted. The ruler was regarded as a god to whom each community owed divine reverence and hence obedience. This homage they paid without offense to their feelings as free citizens. Greek life, with all the noble and beautiful things that it possessed, took root throughout Western Asia and was carried far into the heart of the great continent (see map I, p. 514).

Government of Seleucids: kingship

756. Compared with her two great rivals in Egypt and Asia, Macedonia in Europe seemed small indeed. The tradition of independence still cherished by the Greek states made the Macedonian leadership of the Balkan-Greek peninsula a difficult undertaking. Fighting for their liberty after Alexander's death, the Greek states had proved too weak to maintain themselves against the Macedonian army; they were forced to submit (see map I, p. 514), and the unyielding Demosthenes (§ 717),

Macedonian Empire: revolt of Greek states

whose surrender, along with that of other democratic leaders, was demanded by the Macedonians, took his own life.

Antigonus II repels Gauls and becomes king of Macedonia

757. While the second Antigonus, grandson of Alexander's general, was struggling to establish himself as lord of Macedonia and the Greeks, he was suddenly confronted by a new danger from the far north and west. From France eastward to the lower Danube, Europe was now occupied by a vast group of Indo-European barbarians whom we call Celts or Gauls. They had penetrated into Italy after 400 B.C., and a century later they were pushing far down into the Balkan Peninsula. By 280 B.C. they broke through the northern mountains, and, having devastated Macedonia, they even invaded Greece and reached the sacred oracle of the Greeks at Delphi. The barbarian torrent overflowed also into Asia Minor, where a body of the invaders settled and gave their name to a region afterward called Galatia. Antigonus II completely defeated the barbarians in Thrace and drove them out of Macedonia, of which he then became king (277 B.C.). This overwhelming flood of northern barbarians deeply impressed the Greeks, and left its mark even on the art of the age, as we shall see (§ 771).

Struggle for control of the Eastern Mediterranean

758. After the repulse of the Gauls, Antigonus II took up the problem of restoring his empire and establishing his power. The Egyptian fleet held complete command of the Ægean and thwarted him in every effort to control Greece. As Antiochus in Asia was suffering from the Egyptian fleet in the same way, the two rulers, Antigonus and Antiochus, formed an alliance against Egypt. The energetic Antigonus built a war fleet at vast expense. In a long naval war with the Ptolemies, which went on at intervals for fifteen years, Antigonus twice defeated the Egyptian fleet. As the lax descendants of the earlier Ptolemies did not rebuild the Egyptian fleet, both Macedonia and Asia profited by this freedom of the Eastern Mediterranean. But not long afterward trouble arose in Greece, which involved Macedonia in another long war there.

SECTION 64. THE DECLINE OF GREECE

Commercial decline of Greece

759. Greece was no longer commercial leader of the Mediterranean. The victories of Alexander the Great had opened the vast Persian Empire to Greek commercial colonists, who poured into all the favorable centers of trade. Not only did Greece decline in population, but commercial prosperity and the leadership in trade passed eastward, especially to Alexandria and Antioch and also to the enterprising people of Rhodes and the merchants of Ephesus. As the Greek cities lost their wealth they could no longer support fleets or mercenary armies, and they soon became too feeble to protect themselves.

Rise of leagues

760. They naturally began to combine in alliances or federations for mutual protection. Not long after 300 B.C. two such leagues were already in existence, one on each side of the Corinthian Gulf. On the south side of the gulf was the Achæan League, and on the north side that of the Ætolians. Such a league was in some ways a kind of tiny United States. The league had its general, elected each year and commanding the combined army of all the cities; it had also its other officials, who attended to all matters of defense and to all relations with foreign states outside the league. Each city, however, took care of its own local affairs, like the levying and collecting of taxes. But the two leagues were mostly hostile to each other, and while they were successful for a time in throwing off Macedonian leadership, it was too late for a general federation of all the Greek states, and a United States of the Greeks never existed.

Sparta and Athens

761. One reason for this was that Sparta and Athens refused to join these leagues. The Achæans endeavored to force Sparta into their league, but the gifted Spartan king Cleomenes defeated them in one battle after another. His victories and his reorganization of the state restored to Sparta some of her old-time vigor. The Achæans were obliged to call on Macedonia for help, and in this way Cleomenes was defeated and the Spartans were finally crushed. But the Achæan League was thereafter subject to Macedonia and never enjoyed liberty again. Henceforth the Macedonians were lords of all Greece except the Ætolian League. Meantime, while keeping out of the leagues, Athens preserved her self-government by securing recognition of her neutrality and liberty by the great powers, — first by Egypt and later by Rome. In spite of her political feebleness Athens was still the home of those high and noble things in Greek civilization of which we have already learned something, and to the further study of which we must now turn.

QUESTIONS

Section 63. Discuss the consequences of Alexander's death. Into what main divisions did Alexander's empire fall? Who ruled these divisions? What was the policy of the first Ptolemy? What kind of government did the Ptolemies establish in Egypt. Was it financially better organized than the Greek states?

What was the extent of the Seleucid Empire at first? How were the Seleucids hampered in the Mediterranean? To what region did they give special attention? What kind of government did the Seleucids establish? Were their Greek cities as free as Athens had once been? What form did the authority of the Seleucids take?

What was the first serious obstacle in the way of Macedonian leadership of the Balkan-Greek peninsula? What did Antigonus II accomplish? What was the extent of the Macedonian Empire? (See map I, p. 514.)

Section 64. What were now the leading commercial cities of the Mediterranean? In what direction had commercial leadership shifted? What did the Greeks do? Did a federation of all the Greeks arise?

BIBLIOGRAPHY FOR TOPICAL STUDIES

Geographical knowledge and expansion of trade in the Hellenistic period: BOTSFORD, *Source Book*, pp. 306–308; BURTON, *Discovery of the Ancient World*, pp. 48–61; BURY, in *The Hellenistic Age*, pp. 15–23; TARN, *Hellenistic Civilization*, pp. 140–141, 193–214, 235–236, 246–249.

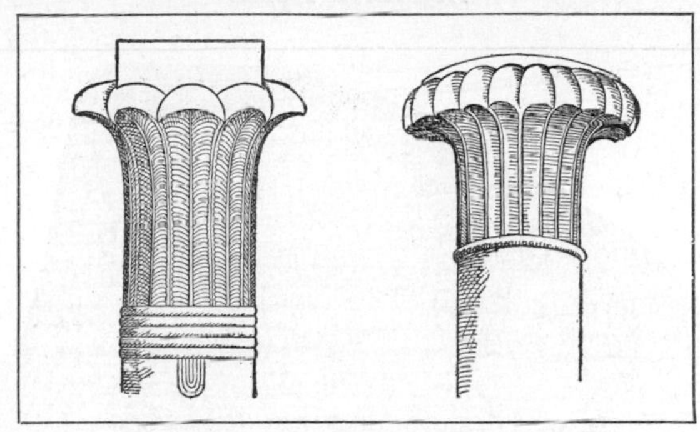

Chapter XXI · *The Civilization of the Hellenistic Age*

Section 65. Cities, Architecture, and Art

Hellenistic Age: supremacy of Greek language

762. The three centuries following the death of Alexander we call the Hellenistic Age, meaning the period in which Greek civilization spread throughout the ancient world, especially the Orient, and was itself much modified by the culture of the Orient. Alexander's conquests placed Asia and Egypt in the hands of Macedonian rulers who were in civilization essentially Greek. Their language was in the main the Greek spoken in Attica. The Orientals found the affairs of government carried on in the Greek language; they transacted business with multitudes of Greek merchants; they found many Greek books, attracting them to read. Attic Greek became the tongue of which every man of education must be master. Thus the strong Jewish community living at Alexandria now found it necessary to translate the books of the Old Testament from Hebrew into Greek, in order that their educated men might read them. While the country people of the East might learn it imperfectly, Attic Greek

Note. The above headpiece shows us the old Egyptian Palm-Tree Capital (on the left) and (on the right) the modification of it as used by the Hellenistic architects at Pergamum. Such an example makes it clear that the idea of taking decorative architectural forms from the vegetable world was acquired by the Greeks from abroad.

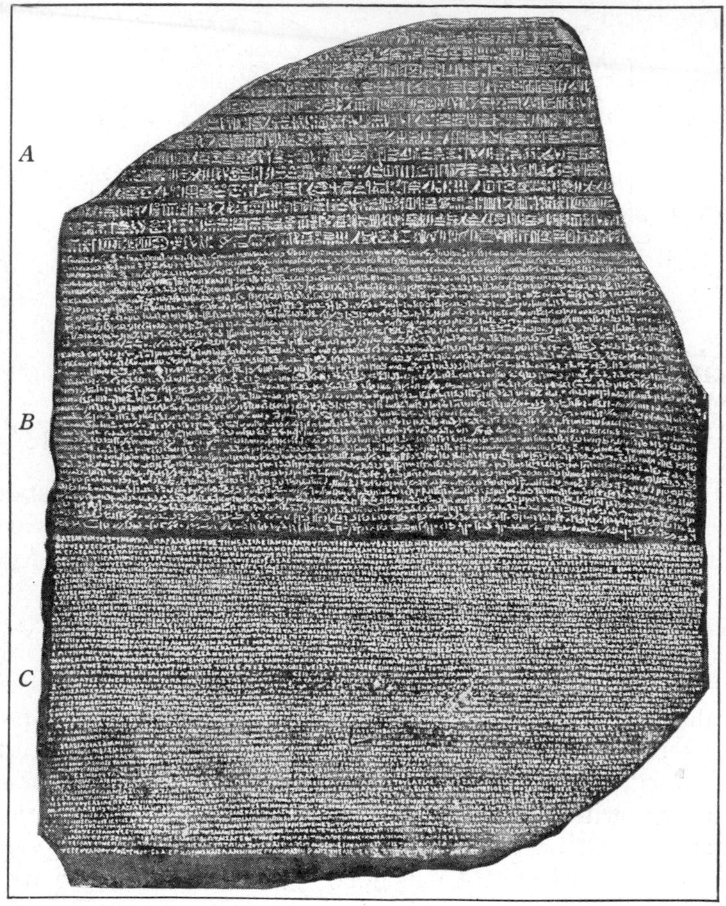

Fig. 203. *The* Rosetta Stone, *bearing the Same Inscription in Greek* (C) *and Egyptian* (A *and* B)*

became, nevertheless, the daily language of the great cities and of an enormous world stretching from Sicily (Fig. 252) and southern Italy eastward on both sides of the Mediterranean and thence far into the Orient.

763. Civilized life in the cities was attended with more comfort and better equipment than ever before. The citizen's house, if he were in easy circumstances, might be built of stone masonry. The old central court was now often surrounded on all four sides by a pleasing colonnaded porch (Fig. 204). Most of the rooms were still small and bare, but the large living room, lighted from the court, might be floored with a bright mosaic pavement, while the walls were plastered and adorned with decorative paintings, or even veneered with marble if the owner's wealth permitted. The furniture was more elaborate and artistic; there might be carpets and hangings; and the house now for the first time possessed its own water supply. The streets also were equipped with drainage channels or pipes, a thing unknown in the days of Pericles.

Improved houses and increased luxury

764. The daily life of the time has been revealed to us, as it went on in Egypt, in a vast quantity of surviving household documents. Among the common people ordinary receipts and other business memoranda were scribbled with ink on bits of broken pottery (Fig. 205), which cost nothing. For more important documents, however, a piece of papyrus paper

---

* This famous INSCRIPTION is in TWO LANGUAGES. It was written in Greek because the language of the government was Greek and also because there were so many Greek-speaking people in Egypt. At the same time, as a public record, it was necessary that it should be read by Egyptians who knew no Greek, just as in some New England factory towns notices are now put up in both English and Italian. The document was therefore first written out with pen and ink, just as we should do it, in the ordinary Egyptian handwriting (demotic). This demotic copy was then cut on the stone, where it occupies the middle (*B*). The priests also wrote out the document in the ancient sacred hieroglyphs, and they put this hieroglyphic form in the place of honor at the top of the stone (*A*), where the two corners have since been broken off and lost. Both of these two forms, then, are Egyptian,— the upper (*A*) corresponding to our print, the lower (*B*) corresponding to our handwriting. The Greek translation of the Egyptian is at the bottom (*C*). The stone was intended as a public record of certain honors which the Egyptian priests were extending to the Greek king, one of the Ptolemies, in 195 B.C. The stone had fallen down and been buried in rubbish for many centuries when the soldiers of Napoleon accidentally found it while digging trenches near the Rosetta mouth of the Nile in 1799. Hence it is called the Rosetta Stone. It was afterward captured by the British and is now in the British Museum. After Champollion had learned the signs in the names of Cleopatra, Ptolemy, and some others, he was finally able to read also the hieroglyphic form of this Rosetta document (*A*), because the Greek translation told him what the hieroglyphic form meant. It was in this way that the Rosetta Stone became the key by which Egyptian hieroglyphic was deciphered. The stone is a slab of black basalt 2 feet $4\frac{1}{2}$ inches wide and 3 feet 9 inches high.

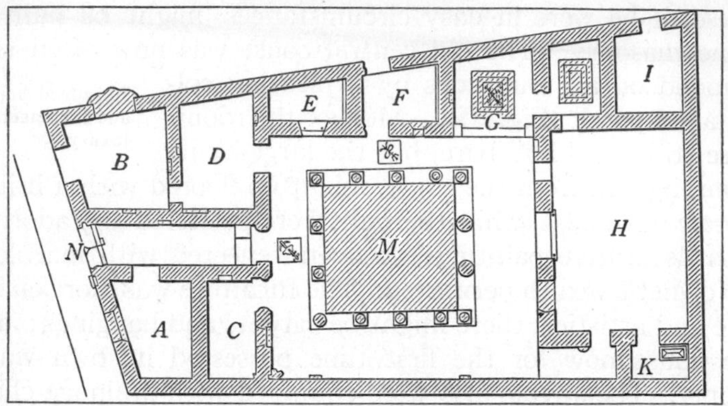

Fig. 204. *Plan of a* House *of a* Wealthy Greek *in the* Hellenistic Age

The rooms are arranged around a central court (*M*) which is open to the sky. A roofed porch with columns (called a peristyle) surrounds the court (cf. Fig. 55). The main entrance is at *N*, with the room of the doorkeeper on the right (*A*). At the corner is a shop (*B*). *C*, *D*, and *E* are for storage and housekeeping. *F* is a back-door entry through which supplies were delivered; it contained a stairway to the second floor. *G* was used as a small living room. It had a built-in divan, and the entire side toward the peristyle was open. The finest room in the house was *H*, measuring about 16 by 26 feet, with a mosaic floor, in seven colors, and richly decorated walls. It was lighted by a large door and two windows. *K* was a little sleeping room, with a large marble bathtub; otherwise the sleeping rooms were all on the second floor, which cannot now be reconstructed. *I* was a second tiny shop. This house was excavated by the French on the island of Delos

Household and business papers preserved in Egypt

was used. Such papers accumulated in the house, just as do our own old letters and papers. In the rainless climate of Egypt they have survived in great numbers in the rubbish heaps now covering the remains of the houses of this age. We can read a father's or a mother's invitation to the wedding of a daughter; the letter of a father to a worthy son absent at school; the repentant confessions of a wayward son who has run away from home; the assurances of sympathy from a friend when a family has lost a son, a father, a mother, or a brother. Indeed, these documents disclose to us the daily intercourse between friends and relatives, just as such matters are revealed by letters which pass between ourselves at the present day. Such word-pictures, penned (with no thought of future readers) by long-vanished fingers, make the distant life of this far-off age seem surprisingly near and real (Fig. 248).

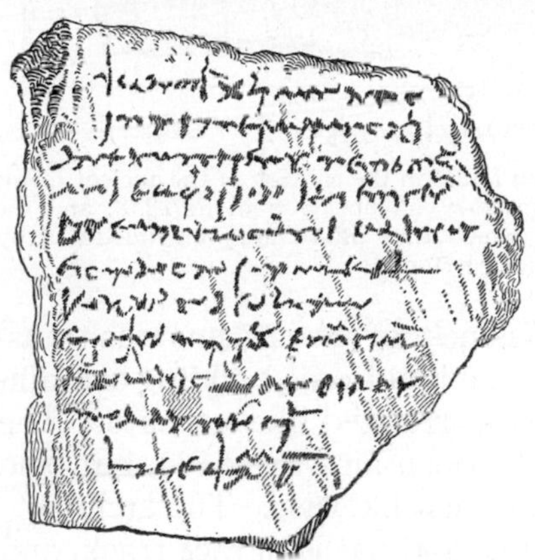

Fig. 205. Potsherd Document *from the Ruins of an Egyptian Town*

Thousands of personal documents of the Hellenistic Age have survived in Egypt. This specimen records a receipt for land rent and closes thus: "Eumelos, the son of Hermulos, being asked to do so, wrote for him, because he himself writes too slowly." The giver of the receipt probably could not write at all, and, to avoid this humiliating confession, says that he writes "too slowly." The hand which Eumelos wrote for him is the rapid-running business hand written by the Greeks of this age, very different from the capital letters which the Greek pottery painters made five centuries earlier (headpiece, p. 342). A modern college student, even though very familiar with printed Greek, would be unable to read it

Equipment of Hellenistic cities; secular public buildings

765. The numerous new cities which this great Hellenistic Age brought forth were laid out on a very systematic plan, with the streets at right angles and the buildings in rectangular blocks (Fig. 207). At Pergamum excavation has uncovered as many as eleven metal water pipes side by side, crossing a street under the pavement. But there never was any system of public street-lighting in the ancient world. In the public buildings also a great change had taken place. In Pericles' time the great state buildings were the temples, but now the architects of the Hellenistic Age began to design large and splendid buildings to house the offices of the government.

Public buildings of a Hellenistic city

766. These fine public buildings occupied the center of the city, where in early Greek and Oriental cities the castle of the king had once stood. Close by was the spacious market square, surrounded by long colonnades; for the Greeks were now making large use of this airy and beautiful form of architecture contributed by

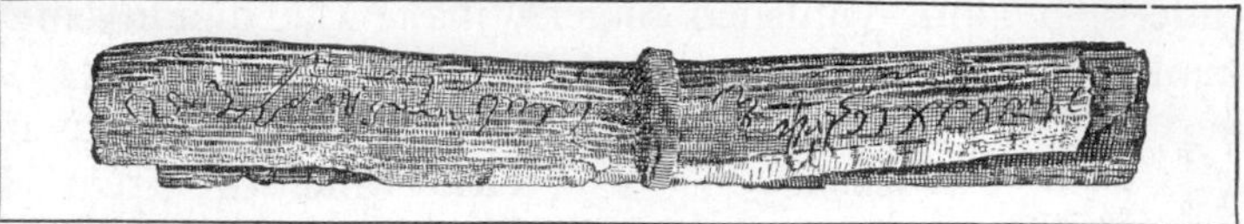

FIG. 206. A PAPYRUS LETTER *rolled up and sealed for Delivery*

Large numbers of such letters have been found in the rubbish of the ancient towns of Egypt. Their appearance when unrolled may be seen in Fig. 248, and the remarkable glimpses into ancient life which they afford are well illustrated by the same letter

Egypt. Here much private business of the citizens was transacted. There was, furthermore, a handsome building containing an audience room with seats arranged like a theater. The Assembly no longer met in the open air (Fig. 175), but held its sessions here, as did the Council likewise. The architects had also to provide gymnasiums and baths, a race track, and a theater. Even a small city of only four thousand people, like Priene in Asia Minor, possessed all these buildings, besides several temples, one of which was erected by Alexander himself. It is very instructive to compare such a little Hellenistic city as Priene with a modern town of four thousand

---

* This little city, when excavated, proved to be almost a second Pompeii, only older. Above *A*, on the top of the cliff, was the citadel with a path leading up to it (*B*). *C* shows the masonry flume which brought the mountain water down into the town. Entering the town, one passed through the gate at *K* and up a straight street to the little provision-market square (*L*). Just above the market was the temple of Athena (*I*), built by Alexander himself. Then one entered the spacious business market (*agora*; *M*), surrounded by fine colonnades with shops behind them, except on one side (under *N*), where there was a stately hall for business and festive occasions, like the basilica halls which were coming in at this time among the Greeks (Fig. 266, 4). Beyond (at *N*) were the offices of the city government, the hall in which the Council and Assembly met, and the theater (*E*). At *G* was the temple of Isis (§ 690), and in the foreground were the gymnasium (*P*) and the stadium (*Q*). The wash-room here still contains the marble basins and the lion-headed spouts from which the water flowed. An attached open hall was used for school instruction and lectures. Above the seats of the stadium (*Q*) was a beautiful colonnade 600 feet long, for pleasure-strolling between the athletic events, to enjoy the grand view of the sea upon which the audience looked down. The houses fronting directly on the street were mostly like the one in Fig. 204, but the finer ones in the region of the theater (*E*) and the temple of Athena (*I*) were of well-joined stone masonry and had no shops in front. Around the whole city was a strong wall of masonry, with a gate at the east (*H*) and at the west (*K*), while along the street outside these gates were the tombs of the ancestors, as at Athens (headpiece, p. 489).

Fig. 207. Restoration of the Hellenistic City of Priene in Asia Minor. (After a Drawing by A. Zippelius) *

inhabitants in America. Our modern houses are much more roomy and comfortable; but our ordinary public buildings, like our courthouses and town halls, make but a poor showing as compared with those of little Priene over two thousand years ago.

Clerestory and arch introduced from Near East

767. On one side of the market there opened a building called a *basilica*, lighted by roof windows, forming a clerestory, which the Hellenistic architects had seen in Egypt. At the same time they had become acquainted with the arch in Asia Minor, whither it had passed from the Fertile Crescent, and they now began occasionally to introduce arches into their buildings. Thus the Near East, which had contributed the colonnade to Greek architecture, now furnished two more great forms, the clerestory and the arch, although the arch was never extensively used by the Greeks.

Alexandria: its commerce and great lighthouse

768. If a little provincial Greek city like Priene possessed such splendid public buildings, an imperial capital and vast commercial city like Alexandria was correspondingly more magnificent. In numbers, wealth, commerce, power, and all the arts of civilization it was now the greatest city of the whole ancient world. Along the harbors stretched extensive docks, where ships which had braved the Atlantic storms along the coasts of Spain and Africa moored beside Oriental craft which had penetrated the gates of the Indian Ocean and gathered the wares of the vast Oriental world beyond. Side by side on these docks lay bars of tin from the British Isles with bolts of silk from China and rolls of cotton goods from India. The growing commerce of the city even required the establishment of government banks. From far across the sea the mariners approaching at night could catch the gleaming of a lofty beacon shining from a gigantic lighthouse tower which marked the entrance of the harbor of Alexandria. This wonderful tower, the tallest building ever erected by a Hellenistic engineer, was a descendant of the old Babylonian tower-temple, to which it was closely related.

769. From the deck of a great merchant ship with a carrying capacity of over four thousand tons the incoming traveler might look cityward beyond the lighthouse and behold the great war fleet of the Ptolemies outlined against the green masses of the magnificent royal gardens. Here, embowered in rich tropical verdure, rose the marble residence of the Ptolemies, occupying a point of land which extended out into the sea and formed the east side of the harbor (see map, p. 498). From the royal parks of the Persian kings and from the villa gardens of the Egyptians the Hellenistic rulers and their architects had learned to appreciate the beauty of parks

Palace park of Ptolemies; Oriental origin of such parks

FIG. 208. *The* LIGHTHOUSE *of the Harbor of* ALEXANDRIA *in the Hellenistic Age*

The harbor of Alexandria (see corner map, p. 498) was protected by an island called Pharos, which was connected with the city by a long causeway of stone. On the island, and bearing its name (Pharos), was built (after 300 B.C.) a lofty stone lighthouse some 445 feet high (that is, over thirty-six stories, like those of a modern skyscraper). It shows how vast was the commerce and wealth of Alexandria only a generation after it was founded by Alexander the Great, when it became the New York or Liverpool of the ancient world, the greatest port on the Mediterranean. The Pharos tower, the first of its kind, was influenced in design by Oriental architecture, and in its turn it furnished the model for the earliest church spires and also for the minarets of the Mohammedan mosques. It stood for about sixteen hundred years, the greatest lighthouse in the world, and did not fall until A.D. 1326. This reconstruction was made by G. G. Woodward from geometrical drawings prepared by Don Modesto Lopez Otero, based on measurements given in a newly discovered mediæval Arabic manuscript. (Courtesy of the Duke of Alba and the *Illustrated London News*)

FIG. 209. GARDEN PAVILION *erected as a* BANQUET HALL *by King Ptolemy II*

The banquet hall itself, which we see in the middle, was over ninety-one feet high, and its roof was supported on gold-covered columns about eighty-six feet high. The rectangular opening in the roof was covered by a magnificent scarlet awning with a white border. Two golden eagles twenty-five feet high surmounted the front of the roof. Around the outside of the surrounding lower gallery were hung scarlet curtains adorned with animal skins. Within the banquet hall, around its three closed sides, were ranged a hundred couches of gold, spread with purple covers and draped with Persian embroideries which hung down between golden sphinxes forming the legs at the corners. Each couch accommodated at least two guests, for whom there were placed individual golden tripod tables with silver bases, while behind the couches were silver basins and pitchers for cleansing the hands. It is important to notice that the Hellenistic architect, working in Egypt, adopted the old Egyptian arrangement of a high roof in the middle and a lower roof on each side, that is, a *clerestory*, affording space for light or windows between the different levels of the two roofs. This building was the link between the temple clerestory of Egypt and the basilica roof of the European cathedrals. Erected as a purely temporary outdoor banquet hall by Ptolemy II, the enormously wealthy son of Alexander the Great's body-guardsman Ptolemy I, the building of course perished long ago, and only a *written* description has made possible the above reconstruction, the work of Franz Studniczka

and gardens artistically laid out and adorned with tropical trees, lakes, fountains, and sculptured monuments. Thus the art of landscape gardening, combined with systematic city planning (an art long familiar to the architects of the Near East), was also being cultivated by Europeans.

FIG. 210. RESTORATION *of the Public Buildings of* PERGAMUM

Pergamum, on the west coast of Asia Minor (see map II, p. 514), became a flourishing city-kingdom in the Third Century B.C. under the successors of Alexander the Great. The dwellings of the citizens were all lower down, in front of the group of buildings shown here. These public buildings stand on three terraces,—lower, middle, and upper. The large *lower* terrace (*A*) was the main market place, adorned with a vast square marble altar of Zeus, having colonnades on three sides, beneath which was a long sculptured band (frieze) of warring gods and giants, which was discovered by excavation and has now been set up in the museum at Berlin (Fig. 212). On the *middle* terrace (*B*), behind the colonnades, was the famous library of Pergamum, where the stone bases of library shelves still survive. The *upper* terrace (*C*) once contained the palace of the king; the temple now standing was built by the Roman emperor Trajan in the Second Century A.D. (After Thiersch)

Public buildings of Alexandria

770. At the other end of the park from the palace were grouped the marble buildings of the Royal Museum, with its great library, lecture halls, exhibition rooms, courts and porticoes, and living rooms for the philosophers and men of science who resided in the institution. In the vicinity was the vast temple of Serapis, the new state god, and nearer the heart of the city were the magnificent public buildings, such as gymnasiums, baths, stadiums, assembly hall, concert hall, market places, and basilicas, all surrounded by the residence quarters of the citizens. Unfortunately not one of these splendid buildings still stands. Even the scanty ruins which survive cannot be recovered,

Fig. 211. A Gallic Chieftain *in Defeat slaying his Wife and Himself*

With one hand he supports his dying wife, and, casting a terrible glance at the pursuing enemy, he plunges his sword into his own breast. The tremendous power of the barbarian's muscular figure is in startling contrast with the helpless limbs of the woman. The beholder feels both terror at the wild impetuosity of the northern barbarian and at the same time involuntary sympathy with his unconquerable courage, which prefers death for himself and his loved one to shameful captivity among the victors

FIG. 212. SCULPTURE *from Hellenistic Pergamum*

Part of the frieze around the altar of Zeus at Pergamum. It pictures the mythical struggle between gods and giants. A giant at the left, whose limbs end in serpents, raises over his head a great stone to hurl it at the goddess on the right

since in most cases the present city of Alexandria overlies them, and its modern buildings are too valuable to disturb.

771. We are more fortunate in the case of Pergamum (map II, p. 514), another splendid city of this age which grew up under Athenian influences. One of the kings of Pergamum defeated and beat off the hordes of Gauls coming in from Europe (§ 757). This achievement greatly affected the art which Attic sculptors, supported by the kings of Pergamum, were creating there. They wrought heroic marble figures of the northern barbarians in the tragic moment of death in battle, with a dramatic power which has never been surpassed (Fig. 211), and the tremendous struggle between gods and giants surrounding the Pergamum altar is the most impressive monument of sculpture produced by ancient Europeans.

Pergamum and its wonderful sculpture

Fig. 213. *The* Death *of* Laocoön *and his* Two Sons

This famous group was wrought some time in the First Century B.C. by Agesander of Rhodes and two other sculptors, perhaps his sons. It shows the priest Laocoön sinking down upon the altar at which he had been ministering, in a last agonizing struggle with the deadly serpents which enfold him and his two sons. It is one of the most marvelous representations of human suffering ever created by art, but it does not move us with such sympathy as the death of the Gallic chieftain (Fig. 211). We should place these works (Figs. 211–213), the sarcophagus reliefs of Alexander (Plate IV), and the mosaic picture of the battle of Issus (Fig. 198) among the supreme creations of ancient art

From an etching by George T. Plowman

FIG. 214. *Greek* TEMPLES *at* PÆSTUM *in Southern Italy*

Pæstum (Greek *Poseidonia*), one of the early Greek colonies in the vicinity of Naples, possesses today the ruins of three Greek temples. The temple of Neptune (Poseidon), the finest of the group, is the best-preserved Greek temple outside of Attica. Built toward the end of the Sixth Century, and perhaps as late as 500 B.C., it is one of the noblest examples of archaic Greek architecture

Athenian art in the Alexander sarcophagus; Rhodian art in the Laocoön

772. It was the works of the Athenian sculptors at Pergamum which especially inspired compositions of tragic and overwhelming power, of violent and thrilling action. Some of these Athenian works have survived. They are best illustrated by the reliefs on a wonderful marble sarcophagus, showing Alexander the Great winning the battle of Issus, and again engaged in a lion hunt (Plate IV). This sculpture of vigorous action in supremely tragic moments was also very beautifully developed by a group of eminent sculptors on the island of Rhodes, which was a prosperous republic in the Hellenistic Age (§ 759). Most of their works have perished, but those which have survived are among the most famous works of sculpture from the ancient world. Particularly important is the group representing the death of the Trojan priest Laocoön and his two sons.

773. The great Greek paintings of this age show the same tendencies as does the sculpture. The painters loved to depict

Painting and mosaic

dramatic and tragic incidents at the supreme moment. Their original works have all perished, but copies of some of them have survived, painted on the walls as interior decorations of fine houses or wrought in mosaic as floor pavement. It is the art of mosaic which has preserved to us the wonderful painting of Alexander charging on the Persian king at Issus, by an unknown Alexandrian painter of the Hellenistic Age.

FIG. 215. HELLENISTIC *Portrait* HEAD *in Bronze*

This magnificent head of an unknown man, with wonderful representation of the hair, was recovered from the bottom of the sea. The eyes are inlaid as in the old Egyptian bronze head (Fig. 52). It is now in the Museum of Athens

774. Both the sculptors and the painters of this age made

Portraiture

wonderful progress in portraiture, and their surviving works now begin to furnish us a continuous stream of portraits, which show us how the great men of the age really looked. Unfortunately these portraits are all works of the *sculptors* in stone or metal, either as statues and busts or as reliefs, especially on medallions and coins; the portraits executed by the *painters* in colors on wooden tablets have all perished. Alexander's favorite painter was Apelles. In one of his portraits of Alexander the horse which the king was riding was said to have been painted with such lifelikeness that on a certain occasion a passing horse trotted up to the painting and whinnied. Later examples of this art of portrait painting have survived, attached to mummies in Egypt.

Section 66. Inventions and Science; Libraries and Literature

775. The keen and wide-awake intelligence of this wonderful age was everywhere apparent, but especially in the application of science to the work and needs of daily life. It was an age of inventions, like our own. An up-to-date man would install an automatic door-opener for the doorkeeper of his house, and a washing machine which delivered water and mineral soap as needed. On his estate olive oil was produced by a press operating with *screw* pressure, for it was at this time that the screw as a mechanical device was invented. Outside the temples the priests set up automatic dispensers of holy water, while a water sprinkler operated by water pressure reduced the danger of fire. The application of levers, cranks, screws, and cogwheels to daily work brought forth cable roads for use in lowering stone from lofty quarries, and water wheels for drawing water on a large scale. A similar endless-chain apparatus was used for quickly raising heavy stone missiles to be discharged from huge missile-hurling war machines, some of which even operated by air pressure. As we go to see the "movies," so the people crowded to the market place to view the marionettes in the automatic theater, in which a clever mechanician presented an old Greek tragedy of the Trojan War in five scenes, displaying shipbuilding, the launch of the fleet, the voyage, with the dolphins playing in the water about the vessels, and finally a storm at sea, with thunder and lightning, amid which the Greek heroes promptly went to the bottom. Housekeepers told stories of the simpler days of their grandmothers, when there was no running water in the house and they had to go out and fetch it a long way from the nearest spring.

Mechanical progress and practical inventions

776. A public clock, either a shadow clock or a water clock, both of them inventions which the Egyptian had had in his garden for over a thousand years, stood in the market place and furnished all the good townspeople with the hour of the day. The Ptolemies or the priests under them attempted to improve the calendar by the insertion, every fourth year, of a leap year with an additional day; but the people could not be roused out of the rut into which usage had fallen, and everywhere they continued to use the inconvenient moon month of the Greeks. There was no system for the numbering of the years anywhere except in Syria, where the Seleucids gave each year a number reckoned from the beginning of their sway.

Time and calendar

FIG. 216. *The* TOWN CLOCK *of Athens in the Hellenistic Age*

This tower, commonly called the Tower of the Winds, now stands among modern houses, but once looked out on the Athenian market place. The arches at the left support part of an ancient channel which supplied the water for the operation of a water clock in the tower. Such clocks were more or less like hourglasses, the flowing water filling a given measure in a given time, like the sand in the hourglass. This tower was built in the last century B.C., when Athens was under the control of Rome

Archimedes

777. The most remarkable man of science of the time was probably Archimedes. He lived in Syracuse, and one of his famous feats was the arrangement of a series of pulleys and levers which so multiplied power that the king was able, by turning a light crank, to move a large three-masted ship standing fully loaded on the dock, and to launch it into the water. After witnessing such feats as this the people easily believed his proud boast, "Give me a place to stand on and I will move the earth." He devised such powerful and dangerous war machines that he greatly aided in defending his native city from capture by the Romans (§ 908). But Archimedes was far more than an inventor of practical appliances. He was a scientific investigator of the first rank. He was able to prove to the king that one of the monarch's gold crowns was not of pure metal, because he had discovered the principle of determining the proportion of loss of weight when an object is immersed in water. He was thus the discoverer of what science now calls specific gravity. Besides his skill in physics he was also the greatest of ancient mathematicians.

Alexandrian scientists

778. Archimedes was in close correspondence with his friends in Alexandria, who formed the greatest body of scientists in the ancient world. They lived together at the Museum, where they were paid salaries and supported by the Ptolemies. With the exception of the Egyptian hospital, or medical school, endowed by Darius, this organization was the first scientific institution (as yet known to us) founded and supported by a government. Without financial anxieties, the Alexandrian scholars could devote themselves to research, for which the halls, laboratories, and library of the institution were equipped. Thus the scientists of the Hellenistic Age, especially this remarkable group at Alexandria, became the founders of systematic scientific research, and their books formed the sum, or body, of scientific knowledge for nearly two thousand years, until the revival of science in modern times.

Mathematics: Euclid and Archimedes

779. The very first generation of scientists at the Alexandrian Museum boasted a great name in mathematics which is still famous among us, — that of Euclid. His complete system of geometry was so logically built up that in modern England Euclid's geometry is still used as a schoolbook, — the oldest schoolbook in use today. Archimedes then for the first time developed what is now called higher mathematics, — certain difficult and advanced mathematical processes the knowledge of which, having in the meantime been lost, had to be rediscovered in modern times.

780. Along with mathematics much progress was also made in astronomy. The Ptolemies built an astronomical observatory at Alexandria, and although it was without telescopes, important observations and discoveries were made. The greatest of the Alexandrian astronomers was Hipparchus.

Astronomy: Hipparchus and Aristarchus

He introduced among the Greek astronomers, and more fully demonstrated, the important fact that the oblique axis of the spinning earth is slowly swinging about like the leaning axis of a wabbling top, — a fact already known to the Chaldean astronomers (§ 277). In the course of his investigations of this fact Hipparchus made a catalogue of nearly eleven hundred stars. He brought to bear on astronomy his unrivaled knowledge of geometry, and especially of trigonometry, a science which he was the first to develop. Believing that the earth is a sphere poised in space, Hipparchus for the first time placed astronomy on a sound scientific basis, in which there was only one important error: he did not accept the conclusion of Aristarchus, an Alexandrian astronomer of little fame who had made one of the greatest discoveries of this age in that he showed that the earth and the planets revolve around the *sun*. Hipparchus made the *earth* the center of his system, about which, he taught, the sun revolved. As a result, for eighteen hundred years all scientists wrongly held that the earth was the center of our universe.

781. At Alexandria astronomy was of great assistance in the study of geography and the problem of the size of the earth.

Astronomy and geography: Eratosthenes computes size of earth

Someone told Eratosthenes, a great mathematical astronomer of Alexandria, that on the longest day of the year (that is, the day when the summer sun, shifting steadily northward, reached its northernmost point) the sunlight shone straight down to the bottom of a well at the First Cataract of the Nile. Eratosthenes saw at once that this fact would enable him to calculate the size of the earth. His calculations gave him about seven thousand eight hundred and fifty miles as the diameter of our earth, — a result surprisingly near correctness.

782. To this notion of the size of the earth much information had been added regarding the extent and character

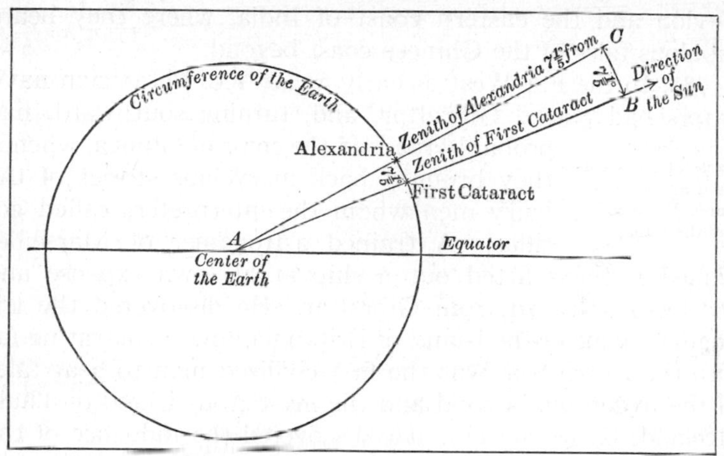

FIG. 217. *Diagram roughly indicating how the* SIZE *of the* EARTH *was first* CALCULATED

The sun standing at noon directly over the First Cataract (line AB) was of course visible also at Alexandria. The result was just the same as if someone had stood at the First Cataract holding vertically upright a surveyor's pole tall enough to be seen from Alexandria. To Eratosthenes at Alexandria the sun was like the top of the pole. With his instruments set up at Alexandria, therefore, Eratosthenes found that the sun over the First Cataract (line AB) was $7\frac{1}{5}$ degrees south of the zenith of his instrument at Alexandria (line AC). The lines AB and AC diverge $7\frac{1}{5}$ degrees at all points, whether in the skies or on earth. Hence Eratosthenes knew that the First Cataract was $7\frac{1}{5}$ degrees of the earth's circumference from Alexandria; that is, the distance between Alexandria and the First Cataract was $7\frac{1}{5}$ degrees of the earth's circumference, or one fiftieth of its total circumference of 360 degrees. Eratosthenes assumed that Alexandria and the First Cataract were on the same meridian, and the actual distance along this meridian between Alexandria and the First Cataract was supposed to be a little less than 500 miles. This distance (– 500 miles), then, was one fiftieth of the earth's circumference, giving a few hundred less than 25,000 miles for the total circumference of the earth, and for its diameter about 7850 miles, which is within 50 miles of being correct

of the inhabited regions reached by navigation and exploration in this age. At home in Greece one geographer undertook to measure the heights of the mountains, though he was without a barometer. The campaigns of Alexander in the Far East had greatly extended the limits where the known world ended. Bold Alexandrian merchants had sailed to India and around its southern tip to

Explorations eastward

Ceylon and the eastern coast of India, where they heard fabulous tales of the Chinese coast beyond.

Explorations westward and northward; Pytheas and the tides

783. In the Far West as early as 500 B.C. Phœnician navigators had passed Gibraltar, and, turning southward, had probably reached the coast of Guinea, whence they brought back marvelous stories of the hairy men whom the interpreters called gorillas. A trained astronomer of Marseilles named Pytheas fitted out a ship at his own expense and coasted northward from Gibraltar. He discovered the triangular shape of the island of Britannia, and, penetrating far into the North Sea, was the first civilized man to hear tales of the frozen sea beyond and the mysterious island of Thule (Iceland) on its margin. He discovered the influence of the full moon on the immense spring tides, and he brought back reports of such surprising things that he was generally regarded as a sensational fable-monger.

Eratosthenes makes the first map with latitude and longitude

784. With a greater mass of facts and reports than anyone before him had ever had, Eratosthenes was able to write a very full geography. His map of the known world (p. 544), including Europe, Asia, and Africa, showed the regions grouped about the Mediterranean with fair correctness, and he was the first geographer who was able to lay out on his map a cross-net of lines indicating latitude and longitude. He thus became the founder of scientific geography.

Botany, zoölogy, anatomy, and medicine

785. In the study of animal and vegetable life Aristotle and his pupils remained the leaders, and the ancient world never outgrew their observations. While their knowledge of botany, acquired without a microscope, was of course limited and contained errors, a large mass of new facts was observed and arranged. In anatomy and medicine the Alexandrians inherited some older Oriental knowledge, just as they had done in astronomy. The Egyptian medical school, endowed two hundred years earlier by Darius the Great, was hardly more than fifty miles distant from Alexandria. The important discoveries which the Alexandrian scientists now made regarding the human brain and the nervous system were without doubt based to no small extent on the knowledge possessed by the earlier Egyptian surgeons. The Ptolemies furnished the Alexandrian scientists with condemned criminals upon whom vivisection was practiced, and the medical men of this Alexandrian laboratory were the first Greeks to undertake the systematic dissection of the human body. In carrying on this dissection they knew that the control of the limbs had its source in the brain, as shown by the old Egyptian surgeons. The Greeks now discovered the nerves and showed that the lines of connection between the whole body and the brain were the nerves. Thus, Herophilus, the greatest of these anatomical Alexandrians, discovered the optic nerve and traced it from the eye to the brain. In this way the brain was shown to be the center of a great system of sensation and of control which we call the nervous system. Although such research came very near to discovering the circulation of the blood, the arteries were still misunderstood to be channels for the circulation of air from the lungs. Alexandria became the greatest center of medical research in the ancient world, and here young men went through long studies to train themselves as physicians, just as they do at the present day.

Earliest state libraries of the Greeks; Alexandrian library

786. Notwithstanding the popularity of the natural sciences there was now also much study of language and of the great mass of older literature. Although the Ancient Near East had long before known royal libraries (§ 263), the first library founded and supported by a Greek government had been formed by the city of Heracleia, on the Black Sea, during the childhood of Alexander the Great (not long before 350 B.C.). Later the kings of Pergamum also founded a very notable library. These efforts were far surpassed by the Ptolemies at Alexandria. They built a library for the Museum (§ 770), where Ptolemy II had over half a million rolls. It finally contained some 700,000 volumes. The art of cataloguing and managing such a great collection of books was

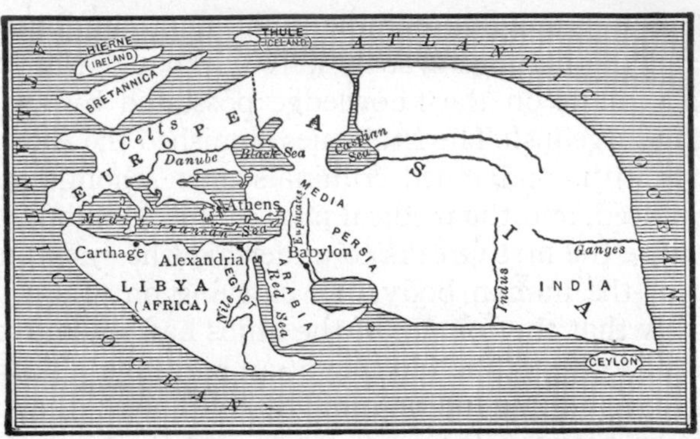

Map of the World *according to* Eratosthenes (200 B.C.)

a new one. A system had to be devised and then put into effect. The work was intrusted by the Ptolemies to a group of learned men directed by a chief librarian. The first chief librarian was Zenodotus of Ephesus. But the actual catalogue was made by the philosopher and poet Callimachus. He listed all the known books of value, both by titles and by authors, and this first great book catalogue filled one hundred and twenty books or sections.

Alexandrian library produces accurate editions: hand copies

787. The immense amount of hand copying required to secure good and accurate editions of famous works for this library gradually created the new science of correct publishing. The copies produced by the librarians and scholars of Alexandria became the standard editions on which other ancient libraries and copyists depended. The Hellenistic world was everywhere supplied with Alexandrian editions, and from these are descended most of the manuscripts now preserved in the libraries of Europe, from which, in turn, have been copied our printed editions of Homer, Xenophon, and other great Greek authors. Unfortunately the library of Alexandria perished, and the earliest example of a Greek book which has survived to us is a roll found in an Egyptian tomb by modern excavators only a few years ago (Fig. 218).

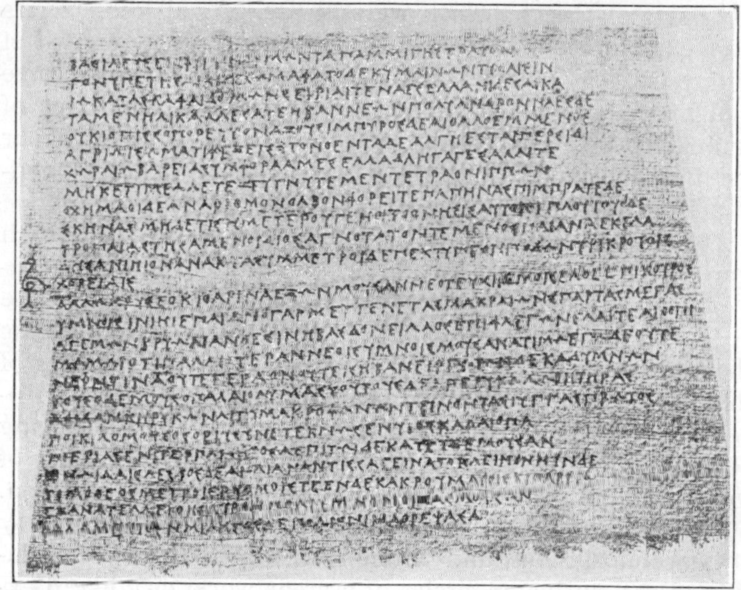

FIG. 218. A PAGE *from the Earliest Surviving* GREEK BOOK

This book contains a poem called *The Persians*, by the Greek poet Timotheos, whose name may be seen in the third line from the bottom, at the beginning of the line. The poem tells the story of the battle of Salamis. Timotheos died 357 B.C., but this copy of the work was written in the lifetime of Alexander the Great. That which we have called a *page* is really a *column* of writing, and the book consisted of a series of such columns side by side on the roll. The column shown here is like those on the rolls which once filled the Alexandrian library

Language study; rise of dictionaries and grammars

788. The new art of editing and arranging the text of books naturally required much language study. Where two old copies differed, the question of which was correct would often arise. Many strange and old words needed explanation, just as when we read Chaucer, and there were constant questions of spelling. The Alexandrian scholars therefore began to make dictionaries. At the same time grammatical questions demanded more and more attention. At last, in 120 B.C., a scholar named Dionysius wrote the first Greek grammar. It contained the leading grammatical terms, such as the names of the parts of speech, which we still use. As all these terms were explained and conveniently arranged in the grammar of Dionysius, his book was used for centuries and thus became the foundation of all later grammars of the languages of civilized peoples, including our own. Such a term as our "subjunctive mode" is simply a translation of the corresponding Greek term created by the Hellenistic scholars.

789. Literature was to a large extent in the hands of such learned men as those of Alexandria. The great librarian Callimachus was a famous poet of the age. These scholars no longer chose great and dramatic themes, like war, fate, and catastrophe, as the subjects of their writing. They loved to picture such scenes as the shepherd at the spring, listening to the music of overhanging boughs, lazily watching his flocks, and dreaming the while of some winsome village maid who has scorned his devotion. Such pictures of country life set in the simplicity and beauty of peaceful hillsides, and wrought into melodious verse, delighted the cultivated circles of a great world city like Alexandria even more than the revered classics of an older day. In such verse the greatest literary artist of the age was a Sicilian named Theocritus, whose idyls have held a place in the world's literature for two thousand years. At the same time the everyday life of the age was also pictured at the theater in a modern form of play known as the new comedy. With many amusing incidents the townsmen saw their faults and weaknesses of character here depicted on the stage, and Menander at Athens, the ablest of such play-writers, gained a great reputation for his keen knowledge of men and his ability to hit them off wittily in clever comedies.

Literature

SECTION 67. EDUCATION, PHILOSOPHY, AND RELIGION

790. In such a cultivated world of fine cities, beautiful homes, sumptuous public buildings, noble works of art, state libraries, and scientific research it was natural that education should have made much progress. The elementary schools, once *private*, were now often *supported by the state.* When the lad had finished at the elementary school, his father allowed him to attend lectures on rhetoric, science, philosophy, and mathematics in the lecture rooms of the gymnasium building.

Education: elementary schools and gymnasiums

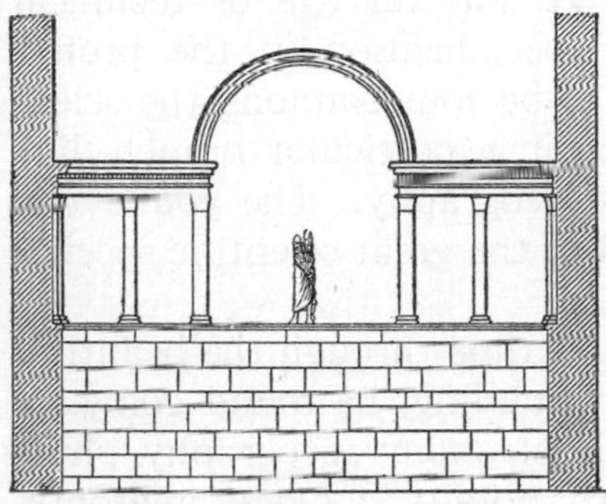

Fig. 219. *Wall of a Gymnasium* Lecture Hall *at* Priene, *still covered with Schoolboys' Names*

This lecture hall opened on the colonnades around the court of the gymnasium at Priene (Fig. 207, *P*). The smooth blocks of marble are scratched with the names of hundreds of schoolboys who heard lectures and classes there twenty-two hundred years ago. In order to set up a permanent claim to his seat a boy would scratch into the wall the words, "Seat of Cleon, the son of Clearchos." When the lower wall was entirely filled with these names, the boys evidently mounted on the benches and then on the backs of comrades to find enough room to write their claims

791. The gymnasium became a place of helpful intellectual stimulus. When the fathers were no longer nimble enough for athletic games, they often sat about in the colonnades watching the contests or idling in groups, discussing the last lecture in science or the latest discovery in the laboratory of the Museum. Here many an argument in science or philosophy might be overheard by the young fellows, fresh from the gymnasium baths, as they wandered out to greet their waiting fathers. Such an atmosphere was one to create great interest in science and philosophy, and often a youth besought his father to give him a few years' higher study at the Museum or at Athens.

Influence of gymnasium toward higher studies

792. Furthermore, in the pursuit of a profession a special training had now become indispensable to a young man's success. Like the medical student, the architect now studied his profession and bent industriously over books that told him how to erect an arch that would be safe and secure, and what were the proper proportions for a column. Young fellows who wished to become engineers studied a host of things in mechanics, like bridge-building and devices for moving heavy bodies. It was an age of technical training. This specialization in the professions was also to be found among the scientists, who now specialized each in a particular branch, like astronomy, or mathematics, or geography. The youth who wished to study science turned to the great scientific specialists at the Alexandrian Museum.

Professional and scientific specialization

793. As he strolled for the first time through the beautiful gardens and into the Museum building, he found going on there lectures on astronomy, geography, physics, mathematics, botany, zoölogy, anatomy, medicine, or rhetoric, grammar, and literature. When he was sufficiently familiar with the *known* facts about these subjects, he could share in the endeavor to discover *new* facts about them. He might cross the court to the halls where the cries of suffering animals told him that vivisection was being practiced; he might climb the tower of the astronomical observatory and sit there night after night at the elbow of some eminent astronomer, or assist Eratosthenes at noonday in taking an observation of the sun for his computation of the earth's size. Or he might withdraw to the quiet library rooms and assist in making up the lists of famous old books, to be put together in Callimachus' great catalogue. If he showed ability enough, he might later be permitted to lecture to students himself, and finally become one of the Museum's group of famous scientific men.

Alexandrian Museum as a university

794. On the other hand, Alexandria was not at first interested in philosophy, out of which science had grown (§ 532). Athens was still the leading home of philosophy. The youth who went there to take up philosophical studies found the successors of Plato still continuing his teaching in the quiet grove of the Academy (§ 704), where his memory was greatly revered. Plato's pupil Aristotle, however, had not been able to accept his master's teachings. After the education of the young

Academy and Peripatetic school at Athens

Alexander, Aristotle had returned to Athens and established a school of his own at the Lyceum (§ 595), where he occupied a terrace called the Walk (Greek, *peripatos*). Here he directed one group of advanced students after another in the arrangement and study of such subjects as anatomy, botany, and zoölogy. All of these groups collected great masses of scientific observations, which were arranged under Aristotle's guidance. The result was a veritable encyclopedia of old and new facts. The work was never completed, and many of the essays and treatises which it included have been lost. When Aristotle died, soon after the death of Alexander, his school declined.

Unrivaled authority of Aristotle's works

795. Aristotle's works formed the greatest attempt ever made in ancient times to collect and state in a clear way the whole mass of human knowledge. They never lost their importance, and they justly gave him the reputation of having possessed the greatest mind produced by the ancient world. In later Europe, particularly in medieval times, men did not try to discover new facts in nature for themselves, but turned to Aristotle's books for the solution of every scientific problem. Indeed, the writings of no other man have ever enjoyed such widespread and unquestioned authority.[1]

Philosophies of practical living: Stoicism and Epicureanism

796. But many Greeks found little satisfaction in the learned researches of Plato's Academy and of Aristotle's Peripatetic school. They desired some teaching which would lead them to a happy and contented frame of mind in living, and enable them to live successfully. To meet this growing desire two more schools of philosophy arose at Athens. The first was founded by an Oriental, a Semite named Zeno, born in Cyprus. He taught in the famous old Painted Porch in the market place of Athens (§ 609). Such a porch was called a *stoa*, and Zeno's school was therefore called the Stoic school. Zeno taught that there was but one good, and that was virtue, and but one evil, and that was moral wrong.

[1] See Robinson, *Medieval and Modern Times*, pp. 252 ff.

The great aim of life should be a tranquillity of soul which comes from virtue and is indifferent both to pleasure and to pain. His followers were famous for their fortitude, and hence our common use of the word "stoicism" to indicate indifference to suffering. The Stoic school was very popular and finally became the greatest of the schools of philosophy. The last school, founded by Epicurus in his own garden at Athens, taught that the highest good was pleasure, both of body and of mind. However, as Epicurus tells us in his letters, one cannot experience pleasure unless one lives "wisely, nobly, and justly," for life which is not so lived is not pleasant. Thus Epicurus sought to instill in his followers certain ideals of serenity and self-sufficiency. It is indeed a tragedy that later men, particularly the Romans, distorted this teaching into a justification for a life of sensual pleasure. The Oriental proverb, "Eat, drink, and be merry, for tomorrow we die," has therefore been commonly applied to them. Hence we still call a man devoted to pleasure, especially in eating, an epicure.

University of Athens and its historic influence

797. These schools lived on the income of property left them by wealthy pupils and friends. The head of the school, with his assistants and followers, lived in quarters having rooms for lectures, books, and study. The most successful of these organizations was that of Aristotle, at least as long as he lived. The Museum of Alexandria was modeled on these Athenian organizations, and they have also become the model of academies of science and of universities ever since. We may regard Hellenistic Athens, then, as possessing a university made up of four departments: the Academy, the Lyceum, the Stoa, and the Garden of Epicurus. Thus, in the day when her political power had vanished, Athens had become even more than Pericles had hoped she might be. Not only was she the teacher of all Greece, but she drew her pupils from all parts of the civilized world.

798. For such highly educated men the beliefs of Stoicism or Epicureanism served as their religion. The gods had, for such men, usually ceased to exist or were explained as merely glorified human beings. A romance writer of the day, a man named Euhemerus, wrote an attractive tale of an imaginary journey which he made to the Indian Ocean, where he found a group of mysterious islands. There, in a temple of Zeus, he found a golden tablet inscribed with a story telling how the great gods worshiped by the Greeks were once powerful kings who had done much for the civilization of mankind, and when they died they had been deified. This story of a novelist of the Hellenistic Age was widely believed, but these gods no longer attracted the reverence of religiously minded men. Moreover, there was now little pressure on any man to keep silence about his beliefs regarding the gods. There was great freedom of conscience, — far more freedom than the Christian rulers of later Europe granted their subjects. The teachings of Socrates would no longer have caused his condemnation by his Athenian neighbors.

Fall of old Greek gods

799. The great multitude of the people had not the education to understand philosophy, nor the means to attend the philosophical schools. Yet gods in some form they must have. With the weakening of faith in the old gods those of the Near East, which we have already seen invading Greek life (§ 690), became more and more popular. So the Ptolemies introduced as their great state god an Oriental deity named Serapis, and they built for him a magnificent temple at Alexandria. From Babylonia the mysterious lore of the Chaldean astrologers was spreading widely through the Mediterranean. It was received and accepted in Egypt, and even Greek science did not escape its influence. Oriental beliefs and Oriental symbols were everywhere. Men had long since grown accustomed to foreign gods, and they no longer looked askance at strange usages in religion. It was in such an age as this that Christianity, an Oriental religion, passed easily from land to land.

Increased popularity of Oriental gods

SECTION 68. FORMATION OF A HELLENISTIC WORLD OF HELLENIC-ORIENTAL CIVILIZATION; DECLINE OF CITIZENSHIP AND THE CITY-STATE

Continuance of Oriental influences in Eastern Mediterranean

800. It is a great mistake to suppose that Marathon and Salamis once and for all banished the influence of the Orient from the Mediterranean, as an impenetrable dam keeps back a body of water. While Alexander's victories and conquests destroyed the military power of the Orient, the daily life and the civilization of the people of the Orient continued to be a permanent force exerting a steady pressure upon the life of the Eastern Mediterranean world, — in commerce, in form of government, in customs and usages, in art, industry, literature, and religion. When Christianity issued from Palestine, therefore, as we shall see, it found itself but one among many other influences from the Orient which were passing westward. Thus, while Greek civilization, with its language, its art, its literature, its theaters and gymnasiums, was Hellenizing the Orient, the Orient in the same way was exercising a powerful influence on the West and was Orientalizing the Eastern Mediterranean world. In this way there was gradually formed an Eastern Mediterranean world of Hellenic-Oriental civilization.

Hellenistic world of Eastern Mediterranean; no citizenship

801. In this larger world the old Greek *city*-citizen, who had made Greek civilization what it was, played but a small part. He felt himself an *individual* belonging in an international world,—a far larger world than the city in which he lived. But this larger world brought home no sense of citizenship in it, for in the great Hellenistic states there was no such thing as *national* citizenship. The city-citizen had no share in guiding the affairs of the great nation or empire of which his city-state was a part. It was as though a citizen of Chicago might vote at the election of a mayor of the city but had no right to vote at the election of a president of the United States. There was not even a name for the empire of the Seleucids, and their subjects, wherever they went, bore the names of their home cities or countries.[1] The conception of "native land" in the national sense was wanting, and patriotism did not exist.

802. The centers of power and progress in Greek civilization had been the *city-states*, but the finest and most influential forces operating within the city-state had now disappeared. So, for example, the old city gods were gone. Likewise the citizen-soldier who defended his city had long ago given way, even in Greece, to the professional soldier who came from abroad and fought for hire. The Greek no longer stood, weapon in hand, ready to defend his home and his city-community against every assault. He found the holding of city offices becoming a profession, as that of the soldier had long been. Losing his interest in the state, he turned to his personal affairs, the cultivation of himself. The patriotic sense of responsibility for the welfare of the city-state which he loved, and the fine moral earnestness which this responsibility roused, no longer animated the Greek mind and quickened it to the loftiest achievements in politics, in art, in architecture, in literature, and in original thought. The Greek city-states, *in competition among themselves*, had developed the highest type of civilization which the world had ever seen, but in this process the city-states themselves had politically perished. In many Greek cities only a discouraged remnant of the citizens was left after the emigration to Asia (§ 759). The cattle often browsed on the grass in the public square before the town hall in such cities of the Greeks. Not even their own Hellas was a unified nation.

Contributions of city-state; end of its usefulness

803. A larger world had engulfed the old Greek city-states, but this Hellenistic world of the *Eastern* Mediterranean had by 200 B.C. reached a point in its own wars and rivalries

[1] It was as though the citizens of the United States were termed Bostonians, New Yorkers, Philadelphians, Chicagoans, etc., or the people of the British Isles were called Londoners, Edinburghers, or Dubliners, and the term "British" did not exist.

where it was to feel the iron hand of a great new military power from the distant world of the *Western* Mediterranean.

Hellenistic world of Eastern Mediterranean under rule of the West

At this point (200 B.C.) we shall therefore be unable to understand the further story of the Eastern Mediterranean until we have turned back and taken up the career of the Western Mediterranean world. There in the West, for some three centuries, the city of Rome had been developing a power which was to unite both the East and the West into a vast empire including the *whole Mediterranean.*

QUESTIONS

Section 65. What was the prevalent language of the Hellenistic Age? What written documents tell us of this age, and how have they been preserved? Describe the new Hellenistic cities. Describe two important examples of sculpture and one of mosaic work in this age.

Section 66. Make a list of scientists and inventors of the Hellenistic Age and tell of the achievements of each. What effect had the Hellenistic libraries on publishing and language study?

Section 67. Discuss education in this age. Where did the young scholar go for advanced study?

Section 68. What kind of world had now grown up in the Eastern Mediterranean? What can you say of civilization there? What had now become of the Greek city-state?

BIBLIOGRAPHY FOR TOPICAL STUDIES

Education and books in the Hellenistic period: BOTSFORD-SIHLER, *Hellenic Civilization,* pp. 598–601; BURY-BARBER, *Hellenistic Age,* pp. 23–24, 31–38, 57, 65–67; MURRAY, *Ancient Greek Literature,* pp. 377, 387–388; POLAND-REISINGER-WAGNER, *Culture of Greece and Rome,* pp. 255–256; TARN, *Hellenistic Civilization,* pp. 82–86, 215–218, 237–239.

CHAPTER XXII · *The Western Mediterranean World and the Roman Conquest of Italy*

SECTION 69. THE WESTERN MEDITERRANEAN WORLD

804. While we have been following the history of the Eastern Mediterranean and the peoples grouped about it, the story of its western shores has largely dropped out of sight. Before we turn to this western world, however, let us endeavor to gain a picture of the Mediterranean world as a whole. We recall that in beginning the story of man we found Stone Age life not only surrounding the entire Mediterranean but likewise

Desert along the south and east of the Mediterranean

NOTE. The above headpiece shows an ancient BRONZE WOLF (Sixth Century B.C.), wrought by Etruscan artists under Greek influence in Italy. The TWO INFANTS nourished by the she-wolf are later additions put there in accordance with the tradition at Rome that the city was founded by these twin brothers, named Romulus and Remus. Their ancestor, so said the tradition, was Æneas (§ 1042), one of the Trojan heroes, who had fled from Troy after its destruction, and after many adventures had arrived in Italy. His son founded and became king of Alba Longa. In the midst of a family feud among his descendants these twin boys, the sons of the War-god, Mars, were born; and after they had been set adrift in the Tiber by the ruling king, their boat gently ran aground at the base of the Palatine Hill, where a she-wolf found and nourished the babes. When they grew up they returned home to Alba Longa, claimed their rights, and eventually founded Rome. Similar legends formed all that the Romans knew of their early history through the period of the kings (see page 571, footnote) and far down into the Republic.

spreading far northward into Europe and southward deep into the heart of Africa. It is important to notice that the drying up of North Africa finally left only a narrow fringe of fertile land between the desert and the Mediterranean Sea. As a home of civilization North Africa was therefore confined to the lower Nile valley and the region opposite Sicily, where the fringe of cultivation is wider. It must be observed, furthermore, that the desiccation, or drying up, included much of Western Asia, and the resulting Asiatic desert extended also along the *east end* of the Mediterranean, leaving little space there for the growth of nations. It was this desert of Western Asia which separated the civilization of Babylonia and Assyria from direct contact with the Mediterranean world. The desiccation of North Africa therefore profoundly altered the Mediterranean world as a whole, for, except in the case of Egypt, it left room for the development of great and powerful civilizations *only along the northern shores of the great sea.* It is, moreover, of enormous importance to us of today in that it eventually forced human development from the south side to the north side of the Mediterranean, so that *Europe* rather than Africa became the home of our ancestors.

The four peninsulas on the north side of the Mediterranean

805. We must now consider the character of the northern shores of the Mediterranean, where great nations could find room for development. If we examine the map (p. 346) we find that the most prominent features on the north side of the Mediterranean are the three peninsulas, — Greece, Italy, and Spain. We recall how Greece and its islands thrust forward and bring the southeastern corner of Europe very near to the ancient civilizations of the Near East. Civilization spreading from the Near East thus reached the easternmost of the three European peninsulas first. Thence it moved westward to the middle one, that is, Italy; and, as we might expect, Spain, the third and westernmost peninsula, was the last to be reached.

Besides these three European peninsulas we must not fail to notice a fourth peninsula on the north side of the Mediterranean. This is Asia Minor, the westernmost extension of Western Asia. When Cyrus conquered Asia Minor, his conquest carried the boundaries of an Oriental empire far westward to the very shores of Europe. We remember that what Cyrus thus did had been going on for ages before his time, as Babylonian civilization spread westward through Asia Minor into Greece. The peninsula of Asia Minor therefore linked the Mediterranean world to that of the Two Rivers.

Mediterranean world, the stage of ancient history

806. The Mediterranean Sea thus stretched out between three continents, with four large peninsulas, all parts of the Highland Zone, lying on its north, and a vast desert extending entirely along its south and east. This sea, together with its shores and adjacent lands, was the chief stage of ancient history. We need to add to it only the Two Rivers, together with Persia on the east, and to remember that the Mediterranean has an extension in the Black Sea. This Mediterranean stage of ancient history was not a small one, for the great sea is almost as long as Europe itself.

Division of Mediterranean into an eastern and a western basin

807. Now the Mediterranean is not a single compact body of water, like the North Sea or one of the American Great Lakes. A land-bridge made up of Italy and Sicily extends almost across this great sea and divides it into two parts, an eastern and a western basin. Although there is almost no difference in climate, the western basin is much farther north than the eastern. A glance at the map (p. 346) shows that the *southern* shore of the western basin is in the same latitude as the *northern* shore of the eastern basin. There are no accepted geographical names for these two basins, but we may call them, for convenience, the Eastern and Western Mediterranean worlds. The story of civilization began very early in the Eastern Mediterranean world (§§ 54 and 403), but civilization was much slower in reaching and improving the life of the Western Mediterranean peoples. Indeed, until the Bronze Age (§ 809) the West had made little advance in civilization since the Stone Age life of the Swiss lake-villages.

808. The most important land in the Western Mediterranean world in early times was Italy. It slopes westward in the main, and thus it faces and belongs to the Western Mediterranean world. The Italian peninsula, thrusting far out into the sea (see map, p. 562), is nearly six hundred miles long, that is, a little longer than England or about half again as long as the peninsula of Florida. Italy[1] is not only four times as large as Greece, but, unlike Greece, it is not cut up by a tangle of mountains into tortuous valleys and tiny plains. The main chain of the Apennines, though crossing the peninsula obliquely in the north, is nearly parallel with the coasts, and many of its outlying ridges are quite so. There are more extensive plains for the cultivation of grain than we find anywhere in Greece; at the same time there is much more room for upland pasturage of flocks and herds. A considerably larger population can be supported in the plains of Italy than in Greece. There are, moreover, fewer good harbors. Hence agriculture and live stock developed much earlier than trade.

Italy: its geography and climate

809. The Late Stone Age has left comparatively few traces in the Italian peninsula, but with the coming of metal the early population of the Western Mediterranean world seems to have increased, and from this period, both in Italy and elsewhere in the West, many more remains have survived. In the Bronze Age eastern civilization first reached the Western Mediterranean world by sea. In Sicily the early tombs have been found to contain many examples of work in bronze, including eastern daggers and especially large numbers of toilet articles, jewelry, and other things, all made by Cretan and Mycenæan craftsmen and undoubtedly brought in by Eastern Mediterranean fleets. It has been thought that colonies of Cretan workmen may even have settled in Sicily and carried on bronze manufacturing there.

Bronze Age civilization expands westward by Mediterranean route

[1] The area of Italy is 91,000 square miles, or, adding the neighboring islands, about 110,000 square miles, that is, almost twice as large as England and Wales together and not quite three times the area of the state of Ohio.

These eastern ships did not stop in Sicily, but passed on westward to Spain, and had introduced metal there before 2000 B.C. Indeed, the Bronze Age civilization which then grew up on the Mediterranean coast of Spain was so strong and flourishing by 1500 B.C. that its trade extended far northward and eastward through southern France and finally into the upper valley of the Danube.

Bronze Age civilization expands westward by Alpine route

810. As a whole the great Italian peninsula was not much affected by this westward spread of Bronze Age civilization in the Mediterranean. Northern Italy first began to feel the influence of the Bronze Age civilization which had developed on the north side of the Alps in the Danube valley. The fertile plains and forest-clad slopes of Italy have always attracted the peoples of northern Europe to forsake their own bleak and wintry lands and migrate to this warm and sunny peninsula in the southern sea. Perhaps as early as 2000 B.C. a people from the north side of the Alps, who had adopted the pile-village mode of life, pushed southward through the Alpine passes and occupied the lakes of northern Italy. The remains of over a hundred of their pile-supported settlements have also been found under the soil of the Po valley, — once a vast morass, which these people reclaimed by erecting their pile dwellings farther and farther out in it. The city of Venice, still standing on piles, although it is now built mostly of stone, is a surviving example of the way the lake-dwellers once built their little wooden houses on piles in the same region. They had their influence on the later Romans, who afterward made their military camps on a plan exactly like that of the Po valley pile-villages (Fig. 220).

Oriental origin of names of metals in Italy

811. When these people reached the Po valley, they had already received metal, for it is found in all their settlements. The forms of their metal work show that it came from the north. Nevertheless the names for the metals which finally survived in Italy clearly show their Oriental origin. Our word "copper" had the form *cuprum* in Italy, from the name of the island of *Cyprus* (ancient *Cuprus*), whose rich mines supplied the Mediterranean lands with copper from very early times. Our word "bronze" is probably derived from the first part of the name of the city of Brondesium (later Brundisium, now called Brindisi) at the back of the heel of Italy, where it was so near the Ægean that it very early received bronze from there.

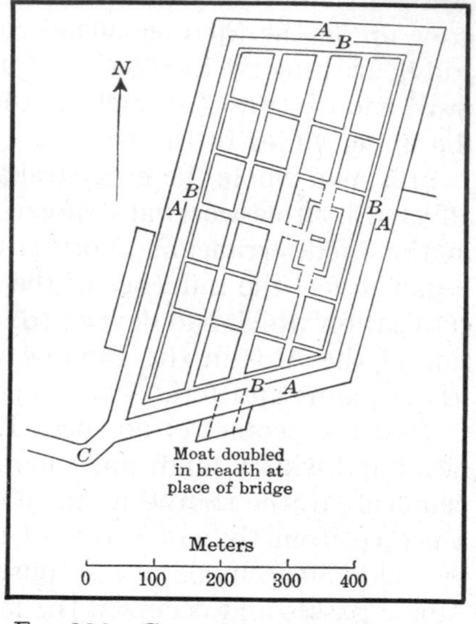

FIG. 220. GROUND PLAN *of a Prehistoric* PILE-VILLAGE *in Northern Italy*

The settlement was surrounded by a moat *A* nearly 100 feet across, filled with water from a connected river *C*. Inside the moat was an earth wall *B* about 50 feet thick at the base. The village thus inclosed was about 2000 feet long, that is, four city blocks. The whole village, being in the marshes of the Po valley, was supported on piles like the lake-villages (Fig. 20). These settlements are called by the Italian archæologists *terramare* (pronounced *ter-rä-mä'rā*)

Western wing of Indo-Europeans enters Italy

812. While the pile-villagers were settling in the Po valley the tribes forming the western end of the Indo-European migration (Fig. 123) began to feel the attractiveness of the warm and verdant hills of Italy. Probably not long after the Greeks had pushed southward into the Greek peninsula (§ 406) other western tribes of Indo-European blood crossed the Balkan Peninsula and, moving westward, entered the beautiful Western Mediterranean world, into which the Italian peninsula extends. They came in successive migrations, but the most important group that settled in the central and southern parts of the peninsula were the Italic tribes, — the earliest Italians. The whole peninsula was finally known by their name, "Italy." Probably within a few centuries they had also overflowed into Sicily.

813. We remember that the Greeks, in conquering the Ægean, took possession of a highly civilized region on the borders of the Near East. This was not the case with the Indo-European invaders of Italy. They found here the old Late Stone Age inhabitants of Italy, who still survived, especially in the north. Besides these barbarian and backward people they found also many settlements of the Mediterranean race, the gifted people who had produced the Cretan civilization and who were already using bronze. But the Indo-European invaders found the Western Mediterranean world still without civilization, for it had no great nations and no powerful and wealthy kings who could undertake great public works. The peoples of the Western Mediterranean world lived in small villages; there were no large fortified cities and no fine buildings. As there was no refined life at a royal court or capital, there were only the simplest arts and industries, no writing, and no literature.

Uncivilized state of Italy and the West

814. The Italic invaders were plain peasant folk, cultivating their little fields and pasturing their flocks. As illiterate peasants they seemed to have slight prospect of great advancement or power. Their chief qualities were a certain steadfastness of purpose, undaunted courage, and a hardihood which nothing seemed to weaken. The Italic tribes were to find this trait very much needed, for besides the pile-village folk they were confronted in Italy by three powerful rivals who had come from the Eastern Mediterranean world, where they had gained all the power in wealth and weapons, military discipline and government organization, which we have seen growing up in the great imperial civilizations of the East. It did not seem probable that the tiny groups of Italic villagers could ever hope to oppose successfully the power and influence of any of these older rivals who had extended their commerce to the West and begun to occupy such a strong position on the shores of the Western Mediterranean. From north to south the three rivals of the Italic tribes were the

Three Western rivals of Italic invaders

THE FOUR RIVAL PEOPLES *of the Western Mediterranean: Etruscans, Italic Tribes, Greeks, and Carthaginians*

Etruscans, the Greeks, and the Phœnicians, whose presence in the Western Mediterranean was due, we recall, to certain movements in the Eastern Mediterranean world (§§ 416, 477, and 436).

First, the Etruscan settlement of Italy

815. The Etruscans settled on the western coast of Italy north of the Tiber. The earliest of them must have arrived not long after their repulse by Ramses III, that is, in the first half of the Twelfth Century B.C.[1] As they pushed inland they were confronted by the pile-village folk and the Italic tribes, whose feeble village organization could not have offered much resistance to the

[1] Ramses III's records call the Etruscans the *T-r-s*, for the Egyptian writing indicates no vowels. The Greeks call their name *Tyrsenians*, in which, after cutting off the ending (*enian*) and disregarding the vowels, we find again the Egyptian *T-r-s*. In the western or Latin name for these people, "Etruscan," the removal of the vowels and the ending (*can*) again gives us the Egyptian *T-r-s*. The eastern origin of the Etruscans has now been proved by the discovery, in 1926, of an Etruscan cemetery on the Greek island of Lemnos.

ITALY
AND ADJACENT LANDS
before
THE SUPREMACY OF ROME
Scale of Miles
0 10 20 30 40 50 100 150
Etruscans
Italians
Carthaginians
Gaul, Liguria, Apulia and Calabria
Greek Colonies are indicated by underlining names in blue
ALPS
CISALPINE GAUL
LIGURIA
ETRURIA
UMBRIA
PICENUM
LATIUM
ILLYRIA
ADRIATIC SEA
CORSICA
APENNINE MTS.
REGION OF PILE VILLAGES
Mt.Cenis
Milan
Genoa
Aquileia
Venice
Rubicon R.
Ariminum
Metaurus R.
Ancona
Sentinum
Asculum
Pisa
Arnus R.
Florence
Lake Trasimene
Clusium
Tiber R.
Ticinus R.
Po R.
ETRUSCANS
Sabines
Æquians
FRENTANI
Veii
Cære
Tibur
Rome
Præneste
Alba Longa
Ostia
Latins
8°
10°
12°
14°
16°
18°
46°
44°
42°

Map Plate, Patented July 5, 1921 · Method of Making Maps, Patented July 5, 1921

invaders. In the course of several centuries, as later colonists of their kindred from the Ægean arrived among them, the Etruscans took possession of north-central Italy from the Tiber to the Arnus.

816. By the Ninth Century B.C. the Etruscans had begun to produce works of art which tell us of the character of their developing civilization. As the earliest civilization that arose in Italy it is important to notice that it came from the Hittite world of Asia Minor and thus brought into Italy an *Oriental* civilization. For instance, the Etruscans introduced the chariot, the arch in building, and divination and foretelling by studying the liver of a sheep. All the early Etruscan works of art were Oriental in character, and their early decorative designs repeat those of Egypt and Assyria. From their Eastern home later Etruscan colonists brought with them the alphabet which had been devised by the Phœnicians. They were therefore not illiterate like their predecessors in Italy. The Etruscans brought also from the East much skill as craftsmen. In Italy they found copper, and in course of time they developed the finest bronze industry in the ancient world of that period. Their goldsmiths too were unrivaled by any in the older countries. Until the arrival of the painted Attic vases not long after 600 B.C., Etruscan pottery also was the best in the West.

Etruscan civilization, the earliest in Italy

817. The leading Etruscans became industrial and commercial princes who did not give up the seafaring life. The triangular basin inclosed by Italy and the three islands — Corsica, Sardinia, and Sicily — finally came to be called the Tyrrhenian, that is, the Etruscan, Sea. From these waters the Etruscans marketed their wares far and wide throughout the Mediterranean. At the same time they also carried on trade with the north through the passes of the Alps. They lived in walled towns, and each town was the home of a powerful Etruscan merchant-lord, who with his wealthy kindred formed the aristocracy which governed the town. There were eventually

Etruscan commercial aristocracy

A

B

FIG. 221. ETRUSCAN TOMBS *at Ancient Cære*

The paved streets are arranged systematically, as in a real city, with the tombs in rows on either side. The tombs are concealed under tumuli consisting of enormous round drums carved out of the natural rock with earth piled on the top to form a conical mound *A*. One enters these tumuli through an opening on a level with the street, and descends by a sloping passage down into galleries which open into a series of large chambers (*B*), carved with architectural details in imitation of houses. The pillars and walls were decorated with representations of household utensils, armor, weapons, and other accessories in the daily life of the Etruscans. The bodies were placed in niches in the walls. In one of these tombs the name of the deceased is inscribed on the wall as *Tarkhnas*, which can be nothing else than Tarquinius, the name preserved in Roman tradition as that of the latest kings of Rome

twelve of these towns, forming a loose federation, which, however, never became a firmly united nation. Etruscan settlements finally extended southward beyond Naples, eastward beyond the Apennines, and northward to the Po valley and the southern slopes of the Alps. This first great civilized race in Italy, evidently not an Indo-European folk, seemed about to take possession of the entire Italian peninsula.

818. Nevertheless the mastery of the Western Mediterranean was a prize for which the other two rivals of the Italic tribes were likewise contending, and we must now follow the three-cornered struggle. The Carthaginians were the *second* of these three rivals. During their great mercantile prosperity, after 1000 B.C., the Phœnicians carried their commerce far into the Western Mediterranean, as we have already learned. On the African coast opposite Sicily they established a flourishing commercial city called Carthage, which was before long the leading harbor in the Western Mediterranean. The Carthaginians soon held the northern coast of Africa westward to the Atlantic. Besides gaining southern Spain they were also absorbing the islands of the Western Mediterranean, especially Sicily.

Second, the Phœnician colony of Carthage

819. The Carthaginians and Etruscans had been facing each other across the Tyrrhenian Sea for over two centuries when the Italic peoples saw their *third* rivals invading the West. They were the Greeks. We have already followed the expansion of the Greeks in the Eighth Century B.C. as they founded their new colonies and city-states along the coast of Sicily and southern Italy (§§ 476–478). The strife among these city-states made the Greeks of the West as unable to unite into a Greek nation as Greece itself had been. The strongest of all these western Greek cities was Syracuse, which took the lead more than once. We recall how the Athenians tried to conquer the West by capturing Syracuse (§ 640).

Third, the western Greeks

820. Although we have spoken of these three peoples — Etruscans, Carthaginians, and Greeks — as the three rivals of the Italic tribes in the West, we have already observed that these Italic tribes were at first too insignificant to do more than watch the rivalry which long remained a three-cornered one, with the Greeks in Sicily and southern Italy maintaining themselves on two fronts against both Carthaginians and Etruscans. We remember how in the famous year of Salamis the Greeks of Syracuse won a great battle against the Carthaginians (§ 551) and saved Sicily from being conquered by Orientals (480 B.C.). Only a few years later it was also Syracuse which met the bold Etruscan sea-rovers as their fleets appeared in the south, and totally defeated them. The western Greeks therefore played an important part in the political situation, — first, by long preventing the Carthaginians from seizing Sicily and southern Italy, and, second, by breaking the sea power of the Etruscans.

Western Greeks repulse Carthaginians and Etruscans

821. By 400 B.C. Dionysius, the Greek tyrant of Syracuse, was building up a powerful empire in Sicily and southern Italy, which looked like a permanent union of the western Greeks into a nation. The successors of Dionysius, however, were not as efficient as he. They called in the great philosopher Plato, and attempted to carry out some of his idealistic theories of government, but the result was a disastrous collapse of the young Syracusan empire (357–354 B.C.). Plato himself expressed the fear that the Greek language was then about to die out in Sicily and that the island would be conquered by the Carthaginians or one of the rising Indo-European tribes of Italy.

Empire of Dionysius of Syracuse and its fall

822. Although the western Greeks, like the homeland, failed to unite in a strong and permanent state, the influence of their civilization in the West was all the more important. Their civilization was essentially the same as that which we have already studied (Chapters XI–XXI). At the very time when Syracuse was victoriously beating back the Carthaginians and Etruscans on two fronts, some of the

Greeks bring civilization into Western Mediterranean world

noblest monuments of Greek architecture were rising in these western cities. Thus great architecture made its first appearance in the Western Mediterranean. The same was true of many other contributions of Greek culture with which we are now familiar. Thus, fifteen hundred years after the Italic tribes had first settled in Italy, there arose on the south of them a wonderful world of civilization, which went on growing and developing until it reached its highest achievements in that Hellenistic culture which brought forth an Archimedes at Syracuse. Let us now turn back to follow the career of the barbarous Italic tribes of central Italy under the leadership of Rome, and watch them slowly gaining organization and power, and finally civilization, as they are dominated first by Etruscan and then by Greek culture.

FIG. 222. ETRUSCAN HELMET *captured by the Greeks of Syracuse in their Victory over the Etruscans at Cumæ in 474 B.C.*

Hiero, the Greek tyrant of Syracuse, dedicated this helmet at Olympia as part of the spoil which he took from the Etruscans in his great naval victory of Cumæ. It is now in the British Museum, and it still bears the dedicatory inscription placed upon it by the Syracusan tyrant twenty-four hundred years ago

SECTION 70. EARLIEST ROME

Tribes of Latium; Alba Longa the leading Latin town

823. On the south or east bank of the Tiber, which flows into the sea in the middle of the west coast of Italy (see map, p. 562), there was a group of Italic tribes known as the Latins. In the days when the Etruscan colonists were still landing on the shores north of the Tiber these Latin tribes had occupied a plain less than thirty by forty miles,[1] that is, smaller than many an English or American county. They called it *Latium*, whence their own name "Latins." Like their Italic neighbors they lived in small, scattered com-

[1] Latium probably contained something over seven hundred square miles.

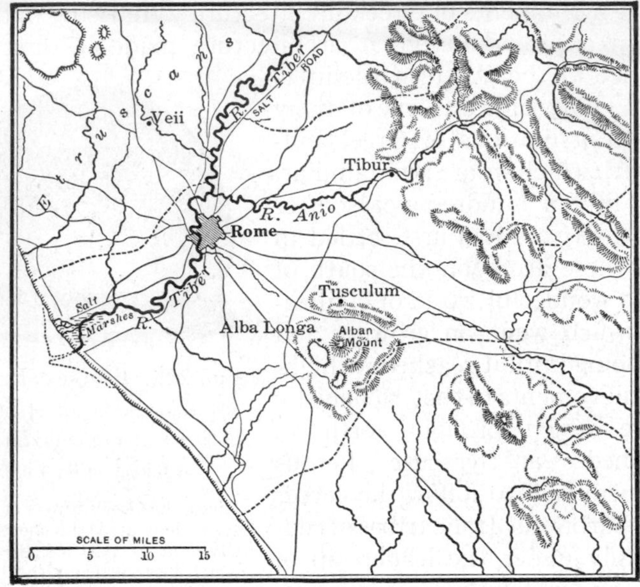

Early LATIUM

munities, cultivating grain and pasturing flocks on the upland. Their land was not very fertile, and the battle for existence developed hardy and tenacious children of the soil. Once a year they went up to the Alban Mount, where all the Latin tribes united in a feast of their chief god, Jupiter, whose rude mud-brick sanctuary was on the mount. Close by was a small town called Alba Longa, whose leadership the Latin tribes followed when they were obliged, as they very often were, to unite and repel the attacks of their hostile neighbors on all sides. They watched very anxiously the growth of the flourishing Etruscan towns on the other side of the Tiber, and they did what they could to keep the Etruscans from crossing to the Latin side.

824. When these Latin peasants needed weapons or tools, they were obliged to carry up a little grain or an ox to a trading post on the south side of the Tiber, just above the

FIG. 223. *The* TIBER *and its* ISLAND *at* ROME

The Tiber is not a large river, but when swollen by the spring freshets it still sometimes floods a large portion of Rome, doing serious damage. The houses which we see on the island are some of them old, but not as old as the ancient Rome we are to study. The bridges, however, are very old. The one on the right of the island was built of massive stone masonry by L. Fabricius in 62 B.C. It has been standing for about two thousand years. Many great Romans, like Julius Cæsar, whose names are familiar to us, must often have crossed this bridge

Emergence of early Rome

coast marshes which extended some ten or twelve miles inland from the river's mouth. Shallow water at this point and an island made an easy crossing of the river, and the metal tools of the early settlers had enabled them to build a staunch bridge here. Overlooking the bridge was a bold hill called the Palatine, and a square stronghold crowning the hill guarded the river crossing. Several neighboring hills bore straggling villages, but the stronghold on the Palatine was their leader. Here, stopped by the shoals and the bridge, moored now and then an Etruscan ship which had sailed up the Tiber, the only navigable river in Italy. On the low marshy ground, encircled by the hills, was an open-air market, beside an old cemetery belonging to the villages. Here in the Forum, as they called this valley market, our Latin peasant could meet the Etruscan traders and exchange his grain or his ox for the metal tools or weapons which he needed. These were now of iron, but he remembered the stories of his fathers, telling how all their tools and weapons were formerly of bronze. The population of the villages was very mixed, — some Latin families who had taken to trading or owned fields near by, Etruscan traders and landowners, and a few oversea strangers of various nationalities, together with many outcasts and refugees from outlying communities.

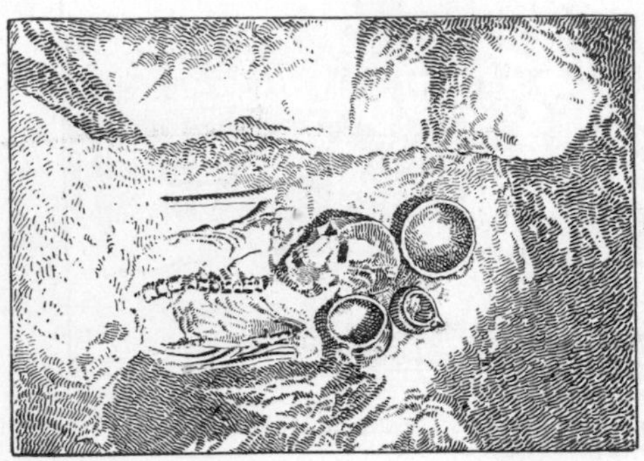

FIG. 224. GRAVE *of Early Villager, found under the* FORUM *at Rome*

Excavations under the Forum (plan, p. 574) have disclosed a cemetery of graves like this. The skeleton which we see here is that of one of the men who lived in the villages on the summits of the neighboring hills, later united to form Rome. The tools, weapons, and pottery found in these graves show that these people lived not many generations after 1000 B.C., in the days when bronze was giving way to iron

825. The fears of the Latin tribes regarding an invasion of the Etruscans were finally realized. We have seen that the Etruscan towns after 800 B.C. stretched far across northern Italy, — a great group of allied city-kingdoms, each with its fortified city. Perhaps as early as 750 B.C. one of their princes crossed the Tiber, drove out the last of the line of Latin chieftains, and took possession of the stronghold on the Palatine. From this place as his castle and palace he gained control of the villages on the hills above the Tiber, which then gradually merged into the city of Rome. These Etruscan kings soon extended their power over the Latin tribes of the Plain of Latium, and the town of Alba Longa by the Alban Mount, which once led the Latins, disappeared. Thus Rome became a city-kingdom under an Etruscan king, like the other Etruscan cities which stretched from Capua far north to the harbor of Genoa. And such it remained for two and a half centuries. Although Rome was

Rome seized by Etruscans (about 750 B.C.)

ruled by a line of Etruscan kings, it must be borne in mind that the population of Latium which these Etruscan kings governed continued to be Latin and to speak the Latin tongue.[1]

FIG. 225. ETRUSCAN CHARIOT *of Bronze*

This magnificent work is the finest surviving product of Etruscan skill in bronze. It was found in an Etruscan tomb and is now in the possession of the Metropolitan Museum of Art in New York. It probably dates from the Sixth Century B.C.

Etruscan civilization in Rome

826. Nevertheless the civilization of Rome became essentially Etruscan, and with the Etruscan kings began a much more civilized life than the city had ever seen before. They introduced important improvements, some of which have lasted till our times. The Forum, the low market valley, was often flooded in the rainy season by stagnant water, forming malaria-breeding pools. The Etruscan kings therefore built a massive masonry drain with an arch forming the roof. The drain carried off the water from the Forum and conducted it into the river, thus

[1] The above presentation makes the line of early kings at Rome (about 750 to about 500 B.C.) exclusively Etruscan. The traditional founding of Rome not long before 750 B.C. would then correspond to its capture and establishment as a strong kingdom by the Etruscans. We possess no written documents of Rome for this early period. Our conclusions are based on a study of archæological remains. If these remains had formed our only evidence, no one could ever have reached any other conclusion than that the kings of Rome were Etruscan. The later Romans themselves, however, with evident disinclination to believe that their early kings had been outsiders, cherished a tradition that their kings were native Romans. This tradition, with many picturesque and pleasing incidents (headpiece, p. 555), has found a place in literature and is still widely believed.

FIG. 226. *A View of the* TIBER *with the* AVENTINE HILL *and the* ETRUSCAN DRAIN

As we look *down* the Tiber in this view we stand not far from our former position looking *up* the river (Fig. 223). The Aventine Hill is at the left. Along its foot, at the water's edge, extend the houses of modern Rome. At this end of this row of houses we see the arched opening of the ancient Etruscan sewer, which served to drain the Forum under which it passed. The Romans called it the *Cloaca Maxima* (chief sewer). Although much altered in later times, its most ancient portions are probably the oldest surviving masonry at Rome

making the city more healthful. This ancient sewer drain built by the Etruscans still survives. On the hill called the Capitol, between the Forum and the Tiber, they built a temple to Jupiter, the state god, which stood for centuries. The earliest architecture known in Rome was Etruscan, and hence it was that Roman architecture differed from that of the Greeks by its constant use of the arch, inherited from the Etruscans.

Etruscan civilization influenced by that of the Greeks

827. Etruscan ships had known Greek waters since Mycenæan days, and the Etruscans were constantly trafficking in the Greek harbors. This intercourse with Greece brought in beautiful Greek pottery, and the Etruscans quickly learned to make similar decorative paintings. Many such paintings still cover the walls of Etruscan tombs and show us how the Etruscans looked, the clothing they wore, and the weapons they carried. Etruscan civilization was finally a composite built up out of their old Eastern Mediterranean culture and Greek civilization. It was this Etruscan civilization, modified by much Greek influence, which shaped the life of Rome after 600 B.C.

FIG. 227. ETRUSCAN STATUE *of an Orator*

This bronze figure is the finest masterpiece of Etruscan art. It may be dated about 300 B.C., and illustrates the spirit which lived on in their art after the political power of the Etruscans had collapsed

Expulsion of Etruscan kings of Rome (about 500 B.C.)

828. Eventually the cruelty and tyranny of the Etruscan rulers caused a revolt, led probably by the Etruscan nobles themselves, and the kings of Rome were driven out. The fugitive king and his followers fled northward to their kinsmen, to Cære. Thus about 500 B.C. the career of Rome under kings came to an end; but the two and a half centuries of Etruscan rule left their mark on Rome, always afterward discernible in architecture, religion, tribal organization, and some other things. Many Etruscans continued to live in Rome and Latium. In the days of Roman splendor some of the greatest families of Rome were of Etruscan descent and were proud of it. For after their expulsion from Rome the Etruscans continued as a powerful and highly civilized federation, although surrounded by dangerous enemies. They lost their northern territory to the invading Gauls (§ 855), and one after another their southern and central towns were captured by the Samnites (§ 858) and the Romans (§§ 853 and 860). At Cære their splendid tombs still survive, and we have many Etruscan inscriptions (§ 816), but unfortunately they have not yet been deciphered.

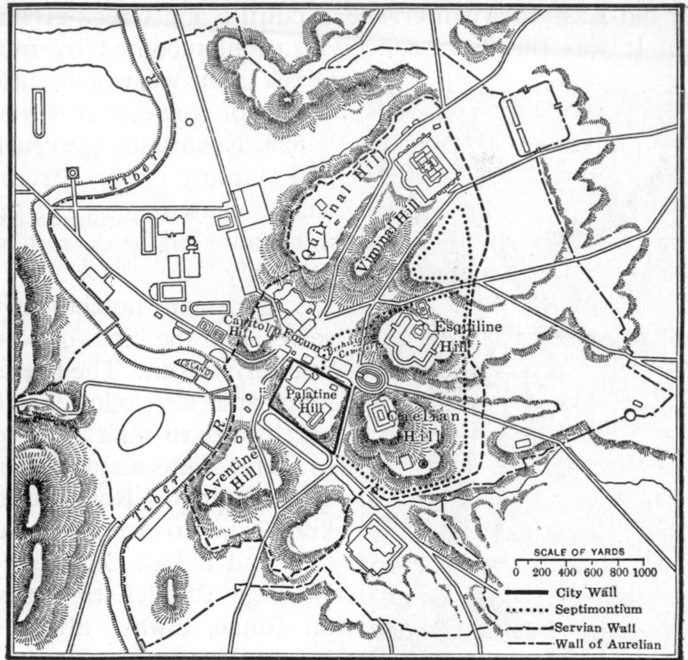

Map of EARLY ROME *showing the Successive Stages of its Growth*

SECTION 71. THE EARLY REPUBLIC: ITS PROGRESS AND GOVERNMENT

Greek alphabet adopted in Rome

829. We have seen that during this Etruscan period Greek influences were equally important in Latium. Down at the dock below the Tiber bridge, ships from the Greek cities of the south were becoming more and more common. Long before the Etruscan kings were driven out, the Roman trader had gradually learned to pick out the names of familiar objects of trade in the bills handed him by the Greek merchants. Ere long the Roman traders too were scribbling memoranda of their own with the same Greek letters, which thus became likewise the Roman alphabet, slightly changed to suit the Latin language. The Oriental alphabet was carried one step farther in the long westward journey which finally made it the alphabet with which this book is printed. In the hands of the Carthaginians and Romans in the West, and the Arameans in the East, the Phœnician alphabet and its descendant alphabets then stretched from India to the Atlantic.

830. There had been at first no *Roman* ships lying at the Tiber docks, but as time passed a Roman mechanic here and there learned to build a ship like those of the Greeks alongside it. As Roman traffic thus grew, it was found very inconvenient to pay bills with grain and oxen while the Greek merchant at the dock paid his bills with copper and silver coins. For a long time, instead of the oxen themselves, rough bars of copper were used, each bearing the figure of an ox. It was not until over a hundred and fifty years after the Etruscan kings had been driven out that the Romans issued actual copper coins (see Fig. 228). Later, as contact with the Greek cities increased, the Romans also began to issue silver coins, using as a basis the Attic drachma (§ 872). In the same way, also, the Romans gradually adopted the Oriental measures of length and of bulk with which the Greeks measured out to them the things they bought.

Greek influence on Roman shipbuilding, money, and measures

831. Greek speech too began to leave its traces in the Latin speech of Rome. The Latin townsmen and peasants learned the Greek words for the clothing offered to them for sale, or for household utensils and pottery and other things brought in by the Greeks. So the Phœnician garment which the Greek merchants called a *kitōn* (§ 433) the Latin peasants called a *ktūn* (ktoon), and in course of time they gave the word a Latin ending *ic* and dropped the *k*, so that it became our familiar word "tunic."

Traces of Greek speech in Rome and Latium

832. But the Greeks also brought in things which could not be weighed and measured like produce, from a realm of which the Roman was beginning to catch fleeting glimpses; for the peasant heard of strange gods of the Greeks, and he was told

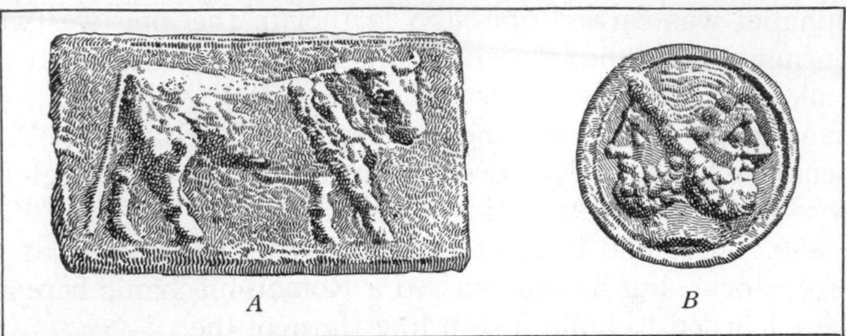

FIG. 228. *Specimens of Early Roman* COPPER MONEY

In the time of Alexander the Great (second half of the Fourth Century B.C.), the Romans began to cast copper in blocks, each block with the figure of an ox upon it (see *A*, above), to indicate its value. The Roman word for cattle (*pecus*) was the origin of their frequent word for property (*pecunia*) and has descended to us in our common word "pecuniary." These blocks were unwieldy, and, influenced by the Greeks, the Romans then cast large disks of copper (*B*, above), which also were very ponderous, each weighing nearly a pound Troy. Hence this coin, called an *as*, was divided into twelve smaller coins, each called an ounce (Roman *uncia*), and there were copper coins of two, three, four, and six *uncias*. When, two generations later, the Romans began to coin silver (see Fig. 230), copper was no longer used for large payments, and the *as* was reduced in size to one sixth its former weight

that they were the counterparts or the originals of his own gods. For him there was a god over each realm in nature and each field of human life: Jupiter was the great Sky-god and king of all the gods; Mars, the patron of all warriors; Venus, the queen of love; Juno, an ancient Sky-goddess, was protectress of women, of birth and marriage, while Vesta, too, watched over the household life, with its hearth fire surviving from the nomad days of the fathers on the Asiatic steppe two thousand years before. Ceres was the goddess who maintained the fruitfulness of the earth, and especially the grain fields (cf. English "cereal"); and Mercury was the messenger of the gods, who protected intercourse and *merc*handising, as his name shows. The streets were full of Greek stories regarding the heroic adventures of these divinities when they were on earth. The Roman learned that Venus was the Greek Aphrodite, Mercury was Hermes, Ceres was Demeter, and so on.

Greek influences, — religion

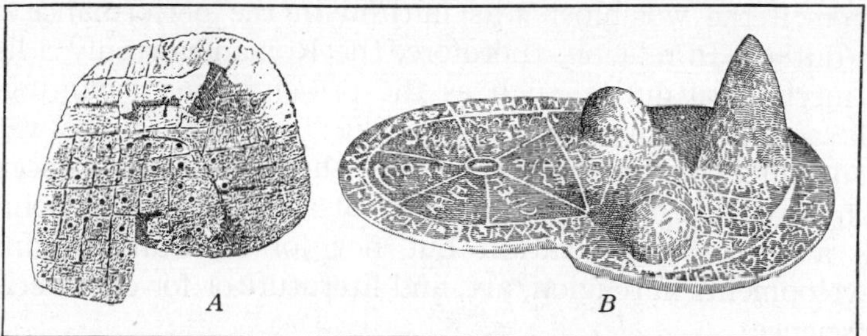

FIG. 229. *Ancient Babylonian Diviner's* BAKED-CLAY MODEL *of* SHEEP'S LIVER (A) *compared with* BRONZE MODEL *of a Liver used by the Etruscans* (B)

The surface of the Babylonian model is marked with lines and holes, indicating the places where the diviner must look for the mysterious signs which disclosed the future. These signs were of course the highly varied natural shapes and markings to be observed in *any* sheep's liver, but the Babylonian believed that these things were signs placed on the liver by the god to whom the sheep had been given, when it was slain as a sacrifice. The meaning of each part of the liver is here written in cuneiform in the proper place. The whole forms a kind of map of the surface and shape of the liver, with written explanations. Absurd as all this seems to us, the art of reading the future in this way was believed in by millions of people, and was finally brought to Italy by the Etruscans (*B*), who had probably received it from the Babylonians by way of Asia Minor

833. This process was aided by the influence of Greek oracles. The oracles delivered by the Greek Sibyl, the prophetess of Apollo of Delphi, were deeply reverenced in Italy. Gathered in the Sibylline books, they were regarded by the Romans as mysterious revelations of the future. Another method of reading the future was brought in by the Etruscans, who were able to discover in the liver of a sheep killed for sacrifice signs which they believed revealed the future (§ 227).

Oracles

834. An art like this appealed to the rather coldly calculating mind of the Roman. As he looked toward his gods he felt no doubts or problems like those which troubled the spirit of Euripides. He lacked the warm and vivid imagination of the Greeks, which had created the beautiful Greek mythology. He was inclined to regard acts of worship as the mere fulfillment of a contract by which the gods must bestow

Mechanical character of Roman religion and the Roman mind

favors if the worshiper was faithful in the performance of his duties. In religion, therefore, the Roman saw only a list of mechanical duties, such as the presentation of offerings, the sacrifice of animals, and the like; and such duties were easily fulfilled. In accordance with this rather legal conception of religion he was fitted for great achievements in political and legal organization but not for new and original developments in religion, art, and literature or for discoveries in science.

Practical sagacity of the Romans

835. Hence it is that in sketching the beginnings of Rome we have found no Homer to picture to us in noble verse the heroic days of her early struggles. Although less gifted than the Greeks, the Romans nevertheless possessed a remarkable ability in applying sober and practical common sense, *enlightened by experience*, to every problem they met. As we shall see, the Romans so contrived their government that it was led and guided by the combined experience of the ripest and most skilled leaders among them. Thus the Roman state was never exposed to the momentary whims of an inexperienced multitude, as in Athens. It was this wisdom and sagacity of the Romans in practical affairs which gave them marked superiority over the Greeks in such matters. Let us now see how Roman political wisdom developed the invincible Roman state.

Elective consuls replace the kings; Roman Republic established

836. When the Etruscan kings were driven out of Rome, about 500 B.C., the nobles, called *patricians*, who had been chiefly instrumental in expelling them, were in control of the government. But none of their number was able to make himself king. Perhaps by compromise with the people, the patricians agreed that two of their number should be *elected* as heads of the state. These two magistrates, called *consuls*, were both to have the same powers; they were to serve for a year only and then give way to two others. To choose them, annual elections were held in an assembly of the weapon-bearing men, largely under the control of the patricians. Nevertheless we must call this new state a republic, of which the consuls were the presidents, for the people had a voice in electing them. But as only patricians could serve as consuls, their government was very oppressive. The people, called the *plebs* (compare our "plebeian"), especially among the Latin tribes, refused to submit to such oppression.

837. The patricians were unable to get on without the help of the peasants as soldiers in their frequent wars. They therefore agreed to give the people a larger share in the government by allowing them in their own assembly to elect a group of new officials called *tribunes*. The tribunes had the right to veto the action of any officer of the government, even that of the consuls themselves. When any citizen was treated unjustly by a consul, he had only to appeal to the tribunes and they could rescind the consul's action and even save a citizen from sentence of death. The tribunes therefore gained great influence, because they could stop the enforcement of any law they thought unjust. Later, as government business increased, their number was also increased.

Tribunes, defenders of the people

838. In the beginning it would seem that almost all the business of government was in the hands of the consuls. They were the commanding generals of the army in war, they had charge of the public funds in the treasury, and they were the judges in all cases at law. It was difficult to combine all these duties. The consuls were often obliged to be absent from Rome for long periods while leading the army, and at such times they were of course unable to give any attention to cases at law, and two citizens having a lawsuit might be obliged to wait until the war was over. Much other ordinary business, like that of the treasury, demanded more time than the consuls could possibly give it. They found it difficult to carry on the volume of business which the government required.

Inability of consuls to attend to all public business

839. This situation made it necessary to create new officers for various kinds of business. To take care of the government funds, treasury officials called *quæstors* were appointed. Two public officers called *censors* were required to keep lists of the people, to assess the amount of taxes each citizen owed, to determine voting rights, and to look after the daily conduct of the people and see that nothing improper was permitted. Our own use of the word "censor" is derived from these Roman officials. For the decision of legal cases a judge called a *prætor* was appointed to assist the consul, and the number of such judges slowly increased. In times of great national danger it was customary to appoint some revered and trustworthy leader as the supreme ruler of the state. He was called a *dictator*, and he could hold his power but a brief period.

Growing body of government officials

840. But a government is called upon to do some other things of great importance besides attending to administrative, financial, and legal business. Important public questions arise which are not mere items of routine business. Examples of such questions are declaring war, restoring peace, and making new laws of all sorts. The consuls had great power and influence in all such matters, but they were much influenced by a council of patricians called the Senate (from Latin *senex*, meaning "old man"), which had existed even as far back as the Etruscan kings, who used to call upon the Senate for advice. Now the patricians enjoyed the exclusive right to serve as consuls, to sit in the Senate, and to hold almost all the offices created to carry on the business of government. The power which the patricians held, therefore, quite unfairly exceeded that of the plebeians.

Public questions and the controlling power of the patricians

841. The tribunes could protect the people from some injustices and save their lives if they were illegally condemned to death, but they could not secure to the citizen all his rights. The tribunes could not recover for the cattle of the people the vanished grass in the public pastures when they had been nipped clean by the great herds of the patricians. The tribunes could not secure for a citizen the right to be elected as consul, or to become a senator, or to marry a patrician's daughter. The struggle

Struggle of plebs and patricians

which had resulted in the appointment of the tribunes, therefore, went on, — a struggle of the common people to win their rights from the wealthy and powerful. It was a struggle like that which we have followed in Athens and the other Greek states, but at Rome it reached a much wiser and more successful settlement. The citizens of Rome manfully stood forth for their rights, and without fighting, civil war, or bloodshed they secured them to a large extent in the course of the first two centuries after the founding of the Republic.

Old laws reduced to writing and the question of new laws

842. They insisted upon a written record of the existing laws, in order that they might know by what laws they were being judged. About fifty years after the establishment of the Republic the earliest Roman laws were reduced to writing and engraved upon twelve tablets of bronze (450 B.C.); but at the same time the people demanded the right to share in the making of *new* laws and to possess an assembly of the people which might itself pass new laws.

Earliest Roman assembly by brotherhoods (*Comitia curiata*)

843. Far back in the days of the kings the people had enjoyed the right to a limited share in the government. To express their opinion they gathered in an assembly called the *Comitia*. It was made up of groups of families or brotherhoods (like the Greek brotherhoods, § 424), each called a *curia*. Hence this assembly was called the *Comitia curiata*. Each such brotherhood assembled and voted by itself, and its decision then counted as one vote. A majority of the brotherhoods decided a question.

Assembly by centuries (*Comitia centuriata*)

844. In the early days of the Republic, when the frequent wars kept the people much together in camp, arrayed in their fighting hundreds, it easily became customary to call them together by these "centuries." Thus a new assembly by centuries arose, called for this reason the *Comitia centuriata*. Owing to the expense of arms and equipment the men of wealth and influence in the centuries far outnumbered the poorer classes. This assembly was therefore controlled by the wealthy and noble classes; they were soon electing the consuls, and ere long they had deprived the old assembly by brotherhoods of all its power.

Tribal assembly (*Concilium plebis tributum* and *Comitia tributa populi*)

845. Under these circumstances a more powerful assembly which at first excluded the patricians had its advantages. Such an assembly was called a *concilium*, and in it the Roman people were assembled by tribes. Every Roman citizen belonged to some tribe to which he or his ancestors had been assigned, but these tribes indicated no distinctions of blood or family; they were merely geographical divisions according to which soldiers were levied, the census taken, and taxes for war collected. Very early the Romans had inclined toward the group vote, for they found it convenient to vote by tribal grouping. This tribal council of the people (*Concilium plebis tributum*) seems gradually to have merged with another tribal assembly, to which the patricians belonged. It was called the *comitia tributa populi*.

Assemblies make laws securing more rights for the people

846. Having shaken off the legal power of the Senate to control their action, the centuriate and tribal assemblies became the lawmaking bodies of the Roman state. Eventually the people were also given voting rights in the centuriate assembly equal to those of the patricians and the wealthy. As a result the people were able to pass laws by which the assemblies gained the right to make laws, and in this way the people gradually secured a fairer share of the public lands and further social rights. Finally, and most important of all, these new laws increased the rights of the people to hold office. In the end Roman citizens elected their plebeian neighbors as censors and quæstors, as judges and at last even as consuls, and they saw men of the people sitting in the Senate.

847. This progress of the people in power brought with it important new developments affecting both society and government. Roman citizens had a deep respect for government and for its officials. The Roman consul appeared in public attended by twelve men called *lictors*, bearing the symbols of state authority. Each man carried a bundle of rods (called *fasces* [1]), suggesting the consul's power to scourge the condemned, and from the midst of the rods rose an ax, symbolizing the consul's legal right to inflict the death penalty. The other officials of high rank were likewise attended by a smaller group of lictors. The consuls and all the higher officials wore white robes edged with purple, a costume which only these men had the right to wear. When a magistrate went out of office, he might assume his official garment from time to time on feast days. There soon grew up a group of once plebeian families, thus distinguished by the public service of its members, to whom the Roman citizens looked up with great respect. When the voters were called upon to select their candidates, they preferred members of these eminent families, especially for the consulship. A new nobility was thus formed, made up of such illustrious families and the old patricians.

New nobility of former magistrates

848. This situation directly affected the Senate, the members of which had formerly been appointed from among the patricians by the consuls. A new law, however, authorized the *censors* to make out the lists of senators, giving the preference to those who had been magistrates. Thus the new nobility of ex-magistrates, formerly plebeians, entered the Senate, bringing in fresh blood from the ranks of the people.

New nobility gains control of Senate

849. As a result of these changes the Senate was made up of the three hundred men of Rome who had gained the most experience in government and in public affairs. When the herald's trumpet echoed from the Forum, and the senators, responding to the call, crowded into the modest assembly hall beside the Forum and took their seats, the consul called them to order. He was president of the Senate, and he and his colleague, the other consul, were the heads of the state, with more power than any senator possessed. From his chair on the platform

Senate gains leadership over the consul

[1] It is from this Latin word that the well-known modern Italian terms *fascism* and *fascisti* have arisen.

the consul looked down into the strong faces of wise and sagacious men, many of whom had already held his high office and knew far more about its duties than he did. Moreover, while he was in office for only a year, the men confronting him held their seats in the Senate for life, and most of them had been conducting public business there for years. The result was that their combined influence, operating steadily for many years, was too strong for the consul. Instead of telling the senators of his own plans and of the laws he desired, he found himself listening to the proposals of the Senate and carrying out the will of the senators. As a result the consul became a kind of senatorial minister, carrying on the government according to instructions from the Senate.

850. In the matter of lawmaking a similar growth of the Senate's influence took place. Although the popular assemblies had the right to make laws, it was not in their power to *propose* a new law. They could vote upon it only after it had been proposed by a *magistrate*, especially by one of the tribunes, who were the presiding officers of the tribal assembly. The influence of the Senate on the magistrates was such that the magistrates discussed with the senators every law to be brought before the assemblies for adoption. The tribunes could stop the operation of any law, and hence the Senate had become accustomed to consult with them before a law was passed. The result was that the tribunes were given membership and seats in the Senate, and so added to the power and influence of that already powerful body.

Senate gains control of lawmaking

851. By far the larger part of the Roman citizens lived too far away to come up to the city and vote. The small minority living in Rome, who could be present and vote at the meetings of the assemblies, were familiar with the faces of the senators and well knew the wisdom, skill, and experience of these old statesmen. They knew also that there was a strong feeling of patriotism among the senators, and, standing at the open doors of the Senate hall, they had heard the voice of many

Roman Senate the supreme leader of the state

a gray-haired ex-consul whom they revered, as it rang through the Forum, in eloquent support of some patriotic measure or in earnest summons to national defense. Feeling too their own ignorance of public affairs, the Roman citizens were not unwilling that important public questions should be settled by the Senate. Thus the Roman Senate became a large committee of experienced statesmen, guiding and controlling the Roman state. They formed the greatest council of rulers that ever grew up in the ancient world, or perhaps in any age. They were a body of aristocrats, and their control of Rome made it an aristocratic state in spite of its republican form. We are now to watch the steady development and progress of Roman power (see maps, p. 591) under the wise and stable leadership of the Senate. We should bear in mind, however, that the Senate's power was a slow growth, continuing during the wars and conquests which we are now to follow.

SECTION 72. THE EXPANSION OF THE ROMAN REPUBLIC AND THE CONQUEST OF ITALY

Latin League and the treaty with Rome

852. It was a tiny nation which began its uncertain career after the expulsion of the Etruscan kings. The territory of the Roman Republic was the mere city with the adjacent fields for a very few miles around. On the other side of the Tiber lived the dreaded Etruscans, and on the Roman side of the river, all around the little republic, lay the lands of the Latin tribes (§ 823), who had combined in what was called the Latin League. The league was independent and did not acknowledge itself subject to Rome, but in their own struggle with their enemies the Latin tribes found the leadership of the city indispensable. The Latin League therefore made a perpetual treaty with Rome, — a treaty uniting the league and the city in a combination for mutual defense under the leadership of Rome. But this arrangement produced only a loose union, not a unified nation. Nevertheless the Roman Senate gave to the citizens of Latium privileges in Rome about equal to those of Roman citizens, and the Latins were therefore ready to fight for the defense of the city whose leadership they followed.

Early struggles of the Republic with Etruscans and Italic tribes

853. For two generations the new republic struggled for the preservation of its mere existence. This struggle against threatening enemies on all its frontiers, especially the Etruscans, was the motive power which stirred the little nation to constant effort, to vigorous life, and to steady growth. Fortunately for the Romans, within a generation after the foundation of the Republic (474 B.C.) the fleet of Syracuse utterly destroyed the Etruscan fleet. Later the Etruscans were attacked in the rear by the Gauls, who were pouring over the Alpine passes into the valley of the Po and were laying waste the Etruscan cities of the north. This weakening of the Etruscans at the hands of their enemies on both north and south probably saved Rome from destruction. It enabled the Romans to maintain a ten years' siege of Veii, a strong southern fortress of the Etruscans only about ten miles by road from Rome. Strangely enough the other Etruscan cities did not come to the aid of Veii, and eventually the Romans captured and destroyed it (396 B.C.). At the same time the Italic tribes surrounding Latium on the south, east, and north were constantly invading and plundering the fields and pastures of the Latin tribes and threatening the city. Rome beat off these marauders and, by establishing a group of colonies along the coast south of the Tiber, formed a buffer against such invasions from the south. By 400 B.C. or a little after, the Romans had conquered and taken possession of a fringe of new territory on all sides, which protected them from their enemies.

854. In the new territory thus gained the Romans planted colonies of citizens, or they granted citizenship or other valuable privileges to the absorbed population. Roman peasants, obligated to bear Roman arms and having a voice in the government, thus pushed out into the expanding borders of Roman territory. This policy of *agricultural* expansion, steadily and consistently followed by the Senate, was irresistible, for it gave to Rome an ever-increasing body of brave and hardy citizen-soldiers, cultivating their own lands and ready at all times to take up the sword in defense of the state which shielded them. The Roman policy was thus in striking contrast with the narrow methods of the Greek republics, which jealously prevented outsiders from gaining citizenship. It was the steady expansion of Rome under this policy which, in a little over two centuries after the expulsion of the Etruscan kings, made the little republic on the Tiber mistress of all Italy (see maps, p. 591).

Agricultural colonization and expansion the Roman policy

855. The second century of Roman expansion opened with a fearful catastrophe which very nearly accomplished the complete destruction of the nation. In the two decades around 400 B.C. the barbarian Gauls, who had been overrunning the territory of the Etruscans, finally reached the lower Tiber, and the Roman army which went out to meet them was completely defeated. The city, still undefended by walls, was entirely at their mercy. They entered at once (perhaps around 390 B.C.), plundering and burning. Only the citadel on the Capitol hill held out against the barbarians. Long afterward Roman tradition told how even the citadel was being surprised at night by a party of Gauls who clambered up the heights, when the sacred geese, kept in a temple close by, aroused the garrison by their cackling, and the storming party was repulsed. Wearied by a long siege of the citadel, the Gauls at length agreed to accept a ransom of gold and to return northward, where they settled in the valley of the Po. But they still remained a serious danger to the Romans.

Capture of Rome by the Gauls

856. As Rome recovered from this disaster it was evident that the city needed fortifications, and for the first time masonry walls were built around it (plan, p. 574). This gave the city a strength it had not before possessed. It gained the southern territory of the Etruscans, now much weakened by the inroads of the Gauls, and it also seized new possessions in the Campanian plain. The high-handed manner in which Rome was now taking new lands seems to have alarmed even the Latin tribes, and they endeavored to break away from the control of the powerful walled city. In the two years' war which resulted the city was completely victorious, and the Roman Senate forced the defeated Latin tribes to break up the Latin League (338 B.C.). The Roman Senate then proceeded to make separate treaties with each of the Latin tribes and did not grant them as many privileges as formerly. Rome thus gained the undisputed leadership of the Latin tribes which was at last to bring her the leadership of Italy.

Latin tribes defeated and Latin League broken up (338 B.C).

857. The year 338 B.C., in which this important event took place, is a date to be well remembered, for it witnessed also the defeat of the Greek cities at the hands of Philip of Macedon. In the same year, therefore, both the Greeks and the Latins saw themselves conquered and falling under the leadership of a single state, — the Greeks under that of Macedonia, the Latins under that of Rome. But in Greece that leadership was in the hands of one man, who might and did perish, while in Italy the leadership of the Latins was in the hands of a whole body of wise leaders, the Roman Senate. In sixty-five years they were now to gain the leadership of all Italy (see maps II, III, and IV, p. 591).

Leadership of Greeks and Latins decided in the same year

858. Meantime another formidable foe, a group of Italic tribes called the Samnites, had been taking possession of the mountains which form the backbone of the Italian peninsula inland from Rome. They had gained some civilization from the Greek cities of the south, and they were able to muster a large army of hardy peasants, very dangerous in war, but they lacked the steadying and continuous leadership of a governing city like Rome. Some of them drifted down into the plains of Campania (see maps, p. 591), where they captured Capua, one of the southern outposts of the Etruscans. Within forty years after the expulsion of the Gauls the Samnites were in hostile collision with

New Samnite enemy

Rome. By 325 B.C. a fierce war broke out, which lasted, with interruptions, for a generation. The Romans lost several battles and in one case were subjected by the Samnites to the ordeal of marching "under the yoke," — a humiliation which the Romans never forgot.[1]

Samnite Wars (325–290 B.C.) and battle of Sentinum (295 B.C.)

859. But the resources of the Roman Senate were not confined to fighting. They gained lands and established Roman colonies on the east of the Apennines and in the plain of Campania. From these new possessions they were able to attack the Samnites from both sides of the mountains (see map II, p. 591). The Samnites attempted a combination of Rome's enemies against her. They succeeded in shifting their army northward and joining forces with both the Etruscans and the Gauls. All central and much of northern Italy was now involved in the war. In the mountains midway between the upper Tiber and the eastern shores of Italy the Roman army met and crushed the combined forces of the allies in a terrible battle at Sentinum (295 B.C.). This battle decided the future of Italy for over two thousand years. It not only gave the Romans possession of central Italy, but it made them the leading power in the whole peninsula (see map III, p. 591).

After Sentinum Rome was mistress of central Italy to the Arnus

860. Henceforth the Etruscans were unable to maintain themselves as a leading power. One by one their cities were taken by the Romans or they entered into alliance with Rome. The Gallic barbarians were beaten off, and the stream of Gallic invasion which was thus forced back in northern Italy by Rome flowed over eastward and southward into the Balkan Peninsula. The settled Gauls, however, continued to hold the Po valley, and the northern boundary of the Roman conquests was along the river Arnus, south of the Apennines. Southward the resistance of the Samnites was easily crushed within five years after the battle at Sentinum.

[1] The defeated troops, in token of their submission, marched under a lance supported horizontally on two upright lances and called a "yoke."

They and the other leading peoples of southern Italy, with the exception of the Greeks there, were forced to enter the Roman alliance. The Romans were supreme from the Arnus to the Greek cities of southern Italy.

Endeavor of western Greeks to unite against Rome

861. Of the three great western rivals the Etruscans had collapsed, and the youthful but powerful new nation of Rome had taken its place as the northern power in the group. Thus the three great rivals in the western world were now the Romans, the Greeks, and the Carthaginians. As for the home cities of the Greeks, they were under the successors of Alexander, fighting among themselves for possession of the fragments of his empire, while Rome was gaining the leadership of Italy. As for the western Greek colonies, four centuries of conflict among themselves had left them still a disunited group of cities fringing southern Italy and Sicily. They had long been fighting with the Italic tribes and other peoples of southern Italy, and a number of the Greek cities of the region had fallen. The survivors, alarmed at the threatening expansion of Roman power, now made another endeavor to unite, and called in help from the outside.

Pyrrhus of Epirus plans to form an empire of the western Greeks

862. The leading city of the Greeks in southern Italy was Tarentum. Unable to secure effective aid from the now declining home cities of Greece, the men of Tarentum sent an appeal to Pyrrhus, the vigorous and able king of Epirus, just across from the heel of Italy. Pyrrhus fully understood the highly developed art of war as it had grown up with Epaminondas and Philip of Macedon. Besides Thessalian horsemen, the best cavalry in the world, he had secured from the Orient a formidable innovation in the form of fighting elephants. With an army of well-trained Greek infantry of the phalanx, and with his well-known talent as a soldier, Pyrrhus was a highly dangerous foe. His purpose was to form a great nation of the western Greeks in Sicily and Italy. Such a nation would have proved a formidable rival of both Rome and Carthage.

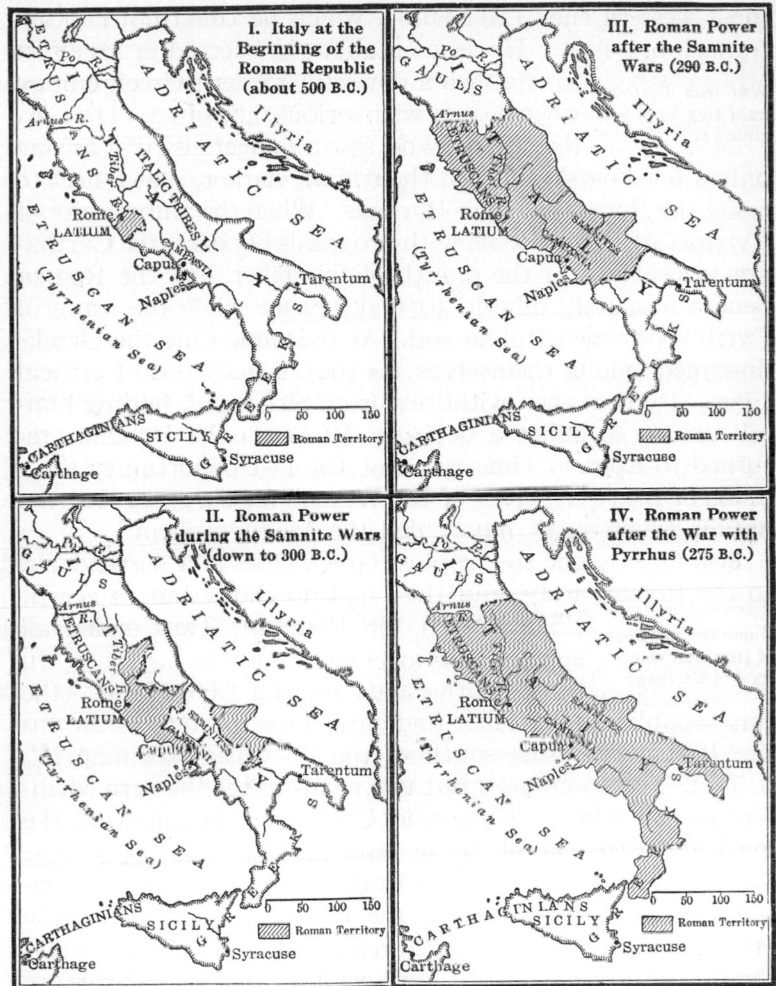

Expansion *of* Roman Power *in Italy*

863. Pyrrhus completely defeated the Romans at Heraclea in 280 B.C., and in the following year they were routed again. Pyrrhus proceeded in triumph to Sicily, where he gained the whole island except the Carthaginian colony on the outermost western end (Lilybæum), which he could not capture for lack of a fleet. He seemed about to succeed in his effort to establish a powerful western Greek empire when he met with serious difficulties. The Carthaginians, who saw a dangerous rival arising only a few hours' sail from their home harbor, sent a fleet to assist the Romans against Pyrrhus. When the ambassador of Pyrrhus arrived at Rome with proposals of peace, the Carthaginian fleet was at the mouth of the Tiber, and the Roman Senate resolutely refused to make peace while the army of Pyrrhus occupied Italian soil. At the same time the Greeks disagreed among themselves, as they usually did at critical times. Pyrrhus then withdrew from Sicily and, finding himself unable to inflict a decisive defeat on the Romans, returned to Epirus. Thus was lost the last opportunity for a union of the Greek cities of the West to form a great Hellenic nation, which might have ruled the Mediterranean.

War with Pyrrhus ended by Carthaginian aid to Rome

864. One by one the helpless Greek cities now surrendered to the Roman army, and they had no choice but to accept alliance with the Romans. Thus ended all hope of a great Greek nation in the West. In two centuries and a quarter (500–275 B.C.) the tiny republic on the Tiber had gained the mastery of the entire Italian peninsula south of the Po valley (see map IV, p. 591). There were now but two rivals in the Western Mediterranean world, — Rome and Carthage. In following the inevitable struggle of these two for the mastery of the Western Mediterranean world during the next two generations, we shall be watching the final conflict between the Western wings of the two great racial lines, — the Semitic and the Indo-European. But before we take up this struggle we must learn more about the character and the civilization of the great Roman power which thus grew up in Italy. These men who won the supremacy of Italy for the little republic on the Tiber were the first generation of Romans about whom sufficient information has survived to make us well acquainted with them.

Rome the mistress of Italy and sole rival of Carthage

QUESTIONS

Section 69. Into what divisions does the Mediterranean fall? Discuss the spread of civilization in the Mediterranean world. Tell about the earliest migrations into Italy and the incoming of metal. What Indo-European tribes came into Italy, and when? Did they find civilization there? With what three rivals were the Italic tribes confronted in Italy? Tell about the coming of the Etruscans. Locate the Carthaginian and Greek settlements in the Western Mediterranean. What did the Greeks accomplish against the Carthaginians and Etruscans? Did the western Greeks unite into a nation?

Section 70. Describe Latium. What tribes settled there? Where was the market of the Latins? Describe the place. What was it called? Who seized it in the Eighth Century B.C.? What line of kings arose? Discuss Etruscan influence on Roman culture.

Section 71. Whence did the Romans gain their alphabet? What other Greek influences can you mention? Who succeeded the Etruscan kings as rulers of Rome? What magistrates did the people elect for their own protection? Who had the exclusive right to serve as consuls and to sit in the Senate? Who had the power to make laws? What new nobility arose? How did they gain control of the Senate? How did the Senate gain the leadership of the state? What can you say of this leadership?

Section 72. What was the relation between Rome and the Latin tribes around it? Describe the colonial policy of the Roman Senate. Tell about the coming of the Gauls. What happened to the Latin League in 338 B.C.? Tell the story of the Roman struggle with the Samnites. What did Tarentum do? Recount the war with Pyrrhus. What happened to the Greeks of Italy after the retirement of Pyrrhus?

BIBLIOGRAPHY FOR TOPICAL STUDIES

Etruscan civilization: BOTSFORD, *Source Book*, pp. 328–329; FRANK, *History of Rome*, pp. 19–29; RANDALL-MACIVER, *The Etruscans*, pp. 18–54, 66–84, 117–130; STRONG, *Art in Ancient Rome*, Vol. I, pp. 12–30.

Legislative and executive powers in the Republic: ABBOTT, *Roman Politics*, pp. 74–95; BOTSFORD, *Source Book*, pp. 348–351, 353–360, 397–401; FRANK, pp. 182–188; *Legacy of Rome*, pp. 94–98; POLAND-REISINGER-WAGNER, *Culture of Greece and Rome*, pp. 295–302; SHOWERMAN, *Rome and the Romans*, pp. 154–173.

CHAPTER XXIII · *The Supremacy of the Roman Republic in Italy and the Rivalry with Carthage*

SECTION 73. ITALY UNDER THE EARLY ROMAN REPUBLIC

865. After the leadership of Italy had been gained by Rome, there were men still living who could remember the Latin war (ended 338 B.C.), when Rome had lost even the surrounding fields of little Latium. Now, sixty-five years later, the city on the Tiber was mistress of *all Italy*. The new power over a large group of cities and states, thus gained within a single lifetime, was exercised by the Roman Senate with the greatest skill and success. Had Rome *annexed* all the conquered lands and endeavored to rule them from Rome, the population of Italy would have been dissatisfied, and constant revolts would have followed. How, then, was Italy to become a nation, controlled by Rome?

Problem of making Italy a nation

866. The Romans began by granting the defeated cities a kind of citizenship. It entitled them to all the protection of the Roman state in carrying on commerce and business, to all the rights of every Roman citizen in the law courts, and, at the same time, to social privileges like that of intermar-

NOTE. The above headpiece represents the beautiful stone SARCOPHAGUS of one of the early SCIPIOS, found in the family tomb on the Appian Way. It is adorned with details of Greek architecture which clearly show that it was done by a Greek artist. Verses in early Latin, on the side of the sarcophagus, contain praises of the departed Scipio.

riage. But this citizenship did not entitle them to vote. In distant communities, however, no one felt the lack of this privilege, for in order to vote it was necessary to go to Rome. Cities and communities controlled by Rome in this way were called "allies." The protection of the powerful Roman state in carrying on business and commerce was of itself a very valuable advantage to the allies. They were therefore willing to place their troops entirely at the disposal of Rome, and likewise all their dealings with foreign peoples. They still had full control of their own local internal affairs except those of the army. In all this Rome wisely granted the different cities very different rights and laid upon them highly varied restrictions. Thus no two cities were likely to feel the same grievances or make common cause against the Roman rule of Italy.

Self-governing local communities made allies

867. Rome had, however, gradually annexed a good deal of territory to pay her war expenses and to supply her increasing numbers of citizens with land. Her own full citizens thus occupied about one sixth of the territory of Italy. It consisted chiefly of the region between the Apennine Mountains and the sea, from Cære on the north to Capua and Cumæ on the south (see map, p. 562). It included likewise some important areas in the Apennines and on the Adriatic coast. It was, furthermore, Rome's policy to sprinkle Roman colonies through the territory of the allies. All Italy was thus more or less dotted with communities of Roman citizens. By these wise measures Rome gained and kept control of Italy.

Communities enjoying full Roman citizenship

868. Rome thus brought into a kind of unity what we may *geographically* call Italy; but an examination of its population will readily show us how far Italy really was from being a *nation*, even though controlled by Rome. Besides the Gauls, whose territory in the Po valley had not yet been taken over by the Romans, there were the conquered Etruscans, who occupied a large part of northern Italy. In the central region were the

Lack of national unity in Italy: diversity of language

Latins and the other Italic tribes. These tribes all spoke related dialects, which were, however, so different that no one tribe could understand any of the others. Finally, in the south were the Greek cities. There was therefore no common language in Italy, even among the Indo-Europeans, and this created a situation very different from that in Greece.

Lack of national unity in Italy: no common traditions

869. Neither did the peoples of Italy possess any common literary inheritance such as the Greeks had in the Homeric poems. Nothing in their history, like the Trojan War in that of the Greeks, had ever given them common traditions. Roman organization had created a kind of United States of Italy, which might after a long time slowly merge into a nation. Meantime these peoples, of course, had no feeling of patriotism toward Rome. Speaking different languages, so that they did not understand one another when they met, they long remained quite distinct.

Italy to become Latin in speech but Greek in civilization

870. In language the future nation was to be Latin, the tongue of the ruling city; geographically it comprised Italy; politically it was Roman.[1] When we consider Rome from the point of view of *civilization*, however, we are obliged to add a fourth name; for, as time went on, Italy was to become in civilization more and more Greek. The Greek cities extended as far north as the plains of Campania, where Rome had early taken Capua, in size the second city of Italy. In the days of the war with Pyrrhus and after, the Roman soldiers had beheld with wonder and admiration the beautiful Greek temples in such cities as Pæstum (Fig. 214) and Tarentum. Here for the first time they saw also fine theaters, and they must have attended Greek plays, of which they understood little or nothing. But the races and athletic games in the handsome stadium of such a Greek city required no interpretation in order to be understood by the sturdy Roman soldiers.

[1] Compare the similar application of three names to the United States. Politically the nation is the United States, geographically it is commonly called America, while the language is English.

871. In southern Italy the Romans had taken possession of the western fringe of the great Hellenistic world, whose wonderful civilization we have already studied. The Romans at once felt the superiority of this new world of cultivated life. When a highborn Roman family like that of the Scipios wished to have carved a beautiful sarcophagus (stone coffin) for their father, they employed a Greek sculptor from the south (headpiece, p. 594). At the same time the temples of Rome began to be laid out on an *oblong* ground plan, like those of the Greeks, and no longer on a *square* ground plan like those of the Etruscans. As Roman power expands we shall see this conquest of the Romans by Greek civilization making greater and greater progress, but it never went so far as to remove all traces of Etruscan civilization. On the contrary, the foundation of Roman civilization remained Etruscan to the end.

Early evidences of Greek art and architecture in Rome

FIG. 230. *A Roman* DENARIUS *of Silver*

After the capture of the Greek cities of southern Italy the Romans began the coinage of silver (268 B.C.)

872. It was as yet chiefly in commerce and in business that Greek influences were evident. Greek merchants from the southern cities now enjoyed Roman protection when they traded in Rome. Greek silver money appeared in greater quantities after the capture of the Greek cities. Copper coins were no longer sufficient for Roman business, and not long after the fall of Tarentum, in 268 B.C., Rome issued her first silver coin. Just as Athens had once done (§ 497), so Rome now began to feel the influence of money, and a moneyed class, largely merchants, arose. They were not manufacturers, as at Athens, and, although possessing some industries, Rome was never noted as a great industrial center.

Greek influence on commerce and coinage; moneyed class

SECTION 74. ROME AND CARTHAGE AS COMMERCIAL RIVALS

873. The old policy of *agricultural* expansion (§ 854) had slowly brought Rome the leadership *within* Italy. A new policy of *commercial* expansion was to bring her into conflict with the Mediterranean world *outside of* Italy. The farmers had looked no farther than the shores of Italy, but the transactions of the Roman merchants reached out beyond those shores. We have seen that when Roman ships issued from the Tiber they entered the Tyrrhenian Sea (§ 817), which is inclosed on the south by Sicily and the Carthaginian coast of Africa. A glance at the map (I, p. 626) shows us how Rome and Carthage faced each other across this triangular sea, where both were now carrying on extensive business.

Commercial expansion of Rome seaward

874. It was indeed a dangerous rival which now confronted Rome across the Tyrrhenian Sea. In the veins of the Carthaginians flowed the blood of those hardy desert mariners of Arabia, the Semitic caravaneers who had made the market places of Babylon the center of ancient eastern trade two thousand years before Rome ever owned a ship. The fleets of their Phœnician ancestors had coursed the Mediterranean in the days when the Stone Age barbarians of Italy were eagerly looking for the merchant of the East and his metal implements. While Rome was an obscure trading village on the Tiber, and before the Greeks ever entered these waters, the Phœnician merchants had explored the Western Mediterranean and had perceived the advantageous position of the commanding projection where the African coast thrusts out toward Sicily. Here, on the northern edge of the region now called Tunis, they had planted the city which had become the commercial queen of the Western Mediterranean and the most powerful rival of Rome.

Early mercantile successes of Semites; foundation of Carthage

875. This advantageous situation gave Carthage unrivaled commercial opportunities. Gradually, as her trade carried her in both directions, she had gained the coast on both sides, — eastward to the frontiers of the Greek city of Cyrene and westward to the Atlantic. It is important to remember at this point that the great desert of Sahara lay behind Carthage and prevented her expansion southward. As she sought room for colonial expansion the desert left Carthage no choice but to look northward to lands in or across the Mediterranean. Her merchants therefore absorbed southern Spain, with its profitable silver mines, and they gained control of the import of British tin by way of the Strait of Gibraltar. Outside of this strait their settlements extended northward along the coast of Spain and southward along the Atlantic coast of Africa to the edge of the Sahara. In this direction Hanno, one of their fearless captains, explored the coast of Africa probably as far as Guinea.

Carthaginian expansion conditioned by desert

876. It was only the incoming of the Greeks which had prevented the Carthaginians from taking possession of the Mediterranean islands upon which their splendid harbor looked out. They usually held a large part of Sicily, the west end of which was almost visible from the housetops of Carthage. They planted their colonies in the islands of Sardinia and Corsica, and they had ports in the Balearic Islands, between Sardinia and Spain. They closed the Strait of Gibraltar and the ports of the islands *to ships from all other cities*. Foreign ships intruding in these waters were promptly rammed and sunk by Carthaginian warships.

Carthaginian expansion in Western Mediterranean islands

877. Unlike Rome the military power of Carthage, supported by the profits from trade, was built up entirely on a basis of money, with which, as long as she prospered, she could support a large mercenary army. She had no farmers cultivating their own land, from whom she could draw an army of citizen-soldiers as did Rome. The rich and fertile region of Tunis just south of Carthage had indeed been taken by the Carthaginians from its native owners. Here the mer-

Commercial prosperity and a mercenary army at Carthage

chant princes of the city developed large and beautiful estates worked by slaves; but such lands, supporting no small farmers, furnished no troops for the army.

878. This was a serious weakness in the organization of the Carthaginian state. The rulers of the city never trusted the army, made up as it was of foreigners, and they always felt some distrust even toward their own generals, although they were, of course, born Carthaginians. The fear lest the generals should endeavor to make themselves kings of Carthage caused much friction between the government and the Carthaginian commanders and was frequently a cause of weakness to the nation. Although there were two elective magistrates called judges at the head of the state, Carthage was really governed by a group of merchant nobles, a wealthy aristocracy whose members formed a council in complete control. They were what the Greeks called an oligarchy, but they were energetic and statesmanlike rulers. Centuries of shrewd guidance on their part made Carthage a great state, far exceeding in power any of the Greek states that ever arose, not excluding Athens.

Carthaginian state

879. But Carthage remained in civilization an Oriental power. Wherever her works of art are dug up today, they show all the earlier limitations of Oriental art and seem to have been little influenced by the Greeks. Only in Sicily did Carthaginian merchants yield to Greek influence, take up coinage, and issue silver money. In Carthage herself they retained the old Oriental use of bars of precious metal. Her merchants finally found it necessary, however, to have some convenient medium of exchange. They issued leather money, the earliest predecessor of paper money, stamped with the seal of the state, guaranteeing its value. In literature their great explorer Hanno wrote an account of his exploration of the Atlantic coast of Africa, and Mago, one of their statesmen, who developed the great farming district of Tunis, wrote a treatise on agriculture which the Roman Senate had translated into Latin. It became the standard book on agriculture in Italy.

Carthaginian civilization

880. In matters of household equipment and city building the Carthaginians were quite the equals of the Greeks. The city of Carthage itself was large and splendid. It was in area three times as large as Rome. Behind wide docks and extensive piers of masonry, teeming with ships and merchandise, the city spread far inland, with spacious markets and busy manufacturing quarters humming with industry. Beyond the dwellings of the poorer craftsmen and artisans rose the stately houses of the wealthy merchants, with luxuriant tropical gardens. Around the whole rose imposing walls and massive fortifications, inclosing the entire city and making its capture almost an impossibility. Behind the great city, outside the walls, stretched a wide expanse of waving palm groves and tropical plantations, dotted with the magnificent country houses of the splendid commercial lords of Carthage, who were to lead the coming struggle with Rome.

City of Carthage

881. Back in the days of the Latin war (ended 338 B.C.), or a little before, when the Roman merchants were still doing a small business, they had been willing that the Senate should make a treaty with Carthage, drawing lines which the ships of neither side should cross. Indeed, about the middle of the Samnite Wars the Roman Senate had made a second treaty with Carthage (306 B.C.), in which it was agreed that no Roman ships should enter the harbors of Sicily and no Carthaginian ships should trade in the ports of Italy. The capture of the Greek cities of Italy by the Romans had left the Greeks of Sicily to face the power of Carthage entirely alone. In times past they had done this with great success (§ 820), but now, unable to unite against Carthage, they were slowly yielding, and the Carthaginians were steadily pushing eastward and absorbing the great island. The merchants of Italy looked over at the busy harbors of Sicily, where so much profitable trade was going on, and it filled them with growing impatience that they were not permitted to do business there. With increasing vexation they realized

Early commercial treaties with Carthage vex Roman merchants

that Rome had gained the supremacy of Italy and pushed her frontiers to the southernmost tip of the peninsula, only to look across and find that the merchant princes of Carthage had made the Western Mediterranean a Carthaginian sea.

Danger to Rome in threatened loss of Strait of Messina

882. Indeed, Carthage was gaining a position which might cut off Rome from communication with even her own ports on the Adriatic side of Italy. To reach them, Roman ships must pass through the Strait of Messina between Italy and Sicily. The advance of Carthage in Sicily might enable her at any time to seize the Sicilian city of Messina and close this strait to Roman ships. We can understand the dread with which Italian merchants looked southward, thinking of the day when Carthaginian warships in the harbor at Messina would stop all traffic between the west coast of Italy and the Adriatic.

War strength of the Romans

883. The Roman Senate without doubt shared these apprehensions. Many a Roman senator must have asked himself the question, What would be Rome's chances of success in a struggle with the mighty North African commercial empire? Rome had little or no navy. The Roman army had been barely able to maintain itself against a modern Hellenistic commander like Pyrrhus. The ancient regulation drawing the soldiers only from among the owners of land had formerly limited the size of the army, but now it was greatly increased in size by the admission of the new class of men having property in money. The introduction of pay for citizens in the army had also increased the possible length of military service among a people still chiefly made up of farmers obliged to return home to plow, sow, and reap. The Romans could thus put a citizen army of over three hundred thousand men into the field. Besides the troops made up of Roman citizens the principle was adopted of having each army include also about an equal number of troops drawn from the allies. This plan, therefore, doubled the number of available troops. Thus enlarged, the Roman army far exceeded in size any other army ever organized in the Mediterranean world.

FIG. 231. *A Roman* SOLDIER *of the* LEGION

The figure of the soldier is carved upon a tombstone erected in his memory by his brother. His offensive weapons are his spear (*pilum*), which he holds in his extended right hand with point upward, and his heavy short sword (*gladius*), which he wears girded high on his right side. As defensive equipment he has a helmet, a leather corselet stopping midway between the waist and knees, and a shield (*scutum*) carried on his left arm

Roman improvements in arms and tactics

884. In arms and tactics the Romans had been able to make some improvements in the Hellenistic art of war. The spear was now employed by the Romans only as the battle opened, when it was hurled into the ranks of the enemy at short range. After this the battle was fought by the Romans with short swords, which were much more easily handled at close quarters than long spears. At the same time the Romans had likewise improved the phalanx, which had thus far been a massive unit possessing as a whole no flexibility, — it had no joints. The Romans gave it joints and flexibility by cutting it up in both directions, that is, lengthwise and crosswise.

Phalanx cut into divisions and maniples

885. They divided the phalanx lengthwise into three divisions,[1] one forming the front, one the middle, and one the rear (Fig. 232). Each division was about six men deep, and there was only a narrow space between the divisions. The front division was made up of the young and vigorous troops, while the older men were placed in the other two divisions. If the steady old troops behind saw that a gap was being made in the front divi-

[1] The word "division" in this discussion is, of course, not employed in a *modern* military sense.

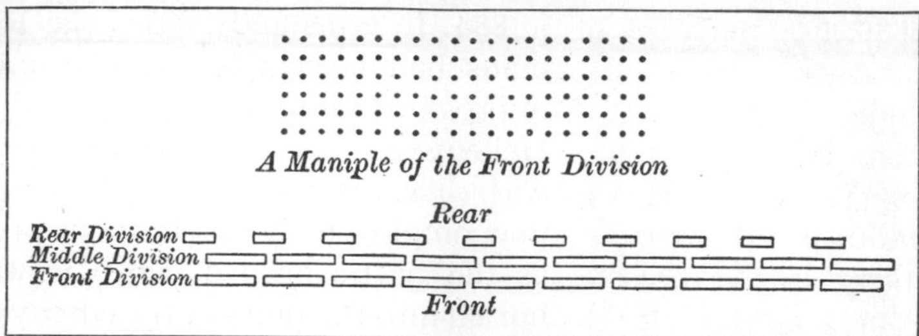

Fig. 232. *Plan of a* Roman Threefold Line *of Battle with Detail of a Single Maniple above it*

Here we see the once solid and indivisible phalanx of the Greeks broken up into three divisions lengthwise (lower diagram) — a front, middle, and rear division — and likewise cut up crosswise into short sections (maniples). In the front and middle divisions these maniples were six men deep and twenty men long (see upper diagram) and half as long in the rear division. These sections (maniples) were so placed that the openings between them did not coincide, but the maniples of the middle division covered the openings, or joints, in the front division

sion, it was the business of the second division to advance at once and fill the gap. This made it necessary to cut up the divisions crosswise into short sections, so that a section could advance without carrying the whole division forward. Such a section of a division had a front about twenty men long, and, being six men deep, each section of a division had a hundred and twenty men. These sections were called *maniples*. Each maniple, in advancing to fill a gap before it, was like a football "back" springing forward to stop a gap in the line before him. But it is important to notice that thus far all three divisions of the phalanx were invariably kept together; they were *inseparable*. The middle and rear divisions were always only *supports of the front division immediately before them*. It had not yet occurred to the Romans to shift the middle or rear division, so that they would fight facing in another direction, or to post them in another part of the field, leaving the first division to fight unsupported. When a great Roman, during the struggle with Carthage, discovered the possibility of thus shifting the middle and rear divisions, a new chapter in the art of war began.

886. For purposes of mustering and feeding an army the Romans divided it into larger bodies called *legions*, each containing usually forty-five hundred men, of whom three hundred were cavalry, twelve hundred were light-armed troops, while the three thousand forming the body of the legion were the heavy-armed men making up the three divisions just described. Each maniple of one hundred and twenty men was divided into two centuries of sixty men each, for a century soon ceased always to contain a hundred men. Each century had a commander called a centurion. A centurion and his century roughly corresponded to our captain and his company.

Legions and centurions

887. Notwithstanding these improvements the Romans did not at first see the importance of a commander-in-chief of long experience, — a man who made warfare his calling and had become a professional military leader like the Hellenistic commanders. Hence the Romans intrusted their armies without hesitation to the command of their consuls, who as presidents of the Republic had often never had any experience in military leadership. Moreover, a consul might be leading his troops just on the eve of battle and find himself deprived of command by the expiration of his term of office. In the Samnite Wars this difficulty had shown the Romans the necessity of extending a consul's military power under such circumstances. When this was done he was called a proconsul. But the Romans were still without professional generals like Xenophon (§ 666). At the same time the introduction of pay for officers and soldiers had made extended service possible, and an experienced body of lower officers such as the centurions had grown up.

Lack of experienced commanding generals

888. In military discipline the Romans surpassed all other peoples of ancient times, for even among the Greek troops there was great lack of discipline. We hear of a Roman father who ordered his son to be executed in the presence of the army, because the young man had, in disobedience of orders, accepted single combat with an enemy and slain him. Even an ex-consul, having won a victory after receiving orders from the dictator not to give battle, was condemned to death by the dictator as the legal consequence of disobedience to a superior. It was only with the greatest difficulty that he was saved by his influential friends. In accordance with the strict system maintained in all their operations it was the invariable practice of a Roman army, when it halted, to construct a square fortified camp surrounded by a ridge of earth bearing a stockade of wooden posts driven into the crest of the ridge. In plan this camp was a descendant of the old prehistoric pile-village of northern Italy.

Roman discipline and the fortified camp

QUESTIONS

Section 73. How did Rome govern the defeated cities of Italy? Was Italy a unified nation? What was the future language of Italy to be? Mention some early Greek influences in Italy.

Section 74. Had agriculture carried the Romans outside of Italy? Was commerce now to do so? Into what triangular sea does the Tiber flow? What great commercial rival of Rome lay on the same sea? Who were the ancestors of the Carthaginians? What region did Carthage commercially control? How did she treat ships of other peoples in this region? Describe the military organization of Carthage. What was the character of the Carthaginian state? What was happening to the Greeks of Sicily? Describe the danger at Messina.

Discuss Roman improvements in arms and tactics. What was the purpose of the legion? How large was it? What was a centurion? Had the Romans any commanding generals of long experience? What can you say about the discipline of a Roman army?

BIBLIOGRAPHY FOR TOPICAL STUDIES

Agriculture in ancient Italy: BOTSFORD, *Source Book*, pp. 404–408; BRITISH MUSEUM, *Guide to Greek and Roman Life*, pp. 168–170; FRANK, *History of Rome*, pp. 78–81, 176–177, 403–405; *Legacy of Rome*, pp. 475–482; SHOWERMAN, *Rome and the Romans*, pp. 251–266.

The Roman army: ABBOTT, *Roman Politics*, pp. 149–152; BOTSFORD, *Source Book*, pp. 374–375; MCCARTNEY, *Warfare by Land and Sea*, pp. 87–110; POLAND-REISINGER-WAGNER, *Culture of Greece and Rome*, pp. 270–278; SHOWERMAN, pp. 453–468; TREBLE-KING, *Everyday Life in Rome*, pp. 100–118.

CHAPTER XXIV · *The Roman Conquest of the Western Mediterranean World*

SECTION 75. THE STRUGGLE WITH CARTHAGE: THE SICILIAN WAR, OR FIRST PUNIC WAR

Opening of Sicilian War at Messina (264 B.C.)

889. Whatever might be the risks involved in a struggle with Carthage, the Romans were soon convinced that it could not be avoided. During a siege of Messina at the hands of the Syracusans one party in the besieged place called in the aid of the Romans, while another party appealed to Carthage. The result was that a Carthaginian garrison quickly occupied the citadel of Messina, and the Carthaginians were then in command of the Strait of Messina. The Romans had long hesitated; but now they took the memorable step, and, responding to the appeal of Messina, a Roman army left the soil of Italy and crossed the sea for the first time in Roman history. The struggle with Carthage had begun (264 B.C.).

890. An alliance with Syracuse soon gave the Romans possession of eastern Sicily, but they were long unable to make much progress into the central and western portion of the island. The chief reason for this was the lack of a strong war fleet. The Romans, therefore, adopting a naval policy like

NOTE. The above fragment of a WALL-PAINTING AT POMPEII shows us a ROMAN WARSHIP, seemingly in battle, for the wreck of another warship is visible at the left. Notice the two steering *oars*, one at each side of the stern, — a device found on Nile ships three thousand years earlier. The rudder had not yet developed from these steering oars.

FIG. 233. *Egyptian* GRAPPLING IRONS, *the Ancestor of the Roman Corvus ("Crow")*

The scene above is taken from the naval battle between the Egyptians and the northern Mediterranean peoples (Fig. 153). From an Egyptian boat (at left) a soldier throws into a boat full of northerners (at the right) a rope to which are attached four large iron hooks. The foremost Egyptian soldiers are poised ready to board the enemy craft, in order quickly to begin a hand-to-hand conflict as soon as the grappling irons have taken hold. This is, so far as is known, the earliest representation of such a boarding device. The Romans ascribed their success against the Carthaginians, in spite of inexperience, to a new boarding grappler which they invented and called a "crow" (*corvus*). It consisted of a heavy upright timber which was made to fall over, with the end on the enemy's rail, where an iron hook attached to the end of the "crow" grappled and held the opposing craft until the Romans could climb over into it. In the hand-to-hand fighting which followed, the sturdy Romans more than made up for their inexperience in seamanship

that of Themistocles (§ 543), determined to build war-ships. The Senate rapidly pushed the building of the new fleet, and in the fifth year of the war it put to sea for the first time. It numbered a hundred and twenty battleships, of which a full hundred were large, powerful vessels with five banks of oars.

The Romans build a fleet

891. In spite of inexperience the Roman fleet was victorious in two successive battles off the coast of Italy. It looked as if the war would be quickly over. The Senate, however, finding that the legions made little progress in Sicily, determined to invade Africa and strike Carthage at home. The invasion was at first very successful, but its progress was unwisely interfered with by the Senate, which recalled one of the consuls with many of the troops. The result was that the remaining consul, with his reduced army, was disastrously defeated. Then one Roman fleet after

Roman victory and disaster at sea

another was destroyed by heavy storms at sea, and one of them was badly defeated by the Carthaginians. The Romans thus lost their newly won command of the sea, and were long unable to make any progress in the war.

892. Year after year the struggle dragged on, while Hamilcar Barca, the Carthaginian commander, was plundering the coasts of Italy with his fleet. The treasury at Rome was empty, and the Romans were at the end of their resources; but by private contributions they succeeded in building another fleet, which put to sea in 242 B.C. with two hundred battleships of five banks of oars. The Carthaginian fleet was defeated and broken up (241 B.C.), and as a result the Carthaginians found themselves unable to send reënforcements across the sea to their army in Sicily.

Final naval victory of the Romans (241 B.C.)

893. They were therefore at last obliged to accept hard terms of peace at the hands of the Romans. The Carthaginians were to give up Sicily and the neighboring islands to Rome, and to pay the Romans as war damages the sum of thirty-two hundred talents (over three and a half million dollars) within ten years. Thus, in 241 B.C., after more than twenty-three years of fighting, the first period of the struggle between Rome and Carthage ended with the victory of Rome.

Peace at the end of the Sicilian War (241 B.C.)

894. The struggle had been carried on till both contestants were completely exhausted. Both had learned much in the art of war, and Rome for the first time had become a sea power. At the same time she had taken a step which forever changed her future and altered her destiny: for the first time she held territory outside of Italy, and from this step she was never able to withdraw. It has been compared with the action of the United States in taking Puerto Rico and the Philippines; for in gaining interests and responsibilities across the sea a nation is at once thrown into conflict with other powers having similar interests, and this conflict of interests never reaches an end, but easily and usually leads from one war to another.

Some results of the Sicilian War

Section 76. The Hannibalic War (Second Punic War) and the Destruction of Carthage

Romans seize Sardinia and Corsica; conquest of the Po valley

895. Both the rivals now devoted themselves to increasing their strength, nor did Rome hesitate to do so at the expense of Carthage. Taking advantage of a revolt among the hired Carthaginian troops in Sardinia, the Romans accepted an invitation from these mercenaries to invade both Sardinia and Corsica; and, in spite of protests from Carthage, only three years after the settlement of peace Rome took possession of these two islands. Rome now possessed three island outposts against Carthage. Some years later the Romans were involved in a serious war by an invasion of the Gauls from the Po valley. The Gauls were disastrously defeated, and their territory was seized by the Romans, who failed to grant the inhabitants any form of citizenship. Thus Roman power was extended northward to the foot of the Alps, and the entire peninsula from the Alps southward was held by Rome (map II, p. 626).

New Carthaginian conquests in Spain; rise of Hannibal

896. To offset this increase of Roman power and to compensate for the loss of the three large islands, the Carthaginian leaders turned to Spain. Here still dwelt the hardy descendants of the Late Stone Age Europeans of the West. Hamilcar, the Carthaginian general, planned to secure the wealth of their silver mines, to enlist the natives in the army, and thus to build up a power able to meet that of Rome. He died before the completion of his plans, but they were taken up by his gifted son Hannibal, who extended Carthaginian rule in Spain as far north as the Ebro River (map II, p. 626). Although only twenty-four years of age, Hannibal was already forming colossal plans for a bold surprise of Rome in her own territory, which by its unexpectedness and audacity should crush Roman power in Italy.

897. Rome, busily occupied in overthrowing the Gauls, had been unable to interfere with the Spanish enterprises of Carthage. She had, however, secured an agreement that Carthage should not advance northward beyond the Ebro River. To so bold and resolute a leader as Hannibal such a stipulation was only an opportunity for a frontier quarrel with Rome in Spain. In the tremendous struggle which followed he was the genius and the dominating spirit. It was a colossal contest between the *nation* Rome and the *man* Hannibal. We may therefore well call it the Hannibalic War.

Frontier quarrel in Spain, Hannibalic War (218–202 B.C.)

898. While the Roman Senate was demanding that the leaders at Carthage disavow his hostile acts, Hannibal, with a strong and well-drilled army of about forty thousand men, was already marching northward along the east coast of Spain (map, p. 612). Several reasons led him to this course. He knew that since the Sicilian War the defeated Carthaginian fleet would be unable to protect his army if he tried to cross by water from Carthage and to land in southern Italy. Moreover, his cavalry, over six thousand strong, was much too numerous to be transported by sea. In southern Italy, furthermore, he would have been met at once by a hostile population, whereas in northern Italy there were the newly conquered Gauls, burning for revenge on the Romans, their conquerors. Hannibal intended to offer them an opportunity for that revenge by enlistment in his ranks. Moreover, he had reports of dissatisfaction among the allies of Rome also, and he believed that by an early victory in northern Italy he could induce the allies to forsake Rome and join him in a war for independence which would destroy Roman leadership in Italy. For these reasons, while the Roman Senate was planning to invade Spain and Africa, they found their own land suddenly invaded by Hannibal from the north.

Reasons for invading Italy by land from the north

899. By clever maneuvering at the Rhone, Hannibal avoided the Roman army, which had arrived there on its way to Spain. The crossing of the Rhone, a wide, deep, and swift river, with elephants and cavalry, and the long detour to avoid the Romans, so delayed Hannibal that it was late

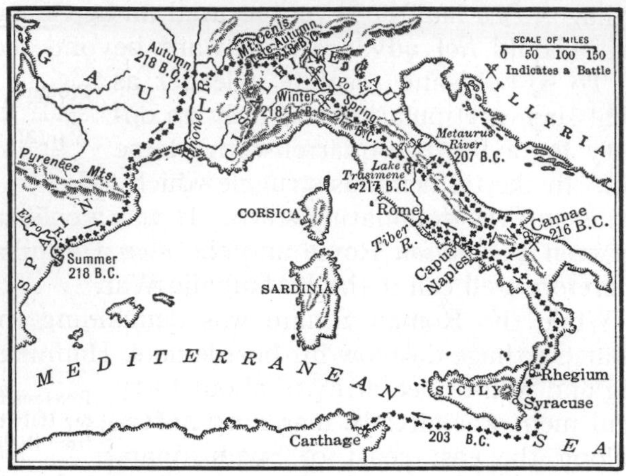

The ROUTE *and* MARCHES *of* HANNIBAL *from* 218 *to* 203 B.C.

The dates indicate the progress of the march. The place where Hannibal crossed the Rhone is unknown, and as indicated above may be quite incorrect, but is given as a surmise. During Hannibal's long stay in southern Italy he made many marches and local movements not indicated in the above sketch. Indeed, we know very little about many of his operations in this region

Hannibal evades the Romans at the Rhone and crosses the Alps

autumn when he reached the Alps (218 B.C.). Overwhelmed by snowstorms, struggling over a steep and dangerous trail (sometimes so narrow that the rocks had to be cut away to make room for the elephants), looking down over dizzy precipices or up to snow-covered heights where hostile natives rolled great stones down upon them, the discouraged army of Hannibal toiled on day after day, exhausted, cold, and hungry. At every point along the straggling line where help was most needed the young Carthaginian was always present, encouraging and guiding his men; but when they issued from the Alpine pass, perhaps Mt. Cenis, into the upper valley of the Po, they had suffered such losses that they were reduced to some thirty-four thousand men.

900. With this little army the dauntless Carthaginian youth had entered the territory of the strongest military power of the time, — a nation which could now call to her defense over seven hundred thousand men, citizens and allies. From this vast number Rome could recruit army after army; but Hannibal, on the other hand, as long as Carthage did not control the sea, could expect no reënforcements from home except through Spain. A military success was necessary at once in order to arouse the hopes of the Gauls and their neighbors and thus secure recruits from among them.

Hannibal's army small compared with Roman resources

901. Hannibal, who was in close contact with a number of Greeks, was thoroughly acquainted with the most highly developed methods of warfare. The exploits of Alexander, who had died a little over a century before Hannibal's invasion of Italy, were familiar to him, and it is not impossible that the fascinating story of Alexander's campaigns was read to the young Carthaginian as he lay with his Greek companions around the camp fires in Italy. Furthermore, we recall that the Roman consuls commanding the Roman armies were simply magistrates like city mayors or civil presidents, often without much more knowledge of handling an army than has a city mayor in our own time. Gifted with little imagination, blunt and straightforward, courageous and eager to meet the enemy at once, the Roman consuls were no match for the crafty young Carthaginian.

Hannibal's military skill superior to that of the Roman consuls

902. By skillful use of his cavalry, in which the Romans were weak, Hannibal at once won two engagements in the Po valley. The Gauls began to flock to his standards, but they were raw, undisciplined troops. He was still outside the barrier of Roman fortresses defending the Apennines, and this he must not fail to pierce without delay. By early spring (217 B.C.), therefore, amid fearful difficulties which would have broken the courage of most commanders, Hannibal successfully passed the belt of Roman strongholds blocking the roads through the Apennines. Even after he had crossed the Arnus, the Roman consul Flaminius had no notion of the Carthaginian advance, though he soon learned that the Carthaginians were between

Hannibal's first three victories

him and Rome. Nevertheless, on the shores of Lake Trasimene, Hannibal easily surprised the army of the unsuspecting consul on the march, ambushed the legions in both front and rear, and cut to pieces the entire Roman army, so that only a handful escaped and the consul himself fell. But a few days' march from Rome, Hannibal might now have advanced directly against the city; but he had no siege machinery, and his forces were not numerous enough for the siege of so strong a fortress. Moreover, his cavalry, in which he was superior to the Romans, would have been useless in a siege. He therefore desired another victory in the hope that the allies of Rome would revolt and join him in attacking the city.

A year of delay and preparation (217–216 B.C.)

903. Hannibal thereupon marched eastward to the Adriatic coast, where he collected numerous horses, much needed by his cavalry, and also secured plentiful provisions, besides an opportunity to drill his Gallic recruits. At this dangerous crisis the Romans appointed a dictator, a stable old citizen named Fabius, whose policy was to wear out Hannibal by refusing to give battle and by using every opportunity to harass the Carthaginians. This policy of caution and delay did not meet with popular favor at Rome. The people called Fabius the "Laggard" (*Cunctator*), a name which ever afterward clung to him, and the new consuls elected for 216 B.C. were urged to take action and destroy the Carthaginian army without more delay. They therefore recruited an army of nearly seventy thousand men and pushed southward toward the heel of the Italian peninsula to meet Hannibal. The Carthaginian deftly outwitted them and, marching to Cannæ, captured the Roman supplies. The consuls were then obliged to give battle or retire for more provisions.

Dispositions at Battle of Cannæ

904. With their fifty-five thousand heavy-armed infantry the consuls were almost twice as strong as Hannibal, who had but thirty-two thousand such troops. On the other hand, Hannibal had about ten thousand horse against six thousand of the Roman cavalry, while both armies were about equally strong in light-armed troops.

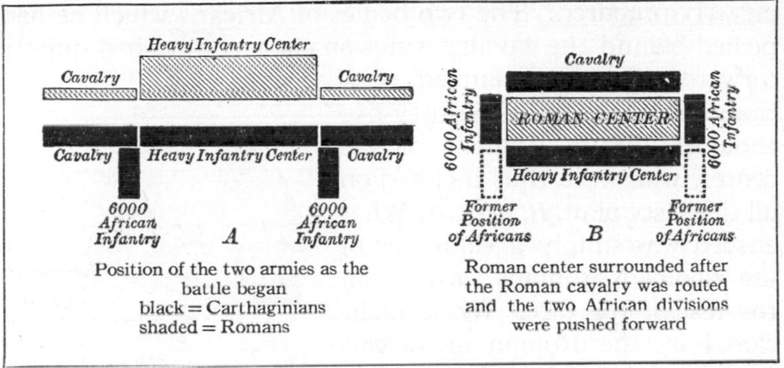

Plan of the BATTLE OF CANNÆ

Varro, the Roman consul, had been merely a successful business man at Rome. He drew up his heavy-armed troops in a deep mass in the center, with a short front. Had he spread them out, so that their superior numbers might form a longer front than that of Hannibal, they might have enfolded and outflanked the Carthaginian army. Both armies divided their cavalry, that it might form the two wings. Instead of massing all his heavy-armed troops in the center to meet the great mass of the Roman center, Hannibal took out some twelve thousand of his heavy-armed African infantry in two bodies of six thousand each and stationed them in a deep column behind each of his cavalry wings (see plan, *A*, above).

Roman army annihilated at Battle of Cannæ (216 B.C.)

905. Hannibal's stronger cavalry put to flight the Roman horse forming both wings. Then as his well-trained horsemen turned back to attack the heavy mass of the Roman center in the rear, he knew that it was too late for the Romans, perceiving their danger, to retreat and escape; for they were caught between the Carthaginian center before them and the Carthaginian cavalry behind them. Only the ends of the trap were open. Then came a great moment in the young Carthaginian's life. With unerring judgment, just at the proper instant, he gave the orders which closed up the ends of the trap he had so cleverly prepared. The two bodies of Africans which he had posted behind the cavalry wings on each side pushed quietly forward till they occupied positions on each side of the fifty-five thousand brave Romans of the center, who were thus inclosed on all sides (see plan, *B*, p. 615). What ensued was simply a slaughter of the doomed Romans, lasting all the rest of the day. When night closed in, the Roman army was annihilated. Ex-consuls, senators, nobles, thousands of the best citizens of Rome, had fallen in this frightful battle. Every family in Rome was in mourning. Of the gold rings worn by Roman knights as an indication of their rank, Hannibal is reported to have sent a bushel to Carthage. Even in modern times pieces of armor have been picked up on the battlefield.

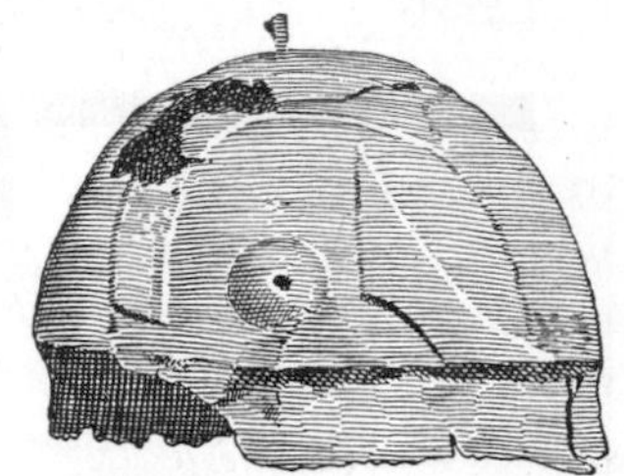

FIG. 234. CARTHAGINIAN HELMET *picked up on the Battlefield at Cannæ*

Revolt of Roman allies; Hannibal calls in the Macedonians

906. Thus this masterful young Carthaginian, the greatest of Semite generals, within two years after his arrival in Italy and before he was thirty years of age, had defeated his giant antagonist in four battles and destroyed three of the opposing armies. He might now count upon a revolt among the Roman allies. Within a few years southern Italy, including the Greek cities, and even Syracuse in Sicily, forsook Rome and joined Hannibal. Only some of the southern Latin colonies held out against him. To make matters worse for Rome, immediately after Cannæ, Hannibal sent messengers to Macedonia, and one of the later Philips then reigning there agreed to send help to the Carthaginians in Italy.

907. In all this Hannibal was displaying the judgment and insight of a statesman combined with amazing ability to meet the incessant demands of the military situation. This required him to lay out campaigns, to drill the inexperienced new recruits, to insure supplies of food and fresh horses for his army, while at the same time he was forced also to find the money with which to pay his turbulent and dissatisfied mercenaries. In carrying out all this work he was untiring, and his eye was everywhere. It was no uncommon thing for some private soldier to wake in the morning and find his young general sleeping on the ground by his side. There was a consuming fire of desire in his soul to save Carthage, and now his glorious victories were drawing together the foes of Rome in a great combination which he believed would bring about the destruction of his country's hated antagonist.

Hannibal's statesmanship and the difficulties of his position

908. But opposing the burning zeal of a single gifted soul were the dogged resolution, the ripe statesmanship, the unshaken organization, and the seemingly inexhaustible numbers of the Romans. It was a battle of giants for the mastery of the Mediterranean; for the victor in this struggle would without any question be the greatest power in the West. Had the successors of Alexander in the Hellenistic Eastern Mediterranean discerned the nature of this gigantic struggle in Italy and been able to combine against Rome, they might now have crushed her forever. But the Roman Senate, with clever statesmanship, made an alliance with the Greeks, thus stirring up a revolt in Greece against the Macedonians and preventing them from furnishing help to Hannibal. In spite of Hannibal's victories the steadiness and fine leadership of the Roman Senate held central Italy loyal to Rome. Although the Romans were finally compelled to place arms in the hands of slaves and mere boys, new armies were formed. With these forces the Romans proceeded to besiege and capture the revolting allied cities one after another. Even the clever devices of Archimedes during a desperate siege (§ 777) did not save Syracuse from being recaptured by the Romans (212 B.C.).

Rome checkmates Macedonia and recovers revolting cities

000. Capua likewise, the second city of Italy, which had gone over to his cause, was besieged by the Romans in spite of all Hannibal's efforts to drive them away. As a last hope he marched upon Rome itself, and with his bodyguard rode up to one of the gates of the great city whose power seemed so unbroken. For a brief time the two antagonists faced each other, and many a Roman senator must have looked over the walls at the figure of the tremendous young Carthaginian who had shaken all Italy as with an earthquake. But they were not to be frightened into offers of peace in this way, nor did they send out any message to him. His army was not large enough to lay siege to the greatest city of Italy, nor had he been able to secure any siege machinery; and he was obliged to retreat without accomplishing anything. Capua was thereupon captured (211 B.C.) by the Romans and was punished without mercy.

Hannibal's fruitless advance to Rome; Romans recapture Capua

910. The hitherto dauntless spirit of the young Carthaginian at last began to feel the crushing weight of Roman confidence. When he had finally been ten years in Italy, he realized that unless powerful reënforcements could reach him his cause was hopeless. His brother Hasdrubal in Spain had gathered an army and was now marching into Italy to aid him. At the Metaurus River, in the region of Sentinum, where the fate of Rome had once before been settled (§ 859), Hasdrubal was met by a Roman army. He was completely defeated and slain (207 B.C.). To the senators, waiting in keenest anticipation at Rome, the news of the victory meant the salvation of Italy and the final defeat of an enemy who had all but accomplished the destruction of Roman power. To Hannibal, anxiously awaiting tidings of his brother and of the needed reënforcements, the first announcement of the disaster and the crushing of his hopes was the head of Hasdrubal hurled into the Carthaginian camp by a Roman messenger.

Hannibal's reënforcements destroyed (207 B.C.)

911. For a few years more Hannibal struggled on in the southern tip of Italy, the only territory remaining of all that he had captured. Meantime the Romans, taught by sad experience, had given the command of their forces in Spain to Scipio, one of the ablest of their younger leaders. He had routed the Carthaginians and driven them entirely out of Spain, thus cutting off their chief supply both of money and of troops. In Scipio the Romans had at last found a general with the masterful qualities which make a great military leader. He demanded of the Senate that he be sent to Africa to inv the dominions of Carthage as Hannibal had invaded of Rome.

Decline of Hannibal's power in Italy, and rise of Scipio

912. By 203 B.C. Scipio had twice defeated the Car ian forces in Africa, and Carthage was forced to call Han home. He had spent fifteen years on the soil of Italy, and the great struggle between the almost exhausted rivals was now to be decided in Africa. At Zama, inland from Carthage, the final battle of the war took place. Hannibal, having insufficient cavalry, foresaw that his weak cavalry wings would be defeated by Scipio's opposing heavy bodies of horsemen. When, as he expected, the Roman cavalry wings disappeared in pursuit of his own fleeing horsemen, the wings of both armies were cleared away for one of those unexpected but carefully planned maneuvers by which the great Carthaginian had destroyed the Roman army at Cannæ. From behind his line Hannibal moved out two divisions in opposite directions, elongating his own line beyond the ends of the Roman line, which he intended to inclose on either side. In football language, Hannibal had ordered his backs to spread out and to execute a play around both the Roman ends at once. The fate of two empires was trembling in the balance as Hannibal's steel trap thus extended its jaws on either side to enfold the Roman army.

Scipio and Hann bal at Zama (202 B.C.); tactics of Hannibal

913. But behind the Roman army there was a mind like that of Hannibal. The keen eye of the Roman commander discovered the flash of moving steel behind the Carthaginian lines. He understood the movement and at once grasped the danger which threatened his army. As a result of Cannæ, Scipio had long before abandoned all Roman tradition and had taught his front division to fight without the support of the rear divisions behind them (§ 885). In football language again, he too had learned to shift his backs and had taught the line to hold without them. The shrewd young Roman commander therefore gave his orders without hesitation. For the first time in history the rear divisions behind the front of a Roman center left the front division to fight alone. As quietly as on a parade march they parted to the left and right and, marching behind the fighting line in opposite directions, took up their posts, extending the Roman front at either end where at first the cavalry wings had been. When Hannibal's spreading divisions pushed out beyond the Roman ends, where they were expected to carry out their "around-the-end" movements, they found facing them a Roman wall of steel, and the battle continued in two parallel lines longer than before. The great Carthaginian had been foiled at his own game by an equally great Roman. When the Roman cavalry returned from their pursuit and fell on the Carthaginian flank, Hannibal beheld his lines crumbling and giving way in final and complete defeat.

Countermoves of Scipio bring the Roman victory at Zama

914. In this great battle we see the conclusion of a long and remarkable development in the art of war, from the wild disorder of entirely undisciplined fighting to the formation of a heavy phalanx of disciplined men, the earliest trained fighting team as it appeared in the Orient (Fig. 90). Then in Europe came the oblique battle front which Philip and Alexander combined with the onset of swiftly moving cavalry. Finally the deep phalanx as used by the Greeks was no longer regarded by the Romans as a rigid, indivisible fighting unit, but was broken up into a fighting line in front and a group of shifting backs behind. On the field of Zama, Scipio and Hannibal had advanced to a new stage in the art of warfare, and had created what is now known as "division tactics," — the art of manipulating an army on the field in *divisions* shifted behind the line of battle as a skillful football leader shifts his backs, trusting to the line to hold while he does so.

New art of war; division tactics

915. The victory of Rome over Carthage made Rome the leading power in the whole ancient world. In the treaty which followed the battle of Zama the Romans forced Carthage to pay ten thousand talents (over $11,000,000) in fifty years and to surrender all her warships but ten triremes. But, what was worse, she lost her independence as a nation, and according to the treaty she could not make war anywhere without the consent of the Romans. Although the Romans did not annex her territory in Africa, Carthage had become a vassal state.

Treaty ending the Hannibalic War (201 B.C.)

916. Hannibal had escaped after his lost battle at Zama. Although we learn of his deeds chiefly through his enemies, the story of his dauntless struggle to save his native country, begun when he was only twenty-four and continued for twenty years, reveals him as one of the greatest and most gifted leaders in all history,— a lion-hearted man, so strong of purpose that only a great nation like Rome could have crushed him. Indeed, Rome now compelled the Carthaginians to expel Hannibal, and, a man of fifty, he went into exile in the East, where we shall find him stirring up the successors of Alexander to combine against Rome.

Fate of Hannibal

917. Such was the commercial ability of the Carthaginians that they continued to prosper even while paying the heavy tribute with which Rome had burdened them. Meantime the new mistress of the Western Mediterranean kept an anxious eye on her old rival. Even the stalwart Romans remembered with uneasiness the invasion of Hannibal. Cato, a famous old-fashioned senator, was so convinced that Carthage was still a danger to Rome that he concluded all his speeches in the Senate with the words, "Carthage must be destroyed." For over fifty years more the merchants of Carthage were permitted to traffic in the Western Mediterranean, and then the iron hand of Rome was laid upon the doomed city for the last time. To defend herself against the Numidians behind her, Carthage

Destruction of Carthage (146 B.C.); Third Punic War

was finally obliged to begin war against them. This step, which the Romans had long been desiring, was a violation of the treaty with Rome. The Senate seized the opportunity at once, and Carthage was called to account. In the three years' war (Third Punic War) which followed, the beautiful city was captured and completely destroyed (146 B.C.). Its territory was taken by Rome and called the Province of Africa. A struggle of nearly one hundred and twenty years had resulted in the annihilation of Rome's only remaining rival in the West (see map III, p. 626).

Rome, supreme in the West, turns eastward

918. Thus the fourfold rivalry in the Western Mediterranean, which had long included the Etruscans and Carthaginians, the Greeks and the Romans, had ended with the triumph of the once insignificant village above the prehistoric market on the Tiber. Racially the western wing of the Indo-European line had proved victorious over that of the Semite line (Fig. 123). The Western Mediterranean world was now under the leadership of a single great nation, the Romans, as the Eastern Mediterranean world had once been under the leadership of the Macedonians. We must now turn back and follow the dealings of Rome with the Hellenistic-Oriental world of the Eastern Mediterranean, which we left (Chap. XXI) after it had attained the most highly refined civilization ever achieved by ancient man.

QUESTIONS

Section 75. How did Rome and Carthage come into conflict? When? Had the Romans any sea power? How did they get it? Give a brief statement of the course of the Sicilian War. What were the main results?

Section 76. What territory did the Romans gain shortly after the Sicilian War? Where did Carthage go for new resources? Who provoked the ensuing war? Describe Hannibal's plan of campaign. Recount his march into Italy. How did his numbers compare with those of Rome? What can you say of his military knowledge? Describe his first three encounters with the Romans. Where did he then go? What did the Romans do? Draw two plans, and tell the story of the battle of Cannæ. What political moves did Hannibal then make? How did the Romans meet them? What course did Rome follow toward her revolting allies? What happened at Capua? What did Hannibal's brother do?

Who was the Roman leader in Spain? Recount the battle of Zama. What advance in the art of warfare was shown there? What were the main results of the Hannibalic War? What became of Hannibal? Recount the destruction of Carthage. How long had the struggle between Rome and Carthage lasted? Who was now leader of the West?

BIBLIOGRAPHY FOR TOPICAL STUDIES

Roman naval development: *Legacy of Rome*, pp. 161–164; McCartney, *Warfare by Land and Sea*, pp. 178–184; Showerman, *Rome and the Romans*, pp. 475–484; Treble-King, *Everyday Life in Rome*, pp. 118–121.

Hannibal the patriot: Botsford, *Source Book*, pp. 383–387; Fowler, *Rome*, pp. 92–110; Frank, *History of Rome*, pp. 111–127; McCartney, *Warfare by Land and Sea*, pp. 113–128, 142–147.

Cato the patriot: Botsford, *Source Book*, pp. 411–415; Dobson, *Ancient Education*, pp. 99–102; Frank, *History of Rome*, pp. 148–162; *Pageant of Greece*, pp. 397–402.

Note. The drawing below shows the harbors of Carthage. Of the city destroyed by the Romans almost nothing has survived. It was rebuilt under Julius Cæsar, but not a great deal remains even of the Roman city.

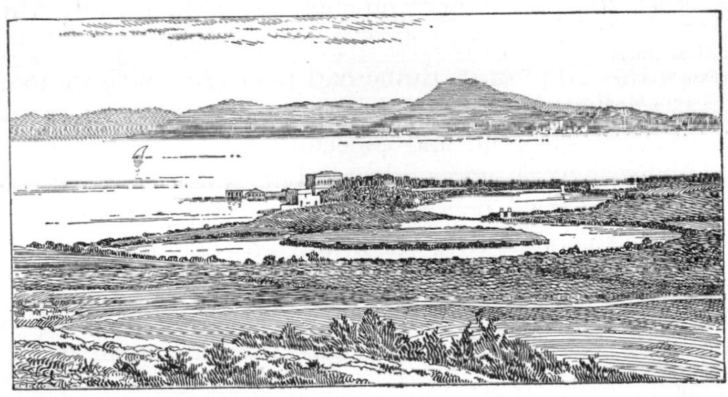

Chapter XXV · *World Dominion and Degeneracy*

Section 77. The Roman Conquest of the Eastern Mediterranean World

Coming conflict between Western and Eastern Mediterranean

919. While the heirs of Alexander were carrying on their ceaseless feuds, plots, wars, and alliances in the Eastern Mediterranean, down to about 200 B.C., the vast power of Rome had been slowly rising in the West. The serious consequences of Rome's growth, and especially of her expansion beyond the sea, were now evident. The Roman Senate could not allow any state on the Mediterranean to develop such strength as to endanger Rome in the way Carthage had done during the Hannibalic War. For this and other reasons the western giant was now to overshadow the whole Hellenistic world of the East and finally to draw the three great states of

NOTE. The relief above, found in the THEATER OF MARCELLUS, built by Augustus (§ 1033), gives us a very vivacious glimpse of a battle between gladiators and wild beasts just as the Romans saw it. The gladiators in this combat wear only a tunic and have no defensive armor except a helmet and a shield. Note the expression of pain on the face of the gladiator at the left, whose arm is being lacerated by the lion.

Alexander's heirs into its grasp. Let us see what the reasons for the first collision were.

920. Hannibal had induced Macedonia to combine with him against Rome (§ 906). This hostile step could not be overlooked by the Romans after the Hannibalic War. Philip, the Macedonian king, was a gifted ruler and an able military commander like his great predecessor, the father of Alexander the Great, a hundred and fifty years earlier. The further plans of this later Philip filled the Senate with anxiety; for he had arranged a combination between himself and Antiochus the Great (the third of the name), the Seleucid king of Syria. By this alliance the two were to divide the dominions of Egypt between them. Because of what he had already done, and also because of what he would do if allowed to go on and gain greatly increased power, the Romans were now obliged to turn eastward and crush Philip of Macedon (map II, p. 626).

Causes of Roman war with Macedon

921. The Greek states had no reason to support the rule of Macedonia over them; Antiochus was too busy seizing the Asiatic territory of Egypt to send any help to Macedonia; and hence, a year after the close of the Hannibalic War, Philip found himself, without strong allies, face to face with a Roman army. By his unusual skill as a commander he evaded the Roman force for some time; but in the end the massive Macedonian phalanx, bristling with long spears, was obliged to meet the onset of the Roman legions, with their deadly short swords and the puzzling divisions behind the lines shifting into unexpected positions which the phalanx was not flexible enough to meet. On the field of Cynoscephalæ (dog's heads), in 197 B.C., the Macedonian army was disastrously routed, and the ancient realm of Alexander the Great became a vassal state under Rome. As allies of Rome the Greek states were then granted their freedom by the Romans.

Battle of Cynoscephalæ (197 B.C.); Macedon a vassal of Rome

922. This war with Macedon brought the Romans into conflict with Antiochus the Great, the Seleucid king, who held a large part of the vast empire of Persia in Asia; for Antiochus now endeavored to profit by Philip's defeat and to seize some of Philip's former possessions which the Romans had declared free. A war with this powerful Asiatic empire was not a matter which the Romans could view without great anxiety. Moreover, Hannibal, expelled from Carthage, was now in Greece with Antiochus, advising him. In spite of the warnings and urgent counsels of Hannibal, Antiochus threw away his opportunities in Greece until the Roman legions maneuvered him back into Asia Minor, whither the Romans followed him, and there the great power of the West for the first time confronted the motley forces of the ancient Orient as marshaled by the successor of Persia in Asia.

Roman conflict with Seleucids after conquest of Macedon

923. The conqueror of Hannibal at Zama was with the Roman army to counsel his brother, another Scipio, consul for the year and therefore in command of the legions. There was no hope for the undisciplined troops of the Orient when confronted by a Roman army under such masters of the new tactics as these two Scipios. At Magnesia the West, led by Rome, overthrew the East, led by the dilatory Antiochus (190 B.C.), and the lands of Asia Minor eastward to the river Halys submitted to Roman control. Under the ensuing treaty Antiochus was not permitted to cross the river Halys westward or to send a warship west of the same longitude. Within twelve years (200–189 B.C.) Roman arms had reduced to the condition of vassal states two of the three great empires which succeeded Alexander in the East,—Macedonia and Syria (see map III, p. 626). As for Egypt, the third, friendship had from the beginning existed between her and Rome. A little over thirty years after a Roman army had first appeared in the Hellenistic world, Egypt acknowledged herself a vassal of Rome (168 B.C.).

Antiochus defeated (190 B.C.); Egypt submits (168 B.C.)

924. Although defeated, the Eastern Mediterranean world long continued to give the Romans much trouble. The quarrels of the eastern states among themselves were constantly carried to Rome for settlement. It became necessary to

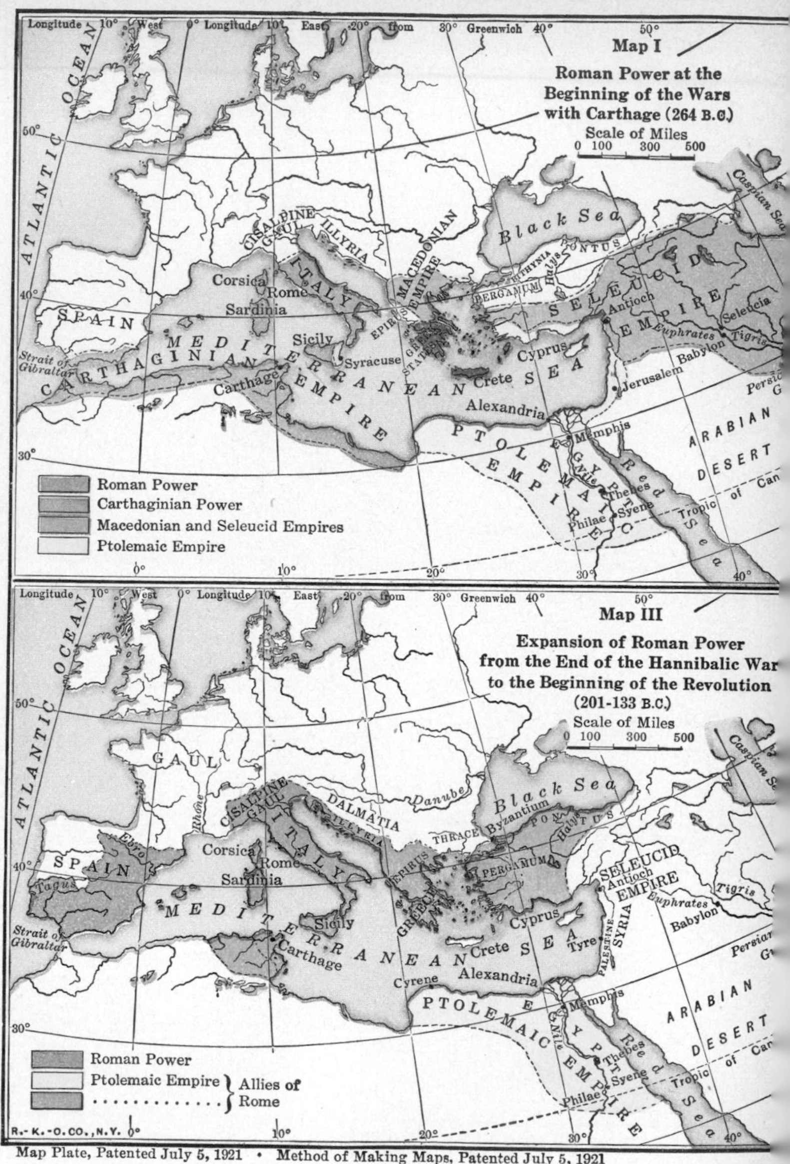

Map Plate, Patented July 5, 1921 • Method of Making Maps, Patented July 5, 1921

SEQUENCE MAP SHOWING THE EXPANSION OF THE ROMAN POWE
TO THE DEATH O

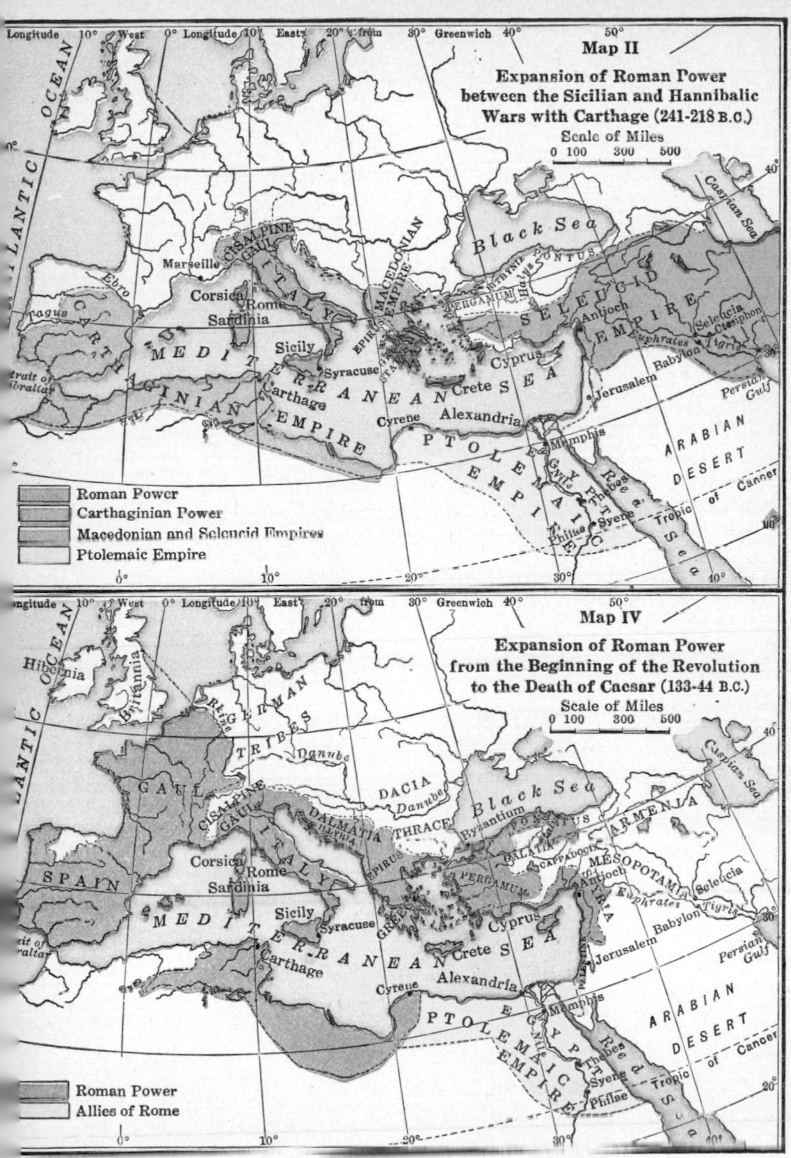

ROM THE BEGINNING OF THE WARS WITH CARTHAGE (264 B.C.)
ESAR (44 B.C.)

destroy Macedonia as a kingdom and to make her a Roman province. At the same time Greek sympathy for Macedonia was made the pretext for greater severity toward the Greeks. Many were carried off to Italy as hostages, and among them no less than a thousand noble and educated Achæans were brought to Rome. When, in spite of this, the Achæan League (§ 760) rashly brought on a war with Rome, the Romans applied the same methods which they were using against Carthage. The same year which saw the destruction of Carthage witnessed the burning of Corinth also (146 B.C.). Greek liberty was of course ended; and while a city of such revered memories as Athens might be given greater freedom, those Greek states whose careers of glorious achievement in civilization we have followed were reduced to the condition of Roman vassals.

Annihilation of Macedon and subjection of Greeks

925. It was little more than three generations since the Republic on the Tiber had taken the fateful step of beginning the conflict with Carthage for the leadership of the West. That struggle had led her into a similar conflict for the leadership of the East. There were old men still living who had talked with veterans of the Sicilian War with Carthage, and the grandsons of the Romans who had fought with Hannibal had burned Carthage and Corinth at the end of the great wars. For nearly a century and a quarter (beginning 264 B.C.) one great war had followed another, and the Roman Republic, beginning these struggles as mistress of Italy only, had in this short space of time (from great-grandfather to great-grandson) gained the political leadership of the civilized world (cf. maps I, II, and III, p. 626).

Rapidity of Roman conquests

926. The Roman Senate had shown eminent ability in conducting the great wars, but now, having gained the supremacy of the Mediterranean world, Rome was faced by the problem of devising successful government for the vast dominions which she had so quickly conquered. In extent they would have reached entirely across the United States. To organize such an em-

Rome's great task of imperial organization

pire was a task like that which had been so successfully accomplished by Darius, the organizer of the Persian Empire. We shall find that the Roman Senate utterly failed in the effort to organize the new dominions. The failure had a most disastrous influence on the Romans themselves and, together with the ruinous effects of the long wars on Italy, finally overthrew the Roman Republic, — an overthrow in which Rome as a nation almost perished. Let us now glance at the efforts of Rome to govern her new dominions, and then observe the effect of the long wars and of world power on the Romans and their life.

SECTION 78. ROMAN GOVERNMENT AND CIVILIZATION IN THE AGE OF CONQUEST

927. The Romans had at first no experience in governing their conquered lands, as the United States had none when it took possession of the Philippines. Most of the conquered countries the Romans organized as provinces, somewhat after the manner of the provinces of the old Persian Empire. The people of a province were not permitted to maintain an army, but they were obliged to pay taxes and, lastly, to submit to the uncontrolled rule of a Roman magistrate who was *governor* of the province. It was chiefly the presence and power of this governor which made the condition of the provinces beyond the sea so different from that of the Roman possessions in Italy. The regulations for the rule of the provinces were made in each case by the Roman Senate, and on the whole they were not oppressive; but the Senate made no provisions for compelling the Roman governor to obey these regulations.

Establishment of Roman provinces

928. Such a governor, enjoying unlimited power like that of an Oriental sovereign, found himself far from home, with Roman troops at his elbow awaiting his slightest command. He had complete control of all the taxes of the province, and he could take what he needed from its people to support his troops and pay the expenses of his government. He usually held office for a single year and was generally without experience in provincial government. His eagerness to gain a fortune in his short term of office, and his complete ignorance of the needs of his province, frequently reduced his government to a mere system of looting and robbery. The Senate soon found it necessary to have laws passed for the punishment of such abuses; but these laws were found to be of little use in improving the situation.

Unlimited power and corruption of Roman provincial governors

929. The effects of this situation were soon apparent in Italy. In the first place, the income of the Roman government was so enormously increased that it was no longer necessary to collect direct taxes from Roman citizens. This new wealth was not confined to the state. The spoils from the wars were usually taken by the victorious commanders and their troops. At the same time the provinces were soon filled with Roman business men. There were contractors called publicans, who were allowed to collect the taxes for the state at a great profit (§ 659) or gained the right to work state lands. We remember the common references to these publicans in the New Testament, where they are regularly classified with "sinners." With them came Roman money-lenders, who enriched themselves by loaning money at high rates of interest to the numerous provincials who were obliged to borrow to pay the extortionate taxes claimed by the Roman governors. The publicans were themselves money-lenders, and all these men of money plundered the provinces worse than the greedy Roman governors themselves. As these people returned to Italy there grew up a wealthy class such as had been unknown there before.

New wealth of Rome

930. Their ability to buy resulted in a vast import trade to supply the demand. From the Bay of Naples to the mouth of the Tiber the sea was white with Roman ships converging on the docks of Rome. The men who controlled all this traffic became wealthy merchants. To handle all the money in circulation, banks were required. During the Hannibalic

War the first banks appeared at Rome, occupying a line of booths on each side of the Forum. After 200 B.C. these booths gave way to a fine basilica like those which had appeared in the Hellenistic cities (Fig. 266, *4*). Here the new wealthy class met to transact financial business, and here large companies were formed for the collection of taxes and for taking government contracts to build roads and bridges or to erect public buildings. Shares in such companies were daily sold, and a business like that of a modern stock exchange developed in the Forum.

Growth of commerce and rise of banking

931. Under these influences Rome changed greatly. With increasing wealth and growing population there was a great increase in the demand for dwellings. Rents at once rose, and land in the city increased in value. Apartments for rent became a good form of paying investment, and as the value of property rose a larger return in rents could be secured by increasing the number of floors. Hence owners began to erect tall buildings with several stories, though these ancient "skyscrapers" were never as tall as ours. It became necessary to limit their height by law, as we do; and when badly built, as they sometimes were, they fell down, as they have been known to do in our own cities.

Rome becomes a profitable real-estate center

932. When a returned governor of Africa put up a showy new house, the citizen across the way who still lived in his father's old house began to be dissatisfied with it. It was built of sun-dried brick, and, like the old settler's cabin of early America, it had but one room. In this room all the household life centered. The stool and spinning outfit of the wife and the bed of the citizen were each assigned to a corner, while the kitchen was simply another corner where the family meals were cooked over an open fire. There was no chimney, and the smoke passed out of a square hole in the middle of the roof. The whole place was so begrimed with smoke that the room was called the *atrium*, a word perhaps connected with the Latin word for "black."

Old-fashioned Roman house

Here, then, the family took their meals, here they slept, and here, in full view of pots and kettles, beds and tables, the master of the house received his friends and transacted his affairs with business or official callers.

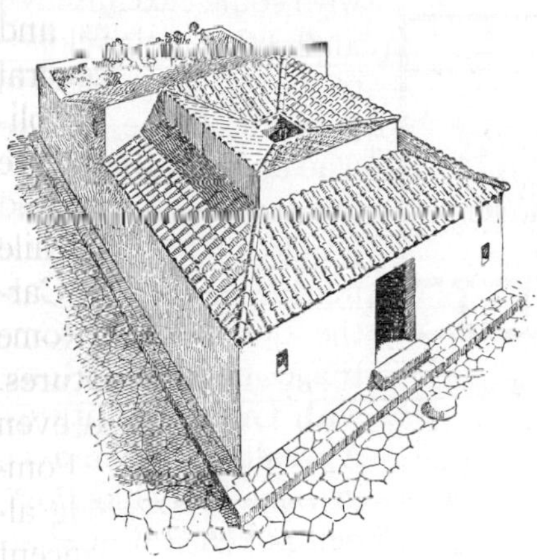

FIG. 235. *An Old Roman* ATRIUM HOUSE

There was no attempt at beautiful architecture, and the bare front showed no adornment whatever. The opening in the roof, which lighted the atrium, received the rainfall of a section of the roof sloping toward it, and this water collected in a pool built to receive it in the floor of the atrium below (Fig. 236, *B*). The tiny area, or garden, shown in the rear was not common. It was here that the later Romans added the Hellenistic peristyle (Fig. 237)

Wealthy Roman's new house and its furnishings

933. The Roman citizen of the new age had walked the streets of the Hellenistic cities. Indeed, he had long before been familiar with the comfort, luxury, and beauty with which the Greek houses of Capua and Naples were filled. As his means increased, therefore, the wealthy Roman added to and enlarged his house. Often there was built a second story, to which the bedrooms and perhaps the dining room could be shifted. The atrium then became a large and stately reception hall where the master of the house could display his wealth in statues, paintings, and other works of art, — the trophies of war from the East. The old Roman houses had been unadorned and had contained nothing but the bare necessities. Carthaginian ambassadors had been amused to recognize at successive dinners in Rome the same silver dishes, which had been loaned around from house to house. Not long before the Carthaginian wars an ex-consul had been fined for having more than ten pounds' weight of silverware in his house. A generation later a wealthy Roman was using, in his household, silverware which weighed some ten thousand pounds. One of the Roman conquerors of Macedonia entered Rome with some two hundred and fifty wagonloads of Greek statues and paintings. The general who crushed the Ætolians carried off over five hundred bronze and marble statues, while the destroyer of Carthage filled all Rome with Greek sculptures. A wealthy citizen even in a small city like Pompeii paved a dining alcove with a magnificent mosaic picture of Alexander in battle (Fig. 198), which had once formed a floor in a splendid Hellenistic house in Alexandria. The finest furniture, carpets, and hangings of the East adorned the houses of the wealthy in Rome.

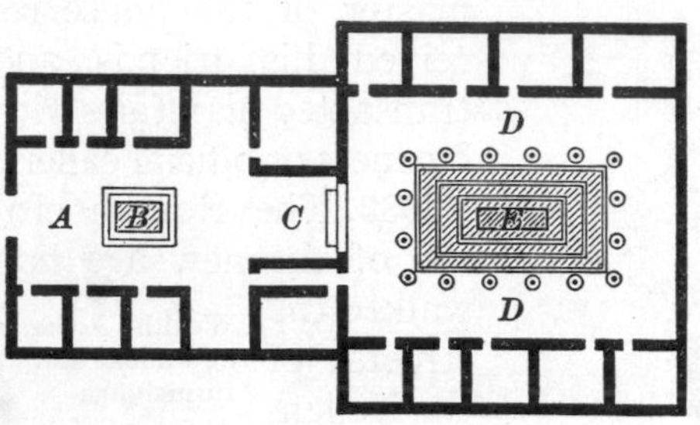

FIG. 236. *Plan of a Roman* HOUSE *with* PERISTYLE

The earliest Roman house had consisted of a single room, the atrium (*A*), with the pool for the rain water (*B*). Then a small alcove, or lean-to, was erected at the rear (*C*), as a room for the master of the house. Later the bedrooms on each side of the atrium were added. Finally, under the influence of Greek life, the garden court (*D*; see Fig. 237), with its surrounding colonnaded porch (peristyle) and a fountain in the middle (*E*), was built at the rear. Then a dining-room, sitting-room, and bedrooms were added, which opened on this court; and, being without windows, they were lighted from the court through the doors. In town houses it was quite easy to partition off a shop, or even a whole row of shops, along the front or side of the house, as in the Hellenistic house (Fig. 204). The houses of Pompeii were almost all built in this way

New conveniences and luxuries of wealthy Roman households

934. All those conveniences which we have found in the Hellenistic dwellings were likewise quickly introduced, such as pipes for running water, baths, and sanitary conveniences. The more elaborate houses were finally equipped with tile pipes conducting hot air for warming the important rooms, the earliest system of hot-air heating yet found. The kitchen was furnished with beautiful bronze utensils, far better than those commonly found in our own kitchens. On social occasions the food on the table included imported delicacies and

Fig. 237. Peristyle *of a* Pompeian House *(below) and its* Egyptian Ancestor *(above; see Fig. 55)*

We must imagine ourselves standing in the Pompeian house (below), with our backs toward the atrium, having immediately behind us the room *C* in Fig. 236. We look out into the court, the garden of the house (Fig. 236, *D*). The marble tables and statues and the marble fountain basin in the middle (Fig. 236, *E*), just as we see them here in the drawing, were all found by the excavators in their places, as they were covered by volcanic ashes over eighteen hundred years ago. Here centered the family life, and here the children played about the court, brightened with flowers and the tinkling music of the fountains

FIG. 238. *Bronze* KITCHEN UTENSILS *excavated at Pompeii*

This kitchen ware used by the cooks of Pompeii was found still lying in the kitchens of the houses as they were uncovered by the excavators. The pieces have been lettered, and the student will find it interesting to make a list of them by name, identifying them by letter and indicating their use as far as possible

luxuries, purchased at enormous expense. A jar of salted fish from the Black Sea cost seventy-five or eighty dollars, and the old-fashioned senator Cato, in a speech in the Senate, protested against such luxury, stating that "Rome was the only city in the world where such a jar of fish cost more than a yoke of oxen."

Numerous household servants chiefly slaves

935. Such luxury required a great body of household servants. There was a doorkeeper at the front door (he was called "janitor" from the Latin word *janua*, meaning "door"), and from the front door inward there was a servant for every small duty in the house, even to the attendant who rubbed down the master of the house after his bath. Almost all these menials were slaves, but it was not always possible to secure a slave as cook, and a wealthy Roman would pay as much as five thousand dollars a year for a really good cook.

936. While the effect of all this luxury introduced from the East was on the whole very bad, nevertheless the former plain, matter-of-fact, prosaic life of the Roman citizen was stimulated and refined both at home and in the Senate hall by the most beautiful creations of Greek genius. Even while eating his dinner the commonplace citizen of Pompeii sat looking at the heroic death of the Persian nobles of Darius. But there were never any *Roman* artists capable of producing such works as these.

Works of Greek art in Rome and their refining influence

937. A Roman senator returning from Alexandria could not but feel that Rome, in spite of some new and modern buildings, was very plain and unattractive, with its simple temples and old public buildings; and he realized that Alexandria was the greatest and most splendid city in the world. Roman emulation was aroused, and forms of Hellenistic architecture, such as the basilica on the Forum, were beginning to appear in Rome. It was not long, too, before a Greek theater was built, improved by the Romans with awnings to keep out the hot sunshine, a curtain in front of the stage, like ours, and seats in the orchestra circle where once the Greek chorus had sung.

Hellenistic architecture in Rome; basilica and theater

938. At the close of the Sicilian War (241 B.C.) a Greek slave named Andronicus, who had been taken as a lad by the Romans when they captured the Greek city of Tarentum, was given his freedom by his master at Rome. Seeing the interest of the Romans in Greek literature, he translated the Odyssey into Latin as a schoolbook for Roman children. For their elders he likewise rendered into Latin the classic tragedies which we have seen in Athens, and also a number of Attic comedies. This worthy Greek, Andronicus, was the first literary man in Europe to attempt artistic translations pos-

Andronicus and his Latin translations of Greek literature

sessing literary finish. He was therefore the founder of the art of literary translation. Through his work the materials and the forms of Greek literature began to enter Roman life.

Old-fashioned Roman schools

939. The Romans had been accustomed to do very little in the way of educating their children. There were no schools at first, but the good old Roman custom had been for the father to instruct his own children. Even when schools arose, there was no literature for the Roman lads to learn, as Greek boys had learned Homer and the other poets. The Roman father's respect for law and order led him to have his son taught the "Twelve Tables" of the law, and recite them to the schoolmaster, as English-speaking children were once taught the Ten Commandments. Such schools had been very poorly equipped; some of them, indeed, were held in the open air in a side street or a corner of the Forum. At best they had met in a bare room belonging to a dwelling house, and there were no schoolhouses.

Greek influences in new education in Rome

940. Gradually parents began to send their children to the schools which the freed Greek slaves of Rome were beginning to open there. Moreover, there was here and there a household which possessed an educated Greek slave, like Andronicus, who might become the tutor of the children, giving regular instruction and teaching his pupils to read from the new primer of Andronicus, as we may call his Latin translation of Homer. Now and then Greek teachers of renown appeared and lectured in Rome. Young Roman nobles thus gained the opportunity of studying rhetoric and public speaking, which they knew to be of great practical use in the career of public office to which they all aspired. Indeed, it was not uncommon for a young Roman of station to complete his higher education at Athens.

941. As Rome gained control of Greece the mingling of Greek and Roman life was increasingly intimate. When a thousand of the leading Achæans were brought to Rome as hostages (§ 924), there was among them a Greek statesman of great refinement and literary culture named Polybius. He was taken into the family of the Scipios, traveled about with them on their great campaigns, and occupied a position of dignity and respect. He witnessed the destruction of both Carthage and Corinth, and finally wrote an immortal history, in Greek, of the great Roman wars. Such cultivated Greeks had a great influence on the finer Romans like the Scipios. Polybius tells how he stood with the younger Scipio and watched the burning of Carthage, while his young Roman lord burst into tears and quoted Homer's noble lines regarding the destruction of Troy.

Influence of cultivated Greeks in Rome; Polybius

942. Such familiarity with the only literature known to the Romans, such daily and hourly intimacy with cultivated Greeks, aroused the impulse toward literary expression among the Romans themselves. To be sure, the Latins, like all peasant peoples, had had their folk songs and their simple forms of verse, but these natural products of the soil of Latium soon disappeared as the men of Latin speech felt the influence of an already highly finished literature. Latin literature, therefore, did not develop along its own lines from native beginnings, as did Greek literature, but grew up on the basis of a great inheritance from abroad. Indeed, we now see, as the Roman poet Horace said, that Rome, the conqueror, was herself conquered by the civilization of the Greeks.

Greek foundations of Latin literature

943. Poets and writers of history now arose in Italy, and educated Romans could read of the great deeds of their ancestors in long epic poems modeled on those of Homer. In such literature were gradually recorded the picturesque legends of early Rome — the story of Romulus and Remus and similar tales — extending down through the early kings (p. 571, note). It is from these sources, now no longer regarded as history, that the early history of Rome used to be drawn. The Greek comedies of Menander (§ 789) attracted the Romans greatly; imitating these, the new Latin play-writers, especially Plautus (died about 184 B.C.) and Terence (died about 159 B.C.), produced

Rise of Latin literature

very clever comedies caricaturing the society of Rome, to which the Romans listened with uproarious delight. Their production on the stage led to the highly developed theater buildings which we have already mentioned.

Publishers, libraries, and the educated class

944. As the new Latin literature grew, papyrus rolls bearing Latin works were more and more common in Rome. Then publishers, in back rooms filled with slave copyists, began to appear in the city. One of the Roman conquerors of Macedon brought back the books of the Macedonian king and founded the first private library in Rome. Wealthy Romans were now providing library rooms in their houses. A group of literary men arose, including the finest of the Roman leaders, and no man could claim to belong to this cultivated world without acquaintance with a well-stocked library of Greek and Latin books. Such Romans spoke Greek almost if not quite as well as Latin. These educated men were finally in sharp contrast to the uneducated mass of the Roman people, and there thus arose the two classes, educated and uneducated, — a distinction unknown in the days of the early farmer Republic.

Section 79. Degeneration in City and Country

Corrupting influence of new luxury; laws against extravagance

945. The new life of Greek culture and luxury brought with it many evils. Even the younger Scipio, an ardent friend of Greek literature and art, expressed his pained surprise at finding Roman boys in a Greek dancing school, learning unwholesome dances, just as many worthy people among us disapprove of the new dances now so widely cultivated. Cato, one of the hardiest of the old-fashioned Romans, denounced the new culture and the luxury which accompanied it. As censor he had the power to stop many of the luxurious new practices, and he spread terror among the showy young dandies and ladies of fashion in Rome. He and other Romans like him succeeded in passing law after law against expensive habits of many kinds, like the growing love of showy jewelry among the women, or their use of carriages where they formerly went on foot. But such laws could not prevent the slow corruption of the people. The old simplicity, purity, and beauty of Roman family life was disappearing, and divorce was becoming common. The greatest days of Roman character were past, and Roman power was to go on growing without the restraining influence of old Roman virtue.

946. This was especially evident in the lives of the uneducated and poorer classes also. To them, as indeed to the vast majority of all classes, Greek civilization was chiefly attractive because of the numerous luxuries of Hellenistic life. The common people had no comprehension of Greek civilization. At the destruction of Corinth Polybius saw Roman soldiers shaking dice on a wonderful old Greek painting which they had torn down and spread out on the ground like a piece of tattered awning. When a cultivated Roman thought to gain popular favor by arranging a program of Greek instrumental music at a public entertainment, the audience stopped the performance and shouted to the musicians to throw down their instruments and begin a boxing match! Contrast this with the Athenian public in the days of Pericles!

Inability of the masses to appreciate Greek literature

947. It was to Roman citizens with tastes like these that the leaders of the new age were obliged to turn for votes and for support in order to gain office. To such tastes, therefore, the Roman nobles began to appeal. Early in the Sicilian War with Carthage there had been introduced the old Etruscan custom of single combats between condemned criminals or slaves, who slew each other to honor the funeral of some great Roman. These combatants came to be called gladiators, from a Latin word *gladius*, meaning "sword." The delight of the Roman people in these bloody displays was such that the officials in charge of the various public feasts, without waiting for a funeral, used to arrange a long program of such combats in the hope of pleasing the people and thus gaining their votes and securing election to future higher offices.

Gladiatorial combats as a political influence

948. These barbarous and bloody spectacles took place at first within a temporary circle of seats, which finally became a great stone structure especially built for the purpose. It was called an amphitheater, because it was formed by placing two (*amphi*) theaters face to face (Fig. 256). Soon afterward combats between gladiators and wild beasts were introduced. The athletic contests which had so interested the Greeks were far too tame for the appetite of the Roman public. The chariot race, however, did appeal to the Romans, and they began to build enormous courses surrounded by seats for vast numbers of spectators. These buildings they called circuses.

Amphitheater for combats, and circuses for chariot races

949. The common people of Rome were thus gradually debased and taught to expect such public spectacles, sometimes lasting for days, as their share of the plunder from the great conquests. At the same time, as their poverty increased, the free food once furnished them by the wealthy classes far exceeded what private donors were able to give. It was therefore taken up by the state, which arranged regular distributions of grain to the populace. Vicious as this custom was, it was far from being so great an evil as the bribery which the candidates for office now secretly practiced. Laws passed to prevent the practice were of slight effect. The only Roman citizens who could vote were those who attended the assemblies at Rome, and henceforth we have only too often the spectacle of a Roman candidate controlling the government that ruled the world by bribing the little body of citizens who attended the Roman assemblies.

Distribution of free grain to the poor; bribery

950. All these practices enormously increased the expenses of a political career. The young Roman who formerly might have demonstrated his ability and his worthy character in some minor office as a claim upon the votes of the community was now obliged to borrow money to pay for a long program of gladiatorial games. In secret he might also spend a large sum in bribing

Expenses of a political career; lack of a civil service

voters. If elected he received no salary, and in carrying on the business of his office he was again obliged to meet heavy expenses. For the Roman government had never been properly equipped with clerks, bookkeepers, and accountants; that is, the staff of public servants whom we call the civil service. The newly elected official, therefore, had to supply a staff of clerks at his own expense. Even a consul sat at home in a household room turned into an office and carried on government business with his own clerks and accountants, of whom one was usually a Greek.

951. The Roman politician now sought office in order that through it he might gain the influence which would bring him the governorship of a rich province. If he finally gained his object, he often reached his province burdened with debts incurred in winning elections in Rome. But the prize of a large province was worth all it cost. Indeed, the consulship itself was finally regarded as merely a stepping-stone to a provincial governorship. When a retired provincial governor returned to Rome, he was no longer the simple Roman of the good old days. He lived like a prince and, as we have seen, surrounded himself with royal luxury. These men of self-interest, who had held the supreme power in a province, were a menace to the Republic, for they had tasted the power of kings without the restraints of Roman law and Roman republican institutions to hamper them.

Dangerous attitude of ex-provincial governors

952. But the evils of the new wealth were not less evident in the *country*. It was not thought proper for a Roman senator or noble to undertake commercial enterprises or to engage in any business. The most respectable form of wealth was land. Hence the successful Roman noble bought farm after farm, which he combined into a great estate or plantation. The capitalists who had plundered the provinces did the same. Looking northward from Rome, the old Etruscan country was now made up of extensive estates belonging to wealthy Romans of the city. Only here and there were still to be found the

Growth of great estates; decline of small farms

little farms of the good old Roman days. Large portions of Italy were in this condition. The small farm seemed in a fair way to disappear as it had done in Greece (§ 662).

953. It was impossible for a wealthy landowner to work these great estates with free hired labor, nor was he obliged to do so. From the close of the Hannibalic War onward the Roman conquests had brought to Italy great numbers of captives of war from Carthage, Spain, Gaul, Macedonia, Greece, and Asia Minor. These unhappy prisoners were sold as slaves. The coast of the Adriatic opposite Italy alone yielded one hundred and fifty thousand captives. An ordinary day laborer would bring about three hundred dollars at auction, a craftsman or a good clerk was much more valuable, and a young woman who could play the lyre would bring a thousand dollars. The sale of such captives was thus enormously profitable. We have already seen such slaves in the households at Rome. The estates of Italy were now filled with them.

Captives of war as slaves

954. Household slavery was usually not attended with much hardship, but the life of the slaves on the great plantations was little better than that of beasts. Worthy and free-born men from the Eastern Mediterranean were branded with a hot iron like oxen, to identify them forever. They were herded at night in cellar barracks, and in the morning were driven like half-starved beasts of burden to work in the fields. The green fields of Italy, where sturdy farmers once watched the growing grain sown and cultivated by their own hands, were now worked by wretched and hopeless creatures who wished they had never been born. When the supply of captives from the wars failed, the Roman government winked at the practices of slave pirates, who carried on wholesale kidnaping in the Ægean and Eastern Mediterranean for years. They sold the victims in the slave market at Delos, whence they were brought by Roman merchants to Italy.

Brutal treatment of plantation slaves

955. Thus Italy and Sicily were fairly flooded with slaves. The brutal treatment which they received was so unbearable that at various places in Italy they finally rose against their masters. Even when they did not revolt, they were a grave danger to public safety. The lonelier roads of Italy were infested with slave herdsmen, lawless ancient cowboys who robbed and slew and in many districts made it unsafe to live in the country or travel the country roads. The conditions in Sicily were worse than in Italy. In central and southern Sicily the revolting slaves gathered, some sixty thousand in number, slew their masters, captured towns, and set up a kingdom. It required a Roman consul at the head of an army and a war lasting several years to subdue them.

Slave revolts and disorders

956. During the uprising of the slaves in Sicily the small farm owners, *free men*, went about burning the fine villas of the wealthy plantation proprietors. The slave rebellion therefore was a revelation of the hatred not only among the slaves but also among the poor farming class of *freemen*, — the hatred toward the rich landowners felt by *all* the lower classes in the country, slave or free. The great conquests and the wealth they brought in had made the rich so much richer and the poor so much poorer that the two classes were completely thrust apart, and they no longer had any common life. Italy was divided into two great social classes dangerously hostile to each other. The bulk of the population of Italy had formerly been small farmers, as we have seen. Let us examine the effect of the great wars on the small farmers.

Hostility between rich and poor, especially the small farmers

957. War seemed a great and glorious thing when we were following the brilliant victories of Hannibal and the splendid triumph of Scipio at Zama. But now we are to see the other side of the picture. Never has there been an age in which the terrible and desolating results of war have so tragically revealed the awful cost of such glory. The happy and industrious families cultivating the little farms which dotted the green hills and plains of Italy had now been helplessly scattered by the storms

Destruction of farms and farm life in Italy by war

of war, as the wind drives the autumn leaves. The campaigns of Hannibal left southern Italy desolate far and wide, and much of central Italy was in little better condition. These devastated districts left lying waste were never again cultivated, and slowly became pasture lands. In regions untouched by invasion, fathers and elder sons had been absent from home for years, holding their posts in the legion, fighting the battles which brought Rome her great position as mistress of the world. If the soldier returned, he often found the monotonous round of farm duties much too tedious after his adventurous life of war abroad. Leaving the plow, therefore, he returned to his place in the legion to resume the exciting life of war and plunder under some great leader whom he loved. Home life and wholesome country influences were undermined and broken up. The mothers, left to bring up the younger children alone, saw the family scattered and drifting away from the little farm, till it was left forsaken.

Small farms bought up by wealthy plantation owners

958. Too often, as the returning soldier approached the spot where he was born, he no longer found the house that had sheltered his childhood. His family was gone and his little farm, sold for debt, had been bought up by some wealthy Roman of the city and absorbed into a great plantation like those which the Romans had found surrounding Carthage. His neighbors, too, had disappeared, and their farms had likewise gone to enlarge the rich man's great estate. Across the hills on a sunny eminence he saw the stately villa, the home of the Roman noble who now owned the farms of all the surrounding country. He cursed the wealth which had done all this, and wandered up to the great city to look for free grain from the government, to enjoy the games and circuses, and to increase the poor class already there.

959. Or, if he found his home and his little farm uninjured, and was willing to settle down to work its fields as of old, he was soon aware that the hordes of slaves now cultivating the great plantations around him were producing grain so cheaply that when he disposed of his harvest he would not receive enough for it to enable him and his family to live. At the same time the markets of Italy were filled with cheap grain from Sicily, Africa, and Egypt. With this imported grain, often given away by the government, he could not compete, and slowly he fell behind; he borrowed money, and his debts increased. Forced to sell the little farm at last, he too wandered into Rome, where he found thousands upon thousands of his kind, homeless, embittered, and dependent upon the state for food.

Farmer unable to compete with slave labor and imported grain

960. The sturdy farmer-citizens who had made up the bulk of the citizenship of Rome, the yeomanry from whom she had drawn her splendid armies — these men who had formed the very substance of the power upon which the Roman Senate had built up its world empire — were now perishing. After the Macedonian wars the census returns showed a steady decline in the number of citizens of the Republic in Italy. At the same time there was serious discontent among the cities of the allies in Italy because they had never been given full citizenship. They saw the government of a world empire in the hands of a corrupt Senate and a small body of more and more brutalized citizens at Rome, and they demanded their share in the control of the great empire to whose armies they had contributed as many troops as the citizens of the Republic had done.

Degeneration and discontent in Italy

961. The wealth and power which Roman world dominion had gained had thus brought Rome and Italy to the verge of destruction. Nor was the situation any better in the most civilized portions of the empire outside of Italy, and especially in Greece. Under the large plantation system, introduced from Asia Minor, where it had grown up under the Persians (§ 355), the Greek farmers had disappeared, as those of Italy were now beginning to do. Add to this condition the robberies and extortions of the Roman taxgatherers and governors, the continuous slave raids of the Ægean pirates, whose pillaging and kidnaping the Roman Republic criminally failed to pre-

Economic and agricultural decline in Greece

vent, the shift of Greek commerce eastward (§ 759), and we have reasons enough for the destruction of business, of agriculture, and of prosperity in the Greek world.

Decline of Hellenistic civilization

962. But that wondrous development of higher civilization which we found in the Hellenistic world was likewise showing signs of decline. The sumptuous buildings forming the great home of science in Alexandria now represented little more than the high aims once cherished and supported by the Macedonian kings of Egypt. For when such state support failed, with its salaries and pensions to scientists and philosophers, the line of scientists failed too. Hence we see how largely science in the Hellenistic Age was rooted in the treasuries of the Hellenistic kings rather than in the minds of the Greek race, as it had been of old, when for sheer love of knowledge the Greek philosopher carried on his studies without such support.

Senate fails to govern the empire; peril to civilization

963. The Mediterranean was now the home of Greek civilization in the East and of Roman civilization in the West, but the failure of the Roman Senate to organize a successful government for the empire they had conquered — a government even as good as that of Persia under Darius — had brought the whole world of Mediterranean civilization perilously near destruction. In the European background, beyond the Alpine frontiers, there were rumblings of vast movements among the northern barbarians, who threatened to descend as of old and completely overwhelm the civilization which for over three thousand years had been slowly built up by Orientals and Greeks and Romans in the Mediterranean world. It now looked very much as if the Roman state were about to perish, and with it the civilization which had been growing for so many centuries. Was civilized man indeed to perish from the earth? Or would the Roman state be able to survive and to preserve civilization from destruction?

964. Rome was a city-state. The finest fruits of civilization in art, literature, science, and thought had been produced under the government of city-states. But among the Greeks this very limited form of state had outlived its usefulness and had over and over again proved its inability to organize and control successfully a larger world, that is, an empire. The city-state of the Roman Republic had now also demonstrated that its limited machinery of government was quite unfitted to rule successfully the vast Mediterranean world which it was now endeavoring to control. Would it be able to transform itself into a great imperial state, with all the many offices necessary to give successful government to the peoples and nations surrounding the Mediterranean? Would it then be able to do for the Mediterranean world what the Oriental empires had once done for a world equally large in Western Asia and Egypt?

Failure of city-state in imperial government

965. We stand at the point where the civilization of the Hellenistic world began to decline, after the destruction of Carthage and Corinth (146 B.C.). We are now to watch the Roman people in the deadly internal struggle which we have seen impending between rich and poor. They had at the same time to continue their rule of the Mediterranean world as best they could while the dangerous internal transformation was going on. In the midst of these grave responsibilities they had also to face the barbarian hordes of the north, whom we have seen shifting southward, beginning at least as far back as 2000 B.C. (and probably earlier), in one migration after another, in a broken line stretching from India westward to the Atlantic. The Romans were now to face similar invasions. In spite of all these threatening dangers we shall see them gaining the needed imperial organization which enabled the Roman state to hurl back the northern barbarians, to hold the northern frontiers for five hundred years, and thus to preserve the civilization which had cost mankind so many centuries of slow progress, — the civilization which, because it was so preserved, has become our own inheritance today. This achievement of Rome we are now to follow in the final chapters of the story of the ancient world.

Responsibility of Rome to organize and defend civilization

QUESTIONS

Section 77. As mistress of the Western Mediterranean world, what was to be Rome's attitude toward the other nations of the Mediterranean? Describe the struggle between Rome and Macedon. By extending her power over Macedon, with what other Eastern empire was Rome in contact? Describe the struggle between Rome and the Seleucid Empire. What then happened to Macedon? to the Greeks? What two splendid cities were destroyed in the same year by the Romans? What can you say of the rapidity of the Roman conquests? Describe the task of government now confronting Rome.

Section 78. Describe the rule of the usual Roman governor. What can you say of the increase of Roman wealth? What was the effect on business at Rome? Describe the changes in the new Roman dwelling house. How was it furnished, and whence did its luxuries often come? What can you say of the servants in a wealthy household? Describe the effect of Greek works of art in Rome. Tell how Greek literature became known in Rome. Describe the old Roman schools. How did educated Greeks affect teaching in Rome? Tell about Polybius. How did Latin literature arise? What can you say of libraries and the educated class?

Section 79. How was the new luxury affecting Roman life? What were the tastes of the ordinary Roman? What can you say about the expenses of a political career? What was happening to small farms? Describe slavery on the large estates. Describe the condition of the small farmers. Describe the situation of Italy as a whole; of Greece and the Ægean world. What was the situation of Hellenistic civilization as a whole? How, then, had Roman leadership of the Mediterranean world succeeded thus far? What three great tasks faced the Roman government?

BIBLIOGRAPHY FOR TOPICAL STUDIES

Social life at Rome: BRITISH MUSEUM, *Guide to Greek and Roman Life*, pp. 103–116, 219–221; DAVIS, *A Day in Rome*, pp. 15–33, 100–121; FOWLER, *Social Life at Rome in the Age of Cicero*, pp. 159–167, 199–203, 263–284; *Legacy of Rome*, pp. 209–227; MCDANIEL, *Roman Private Life*, pp. 116–167; SHOWERMAN, *Rome and the Romans*, pp. 137–147, 362–382; TREBLE-KING, *Everyday Life*, pp. 43–50.

Roman slaves: BRITISH MUSEUM, *Guide to Greek and Roman Life*, pp. 13–14; DAVIS, *A Day in Rome*, pp. 122–138; *Influence of Wealth in Imperial Rome*, pp. 205–224; FOWLER, *Social Life at Rome*, pp. 204–236; *Legacy of Rome*, pp. 227–231, 485–491; MCDANIEL, *Roman Private Life*, pp. 26–40.

Chapter XXVI · *A Century of Revolution and the End of the Republic*

Section 80. The Land Situation and the Beginning of the Struggle between Senate and People

Dangerous situation to be met by the Senate

966. We must now recall the problems, noticed at the close of the last chapter, demanding settlement by the Roman Senate. In Italy there was, in the first place, the perilous condition of the surviving farmers and the need of increasing in some way their numbers and their farms. Equally dangerous was the discontent of the Italian allies, who had never been given the vote or the right to hold office. The problems outside of Italy were not less pressing. They likewise were two in number. There were, first, the thoroughgoing reform of provincial government and the creation of a system of honest and successful administration of the vast Roman conquests, and, second, the settlement of the frontier boundaries and the repulse of the invading barbarians who were threatening to crush the Mediterranean world and its civilization, as the prehistoric Greeks, pushing in from the north, had crushed Ægean civilization.

Note. The above headpiece shows us the two sides of a Coin issued by Brutus, one of the leading assassins of Julius Cæsar. On one side the coin bears the head of Brutus, accompanied by his name and the title "Imperator" (abbreviated to IMP). On the other side are two daggers, intended to recall the assassination of Cæsar, and between them appears the cap of liberty, to suggest the liberty which the Romans supposedly gained by his murder. In order that the meaning of all this might be perfectly clear, there appears, below, the inscription EID MAR, which means the Ides of March (the Roman term for the fifteenth of March), the date of Cæsar's murder (§ 1008).

Faults of Senate; lack of legal basis for their power

967. The Senate which was to meet this dangerous situation had been in practical control of the Roman government since the days of the Samnite War. The senators now formed an oligarchy of selfish aristocrats, as in the Greek cities (§ 654). Yet there were no laws creating the powers of the Senate. It was merely by their great prestige and their combined influence as leading men and former magistrates that the senators maintained their control. The *legal* power of the Roman state really rested in the hands of the Roman people, gathered in their assemblies (§ 846), and this power had never been surrendered to the Senate by any vote or any law.

Landless farmers; Senate and people struggle for lands

968. The crying needs of the farming class in Italy failed to produce any effect upon the blinded and selfish aristocrats of the Senate as a whole. Even before the Hannibalic War the need of newly distributed farm lands was sorely felt. Led by the brave Flaminius, who afterward, as consul, fell at the head of his army in Hannibal's ambush at Trasimene, the Assembly had passed a law in defiance of the Senate, providing for a distribution of public lands which the senators desired for themselves and their friends of the noble class. As a result Flaminius was always hated by the senatorial party, and ever after was regarded as the popular leader who had opened the struggle between people and Senate and, having thus shown the people their power, had begun the dangerous policy of allowing the unstable populace to control the government. The conflict between Senate and people had subsided during the Hannibalic War; but when this great danger had passed, it would seem that a tribune named Licinius, who understood the needs of the people, had succeeded in having a law passed by the Assembly which forbade any wealthy citizen to hold over five hundred acres of the public lands or to pasture more than a hundred cattle or five hundred sheep on these lands. These Licinian laws, however, had become a dead letter.[1]

[1] The usually accepted earlier date for the Licinian laws (376 B.C.) is quite impossible, nor is the date above suggested at all certain.

969. In gaining control of Italy, Rome had finally annexed about half of the peninsula, and no more land could now be taken without seizing that of the Italian allies. About a decade before the destruction of Carthage and Corinth the last Roman colony had been founded. The only way to secure new farms for assignment to landless farmers was by making the Licinian laws effective, that is, by taking and assigning to farmers the public lands already belonging to the state, — what are called government lands in the United States. But for generations these lands had been largely held under all sorts of arrangements by wealthy men, and it was sometimes difficult to decide whether a noble's estate was his legal property or merely public land which he was using. Under these circumstances we can easily imagine with what stubbornness and anger great landholders of the senatorial party would oppose any effort to redistribute the public lands on a basis fair to all.

Absorption of public lands by nobles

970. Flaminius had taught the people their power. Since then they had lacked a skillful leader. The unselfish patriot who undertook to become the leader of the people and to save Italy from destruction by restoring the farmer class was a noble named Tiberius Gracchus. He was a grandson of the elder Scipio, the hero of Zama, and his sister had married the younger Scipio. Elected tribune (133 B.C.), he used to address the people with passionate eloquence and tell them of their wrongs: "The beasts that prowl about Italy have holes and lurking places, where they may make their beds. You who fight and die for Italy enjoy only the blessings of air and light. These alone are your heritage. Homeless, unsettled, you wander to and fro with your wives and children. . . . You fight and die to give wealth and luxury to others. You are called the masters of the world; yet there is no clod of earth that you can call your own."

Tiberius Gracchus, tribune (133 B.C.)

971. As tribune, Tiberius Gracchus submitted to the Assembly a law for the reassignment of public lands and the protection and support of the farming class. It was a statesmanlike and moderate law. It called for little if anything more than what was already demanded by the Licinian laws. It was an endeavor to do for Italy what Solon had done for Attica (§ 506), and was decidedly more moderate than the legislation of Solon. After a tragic struggle in which the new tribune resorted to methods not strictly legal, he succeeded in passing his law. In the effort to secure reëlection, that he might insure the *enforcement* of his law, Gracchus was slain by a mob of senators, who rushed out of the Senate house and attacked the tribune and his supporters. This was the first murderous deed introducing a century of revolution and civil war (133–30 B.C.), which terminated in the destruction of the Roman Republic.

Land laws of Tiberius Gracchus; his death (132 B.C.)

972. Ten years after the tribunate of Tiberius Gracchus his younger brother Gaius gained the same office (123 B.C.). He not only took up the struggle on behalf of the landless farmers, but made it his definite object to attack and weaken the Senate. He endeavored to enlist on the side of the people every possible enemy of the Senate. He therefore organized the capitalists and men of large business affairs, who of course were not senators. Because of their wealth they had always furnished their own horses and served in the army as horsemen. They were therefore called knights or, as a group, the equestrian order. Gaius Gracchus secured the support of these men by obtaining for them the right to collect the taxes in Asia, and he gave them great power by founding a court made up of knights for the trial of dishonest and extortionate Roman governors appointed by the Senate. At the same time he proposed to give to the Italian allies the long-desired full citizenship, — a proposal which angered the people as much as it did the Senate. His efforts finally resulted in a riot in which he was killed (121 B.C.), as his brother had been.

Gaius Gracchus attacks the Senate; his death (121 B.C.)

Section 81. The Rise of One-Man Power: Marius and Sulla

973. The weakness in the reforms of the Gracchus brothers lay chiefly in their unavoidable reliance upon votes, that is, upon the unstable support of the people at the elections and at the meetings of the popular assembly. It was difficult to hold the interest of the people from election to election. In the Gracchan elections, when work on the farms was pressing, the country people around Rome would not take the time to go up to the city and vote, although they were the very ones to be benefited by the Gracchan laws. The work of Flaminius, and especially of the Gracchi, had taught the people to look up to a leader. This tendency was the beginning of one-man power. But the leader to whom the people now turned was not a magistrate, as the Gracchi had been, but a *military commander*.

Unreliability of popular support

974. Meantime the blindness and corruption of the Senate offered the people more than one opportunity for gaining power. The misrule of the Senate abroad was now so scandalous that the people seized this opportunity. In a war between Rome and Jugurtha, ruler of the great kingdom of Numidia, beside Carthage in North Africa, the African king, knowing the weakness of the Romans of this age, succeeded in bribing the consul, and thus inflicted a crushing defeat on the Roman army. The war then dragged disgracefully on. These events so incensed the people of Rome that, in spite of the fact that the Senate's commander, at this time an able and honest consul named Metellus, had finally met and defeated Jugurtha, the Assembly passed a law appointing their own general to supersede Metellus. The *people* thus assumed charge of a great foreign enterprise, and, what was more important, *the people by this action seized control of the army*. The Senate was unable to prevent the Assembly's action from going into effect. The interests of the people were no longer dependent wholly upon civil magistrates, changing

War with Jugurtha; appointment of a general by the people

from election to election, but upon military force under a leader who might be given a long command.

975. The commander on whom the people relied was himself a man of the people, named Marius, who had once been a rough plowboy. He was fortunately an able soldier, and he quickly brought the war with Jugurtha to an end, after the Senate's leaders had allowed it to drift on for six years. When the news of his victory reached Rome, the people, before his return, promptly elected him consul for the second time. In 104 B.C. he returned to Rome, and the people beheld the captive Numidian king led through the streets in chains. Meantime the two powerful tribes of German barbarians, the Cimbrians and the Teutons, combined with Gauls, had been shifting southward and crossing the northern frontiers of the Roman possessions. In Gaul and on the Gallic frontiers six Roman armies, one after another, had been disastrously defeated. It looked as if the Roman legions had at last met their match. There was great anxiety in Rome, and the people determined to reëlect Marius consul and send him against the terrible northern barbarians. Meeting the Teutons in southern Gaul, the people's hero not only defeated but practically destroyed the first German host (102 B.C.). Shortly afterward, when the Cimbrians had finally succeeded in crossing the Alps into the Po valley, Marius met and crushed them also. A soldier of the people had saved Rome.

Marius, the people's general, defeats Jugurtha and Germans

976. Not only was Marius an able soldier, but he was also a great organizer, and he introduced changes in the Roman army which were epoch-making both in the history of warfare and in the political history of Rome. In order to secure sufficient men for the legions, he abolished the old custom of allowing only citizens of property to serve in the army, and took in the poor and the penniless. Such men soon became professional soldiers. As once in Greece (§ 665), so now in Rome, the day of the citizen-soldier had passed. The long wars had made many a Roman citizen practically a profes-

Property qualification for the army abolished; professional army

sional soldier, as we have noticed. The army of Marius was largely a professional army; and although the obligation to serve in the army still rested on every Roman citizen, it was less and less rigidly enforced.

Cohort as tactical unit devised by Marius

977. The youths who permanently took up the life of the soldier could be so well drilled that they were able to carry out maneuvers impossible for an army made up of citizens serving for a limited time. Marius therefore completely reorganized the legion. He raised its numbers from forty-five hundred to six thousand. He divided each six thousand into ten groups of six hundred each. Such a body of six hundred was called a *cohort*. It formed the unit in the shifting maneuvers which, as we have seen, meant victory or defeat in battle (§ 914). So perfectly drilled and so fearless were these units that the cohorts would move about the field with the precision of clockwork and with complete confidence in the plan of the commander, just as the individuals in a perfectly trained football squad respond almost automatically to the signal. The production of the cohort, as we shall see, made it possible to complete the final chapter in the development of the art of warfare in ancient times.

Failure of Marius as a statesman; Senate regains leadership

978. But in spite of his ability as a soldier and as an army organizer, Marius was not a statesman. Having risen from the ranks, he was at heart a rough Roman peasant. He hated the aristocrats of the city; he did not know how to deal with them, nor did he understand the leadership of the popular party which had given him his great military commands. Elected consul for the sixth time in the year 100 B.C., he failed utterly to control the leaders of his party in the political struggles in Rome. They went to such excesses that two of them were slain in a riot. Moderate men were estranged from the cause of the people, and the Senate gained the upper hand again. Marius retired in disgrace, but his leadership had revealed to the people how they might gain control over the Senate by combining on a *military* leader, whose power, therefore, consisted not in the peaceful enforcement of the laws and usages of the Roman state but in the illegal application of military force.

Disunion in Italy and discontent of Italian allies

979. Meantime the struggle between Senate and people was complicated by the increasing discontent of the Italian allies. They had contributed as many troops to the conquering armies as had Rome herself, and now they were refused any voice in the control of the conquered territory or any share in the immense wealth which they saw the Romans drawing from it. The wise and liberal policy of the ancient Senate in freely granting citizenship to communities in newly acquired Italian territory had been long abandoned, which reminds us of the Athenians in the later years of Pericles. Before the different communities of Italy had had time to merge into a nation, they had been forced into a long series of foreign wars which had made vast conquests. But the possession of these conquests had corrupted and blinded the Senate and the governing community at Rome. By this sudden wealth and power Rome had been raised above all feeling of fellowship with the other communities of Italy. The great peninsula was still filled with disunited communities, and there now rested upon Rome the obligation to make Italy a nation.

Exclusiveness of Romans; assassination of Drusus (91 B.C.)

980. There were, happily, some Roman leaders with the insight of statesmen, who perceived this great need and who planned that the Italian allies should receive citizenship. Among them was a wealthy, popular, and unselfish noble named Drusus, who gained election as tribune and began measures leading to the enfranchisement of the Italian allies. But so fierce and savage was the opposition aroused that this great Roman statesman was attacked while on the street and stabbed. The opposition to Drusus and his plans was by no means confined to the Senate. The common people of Rome were likewise jealous of their ancient privileges, and the wealthy men of the new equestrian order were equally unwilling to share their opportunities of plundering the provinces. The Italian allies therefore soon saw the hopelessness of an appeal to Rome for their rights. Immediately after the assassination of Drusus the leading Italian peoples of central and southern Italy revolted and formed a new state and government of their own, with a capital at a central town which they impressively renamed Italica (90 B.C.).

981. In the war (often called the Social War) which followed, the army of Rome was at first completely defeated; and although this reverse was in a measure retrieved, the strength of the allies could not be broken. Seeing the seriousness of the situation, the Roman politicians tardily took action and granted the desired citizenship. The Italian alliance then broke up, and the Italian communities reëntered the Roman state. Yet they entered it as distant wards of the city on the Tiber. The citizens residing in these distant wards could not vote or take any part in the government unless they journeyed to Rome to do so. This situation was of course an absurdity, and again illustrated the inability of an ancient city-state to furnish the machinery of government for a large nation, not to mention a world empire. Nevertheless Italy was on the way to become a nation unified in government and in speech.

War with allies (90–88 B.C.); citizenship given to all Italy

982. A very threatening war was now breaking out in Asia Minor. Wealthy senators and other Romans of the moneyed class who ruled Rome had many financial interests in this region, and this led them to dread a war there and to stop it as soon as possible. Among the officers of Marius there had been a very successful soldier named Sulla, who was chosen consul for the year after the war with the allies. The Senate now selected him to command in Asia Minor. But the leaders of the people would not accept the Senate's appointment, and, just as in the war against Jugurtha, they passed a law electing Marius to command in the coming war in Asia Minor. Now Marius had no army at the moment, but Sulla was still at the head of the army he had been leading

Sulla as consul, using the army, defeats the will of the people

against the Italian allies. He therefore ignored the law passed by the people and marched on Rome with his troops. For the first time a Roman consul took possession of the city by force. The Senate was now putting through its will with an army, as the Assembly had done before. Sulla forced through a new law by which the Assembly would always be obliged to secure the consent of the Senate before it could vote on any measure. Having thus destroyed the power of the people legally to oppose the will of the Senate, Sulla marched his army to Asia Minor.

People in control in Sulla's absence; fighting in Rome

983. The Senate had triumphed, but with the departure of Sulla and his legions the people refused to submit. There was fighting in the streets, and the senatorial troops fell upon the new Italian citizens as they voted in the Forum, and slew them by hundreds. In the midst of these deeds of violence Marius, who had escaped to Africa, returned at the head of a body of cavalry. He joined the popular leaders and, entering Rome, began a frightful massacre of the leading men of the senatorial party. The Senate, the first to sow seeds of violence in the murder of Tiberius Gracchus, now reaped a fearful harvest. Marius was elected consul for the seventh time; but he died a few days after his election (86 B.C.), leaving the people to rule in Rome until the day of reckoning which was sure to come on the return of Sulla.

Sulla's campaign against Mithradates

984. The war which had called Sulla to Asia Minor was due to the genius of Mithradates, the gifted young king of Pontus (see map IV, p. 626). He had prospered by taking advantage of Roman misrule in the East. He had rapidly extended his kingdom to include a large part of Asia Minor, and such was the deep-seated discontent of the Greek cities under Roman rule that he was able to induce the Greek states of Asia Minor and some in Greece to join him in a war against Rome. Even Athens, which had suffered least, supported him. The Romans, busily occupied with civil war at home, were thus suddenly confronted by a foe in the East who seemed as dangerous as Carthage had once been. Sulla besieged Athens, recovered European Greece, and drove the troops of Mithradates back into Asia. Thereupon, crossing to Asia Minor, he finally concluded a peace with Mithradates. He laid an enormous indemnity of twenty thousand talents on the Greek cities of Asia Minor. Then, leaving them to the tender mercies of the Roman money-lenders and to the barbarous raids of the eastern pirates, Sulla returned to Rome.

985. On the way thither the Roman army of Sulla defeated the Roman armies of the people one after another. Finally, outside the gates of the city, Sulla overthrew the last army of the people and entered Rome as master of the state, without any legal power to exercise such mastery. By means of his army, however, he forced his own appointment as dictator, with far greater powers than any dictator had ever before possessed (82 B.C.). His first action was to begin the systematic slaughter of the leaders of the people's party and the confiscation of their property. Rome passed through another reign of terror like that which followed the return of Marius. The hatreds and the many debts of revenge which Sulla's barbarities left behind were later a frequent source of disturbance and danger to the state.

Sulla defeats the armies of the people and becomes dictator (82 B.C.)

986. Then Sulla forced the passage of a whole series of new laws which deprived the Assembly and the tribunes of their power and gave the supreme leadership of the state to the Senate, the body which had already so disastrously failed to guide Rome wisely since the great conquests. Some lesser reforms of value Sulla did introduce, but a policy based on the supremacy of the Senate was doomed to failure. To Sulla's great credit he made no attempt to gain permanent control of the state, but on the completion of his legislation he retired to private life (79 B.C.)

Sulla takes power from the people and gives the Senate leadership

Section 82. The Overthrow of the Republic: Pompey and Cæsar

987. Following the death of Sulla a year after his retirement, agitation for the repeal of his hateful laws, which bound the people and the tribunes hand and foot, at once began. To accomplish this the people had now learned that they must make use of a military leader. The Senate had been ruling nine years in accordance with Sulla's laws when the popular leaders found the military commander whom they needed. He was a former officer of Sulla, named Pompey, who had recently won distinction in Spain, where he had been sent by the Senate to overthrow a still unsubdued supporter of Marius. He was elected consul (70 B.C.), chiefly because he agreed to repeal the obnoxious laws of Sulla, and he did not fail to carry out his promise. This service to the people now secured to Pompey a military command of supreme importance.

People elect Pompey consul and regain political power

988. Such was the neglect of the Senate to protect shipping that the pirates of the east, chiefly from Cilicia, had overrun the whole Mediterranean (§ 954). They even appeared at the mouth of the Tiber, robbing and burning. They kidnaped Roman officials on the Appian Way, but a few miles from Rome, and they finally captured the grain supplies coming in to Rome from Egypt and Africa. In 67 B.C. the Assembly of the people passed a law giving Pompey supreme command in the Mediterranean and for fifty miles back from its shores. He was assigned two hundred ships and allowed to make his army as large as he thought necessary. No Roman commander had ever before held such far-reaching and unrepublican power.

Pompey's appointment against the pirates of the Mediterranean

989. In forty days Pompey cleared the Western Mediterranean of pirates. He then sailed eastward, and in seven weeks after his arrival in the Ægean he had exterminated the Cilician sea robbers likewise and burned their docks and strongholds. The next year his command was enlarged to include also the leadership in a new war against Mithradates which had been going on with satisfactory results under Lucullus, a Roman commander of the greatest ability. Lucullus had already broken the power of Mithradates and also of the vast kingdom of Armenia, under its king, Tigranes. Pompey therefore had little difficulty in subduing Mithradates, and had only to accept the voluntary submission of Tigranes. He crushed the remnant of the kingdom of the Seleucids (§ 753) and made Syria a Roman province. He entered Jerusalem and brought the home of the Jews under Roman control. Before he turned back, the legions under his leadership had marched along the Euphrates and had looked down upon the Caspian. There had been no such conquests in the Orient since the Macedonian campaigns, and to the popular imagination Pompey seemed a new Alexander marching in triumph through the East.

Pirates exterminated and Orient conquered by Pompey (67–62 B.C.)

FIG. 239. BUST *said to be a Portrait of* JULIUS CÆSAR

The ancient portraits commonly accepted as those of Julius Cæsar are really of uncertain identity

990. Meantime a new popular hero had arisen at Rome. He was a nephew of Marius, named Julius Cæsar, born in the year 100 B.C., and thirty years old in Pompey's consulate. He had supported all the legislation against the laws of Sulla and in favor of Pompey's appointment to his great command. He took up the cause of Marius and exalted his memory in public speeches so that he quickly gained a foremost place among the leaders of the people. The hatreds aroused by

Rise of Cæsar and his support of Catiline

Sulla's executions and confiscations had left a great number of revengeful and dissatisfied men, who to no small extent made up the following of Cæsar. Among Cæsar's political friends was a nobleman named Catiline. He was the leader of a good many undesirable followers, but Cæsar was supporting him and another friend for election to the consulship.

Overthrow of Catiline and success of Cicero

991. Popular distrust of Cæsar's purposes, and Catiline's evil reputation, led to the defeat of Catiline and to the election of Cicero, a comparatively new man, but the ablest orator and one of the most gifted literary men of the age. By the formation of a new middle-class party from the Italian communities, which should stand between the Senate and the people, Cicero dreamed of a restoration of the old Republic as it had once been. Catiline, meantime, burdened with debts and rendered desperate by the loss of the election, gathered about him all the dissatisfied bankrupts, landless peasants, Sulla's veterans, outlaws, and slaves,—the debased and lawless elements of Italy seeking an opportunity to rid themselves of debt or to better their situation. Foiled by Cicero in an attempt to seize violent control of the government, the reckless Catiline died fighting at the head of his motley following. Cicero's overthrow of Catiline brought him great power and influence and made his consulship (63 B.C.) one of brilliant success. Cæsar, on the other hand, was suspected of connection with the uprising of Catiline. This suspicion, whether just or unjust, proved to be a serious setback in his political career.

Triumvirate of Pompey, Cæsar, and Crassus; Cæsar as consul

992. Just at this juncture Pompey returned to Italy clothed in splendor as the great conqueror of the Orient. He made no attempt to influence the political situation by means of his army, the command of which he relinquished. But he needed political influence to secure the Senate's formal approval of his arrangements in Asia Minor, and a grant of land for his troops. For two years the Senate refused Pompey these concessions. Meantime Cæsar stepped forward in Pompey's support, and the two secured for their plans the support of a very wealthy Roman nobleman named Crassus. The plan was that Cæsar should run for the consulship and, if successful, secure the two things which we have seen Pompey needed. This private alliance of these three powerful men (called a triumvirate) gave them the control of the situation. As a result Cæsar was elected consul for the year 59 B.C.

993. The consulship was but a step in Cæsar's plans. Having secured for Pompey the measures which he desired, Cæsar fearlessly put through new land laws for the benefit of the people, and then provided for his own future career. It was clear to him that he must have an important military command in order to gain an army. He saw a great opportunity in the West, like that which had been given Pompey in the Orient. Rome still held no more than a comparatively narrow strip of land along the coast of what is now southern France. On its north was a vast country occupied by the Gauls, and this region of Gaul was now sought by Cæsar. He had no difficulty in securing the passage of a law which made him for five years governor of Illyria and of Gaul on both sides of the Alps, — that is, the valley of the Po in northern Italy, which we remember had been occupied by the Gauls (§ 855), and also farther Gaul beyond the Alps, as just described.

Cæsar secures government of Gaul on both sides of the Alps

994. Cæsar took charge of his new province early in 58 B.C., and at once showed himself a military commander of surpassing skill. Not only did he possess the keenest insight into the tactical maneuvers which win victory on the field of battle itself, but he also understood at a glance the resources and abilities of a people and their armies. He knew that the greatest problem facing a commander was to keep his army in supplies and to guard against moving it to a point where it was impossible either to carry with it the supplies for feeding it or to find them on the spot. So efficient was his own great organization that he knew he could transport supplies more successfully than could the barbarian Gauls. He perceived

Cæsar's military skill and plan of operations in Gaul

that no great barbarian host could be kept long together in one place, because they did not possess the organization for carrying with them, or securing later, enough food to maintain them long. When the necessity of finding provisions had forced them to separate into smaller armies, then Cæsar swiftly advanced and defeated these smaller divisions.

Cæsar's conquest of Gaul (58–50 B.C.)

995. By this general plan of operations, in eight years of march and battle he subdued the Gauls and conquered their territory from the ocean and the English Channel eastward to the Rhine. He checked a dangerous invasion of Gaul by the Germans, and, astonishing them by the skill and speed with which he built a bridge over the Rhine, he invaded their country and established the frontier of the new Gallic province at the Rhine. He even crossed the Channel and carried an invasion of Britain as far as the Thames. He added a vast dominion to the Roman Empire, comprising in general the territory of modern France and Belgium. We should not forget that his conquest brought into France the Latin language, from which French speech has descended (see map IV, p. 626).

Cæsar's view of the situation as a statesman

996. Cæsar had shown himself at Rome a successful politician. In Gaul he proved his ability as a brilliant soldier. Was he also a great statesman, or was he, like Pompey, merely to seek a succession of military commands and to accomplish nothing to deliver Rome from being a cat's-paw of one military commander after another? Cæsar's understanding of the situation at Rome was perfectly clear and had been so from the beginning. He was convinced that the foreign wars and the rule of the provinces had introduced into Roman government the ever-returning opportunity for a man of ability to gain military power which could not be controlled by the state. It was of no use to bring in a new political party, as Cicero hoped to do, and to pit mere *votes* against the flashing swords of the legions; for the old machinery of government furnished by the Republic possessed no means of preventing the rise of one ambitious general after another to fight for control of the state as Marius and Sulla had done. The Republic could therefore never again restore order and stable government for Italy and the empire. Herein Cæsar showed his superiority as a statesman over both Sulla and Cicero.

Cæsar publishes an account of his Gallic Wars

997. The situation therefore demanded an able and patriotic commander with an army behind him, who should make himself the undisputed and permanent master of the Roman government and subdue all other competitors. Consistently and steadily Cæsar pursued this aim, and it is no reflection upon him to say that it satisfied his ambition to do so. One of his cleverest moves was the publication of the story of his Gallic campaigns, which he found time to write even in the midst of dangerous marches and critical battles. The tale is narrated with the most unpretentious simplicity. Although it is one of the greatest works of Latin prose, the book was really a political pamphlet, intended to convey to the Roman people a vivid impression of the vast conquests and other services which they owed to their governor in Gaul. It did not fail of its purpose. At present it is the best-known Latin reading book for beginners in that language.

Pompey at Rome takes up the cause of the Senate

998. When Cæsar's second term as governor of Gaul drew near its end, his supporters in Rome, instructed by him, were arranging for his second election to the consulship. The Senate was dreading his return to Italy and was putting forth every effort to prevent his reëlection as consul. The experience in the time of Marius had taught the Senate what to fear when a victorious commander returned to Rome to avenge their opposition to the people. They must have a military leader like Sulla again. Meantime Crassus, the wealthy member of the triumvirate, had been slain in a disastrous war against the Parthians, beyond the Euphrates, and the group had broken up, thus freeing Pompey. In the midst of great confusion and political conflict in Rome the leading senators now made offers to Pompey, in spite of the fact that he had received his great command from the Assembly of the people and had been a leader of the popular party. He was no statesman and had no plans for the future of the state. He was simply seeking control of an army. The result was that he undertook to defend the cause of the Senate and support the enemies of the people. What should have been a lawful political contest again became a military struggle between two commanding generals, Cæsar and Pompey, like that between Marius and Sulla a generation earlier.

Cæsar and his army of professional soldiers

999. Cæsar endeavored to compromise with the Senate, but on receiving as their reply a summons to disband his army, he had no hesitation as to his future action. The professional soldiers who now made up a Roman army had no interest in political questions, felt no responsibility as citizens, and were conscious of very little obligation or attachment to the state. On the other hand, they were usually greatly attached to their commanding general. The veterans of Cæsar's Gallic campaigns were unswervingly devoted to him. When he gave the word, therefore, his troops followed him on the march to Rome without a moment's hesitation, to draw their swords against their fellow Romans forming the army of the Senate under Pompey. Cæsar and his troops at once crossed the Rubicon, the little stream which formed the boundary of his province toward Rome. Beyond this boundary Cæsar had no legal right to lead his forces, and in crossing it he had taken a step which became so memorable that we still proverbially speak of any great decision as a crossing of the Rubicon.

Cæsar takes Rome and is elected consul (49 B.C.)

1000. The swiftness of Cæsar's lightning blows was always one of the greatest reasons for his success. Before the Senate's message had been an hour in his hands, Cæsar's legions were on the march from the Po valley toward Rome (49 B.C.). Totally unprepared for so swift a response on Cæsar's part, the Senate turned to Pompey, who informed them that the forces at his command could not hold Rome against Cæsar. Indeed, there was at the moment no army in the empire capable of meeting Cæsar's veteran legions with any hope of victory. Pompey retreated, and as Cæsar approached Rome the majority of the senators and a large number of nobles fled with Pompey and his army. By skillful maneuvers Cæsar forced Pompey and his followers to forsake Italy and cross over to Greece. Cæsar's possession of Rome made it possible for him to be elected consul, and then to assume the rôle of lawful defender of Rome against the Senate and the army of Pompey.

Pompey's power; Cæsar captures Pompey's army in Spain

1001. His position, however, was not yet secure. Pompey, in the eyes of the Orient, was the greatest man in Rome. He could muster all the peoples and kingdoms of the East against Cæsar. Furthermore, he now held the great fleet with which he had suppressed the pirates, and he was thus master of the sea. With all the East at his back, he was improving every moment to gather and discipline an army with which to crush Cæsar. Furthermore, Pompey's officers still held Spain since his recovery of it from the followers of Marius. Cæsar was therefore obliged to reckon with the followers of Pompey on both sides, east and west. He determined to deal with the west first. With his customary swiftness he was in Spain by June (49 B.C.). Here he met the army of Pompey's commanders with maneuvers of such surprising cleverness that in a few weeks he cut off their supplies, surrounded them, and forced them to surrender without fighting a battle.

Cæsar crosses over into Greece and surprises the senatorial party

1002. Having heard of Cæsar's departure into Spain, Pompey and his great group of senators and nobles had been preparing at their leisure to cross over and take possession of Italy. Before they could even begin the crossing, Cæsar had returned from Spain victorious, and to their amazement, in spite of the fact that they controlled the sea, he embarked at Brundisium, evaded their warships, and landed his army on the coast of Epirus. Forced by lack of supplies to divide his army, he left a part of his troops so exposed that they suffered a dangerous reverse. In the end, however, in spite of his inferior numbers, he accepted battle with Pompey at Pharsalus in Thessaly (48 B.C.).

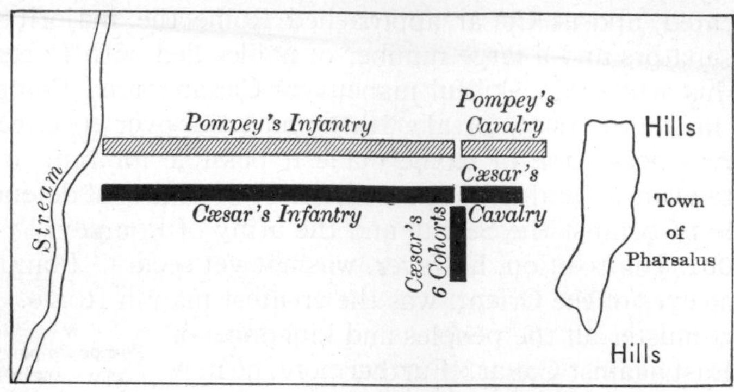

Plan of the BATTLE OF PHARSALUS

1003. Pompey's plan for the battle was skillfully made, but it was not clever enough to outwit the greatest commander of the age. It consisted in drawing up his line so that a small stream would protect his right wing, in order that he might throw *all* his cavalry to his left wing. Probably twice as strong as Cæsar's right wing, which it faced, Pompey's cavalry was expected to cut its way victoriously through, and then, passing around Cæsar's right end, to attack his legions in the rear. As the two armies approached each other Cæsar perceived Pompey's plan of battle. He at once shifted six of his best cohorts, over three thousand men, to his right end, where they were screened by his own cavalry from discovery by the enemy (see plan, above). The position of these six cohorts may be compared to that of an unobserved football player crouching on the right side lines to receive the ball. Cæsar then ordered his cavalry, mostly Gauls and Germans, to retreat as Pompey's horsemen attacked them. As they retreated Pompey's unsuspecting cavalry followed and pushed forward into Cæsar's cleverly devised trap; for when Cæsar's six cohorts swiftly dropped in behind them, Pompey's horsemen were caught between the six cohorts behind and Cæsar's cavalry in front, and they were quickly cut to pieces. Cæsar's cavalry then

Battle of Pharsalus (48 B.C.)

swept swiftly around the enemy's now undefended left end and attacked Pompey's legions in the rear. As Cæsar threw in his reserves against the hostile center at the same moment, the whole senatorial army was driven off the field in flight. Its remnants surrendered the next morning.

1004. This battle represented the highest development of military art in the ancient world, and it never passed beyond the masterful skill of the victor of Pharsalus. Pompey, crushed by the first defeat of his life, escaped into Egypt, where he was basely murdered. Cæsar, following Pompey to Egypt, found ruling there the beautiful Cleopatra, the seventh of the name and the last of the Ptolemies. The charms of this remarkable queen and the political advantages of her friendship met a ready response on the part of the great Roman. Here Cæsar displayed probably the most serious weakness in his career as he tarried in Alexandria, dallying with this charming and gifted woman for three quarters of a year (from October, 48 B.C., to June, 47 B.C.). We know little of the operations and battles by which Cæsar overthrew his opponents in Asia Minor. It was from there that he sent his famous report to the Senate: "I came, I saw, I conquered" (*veni, vidi, vici*). He was equally triumphant in the African province behind Carthage, and finally also in Spain. These, the only obstacles to Cæsar's complete control of the empire of the western world, were all disposed of by March, 45 B.C., a little over four years after he had first taken possession of Italy with his army (map IV, p. 626).

Cæsar completes conquest of Mediterranean world (48–45 B.C.)

1005. Cæsar used his power with great moderation and humanity. From the first he had taken special pains to show that his methods were not those of the bloody Sulla. He gratified no personal revenge, and he preserved the life of the gifted Cicero in spite of his hostility. It is clear that he intended his own position to be that of a Hellenistic sovereign like Alexander the Great. Nevertheless he was too wise a statesman to abolish at once the outward forms of the Republic. He pos-

Cæsar's moderation and his own position

sessed all the real power, and the Republic was doomed; for there was no one in Rome to gainsay this mightiest of the Romans. He had himself made dictator for life, and assumed also the powers of the other leading offices of the state.

Cæsar's reorganization of state and empire

1006. Cæsar lived only five years (49–44 B.C.) after his first conquest of Italy (49 B.C.). Of this period, as we have seen, four years were almost wholly occupied with campaigns. He was therefore left but little time for the colossal task of reshaping the Roman state and organizing the vast Roman Empire, the task in which the Roman Senate had so completely failed. Sulla had raised the membership of the Senate from three hundred to six hundred. Cæsar did not abolish the ancient body, but he greatly increased its numbers, filled it with his own friends and adherents, and even installed former slaves and foreigners among its members. He thus destroyed the public respect for it, and it was entirely ready to do his bidding. The new Senate could not obstruct him, and hence the whole projected administration of the provinces centered in him and was permanently responsible to him. The election of the officials of the Republic went on as before, but he began far-reaching reforms of the corrupt Roman administration. In all this he was launching the Roman Empire. He was, in fact, its first emperor, and only his untimely death continued the death struggles of the Republic for fifteen years more.

Cæsar's vast plans and improvements

1007. He sketched vast plans for the rebuilding of Rome, for magnificent public buildings, and for the alteration of the plan of the city, including even a change in the course of the Tiber. He laid out great roads along the important lines of communication, and he planned to cut a sea canal through the Isthmus of Corinth. He completely reformed the government of cities. He put an end to centuries of inconvenience with the Greco-Roman moon-calendar by introducing into Europe the practical Egyptian calendar, which we are still using, though with inconvenient Roman alterations. The imperial sweep of his plans included far-reaching conquests into new lands, like the subjugation of the Germans. Had he carried out these plans, the language of the Germans today would be a descendant of Latin, like the speech of the French and the Spanish.

1008. The eighteenth of March, 44 B.C., was set as the date for Cæsar's departure for the Orient on a great campaign against the Parthians east of the Euphrates, where he was without doubt expecting to repeat the achievements of Alexander and especially to establish a safe eastern frontier, so dangerously exposed by the defeat of Crassus. But there were still men in Rome who were not ready to submit to the rule of one man. On the fifteenth of March, three days before the date arranged for his departure, and only a year after he had quelled the last disturbance in Spain, these men struck down the greatest of the Romans. If some of the murderers of this just and powerful statesman, who was for the first time giving the unhappy peoples of the Mediterranean world a government alike just, honest, and efficient, — if some of his murderers, like Brutus and Cassius, fancied themselves patriots overthrowing a tyrant, they little understood how vain were all such efforts to restore the ancient Republic. World dominion and its military power had forever demolished the Roman Republic, and the murder of Cæsar again plunged Italy and the empire into civil war. The death of Alexander the Great interrupted in mid-career the conquest of a world empire stretching from the frontiers of India to the Atlantic Ocean. The bloody deed of the Ides of March, 44 B.C., stopped a similar conquest by Julius Cæsar, — a conquest which would have subjected Orient and Occident to the rule of a single sovereign. A like opportunity never arose again, and Cæsar's successor had no such aims.

Assassination of Cæsar (March 15, 44 B.C.) and its results

Section 83. The Triumph of Augustus and the End of the Civil War

1009. Over in Illyria the terrible news from Rome found the murdered statesman's grand-nephew Octavian, a youth of eighteen, quietly pursuing his studies. A letter from his mother, brought by a secret messenger, bade him flee far away eastward without delay, in order to escape all danger at the hands of his uncle's murderers. The youth's reply was to proceed without a moment's hesitation to Rome. This statesmanlike decision of character reveals the quality of the young man as he showed it both then and for years to follow.

Youth of Cæsar's nephew Octavian (Augustus)

1010. On his arrival in Italy, Octavian learned that he had been legally adopted by Cæsar and also made his sole heir. His bold claim to his legal rights was met with refusal by Mark Antony, Cæsar's fellow consul and one of his closest friends and supporters, who had taken possession of Cæsar's fortune and as consul could not be easily forced. By such men Octavian was treated with patronizing indulgence at first, — a fact to which he owed his life. He was too young to be regarded as dangerous. But his young shoulders carried a very old head; he slowly gathered the threads of the tangled situation in his clever fingers, not forgetting the lessons of his adoptive father's career. The most obvious lesson was the necessity of military power. He therefore rallied a force of Cæsar's veterans, and two legions of Antony's troops also came over to him. Then playing the game of politics, with military power at his back and none too scrupulous a conscience, he showed himself a statesman no longer to be ignored.

Early career of Octavian

1011. By skillful manipulation of the situation at Rome Octavian forced his own election as consul when only twenty years of age (43 B.C.). He was then able to form an alliance composed of himself and the other two most powerful leaders — Antony (Cæsar's old follower) and Lepidus. This second triumvirate was officially

Second triumvirate

recognized by vote of the people. To obtain the money for carrying on their wars and establishing themselves, the three began at once a Sulla-like reign of terror, with confiscation of property and murder of their enemies. Among them the great orator Cicero, who had endeavored to preserve the old Republic, was assassinated by Antony's brutal soldiers. He was the last of the orator-statesmen of Rome, as Demosthenes had been in Athens (§ 756). But the Republic was still supported by the two leading murderers of Cæsar, — Brutus and Cassius. They were at the head of a powerful eastern army, like that of Pompey, and were encamped at Philippi in Macedonia. As soon as they could leave Rome, Octavian and Antony moved against Brutus and Cassius, and in a great battle at Philippi the last defenders of the Republic were completely defeated (42 B.C.).

FIG. 240. *Portrait of* AUGUSTUS *(now in the Museum of Fine Arts, Boston)*

Octavian gains Italy and the West (42–35 B.C.)

1012. The two victors then divided their domains: Octavian was to return to Italy and endeavor to crush the enemies of the triumvirate in the West; Antony was to remain in the East and bring it again under full subjection to Rome. In the West a rebellious son of Pompey, who seized Sicily and held control of the sea with his fleet, was finally crushed by Octavian. Lepidus, the third triumvir, was powerless, for he had early been forced into an inferior position. Within ten years after Cæsar's assassination Octavian, although only twenty-eight, had gained complete control of Italy and the West.

1013. Antony, meantime, had shown that he had no ability as a serious statesman. His prestige was also greatly dimmed by a disastrous campaign against the Parthians. Dazzled by the attractions of Cleopatra, he was now living in Alexandria and Antioch, where he ruled the East as far as the Euphrates like an Oriental sovereign. With Cleopatra as his queen he maintained a court of sumptuous splendor, like that of the Persian kings in the days of their empire. Cleopatra, who had once hoped to rule Rome as Cæsar's queen, was now cherishing similar hopes as the favorite of Antony. The tales of all this made their way to Rome and did not help Antony's cause in the eyes of the Roman Senate. Octavian easily induced the Senate, for this and other reasons, to declare war on Cleopatra, and thus he was able to advance against Antony. As the legions of Cæsar and Pompey, representing the East and the West, had once before faced each other on a battlefield in Greece, so now Octavian and Antony, the leaders of the East and the West, met at Actium on the west coast of Greece. A naval battle was fought, with the land forces as spectators. Before the battle was over, the soldiers of Antony saw their leader and his Oriental queen forsaking them in flight as Cleopatra's gorgeous galley, followed by her splendid royal flotilla, swept out to sea carrying the cowardly Antony to Egypt. The outcome was a sweeping victory for the heir of Cæsar.

Octavian overthrows Antony and gains the East (31 B.C.)

1014. The next year Octavian landed in Egypt without resistance worth mentioning and took possession of the ancient land. Antony, probably forsaken by Cleopatra, took his own life. The proud queen was unwilling to undergo the crushing humiliation of gracing Octavian's triumph at Rome, two of whose rulers had yielded to the power of her charm and her personality, and she too died by her own hand. She was the last of the Ptolemies (§ 751), the rulers of Egypt for nearly three hundred years, — since Alexander the Great. Octavian therefore made Egypt Roman territory (30 B.C.). To the West, which he already controlled, Octavian had now added also the East. The lands under his control girdled the

Octavian seizes Egypt and ends a century of revolution (133–30 B.C.)

Mediterranean, and the entire Mediterranean world was under the power of a single ruler. Thus at last the unity of the Roman dominions was restored, and an entire century of revolution and civil war, which had begun in the days of the Gracchi (133 B.C.), was ended (30 B.C.).

1015. Octavian's success marked the final triumph of one-man power in the entire ancient world, as it had long ago triumphed in the Orient. The century of strife which Octavian's victory ended was now followed by two centuries of profound peace, broken by only one serious interruption. These were the first two centuries of the Roman Empire, beginning in 30 B.C.[1] We shall now take up the two centuries of peace in the two following chapters.

Beginning of two centuries of peace

QUESTIONS

Section 80. What problems beset the Roman state in Italy? outside of Italy? What can you say of the ability and the legal right of the Senate to meet these problems? How did the Licinian laws attempt to aid the people? What was the condition of the government lands? What did Tiberius Gracchus tell the people? Describe his efforts to aid the people, and the result. Recount the work of Gaius Gracchus, and the result.

Section 81. What was the chief reason for the failure of the Gracchus brothers? Toward what kind of power did their leadership tend? How did the people gain control of the army in the war with Jugurtha? Recount the victories of Marius against Jugurtha and the northern barbarians. Give an account of his new military measures. How did Marius succeed as a statesman? What was now the feeling of the Italian allies toward Rome? What can you say of Drusus? What happened on the death of Drusus? What was the result of the war with the allies? Describe the rise of Sulla. How did he defeat the will of the people? Recount Sulla's campaign against Mithradates. What happened on Sulla's return to Italy? What was the policy of Sulla, and how did he put it through?

Section 82. How did the people succeed in throwing off the rule of the Senate? What great command did they give to Pompey?

[1] It should be noticed that these two centuries of peace began thirty years before the first year of the Christian Era, and hence do not correspond exactly with the first two centuries of this era.

Recount his operations against the pirates and in the Orient. Tell about the rise of Julius Cæsar. Recount the rise of Cicero and his defeat of Catiline. How did Cæsar secure election as consul? Recount his campaign in Gaul. What was his view of the political situation of Rome? What did the Senate do to thwart Cæsar? What was the result of Cæsar's advance on Rome? Describe the battle of Pharsalus. Recount briefly the achievements of Cæsar after his triumph. Tell the story of his death and its results.

Section 83. Tell the story of Octavian until the battle of Philippi. How did Octavian gain the East? What great world did he then control? What kind of power had triumphed at the end of a century of revolution?

BIBLIOGRAPHY FOR TOPICAL STUDIES

Business and trade in Rome: ABBOTT, *Common People of Ancient Rome*, pp. 205–234; DAVIS, *A Day in Rome*, pp. 220–253; *Influence of Wealth*, pp. 105–122; FOWLER, *Social Life at Rome*, pp. 42–66; FRANK, *History of Rome*, pp. 375–403; SHOWERMAN, *Rome and the Romans*, pp. 234–250; STRONG, *Art in Ancient Rome*, Vol. I, pp. 171–172.

The meaning of Roman citizenship: ABBOTT, *Roman Politics*, pp. 103–108; FOWLER, *Rome*, pp. 132–134; SHOWERMAN, *Rome and the Romans*, pp. 103–105, 448–449.

Julius Cæsar as a general and statesman: BOTSFORD, *Source Book*, pp. 450–454; BUCHAN, *Julius Cæsar*, pp. 80–111, 141–156, or FOWLER, *Julius Cæsar*, pp. 148–160, 326–357; FOWLER, *Rome*, pp. 176–180; FRANK, *History of Rome*, pp. 302–313; MCCARTNEY, *Warfare by Land and Sea*, pp. 131–140.

NOTE. The sketch below shows us a corner of a Roman library. The books are all in the form of rolls, arranged in large pigeonhole sections, with the ends pointing outward and bearing tags containing the titles of the books. Thus the librarian was able to find a given book quickly or to return it to the shelves at the proper place, as he is engaged in doing in this relief.

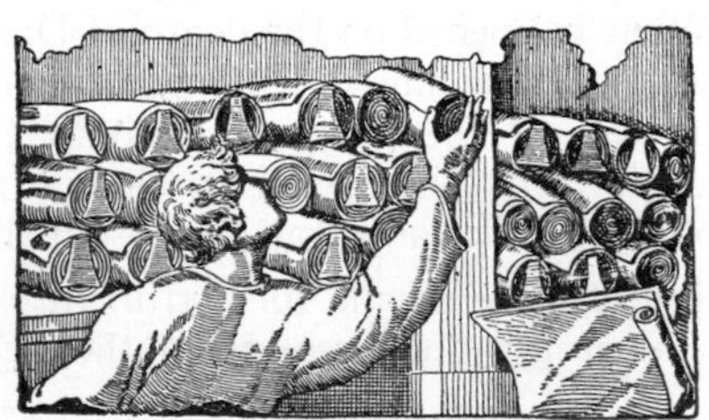

PART V · THE ROMAN EMPIRE

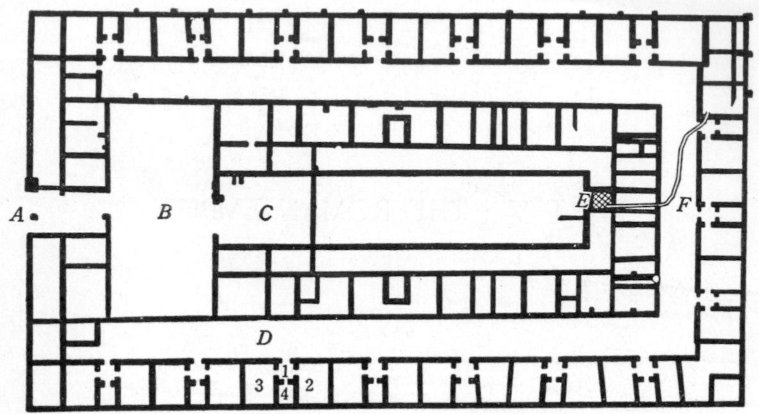

The Roman Military Hospital *at* Novæsium *(near Neuss, in the Prussian Rhine Province), about* A.D. 100

While the scientific progress made in medicine after the Sixth Century B.C. was of Greek origin, yet it was during the Roman Empire that the Greek and Greek-trained physicians made certain improvements in the *practice* of medicine. These improvements were principally in organization, in development of surgical implements, and in sanitation. The greatest physician of Roman times was the Greek Galen, from Asia Minor. It seems evident from his books that the ideas of sanitation which Rome developed made the doctors of the Roman Empire perhaps the cleanest group of doctors in antiquity. The ground plans of the hospital excavated at Novæsium well illustrate the above three points in the progress of medicine in the Roman Empire. The Empire was very particular about the health of the soldiers. Indeed, the doctors of such a well-regulated Roman military hospital as that at Novæsium, around the end of the First Century A.D., would have been shocked at the horrors which Florence Nightingale found at the Scutari barrack hospital in the Crimean War in A.D. 1854. The hospital at Novæsium was about 165 feet wide by 295 feet long. The arrangement, as may be seen from the diagram above, was very similar to the corridor system in modern hospitals. The entrance corridor, beginning at *A*, led into the court *B*, which probably held a reservoir for rain water. Room *C* was perhaps the dining-hall. There are some seventeen suites distributed along the main corridor, like the one at *D*. Apparently one entered the anteroom No. *1*, opening off the corridor, and could immediately shut the door to keep drafts and noise from the sickrooms *2* and *3*. In the small room *4* the attendant probably sat, and clothes and supplies could also be stored there. The room *E* was apparently for the disposal of waste, as it contains a brick tile covering under which begins the channel *F*, which seems to have continued on to the outside of the building. Many surgical implements were found scattered throughout the ruins of the building. (After Meyer-Steinig)

Chapter XXVII · The First of Two Centuries of Peace: The Age of Augustus and the Successors of his Line

Section 84. The Rule of Augustus (30 B.C.–A.D. 14) and the Beginning of Two Centuries of Peace

1016. When Octavian returned to Italy, he was received with the greatest enthusiasm. A veritable hymn of thanksgiving arose among all classes at the termination of a century of revolution, civil war, and devastation. The great majority of Romans now felt that an individual ruler was necessary for the control of the vast Roman dominions. Octavian therefore entered upon forty-four years of peaceful and devoted effort to give to the Roman Empire the organization and government which it had so long lacked. His most difficult task was to alter the old form of government so as to make a legal place for the power he had taken by military force. Unlike Cæsar, Octavian felt a sin-

Octavian's moderate policy

NOTE. The above headpiece shows a restoration of a magnificent marble inclosure containing the ALTAR OF AUGUSTAN PEACE, erected by order of the Senate in honor of Augustus. The inclosure was open to the sky, and its surrounding walls, of which portions still exist, are covered below by a broad band of ornamental plant spirals, very sumptuous in effect. Above it is a series of reliefs, of which the one on the right of the door pictures the legendary hero Æneas bringing an offering to the temple of the Roman household gods (*Penates*) which he carried from Troy to Latium (footnote, p. 571).

cere respect for the institutions of the Roman Republic and did not wish to destroy them or to gain for himself the throne of an Oriental sovereign. During his struggle for the mastery heretofore, he had preserved the forms of the Republic and had been duly elected to his great position.

Organization of the Roman state by Octavian

1017. Accordingly, on returning to Rome, Octavian did not disturb the Senate, but did much to strengthen it and improve its membership. Indeed, he voluntarily handed over his powers to the Senate and the Roman people in January, 27 B.C. The Senate thereupon, realizing by past experience its own helplessness and knowing that it did not possess the organization for ruling the great Roman world successfully, gave him officially the command of the army and the control of the most important frontier provinces. Besides these vast powers he held also the important rights of a tribune (§§ 837, 850), and it was chiefly on this last office that he based his legal claim to his power in the state.

Titles of new ruler

1018. At the same time the Senate conferred upon him the title of *Augustus*, that is, "the august." The chief name of his office was *Princeps*, that is, "the first," meaning the first of the citizens. Another title given the head of the Roman Empire was an old word for director or commander, namely, *Imperator*, from which our word "emperor" is derived. Augustus, as we may now call him, regarded his position as that of an official of the Roman Republic appointed by the Senate. Indeed, his appointment was not permanent but for a term of years, after which he was reappointed.

Dual character of new state; waning power of Senate

1019. The Roman Empire, which here emerges, was thus under a dual government of the Senate and the Princeps, whom we commonly call the emperor. The clever Augustus had done what his illustrious foster father, Julius Cæsar, had thought unnecessary: he had conciliated those Romans who still cherished the old Republic. The new arrangement was officially a restoration of the Republic. But this dual state in which Augustus endeavored to preserve the old Republic was not well balanced: the Princeps held too much power to remain a mere appointive official. His powers were more than once increased by the Senate during the life of Augustus, — not on his demand, for he always showed the Senate the most ceremonious respect, but because the Senate could not dispense with his assistance. At the same time the old powers of the Senate could not be maintained reign after reign when the Senate controlled no army.

1020. The Princeps was the real ruler, because the legions were behind him, and the so-called republican state created by Augustus tended to become a military monarchy, as we shall see. All the influences from the Orient were in the same direction. Egypt was in no way controlled by the Senate, but remained a private domain of the emperor. In this, the oldest state on the Mediterranean, the emperor was king in the Oriental sense. He collected its huge revenues and ruled there as the Pharaohs and Ptolemies had done. His position as absolute monarch in Egypt influenced his position as emperor and his methods of government everywhere. Indeed, the East as a whole could understand the position of Augustus only as that of a king, and this title they at once applied to him. This also had its influence in Rome.

Oriental influences toward military monarchy

1021. The empire which Rome now ruled consisted of the entire Mediterranean world, or a fringe of states extending entirely around the Mediterranean and including all its shores. But the frontier boundaries, left almost entirely unsettled by the Republic, were a pressing question. There was a natural boundary in the south, the Sahara, and also in the west, the Atlantic; but on the north and east further conquests might be made. In the main Augustus adopted the policy of organizing and consolidating the Empire *as he found it*, without making further conquests. In the east his boundary thus became the Euphrates, and in the north the Danube and the Rhine. The Rhine and the Danube formed an angle in the

Peace policy of Augustus; frontiers

frontier which was not favorable for defense, and late in his reign Augustus seems to have made an effort to push forward to the Elbe (see map I, p. 722). This would have given the Empire a more nearly straight boundary, extending from the Black Sea to Denmark in a line from the southeast to the northwest. Whatever the intentions of Augustus may have been, the Roman army was terribly defeated by the barbarous German tribes, and the effort was abandoned. The northern boundary of the Empire was then made a line of provinces west of the Rhine and south of the Danube, extending from the North Sea to the Black Sea.[1]

1022. For the defense of these vast frontiers it was necessary to maintain a large standing army. Nevertheless the army, now carefully reorganized by Augustus, was not as large as the armies which had grown up in the civil wars. Augustus first reduced it to eighteen legions, but later raised it to twenty-five. It probably contained, on the average, about two hundred and twenty-five thousand men. The army was now recruited chiefly from the provinces, and the foreign soldier who entered the ranks received citizenship in return for his service. Thus the fiction that the army was made up of citizens was maintained. But the tramp of the legions was heard no more in Italy; henceforth they were posted far out on the frontiers, and the citizens at home saw nothing of the troops who defended them.

The army

1023. At the accession of Augustus the Roman Empire, from Rome outward to the very frontiers of the provinces, was sadly in need of restoration and opportunity to recuperate. The cost of the civil wars had been borne by the provinces. The eastern dominions, especially Greece, where the most important fighting of the long civil war had occurred, had suffered severely. For a century and a half before the great battles of the civil war the provinces had been oppressed, — excessively overtaxed or

Sufferings of the provinces

[1] Some historians adopt the view that Augustus never really intended or attempted to conquer to the Elbe.

tacitly plundered (§ 928). Barbarian invaders had seized the undefended cities of Greece and had even established robber states for plundering purposes. Greece herself never recovered from the wounds then suffered, and in general the Eastern Mediterranean had been greatly demoralized. The civilized world was longing for peace.

1024. Augustus therefore now undertook to do for the Mediterranean world what five hundred years earlier Darius had done for the Persian Empire, when it was even larger than the Roman Empire. But the task of Augustus demanded the organization of a much more highly civilized world than that of the Persian Empire, including a vast network of commerce in the Mediterranean such as no earlier age had ever seen. Great peoples and nations had to be officially taken into the Empire and given honest and efficient government. Some of them had old and successful systems of government; others had no government at all. Egypt, for example, had long before possessed the most highly organized administration in the ancient world; but regions of the West, like Gaul, had as yet no system of government. All this Augustus endeavored to do.

Great task of Augustus: organization of provinces

1025. Under the Republic the governor of a province not only served for a short term but was also without experience. His unlimited power, like that of an absolute monarch, made it impossible for the consuls, changing every year at home, to control him. The governor of a province was now appointed by the permanent ruler at Rome, and such a governor knew that he was responsible to that ruler for wise and honest government of his province. He knew also that if he proved successful he could hold his post for years or be promoted to a better one. There thus grew up under the permanent control of Augustus and his successors a body of provincial governors of experience and efficiency. The small group of less important provinces still under the control of the Senate, although they continued to suffer to some extent under the old system, also felt the influence of the improved methods.

Improved system of governors of provinces

1026. In the days of the Republic no one had ever tried to settle how much money was needed to carry on the government and how much of this sum each province ought justly to pay in the form of taxes. Augustus proceeded to put together huge census lists and property assessments, by which to determine the population and the total value of the property in each province. When this great piece of work was done, he could determine exactly how much tax each province should justly pay. He decreed that the inhabitants of the provinces were to pay two kinds of direct taxes, one on land and one on personal property, besides customs duties and various internal-revenue taxes. Augustus had complete control of the vast sums which he thus received in taxes, and his use of them was wise and just. Much of this money went back to the provinces to pay for necessary public works, like roads, bridges, aqueducts, and public buildings. In making all these financial arrangements Augustus learned much from Egypt.

Finances of the Empire regulated for the first time

1027. Thus at last two centuries of Roman mismanagement of the provinces ended, and the obligation of Rome to give good government to her dependencies was finally fulfilled. The establishment of just, stable, and efficient control by the government at once produced a profound change, visible in many ways, as we shall see (§§ 1030–1043), but especially in business. Men of capital no longer kept their money timidly out of sight but put it at once into business ventures. The rate of interest under the last years of the Republic had been 12 per cent, but as money now became more plentiful the interest rate quickly sank to 4 per cent.

Beneficial effect of new and efficient government

1028. The great Mediterranean world under the control of Rome now entered upon a new age of prosperity and development unknown before, when the nations along its shores were still fighting each other in war after war. A process of unification began which was to make the Mediterranean *world* a Mediterranean *nation*. The national threads of our historical narrative have heretofore been numerous, as we have followed the stories of the Oriental nations, of Athens, Sparta, Macedonia, Rome, Carthage, and others. For a long time we have followed these narratives separately like individual strands, but now they are to be twisted together into a single thread of national history, that of the Roman Empire. The great exceptions are the German barbarians in the north and the unconquered Orient east of the Euphrates.

Mediterranean *world* on the way to become a Mediterranean *nation*

SECTION 85. THE CIVILIZATION OF THE AUGUSTAN AGE

1029. In the new Mediterranean nation thus growing up it was the purpose of Augustus that Italy should occupy a superior position as the imperial leader of all the peoples around the Mediterranean. Italy was not to sink to the level of these peoples nor to be merely one of them. We have seen the sturdy virtues of earlier Roman character undermined and corrupted by sudden wealth and power before Italy had had a chance to become a nation. Augustus made a remarkable effort to undo all this damage and restore the fine old days of rustic Roman virtue, the good old Roman customs, the beliefs of the fathers. To meet increasing divorce, laws designed to add to the permanence of marriage were passed. The Oriental gods, so common for centuries in Greece and long widespread in Italy, were to be banished. The people were urged to awaken their declining interest in the religion of their fathers, and the old religious feasts were celebrated with greater splendor and impressiveness. At the same time the state temples, which had frequently fallen into decay, were repaired; new ones were built, especially in Rome; and the services and usages of Roman state religion were everywhere revived.

Augustus attempts the restoration of old Roman life

1030. Tendencies like those which had changed the Roman people lie too deep in the life and the nature of men to be much altered by the power of a government or the pressure of new laws. It was a new world in which the Romans of the Augustan Age were living. The more Augustus applied his own power to modify the situation, the more noticeable became the contrast between the Augustan Age and the old days before one-man power arose. Under Augustus, Rome for the first time received organized police, a fire department, a water department, and a fully organized office for the government sale of grain. Augustus himself boasted that he found Rome a city of brick and left it a city of marble. To the visitor at Rome, therefore, the new age proclaimed itself in imposing new buildings; for republican Rome had lacked the magnificent monumental theaters and gymnasia, libraries and music halls, which had long adorned the greater Hellenistic cities. It had also, of course, possessed no royal palace like that at Alexandria. Architecturally Alexandria was still the most splendid city of the ancient world.

New Rome

1031. The great architectural works which Augustus now began made Rome the leading art center of the ancient world. His building plans were in the main those which his adoptive father, the Great Dictator, had himself either laid out or already begun. On the Palatine Hill, Augustus united several dwelling houses, already there, into a palace for his residence. It was very simple, and the quiet taste of his sleeping room, which long survived the rest of the building, was the admiration of later Romans. From this royal dwelling on the *Palatine* arose our English word "palace." A new and sumptuous temple of Apollo surrounded by colon-

Rome the greatest art center; Palatine buildings of Augustus

* The SACRED WAY passed the little circular temple of Vesta (*A*) and reached the Forum at the Arch of Augustus (*B*) and the Temple of the Deified Julius Cæsar (*C*). On the right was the old Basilica of Æmilius (*D*), and on the left the new Basilica of Julius Cæsar (*E*). Opposite this, across the old Forum market place (*F*), was the new Senate House (*G*) planned by Julius Cæsar. At the upper end of the Forum was the new speaker's platform (*H*); near it Septimius Severus later erected his crude arch (*I*). Beyond rises the Capitol, with the Temple of Saturn (*J*) and the Temple of Concord (*K*) at its base; above, on its slope, is the Tabularium (*L*), a place of public records; and on the summit of the Capitol the Temple of Jove (*M*). The subsequent growth of the emperors' Forums on the north may be seen in Fig. 242, where the same lettering is repeated and continued.

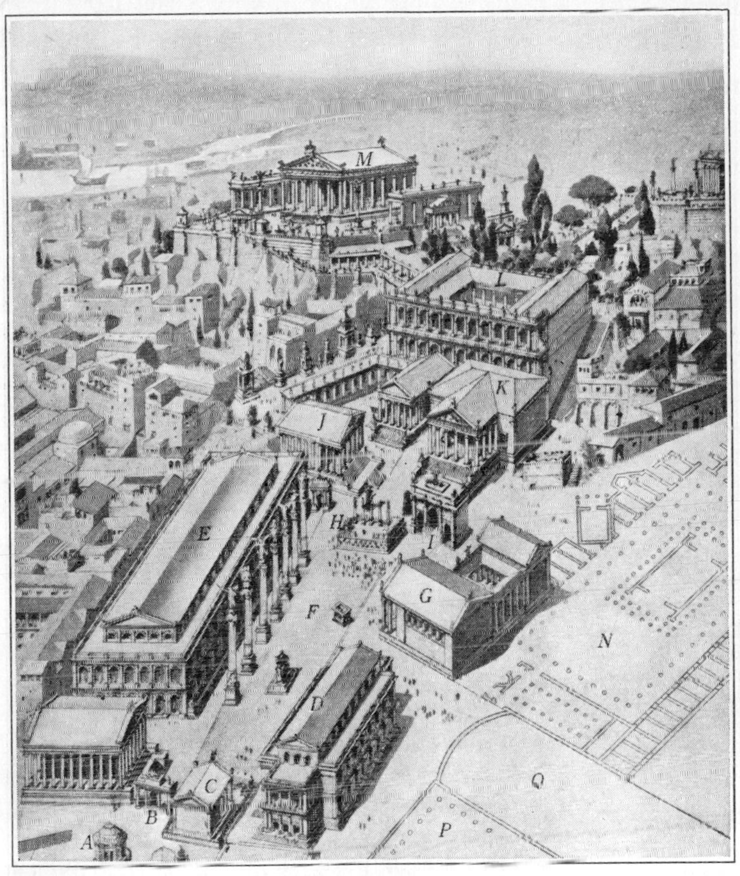

FIG. 241. *The* ROMAN FORUM *and its Public Buildings in the Early Empire*

We look across the ancient market place (*F*; see § 824) to the Tiber, with its ships, at the head of navigation. On each side of the market place, where we see the buildings *E*, *J*, and *D*, *G*, *I*, were once rows of little wooden booths for selling meat, fish, and other merchandise. After the beginning of the Carthaginian wars these booths were displaced by fine buildings, like the basilica hall *D*, built not long after 200 B.C. Note the square ground plans (*J*, *M*) and the arches showing Etruscan influence, the Attic roofs and colonnades, and the clerestory windows (*D*, *E*) copied from the Hellenistic cities. See complete key on opposite page, footnote.* (After Luckenbach)

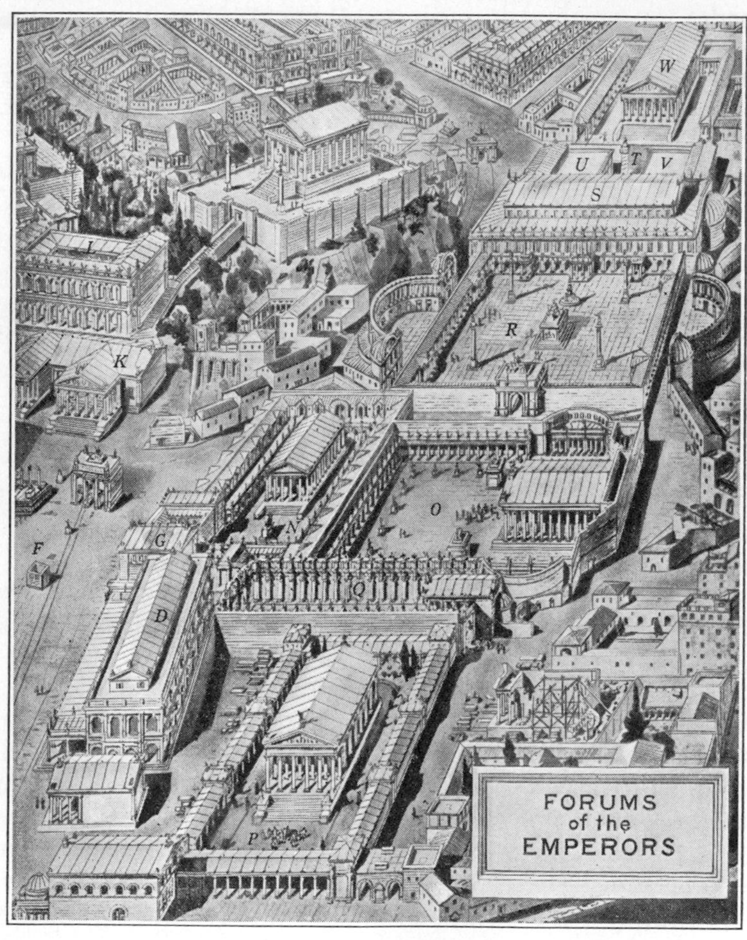

FIG. 242. *The* FORUMS *of the* EMPERORS, *continuing the View of the Old Forum in Fig.* 241

The plan (p. 701) shows how the forums of the emperors formed a connecting link uniting the old Roman Forum (*F*) with the magnificent new buildings of the Campus Martius, like the Theater of Pompey, Baths of Agrippa, Pantheon, etc. In order to make this connection, Trajan cut away the ridge joining the Capitol Hill and the Quirinal Hill to a depth of 100 feet. The summit of his column (*T*) still marks the former height of the ridge. Little now remains of all this magnificence. See discussion of buildings on opposite page, footnote.* (After L. Levy (Luckenbach))

nades, in which the emperor installed a large library, was erected within easy reach of his palace doors.

New buildings in Forum and vicinity

1032. The palace looked down upon an imposing array of new marble buildings surrounding the ancient Forum. Nearest the palace the magnificent basilica business hall erected by Cæsar, left unfinished and then damaged by fire, was now restored and completed by Augustus. He erected also a new Senate building, planned but never built by Cæsar, opposite the new basilica. Facing the end of the Forum the emperor now built a temple, for the worship of his deified foster father, known as the temple of the Divine Julius; and at the opposite end of the Forum Augustus placed a magnificent speaker's platform of marble. Behind the ground intended by him for the new Senate building Cæsar had built a new forum called the Forum of Cæsar; but the growing business of the city led Augustus to construct a third forum, known as the Forum of Augustus, which he placed next to that of Cæsar.

First theaters and baths; Altar of Peace

1033. The first stone theater in Rome had been built by Pompey about twenty-five years before the accession of Augustus. The emperor, therefore, erected a large and magnificent theater which he named the Theater of Marcellus, after his deceased son-in-law Marcellus. At the same time Agrippa, the ablest of the generals and ministers of Augustus, erected the first fine public baths in Rome, for which he was given space in the Field of Mars, an old drill ground. In connection

---

* The SENATE HOUSE OF JULIUS CÆSAR (*G*) and his new FORUM (*N*) extended from the old Forum northward, occupying the ground where once the Assembly of the Roman people (*Comitia*) had been accustomed to meet. The northern addition to the old Forum was still further extended by the Forum of Augustus (*O*). The great emperors of the First and Second Centuries continued this expansion first southeast (*P*, *Q*) and then northwest (*R*, *S*, *T*, *U*, *V*, *W*). In the First Century Vespasian built the beautiful Forum of Peace (*P*), and the aged Nerva inserted his long, narrow Forum (*Q*); while in the Second Century Trajan built the most magnificent of all the forums (*R*), with a vast basilica (*S*, called Basilica Ulpia) beside it, and beyond it his two libraries (*U*, *V*; see § 1000), with his wonderful column (*T*, see Fig. 240) between them. In Trajan's honor Hadrian then built a temple (*W*), completing this line of the most magnificent buildings the ancient world ever saw.

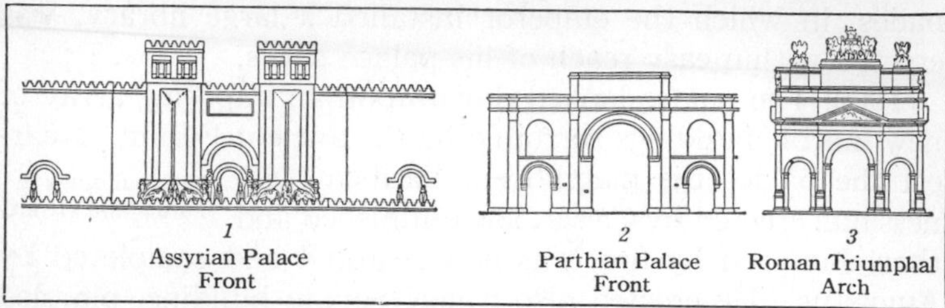

FIG. 243. *The Roman* TRIUMPHAL ARCH *and its* ORIENTAL ANCESTORS

The imposing front of the Assyrian palace (*1*), with its tall arch in the middle and a lower arch on each side, was continued by the Parthians (*2*), and at the same time they shifted the side arches nearer to the middle arch. The arch made its way slowly westward, although the Greeks were very reluctant to adopt it and did not make full use of it until they were Christianized and began to employ it in their churches. The Romans, on the contrary, were influenced by the Etruscans, who brought the arch with them from Asia Minor. Hence we found it in Rome early, and the triumphal arch of Augustus and other arches of this kind built by the Romans (*3*) were descendants of the Assyrian palace front, with a tall arch in the middle and lower arches on each side, just as widely traveled Romans had seen it in the East

with it were other splendid public buildings added by Agrippa, and a spacious open square for the Assembly of the people. At the same time the Senate showed its appreciation of the new era of peace by erecting a large and beautiful marble Altar of Peace (headpiece, p. 679).

Influence of Greece and the Orient on Roman architecture

1034. In this new architecture of Rome, Greek models were the controlling influence. Nevertheless, Oriental influences also were very prominent. Greek architecture did not employ the arch so long used in the Orient, but the architects of Rome now gave it a place of prominence along with the colonnade, as the two leading features of their buildings. It was through these Roman buildings that the arch gained its important place in our own modern architecture. Augustus seems to have been much interested in the monuments of the ancient Oriental world, which he more than once visited. His triumphal arch was arranged with three gates like the Assyrian palace front. He carried away from the Nile a number of Egyptian obelisks and set them up in Rome, and

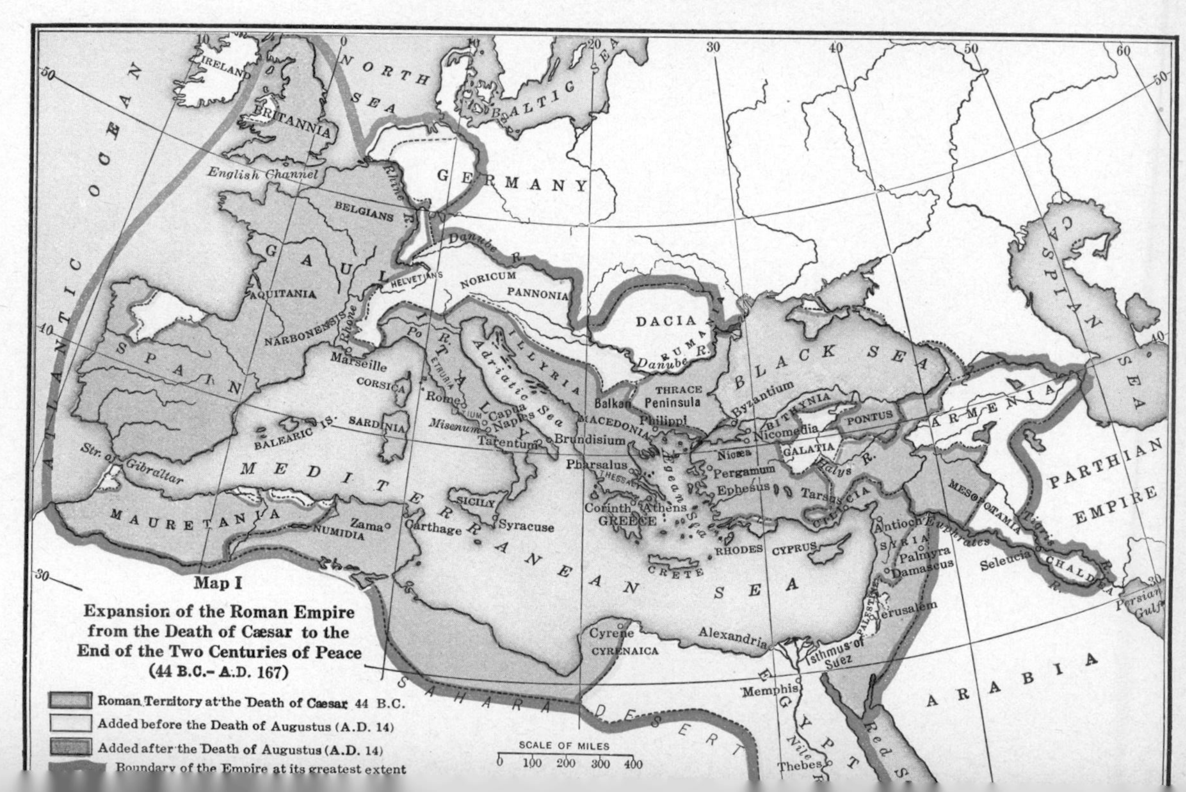

Map I

Expansion of the Roman Empire from the Death of Cæsar to the End of the Two Centuries of Peace (44 B.C.- A.D. 167)

Roman Territory at the Death of Caesar 44 B.C.

Added before the Death of Augustus (A.D. 14)

Added after the Death of Augustus (A.D. 14)

Boundary of the Empire at its greatest extent

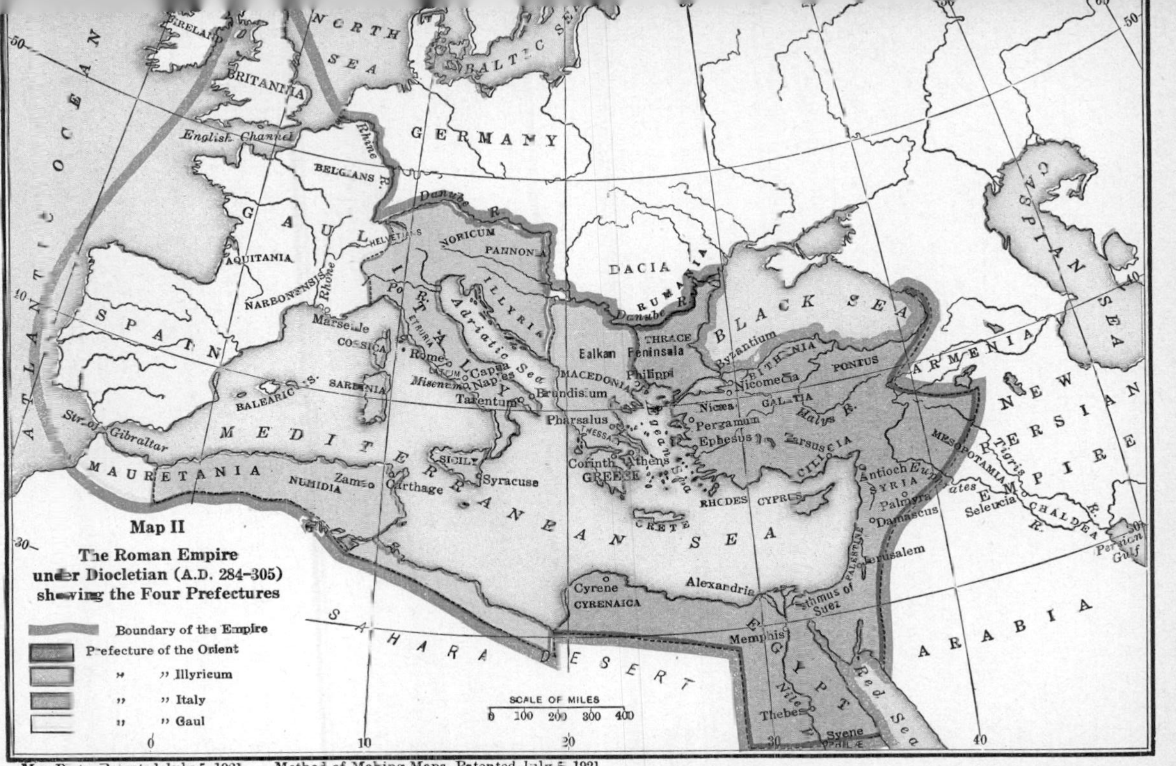

Map Plate, Patented July 5, 1921 · Method of Making Maps, Patented July 5, 1921

SEQUENCE MAP SHOWING TERRITORIAL GAINS AND LOSSES OF THE ROMAN EMPIRE FROM THE DEATH OF CÆSAR (44 B.C.) TO THE DEATH OF DIOCLETIAN (A.D. 305)

FIG. 244. PYRAMID-TOMB *of a Roman Nobleman*

Wealthy Romans familiar with the East might erect a tomb of Oriental form, as the family of this nobleman Cestius did. His pyramid-tomb, when built (in the reign of Augustus), stood outside of the city, but nearly three hundred years later it was included in the wall (seen here on each side of the pyramid) erected around the city by Aurelian for the protection of Rome against the barbarian invasions (§ 1135)

in building his own family tomb he selected a design from the Orient. One of the noble families of Rome even built a pyramid as a tomb, and it still stands on the outskirts of the city.

1035. While architecture flourished in Rome, sculpture was less cultivated. Beautiful sculpture, following old models, might still be produced, but there were no creative sculptors in Rome like those whom we have met in Athens. Painting as an independent art had ceased to be practiced. There was not a single great painter in Rome, and the painting which was practiced was merely that of wall decoration as we see it in the houses of Pompeii, which we are yet to visit.

Complete lack of initiative in sculpture and painting at Rome

1036. If Rome was a borrower in art, she was even more so in science. Rome had no such men as Archimedes and Eratosthenes. When Agrippa, Augustus's powerful minister, drew up a great map of the world, all he had in view was the practical use of the map by Roman governors going out to their provinces or by merchants traveling with goods. Hence the roads were elaborately laid out, not on a fixed scale but so that there would be space enough along each road for the names of all the towns situated along it and for all the distances in miles between towns, which were inserted in figures on the map. Such a map was without doubt convenient; but it entirely lacked the network of latitude and longitude so carefully worked out by Eratosthenes, and for this reason the shapes of the countries and seas were so distorted that none of the readers of this book would be able to find anything or recognize familiar countries.

Lack of science at Rome; Agrippa's map of the world

1037. The leading geography of the time was written by a Greek living in Rome, named Strabo. It was a delightful narrative of wide travels mingled with history; and although sadly lacking in scientific method, it was for many centuries the world's standard geography, and may still be read with great pleasure and profit as an ancient book of travel. The work of Strabo, however, is a landmark disclosing the decline of ancient science and the end of that great line of scientists whose achievements made the Hellenistic Age the greatest age of science in the early world.

Strabo and geography; decline of science

1038. Indifference to science at Rome was in marked contrast with Roman interest in literature. The greatest of the leading Romans displayed in some cases an almost pathetic devotion to literary studies, even while weighed down with the heaviest responsibilities. Cæsar put together a treatise on Latin speech while crossing the Alps in a palanquin, when his mind must have been filled with the problems of his great wars in Gaul. He dedicated the essay to Cicero, the greatest master of Latin prose. Such men as these had studied in Athens or Rhodes and were deeply versed in the finest works of Greek learning and literature. Cæsar and Cicero

Educated Romans the most cultivated men of the ancient world

and the men of their class spoke Greek every day among themselves, perhaps more than they did Latin. In these men Hellenistic civilization and Roman character had mingled to produce the most cultivated minds of the ancient world. Among the educated men in the declining Greek communities of the East, none could rival these finest of the Romans in cultivation or in power of mind. Indeed, Greece never produced men of just this type, who exhibited such a combination of gifts,— the highest ability both in public leadership and in literary achievement.

Cicero the type of highly educated man of the late Republic

1039. Of literary studies Cicero said: "Such studies profit youth and rejoice old age; while they increase happiness in good fortune, they are in affliction a consolation and a refuge; they give us joy at home and they do not hamper us abroad; they tarry with us at night time and they go forth with us to the countryside." Thus spoke the most cultivated man Rome ever produced, and the ideals of the educated man which he himself personified have never ceased to exert a powerful influence upon educated men in all lands. When he failed as a statesman, a career for which he did not possess the necessary firmness and practical insight, he devoted himself to his literary pursuits. As the greatest orator in Roman history he had already done much to perfect and beautify Latin prose in the orations which he delivered in the course of his career as a lawyer and a statesman. But after his retirement he produced a group of remarkable essays on oratory, besides a series of treatises on conduct,— such matters as friendship, old age, and the like; and he left behind also several hundred letters which were preserved by his friends. As one of the last sacrifices of the civil wars Cicero had fallen by the hands of Antony's brutal soldiery, but his writings were to exert an undying influence. They made Latin speech one of the most beautiful instruments of human expression; and as an example of the finest literary style, they have influenced the best writing in all the languages of civilization ever since.

1040. Augustus and a number of the leading men about him had known Cicero. For them that commingling of Greek and Roman civilization which might well be called Ciceronian became the leading cultural influence in their lives. The Ciceronian culture of the last days of the dying Republic thus became the ideal of the early Empire and the Augustan Age. Augustus had early established two libraries in Rome, and one of them contained the greatest collection of both Greek and Latin books in the ancient world. Men steeped in this Greco-Roman culture now began to feel the influence of the great events which had built up the vast Roman Empire. As at Athens in the days of the greatest Athenian power, so the vision of the greatness of the state stirred the imagination of thinking men. Livy wrote an enormous history of Rome from the earliest times, that is to say, from the Trojan War to the reign of Augustus, in one hundred and forty-two rolls, — a work which cost him forty years of labor. While it was beautiful literature, and the fragments which survive still form fascinating reading, it was very inaccurate history. The careful historical method that had made Thucydides (§ 700) the greatest of ancient historians had disappeared.

Augustan Age and literature: Livy

1041. In the last days of the Republic, in spite of turbulence and civil war, Cicero and the men of his time had perfected Latin *prose*. On the other hand, the greatest of Latin *poetry* arose under the inspiration of the early Empire and the universal peace established by Augustus. Horace, the leading poet of the time, had been a friend of the assassins of Cæsar, and he had faced the future Augustus on the battlefield of Philippi. After a dangerous struggle he had saved himself and at last found security in the era of peace. Having lived through many dangers to rejoice in the general peace, he gained the forgiveness and friendship of Augustus. In his youth, although only the son of a freedman of unknown race, he had studied in Greece, and he knew the old Greek lyric poets, who had suffered danger and disaster as he himself had done. With

Rise of poetry in the Augustan Age: Horace

the haunting echoes of old Greek poetry in his soul, he now found his own voice. Then he began to write of the men and the life of his own time in a body of verse which forms for us an undying picture of the Romans in the days of Augustus. The poems of Horace will always remain one of the greatest legacies from the ancient world, — a treasury of Roman life as pictured by a ripe and cultivated mind, unsurpassed even in the highly developed literature of the Greeks.

1042. Virgil, the other great poet of the Augustan Age, had from the beginning been a warm admirer of the great Cæsar and the young Octavian. When the civil war had deprived Virgil of his ancestral farm under the shadow of the Alps in the north, it was restored to him by Augustus. Here, as he looked out upon his own fields, the poet began to write verses like those of Theocritus (§ 789), reflecting to us in all its poetic beauty the rustic life of his time on the green hillsides of Italy. But these imitations of Greek models would never have given Virgil his place as one of the greatest poets of the world. As time passed he gained an exalted vision of the mission of Rome, and especially of Augustus, as the restorer of world peace. More than one Latin epic was already in circulation (§ 943); but in order to give voice to his vision Virgil now undertook the creation of another epic, in which he pictured the wanderings of the Trojan hero Æneas from Asia Minor to Italy, where, in the course of many heroic adventures, he founded the royal line of Latium (headpiece, p. 555). From him, according to the story, were descended the Julian family, the Cæsars, whose latest leader, Augustus, had saved Rome and established a world peace.

Virgil and the Æneid

1043. Unlike the Homeric epics, Virgil's Æneid, as it is called, was not the outgrowth of a heroic age. It was a tribute to Augustus, whom the poem artistically placed against a glorious background of heroic achievement in the Trojan Age, just as Alexander the Great had contrived to do for himself (§ 723). The Æneid was therefore the product of a self-conscious literary

Character of the Æneid

age, — the highly finished work of a literary artist who now took his place with Horace as one of the great interpreters of his age. Hardly so penetrating a mind as his friend Horace, Virgil was perhaps an even greater master of Latin verse. Deeply admired by the age that produced it, the Æneid has ever since been one of the leading schoolbooks of the civilized world, and has had an abiding influence on the best literature of later times.

Account of his deeds left by Augustus in Ancyra monument

1044. Augustus himself also left an account of his deeds. When he was over seventy-five years old, as he felt his end approaching, he put together a narrative of his career, which was engraved on bronze tablets and set up before his tomb. In the simple dignity of this impressive story we see the career of Augustus unfolding before us in one grand achievement after another, rising, like a panorama of successive mountain peaks, in a vision of such grandeur as to make the document probably the most impressive brief record of a great man's life which has survived to us from the ancient world. Almost with his last breath Augustus penned the closing lines of this remarkable document, and on the nineteenth of August, the month which bears his name, in the year A.D. 14, the first of the Roman emperors died.

SECTION 86. THE LINE OF AUGUSTUS AND THE END OF THE FIRST CENTURY OF PEACE (A.D. 14–68)

Four successors of the line of Augustus (A.D. 14–68)

1045. Augustus had been in supreme control of the great Roman world for forty-four years, that is, nearly half a century. Four descendants of his family, either by blood or by adoption, were to rule for more than another half-century and thus to fill out the first century of peace. The prejudice against one-man power was still so strong that the writers of this age and their successors have transmitted to us very unfair accounts of these four rulers. Two of them were indeed deserving of the contempt in which they are still held, but the other two were in many respects able rulers who did much to improve the developing government of the Empire.

1046. Augustus had never put forward a law providing for the appointment of his successor or for later successors to his position. Any prominent Roman citizen might have aspired to the office. Augustus left no son, and one after another his male heirs had died, among them his grandsons, the sons of his daughter Julia. He had finally been obliged to ask the Senate to associate with him his stepson Tiberius, his wife's son by an earlier marriage. Before the death of Augustus, Tiberius had therefore been given joint command of the army and also the tribune's power. The Senate, therefore, at once appointed him to all his stepfather's powers, and without any limit as to time.

Question of succession; Tiberius

1047. Tiberius was an able soldier and an experienced man of affairs. He gave the provinces wise and efficient governors and showed himself a skilled and successful ruler. He did not, however, possess his stepfather's tact and respect for the old institutions. He found it very vexatious to carry on joint rule with a Senate whose power was in reality little more than a fiction. He felt only contempt for the Roman nobles who publicly did him homage and secretly slandered him or plotted his downfall. He likewise despised the Roman populace. Under Augustus they had continued to go through the form of electing magistrates and passing laws as in the days of the Republic, but of course both the magistrates they elected and the laws they passed had been those proposed to the assemblies by Augustus. Tiberius, however, no longer allowed the Roman rabble to go through the farce of voting on what the emperor had already decided, and even the appearance of a government by the Roman people thus finally disappeared forever. To complete his unpopularity in Rome, Tiberius also practiced strict economy in government and much reduced the funds devoted to public shows for the amusement of the people. Universally hated in Rome, greatly afflicted also by bereavements and disappointments in his private life,

Efficient reign of Tiberius (A.D. 14–37)

Tiberius left the city and spent his last years in a group of magnificent villas on the lofty island of Capri, overlooking the Bay of Naples, where he died a disappointed man (A.D. 37).

Caligula (A.D. 37–41)

1048. As Tiberius had lost his son, the choice for his successor fell upon Gaius Cæsar, a great-grandson of Augustus, nicknamed Caligula ("little boot") by the soldiers among whom he was brought up. A young man of only twenty-five years, and at first very popular in Rome, Caligula was so transformed by his sense of vast power and by long-continued dissipation that his mind was crazed. He made his horse a consul, and the enormous wealth saved for the state by Tiberius he squandered in reckless debauchery and absurd building enterprises. In the midst of confiscation and murder this mockery of a reign was brought to a sudden close by Caligula's own officers, who put an end to his life in his palace on the Palatine after he had reigned only four years.

Accession of Claudius (A.D. 41)

1049. The imperial guards, ransacking the palace after the death of Caligula, found in hiding the trembling figure of a nephew of Tiberius and uncle of the dead Caligula, named Claudius. He had always been merely tolerated by his family as a man both physically and mentally inferior. He was now fifty years old, and there is no doubt that he was weak-kneed both in body and in character. But the guards hailed him as emperor, and the Senate was obliged to consent. Claudius was a great improvement upon Caligula, although he was easily influenced by the women of his family and the freedmen officials whom he had around him. The palace therefore soon became a nest of plots and intrigues, in which slander, banishment, and poison played their evil parts.

1050. Nevertheless Claudius accomplished much for the Empire and devoted himself to its affairs. He conducted in person a successful campaign in Britain, and for the first time made its southern portion a province of the Empire. Britain remained a Roman province for three and a half centuries. At Rome, Claudius was greatly interested in build-

FIG. 245. *The* AQUEDUCT *of the Emperor Claudius*

This wonderful aqueduct, built by the Emperor Claudius about the middle of the First Century A.D., is over 40 miles long. About three fourths of it is subterranean, but the last 10 miles consists of tall arches of massive masonry, as seen here, supporting the channel in which the water flowed till it reached the palace of the emperor on the Palatine. In plan it is derived from the older aqueducts which the Romans had seen in the Near East (see Fig. 106). The ancient Roman aqueducts were so well built that four of them are still in use at Rome, and they convey to the city a more plentiful supply of water than any great modern city elsewhere receives

ings and practical improvements. He built two vast new aqueducts, together nearly a hundred miles in length, furnishing Rome with a plentiful supply of fresh water from the mountains. At the same time his own officials, chiefly able Greek freedmen who were aiding him in his duties, were beginning to form a kind of cabinet destined finally to give the Empire for the first time a group of efficient ministers whom we should call the Secretary of the Treasury, the Secretary of State, and so on.

Enlightened rule of Claudius; Britain conquered; ministers of state

1051. The inability of Claudius to select wisely and to control those who formed his circle was the probable cause of his death. It was also the reason why Agrippina, the last of his wives, was able to push aside the son of Claudius and gain the throne for her own son Nero as the successor of Claudius. Not only on his mother's side but also on his father's Nero was descended from the family of Augustus. His mother had intrusted his education to the philosopher Seneca, and for the first five years of his reign, while Seneca was his chief minister, the rule of Nero was wise and successful. When palace plots and intrigues, in which Seneca was not without blame, had removed this able minister from the court and had also banished Nero's strong-minded mother, Agrippina, he cast aside all restraint and followed his own evil nature in a career of such vice and cruelty that the name of Nero has ever since been regarded as one of the blackest in all history.

Claudius probably assassinated; accession of Nero (A.D. 54)

1052. Nero was devoted to art and wished personally to practice it. While the favorites of the palace carried on the government he toured the principal cities of Greece as a musical composer, competing for prizes in dancing, singing, and chariot races. As the companion of actors, sportsmen, and prize fighters he even took part in gladiatorial exhibitions. Becoming more and more entangled in the meshes of court plots, his cowardly and suspicious nature led him to condemn his old teacher, Seneca, to death and to cause the assassination of the son of Claudius and of many other innocent and deserving men. In the same way he was persuaded to take the life of his wife, and, to crown his infamy, even had his own mother assassinated. At the same time his wild extravagance, his excessive taxation in some of the provinces, and his murders among the rich and noble were stirring up dangerous resentment which was to result in his fall.

Infamy of Nero's reign

1053. A great disaster, meantime, took place in Rome. A fire broke out among the cheap wooden buildings around the circus. It swept over the Palatine Hill, destroying the palace of Augustus, leaving only his sleeping room, and then passed on through the city. It burned for a week, wiping out a large portion of the city, and then, breaking out again, increased the damage.

Great fire at Rome (A.D. 64); Nero's palace

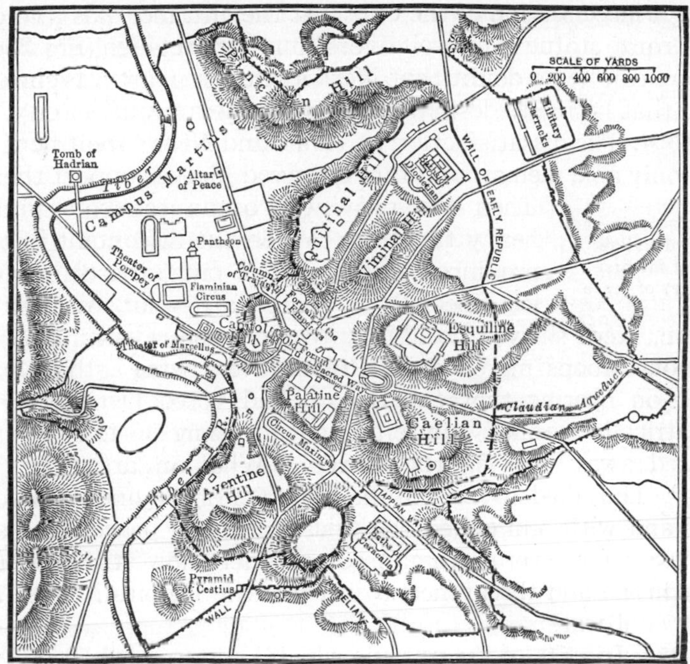

Map of Rome *under the* Emperors

Dark rumors ran through the streets that Nero himself had set fire to the city that he might rebuild it more splendidly, and gossip told how he sat watching the conflagration while giving a musical performance of his own on the destruction of Troy. There is no evidence to support these rumors. Under the circumstances Nero himself welcomed another version, which accused the Christians of having started the fire, and he executed a large number of them with horrible tortures. At vast expense, to which much of his excessive taxation was due, he undertook the rebuilding of the city, and he erected an enormous palace for himself called the Golden House, extending across the ground where the Colosseum now stands, from the east end of the Forum eastward and northeastward across the Esquiline Hill and over a large section of the city. At the entrance was a colossal bronze statue of himself over a hundred feet high (Fig. 256). There can be no doubt that Nero's interest in art was sincere and that he really desired to make Rome a beautiful city.

Nero's death ends the Julian line; end of the first century of peace

1054. The dissatisfaction at Rome and Nero's treatment of the only able men around him deprived him of support there. Then the provinces began to chafe under heavy taxation. When the discontent in the provinces finally broke out in open revolt, led especially by Galba, a Roman governor in Spain, Nero showed no ability to meet the revolt. The rebellious troops marched on Rome. Nero went into hiding, and, on hearing that the Senate had voted his death, he theatrically stabbed himself; attitudinizing to the last, he passed away uttering the words, "What an artist dies in me!" Thus died, in A.D. 68, the last ruler of the line of Augustus, and with him ended the first century of peace (30 B.C.–A.D. 68); for several Roman commanders now struggled for the throne and threatened to involve the Empire in another long civil war.

Progress during the rule of the Julian line; deification of emperors

1055. In spite of the misrule which had attended the reigns of two of the line of Augustus, the good accomplished in the reigns of Tiberius and Claudius could not be wholly undone. Both at Rome and in the provinces the government had been much improved. But, as we have seen, the Roman state was fast becoming a monarchy in which the crown was bequeathed from father to son. This process had been hastened by the fact that the Cæsars, as the emperors were now called, had gained a position of unique reverence. Beginning with Julius Cæsar, the emperors,[1] like Alexander the Great, were deified, and their worship was widely practiced throughout the Empire. It was indeed an obligation of citizenship to pay divine homage to the emperor. The supreme place

[1] Besides Julius Cæsar and Augustus, Claudius was the only emperor of the Julian line who was deified. Tiberius failed of it because of his unpopularity, and Caligula and Nero, of course, because of their infamous characters.

which he now occupied was not to be endangered by the brief struggles which followed the death of Nero; and the wide rule of the Roman emperor, even after the fall of Julius Cæsar's line, was to maintain another century of prosperity and peace. To this second century of peace in the Roman Empire we must devote another chapter.

QUESTIONS

Section 84. What was Augustus's attitude toward the Republic? What chief offices and powers did he receive? What were his titles? What body was continuing the power of the Republic? Who was the real ruler? What was the policy of Augustus on the frontiers? How did Augustus improve the rule of the provinces? Describe his financial improvements and the beneficial effects of efficient government on business.

Section 85. What kind of life did Augustus desire for Italy? How had Rome become a new world? What improvements did Augustus introduce in the city? What architectural influences prevailed? What work did Strabo produce? Tell about the attitude of educated Romans toward literature. What has been the influence of the writing of Cicero? What can you say of Livy? of Horace? of Virgil? What remarkable narrative did Augustus himself write?

Section 86. How long were Augustus and the four following rulers of his line in power? Who succeeded Augustus? What became of the old power of the people under Tiberius? Describe the accession of Claudius. What did he accomplish? How had Nero been educated? Describe his reign and character. What catastrophe overtook Rome? What period closed with the death of Nero? Give its date. What exalted station was given to the Roman emperors?

BIBLIOGRAPHY FOR TOPICAL STUDIES

Roman maps: BURTON, *Discovery of the Ancient World*, pp. 67–68, 98–100, 108–110; *Legacy of Rome*, pp. 157–159, 304–314; STRONG, *Art in Ancient Rome*, Vol. I, pp. 60–61.

Roman historical sculpture and portraits: *Legacy of Rome*, pp. 414–427; STRONG, *Art in Ancient Rome*, Vol. I, pp. 183–190, Vol. II, pp. 71–87, 106–108, 122–126, 157–165, 188–198.

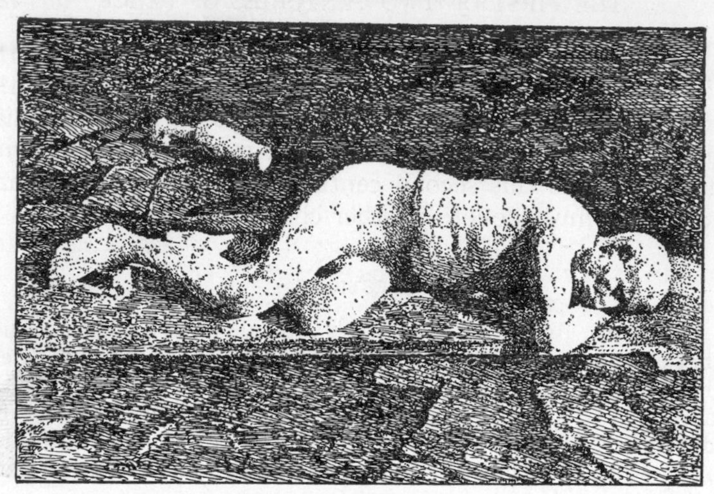

CHAPTER XXVIII · *The Second Century of Peace and the Civilization of the Early Roman Empire*

SECTION 87. THE EMPERORS OF THE SECOND CENTURY OF PEACE (BEGINNING A.D. 69)

Advent of second century of peace with triumph of Vespasian

1056. For about a year after the death of Nero the struggle among the leading military commanders for the throne of the Cæsars threatened to involve the Empire in another long civil war. Fortunately the troops of Vespasian, a very able commander in the East, were so strong that he was easily victorious, and in A.D. 69 he was declared emperor by the Senate. With him, therefore, began a second century of peace

NOTE. The above headpiece shows us the body of a CITIZEN OF POMPEII who perished when the city was destroyed by an eruption of Vesuvius in A.D. 79. The fine volcanic ashes settled around the man's body, and these, soaked by rain, made a cast of his figure before it had perished. After the body had decayed it left in the hardened mass of ashes a hollow mold, which the modern excavators poured full of plaster. They thus secured a cast of the figure of the unfortunate man just as he lay smothered by the deadly ashes which overwhelmed him over eighteen and a half centuries ago.

under a line of able emperors who brought the Empire to the highest level of prosperity and happiness. We shall first sketch the political and military activities of these emperors and then turn to the life and civilization of the Empire as a whole during the second century of peace.

Rebellion of the Jews and the destruction of Jerusalem (A.D. 70)

1057. Even though remote wars broke out on the frontiers or in distant provinces, they did not disturb the peace of the Empire as a whole. Before his election as emperor, Vespasian had been engaged in crushing a revolt of the fanatical Jews in Palestine, and the next year his able son Titus captured and destroyed Jerusalem amid frightful massacres which exterminated large numbers of the rebellious Jews (A.D. 70). It was later found necessary to forbid all Jews from entering their beloved city, consecrated by so many sacred memories; and it was made a Roman colony under a different name. Judea at the same time became a Roman province.

Tasks of emperors: frontier defenses; government organization

1058. Two great tasks were accomplished by the emperors of the age we are discussing: first, that of perfecting the system of defenses on the frontiers, and, second, that of more fully developing the government and administration of the Empire. Let us look first at the frontiers. On the south the Empire was protected by the Sahara and on the west by the Atlantic, but on the north and east it was open to attack. The shifting German tribes constantly threatened the northern frontiers, while in the east the frontier on the Euphrates was made chronically unsafe by the Parthians, the only civilized power still unconquered by Rome (see map I, p. 722).

Roman Empire the bulwark of civilization against the northerners

1059. The pressure of the barbarians on the northern frontiers, which we recall in the time of Marius, was the continuance of the vast movement with which we are already acquainted, — the tide of migration which long before had swept the Indo-European peoples to the Mediterranean and had carried the Greeks and the Romans into their two Mediterranean peninsulas. Mediterranean civilization was thus

FIG. 246. *The Emperor* TRAJAN SACRIFICING *at his New Bridge across the Danube*

In the background we see the heavy stone piers of the bridge, supporting the wooden upper structure, built with strong railings. In the foreground is the altar, beside which the emperor stands at the right, with a flat dish in his right hand, from which he is pouring a libation upon the altar. At the left of the altar stands a priest, naked to the waist and leading an ox to be slain for the sacrifice. A group of the emperor's officers approach from the left, bearing army standards. The scene is sculptured with many others on the column of Trajan at Rome, and is one of the best examples of Roman relief sculpture of the Second Century

in constant danger of being overwhelmed from the north, just as the splendid Ægean civilization was once submerged by the incoming of the Greeks. The great problem for future humanity was whether the Roman emperors would be able to hold off the barbarians long enough so that in course of time these rude northerners might gain enough of Mediterranean civilization to respect it, and to preserve at least some of it for mankind in the future.

Flavian emperors strengthen the northern frontiers (A.D. 69–96)

1060. The Flavian family, as we call Vespasian and his two sons, Titus and Domitian, did much to make the northern frontiers safe. After the mild and kindly rule of Titus, his brother Domitian adopted the frontier lines laid down by Augustus and planned their fortification with walls wherever necessary. He began the protection of the exposed border between the upper Rhine and the upper Danube. In

FIG. 247. RESTORATION *of the Roman* FORTIFIED WALL *on the German Frontier*

This masonry wall, some three hundred miles long, protected the northern boundary of the Roman Empire between the upper Rhine and the upper Danube, where it was most exposed to German attack. At short intervals there were blockhouses along the wall; at points of great danger, strongholds and barracks (Fig. 249) for the shelter of garrisons

Britain, Domitian even pushed the frontier farther northward and then erected a line of defenses. But on the lower Danube he failed to meet the dangerous power of the growing kingdom of Dacia. He even sent gifts to the Dacian king, intended to keep him quiet and satisfied. By this unwise policy Domitian created a difficult problem in this region, which had to be solved by his successors.

Trajan conquers Dacia, on the lower Danube (A.D. 106)

1061. The brief and quiet reign of the senator Nerva, who was selected by the Senate to succeed Domitian (A.D. 96), left the whole dangerous situation on the lower Danube to be met by the brilliant soldier Trajan, who followed Nerva in A.D. 98. He quickly discerned that there would be no safety for the Empire along the Danube frontier except by crossing the river and crushing the Dacian kingdom. Bridging the Danube with boats and hewing his way through wild forests, Trajan led his army through obstacles never before overcome by Roman troops. He captured one stronghold of the Dacians after another, and in two wars finally destroyed their capital. Thereupon the Dacian king and his leading men took their own lives. Trajan built a massive stone bridge across the Danube, made Dacia a Roman province, and sprinkled plentiful Roman colonies on the north side of the great river. The descendants of these colonists in the same region still call themselves *Rumanians* and their land *Rumania*, a form of the word "Roman." Trajan's vigorous policy quieted all trouble along the lower Danube for a long time.

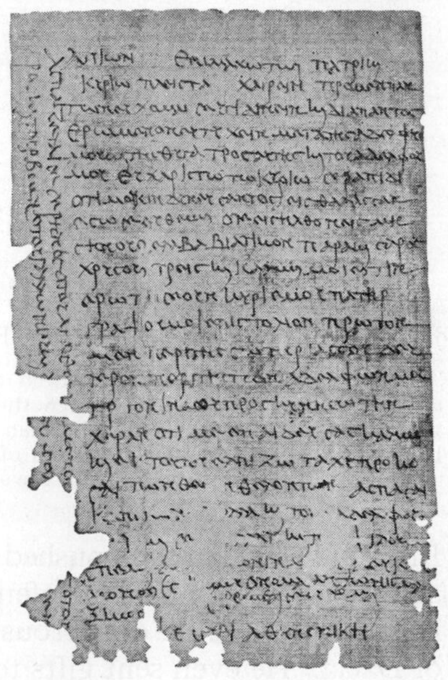

Fig. 248. Letter of Apion, *a Young Soldier in the Roman Army, to his Father, Epimachos, in Egypt* *

Trajan's war with the Parthians (A.D. 115–117)

1062. The military glory of Rome, which had declined since the days of Cæsar, revived in splendor under this great soldier-emperor. Trajan next turned his attention to the eastern frontier, extending from the east end of the Black Sea southward to the Peninsula of Sinai. In the northern section of this frontier a large portion of the boundary was formed by the upper Euphrates River. Rome thus held the western half of the Fertile Crescent, but it had never conquered the eastern half, which included Assyria and Babylonia (see map I, p. 722). Here the powerful kingdom of the Parthians, kindred of the Persians, had maintained itself with ups and downs since the days of the early Seleucids,— for three hundred and fifty years. Twice before they had defeated Roman expeditions sent against them. Trajan, however, dreamed of a great Oriental empire like that of Alexander. He led an army against the Parthians and defeated them. He added Armenia, Mesopotamia, and Assyria to the Empire as new provinces. He visited the ruins of Babylon to behold the spot where, four hundred and forty years before, Alexander had died; but he said he "saw nothing worthy of such fame, but only heaps of rubbish, stones, and ruins." Then a sudden rebellion in his rear forced him to a dangerous retreat. Weakened by sickness and bitterly realizing that his great expedition was a failure, he died in Asia Minor while returning to Rome (A.D. 117).

1063. Trajan's successor, Hadrian, was another able soldier, but he had also the judgment of a statesman. He made no effort to continue Trajan's conquests in the East. On the contrary, he wisely gave them all up except the Peninsula of Sinai, and brought the frontier back to the Euphrates.

---

* This Egyptian youth, APION, having enlisted in the Roman army in company with other boys from his little village in Egypt, bade his family good-by and embarked on a great government ship from Alexandria for Italy. After a dangerous voyage he arrived safely at Misenum, the Roman war harbor near Naples, and hastened ashore in his new uniform to have a small portrait of himself painted and to send his father the letter on the opposite page. It was written for him in Greek, on papyrus, in a beautiful hand by a hired public letter-writer, and reads as follows (with the present author's explanations in brackets): "Apion to Epimachos his father and lord, many good wishes! First of all I hope that you are in good health, and that all goes well with you and with my sister and her daughter and my brother always. I thank the lord Serapis [a great Egyptian god] that he saved me at once when I was in danger in the sea. When I arrived at Misenum, I received from the emperor three gold pieces [about fifteen dollars] as road money, and I am getting on fine. I beg of you, my lord father, write me a line, first about your own well-being, second about that of my brother and sister, and third in order that I may devotedly greet your hand, because you brought me up well and I may therefore hope for rapid promotion, the gods willing. Give my regards to Capiton [some friend] and my brother and sister and Serenilla and my friends. I send you by Euktemon my little portrait. My [new Roman] name is Antonius Maximus. I hope that it may go well with you." On the left margin, where we see two vertical lines inserted, just as *we* are accustomed to insert them, Apion's chums (the other village boys who enlisted with him) sent home their regards. Folded and sealed as in Fig. 206, the letter went by the great Roman military post, arrived safely, and was read by the young soldier's waiting father and family in the little village on the Nile over seventeen hundred years ago. Then, years later, after the old father had died, it was lost in the household rubbish, and there the modern excavators found it among the crumbling walls of the house. The ancient letter had some holes in it; but with it was another letter written by our soldier to his sister years later, after he had long been stationed somewhere on the Roman frontier and had a wife and children of his own. And that is all that the rubbish heaps of the village on the Nile have preserved of this lad who entered the army of the great Roman Empire in the Second Century A.D.

But he retained Dacia and strengthened the whole northern frontier, especially the long barrier reaching from the Rhine to the Danube, where the completion of the continuous wall was largely due to him. He built a similar wall along the northern boundary across Britain. The line of both these walls is still visible. As a result of these wise measures and the impressive victories of Trajan the frontiers were safe and quiet for a long time. Nor was there any serious disturbance until a great overflow of the northern barbarians (A.D. 167), in the reign of Marcus Aurelius, brought to an end the second century of peace.

Hadrian (A.D. 117–138) completes the frontier defenses

1064. Under Trajan and Hadrian the army which defended these frontiers was the greatest and most skillfully managed organization of the kind which the ancient world had ever seen. Drawn from all parts of the Empire, the army now consisted of all possible nationalities, like the British army in the World War. A legion of Spaniards might be stationed on the Euphrates, or a group of youths from the Nile might spend many years in sentry duty on the wall that barred out the Germans. Although far from home, such young men were enabled to communicate easily with their friends at home by a very efficient military postal system covering the whole Empire like a vast network. We are still able to hold in our hands the actual letters written from a northern post by a young Egyptian recruit in the Roman army to his father and sister in a distant little village on the Nile. When not on sentry duty somewhere along the frontier line, such a young soldier lived with his comrades in one of the large garrisons maintained at the most important frontier points, with fine barracks and living quarters for officers and men. The discipline necessary to keep the troops always ready to meet the barbarians outside the walls was never relaxed. Besides regular drill the troops were also employed in making roads, erecting bridges and public buildings, repairing the frontier walls, and especially in building vast aqueducts, which they had first seen in the East (Fig. 106).

Army under Trajan and Hadrian

FIG. 249. *Glimpses of a Roman* FRONTIER STRONGHOLD

Above, at the left, the main gate of the fort; the other three views show the barracks (cf. Fig. 247). (Restored after Waltze-Schulze)

Organization of efficient government departments

1065. Meantime the Empire had been undergoing important changes within. The emperors developed a system of government departments already foreshadowed in the time of Claudius. To manage them, they appointed Roman knights. Thus there grew up a body of experienced administrators, as heads of departments and their helpers, who carried on the government of the Empire. It was the wise and efficient Hadrian who accomplished the most in perfecting this organization of the government business. Thus after Rome had been for more than three centuries in control of the Mediterranean world, it finally possessed a well-developed government organization such as had been in operation in the Orient since the days of the pyramid-builders.

1066. Among many changes one of the most important was the abolition of the system of "farming" taxes, to be collected by private individuals, — a system which had caused both the Greeks and the Romans much trouble. Government tax-collectors now gathered in the taxes of the great Mediterranean world. It is interesting to recall that such a system had been fully organized on the Nile over three thousand years before the Romans possessed it.

Change from private tax-farmers to government tax-collectors

1067. With the complete control of these departments entirely in his own hands, the power of the emperor had much increased. From being the first citizen of the state, like Augustus, ruling jointly with the Senate, the emperor had thus become a sovereign whose power was so little limited by the Senate that he was not far from being an absolute monarch. Furthermore, the emperors of the second century of peace secured laws and regulations which made the rule of the emperor legal, although they unfortunately passed no laws providing for a successor on the death of an emperor, and dangerous conflict might ensue whenever an emperor died.

Increased power of emperor and decline of Senate

1068. At the same time an important change in the position of Italy was taking place. The condition of the farmers was now so bad that there was danger of the complete disappearance of free population in the country districts of Italy. Two of the emperors, Nerva and Trajan, even set aside large sums as capital to be loaned at a low rate of interest to farmers needing money. This interest was to be used to support poor free children in the towns of Italy, in the hope that a new body of free country people might be thus built up. This remarkable effort, one of the earliest known government plans for "farm relief," like that undertaken by the United States in 1933, was, however, not successful. As Italy was, furthermore, not a manufacturing country, its citizenship declined. Meantime a larger idea of the Empire had displaced the conception of Augustus, who had desired to see the Empire a group of states led and dominated by Italy. Whole provinces, especially in the West, had been granted citizenship, or a modified form of it, by the emperors. Influential citizens in the prov-

Italy loses its leadership and drops to level of provinces

inces were often given high rank and office at Rome. As a result there had now grown up a Mediterranean nation, as we have seen it foreshadowed even in the time of Augustus, and Italy dropped to a level with the provinces.

1069. Not only did the subjects of this vast state pay their taxes into the same treasury, but they were now controlled by the same laws. The lawyers of Rome under the emperors whom we are now discussing were the most gifted legal minds the world had ever seen. They expanded the narrow *city*-law of Rome that it might meet the needs of the whole Mediterranean world. They laid the foundations for a vast imperial code of laws, the greatest work of Roman genius. In spirit these laws of the Empire were most fair, just, and humane. Antoninus Pius, the kindly emperor who followed Hadrian, maintained that an accused person must be held innocent until proved guilty by the evidence, a principle of law which has descended to us and is still part of our own law. In the same spirit was the protection of wives and children from the arbitrary cruelty of the father of the house, who in earlier centuries had held the legal right to treat the members of his family like slaves. Even slaves now enjoyed the protection of the law, and the slave could not be put to death by the master as formerly. We should notice, however, that in some important matters the Roman law treated a citizen according to his social rank, showing partiality to the noble in preference to the common citizen. These laws did much to unify the peoples of the Mediterranean world into a single nation; for they were now regarded by the law not as different nations but as subjects of the same great state, which extended to them all the same protection of justice, law, and order. At the same time the earlier laws long developed by the older city-states were not interfered with by Rome where they did not conflict with the interests of the Empire.

Rise of a system of law for the whole Empire

1070. The Empire as a whole was still organized in provinces, which steadily increased in number. Within each province by far the large majority of the people lived in towns and cities. Such a city and its outlying communities formed a city-state like that which we found in early Greece. Each city had the right to elect its own governing officials and to carry on its own local affairs. The people still took an interest in local affairs, and there was a good deal of rivalry for election to the public offices. On the walls at Pompeii we still find the appeals of rival candidates for votes. At the same time each city was under the sovereignty of the Roman Empire and the control of the Roman governor of the province.

Government of the provinces; the people's interest in public affairs

1071. Able and conscientious governors were now controlling affairs all over the Empire. The letters written to Trajan by the younger Pliny, governor of Bithynia in Asia Minor, regarding the interests of his province reveal to us both his own faithfulness and the enormous amount of provincial business which received the emperor's personal attention. Such attention by emperors like Trajan and Hadrian relieved the communities of much responsibility for their own affairs. Hadrian traveled for years among the provinces and became very familiar with their needs. Hence the local communities inclined more and more to depend upon the emperor, and interest in public affairs declined. Along with growing imperial control of the provinces there thus began a decline in the sense of responsibility for public welfare. This was eventually a serious cause of general decay, as we shall see.

Control of the provinces by emperors; decline of the people's interest

Section 88. The Civilization of the Early Roman Empire: the Provinces

1072. Here was a world of sixty-five to a hundred million souls girdling the entire Mediterranean. Had human vision been able to penetrate so far, we might have stood at the Strait of Gibraltar and followed these peoples as our eyes swept along the Mediterranean coasts through Africa, Asia, and Europe, and thus back to the strait again. On our right in Africa would have been

Peoples of the Roman Empire

Moors, North Africans, and Egyptians; in the eastern background, Arabs, Jews, Phœnicians, Syrians, Armenians, and Hittites; and as our eyes returned through Europe, Greeks, Italians, Gauls, and Iberians (Spaniards); while north of these were the Britons and some Germans within the frontier lines. All these people were of course very different from one another in native manners, clothing, and customs, but they all enjoyed Roman protection and rejoiced in the far-reaching Roman peace. For the most part, as we have seen, they lived in cities, and the life of the age was prevailingly a city life.

1073. Fortunately one of the provincial cities has been preserved to us with much that we might have seen there if we could have visited it nearly two thousand years ago. The little city of Pompeii, covered with volcanic ashes in the brief reign of Titus, still shows us the very streets and houses, the forum and the public buildings, the shops and the markets, and a host of other things very much as we might have found them if we had been able to visit the place before the disaster (A.D. 79). We can look down long streets where the chariot wheels have worn deep ruts in the pavement; we can enter dining-rooms with charming paintings still on the walls (Fig. 192); we can look into the bakers' shops with the charred bread still in the ovens and the flour mills standing silent and deserted; or we can peep into kitchens with the cooking utensils still scattered about and the cooking hearth in perfect order for building another fire. The very life of the people in the early Roman Empire seems to rise before us as we tread the now silent streets of this wonderfully preserved place.

Pompeii, provincial city of early Roman Empire

1074. Pompeii was close beside the Greek cities of southern Italy, and we at once discover that the place was essentially Hellenistic in its life and art. Indeed, from southern Italy eastward we should have found the life of the world controlled by Rome to be simply the natural outgrowth of Hellenistic life and civilization. In some matters there had been great progress. This was especially true of intercourse and rapid

Improved means of intercourse: Roman roads and bridges

FIG. 250. *A* STREET *in Ancient* POMPEII *as it appears Today*

The pavement and sidewalk are in perfect condition, as when they were first covered by the falling ashes. At the left is a public fountain, and in the foreground is a street crossing. Of the buildings on this street only half a story still stands, except at the left, where we see the entrances of two shops, with the tops of the doors in position and the walls preserved to the level of the second floor above

communication. Everywhere the magnificent Roman roads, massively paved with smooth stone, like a town street, led straight over the hills and across the rivers by imposing bridges. Some of these bridges still stand and are in use today (Fig. 254). Near the cities there was much traffic on such a highway.

Traffic on a Roman highway

1075. One met the ponderous coach of the Roman governor, perhaps returning from his province to Rome. The curtains are drawn and the great man is comfortably reading or dictating to his stenographer. Behind him trots a peddler on a donkey, which he quickly draws to one side to make room for a cohort of Roman legionaries marching with swinging stride, their weapons gleaming through a cloud of dust. Following them rides an officer accompanied by a shackled prisoner going up to Rome for trial. He is a Christian teacher named Paul. A young dandy, exhibiting the paces of his fine horse to two ladies riding in a palanquin, grudgingly vacates the road before a rider of the imperial post who comes clattering down the next hill at high speed. Often the road is cumbered with long lines of donkeys, laden with bales of goods, or with caravans of heavy wagons creaking and groaning under their heavy loads of merchandise, — the freight trains of the Roman Empire. As for passenger trains, the traveler must resort to the horse coach or small special carriage or ride his own horse. The speed of travel and communication was fully as high as that maintained in Europe and America a century ago, before the introduction of the steam railway, and the roads were better.

1076. Indeed, the good Roman roads showed marked advance over those of the Hellenistic Age. By sea, however, the chief difference was the freedom from the old-time pirates (§ 988). From the splendid harbor laid out at the mouth of the Tiber by Claudius the traveler could take a large and comfortable ship for Spain and land there in a week. The Roman whose son was studying in Athens dispatched a bank draft for the youth's university expenses, and a week later the boy could be spending the money. A Roman merchant could send a letter to his agent in Alexandria in ten days. The huge government corn ships that plied regularly between the Roman harbors and Alexandria were stately vessels carrying several thousand tons. They could accommodate an Egyptian obelisk, weighing from three to four hundred tons, which the emperor desired to erect in Rome, besides a large cargo of grain and several hundred passengers. Good harbors had everywhere been equipped with docks, and lighthouses modeled on that at Alexandria guided the mariners into every harbor. In winter, however, sea traffic stopped.

Navigation and shipping

1077 Under these circumstances business flourished as never before. The good roads led merchants to trade be-

FIG. 251. BAKERY *with* MILLSTONES *still in Position at Pompeii*

In a court beside the bakery we see the mills for grinding the baker's flour. Each mill is an hourglass-shaped stone, which is hollow, the upper part forming a funnel-shaped hopper into which the grain is poured. The lower part of the stone is an inverted funnel placed over a cone-shaped stone inside it. The grain drops between the inner stone and the outer, and when the outer stone is turned by a long timber inserted in its side, the grain is ground between the two

yond the frontiers and to find new markets. Goods found their way from Italy even to the northern shores of Europe and Britain, whence great quantities of tin passed up the Seine and down the Rhône to Marseilles. At the other end of the Empire the discovery of the seasonal winds in the Indian Ocean led to a great increase of trade with India, and there was a fleet of a hundred and twenty ships plying regularly across the Indian Ocean between the Red Sea and the harbors of India. The wares which they brought crossed the desert by caravan from the Red Sea to the Nile and were then shipped west from the docks of Alexandria, which still remained the greatest commercial city on the Mediterranean, — the Liverpool of the Roman Empire. It shipped, besides

Commerce from Atlantic to India and from Baltic to Mediterranean

East Indian luxuries, Egyptian papyrus, linen, rich embroideries, the finest of glassware, great quantities of grain for Rome, and a host of other things. There was a proverb that you could get everything at Alexandria except snow. Along the northern roads of the Eastern world was the caravan connection with China, which continued to bring silk goods to the Mediterranean. It will be seen, then, that a vast network of commerce covered the ancient world from the frontiers of China and the coast of India on the east to Britain and the harbors of the Atlantic on the west.

1078. Both business and pleasure now made travel very common, and a wide acquaintance with the world was not unusual. The Roman citizen of means and education made his tour of the Mediterranean much as the modern sight-seer does. Having arrived in the provincial town, however, he found no good hotels, and if he did not sleep in his own roomy coach or a tent carried by his servants, he was obliged to pass the night in untidy rooms over some shop the keeper of which entertained travelers. More often, however, the traveler of birth and means brought with him letters of introduction, which procured him entertainment at some wealthy private house.

Frequency of travel but lack of hotels

1079. For even in the provincial town the traveler found a group of successful men of business and public affairs who had gained wealth and had been given the rank of Roman knights. Among them, now and again, was one of special prominence who had been given senatorial rank by the emperor. Below the senators and knights there was a free population of merchants, shopkeepers, artisans, and craftsmen. Following a custom as old as the end of the Athenian Empire, these men were organized into numerous guilds, societies, and clubs, each trade or calling by itself. These societies were in some ways much like our labor unions. They were chiefly intended for the mutual benefit of the members in each occupation. Some of them also aided in social life, in the celebration of popular holidays; and the society treasury paid the funeral expenses when a

Society in the provinces

member died, just as some societies among us do. As likely as not the richest and most influential man of the place was a freedman. There were in every large town a great number of freedmen, and they carried on an important share of the business of the Empire.

Fig. 252. Scribblings *of Sicilian* Schoolboys *on a Brick in the Days of the Roman Empire*

In passing a brickyard these schoolboys of 1700 years ago amused themselves by scribbling school exercises in *Greek* on soft clay bricks before they were baked. At the top a little boy who was still making capitals carefully wrote the letter *S* (the Greek Σ) ten times, and under it the similar letter *K*, also ten times. Then he wrote "turtle" (ΧΕΛΩΝΑ), "mill" (ΜΥΛΑ), and "pail" (ΚΑΔΟΣ), all in capitals. An older boy then pushed the little chap aside and proudly demonstrated his superiority by writing in two lines an exercise in tongue gymnastics (like "Peter Piper picked a peck of pickled peppers," etc.) which in our letters is as follows:

Nai neai nea naia neoi temon, hōs neoi ha naus

This means: "Boys cut new planks for a new ship, that the ship might float." A third boy then added two lines at the bottom. The brick illustrates the spread of Greek as well as provincial education under the Roman Empire

Public benefactions and schools in the provinces

1080. The traveler walking about such a town discovered everywhere impressive evidences of the generous interest of the citizens. There were fountains, theaters, music halls, baths, gymnasiums, and schools, erected by wealthy men and given to the community. Among such men the most celebrated was Herodes Atticus, who built a magnificent concert hall (Fig. 180, *I*) for Athens. He has been called the Andrew Carnegie of his time. In the market place were statues of such donors, with inscriptions expressing the gratitude of the people. The boys and girls of these towns found open to them schools with teachers paid by the government, where all those ordinary branches of study which we have found in the Hellenistic Age were taught. The boy who turned to business could engage a stenographer to teach him shorthand, and the young man who wished higher instruction could still find university teachers at Alexandria and Athens, and also at a number of younger universities in both East and West, especially the new university established by Hadrian at Rome and called the Athenæum. Thus the cultivated traveler found men of education and literary culture wherever he went.

1081. To such a traveler wandering in Greece and looking back some six hundred years to the Age of Pericles or the Persian wars of Athens, Greece seemed to belong to a distant and ancient world, of which he had read in the histories of Thucydides and Herodotus. Dreaming of those ancient days when Rome was a little market town on the Tiber, he might wander along the foot of the Acropolis and catch a vision of vanished greatness as it was in the days of Themistocles and Pericles. He could stroll through the porch of the Stoics (§ 796) and renew pleasant memories of his own student days when as a youth his father had permitted him to study there; or he might take a walk out to the Academy, where he had once listened to the teachings of Plato's successors.

Roman traveler in the East: Greece and Athens

1082. At Delphi too he found a vivid story of the victories of Hellas in the days of her greatness, — a story told in marble treasuries and votive monuments, the thanksgiving gifts of the Greeks to Apollo. As the Roman visitor stood there among the thickly clustered monuments he noticed many an empty pedestal, and he recalled how the villas of his friends at home were now adorned with the statues which had once occupied those empty pedestals. The Greek cities which had brought forth such things were now poor and helpless, commercially and politically, in spite of the rich heritage of civilization which they had bequeathed to the Romans.

Roman traveler in the East: Delphi

1083. As the traveler passed eastward through the flourishing cities of Asia Minor and Syria he might feel justifiable pride in what Roman rule was accomplishing. In the western

FIG. 253. *Roman* AMPHITHEATER *seen across the Huts of a Modern North African Village*

The town which once supported a public place of amusement like this has given way to a squalid village, and the whole region west of Carthage has to a large extent relapsed into barbarism

half of the Fertile Crescent, especially on the east of the Jordan, where there had formerly been only a nomad wilderness, there were now prosperous towns, with long aqueducts, with baths, theaters, basilicas, and imposing public buildings, of which the ruins even at the present day are astonishing. All these towns were not only linked together by the fine roads we have mentioned, but they were likewise connected with Rome by other fine roads leading entirely across Asia Minor and the Balkan Peninsula.

Roman traveler in the East: Asia Minor and Syria

1084. Beyond the desert behind these towns lay the troublesome Parthian Empire. The educated Roman had read how over five hundred years earlier Xenophon, and later Alexander the Great, had passed by the heaps of ruins which were once Nineveh out yonder on the Tigris, and he knew from several Greek histories and the report of Trajan that the ruinous buildings of Babylon lay still farther down toward the sea on the Euphrates. Trajan's effort to conquer all that country

Roman traveler in the East: Parthia, Assyria, and Babylonia

FIG. 254. ROMAN BRIDGE *and* AQUEDUCT *near Nîmes, France*

This structure was built by the Romans about the year A.D. 20 to supply the Roman colony of Nemausus (now called Nîmes), in southern France, with water from two excellent springs 25 miles distant. It is nearly 900 feet long and 160 feet high, and carried the water over the valley of the river Gard. The channel for the water is at the very top, and one can still walk through it. The miles of aqueduct on either side of this bridge and leading to it have almost disappeared

having failed, the Roman traveler made no effort to extend his tour beyond the frontier out into these foreign lands.

Roman traveler in the East: Egypt

1085. But he could take a great Roman galley at Antioch and cross over to Alexandria, where a still more ancient world awaited him. In the vast lighthouse (§ 768), over four hundred years old and visible for hours before he reached the harbor, he recognized the model of the Roman lighthouses he had seen. Here our traveler found himself among a group of wealthy Greek and Roman tourists on the Nile. As they left the magnificent buildings of Hellenistic Alexandria their voyage up the river carried them at once into the midst of an earlier world, — the earliest world of which they knew. All about them were buildings which were thousands of years old before Rome was founded. Like our modern fellow citizens touring the same land, many of them were merely curious idlers of the fashionable world. They berated the slow mails and languidly discussed the latest news from Rome while with indolent curiosity they visited the pyramids of Gizeh, lounged along the temple lakes and fed the sacred crocodiles, or spent a lazy afternoon carving their names on the colossal statues which overshadowed the plain of Egyptian Thebes, where Hadrian himself listened to the divine voice which issued from one of the statues every morning when the sun smote upon it. And here we still find their scribblings at the present day. But the thoughtful Roman, while he found not a little pleasure in the sights, took note also that this land of ancient wonders was filled as of old with flocks and herds and vast stretches of luxuriant grainfields, which made it the granary of Rome and an inexhaustible source of wealth for the emperor's private purse.

Ancient civilization in the East; later in the Roman West

1086. The Eastern Mediterranean then was regarded by the Romans as *their* ancient world, long possessed of its own ancient civilization, Greek and Oriental. There the Roman traveler found Greek everywhere, and spoke it as he traveled; but when he turned away from the East and entered the Western Mediterranean, he found a much more modern world, with vast regions where civilization was a recent matter, just as it is in America. Thus throughout North Africa, west of Carthage, throughout Spain, Gaul, and Britain, the Romans had at first found only rough settlements, but no cities and no real architecture. Indeed, these western lands, the America of the ancients, when first conquered by Rome, had not advanced much beyond the stage of the Late Stone Age settlements of several thousand years earlier, except here and there, where they had come into contact with the Greeks or Carthaginians.

Roman cities of the West and their surviving buildings

1087. Seneca, one of the wisest of the Romans, said, "Wherever a Roman has conquered, there he also lives." This was especially true of the West. Roman merchants and Roman officials were everywhere, and many of the cities were Roman colonies. The language of civilized intercourse in all the West was Latin, the language of Rome, whereas east of Sicily the traveler heard only Greek. In this age western Europe had for the

FIG. 255. RESTORATION *of Roman* TRIUMPHAL ARCH *at Orange, France*

Having once adopted this form of monument, the Romans built many such handsome arches to commemorate important victories. There were naturally a number at Rome. Of those built in the chief cities of the Empire several still remain. The one pictured above was built at the Roman colony of Arausio (now called Orange), on the river Rhone, to celebrate a victory over the Gauls in A.D. 21. Modern cities have erected similar arches; for example, Paris, Berlin, London, and New York

first time been building cities; but it was under the guidance of Roman architects, and their buildings looked like those at Rome. In North Africa, between the desert and the sea, west of Carthage, the ruins of whole cities with magnificent public buildings still survive (Fig. 253) to show us how Roman civilization reclaimed regions little better than barbarous before the Roman conquest. Similar imposing remains survive in western Europe, especially southern France. We can still visit and study massive bridges, spacious theaters, imposing public monuments, sumptuous villas, and luxurious public baths, — a line of ruins stretching from Britain through southern France and Germany to the northern Balkans.

Whole Mediterranean world at last highly civilized

1088. Just as the communities of Roman subjects once girdled the Mediterranean, so the surviving monuments and buildings which they used still envelop the great sea from France and Spain eastward to Jerusalem, and from Jerusalem westward to Morocco. They reveal to us the fact that, as a result of all the ages of human development which we have studied, the whole Mediterranean world, west as well as east, had now risen to a high civilization. Such was the picture which the Roman traveler gained of that great world which his countrymen ruled: in the center the vast midland sea, and around it a fringe of civilized countries surrounded and protected by the encircling line of legions. They stretched from Britain to Jerusalem, and from Jerusalem to Morocco, like a dike restraining the stormy sea of barbarians outside, which would otherwise have poured in and overwhelmed the results of centuries of civilized development. Meantime we must return from the provinces to the great controlling center of this Mediterranean world, to Rome itself, and endeavor to learn what had been the course of civilization there since the Augustan Age, that is, for the last three quarters of the two centuries of peace.

SECTION 89. THE CIVILIZATION OF THE EARLY ROMAN EMPIRE: ROME

Public buildings of Rome: Colosseum

1089. The visitor in Rome at the close of the reign of Hadrian found it the most magnificent monumental city in the world of that day. It had by that time quite surpassed Alexandria in size and in the number and splendor of its public buildings. At the eastern end of the Forum, on ground once occupied by Nero's Golden

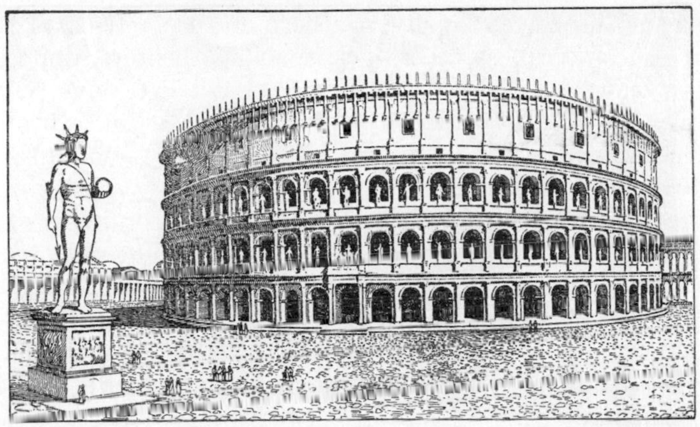

FIG. 256. *The Vast* FLAVIAN AMPHITHEATER *at Rome; now called the Colosseum*

This enormous building, one of the greatest in the world, was an oval arena surrounded by rising tiers of seats, accommodating nearly fifty thousand people. We see here only the outside wall as restored. Built by Vespasian and Titus, it was completed in A.D. 80. At the left is the colossal bronze statue of Nero, which originally stood in this vicinity near the entrance of his famous Golden House. (Restored after Luckenbach)

House, Vespasian erected a vast amphitheater (now known as the Colosseum) for gladiatorial combats. It was completed and dedicated by his son Titus, who arranged, for the forty-five thousand spectators whom it held, a series of bloody spectacles lasting a hundred days. Although now much damaged, it still stands as one of the greatest buildings in the world. At the same time Vespasian completed the rebuilding of the city after the great fire of Nero's reign.

New forums of the emperors

1090. It was especially in and alongside the old Forum that the grandest buildings of the Empire thus far had grown up. The business of the great world capital led Vespasian and Nerva to erect two more magnificent forums (Fig. 242). These two, with the two of Cæsar and Augustus, formed a group of four new forums along the north side of the old Forum. At the northwest end of this group of four Trajan built another, that is, a fifth new forum, which surpassed in magnificence anything which the Medi-

Fig. 257. *Interior View of the* Dome *of the* Pantheon, *built at Rome by Agrippa and Hadrian*

The first building on this spot was erected by Agrippa, Augustus's great minister, but it was completely rebuilt, as we see it here, by Hadrian. The circular hole in the ceiling is 30 feet across; it is 142 feet above the pavement, and the diameter of the huge dome is also 142 feet. This is the only ancient building in Rome which is still standing with walls and roof in a perfectly preserved state. It is thus a remarkable example of Roman skill in the use of concrete (§ 1091). At the same time it is one of the most beautiful and impressive domed interiors ever designed. (Compare the church of St. Sophia, p. 766)

terranean world had ever seen before. On one side was a vast new business basilica, and beyond this rose a mighty column, richly carved with scenes picturing Trajan's brilliant campaigns. On each side of the column was a library building, one for Greek and one for Latin literature. The column still stands beside one of the busy streets of modern Rome, but little of the other magnificent buildings has survived.

1091. In the buildings of Trajan and Hadrian the architecture of Rome reached its highest level of splendor and beauty, and also of workmanship. Sometime in the Hellenistic Age architects had begun to employ increasing quantities of cement concrete, though it is still uncertain where or by whom the hardening properties of cement were discovered.

Under Hadrian and his successors the Roman builders completely mastered the art of making colossal casts of concrete. The domed roof of Hadrian's Pantheon is a single enormous concrete cast, over a hundred and forty feet across. The Romans, therefore, eighteen hundred years ago, were employing concrete on a scale which we have only recently learned to imitate, and after all this lapse of time the roof of the Pantheon seems to be as safe and stanch as it was when Hadrian's architects first knocked away the posts which supported the wooden form for the great cast. The mausoleum erected by Hadrian is the greatest of all Roman tombs and for several generations was the burial place of the emperors. It survives as one of the great buildings of Rome.

Roman concrete: Pantheon and Hadrian's tomb

1092. The *relief* sculpture adorning all these monuments is the greatest of Roman art. The reliefs covering Trajan's column display greater power of invention than Roman art ever showed elsewhere. Of *statue* sculpture, however, the vast majority of the works now produced were copies of the masterpieces of the great Greek sculptors. Many such famous Greek works, which perished long ago, are now known to us only in the form of surviving copies made by the Roman sculptors of this age and discovered in modern excavations in Italy. The portrait sculptors followed the tendencies which they had inherited from the Hellenistic Age. Their portraits of the leading Romans are among the finest works of the kind ever wrought.

Roman sculpture

1093. In painting, the wall decorators were almost the only surviving practicers of the art. They merely copied the works of the great Greek masters of the Hellenistic Age over and over again on the walls of Roman houses. Portrait painting, however, flourished, and the hack portrait painter at the street corner, who did your portrait quickly for you on a tablet of wood, was almost as common as our own portrait photographer. Perfectly preserved examples of such work have been excavated in the Nile valley.

Roman painting

1094. There was now a larger educated public at Rome than ever before, and splendid libraries, maintained by the state, were accessible to all. Authors and literary men were also liberally supported by the emperors. Nevertheless, even under these favorable circumstances not a single genius of great creative imagination arose. Just as in sculpture and painting, so now in literature, the leaders were content to imitate or copy the great works of the past. Real progress in literature had therefore ceased. The leadership in such matters, held for a brief time by Rome in the Augustan Age, had now returned to Athens, where the emperors had endowed the four schools of philosophy (§ 797) as a government university. Nevertheless Rome was still a great influence in literature; the leading literary men of the Empire desired to play a part there, and when a philosopher or teacher of rhetoric published his lectures in book form, he was proud to place under the title the words "Delivered at Rome."

Leadership in literature passes from Rome back to Athens

Fig. 258. *Portrait of an* Unknown Roman

This terra-cotta head is one of the finest portraits ever made. It represents one of the masterful Roman lords of the world, and shows clearly in the features those qualities of power and leadership which so long maintained the supremacy of the Roman Empire. (Courtesy of the Museum of Fine Arts, Boston)

1095. While poetry had declined, prose writers were still productive. Nero's able minister Seneca (§ 1051) wrote very attractive essays and letters on personal character and conduct. They show so fine an appreciation of the noblest human traits that many have thought he had secretly adopted Christianity. His style became so influential that it displaced that of Cicero for a long time. The new freedom of speech which arose under the liberal emperors after the death of Domitian permitted Tacitus to write a frank history of the Empire from the death of Augustus to the death of Domitian (from A.D. 14 down to A.D. 96). Although he allowed his personal prejudices to influence him, so that he has given us a very dark picture of the Julian emperors, his tremendous power as a writer resulted in the greatest history ever put together by a Roman. Among his other writings was a brief account of Germany, which furnishes us our first full glimpse into the life of the peoples of northern Europe. The letters which at this time passed between the younger Pliny and the emperor Trajan (§ 1071) are among the most interesting literature of the ancient world. They remind us of the letters of Hammurapi of Babylon, some twenty-two hundred years earlier.

Latin prose writers: Seneca, Tacitus, and the younger Pliny

1096. With these writers in Latin we should also associate several immortal works by Greeks of the same age, though they did not live at Rome. In the little village of Chæronea, in Bœotia, where Philip of Macedon crushed the Greeks, Plutarch at this time wrote his remarkable series of lives of the greatest men of Greece and Rome, placing them in pairs, a Greek and a Roman together, and comparing them. Although they contain much that belongs in the world of romance, they form an imperishable gallery of heroes which has held the interest and the admiration of the world for eighteen centuries. At the same time another Greek, named Arrian, who was serving as a Roman governor in Asia Minor, collected the surviving accounts of the life of Alexander the Great. He called his book the Anabasis of Alexander, after the Anabasis of Xenophon, whom he was imitating in accordance with the imitative spirit of the age. Arrian was only a passable writer of prose and certainly not a great historian, but without his compilation we should know very little about Alexander the Great. A huge guidebook of Greece, telling the reader all about the buildings and monu-

Greek prose writers: Plutarch, Arrian, and Pausanias

ments still standing at that time in the leading Greek towns, like Athens, Delphi, and Olympia, was now put together by Pausanias. It furnishes us an immortal picture book in words, showing ancient Greece in all its splendor of statues and temples, theaters and public buildings.

Lack of science at Rome: Pliny's *Natural History*

1097. In science the Romans continued to be collectors of the knowledge gained by the Greeks. During a long and successful official career the elder Pliny devoted himself with incredible industry to scientific studies. He made a vast collection of the facts, then known to science, to be found in books, chiefly Greek. He put them all together in a huge work which he called *Natural History*, — really an encyclopedia. He was so deeply interested in science that he lost his life in the great eruption of Vesuvius as he was trying both to study the tremendous event at short range and (as admiral of the fleet) to save the fleeing people of Pompeii. But Pliny's *Natural History* did not contain any new facts of importance discovered by the author himself, and it was marred by many errors in matters which Pliny misunderstood. Nevertheless, for hundreds of years, until the revival of science in modern times, Pliny's work was, next to Aristotle, the standard authority referred to by all educated Europeans. Thus men fell into an indolent attitude of mind and were satisfied merely to learn what earlier discoverers had found out. This attitude never would have led to the discovery of the size of the earth as determined by Eratosthenes, or in modern times to X-ray photographs or wireless telegraphy.

End of investigative science at Alexandria; Ptolemy

1098. A great astronomer and geographer of Alexandria, named Ptolemy, who flourished under Hadrian and the Antonines, was the last of the famous scientists of the ancient world. He wrote, among other works, a handbook on astronomy, for the most part a compilation from the works of earlier astronomers. In it he unfortunately adopted the conclusion that the sun revolved around the earth as a center. His book became a standard work, and hence this mistaken view of the

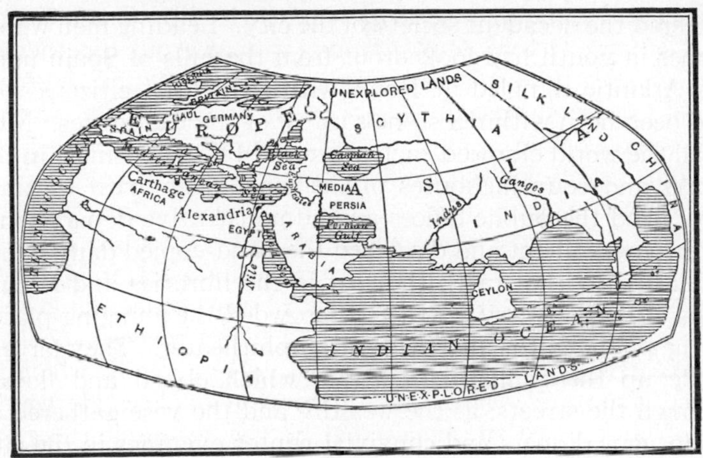

Map of the WORLD *according to the Astronomer and Geographer* PTOLEMY
(Second Century A.D.*)*

solar system, called the Ptolemaic system, was everywhere accepted by the later world. It was not until four hundred years ago that the real truth, already long before discovered by the Greek astronomer Aristarchus (§ 780), was rediscovered by the Polish astronomer Copernicus. It was a further sign of the decline of science that Ptolemy even wrote a book on Babylonian astrology. Knowledge of the spherical form of the earth as shown by Ptolemy and earlier Greek astronomers reached the travelers and navigators of later Europe, and finally led Columbus to undertake the voyage to India and the East *westward*, — the voyage which resulted in the discovery of America.

Cosmopolitan life of Rome

1099. The position of educated Greeks at Rome was very different from what it had been under the Republic, when such men were slaves or teachers in private households. Now they were holding important positions in the government or as teachers and professors paid by the government. The city was no longer Roman or Italian; it had become Mediterranean, and many worthy families from the provinces, settling in Rome, had greatly bettered the decadent society of the city. Leading men whose homes in youth had looked out from the hills of Spain upon the Atlantic mingled at Rome with influential citizens who had been born within a stone's throw of the Euphrates. Men of all the world elbowed each other and talked business in the banks and countinghouses of the magnificent new forums; they filled the public offices and administrative departments of the government and discussed the hand-copied daily paper published by the state; they sat in the libraries and lecture halls of the university, and they crowded the lounging places of the public baths and the vast amphitheater. They largely made up the brilliant social life which ebbed and flowed through the streets, as the wealthy and the wise gathered at sumptuous dinners and convivial winter evenings in the city itself or indolently killed time loafing about the statue-filled gardens and magnificent country villas overlooking the Bay of Naples, where the wealthy Romans spent their summer leisure. We call such all-inclusive, widely representative life "cosmopolitan," — a word of Greek origin meaning "world-cityish."

Incoming of Oriental luxuries

1100. This converging of all the world at Rome was evident in the luxuries now enjoyed by the rich. The outward life, houses, and costumes of the wealthy were, on the whole, not much changed from that which we found toward the close of the Republic. Luxury and display had somewhat increased, and in this direction Oriental rarities now played a noticeable part. Roman ladies were decked with diamonds, pearls, and rubies from India, and they robed themselves in shining silks from China. The tables of the rich were bright with peaches and apricots, now appearing for the first time in the Roman world. Roman cooks learned to prepare rice, formerly a delicacy required only by the sick. Horace had amusingly pictured the distress of a miserly Roman when he learned the price of a dish of rice prescribed by his physician. Instead of sweetening their dishes with honey as formerly, Roman households began to find a new product in the market place known as "sakari"; for so the report of a venturesome Oriental sailor of the First Century A.D. calls the sirup of sugar cane which he brought by water from India into the Mediterranean for the first time. It gave the Romans their word for sugar, *saccharum*, and is the earliest mention of sugar in history. These new things from the Orient were beginning to appear in Roman life just as the potatoes, tobacco, and Indian corn of America found their way into Europe after the voyages of Columbus had disclosed a new western world.

Section 90. The Popularity of Oriental Religions and the Spread of Early Christianity

Decline of intellectual life; Roman religion

1101. The life of the Orient was at the same time continuing to bring into the Mediterranean other things less easily traced than rice or sugar but much more important in their influence on the Roman world. The intellectual life of the Empire was steadily declining, as we have seen indicated by literature and science. Philosophy was no longer occupied with new thoughts and the discovery of new truths. Such philosophy had given way to the semi-religious systems of living and ideas of right conduct taught by the Stoics and Epicureans. Thoughtful Romans read Greek philosophy of this kind in the charming treatises of Cicero or the discussions of Seneca. Such readers had given up the old Roman gods and accepted these philosophical precepts of daily conduct as their religion. But this teaching was only for the highly educated and intellectual class.

Egyptian religion in Europe

1102. Nevertheless such men sometimes followed the multitude and yielded to the fascination of the mysterious religions coming in from the East. Even in Augustus's time the Roman poet Tibullus, absent on a military campaign which sickness had interrupted, wrote to his fiancée Delia in Rome: "What does your Isis for me now, Delia? What avail me those brazen sistrums [1] of hers,

[1] Egyptian musical instruments played by shaking in the hand.

FIG. 259. *The* TEMPLE *of* ISIS *at Pompeii*

Even the little town of Pompeii had its temple of Isis, as did also the little Hellenistic city of Priene (Fig. 207). It has here been restored after Mau

so often shaken by your hand? . . . Now, now, goddess, help me; for it is proved by many a picture in thy temples that man may be healed by thee." Tibullus and his fiancée belonged to the most cultivated class, but they had taken refuge in the faith of the Egyptian Isis. When Hadrian's handsome young Greek friend Antinoüs was drowned in the Nile, the emperor erected an obelisk at Rome in his memory, with a hieroglyphic inscription announcing the beautiful youth's divinity and his union with Osiris. Attached to Hadrian's magnificent villa near Rome was an Egyptian garden, sacred chiefly to Isis and Osiris and filled with their monuments. Plutarch wrote an essay on Isis and Osiris which he dedicated to a priestess of Isis at Delphi. Since the days of the early Empire, multitudes had taken up this Egyptian faith, and temples of Isis were to be found in all the larger cities. Today tiny statuettes and other symbols of the Egyptian goddess are found even along the Seine, the Rhine, and the Danube.

1103. The Earth-Mother of Asia Minor (§ 330), with her consort Attis, also gained the devotion of many Romans.

In the army the Persian Mithras, a god of light (§ 366), was a great favorite, and many a legion had its underground chapel where its members celebrated his triumph. All these faiths had their "mysteries," consisting chiefly of dramatic presentations of the career of the god, especially his submission to death, his triumph over it, and his ascent to everlasting life. It was believed that to witness these things and share in the holy ceremonies of initiation would bring to all initiates deliverance from evil and power to share in the endless life of the god and to dwell with him forever.

The Earth Mother; Mithras; Oriental mysteries popular

1104. The old Roman faith had little to do with conduct and held out to the worshiper no such hopes of future blessedness. Throughout the great Roman world men were longing for some assurance regarding the life beyond the grave, and in the midst of the trials and burdens of this life they wistfully sought the support and strength of a divine protector. Little wonder that the multitudes were irresistibly attracted by the comforting assurances of these Oriental faiths and the blessed future insured by their "mysteries"! At the same time it was believed possible to learn the future of every individual by the use of Babylonian astrology. Even the astronomer Ptolemy wrote a book on it. The Orientals who practiced it were called Chaldeans, or Magi (whence our words "magic" and "magician"); and everyone consulted them.

Decline of Roman religion and the old gods

1105. The Jews too, now that their temple in Jerusalem had been destroyed by the Romans, were to be found in increasing numbers in all the larger cities. Strabo, the geographer, said of them, "This people has already made its way into every city, and it would be hard to find a place in the habitable world which has not admitted this race and been dominated by it." The Roman world was becoming accustomed to their synagogues; but the Jews refused to acknowledge any god besides their own, and their exclusiveness brought them disfavor and trouble with the government.

Judaism

1106. Among all these faiths of the East the common people were more and more inclining toward one, whose teachers told how their Master, Jesus, a Hebrew, was born in Palestine, the land of the Jews, in the days of Augustus. Everywhere they told the people of his vision of human brotherhood and of divine fatherhood, surpassing even that which the Hebrew prophets had once discerned. This faith he had preached for a few years in the Aramaic language of his countrymen, till he incurred their hatred; and in the reign of Tiberius they had brought charges against him, accusing him of political conspiracy, before the Roman governor, Pontius Pilate, who had allowed him to be put to death.

Rise of Christianity

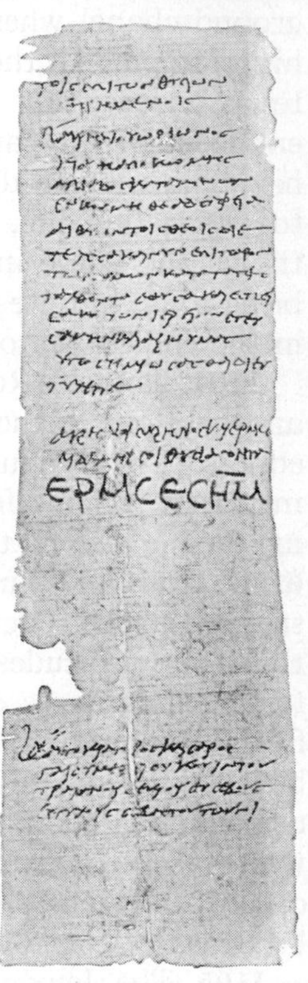

Fig. 260. Certificate *showing that a Roman Citizen had sacrificed to the Emperor as a God* *

1107. A Jewish tentmaker of Tarsus named Paul, a man of passionate eloquence and unquenchable love for his Master, passed far and wide through the cities of Asia Minor and Greece, and even to Rome, proclaiming his Master's teaching. He left behind him a line of devoted communities stretching from Palestine to Rome. Certain letters which he wrote in Greek to his followers were circulating widely among them and were read with eagerness. At the same time a narrative of the Master's life had also been written in Aramaic, the language in which he had preached. This perished, but Greek accounts drawing upon the Aramaic narrative also appeared and were now widely read by the common people. There were finally *four*

Paul and the foundation of the earliest churches; New Testament

leading biographies of Jesus in Greek, which came to be regarded as authoritative, and these we call the Four Gospels. Along with the letters of Paul and some other writings they were later put together in a Greek book now known in the English translation as the New Testament.

1108. The other Oriental faiths, in spite of their attractiveness, could not offer to their followers the consolation and fellowship of a life so exalted and beautiful, so full of brotherly appeal and human sympathy, as that of the new Hebrew Teacher. In the hearts of the toiling millions of the Roman Empire his simple summons, "Come unto me all ye that labor and are heavy laden," proved a mightier power than all the edicts of the Roman emperors. The slave and the freedman, the artisan and the craftsman, the humble and the despised in the huge barracks which sheltered the poor in Rome, listened to this new mystery from the East, as they thought it to be; and as time passed, multitudes responded and found joy in the hopes which it awakened. In the second century of peace it was rapidly outstripping the other religions of the Roman Empire.

Superiority of Christianity over other Oriental religions

1109. The officers of government often found these early converts not only refusing to sacrifice to the emperor as a god (§ 1055) but also openly prophesying the downfall of the Roman state. The early Christians were therefore more than once called upon to endure cruel persecution. Their religion seemed incompatible

Rome persecutes early Christians

* Excavators in the ruins of Egyptian villages have discovered over a score of such certificates, each written on a strip of papyrus. This specimen states that a citizen named Aurelius Horion, living in the village of Theadelphia in Egypt, appeared before a government commission and not only affirmed that he had always been faithful in the worship of the gods, but also, in the presence of the commission and of witnesses, offered sacrifice (a slaughtered animal), presented a drink offering, and likewise consumed a portion of these offerings. In the middle we see the heavy black signature of the presiding official, and at the bottom in four lines the date, corresponding to our A.D. 250. Every Roman citizen at this time, no matter what his religion might be, was obliged to possess such a certificate and to show it on demand. It was called a *libellus*, and the owner of it was called a *libellaticus*. (Compare our word "libel.") A Christian who would resort to such a means of escaping persecution by the government was greatly despised by the faithful, who refused to comply.

with good citizenship, since it forbade them to show the usual respect for the emperor and the government.

Organization of churches and the revival of popular leadership

1110. Nevertheless their numbers steadily grew, and each new Christian group or community organized itself into an assembly of members called an *ecclesia*, or, as we say, a church. *Ecclesia* was the old Greek word for Assembly of the People, and in these new assemblies, or churches, men of ability were now beginning to find those opportunities for leadership and power which the decline of citizenship in the old city-republics no longer offered. The leaders of the *churches* were soon to be the strong men of the people and to play a *political* as well as a *religious* rôle.

SECTION 91. THE END OF THE SECOND CENTURY OF PEACE

Decline of Mediterranean civilization; Antoninus Pius and Marcus Aurelius

1111. In spite of outward prosperity, especially suggested by the magnificent buildings of the Empire, Mediterranean civilization was declining in the second century of peace. The decline became noticeable in the reign of Hadrian. The just and kindly Antoninus (who followed Hadrian in A.D. 138), called by the Romans "the Pious," showed hardly enough energy to maintain the foreign prestige of the Empire, even though he strengthened the walls along the northern frontier. His successor, the noble Marcus Aurelius, therefore had to face a very serious situation (A.D. 161). The Parthians, encouraged by the easy-going reign of Antoninus Pius, made trouble on the eastern frontier, and Marcus Aurelius was obliged to fight them in a four years' war before the frontier was safe again.

1112. When the Roman troops returned from this war, they brought back with them a terrible plague which destroyed multitudes of men at the very moment when the Empire most needed them; for at this juncture the barbarian hordes in the German north broke through the frontier defenses (Fig. 247), and for the first time in two centuries they poured down into Italy (A.D. 167). The two centuries of peace were ended. At the same time the finances of the Empire were so low that the emperor was obliged to sell the crown jewels to raise the money necessary for equipping and supporting the army. With little intermission, until his death in A.D. 180, Marcus Aurelius maintained the struggle against the Germans in the region later forming Bohemia. Indeed, death overtook him while he was still engaged in the war. But in spite of his victory over the barbarians he was unable to sweep them entirely out of the northern regions of the Empire. He finally took the dangerous step of allowing some of them to remain as farmer colonists on lands assigned to them inside of the frontier. Very serious consequences resulted.

Marcus Aurelius stops the barbarian invasion (A.D. 167–180)

1113. Nevertheless the ability and enlightened statesmanship of Marcus Aurelius are undoubted. Indeed, they were only equaled by the purity and beauty of his personal life. He regarded his exalted office as a sacred trust to which he must be true, in spite of the fact that he would have greatly preferred to devote himself to reading, study, and philosophy, which he deeply loved. Amid the growing anxieties of his position, even as he sat in his tent and guided the operations of the legions among the forests of Bohemia in the heart of the barbarous north, he found time to record his thoughts and leave to the world a little volume of meditations written in Greek. As the aspirations of a gentle and chivalrous heart toward pure and noble living these meditations are among the most precious legacies of the past. He was the last of a high-minded succession, the finest spirit among all the Roman emperors. There was never another like him on the imperial throne. But no ruler, however pure and unselfish his purposes, could stop the processes of decline going on in the midst of the great Roman world. Following the two centuries of peace, therefore, was to come a fearful century of revolution, civil war, and anarchy, from which a very different Roman world was to emerge.

Character of Marcus Aurelius

QUESTIONS

Section 87. Did the struggle at the death of Nero long endanger the peace of the Empire? What two great tasks were awaiting the emperors? What did Domitian do for the frontiers? Describe the military exploits of Trajan. How did Hadrian treat the conquests of Trajan? What can you say of the Roman army under Trajan and Hadrian? How was the management of the government improved? How did this affect tax-collecting? What can you say of agricultural conditions in Italy? How were the laws improved?

Section 88. Give an imaginary bird's-eye view of the Roman Empire from Gibraltar to the Euphrates. Where did the Roman's ancient world lie?

Section 89. Describe the Colosseum. What can you say of Roman use of cement in architecture? What had happened to literature in Rome since Augustus? Tell about the Latin prose writers; the Greek prose writers. What can you say of science in the Roman Empire?

Section 90. What can you say of religious life at Rome? of incoming Oriental religions? What can you say of the Jews at this time? Describe the rise of Christianity and the work of Paul. What practical difficulty did the Christians meet in their relations with the Roman government?

Section 91. What events ended the second century of peace? What can you say of the mind and character of Marcus Aurelius?

BIBLIOGRAPHY FOR TOPICAL STUDIES

Travel and the Roman road system: DAVIS, *Influence of Wealth*, pp. 95–105; *Legacy of Rome*, pp. 141–157, 464–465; MCDANIEL, *Roman Private Life*, pp. 168–178; QUENNELL, *Everyday Life in Roman Britain*, pp. 93-100; SHOWERMAN, *Rome and the Romans*, pp. 485–502.

The eruption of Vesuvius, and Pliny the Elder: *Art and Archæology*, Vol. 29 (1930), pp. 51–55, 75; MAGOFFIN, *Lure and Lore of Archæology*, pp. 27–30.

Roman provinces: *Art and Archæology*, Vol. 35 (1934), pp. 3–17; QUENNELL, *Everyday Life in Roman Britain*, pp. 17–68; SHOWERMAN, *Rome and the Romans*, pp. 545–556.

Chapter XXIX · *A Century of Revolution and the Division of the Empire*

Section 92. Internal Decline of the Roman Empire

1114. We have seen good government, fine buildings, education, and other evidences of civilization more widespread in the second century of peace than ever before. Nevertheless the great Empire which we have been studying, although in a condition seemingly so favorable, was suffering from an inner decay whose symptoms, at first hidden, were fast becoming

Signs of inner decay: former decline of farming continues

Note. The above headpiece shows us the surviving ruins of the Royal Palace at Ctesiphon, on the Tigris, once the capital of New Persia. The huge vault on the right was built over the enormous hall below, without any supporting timbers during the course of construction. It is 84 feet across and is the largest masonry vault of its age still standing in Asia. Here the magnificent kings of New Persia held their splendid court, imitated by the weak Roman emperors at Constantinople. Situated almost within sight of Babylon, Ctesiphon was but one in a succession of powerful capitals occupying the river crossing on the great highway between Asia Minor and the East (map, p. 754): Akkad (§ 195), Babylon (§ 211), Seleucia, Ctesiphon, and, finally, Baghdad (§ 1192).

more and more evident. In the first place, the decline of farming, so noticeable before the fall of the Republic, had gone steadily on.

Spread of Oriental domain system of land ownership; villas

1115. In spite of the heavy taxes imposed upon it, land had continued to pass over into the hands of the rich and powerful. The Oriental system of confining land-ownership to large domains held by the state and a few individuals had also a strong influence. From Asia Minor, where it was wide-spread under the Persians, this system had passed to Greece. The Romans had found it also in Africa, the province behind Carthage. Already in Nero's time, half of this province was made up of six domains, held by only six great landlords. Such a great estate was called a *villa*; and the system of villa estates, having destroyed the small farmers of Italy, was likewise destroying them in the provinces. Villas now covered not only Italy but also Gaul, Britain, Spain, and other leading provinces.

Rise of *coloni*

1116. Unable to compete with the great villas, and finding the burden of taxes unbearable, most of the small farmers gave up the struggle. A man in this plight would often enter upon an arrangement which made him the *colonus* of some wealthy villa-owner. By this arrangement the farmer and his descendants were forever bound by law to the land which they worked, and they passed with it from owner to owner when it changed hands. While not actually slaves, they were not free to leave or go where they pleased; and without any prospect of bettering themselves or any opportunity for their children ever to possess their own lands, these men lost all energy and independence and were very different from the hardy farmers of early Rome. As we shall see, many northern barbarians also became *coloni* within the frontiers of the Empire.

1117. The great villas once worked by slaves were now cultivated chiefly by these *coloni*. With the end of the long wars the captives who had been sold as slaves were no longer obtainable, and slaves had steadily diminished in numbers. Their condition had also much improved, and the law now protected them from the worst forms of cruelty once inflicted upon them. We have already noticed the growing practice of freeing slaves, which made freedmen so common throughout the Empire that they were playing an important part in manufactures and business.

Decline of slavery, and improvement in the condition of slaves

1118. Multitudes of the country people, unwilling to become *coloni*, forsook their fields and turned to the city for relief. Many did so because neglect of fertilization, as well as long-continued cultivation, had exhausted their land and it would no longer produce crops. Great stretches of unworked and weed-grown fields were no uncommon sight. As a result the amount of land under cultivation continually decreased, and the ancient world was no longer raising enough food to feed itself properly. The scarcity was felt most severely in the great centers of population like Rome, where prices had rapidly gone up.

Decrease in extent of cultivated lands; scarcity of food

1119. Offers by the emperor to give land to anyone who would undertake to cultivate it failed to increase the amount of land under the plow. Even under the wisest emperors the government was therefore entirely unable to restore to the country districts the hardy yeomen, the brave and independent farmers, who had once formed the basis of Italian prosperity, — the men who, in the ranks of the legion, had laid the foundation of Roman power. The destruction of the small farmers and the inability of Rome to restore them formed the leading cause among a whole group of causes which brought about the decline and fall of this great empire.

Rome's inability to bring back the small farmers

1120. The country people who moved to Rome were only bringing about their own extermination as a class. The large families which country life favors were no longer reared, the number of marriages decreased, and the population of the Empire shrank. Debased by the life of the city, the former sturdy yeoman lost his in-

Debasing influences of city life

dependence in an eager scramble for a place in the waiting line of city poor, to whom the government distributed free grain, wine, and meat. The time which should have been spent in breadwinning was worse than wasted among the cheering multitudes at the chariot races, bloody games, and barbarous spectacles. Notwithstanding the fine families who moved to Rome from the provinces under the liberal emperors of the Second Century A.D., the city became a great hive of shiftless population supported by the state with money which the struggling agriculturist was taxed to provide. The same situation was in the main to be found in all the leading cities.

Decline of citizenship in the cities

1121. In spite of outward splendor, therefore, these cities too were declining. They had now learned to depend upon Rome to care for them even in their own local affairs, and their citizens had rapidly lost all sense of public responsibility. The helpful rivalry between neighboring city-states too had long ago ceased. Everywhere the leading men of the cities were indifferently turning away from public life. Moreover, Rome was beginning to lay greater financial obligations upon the leading men of such cities, and it was becoming increasingly difficult to find men willing to assume these burdens. Responsible citizenship, which does so much to develop the best among the citizens in any community and which had earlier so sadly declined in Greece (§ 802), was passing away, never to reappear in the ancient world.

Decline of business

1122. At the same time the financial and business life of the cities was also declining. The country communities no longer possessed a numerous purchasing population. Hence the country market for goods manufactured in the cities was so seriously reduced that city industries could no longer dispose of their products. They rapidly declined. The industrial classes were thrown out of work and went to increase the multitudes of the city poor. City business was also much hurt by a serious lack of precious metals for coining money.

1123. Many of the old silver and gold mines around the Mediterranean now seem to have been worked out. Wear in circulation, loss by shipwreck, private hoards, and considerable sums which went to pay for goods in India and China, or as gifts to the German barbarians, — all these causes aided in diminishing the supply of the precious metals. The government was therefore unable to secure enough to coin the money necessary for the transaction of business. The emperors were obliged to begin mixing in an increasing amount of less valuable metals and coining this cheaper alloy. The Roman coin collections in the European museums show us that the coins of Augustus were pure, while those of Marcus Aurelius contain 25 per cent of alloy. Two generations after Marcus Aurelius there was only 5 per cent of silver in a government coin. A *denarius*, the common small coin, worth nearly twenty cents under Augustus, a century after the death of Marcus Aurelius was worth only half a cent. This was the result of a process of monetary debasement, such as the United States, for very different reasons, began in 1933.

Lack of precious metals for coinage; debasement of coins

1124. Even Marcus Aurelius had trouble in finding enough money to pay his army. As soon as this difficulty became serious it paralyzed the government and demoralized the army. It was impossible to maintain a paid army without money. As it became quite impossible to collect taxes in money, the government was obliged to accept grain and produce as payment of taxes, and great granaries and storehouses began to take the place of the treasury as in ancient Egypt. Here and there the army was paid in grain. On the frontiers, for lack of other pay, the troops were assigned lands, which of course did them no good unless they could cultivate them. Then they were allowed to marry and to live with their families in little huts on their lands near the frontier. Called out only occasionally for drill or to repel a barbarian raid, they soon lost all discipline and became merely feeble militia, called by the Roman government "frontiersmen" (*limitanei*).

Decline of army; frontier legions become militia

1125. Even under Marcus Aurelius a governor of a province had started a serious rebellion. Hence the emperor was now obliged to keep a standing army in Italy. These legions had become much smaller, and they were made up increasingly of barbarians, especially Germans and the uncivilized natives of the northern Balkans, among whom the Illyrians took the lead. The Roman citizen was now a rarity in the ranks, and it soon became necessary to allow the barbarians to fight in their own massed formations, to which they were accustomed. The discipline of the legion, and the legion itself, disappeared, and with it the superior military power of Rome was gone. The native ferocity and reckless bravery of uncivilized hordes, before which the unmilitary Roman townsmen trembled, were now the power upon which the Empire relied for its protection.

Standing army in Italy, and its decline

1126. This degeneration of the army was much hastened by a serious imperfection in the organization of the Roman state, left there by Augustus. This was the lack of a legal and long-practiced method of choosing a new emperor and transferring the power from one emperor to the next, and thus maintaining from reign to reign, without a break, the supreme authority in the Roman state. The troops found that they could make a new emperor whenever the old emperor's death gave them an opportunity. For an emperor so made they had very little respect, and if he attempted to enforce discipline among them, they put him out of the way and appointed another. Rude and barbarous mercenary soldiery thus became the highest authority in the state.

Lack of a law of succession leads to demoralization of army and state

1127. Finally, the spread of civilization to the provinces had made them feel that they were the equals of Rome and Italy itself. Even under the Republic there had been much foreign blood in the peninsula. Horace himself was the son of a freedman, of nobody knows what race. Italy was now largely foreign in population. Trajan and Hadrian were Spaniards, and more than one province furnished the Empire with its ruler.

Competition between Italy and the provinces

When, in A.D. 212, citizenship was granted to all free men within the Empire, in whatever province they lived, the leveling of distinctions gave the provinces more and more opportunity to compete for leadership.

Section 93. A Century of Revolution

1128. These forces of decline were swiftly bringing on a century of revolution which was to shipwreck the civilization of the early world. This fatal century began with the death of Marcus Aurelius in A.D. 180. The assassination of his unworthy son Commodus, who reminds us of Nero, gave the opportunity for a struggle among a group of military usurpers. From this struggle a rough but successful soldier named Septimius Severus emerged triumphant. It was he who found himself obliged to settle the frontier troops on their own lands, with the resulting demoralization of the army (§ 1124). He systematically filled the highest posts in the government with military leaders of low origin. Thus, both in the army and in the government, the ignorant and often foreign masses were gaining control. Nevertheless the energy of Severus was such that he led his forces with success against the Parthians in the East, and even recovered Mesopotamia. But the arch which he erected to commemorate his victories, and which still stands in the Forum at Rome, reveals in its barbarous sculptures the fearful decline of culture in Italy. The Roman artists who wrought these rude reliefs were the grandsons of the men who had so skillfully sculptured the column of Trajan.

Revolution begins; decline under Septimius Severus (A.D. 193–211)

1129. The family of Septimius Severus maintained itself for a time, and it was his son Caracalla who conferred citizenship on all free men in the Empire in A.D. 212. But when the line of Severus ended (A.D. 235), the storm broke. The barbaric troops in one province after another set up their puppet emperors to fight among themselves for the throne of the Mediterranean world. The proclamation of a new emperor

Line of Severus ends (A.D. 235); wars among provincial emperors

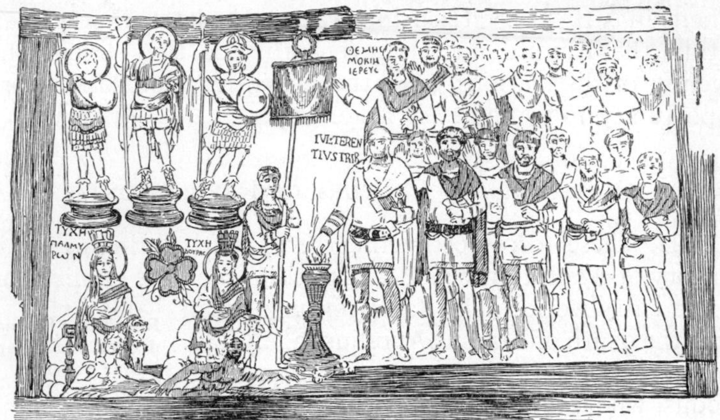

Fig. 261. Roman Garrison *of Septimius Severus* worshiping Oriental Gods *on the Euphrates Frontier*

This is the easternmost representation of Roman soldiers ever discovered. At the left, standing on three pedestals and leaning on their spears, are the three gods of Palmyra; below them are two seated goddesses of Fortune. Their names are written over them in Greek, and we learn that the one at the left is "Fortuna of Palmyra" and the other is "Fortuna of Dura," the name of the city where this garrison was posted. Near the middle, before a small burning altar, stands the Roman commander, whose name is written beside him, "Julius Terentius, the Tribune." He is dropping incense on the fire. Before him is posted the standard-bearer, holding the red standard of a Roman army, while behind the commander is a group of the garrison legionaries who have been stationed here by Septimius Severus. It was natural that these soldiers should want to gain the favor of the local goddess of Fortune, and also of the divinities of Palmyra, which was about one hundred and forty miles away. It is important to note that these five Oriental divinities all have the golden disk, or aureole, behind their heads to indicate their divine character (§ 1175). The scene is a wall painting discovered by the Oriental Institute Expedition of The University of Chicago in the fortress of Dura, on the middle Euphrates, about forty miles outside of the frontier later established by Diocletian. (Drawing by courtesy of Franz Cumont)

would be followed again and again by news of his assassination. From the leaders of the barbaric soldier class, after the death of Commodus, the Roman Empire received eighty rulers in ninety years. One of these rulers of a day, in A.D. 248, went through the mockery of celebrating the thousand years' jubilee of the traditional founding of Rome.

1130. Most of these so-called emperors were not unlike the revolutionary bandits who proclaim themselves presidents of the small republics of Central America. For fifty years there was no public order, as the plundering troops tossed the scepter of Rome from one soldier-emperor to another. Life and property were nowhere safe; turbulence, robbery, and murder were everywhere. The tumult and fighting between rival emperors hastened the ruin of all business; and as the affairs of the nation passed from bad to worse, national bankruptcy ensued. In this tempest of anarchy during the Third Century A.D. the civilization of the ancient world suffered final collapse. The supremacy of mind and of scientific knowledge won by the Greeks in the Third Century B.C. (§ 778) yielded to the reign of ignorance and superstition in these social disasters of the Third Century of the Christian Era.

Fifty years of anarchy and the collapse of higher civilization

1131. As the Roman army weakened, the northern barbarians were quick to perceive the helplessness of the Empire. In the east the Goths, one of the strongest German tribes, took to the water, and their fleet passed out of the Black Sea into the Mediterranean. While they devastated the coast cities far and wide, other bands pushed down through the Balkan Peninsula and laid waste Greece as far as the Peloponnese. Even Athens was plundered. The barbarians penetrated far into Italy; in the west they overran Gaul and Spain, and some of them even crossed to Africa. In Gaul they burned city after city, and their leaders stood by and laughed in exultation as they saw the flames devouring the beautiful buildings of these Roman towns.

Barbarian raids

1132. Under these circumstances, when the people of the plundered lands saw that the Empire could no longer defend them, they organized for their own defense. In this way Gaul, for example, became an independent nation living under its own rulers for years in this terrible century. Its people repulsed the barbarians and slowly rebuilt their burned cities. They dared not spread out the city as before, but, grouping all the buildings close together, they built the town com-

Gaul rebuilds its cities during a temporary independence

pactly and surrounded it with a massive wall made largely of blackened blocks of stone taken from the ruined buildings burned by the barbarians. In no less than sixty cities of France today sections of these heavy walls, when taken down to make room for modern improvements, are found to contain these smoke-blackened blocks. Far outside the city walls containing these blocks, excavation has revealed to us the foundations of the splendid Roman structures from which the blocks came and which formed the once larger city destroyed by the barbarians.

Rise of New Persia (A.D. 226) under her Sassanian kings

1133. At the same time a new danger had arisen in the East. A revival of patriotism among the old Persian population had resulted in a vigorous restoration of their national life. Their leaders, a family called Sassanians (or Sassanids), overthrew the Parthians (A.D. 226) and furnished a new line of enlightened Persian kings. As they took possession of the Fertile Crescent and established their capital at Ctesiphon on the Tigris, not far north of Babylon, a new Orient arose on the ruins of seemingly dead and forgotten ages. Noble examples of Persian architecture (p. 743), though influenced by Greek art, again looked down on the Tigris and Euphrates; beautiful works of the Persian artist and craftsman again began to appear; and the revered religion of Zoroaster took on new life. We have in this movement a last revival of that old Iranian race which produced the religion of Zoroaster and built up the vast Persian Empire. The Sassanian kings organized a much more powerful state than that of the Parthians which they had overthrown, and they regarded themselves as the rivals of the Romans for the empire of the world (tailpiece, p. 765). The old rivalry between the Orient and the West, as in the days of Greece and Persia, was now continued, with Rome as the champion of the West and with this New Persia as the leader of the East (see map II, p. 722).

1134. Just as the family of Severus was declining, this empire of New Persia rose into power as a dangerous foe of the Roman Empire. From this time on, the Roman dominion was seriously threatened on two fronts, north and east. As in Gaul, so in the East, the rise of a usurper within the Roman Empire for a time saved the region from absorption by the outside enemy. One of the eastern governors, using Palmyra as a center, gained his independence and defended the eastern frontier on his own account. After his death his widow, the beautiful Zenobia, ruled at Palmyra as queen of the East, over a realm which included Asia Minor, Syria, and Egypt. Her kingdom served for a time as a buffer state, protecting the Roman Empire from attack by New Persia.

Palmyra a buffer state against New Persia; Zenobia

1135. With a powerful Oriental state under Zenobia holding the Eastern Mediterranean lands, and an able senator named Tetricus, master of Gaul, Britain, and northern Spain, ruling the West as an independent emperor, it looked as if the Roman Empire were about to fall to pieces. The anarchy which we have already noticed within the Empire was at its worst when one of the soldier-emperors, named Aurelian (A.D. 270–275), advanced against Zenobia, defeated her army, captured Palmyra, and took the queen prisoner. Similar success in Gaul enabled him to celebrate a gorgeous triumph in Rome, with Zenobia and Tetricus led through the streets of the city along with the other captives who adorned his triumph. Aurelian restored some measure of order and safety; but in order to protect Rome from the future raids of the barbarians, he built entirely around the great city the massive wall (Fig. 244) which still stands, — a confession of the dangerous situation of Rome in the Third Century A.D. It was a little over a century after the death of Marcus Aurelius when the emperor Diocletian restored what looked like a lasting peace (A.D. 284).

Aurelian recovers the East and Gaul; peace under Diocletian

1136. If at this point we look back some four hundred years over the history of Rome since she became mistress of the world, we discern three great periods.[1] With the foundation

[1] Periods of history do not end or begin abruptly. The dates given merely suggest the points at which the transition from period to period was very evident.

of the Empire by Augustus there began two centuries of peace, and this period of peace was both preceded and followed by a century of revolution. We have thus had a century of revolution, two centuries of peace, and then a second century of revolution. The first century of revolution (that is, about 133–30 B.C.) led from the Gracchus brothers to the triumph of one-man power and the foundation of the Empire by Augustus. The two centuries of peace (that is, about 30 B.C. to nearly A.D. 170) beginning with the foundation of the Empire by Augustus continued into the reign of Marcus Aurelius. The second century of revolution (that is, about A.D. 180 to about A.D. 284) led from the enlightened reign of Marcus Aurelius to Oriental despotism under Diocletian. Thus four centuries of Roman imperialism, after bringing forth such masterful men as Sulla and Julius Cæsar, had passed through various stages of one-man power, to end in despotism. We are now first to examine that despotism and then to see how it was overwhelmed by two centuries of barbarian invasions from the north, while at the same time it was also crushed by the reviving power of the Orient, whose assaults were to last many centuries more (study map, p.787).

Four centuries of Roman imperialism, culminating in Diocletian

SECTION 94. THE ROMAN EMPIRE AN ORIENTAL DESPOTISM

1137. The world which issued from the disasters of this second revolution, toward the end of the Third Century A.D., under Diocletian was one totally different from that which Augustus and the Roman Senate had ruled three centuries before. Diocletian deprived the shadowy Senate of all power, except for the municipal government of the city of Rome. The Roman Senate, now reduced to a mere city council, a board of aldermen, disappeared from the stage of history. The emperor thus became for the whole Roman world what he had always been in Egypt, — an absolute

Diocletian (A.D. 284–305); the Empire an Oriental despotism

Map Plate, Patented July 5, 1921 • Method of Making Maps, Patented July 5, 1921

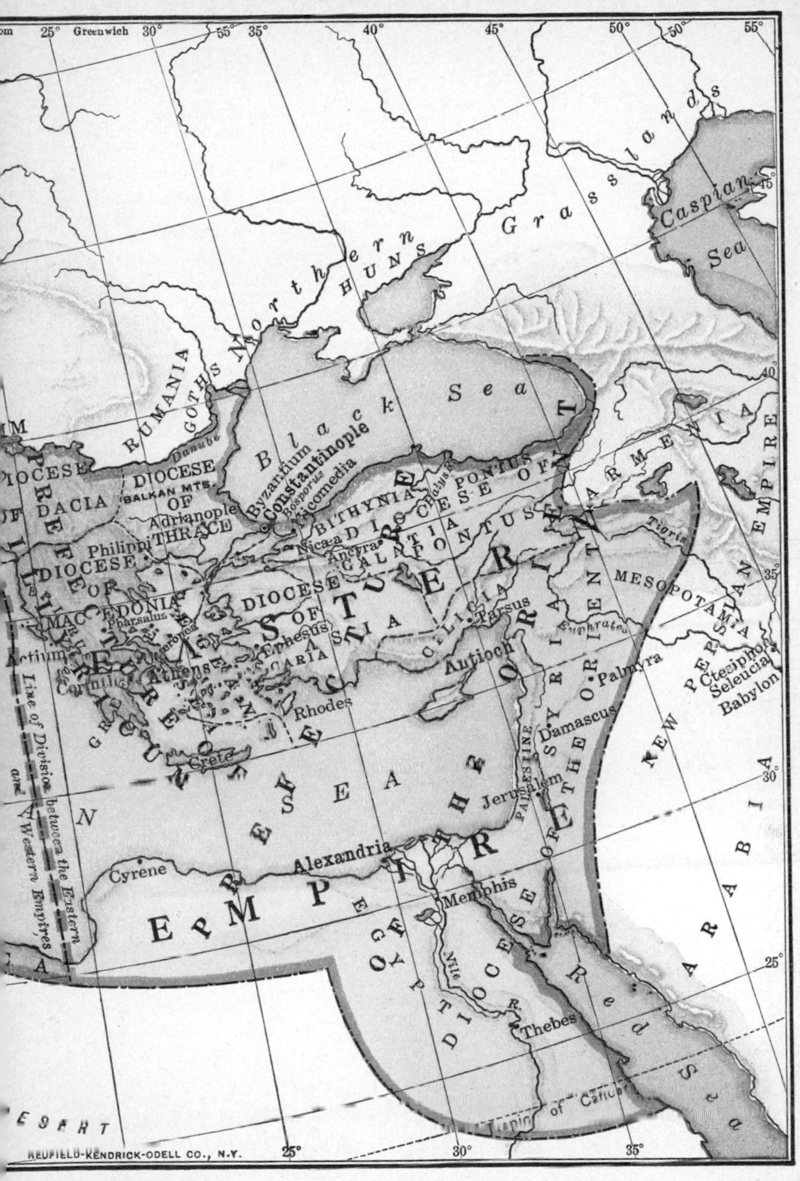
Greenwich
Northern
HUNS
Grasslands
Caspian
Sea
Black Sea
RUMANIA
GOTHS
Danube
DIOCESE OF DACIA
DIOCESE
BALKAN MTS.
OF
THRACE
Adrianople
Byzantium
Constantinople
Bosporus
Nicomedia
BITHYNIA
DIOCESE OF PONTUS
Halys
Nicaea
Ancyra
GALATIA
Philippi
DIOCESE OF MACEDONIA
Pharsalus
Actium
Corinth
Athens
DIOCESE OF ASIA
Ephesus
CARIA
Rhodes
Crete
CILICIA
Tarsus
Antioch
ARMENIA
Tigris
MESOPOTAMIA
Euphrates
Palmyra
Ctesiphon
Seleucia
Babylon
NEW PERSIAN EMPIRE
Damascus
SYRIA
PALESTINE
Jerusalem
Alexandria
Cyrene
Memphis
Nile R.
Thebes
EGYPT
Red Sea
ARABIA
Line of Division between the Eastern and Western Empires
EASTERN EMPIRE
DIOCESE OF THE ORIENT
DIOCESE OF EGYPT
PREFECTURE OF ILLYRICUM
GREECE
SEA
KENDRICK-ODELL CO., N.Y.

monarch, with none to limit his power. The state had been completely militarized and orientalized. With the unlimited power of the Oriental despot the emperor now assumed also its outward symbols, — the diadem, the gorgeous robe embroidered with pearls and precious stones, the throne and footstool, before which all who came into his presence must bow down to the dust.

1138. Archæological research has shown that the gorgeous costume in which the Roman emperor now decked himself was copied from that of the Sassanian kings of New Persia. The Roman leaders had seen much of this new empire of the East for two generations, and from its brilliant Oriental court these outward matters of royal costume, court symbols, and customs were adopted. Oriental influence on Roman beliefs, such as we have seen in the spread of the worship of the Persian god Mithras, was now also affecting the notion of the divinity of the emperor. In these things we recognize a further stage in that commingling of East and West begun by Alexander the Great over six hundred years before. Indeed, the Roman Empire had now become like a vast sponge absorbing the life and civilization of the Orient.

New Persian influence; triumph of Oriental influences

1139. As a divinity the emperor had now become an Oriental Sun-god, and he was officially called the Invincible Sun. His birthday, the same as that of the Sun-god himself, was on the twenty-fifth of December; that is, about the date when the sun each year begins to turn northward after it has reached its southernmost limit. It was a long time before this day became the Christmas feast of the early Christians. The inhabitants of each province might revere their particular gods, undisturbed by the government, but all were obliged as good citizens to join in the official sacrifices to the head of the state as a god. With the incoming of this Oriental attitude toward the emperor the long struggle for democracy, which we have followed through so many centuries, ended in the triumph of Oriental despotism.

Emperor an Oriental Sun-god; despotism; end of democracy

Diocletian resides in the East and appoints an emperor of the West

1140. The necessity of leading the army against New Persia, the new Oriental enemy, carried the emperor much to the East. The result was that Diocletian resided most of the time at Nicomedia, in Asia Minor. As a natural consequence the emperor was unable to give close attention to the West. Following some earlier examples, and perhaps remembering the two consuls of the old Republic, Diocletian therefore appointed another emperor to rule jointly with himself, to give his attention to the West. The second emperor was to live at Milan, in the Po valley, really the most important region of Italy. All government edicts, whether issued in the East or in the West, were signed by both emperors, and it was not Diocletian's intention to divide the Roman Empire, any more than it had been the purpose to divide the Republic in electing two consuls. The final result was nevertheless the division of the Roman Empire into East and West, just as it had once been divided by the war between Cæsar in the West and Pompey in the East, or the similar conflict between Octavian in the West and Antony in the East.

Diocletian's arrangements for succession

1141. In order to avoid the recurrence of civil war at the death of an emperor, Diocletian sought to arrange the transfer of power from one emperor to the next. He and his fellow emperor each bore the title of "Augustus." The two Augustuses appointed two subordinates, to be called Cæsars. There were thus two emperors, or Augustuses, and two subordinate emperors, or Cæsars, intended to be somewhat like vice presidents; for it was provided that at the death or resignation of either Augustus one of the Cæsars should at once take his place as Augustus, and another Cæsar was then to be appointed. These arrangements display little statesmanship, and there was no possibility of their permanence.

1142. In accordance with this organization, involving four rulers, the provinces of the Empire, over a hundred in number, were divided into four great groups, or prefectures (see map, p. 754), with a prefect over each. Still smaller groups of provinces, twelve in number, were called *dioceses*, mostly ruled by *vicars*, the subordinates of the prefects, while under the vicars were the governors of the separate provinces. The business of each province was organized in the hands of a great number of local officials graded into many successive ranks and classes from high to low. There was an unbroken chain of connection from the lowest of these up through various ranks to the governor, the vicar, and the prefect, and finally to the emperor himself.

Diocletian's administrative organization

1143. The financial burden of this vast organization, begun under Diocletian and completed under his successors, was enormous, for this multitude of government officials and the clamorous army had all to be paid and supported. It was a great expense also to maintain the luxurious Oriental court of the emperor, surrounded by his innumerable palace officials and servants. But now there were *four* such imperial courts instead of one. At the same time it was still necessary to supply "bread and circuses" for the populace of the towns. In regard to taxation the situation had grown steadily worse since the reign of Marcus Aurelius. The amount of a citizen's taxes continued to increase until finally little that he possessed was free from taxation.

Oppressive taxation

1144. When the scarcity of coin forced the government to accept grain and produce from the delinquent taxpayer, taxes had become a mere share in the yield of the lands. The Roman Empire thus sank to a primitive system of taxation already thousands of years old in the Orient. It was now customary to oblige a group of wealthy men in each city to become responsible for the payment of the entire taxes of the district each year; and if there was a deficit, these men were forced to make up the lacking balance out of their own wealth. The penalty of wealth seemed to be ruin, and there was no motive for success in business when such prosperity meant ruinous overtaxation.

Bad methods of tax collection

1145. Many a worthy man secretly fled from his lands to become a wandering beggar or even to take up a life of robbery and violence. The Roman Empire had already lost, and had never been able to restore, its prosperous *farming class*. It now lost likewise the enterprising and successful *business men* of the middle class. Diocletian therefore endeavored to force these classes to continue their occupations. He enacted laws forbidding any man to forsake his lands or occupation. The societies, guilds, and unions into which the men of various occupations had long been organized were now gradually made obligatory, so that no one could follow any calling or occupation without belonging to such a society. Once a member he must always remain in the occupation it implied.

Diocletian attempts to enforce the permanence of callings

1146. Thus under this Oriental despotism there disappeared in Europe the liberty for which men had striven so long, and the once free Roman citizen had no independent life of his own; for the will of the emperor had now become law, and as such his decrees were dispatched throughout the length and breadth of the Roman dominions. Even the citizen's wages and the prices of the goods he bought or sold were as far as possible fixed for him by the state. The emperor's innumerable officials kept an eye upon even the humblest citizen. They watched the grain dealers, butchers, and bakers, and saw to it that they properly supplied the public and never deserted their occupation. In some cases the state even forced the son to follow the profession of his father. In a word, the Roman government now attempted to regulate almost every interest in life, and wherever the citizen turned he felt the control and oppression of the state.

Disappearance of liberty and free citizenship

1147. Staggering under his crushing burden of taxes, in a state which was practically bankrupt, the citizen of every class had now become a mere cog in the vast machinery of the government. He had no other function than to toil for the state, which exacted so much of the fruit of his labor that he was fortunate if it

Every citizen a toiler for the state

proved barely possible for him to survive on what was left. As a mere toiler for the state he was finally where the peasant on the Nile had been for thousands of years. The emperor had become a Pharaoh, and the Roman Empire a colossal Egypt of ancient days.

Rome's mission to preserve part of ancient civilization

1148. The century of revolution which ended in the despotic reorganization by Diocletian completely destroyed the creative ability of ancient men in art and literature, as it likewise crushed all progress in business and affairs. In so far as the ancient world was one of progress in civilization, its history was ended with the accession of Diocletian. Nevertheless the Roman Empire had still a great mission before it in the preservation of at least something of the heritage of civilization which it was to hand down the centuries to us of today. Moreover, it was out of the fragments of the Roman Empire that the nations of modern Europe grew up. We are now to watch it, then, as it falls to pieces, still mechanically maintaining its hold upon its mighty heritage from the past and furnishing the materials, as it were, out of which our world of today has been built up.

SECTION 95. THE DIVISION OF THE EMPIRE AND THE TRIUMPH OF CHRISTIANITY

Shift of the center of power from Italy to the Balkan Peninsula

1149. Under Diocletian, Italy had been reduced to the position of a taxed province, and had thus lost the last vestige of superiority over the other provinces of the Empire. The dangerous flood of German barbarians along the lower Danube and the threatening rise of New Persia had drawn the emperor into the northeast corner of the Empire. During the century of revolution just past, the Illyrian soldiers of the Balkan Peninsula had filled the army with the best troops and furnished more than one emperor. An emperor who had risen from the ranks of provincial troops in the Balkans felt little attachment to Rome. Not only had Rome ceased to be

FIG. 262. VIEW *across the* BOSPORUS *from Europe to Asia*

This view places us on the *European* shore of the Bosporus, and we look eastward to the *Asiatic* shore, with the mountains behind rising to the table-land of central Asia Minor. Just south of us (at the right) on the same shore is Constantinople; a little to the north (the left) is the place where Darius the Great probably built his bridge when he first invaded Europe to conquer the Scythians. The towers and walls before us are part of a fortress built by the Turkish conquerors when they crossed from Asia for the conquest of Constantinople in A.D. 1453. For ages this intercontinental crossing has been the commercial and military link between Europe and Asia

the residence of an emperor, but the center of power had clearly shifted from Italy to the Balkan Peninsula. The movement was the outcome of a reviving respect for the East and a long-growing interest in the Balkan Peninsula, observable even as early as Hadrian, who spent vast sums in the beautification of Athens. After the struggles following Diocletian's death — struggles which his arrangements for the succession failed to prevent — the Emperor Constantine the Great emerged victorious (A.D. 324). He did not hesitate to turn to the eastern edge of the Balkan Peninsula and establish there a new Rome as his residence.

1150. The spot which he selected showed him to be a far-seeing statesman. He chose the ancient Greek town of Byzantium, on the European side of the Bosporus, — a mag-

FIG. 263. *Ancient* MONUMENTS *in Constantinople*

The obelisk in the foreground (nearly 100 feet high) was first set up in Thebes, Egypt, by the conqueror Thutmose III; it was erected here by the Roman emperor Theodosius. The small spiral column at the right is the base of a bronze tripod set up by the Greeks at Delphi in commemoration of their victory over the Persians at Platæa. The names of thirty-one Greek cities which took part in the battle are still to be read, engraved on this base. These monuments of ancient Oriental and Greek supremacy stand in what was the Roman horse-race course when the earlier Greek city of Byzantium became the eastern capital of Rome. Finally, the great mosque behind the obelisk, with its slender minarets, represents the triumph of Islam under the Turks, who took the city in A.D. 1453

nificent situation overlooking both Europe and Asia, and fitted to be a center of power in both. In placing his new capital here Constantine established a city the importance of which was equaled only by Alexandria in Egypt. The emperor stripped many an ancient city of its great monuments to employ them in beautifying his splendid residence. By A.D. 330 the new capital on the Bosporus was a magnificent monumental city, worthy to be the successor of Rome as the seat of the Mediterranean empire. It was renamed Constantinople ("Constantine's city"), after its founder.[1]

Constantine (A.D. 324–337) makes Constantinople the capital

[1] The Arabic form of this name is *Stambūl*, from which the official Turkish form *Istanbūl* is derived.

1151. The transfer of the capital of the Roman Empire to the east side of the Balkan Peninsula was a decided triumph for the older civilization of the Eastern Mediterranean; but it meant the separation of East and West, — the cutting of the Roman Empire in two. Although the separation did not take place abruptly, yet, within a generation after Constantinople was founded, the Roman Empire had in fact, if not in name, become two states, and they were never more than temporarily united again. Thus the founding of Constantinople sealed the doom of Rome and the Western Mediterranean lands of the empire. For a time the eastern half of the Empire ruled by Constantinople was greatly strengthened by Diocletian's reorganization. Nevertheless it too was doomed to steady decline. We have seen that citizenship in the Roman Empire no longer meant a share in the control of public affairs. Able men of affairs were no longer arising among such citizens except as the army raised one of its commanders to the position of emperor. Peaceful civil life was no longer producing statesmen to control government affairs as in the days of the Roman and Greek republics.

Separation of East and West; continuance of decline

1152. In this situation, as the Christian churches steadily increased in numbers and their influence grew, they more and more needed the guidance of able men. The management of the great Christian communities and their churches called for increasing ability and experience. Public discussion and disputes in the church assemblies enabled gifted men to stand forth, and their ability brought them position and influence. The Christian church thus became a new arena for the development of statesmanship, and church statesmen were soon to be the most influential men of the age, at a time when the civil responsibilities of the old democracies had long since ceased to produce such men.

Churches a new arena for the rise of able men

1153. These officers of the church gradually devoted themselves more and more to church duties until they had no time for anything else. Thus they came to be distinguished from the other members and were called the *clergy*, while the people who made up the membership were called the *laymen* or the *laity*. The old men who cared for the smaller country congregations were finally called merely *presbyters*, a Greek word meaning "old men"; our word "priest" is derived from this Greek term. Over the group of churches in each city a leading priest gained authority as bishop. In the larger cities these bishops had such influence that they became archbishops, or head bishops, having authority over the bishops in the surrounding cities of the province. These church arrangements were modeled to a large extent on those of the Roman government, from which such terms as "diocese" were borrowed. Thus Christianity, once the faith of the weak and the despised, became a powerful organization, strong enough to cope with the government.

Organization of the church; priests, bishops, and archbishops

1154. The Roman government began to see the uselessness of persecuting the Christians. The struggle to suppress them was one which decidedly weakened the Roman state at a time when the long disorders of the century of revolution made the emperors feel their weakness. After the retirement of Diocletian his "Cæsar" Galerius, feeling very probably the dangers threatening Rome from *without* and the uselessness of the struggle against the Christians *within*, issued a decree, in A.D. 311, by which Christianity was legally recognized. Its followers received the same legal position granted to the worshipers of the old gods. This decree was also maintained by Constantine, and under his direction the first great assembly, or council, of all the churches of the Roman world was held at Nicæa, in northwestern Asia Minor.

Christianity placed on legal basis with other religions

1155. The victory of Christianity was not yet final, however. After Constantine's sons and nephews had spent years in fighting for the crown, which one of the sons held for a time, the survivor among the group was Constantine's nephew Julian, the ablest emperor since the second century of peace. Like Marcus Aurelius he was a philosopher on the throne, for he was devoted to the old literature and philosophy of the Greeks. He therefore renounced Christianity and did all that he could to retard its progress and to restore Hellenistic religion and civilization. He was an able general also. He defeated the German barbarians in the West, but while leading his army in the East against the New Persians he died. The church called him Julian the Apostate; he was the last of the Roman emperors to oppose Christianity.

Julian the Apostate (A.D. 361–363)

QUESTIONS

Section 92. In spite of seeming prosperity, what was now the real condition of the Roman Empire? Describe the system of *coloni.* What was now the condition of slavery? What can you say of the extent of cultivated lands and the food supply? Discuss city life; the decline of business. Discuss the supply of precious metals and money. How did this difficulty affect the army? What was the effect of the lack of a law of succession on the army? What was now Italy's situation in the Empire?

Section 93. Tell what happened after the death of Marcus Aurelius. Describe the conditions following the time of the family of Septimius Severus. What did the northern barbarians do? What happened in Gaul? Describe the rise of New Persia. Tell about Palmyra and Zenobia. What did Aurelian do? Who ended the century of revolution, and when?

Section 94. How did Diocletian treat the Roman Senate? What did the Roman emperor become? What became of democracy? What can you say about the emperor's place of residence? What arrangements for the succession did Diocletian make? Tell about his administrative organization. What can you say of taxation under Diocletian? How did this affect men of means? What two classes of men had the Empire now lost? What can you say of liberty and free citizenship?

Section 95. Where had the center of power shifted? Who triumphed in the struggles following Diocletian's death? Where did he establish the new eastern Rome? What was the effect upon old Rome? upon the Empire? What can you say of the opportunities offered by the church to able men? How did Christianity gain legal recognition? When? Tell about Julian the Apostate.

BIBLIOGRAPHY FOR TOPICAL STUDIES

Regulation of prices, "relief," and benefactions, in the Hellenistic-Roman world: ABBOTT, *Common People of Ancient Rome*, pp. 145–204; *Roman Politics*, pp. 152–159; BOTSFORD, *Source Book*, pp. 417–423, 476–477, 505, 530–531; DAVIS, *Influence of Wealth*, pp. 248–276; FOWLER, *Social Life at Rome*, pp. 32–39; TARN, *Hellenistic Age*, pp. 91–95.

Zenobia and Palmyra: *Museum Journal of the University of Pennsylvania*, Vol. XVIII (1927), pp. 325–350; WRIGHT, *Palmyra and Zenobia*, pp. 74–94, 109–170.

NOTE. The relief scene below shows us Shapur, the victorious king of New Persia, proudly seated on his horse as the Roman emperor Valerian (at the left) kneels with hands extended to beg for mercy from the Oriental conqueror, who had defeated and captured him A.D. 258. This sculpture is the easternmost representation of a Roman emperor. As sovereign of a new and revived Persia, Shapur showed a fine realization that his triumph was the renewal of ancient Persian glory; for he sent his sculptors to Persepolis, and there they carved this monument of Oriental triumph at the foot of the cliff under the splendid tomb where Darius the Great had been buried almost seven hundred and fifty years earlier (see Fig. 136). Shapur's victory and his monument were the Oriental reply to Alexander the Great, a Western conqueror, who had burned Persepolis nearly six centuries before.

Chapter XXX · The Triumph of the Barbarians and the End of the Ancient World

Section 96. The Barbarian Invasions and the Fall of the Western Empire [1]

Danger from the barbarians

1156. We have often met the Indo-European barbarians who occupied northern Europe, behind the civilized belt on the north of the Mediterranean. Since the days of the Stone Age men this northern region had never advanced to a high civilization. Its barbarian peoples had been a frequent danger to the fringe of civilized

[1] This account of the absorption of the western part of the ancient world by the barbarians is here necessarily very brief. A fuller presentation of this period will be found in Robinson's *Medieval and Modern Times* (chaps. ii-v), a book which continues this volume.

NOTE. The above headpiece shows us the interior of the famous CHURCH OF ST. SOPHIA, built at Constantinople by Justinian from A.D. 532 to 537. The first church on this spot was of the usual basilica form, but Justinian's architects preferred an Oriental dome. They therefore roofed the great church with a gigantic dome, 183 feet high at the center, sweeping clear across the

nations along the Mediterranean. We recall how the Gauls overwhelmed northern Italy, even capturing Rome, and how they then overflowed into the Balkan Peninsula and Asia Minor. We remember the terror at Rome when the Germans first came down, and how they were defeated only by a supreme effort under the skillful soldier Marius.

Roman army disorganized; the barbarians raid the Empire

1157. By superior organization the Romans had been able to feed and to keep together at a given point for a long time a larger number of troops than the barbarians. This was the secret of Cæsar's success against them. During the century of revolution after the reign of Marcus Aurelius, Roman army organization had gone to pieces, and the barbarians raided the lands of the Empire without hindrance. After such raids they commonly withdrew. By the time of Diocletian, however, they were beginning to form permanent settlements within the limits of the Empire, and there followed two centuries of barbarian migration in the course of which they took possession of the entire Western Mediterranean world.

German peoples at home

1158. The Germans were a fair-haired, blue-eyed race of men of towering stature and terrible strength. In their native forests of the north each German people or nation occupied a very limited area, probably not over forty miles across, and in numbers such a people had not usually more than twenty-five or thirty thousand souls. They lived in villages, each of about a hundred families, and there was a head man over each village. Their homes were but slight huts, easily moved. They had little interest in

audience room and producing the most imposing vaulted interior now surviving from the ancient world. Justinian is said to have expended 18 tons of gold and the labor of 10,000 men in the erection of the building. Since the capture of Constantinople by the Turks (A.D. 1453) the vast church has served as a Mohammedan mosque. The gorgeous mosaics with which the magnificent interior was adorned were covered with whitewash and modern decorative designs, and large circular shields bearing the monogram of the Sultan were hung against the walls. Under the enlightened rule of Ghazi Mustafa Kemal permission has been granted for cleaning these Christian mosaics, and the work is now being carried on by American archæologists, with very important results. (See Fig. 269.)

farming the fringe of fields around the village, much preferring their herds, and they shifted their homes often. They possessed no writing and very little in the way of industries, manufactures, or commerce. A group of noble families furnished the leaders (dukes), or sometimes kings, governing the whole people.

German peoples in migration and war

1159. Hardened to wind and weather in their raw northern climate, they yielded to their native fearlessness and love of war and plunder, which often led them to wander, followed by their wives and families in heavy wagons. An entire people might comprise some fifty villages, but each village group remained together, protected by its body of about a hundred warriors, the heads of the village families. When combined, these hundreds made up an army of five or six thousand men. Each hundred held together in battle, as a fighting unit. They all knew each other; the village head man, the leader of the group, had always lived with them; the warrior in the tumult of battle saw all about him his friends and relatives, the sons of his brothers, the husbands of his daughters. In spite of lack of discipline these fighting groups of a hundred men, united by such ties of blood and daily association, formed battle units as terrible as any ever seen in the ancient world. Their eager joy in battle and the untamed fierceness of their onset made them irresistible.

Germans permitted to settle in the Empire and to serve in the army

1160. The highly organized and carefully disciplined Roman legions, which had gained for Rome the leadership of the world, were now no more. Legions made up of the peace-softened townsmen of Diocletian's time, even if they had existed, would have given way before the German fighting groups as chaff is driven before the wind. Hopeless of being able to drive the Germans back, the emperors had allowed them to settle within the frontiers. Indeed, the lack of men for the army had long since led the emperors to hire the Germans as soldiers, and Julius Cæsar's cavalry had been largely barbarian. A more serious step was the admission of *entire*

German peoples to live in the Empire in their accustomed manner. The men were then received into the Roman army; but they remained under their own German leaders and they fought in their old village units, for it was only as the Roman army was made up of the German fighting units that it had any effectiveness. Barbarian life, customs, and manners were thus introduced into the Empire, and the Roman army as a whole was barbarian. At the same time the German leaders of such troops were recognized as Roman officers.

Chief German peoples; Julian defeats them at Strassburg

1161. Along the lower Rhine there lived under a king a powerful group of German peoples called the Franks. The Vandals, also in the north, had long borne an evil reputation for their destructive raids. South of them the Alemanni had frequently moved over the frontiers, and on the lower Danube the Goths were a constant danger. Constantine's nephew Julian had gained a fierce battle against the Germans at Strassburg (A.D. 357), and had thus stopped the Franks and Alemanni at the Rhine. He established his headquarters at Paris, where he still continued to read his beloved books in the midst of the campaign. The philosopher-emperor's stay at Paris, almost sixteen centuries ago, for the first time brought clearly into history that important city of future Europe.

German peoples gain some civilization; writing and Christianity

1162. This constant commingling of the German peoples with the civilized communities of the Empire was gradually softening their northern wildness and giving them not only familiarity with civilization but also a respect for it. Their leaders, who held office under the Roman government, came to have friends among highborn Romans. Such leaders sometimes married educated Roman women of rank, even close relatives of the emperors. Some of them, too, were converted to Christianity. An educated Goth named Ulfilas translated the New Testament into Gothic, a language akin to German. As the Germanic peoples possessed no writing, he was obliged to devise an alphabet from Greek and Latin for writing Gothic. He thus produced the earliest surviving example of a written Germanic tongue and aided in converting the northern peoples to Christianity.

Romans defeated at Adrianople; a century of barbaric migrations

1163. At this juncture barbarians of another race, having no Indo-European blood in their veins, had been penetrating Europe from Asia. These people were the Huns. They were the most destructive of all the barbarian invaders. They pushed down upon the lower Danube, and the West Goths (often called Visigoths), fleeing before them, begged the Romans for permission to cross the Danube and settle in the Empire. Valens, who had followed Julian as emperor of the East, gave them permission to do so. Thereupon friction between them and the Roman officials caused them to revolt. In the battle which ensued at Adrianople (A.D. 378), although the Goths could not have had an army of over fifteen thousand men, the Romans—or, rather, the Germans fighting for them — were defeated, and the emperor Valens himself was killed. Henceforth the helplessness of the Roman Empire was evident to all the world. This movement of the West Goths and the battle of Adrianople were the beginning of a century of continuous migration in which the Western Empire was slowly absorbed by the barbarians and broken up into German kingdoms under German military leaders.

Theodosius (A.D. 379–395) restores the Empire

1164. Theodosius, who succeeded Valens at Constantinople, was the last of the great emperors to unite and rule the whole Roman Empire. He came to an understanding with the West Goths, allowing them to settle where they were, taking them into his army, and giving their leaders important posts in the government. But it was only by using the able and energetic Germans themselves as his ministers and commanders that he was able to maintain his empire. He even gave his niece in marriage to his leading military commander, a Vandal named Stilicho; and at his death, in A.D. 395, Theodosius intrusted to this able German the care of his two young sons, Honorius and Arcadius.

1165. Theodosius divided the Empire between these two youths, giving to Arcadius the East and to Honorius the West. The Empire was never to be united again. Indeed, after the appearance of these two young emperors the dismemberment of the Western Empire went rapidly forward, and in two generations resulted in the disappearance of both the western emperor and his Empire (see map, p. 770).

Division of empire at death of Theodosius (A.D. 395)

1166. From the Danube and the Rhine the movement of the barbarians southward and westward went on. Led by their king, Alaric, the West Goths first pushed down from the Danube into the Balkan Peninsula and advanced plundering into Greece, where they even took Athens. Here the German Stilicho, leading German troops, confronted the German (Gothic) invasion and forced it back. Driving their wagons piled high with the plunder of Greece, Alaric led his West Goths into Illyricum, where Arcadius made him official commander. When the faithful Stilicho had been executed on a charge of treason by Honorius, there was no one to oppose Alaric in his invasion of Italy. In A.D. 410 the emperor of the West was thus obliged to look on helplessly while the Gothic host captured and plundered Rome itself.[1] Indeed, when the West Goths, after the death of Alaric, retired from Italy into southwestern Gaul, and later into Spain, Honorius was obliged to recognize the West Gothic kingdom which they set up there (see map, p. 770).

West Goths invade Greece, take Rome (A.D. 410), and settle in Gaul

1167. While these movements of the West Goths were going on after A.D. 400, the Vandals and two other German peoples had crossed the Rhine and, advancing through Gaul, had penetrated into Spain, where these three peoples now set up three German kingdoms. These kingdoms, like that of the West Goths in Spain, acknowledged that they were vassals of Honorius as emperor of the West. Not long after

Vandal kingdoms in Spain and in Africa; Burgundians in Gaul

[1] Not long after 400 B.C. Rome was captured by the *Gauls* (§ 855), and a few years after A.D. 400 it was captured by the *Goths*.

their settlement in Spain the Vandals sailed across the Strait of Gibraltar and seized the Roman province of Africa (A.D. 429). The African kingdom of the Vandals was likewise recognized by the western emperor. A little later the German Burgundians had pushed in beside the West Goths and set up a kingdom in southeastern Gaul.

Western Empire loses Britain and dwindles to Italy

1168. Meantime German peoples located along the North Sea had taken to the water and were landing in the island of Britain. While Alaric was sacking Rome the last Roman soldiers were being withdrawn from the island, and within a generation afterward the German tribes of the Angles and Saxons were setting up kingdoms there which did not acknowledge the sovereignty of Rome. A rival emperor in Gaul was obliged to let the island go, nor could the feeble emperor of the West, in Italy, ever recover it. He was equally helpless as far as any real power over the western German kingdoms was concerned. Within a generation after A.D. 400 the Western Empire had therefore dwindled to Italy itself, and even there the emperor of the West was entirely in the hands of his German officials and commanders.

West invaded by Huns; Rome taken by Vandals (A.D. 455)

1169. In this condition of weakness Italy was subjected to two more serious invasions. The Eastern Empire had not been able to control the Huns who had forced the West Goths across the Danube. For two generations since then the kingdom of the Huns had steadily grown in power, until their king, Attila, governed an empire extending from southern Russia to the Rhine. He laid the Eastern Empire under tribute, and by A.D. 450 he and his terrible barbarian host were sweeping down upon Italy in the most destructive invasion which the south ever suffered. The West Goths, with other western Germans, however, rallied to the assistance of the western emperor against the common enemy, and in a terrible battle at Châlons, in France, Attila was defeated in A.D. 451. He retreated eastward, and two years later, as he was invading Italy, he died. The Hunnish empire fell to pieces, never to trouble Europe again. Hardly had Rome thus escaped when the Vandals crossed over from Carthage to Sicily and Italy, and in A.D. 455 they captured Rome. Although they carried off great quantities of spoil, they spared the magnificent buildings of the city, as Alaric and his West Goths had also done forty-five years earlier (see map, p. 770).

Last emperor at Rome displaced by German leader Odoacer (A.D. 476)

1170. In Italy (all that was left of the Western Empire) the German military leaders possessed all the power and made and unmade emperors as they pleased. But these *seeming* emperors of the West were now to disappear. By a remarkable coincidence the last to bear the title was called Romulus Augustulus, that is, Romulus, "the little Augustus." He thus bore the names both of the legendary founder of Rome itself and of the founder of the Roman Empire. He was quietly set aside by the German soldiery, who put Odoacer, one of their number, in his place. Thus, in A.D. 476, two generations after Theodosius, the last of the western emperors disappeared. The line of emperors at Rome therefore ended a little over five hundred years after it had been established by Augustus. The German leaders in Italy sent word to the eastern emperor at Constantinople that they acknowledged the sovereignty of the eastern emperor, who then authorized Odoacer to rule with the title of "patrician."

East Gothic kingdom established in Italy by Theodoric

1171. Meantime another great migration of the barbarians again altered the situation in the West. An eastern branch of the Goths, whom we call, therefore, the East Goths (Ostrogoths), had remained along the Danube for two generations after their kindred the West Goths had departed. Then they also shifted westward and southward into Italy, where, in A.D. 493, their king Theodoric the Great displaced Odoacer and made himself king of a strong East Gothic kingdom in Italy. Although he was unable even to read, Theodoric was a wise and highly civilized ruler, and under him Italy began to recover from her misfortunes. His power finally included, besides Italy and Sicily, part of Gaul and Spain; and at one time it seemed that the Western Empire was about to be restored under a German emperor. Such a restoration of the West was prevented, however, by the rise of Justinian, the last of the great emperors of the East at Constantinople.

FIG. 264. HALL *of an* EGYPTIAN TEMPLE *altered into a Christian Church*

After Theodosius closed the temples of the old gods, over fifteen hundred years ago, they were gradually forsaken, or the huts and sun-dried brick hovels of the poor were crowded into them. In some cases a temple hall was converted into a Christian church, as in the Luxor Temple at Thebes in Egypt. The arched niche that we see here was cut into the wall for the pulpit of the preacher. The pagan relief scenes on the walls were covered with plaster on which Christian saints were painted. This Christian plaster, visible just at the left of the left-hand column, has now largely fallen off, and (still farther to the left) the pictures of the old Egyptian gods have emerged again, to find their former worshipers all vanished

Justinian's partial reconquest of the West

1172. After the death of Theodosius (A.D. 395) the Eastern Empire had been under the rule of weaklings. But Justinian, who was crowned at Constantinople in A.D. 527, only a generation after the rise of Theodoric, was a gifted and energetic ruler. His dream was the restoration of the united Empire. With the aid of his able general Belisarius he endeavored to reconquer the West. Belisarius overthrew the Vandal kingdom in the province of Africa and then passed over into Italy, where he finally crushed the kingdom of the East Goths. Although disturbed by a serious revolt in Italy, the eastern emperor's authority was restored in Italy, Sicily, Africa, and southern Spain. But Justinian showed very poor judgment in supposing that the Eastern Empire possessed the power again to rule the whole Mediterranean world. His destruction of the East Gothic kingdom in Italy left the peninsula helpless before the next wave of barbaric migration, nor were his successors able to maintain his conquests.

1173. But if political unity failed, the emperor's large plans did succeed in establishing a great judicial or legal unity. He employed a very able lawyer named Tribonian to gather together all the numerous laws which had grown up in the career of Rome since the age of the Twelve Tablets (§ 842), a thousand years before. Justinian was the Hammurapi of the Roman Empire, and the vast body of laws which he collected represented the administrative experience of the most successful rulers of the ancient world. Almost every situation arising in social life, in business transactions, or in legal proceedings had been met and settled by Roman judges. The collection of their decisions by Justinian was called a digest. Justinian's Digest became the foundation of law for later ages, and still remains so to a large extent in the government of the civilized peoples of today.

Justinian's code compiled

1174. Under Justinian, Constantinople enjoyed wide recognition, and the emperor gave lavishly for its beautification. But it was no longer for the erection of temples to the old gods, or for basilicas and amphitheaters, that he gave his wealth. The old world of Greek civilization had received its last support from Julian, two centuries earlier. Theodosius, the last emperor to rule the entire Empire, had forbidden the worship of the old gods and issued a decree closing all their temples. Since A.D. 400 the splendid temples of the gods, fringing the Mediterranean and extending far up the Nile, had been deserted and desolate as they are today, or had been altered for use as Christian churches. The last blow to what the church regarded as Greek paganism was now struck by Justinian, who closed the schools of philosophy forming the university at Athens. The buildings

End of old temples

A

B

Fig. 265. Comparison *of Oriental* Wall Paintings *of* a.d. 100 *from Dura, on the Euphrates* (A), *with Sixth-Century* Mosaics *of Justinian at Ravenna* (B) *

to which the emperor now devoted his wealth were churches. The vast church of Saint Sophia, which he built at Constantinople, still stands, the most magnificent of the early churches of the East (headpiece, p. 766).

1175. The Christian church carried over into its life and its outward forms the old Oriental civilization out of which it had come. Justinian's great church of St. Sophia, as we have already seen, was roofed with a dome of the old Babylonian type. Its interior walls were originally decorated with pictures of the saints and apostles and the Holy Family, which any Oriental would have considered to be his ancient gods; for each of the figures had painted in bright gold, behind its head, a shining disk, or *aureole*, the halo worn by the Oriental gods as we have seen them worshiped by the Roman soldiers doing garrison duty on the Euphrates. Even as far west as Italy the arrangement and style of the figures in such church paintings clearly disclose Oriental influence of the later period called Byzantine, after "Byzantium," the old Greek name of Constantinople (see Fig. 265). An essential usage of the church service was the burning of incense, which had lifted the prayers of the priests upward to the sky-gods in the temples of Egypt three thousand years before Christ. Finally, the Christian religion itself was of Oriental origin, and its movement westward was but a part and a continuation of that enormously old westward drift of civilization of which we have now seen so many evidences.

Oriental civilization in the church

---

* The painting (*A*) shows at the right five members of a noble family of Dura, and at the left three officiating priests of *Zeus-Baal*. All eight figures are grouped in a long row across the observer's line of vision. Each figure faces straight ahead. The bodies are balanced with the weight on the left foot and both feet turned out. The position of the feet (one sometimes resting on the other) shows that the feet do not touch the floor, and the figures seem to float in the air like phantoms. There is a crowding and a complete disregard of spatial relations. The mosaic (*B*), below, displays the same grouping of the figures of the emperor Justinian and his attendants conducting a *Christian* ceremony in company with the bishop Maximian and priestly officiants. Here we observe the same characteristics as at Dura. If the two pictures are studied closely, the many similarities show that the Dura paintings are the ancestors of the Ravenna mosaics. When, therefore, the Dura paintings were recovered by the Oriental Institute of The University of Chicago in 1920, the lost Oriental ancestry of Byzantine art, and therefore of early Christian art, was disclosed.

1176. Just as the church of St. Sophia shows its Oriental origin in its architecture, so did the teachings of the church in the Eastern Empire. The efforts of Justinian to unite East and West failed to a large extent because of the jealousy of the Oriental churches and the power of the Western Church. A division was therefore steadily developing between the Eastern (Greek) Church and the Western (Latin) Church; for while the dismemberment of the Western Empire, which we have followed, was still going on, there was arising at Rome an emperor of the church, who was in no small degree the heir to the lost power of the western emperor. As there had been an Empire of the East and an Empire of the West, so there were to be also a Church of the East and a Church of the West. To the Western Church we must now turn.

Division of church into East and West

Section 97. The Triumph of the Roman Church and its Power over the Western Nations

1177. The venerable city of Rome, with its long centuries as mistress of the world behind it, had gained a position of unique respect and veneration even among the barbarians. The Goths and the Vandals had stood in awe and reverence under the shadow of its magnificent public buildings. They had left them uninjured, and in all its monumental splendor Rome was still the greatest city of the world, rivaled only by Constantinople and Alexandria, the two other imperial cities. It was natural that the bishop of Rome should occupy a position of unusual power and respect. When the West Goths were threatening the city, and also in other important crises caused by the incoming of the barbarians, the bishop of Rome had more than once shown an ability which made him the leading statesman of Italy, if not of the West. There is no doubt that his influence had much to do with the respect which the West Goths and the Vandals had shown the city in sparing its buildings.

Unique position of Rome and of the bishop of Rome

Map Plate, Patented July 5, 1921 • Method of Making Maps, Patented July 5, 1921

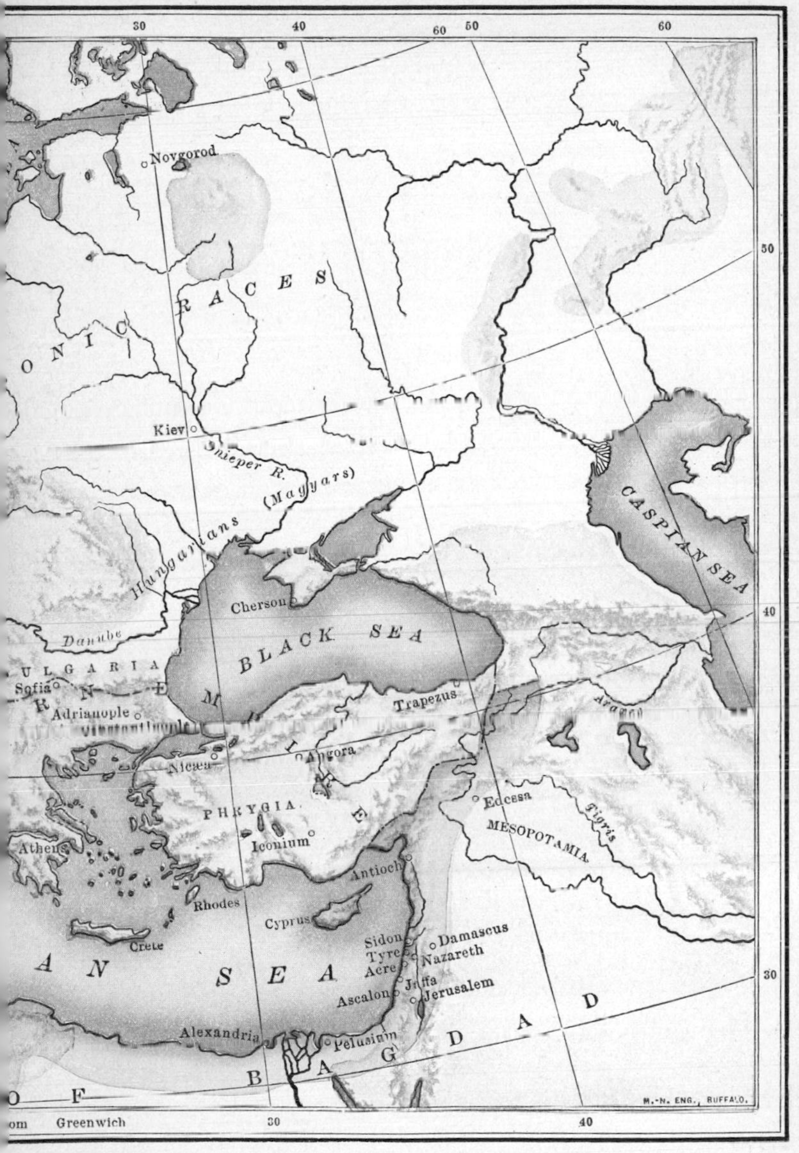

Novgorod
ONIC RACES
Kiev
Dnieper R.
(Magyars)
Hungarians
Danube
BULGARIA
Sofia
Adrianople
Cherson
BLACK SEA
CASPIAN SEA
Trapezus
Angora
Nicaea
PHRYGIA
Iconium
Athens
Rhodes
Crete
Cyprus
Antioch
Edessa
Tigris
MESOPOTAMIA
Sidon
Tyre
Acre
Damascus
Nazareth
Jaffa
Jerusalem
Ascalon
Alexandria
Pelusium
AN SEA
BAGDAD
M.-N. ENG., BUFFALO.
Greenwich

1178. At the same time the church throughout the West had early produced able men. This was especially true in Africa, the province behind Carthage, where the leading early Christian writers had appeared. The bishop of Carthage was soon a serious rival of the bishop of Rome, and their rivalry in Christian times curiously reminds us of the long-past struggle between the two powerful cities. Here in Africa in the days of Theodosius, Augustine (A.D. 354–430), the greatest of the thinkers of the early church, had arisen. Not at first a Christian, the young Augustine had been devoted to Greek philosophy and learning. At the same time he gave way to evil habits and uncontrolled self-indulgence. As he gained a vision of spiritual self-denial his faithful Christian mother, Monica, followed him through all the tremendous struggle and distress of mind from which he emerged at last into a triumphant conquest of his lower nature and the devotion of his whole soul to Christianity. In a volume of *Confessions* he told the story, which soon became the never-failing guide of the tempted in the Christian church. Along with the *Meditations* of Marcus Aurelius it belongs among the most precious revelations of the inner life of a great man which we have inherited.

Early rise of influential men in the African church: Augustine

1179. In the days after Alaric had plundered Rome, when earthly government seemed to totter, Augustine also wrote a great treatise which he called *The City of God*, meaning the government of God. Opposed to the governments of this world and superior to them, he pictured an invisible kingdom of God, to which all Christian believers belonged. But this invisible kingdom was, after all, hardly distinguished by Augustine from the visible organized church, with its bishops and priests. To the authority of this eternal kingdom — that is, to the authority of the church — all believers were urged by Augustine to submit without reservation. In the teaching of Augustine, therefore, the church gained complete control over the beliefs of men. This was at the very same time when the Edict of Theodosius was closing the temples of the

Augustine's *City of God*; church and state end free thought

old gods. The state was thus assuming the power to suppress all other beliefs, and henceforth it maintained its power over both the bodies and the minds of its subjects. In accordance with this idea Justinian had closed the university at Athens in order to stop freedom of thought and the teaching of the old philosophy. To the authority of the state over the beliefs of its people Augustine added the authority of the church. Thus ended all intellectual liberty in the ancient world.

Growing power of the church of Rome

1180. Augustine, moreover, recognized the leadership of the church at Rome, and thus added his influence to a tendency already long felt by all. For it was widely believed that Christ had conferred great power in the church upon the Apostle Peter. Although it was known that Paul had also worked in Rome, early tradition told how Peter had founded the church there and become its bishop. It was also widely held that Peter had transferred his authority to his successors as bishops at Rome. Tradition thus aided in establishing the supremacy of the Roman bishop.

Missionary monks extend the power of the Roman church in the north

1181. As increasing numbers of men withdrew from worldly occupations and gathered in communities, called monasteries, to lead holy lives or to help carry the Christian faith to the northern barbarians, these beliefs regarding the church of Rome went with them. Such monks, as they were called, taught the barbarians that the church also had power over the life hereafter. Dreading frightful punishments beyond the grave, the superstitious peoples of the north submitted readily to such influences, and the church gained enormous power over the barbarians. It was a power wielded more and more exclusively by the bishop of Rome.

Value of the influence of the church over the barbarians

1182. When the power of the Roman Empire was no longer able to restrain the barbarians, the influence of the church held them in check. The church gradually softened and modified the fierce instincts of barbarian kings ruling over barbarian peoples. The barrier of Roman organization and of Roman legions which had protected Mediterranean civilization had given way; but the church, taking its place, made possible the transference of power from the Roman Empire to the barbarians in the West, without the complete destruction of our heritage of civilization bequeathed us by Greece and Rome.

1183. Less than a generation after the death of Justinian a gifted bishop of Rome named Gregory, commonly called Gregory the Great, showed himself to be a statesman of such wisdom and ability that he firmly established the leadership of the Roman church. Italy, left defenseless by Justinian's destruction of the East Gothic kingdom, was thereupon invaded by the Lombards ("Longbeards"), the least civilized of all the German barbarians, who easily took possession of the Po valley. The Lombards were divided into small and rather weak communities. Thus the fallen Western Empire was not followed by a powerful and enduring nation in Italy, and this gave to the bishops of Rome the opportunity, so well used by Gregory, to make themselves the leaders of Italy. It was this great church ruler, also, who sent missionary monks to Britain and thus established Christianity in England two centuries after the Roman legions had left it.

Gregory the Great, bishop of Rome (A.D. 590–604)

1184. The influence of the Roman church was likewise extended among the powerful Franks, a group of German tribes on the lower Rhine. Their king, Clovis, accepted Christianity not long before A.D. 500. He succeeded in welding together the Frankish tribes, and the kingdom he left had been steadily growing for over a century before Gregory's time. After Gregory's death this Frankish kingdom included a large part of western Europe, embracing, besides western Germany, the countries which we now call Holland, Belgium, and France. By the middle of the Sixth Century the Frankish kings had fallen under the influence of a family of their own powerful household stewards called "Mayors of the Palace," who at last really held the ruling power, though in the name of the king. After A.D. 700 the Mayor of the Palace, who actually governed the great Frankish kingdom, was Charles Martel. He

Rise of Franks; "Mayors of the Palace"

saved Europe from being overrun by the Moslems (A.D. 732), and his descendants became the greatest kings of the Franks.

Charlemagne's alliance with the Pope; his coronation (A.D. 800)

1185. By combining with the bishop of Rome, whom we may now call the Pope, the new Frankish kings gained the dominion of western Europe. They assisted the Pope by subduing the unruly Lombards in Italy, and conquered a large part of modern Germany, besides northern Spain. Charlemagne, the grandson of Charles Martel, ruled an empire consisting of western Germany, France, Italy, and northern Spain. He was the most powerful European sovereign of his time, and in A.D. 800 he was crowned by the Pope at Rome as Roman emperor, theoretically supposed to succeed the line of emperors headed by Augustus. The emperor Charlemagne was an enlightened ruler who desired to do all that he could for the education and well-being of his people. The civilization which he tried to spread, although it was very limited, was what was left of old Roman life and organization, which had been preserved largely through the influence of the church.

Preservation of Latin literature by the church

1186. The church had been founded in the beginning chiefly among the lowly and the ignorant. It had originally been without higher Greek civilization, learning, and art. Gradually it gained also these things, as men like Augustine arose. It is chiefly to the libraries of the monks in the monasteries, and to their practice of copying ancient literary works, that we owe the preservation of such Latin literature as has survived. Today our oldest and most important copies of such things as Virgil's Æneid are manuscripts written on parchment, which were preserved in the libraries of the Christian monks.

Basilica church and its Oriental ancestor

1187. Art was slow to rise among early Christians, and for a thousand years or more there were no Christian painters or sculptors to be compared with those of Greece. On the other hand, the need for places of sacred assembly led to the rise of great architects among the early Christians. Influenced chiefly by the old business basilica, they devised noble and impressive

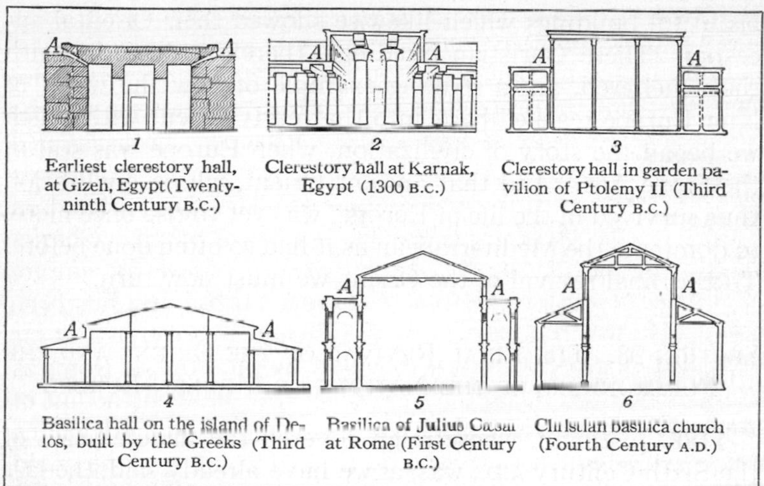

1 Earliest clerestory hall, at Gizeh, Egypt (Twenty-ninth Century B.C.)

2 Clerestory hall at Karnak, Egypt (1300 B.C.)

3 Clerestory hall in garden pavilion of Ptolemy II (Third Century B.C.)

4 Basilica hall on the island of Delos, built by the Greeks (Third Century B.C.)

5 Basilica of Julius Cæsar at Rome (First Century B.C.)

6 Christian basilica church (Fourth Century A.D.)

FIG. 266. *The* BASILICA CHURCH *and its Oriental Ancestors*

A central aisle with roof windows (*A*) in the side walls, forming a clerestory and occupying the difference in level between the higher roof over the central aisle (nave) and the lower roof over the side aisles, with a resulting division of the building into three aisles, — this arrangement is the chief characteristic of the basilica cathedral. We found the earliest hint of such an arrangement at the pyramids of Gizeh, shown in cross section above (*1*). Its clerestory windows (*AA*), built in the Twenty-ninth Century B.C., were mere light chutes. In the course of fifteen hundred years these light chutes were developed by the Egyptian architects into tall, stately clerestory windows, as at Karnak (*2, AA*). The Hellenistic architect, working in Egypt, adopted the old Egyptian arrangement of a high roof in the middle and a lower roof on each side for the garden pavilion of Ptolemy II (*3, AA*). In the same age the Greeks adopted the form and combined it with their sloping roofs, as shown here in a business hall excavated by the French on the island of Delos (*4, AA*). It was the Greeks who gave this form of hall its name "basilica." In Rome it was in use in the Second Century B.C. in the Forum, and we have put in the above series the great basilica of Julius Cæsar (*5*). Finally, these business basilica halls of the Greeks and Romans influenced the early Christian architects to adopt a similar form for their churches (*6*). We thus have an architectural development of some thirty-four hundred years leading from the early Near East, nearly 3000 B.C., to the Christian churches of the Fourth Century A.D.

assembly rooms for the early congregations in the days of Constantine. In Fig. 266 we can trace the architectural development from the earliest known clerestory at the pyramids of Gizeh to the Christian basilica church or cathedral. Thus the faith of Jesus, an Oriental teacher, was sheltered in beautiful buildings which likewise showed their Oriental ancestry. These Christian buildings, therefore, like the faith they sheltered, are a striking example of how the world of later Europe reached back into that early Orient with which we began the story of civilization, when Europe was still in the Stone Age. And that ancient Orient, whose civilization thus survived in the life of Europe, was yet to rise once more, to dominate the Mediterranean as it had so often done before. To this final revival of the Orient we must now turn.

Section 98. The Final Revival of the Orient and the Forerunners of the Nations of Modern Europe

Decline of the Eastern Empire after Justinian

1188. Justinian, whose reign covered the middle years of the Sixth Century A.D., was, as we have already said, the last great ruler of the Eastern Empire. His endeavors to reunite the Empire and to adorn his capital both proved very disastrous. He spent the strength of his Empire in trying to regain the West when he needed all his resources to defend himself against the New Persians, who assailed the eastern frontier in war after war. His great buildings, especially the magnificent church of Saint Sophia, required so much money that his treasury was emptied and the government was bankrupt. From the mistakes of Justinian the Eastern Empire never recovered, and at his death it entered upon an age of steady decline.

Invasion of Slavs; Eastern Empire no longer Roman

1189. Meantime a new invasion of barbarians was bringing in the Slavs, a non-German group of Indo-European peoples. They poured into the Balkan Peninsula to the gates of Constantinople and even down into Greece. They were soon holding much the same territory in these regions which they still occupy. Under these circumstances the Eastern Empire at Constantinople, although it was without interruption the direct descendant of the Roman Empire, was no longer Roman. The Eastern Empire became what it was in population and civilization, a mixed Greek-Slavic-Oriental state.

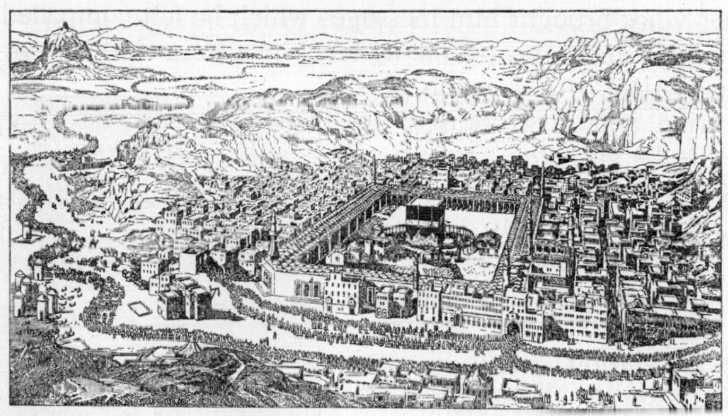

FIG. 267. *A Bird's-eye View of* MECCA *and its Mosque*

Mecca is one of the few towns in the barren Arabian peninsula; for by far the great majority of the Arabs live as roving shepherds and not in towns. Mecca had been a sacred place long before the time of Mohammed, and the people had been accustomed to come there as pilgrims, to do homage to a sacred black stone. Mohammed did not interfere with these customs. After his death the Moslems built a large court modeled on a colonnaded Greek market place. This structure was the simplest form of mosque. Over the black stone they erected a square shelter called the *Kaaba*, which we see in the middle of the mosque court. To this place the Moslem believers still come in great numbers every year as pilgrims. Our sketch shows an exaggerated representation of the procession of pilgrims. In his later years Mohammed lived at Medina, over 200 miles north of Mecca, and the pilgrims also visit his tomb there

Mohammed (A.D. 570–632); founding of Islam

1190. Moreover, a vast section of the eastern emperor's dominions lay in the Orient. Of these eastern dominions a large part was now about to be invaded and seized by a great Semitic migration like those which we have repeatedly seen as the nomads of the Arabian Desert were led by Sargon or the rulers of Hammurapi's line into Babylonia, or as the Hebrews swept in from the desert and seized the towns of Palestine. The last and the greatest movement of the Semitic barbarians was now about to take place. Not long after the death of Justinian there was born in Mecca in Arabia a remarkably gifted lad named Mohammed. As he grew up he believed, like so many Semitic teachers, that a commanding voice spoke within him as he wandered in the wilderness. This inner voice brought him messages which he felt compelled to communicate to his people as teachings from God, whom he called *Allah.* After much persecution and great danger to his life he gathered a group of faithful followers about him; and when he died, in A.D. 632, he had established a new religion among the Arabs, which he had called *Islam*, meaning "reconciliation," that is, reconciliation to Allah, the sole God. The new believers he had called *Muslims*, or, as we spell it, Moslems, meaning "the reconciled." By us they are often called Mohammedans, after their prophet. After Mohammed's death the Moslem leaders gathered together his teachings, till then uncollected, and copied them to form a book called the Koran, the Bible of the Moslems.

FIG. 268. *A Page of a Manuscript Copy of the* KORAN

This writing has descended from the ancient alphabet of the Phœnicians, and, like it, is still written and read from right to left. The Arab writers love to give it decorative flourishes, producing a handsome page. The rich decorative border is a good example of Moslem art. The whole page was done by hand. In such hand-written books as these the educated Moslems wrote out translations of the books of the great Greek philosophers and scientists, like Aristotle; for example, one of the most valuable of the books of Ptolemy, the Greek astronomer (§ 1098), and of Hero, the great physicist, we now possess only in Arabic translations. At the same time the Moslems wrote their own treatises on algebra, astronomy, grammar, and other sciences in similar books, to which the West owes much

Rise of the Oriental empire of the Moslems

1191. The leaders who inherited the power of Mohammed were called *caliphs*, a word meaning "substitute." As rulers they proved to be men of the greatest ability. They organized the untamed desert nomads, who now added a burning religious zeal to the wild courage of barbarian Arabs. This combination made the Arab armies of the

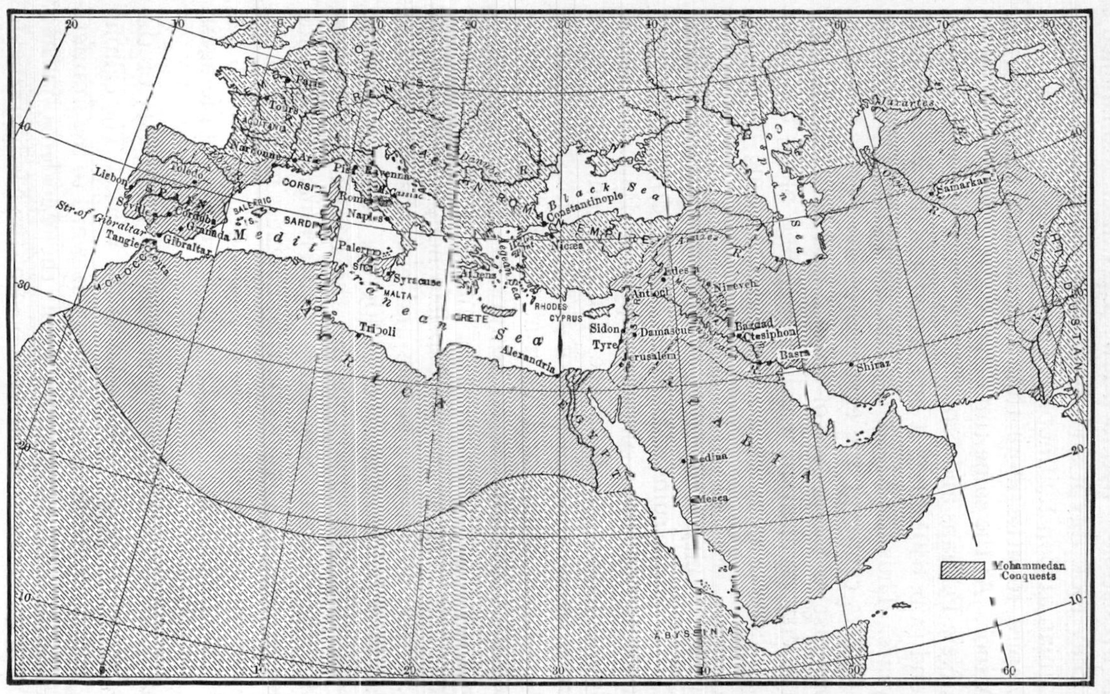

The MOHAMMEDAN CONQUESTS at their Greatest Extent, about the Year 750 (indicated by Oblique Shading, Unbroken Lines)

caliphs irresistible. Within a few years after Mohammed's death they took Egypt and Syria from the feeble successors of Justinian at Constantinople. They thus reduced the Eastern Empire to little more than the Balkan Peninsula and Asia Minor. At the same time the Arabs crushed the empire of the New Persians and brought the Sassanian line of kings to an end (A.D. 640), after it had lasted a little over four hundred years. Thus the Moslems built up a great Oriental empire, with its center at the east end of the Fertile Crescent.

Moslem Arabs learn city civilization along the Fertile Crescent

1192. Just as the people of Sargon and Hammurapi took over the city civilization which they found along the lower Euphrates, so now in the same region the Moslem Arabs of the desert took over the city civilization of the New Persians. With the ruins of Babylon looking down upon them the Moslems built their splendid capital at Baghdad, beside the New Persian royal residence of Ctesiphon. They built, of course, under the influence of the ancient structures of Egypt, Babylon, Persia, and Assyria. The Babylonian tower-temples or Christian church towers of similar character showed them the first models of the minarets with which they adorned their mosques, as the Moslem houses of prayer are called. Here, as Sargon's people and also the Persians had done so long before, the once wandering Arabs learned to read and write, and could thus put the Koran into writing. Here, too, they learned the business of government and became experienced rulers. Thus beside the shapeless mounds of the older capitals, Akkad, Babylon, Seleucia, and Ctesiphon, the power and civilization of the Orient rose into new life again for the last time.

Moslems advance westward; battle of Tours (A.D. 732)

1193. Eventually Baghdad became the finest city of the East and one of the most splendid in the world. The caliphs extended their power eastward to the frontiers of India. Westward the Moslems pushed along the African coast of the Mediterranean, as their Phœnician kindred had done before them. It was the Moslem overthrow of Carthage and its bishop which now

FIG. 269. *Newly* UNCOVERED MOSAICS *in the* CHURCH OF ST. SOPHIA *showing the* EMPEROR OF THE EASTERN *(or Byzantine)* EMPIRE *kneeling in Adoration before* CHRIST

This scene is one of the Christian mosaics recently uncovered by the Byzantine Institute of America in the mosque-church of St. Sophia, at Istanbul (note, p. 767). The emperor is probably Leo VI (A.D. 886–912), identified by the likeness of the face to his image as found on coins, as well as by his costume, a description of which, made by his own son, is still extant. The book in the hand of the Christ is represented as open and facing us. The inscription reads: "Peace be with you. I am the Light of the World." The magnificent throne shows clearly its descent from New Persian originals. The beautiful coloring of the bits of glass and marble and the gold and silver cubes composing these mosaics, as well as the artistic excellence of the composition, confirm the importance of this contribution to the history of art resulting from the baring of the Byzantine mosaics in St. Sophia. (Courtesy of Mr. Thomas Whittemore and the Byzantine Institute)

relieved the bishop of Rome (the Pope) of his only dangerous rival in the West. Only two generations after the death of Mohammed the Arabs crossed over from Africa into Spain (A.D. 711). As they moved on into France they threatened to girdle the entire Mediterranean. At the battle of Tours (A.D. 732), however, just a hundred years after the death of Mohammed, the Moslems were unable to crush the Frankish army under Charles Martel. They withdrew permanently from France into Spain, where they established a western Moslem kingdom which we call Moorish. The magnificent buildings which it left behind are the most splendid in Spain today.

Leadership of Moslem civilization

1194. The Moorish kingdom developed a civilization far higher than that of the Franks, and indeed the highest of that age in Europe. Thus while Europe was sinking into the ignorance of the Middle Ages the Moslems were the leading students of science, astronomy, mathematics, and grammar. There was soon much greater knowledge of these matters among the Moslems than in Christian Europe. Such Arabic words as *algebra* and the written form of our numerals, which we received from the Arabs, suggest to us how much we owe to them.

Emergence of the forerunners of the nations of modern Europe

1195. As we look out over this final world situation we see, lying in the middle, the remnant of the Roman Empire ruled by Constantinople, holding little more than the Balkan Peninsula and Asia Minor, while on one side was the lost West, made up of the German kingdoms of the former northern barbarians, and on the other side was the lost East, then part of the great Oriental empire of the caliphs of Baghdad. Looking at Europe without the East, we discover that there was at its western end a *Moslem* Oriental kingdom (the Moors), while at its eastern end there was a *Christian* Oriental state (Constantinople). Between these lay chiefly the German states, later to be consolidated into the empire of Charlemagne, with vast masses of Slavs on the east of it and detached German peoples in the outlying island of Britain. Out of these fragments of the Roman Empire and the newly formed nations of the north the nations of modern Europe came forth. In France and the two southern peninsulas of Spain and Italy, Latin speech survived among the people, to become French, Spanish, Portuguese, and Italian, while in the island of Britain the German language spoken by the invading Angles and Saxons mingled with much Latin and French to form our own English speech, written with Roman letters inherited from Greece, Phœnicia, and Egypt.

1196. Thus Rome left her stamp on the peoples of Europe, still evident not only in the languages they use but also in many other important matters of life, and especially in law and government. In Roman law, still a power in modern government, we have the great creation of Roman genius, which has more profoundly affected the later world than any other Roman institution. Another great achievement of Rome was the universal spread of that international civilization brought forth by Greece under contact with the Orient. Rome gave to that civilization the far-reaching organization which under the Greeks it had lacked. That organization, though completely transformed into Oriental despotism, endured for five centuries and long withstood the barbarian invasions from the north, which would otherwise have overwhelmed the disorganized Greek world long before. The Roman state was the last bulwark of civilization intrenched on the Mediterranean against the Indo-European barbarians. But the bulwark, though shaken, did not fall solely, or even chiefly, because of hostile assaults from *without*: it fell chiefly because of decay within.

Surviving influences of Rome in later Europe

1197. Nor did it fall everywhere; for, as we have seen, a fragment of the vast Empire still survived in the East. The emperors ruling at Constantinople traced their predecessors back in an unbroken line to Augustus, and they ruled as his successors. Founded on the site of an ancient Greek city, lying in the midst of the Greek East, Constantinople had always been Greek in both language and civilization. But at the same time, as we have seen, it was largely Oriental also. Notwithstanding this, it never wholly lost the tradition of old Greek culture. Learning, even though of a mechanical type, never died out there as it did so completely in the West; nor did art ever fall so low. As Rome declined, Constantinople became the greatest and most splendid city of Europe,

Survival of a fragment of the Empire at Constantinople

exciting the admiration and surprise of all visitors from the less civilized West. Thus the last surviving fragment of the Empire, which by right of succession might still continue to call itself Roman, lived on for a thousand years after the Germans had completely conquered the West. Nor did the Germans ever gain Constantinople; for in 1453 this last remnant of the Roman Empire fell into the hands of the Turks, who have held it ever since.

SECTION 99. RETROSPECT

1198. Besides the internal decay of Rome and the triumph of the Christian church the other great outstanding feature of the last centuries of the Roman Empire was the incoming of the barbarians, with the result that while Mediterranean civilization steadily declined, it nevertheless slowly spread northward, especially under the influence of the church, till it transformed the ruder life of the north. There in the region of western and northern Europe, among the crumbling monuments of the Stone Age, Christian churches now began to rise. Books and civilized government, once found only along the Mediterranean, reached the northern shores of Europe, where grass and great forest trees were growing over the graves of the Stone Age Norsemen. What a vast sweep of the human career rises before our imagination as we picture the first church spires among the massive tombs of Stone Age men.

Northern Europe from fist-hatchet to Christian civilization

1199. We have watched early man all around the Mediterranean through thousands of years of Stone Age savagery and barbarism. Toward the end of that struggle we saw the first civilization emerging in the Orient. One by one the first great civilized nations stood forth and took their places as if to play their parts on the vast stage of the Near East extending around the eastern end of the Mediterranean, from the Nile, through Babylonia and Assyria, to the Hittites in Asia Minor.

Long struggle of civilization and barbarism

Then on the borders of the Orient, against this background of great Oriental civilizations, we saw the Stone Age Europeans of the Ægean receiving civilization from the Nile and thus developing a wonderful civilized world of their own.

Then we beheld that far-flung northern line of Indo-European migration, stretching from the Balkans to India, shifting slowly southward through the Highland Zone to overwhelm the Mediterranean and the Fertile Crescent. The *west* end of that Indo-European migration, made up of barbarian Greeks, swept down upon the remarkable Ægean civilization, the earliest in Europe, and destroyed it. Writing, art, architecture, and shipbuilding, which had arisen on the borders of southeastern Europe, passed away, and civilization in Europe perished at the hands of the Greek nomads from the north. Civilization would have been lost entirely had not the Orient, where it was born, now preserved it. Southeastern Europe, controlled by the Greeks, was therefore able to make another start, and from the Orient it again received writing, art, architecture, shipbuilding, and many other things which make up civilization.

After having thus halted civilization in Europe for over a thousand years, the Greeks left behind their early barbarism, and, developing a noble and beautiful culture of their own, they carried civilization to the highest level it ever attained. They checked the invasion of Europe by the *east* end of the Indo-European migration which had founded the Persian Empire, and, led by Alexander the Great, they destroyed the Persian Empire and carried Greek civilization to the borders of India. Then, as the Indo-European barbarians from the north again descended to the Mediterranean, Roman organization prevented civilization from being destroyed for the second time. Thus enough of the civilization which the Orient, the Greeks, and the Romans had built up was preserved, so that after long delay it rose again in Europe to become what we now find it.

1200. Today, marking the successive stages of that long career, the stone fist-hatchets lie deep in the river gravels of

Egypt and France; the furniture of the pile-villages rests at the bottom of the Swiss lakes; the majestic pyramids and temples announcing the dawn of civilization rise along the Nile; the silent and deserted city-mounds by the Tigris and Euphrates shelter their myriads of clay tablets; the palaces of Crete look out toward the sea they once ruled; the Hittite cities yield up the wonderful story of their newly deciphered writing; the noble temples and sculptures of Greece still proclaim the new world of beauty and freedom first revealed by the Greeks; the splendid Roman roads and aqueducts assert the supremacy and organized control of Rome; and the Christian churches proclaim the new ideal of human brotherhood. These things still reveal something of the fascinating trail along which our ancestors came, and in following that trail we have recovered portions of the earliest chapters in the marvelous human story which we call ancient history. But excavation and discovery must go on for generations, or more probably for centuries, before all the surviving evidences that reveal the human story are in our hands.

The trail which we have followed to recover ancient history

QUESTIONS

Section 96. Describe the German peoples at home; in migration and war. Describe the incoming of the West Goths and the results. Describe the two great barbarian invasions of Italy in the middle of the Fifth Century A.D., and the end of the line of emperors at Rome. Describe Justinian's Digest. What had happened to the old religions? What did Justinian do about Greek philosophy? Discuss the Oriental influences within the church. Describe the division of the church.

Section 97. Tell about Augustine and his writings. Describe the growing power of the church at Rome. Sketch the story of the Franks and their alliance with the bishop of Rome. What elements of culture had the church now gained? What form did early church architecture have, and whence did it come?

Section 98. Tell the story of Mohammed. What did his successors accomplish in civilization? in conquest? Describe briefly the world situation which resulted. What influences did the Roman Empire leave behind?

Section 99. Where did mankind first gain civilization? What happened when the Greeks came into Europe? Where was civilization then preserved? Who carried it to its highest level? By whom was it almost destroyed for the second time? What organization saved it?

BIBLIOGRAPHY FOR TOPICAL STUDIES

Roman law: ABBOTT, *Roman Politics*, pp. 95–103; BAYNES, *Byzantine Empire*, pp. 191–206; *Legacy of Rome*, pp. 173–181; SHOWERMAN, *Rome and the Romans*, pp. 503–522.

The trade of the Eastern Empire: BAYNES, pp. 207–220.

NOTE. The scene below shows us the condition of Europe at least fifty thousand years ago, in the Early Stone Age (§§ 9–14), when man began the long upward climb which carried him through all the ages of developing and declining civilization which we have been following.

BIBLIOGRAPHY

It has not been possible in this bibliography to mention all of even the important books which might be listed. It is important to include such books as the teacher has some chance of procuring. It not infrequently happens that the best account of a particular period or topic is in a foreign language or in a rare publication, such as a doctor's dissertation, which could be found only in one of our largest libraries. All such titles, however valuable, are omitted from this list.

CHAPTERS I–II

Antiquity, 1927–   (Assistant Editor, 24 Parkend Road, Gloucester, England). AVEBURY, Sir J. L., *Prehistoric Times* (7th ed., N.Y., 1913). BRITISH MUSEUM, *Flints* (London, 1928). BURKITT, M. C., *Old Stone Age* (Cambridge University Press, 1933), *Our Early Ancestors* (Cambridge University Press, 1929); *Our Forerunners* (London, 1924). BUXTON, L. H. D., *Primitive Labour* (London, 1924). CHILDE, V. G., *The Most Ancient East* (N.Y., 1929). CLELAND, H. F., *Our Prehistoric Ancestors* (N.Y., 1928). COLE, F. C., *The Long Road from Savagery to Civilization* (N.Y., 1933). DAVISON, D., *Our Prehistoric Ancestors* (London, 1926). DAWSON, C. H., *Age of the Gods* (London, 1933). GARDNER, H., *Art through the Ages* (N.Y., 1926), chap. i. HIBBEN, T., *The Carpenter's Tool Chest* (Philadelphia, 1933). KROEBER, A. L., *Anthropology* (N.Y., 1923). KUMMER, F., *First Days of Knowledge* (N.Y., 1923). MACALISTER, R. A., *A Text-book of European Archæology* (Cambridge, 1921). MACCURDY, G. G., *Human Origins* (2 vols.; N.Y., 1924). MAGOFFIN, R. V. D., and DUNCALF, F., *Ancient and Medieval History* (N.Y., 1934). MARETT, R. R., *Anthropology* (N.Y., 1912). MORGAN, J. M. DE, *Prehistoric Man* (N.Y., 1925). MORGAN, L. H., *Ancient Society* (N.Y., 1878). OBERMAIER, H., *Fossil Man in Spain* (Yale University Press, 1924). OSBORN, H. F., *Man Rises to Parnassus* (Princeton University Press, 1928); *Men of the Old Stone Age* (3d ed., N.Y., 1919). PARSONS, G., *The Stream of History* (N. Y., 1928). PEAKE, H. J. E., and FLEURE, H. J., *Hunters and Artists* (Yale University Press, 1927). QUENNELL, M. and C. H. B., *Everyday Life in Prehistoric Times* (2d ed., London, 1931). RENARD, G. F., *Life and Work in Prehistoric Times* (N.Y., 1929). SOLLAS, W. J., *Ancient Hunters and their Modern Representatives* (3d ed., N.Y., 1924). TYLER, J. M., *The New Stone Age in Northern Europe* (London, 1921). WILDER, H. H., *Man's Prehistoric Past* (rev. ed., N.Y., 1923).

CHAPTERS III–IV

***A.* Histories.** BREASTED, J. H., *History of the Ancient Egyptians* (N.Y., 1913); *History of Egypt* (2d ed., N.Y., 1924). *Cambridge Ancient History* (Cambridge University Press), Vols. I and II, *passim* (Vol. I, 2d ed., 1928; Vol. II, 1926). HALL, H. R. H., *The Ancient History of the Near East* (7th ed., London, 1927). QUIBELL, A. A., *Egyptian History and Art* (N.Y., 1923). ROSTOVTZEFF, M. I., *A History of the Ancient World* (Oxford, 1926), Vol. I.

***B.* Art and archæology.** BELL, E., *The Architecture of Ancient Egypt* (London, 1915). BOSTON MUSEUM OF FINE ARTS, *Bulletin*, 1903–   . BRITISH MUSEUM,

A General Introductory Guide to the Egyptian Collections (London, 1930). *Cambridge Ancient History,* Vol. I, chap. xvi; Vol. II, chap. xv. CAPART, J., *Egyptian Art* (London, 1923); *Lectures on Egyptian Art* (University of North Carolina Press, 1928). CLARKE, S., and ENGELBACH, R., *Ancient Egyptian Masonry* (Oxford University Press, 1930). CROSS, L. (Ed.), *Pre-Greek Art* (Student Series M of The University Prints, Cambridge, Mass., 1925). FECHHEIMER, H., *Die Plastik der Ägypter* (Berlin, 1920). GARDNER, H., *Art through the Ages,* chaps. ii–iii. MASPERO, SIR G., *Art in Egypt* (Ars Una: Species Mille. General History of Art series, N.Y., 1930). METROPOLITAN MUSEUM OF ART (New York), *Bulletin,* 1905– . MURRAY, M. A., *Egyptian Sculpture* (London, 1930). NELSON, H. H., and HOLSCHER, U., *Medinet Habu Reports* (University of Chicago Press, 1931). PETRIE, SIR W. M. F., *The Arts and Crafts of Ancient Egypt* (Edinburgh and London, 1923). ROSS, SIR E. D., *The Art of Egypt through the Ages* (London, 1931). WEIGALL, A., *Ancient Egyptian Works of Art* (London, 1924).

C. **Mythology and religion.** BREASTED, J. H., *The Dawn of Conscience* (N.Y., 1933); *Development of Religion and Thought in Ancient Egypt* (N.Y., 1912). *Cambridge Ancient History,* Vol. I, chap. ix; Vol. II, chap. ix. GARDINER, A., article "Egypt: Ancient Religion" in *Encyclopædia Britannica* (11th ed.). PETRIE, SIR W. M. F., *Religious Life in Ancient Egypt* (London, 1924). SHORTER, A. W., *An Introduction to Egyptian Religion* (London, 1931).

D. **Social life.** BLACKMAN, A. M., *Luxor and its Temples* (London, 1923). ERMAN, A., *Life in Ancient Egypt* (N.Y., 1894) (new edition in German by Ranke, Tübingen, 1923). GLANVILLE, S. R. K., *Daily Life in Ancient Egypt* (London, 1930); *The Egyptians* (London, 1933). SHORTER, A. W., *Everyday Life in Ancient Egypt* (London, 1932).

E. **Excavation and discovery.** BAIKIE, J., *A Century of Excavation in the Land of the Pharaohs* (N.Y., 1924); *Egyptian Papyri and Papyrus-Hunting* (N.Y., 1925). CARTER, H., and MACE, A. C., *The Tomb of Tut-ankh-amen* (3 vols.; N.Y., 1923–1933). *Journal of Egyptian Archæology* (Egypt Exploration Society; Secretary, American Branch, Riverbank Lodge, Antrim, New Hampshire), 1914– . PETRIE, SIR W. M. F., *Seventy Years in Archæology* (London, 1931).

F. **Original sources in English.** BREASTED, J. H., *Ancient Records of Egypt* (5 vols.; University of Chicago Press, 1906–1907); *The Edwin Smith Surgical Papyrus* (Oxford University Press, 1930). ERMAN, A., *The Literature of the Ancient Egyptians* (London, 1927). MASPERO, SIR G., *Popular Stories of Ancient Egypt* (N.Y., 1915). PEET, T. E., *A Comparative Study of the Literatures of Egypt, Palestine, and Mesopotamia* (Oxford University Press, 1931). PETRIE, SIR W. M. F., *Egyptian Tales, Translated from the Papyri* (London, 1913).

G. **The monuments as they are today.** BAIKIE, J., *Egyptian Antiquities in the Nile Valley* (London, 1932). BORCHARDT, L., and RICKE, H., *Egypt: Architecture, Landscape, Life of the People* (London, 1930). BREASTED, J. H., *Egypt through the Stereoscope; a Journey through the Land of the Pharaohs* (Keystone View Co., Meadville, Pa., 1908; 100 views, with guidebook and maps). MURRAY, M. A., *Egyptian Temples* (London, 1931).

CHAPTERS V–VI

A. **Histories.** *Cambridge Ancient History,* Vols. I, II, and III (1929), *passim.* DELAPORTE, L. J., *Mesopotamia* (N.Y., 1925). DOUGHERTY, R. P., *Nabonidus and Belshazzar* (Yale University Press, 1929). GADD, C. J., *History and Monuments of Ur* (N.Y., 1929). GOODSPEED, G. S., *History of the Babylonians and Assyrians* (N.Y., 1917). HALL, H. R. H., *Ancient History of the Near East.* JOHNS, C. H. W., *Ancient Babylonia* (N.Y., 1913); *Ancient Assyria* (Cambridge University Press, 1912). KING, L. W., *History of Babylon from Foundation of Monarchy to Persian Conquest* (N.Y., 1915); *History of Sumer and Akkad* (London, 1916). OLMSTEAD,

A. T. E., *History of Assyria* (N.Y., 1923); *Western Asia in the Days of Sargon of Assyria* (N.Y., 1908). ROGERS, R. W., *History of Babylonia and Assyria* (6th ed., N.Y., 1915). ROSTOVTZEFF, M., *History of the Ancient World*, Vol. I. WOOLLEY, C. L., *The Sumerians* (Oxford, 1928).

***B.* Art and archæology.** BELL, E., *Early Architecture in Western Asia* (London, 1924), chaps. i–iv, vii–x. *Cambridge Ancient History*, Vols. I–II, *passim*. CROSS, L. (Ed.), *Pre-Greek Art*. FRANKFORT, H., *Archæology and the Sumerian Problem* (University of Chicago Press, 1932). GARDNER, H., *Art through the Ages*, chap. iv. HARCOURT-SMITH, S., *Babylonian Art* (N.Y., 1928). MEISSNER, B., *Babylonien und Assyrien* (2 vols.; Heidelberg, 1920–1925) (invaluable to teachers who read German). OLMSTEAD, A. T. E., "A Visit to Babylon," in *History Teacher's Magazine*, Vol. VIII (1917), pp. 79–81. PATERSON, A., *Assyrische Skulpturen* (Haarlem, Holland, 1901–1907; Kleinmann, London; plates, with descriptions in German, French, and English).

***C.* Mythology and religion.** *Cambridge Ancient History*, Vol. III, chap. xi. JASTROW, M., *Aspects of Religious Belief and Practice in Babylonia and Assyria* (N.Y., 1911).

***D.* Social life.** JASTROW, M., *The Civilization of Babylonia and Assyria* (Philadelphia, 1915). MEISSNER, B., *Babylonien und Assyrien*. SAYCE, A. H., *Babylonians and Assyrians: Life and Customs* (N.Y., 1899).

***E.* Excavation and discovery.** *American Journal of Archæology* (Baltimore), 1885– . KOLDEWEY, R., *The Excavations at Babylon* (London, 1914). *Museum Journal of the University of Pennsylvania*, 1910– . ROGERS, R. W., *History of Babylonia and Assyria*, Vol. I. THOMPSON, R. C., and HUTCHINSON, R.W., *A Century of Exploration at Nineveh* (London, 1929). WOOLLEY, C. L., *Ur of the Chaldees; a Record of Seven Years of Excavation* (London, 1929).

***F.* Original sources in English.** BOTSFORD, G. W. and L. S., *Source Book of Ancient History* (N.Y., 1913), chap. iii. JOHNS, C. H. W. (Tr.), *The Oldest Code of Laws in the World* (Edinburgh, 1911). KING, L. W. (Tr.), *Letters and Inscriptions of Hammurabi* (London, 1900), Vol. III. LUCKENBILL, D. D., *Ancient Records of Assyria and Babylonia* (2 vols.; University of Chicago Press, 1926–1927). SAYCE, A. H., *Records of the Past* (6 vols.; London, 1889–1893). SMITH, S., *Babylonian Historical Texts relating to the Capture and Downfall of Babylon* (London, 1924).

***G.* The monuments as they are today.** The buildings surviving in Babylonia and Assyria are in a ruinous state. Photographs of sites in Mesopotamia may be obtained from the Keystone View Co., Meadville, Pa.

CHAPTER VII

***A.* Histories.** BAILEY, A. E., and KENT, C. F., *History of the Hebrew Commonwealth* (N.Y., 1920). BAYNES, N. H., *Israel amongst the Nations* (Student Christian Movement, London, 1927). BLUNT, A. W. F., *Israel in World History* (Oxford University Press, 1927). GOLUB, J. S., *In the Days of the First Temple* (Cincinnati, 1931). GOODSPEED, E. J., *The Story of the Old Testament* (University of Chicago Press, 1934). KENT, C. F., *History of the Hebrew People* (N.Y., 1906; Vol. I, 10th ed.; Vol. II, 9th ed.); *A History of the Jewish People during the Babylonian, Persian, and Greek Periods* (N.Y., 1927); *The Kings and Prophets of Israel and Judah* (N.Y., 1909). KITTEL, R., *Great Men and Movements in Israel* (N.Y., 1929). KNOPF, C. S., *The Old Testament Speaks* (N.Y., 1933). KNOTT, L. A., *Student's History of the Hebrews* (N.Y., 1927). LODS, A., *Israel, from its Beginnings to the Middle of the Eighth Century* (London, 1932). MACALISTER, R. A. S., *History of Civilization in Palestine* (N.Y., 1921). NOYES, C. E., *The Genius of Israel* (Boston, 1924). OLMSTEAD, A. T., *History of Palestine and Syria to the Macedonian Conquest* (N.Y., 1931). PERITZ, I. J., *Old Testament History* (N.Y., 1923). PRICE, I. M., *The Dramatic Story of Old Testament History* (N.Y., 1929); *The Monuments and* *the Old Testament* (Philadelphia, 1925). SMITH, SIR G. A., *The Historical Geography of the Holy Land* (25th ed., 1932).

***B.* Mythology and religion.** BARTON, G. A., *Religion of Israel* (2d ed., University of Pennsylvania Press, 1928). BUDDE, K. F. R., *Religion of Israel to the Exile* (N.Y., 1899). CADMAN, S. P., *The Prophets of Israel* (N.Y., 1933). CHAMBERLIN, G. L., *Hebrew Prophets* (University of Chicago Press, 1911). CHEYNE, T. K., *Jewish Religious Life after the Exile* (N.Y., 1915). COOK, S. A., *Religion of Ancient Palestine in the Light of Archæology* (Oxford University Press, 1930). GRAHAM, W. C., *The Prophets and Israel's Culture* (University of Chicago Press, 1934). OXTOBY, F. B., *Israel's Religious Development* (Philadelphia, 1927). PEAKE, A. S., *Religion of Israel* (London, 1908). PEDERSEN, J., *Israel; its Life and Culture* (London, 1926). SMITH, H. P., *Religion of Israel* (N.Y., 1928). SMITH, J. M. P., *The Prophet and his Problems* (N.Y., 1923). WOOD, W. C., *Religion of Canaan from Earliest Times to Hebrew Conquest* (Newmarket, Ontario, 1916; offprint of *Journal of Biblical Literature*).

***C.* Excavation and discovery.** ALBRIGHT, W. F., *The Archæology of Palestine and the Bible* (N.Y., 1932). BARTON, G. A., *Archæology and the Bible* (5th ed., American Sunday-School Union, Philadelphia, 1927). GARSTANG, J., *Foundations of Bible History: Joshua, Judges* (N.Y., 1931). JACK, J. W., *Samaria in Ahab's Time* (N.Y., 1929). MACALISTER, R. A. S., *A Century of Excavation in Palestine* (N.Y., 1926). PEET, T. E., *Egypt and the Old Testament* (London, 1924). WOOLLEY, C. L., *Excavations at Ur and the Hebrew Records* (London, 1929).

***D.* Social life.** BUDDEN, C. W., and HASTINGS, E., *Local Colour of the Bible* (3 vols.; Edinburgh, 1922–1925). HENRY, L. I., *Paul, Son of Kish* (University of Chicago Press, 1923). HUNTING, H. B., *Hebrew Life and Times* (N.Y., 1921). SMITH, J. M. P., *The Prophets and their Times* (University of Chicago Press, 1925).

***E.* Literature.** *Abingdon Bible Commentary* (N.Y., 1929). BOTSFORD, G. W. and L. S., *A Source Book of Ancient History*, chap. iv. CORNILL, C. H., *Introduction to the Canonical Books of the Old Testament* (N.Y., 1907). FOWLER, H. T., *History of the Literature of Ancient Israel* (N.Y., 1922). GENUNG, J. F., *Guidebook to the Biblical Literature* (Boston, 1919). LEWIS, F. G., *How the Bible Grew* (University of Chicago Press, 1919). *Old Testament* in the Revised Version. PEAKE, A. S., *Commentary on the Bible* (N.Y., 1920). PENNIMAN, J. H., *Book about the English Bible* (University of Pennsylvania Press, 1931). ROGERS, R. W., *Cuneiform Parallels to the Old Testament* (2d ed., N.Y., 1926). SANDS, P. C., *Literary Genius of the Old Testament* (Oxford University Press, 1932). WILD, L. H., *Literary Guide to the Bible* (rev. ed., N.Y., 1925).

***F.* Palestine, its people and monuments as they are today.** BAIKIE, J., *Ancient Jerusalem* (N.Y., 1930). CROSBY, R. L., *Geography of Bible Lands* (N.Y., 1921). ELMENDORF, D. L., *A Camera Crusade through the Holy Land* (N.Y., 1912). HURLBUT, J. L., *Traveling in the Holy Land through the Stereoscope* (the Keystone View Co., Meadville, Pa., 1900; 100 views, with guidebook and maps). PREISS, L., and ROHRBACH, P., *Palestine and Transjordania* (N.Y., 1926).

CHAPTER VIII

***A.* Histories.** AHL, A. W., *Outline of Persian History* (N.Y., 1922). *Cambridge Ancient History*, Vols. II, III, IV (1926), and VI (1927), *passim*. COWLEY, A. E., *The Hittites* (Oxford University Press, 1920). GROUSSET, R., *Civilizations of the East* (N.Y., 1931), pp. 112–133. HALL, H. R. H., *The Near East*. HOGARTH, D. G., *The Ancient East* (N.Y., 1915). HUART, C. I., *Ancient Persia and Iranian Civilization* (N.Y., 1927). MEYER, E., *Reich und Kultur der Chetiter* (Berlin, 1914). ROGERS, R. W., *History of Ancient Persia* (N.Y., 1929). ROSS, SIR E. D., *The Persians* (Oxford University Press, 1931). SAYCE, A. H., *The Hittites; the Story* *of a Forgotten Empire* (rev. ed., London, 1925). SYKES, SIR P. M., *A History of Persia* (2d ed., London, 1921), Vol. I.

***B*. Art and archæology.** BELL, E., *Early Architecture in Western Asia*, chaps. v–vi, xi. BRITISH MUSEUM (Department of British and Mediæval Antiquities), *Treasure of the Oxus* (2d ed., London, 1926). PERROT, G., and CHIPIEZ, C., *History of Art in Persia* (N.Y., 1892). SARRE, F. P. T., *Kunst des alten Persien* (Berlin, 1922) (valuable for plates). WEBER, O., *Die Kunst der Hethiter* (Berlin, 1922) (valuable for plates). WOOLLEY, C. L., *Dead Towns and Living Men* (Toronto, 1932).

***C*. Mythology and religion.** CARNOY, A., *Iranian Mythology* (Boston, 1917). EAKIN, F., *Revaluing Scripture* (N.Y., 1928), chap. iv. MOULTON, J. H., *Early Religious Poetry of Persia* (N.Y., 1911).

***D*. Social life.** GLOVER, T. R., *From Pericles to Philip* (4th ed., London, 1926), chap. vii. JACKSON, A. V. W., *Zoroaster, the Prophet of Ancient Iran* (N.Y., 1899). RAWLINSON, G., *Seven Great Monarchies*: "The Fifth Monarchy: Persia" (N.Y., 1885).

***E*. Exploration and discovery.** BREASTED, CHARLES, "Exploring the Secrets of Persepolis," in the *National Geographic Magazine*, Vol. 64 (1933), pp. 381–420. GARSTANG, J., *The Hittite Empire* (London, 1929); *The Land of the Hittites* (N.Y., 1910). GELB, I., *Hittite Hieroglyphs* (University of Chicago Press, 1931). HERZFELD, E. E., *Archäologische Mitteilungen aus Iran* (Berlin, 1929–1930), Vol. I, pp. 4–40 and Pls. 1–30; *A New Inscription of Xerxes from Persepolis* (University of Chicago Press, 1932). HOGARTH, D. G., *Kings of the Hittites* (Oxford University Press, 1926). JACKSON, A .V. W., *Persia, Past and Present* (N.Y., 1909). OSTEN, H. H. VON DER, *Discoveries in Anatolia, 1930–31* (University of Chicago Press, 1933). SCHMIDT, E. F., *Anatolia through the Ages* (University of Chicago Press, 1931). STURTEVANT, E. H., "The Hittite Tablets from Boghaz Kevi," in *Classical Weekly*, Vol. XVIII, No. 22 (April 20, 1925).

***F*. Original sources in English.** BOTSFORD, G. W. and L. S., *Source-Book of Ancient History*, chap. v. DARMESTETER, J. (Tr.), *Zend-Avesta* (Christian Literature Co., N.Y., 1898). TOLMAN, H. C., *The Behistan Inscription of King Darius* (Vanderbilt University Studies, Nashville, Tenn., 1908).

CHAPTERS IX–XVIII

***A*. Ægean civilization.** BAIKIE, J., *Sea-Kings of Crete* (4th ed., London, 1926). BELL, E., *Prehellenic Architecture in the Ægean* (London, 1926). BOSSERT, H. T., *Alt Kreta* (2d ed., Berlin, 1923) (valuable for illustrations). BURN, A. R., *Minoans, Philistines, and Greeks, B.C. 1400–900* (N.Y., 1930). BURROWS, R. M., *Discoveries in Crete* (London, 1907). EVANS, SIR A. J., *Palace of Minos* (3 vols.; London, 1921–1928). GARDNER, H., *Art through the Ages*, chap. v. GLASGOW, G., *The Minoans* (London, 1923). GLOTZ, G., *The Ægean Civilization* (N.Y., 1925). HALL, H. R. H., *The Civilization of Greece in the Bronze Age* (London, 1928). HAWES, C. H. and H. B., *Crete, the Forerunner of Greece* (4th ed., N.Y., 1922). NILSSON, M. P., *Homer and Mycenæ* (London, 1933); *The Minoan-Mycenæan Religion and its Survival in Greek Religion* (Lund, 1927); *Mycenæan Origin of Greek Mythology* (University of California Press, 1932). SHUCHHARDT, K., *Schliemann's Excavations* (N.Y., 1891). TOLMAN, H. C., and SCOGGIN, G. C., *Mycenæan Troy* (N.Y., 1903).

***B*. General and political histories.** ABBOTT, E. A., *Pericles and the Golden Age of Athens* (N.Y., 1903). ABBOTT, G. F., *Thucydides, a Study in Historical Reality* (London, 1925). ALLCROFT, A. H., *Sparta and Thebes: a History of Greece, 404–362 B.C.* (London, 1895). ALLCROFT, A. H., and MASON, W. F., *History of Sicily from 491–289 B.C.* (London, 1912). BOTSFORD, G. W., *Hellenic History* (N.Y., 1924); *History of Ancient World* (N.Y., 1921). BURY, J. B., *History of Greece*

(2d ed., London, 1924). BURY, J. B., and KIMBALL, E., *Students' History of Greece* (N.Y., 1916). *Cambridge Ancient History* (Vol. V, 1927), Vols. I–VI, *passim.* CARPENTER, R., *The Greeks in Spain* (N.Y., 1925). CARY, M., *Documentary Sources of Greek History* (Oxford, 1927). CURTIUS, E., *History of Greece* (5 vols.; N.Y., 1902). FLEMING, W. B., *History of Tyre* (Columbia University Press, 1915). FREEMAN, E. A., *History of Sicily* (4 vols.; Oxford, 1891–1894). GOODSPEED, G. S., *History of the Ancient World* (N.Y., 1912). GRANT, A. J., *Greece in the Age of Pericles* (N.Y., 1897). GROTE, G., *History of Greece* (10 vols.; London, 1904–1907). GRUNDY, G. B., *The Great Persian War* (London, 1901); *History of the Greek and Roman World* (London, 1926); *Thucydides and the History of his Age* (London, 1911). HALL, H. R. H., *Ancient History of the Near East.* HENDERSON, B. W., *The Great War between Athens and Sparta* (London, 1927). HOLM, A., *History of Greece* (4 vols.; N.Y., 1899–1900). JAMES, H. R., *Our Hellenic Heritage* (N.Y., 1927). KELLER, A. G., *Colonization* (Boston, 1908). MACALISTER, R. A. S., *The Philistines* (London, 1913). MCCARTNEY, E. S., *Warfare by Land and Sea* (Boston, 1923). MILLS, D., *Book of the Ancient Greeks* (N.Y., 1925). MYRES, J. L., *Dawn of History* (London, 1915). RAWLINSON, H. G., *Bactria* (London, 1912). ROSTOVTZEFF, M. I., *History of the Ancient World,* Vol. I. SANKEY, C., *Spartan and Theban Supremacies* (N.Y., 1899). SEIGNOBOS, M. J. C., *History of Ancient Civilization* (N.Y., 1910). SELTMAN, C. T., *Athens, its History and Coinage before the Persian Invasion* (Cambridge University Press, 1924). SHUCKBURGH, E. S., *Greece from the Coming of the Hellenes to A. D. 14* (London, 1905). WELLS, J., *Studies in Herodotus* (Oxford, 1923). WESTERMANN, W. L., *Story of Ancient Nations* (N.Y., 1912). WHIBLEY, L., *Political Parties in Athens during the Peloponnesian War* (2d ed., Cambridge University Press, 1889).

***C.* Constitutional and institutional histories.** BONNER, R. J., *Aspects of Athenian Democracy* (University of California Press, 1933). CALHOUN, G. M., *Athenian Clubs in Politics and Litigation* (University of Texas, 1913); *Growth of Criminal Law in Ancient Greece* (University of California Press, 1927). FERGUSON, W. S., *Greek Imperialism* (Boston, 1913). FOWLER, W. W., *The City-State of the Greeks and Romans* (London, 1926). FREEMAN, E. A., *History of Federal Government in Greece and Italy* (2d ed., N.Y., 1893). GILBERT, G., *The Constitutional Antiquities of Sparta and Athens* (N.Y., 1895). GLOVER, T. R., *Democracy in the Ancient World* (N.Y., 1927). GREENIDGE, A. H. J., *Handbook of Greek Constitutional History* (London, 1920). HALLIDAY, W. R., *The Growth of the City State* (London, 1923). HAMMOND, B. E., *Political Institutions of the Ancient Greeks* (London, 1895). PHILLIPSON, C., *International Law and Custom of Ancient Greece and Rome* (2 vols.; London, 1911). TOD, M. N., *International Arbitration amongst the Greeks* (Oxford, 1913). URE, P. N., *The Origin of Tyranny* (Cambridge University Press, 1922). WHIBLEY, L., *Greek Oligarchies* (N. Y., 1896). ZIMMERN, A. E., *Greek Commonwealth* (5th ed., Oxford, 1931).

***D.* Economic and social life.** ABRAHAMS, E. B., *Greek Dress* (London, 1908). BECKER, W. A., *Charicles: or Illustrations of the Private Life of the Ancient Greeks* (8th ed., London, 1911). BLÜMNER, H., *Home Life of the Ancient Greeks* (3d ed., N.Y., 1910). BRITISH MUSEUM, *A Guide to the Exhibition illustrating Greek and Roman Life* (London, 1929). CALHOUN, G. M., *The Ancient Greeks and the Evolution of Standards in Business* (Boston, 1926); *Business Life of Ancient Athens* (University of Chicago Press, 1926). DAVIS, W. S., *A Day in Old Athens* (N.Y., 1914). DOBSON, J. F., *Ancient Education and its Meaning to Us* (N.Y., 1932). DONALDSON, SIR J., *Woman: her Position and Influence in Ancient Greece and Rome* (N.Y., 1907). FREEMAN, K. J., *Schools of Hellas* (3d ed., London, 1932). GARDINER, E. N., *Athletics of the Ancient World* (Oxford, 1930); *Greek Athletic Sports and Festivals* (London, 1910). GLOTZ, G., *Ancient Greece at Work* (N.Y., 1926). GUHL, E. K., and KONER, W., *Life of the Greeks and Romans* (tr. from 3d German ed., N.Y., 1898). GULICK, C. B., *Life of the Ancient Greeks* (N.Y., 1929);

Modern Traits in Old Greek Life (N.Y., 1927). JONES, W. H. S., *Greek Morality in Relation to Institutions* (London, 1906). KELLER, A. G., *Homeric Society* (N.Y., 1902). LIVINGSTONE, R. W. (Ed.), *Legacy of Greece* (Oxford, 1921). MCCLEES, H., *Daily Life of the Greeks and Romans as illustrated by the Classical Collections* (Metropolitan Museum of Art, N.Y., 1925). MAHAFFY, SIR J. P., *Social Life in Greece* (7th ed., N.Y., 1898). QUENNELL, M. and C. H. B., *Everyday Things in Homeric Greece* (London, 1929). SEYMOUR, T. D., *Life in the Homeric Age* (N.Y., 1908). TOYNBEE, A. J., *Greek Civilisation and Character* (N.Y., 1924). TREVER, A. A., *A History of Greek Economic Thought* (University of Chicago Press, 1916). TUCKER, T. G., *Life in Ancient Athens* (N.Y., 1929). WHIBLEY, L., *Companion to Greek Studies* (4th ed., Cambridge University Press, 1931). WRIGHT, F. A., *Greek Social Life* (N.Y., 1925).

***E.* Religion and mythology.** ADAM, J., *The Religious Teachers of Greece* (Edinburgh, 1923). BULFINCH, T., *Age of Fable* (Everyman's Library, N.Y., 1916). FAIRBANKS, A., *Handbook of Greek Religion* (N.Y., 1910); *Mythology of Greece and Rome* (N.Y., 1907). FARNELL, L. R., *The Cults of the Greek States* (5 vols.; Oxford, 1896–1909); *Higher Aspects of Greek Religion* (London, 1912); *Outline-History of Greek Religion* (London, 1921). GAYLEY, C. M., *The Classic Myths in English Literature and in Art* (Boston, 1911). HARRISON, J. E., *Mythology* (Boston, 1924); *Myths of Greece and Rome* (Benn's Sixpenny Library, London, 1928); *Religion of Ancient Greece* (London, 1921). HOWE, G., and HARRER, G. A., *Handbook of Classical Mythology* (N.Y., 1929). MOORE, C. H., *The Religious Thought of the Greeks from Homer to the Triumph of Christianity* (Harvard University Press, 1925). MURRAY, SIR G., *Five Stages of Greek Religion* (Oxford University Press, 1925). NILSSON, M. P., *History of Greek Religion* (Oxford, 1925). SABIN, F. E., *Classical Myths that Live Today* (N.Y., 1927). ZIELINSKI, T., *Religion of Greece* (London, 1926).

***F.* Art and archæology.** *American Journal of Archæology*, 1885– . *Art and Archæology*, 1914– . BEAZLEY, J. D., and ASHMOLE, B., *Greek Sculpture and Painting* (N.Y., 1932). BELL, E., *Hellenic Architecture* (London, 1920). *Classical Weekly*, 1907– . FOWLER, H. N., WHEELER, J. R., and STEVENS, G. P., *Handbook of Greek Archæology* (N.Y., 1909). GARDNER, E. A., *Greece and the Ægean* (London, 1933); *Handbook of Greek Sculpture* (2d ed., London, 1920); *Six Greek Sculptors* (London, 1925). GARDNER, H., *Art through the Ages*. GARDNER, P., *New Chapters in Greek Art* (Oxford, 1926). GARDNER, P., and BLOMFIELD, SIR R., *Greek Art and Architecture* (London, 1922). HOPPIN, J. G., *A Handbook of Attic Red-Figured Vases* (2 vols.; Harvard University Press, 1919); *A Handbook of Greek Black-Figured Vases* (Paris, 1924). HUDDILSTON, J. H., *Lessons from Greek Pottery* (N.Y., 1902). JOHNSON, F. P., *Lysippos* (Duke University Press, 1927). JONES, H. S., *Select Passages from Ancient Writers Illustrative of History of Greek Sculpture* (London, 1895). *Journal of Hellenic Studies* (London), 1880– . LAMB, W., *Greek and Roman Bronzes* (London, 1929). LAWRENCE, A. W., *Classical Sculpture* (N.Y., 1929). LEAF, W., *Troy* (London, 1912). MAGOFFIN, R. V. D., *The Lure and Lore of Archæology* (Baltimore, 1930). MARSHALL, F. H., *Discovery in Greek Lands: a Sketch of the Principal Excavations and Discoveries of the Last Fifty Years* (Cambridge University Press, 1920). MICHAELIS, A. T. F., *A Century of Archæological Discoveries* (London, 1908). PFUHL, E., *Masterpieces of Greek Drawing and Painting* (N.Y., 1926). POLAND, F., REISINGER, E., and WAGNER, R., *The Culture of Ancient Greece and Rome* (Boston, 1926). POULSEN, F., *Delphi* (London, 1920). POWERS, H. H., *The Hill of Athena* (N.Y., 1924). RICHTER, G. M., *The Craft of Athenian Pottery* (Yale University Press, 1923); *Handbook of the Classical Collection* (new and enlarged ed., Metropolitan Museum of Art, N.Y., 1927). ROBERTSON, D. S., *Handbook of Greek and Roman Architecture* (Cambridge University Press, 1929). ROSE, H. J., *Primitive Culture in Greece* (N.Y., 1925). TARBELL, F. B., *History of Greek Art* (N.Y., 1927). WALTERS, H. B., *History of*

Greek Pottery (London, 1905). Whibley, L., *A Companion to Greek Studies* (4th ed., Cambridge University Press, 1931).

G. **Literature, philosophy, and science.** Allen, J. T., *Stage Antiquities of the Greeks and Romans* (N.Y., 1927). Benn, A. W., *Early Greek Philosophy* (London, 1909); *Philosophy of Greece* (London, 1898). Bowra, C. M., *Tradition and Design in the Iliad* (Oxford, 1930). Brett, G. S., *Psychology, Ancient and Modern* (N.Y., 1928). Burnet, J., *Greek Philosophy* (London, 1914), Part I. Burt, B. C., *Brief History of Greek Philosophy* (Boston, 1896). Burton, H. E., *The Discovery of the Ancient World* (Harvard University Press, 1932). Cary, M., and Warmington, E. H., *The Ancient Explorers* (London, 1929). Croiset, M., *Hellenic Civilization* (N.Y., 1925). Dresser, H. W., *A History of Ancient and Medieval Philosophy* (N.Y., 1926). Fowler, H. N., *History of Ancient Greek Literature* (new and revised ed., N.Y., 1928). Haigh, A. E., *Attic Theatre* (3d ed., rev. by A. W. Pickard-Cambridge, Oxford, 1907). Hamilton, E., *The Greek Way* (London, 1930). Jebb, Sir R. C., *Attic Orators* (London, 1893); *Greek Literature* (N.Y., 189–); *Growth and Influence of Classical Greek Poetry* (N.Y., 1894). Jevons, F. B., *History of Greek Literature* (N.Y., 1900). Lang, A., *Homer and the Epic* (N.Y., 1893); *Homer and his Age* (N.Y., 1906). Leaf, W., *Homer and History* (N.Y., 1915). Mackail, J. W., *Lectures on Greek Poetry* (new ed., N.Y., 1926). Murray, Sir G., *Aristophanes and the War Party* (London, 1919); *History of Ancient Greek Literature* (Appleton's Dollar Library, N.Y., 1927); *Rise of the Greek Epic* (3d ed., Oxford, 1924). Norwood, C., and Duff, J. W., *Writers of Greece and Rome* (Oxford University Press, 1925). Powell, J. U. (Ed.), *New Chapters in the History of Greek Literature* (3d series, Oxford, 1933). Sandys, Sir J. E., *History of Classical Scholarship* (3d ed., Cambridge University Press, 1921), Vol. I. Shorey, P., *What Plato Said* (University of Chicago Press, 1933). Singer, C., *Greek Biology and Greek Medicine* (Oxford, 1922). Symonds, J. A., *Studies of the Greek Poets* (3d ed., London, 1920). Taylor, A. E., *Plato, the Man and his Work* (N.Y., 1929). Taylor, H. O., *Greek Biology and Medicine* (Boston, 1922). Taylor, M. E. J., *Greek Philosophy* (Oxford University Press, 1924). Tozer, H. F., *History of Ancient Geography* (Cambridge University Press, 1897). Ullman, B. L., *Ancient Writing and its Influence* (N.Y., 1932). Wardeke, J. M., *The Searching Mind of Greece* (N.Y., 1930).

H. **Source selections.** Botsford, G. W. and L. S., *Source Book of Ancient History*. Botsford, G. W., and Sihler, E. G., *Hellenic Civilization* (N.Y., 1924). Cornford, F. M., *Greek Religious Thought from Homer to the Age of Alexander* (N.Y., 1923). Fling, F. M., *Source Book of Greek History* (Boston, 1909). Hill, Mrs. Ida C. (Thallon), *Readings in Greek History* (Boston, 1914). Howe, G., and Harrer, G. A., *Greek Literature in Translation* (N.Y., 1924). Livingstone, R. W. (Ed.), *Pageant of Greece* (Oxford, 1923).

I. **Authors in translation.** Æschylus, The Persians (L. Campbell (Tr.), World's Classics, London, 1925); complete works (H. W. Smyth (Tr.), Loeb Classical Library, N.Y., 1922–1926). Alcæus, songs (J. S. Easby-Smith (Tr.), Washington, 1901). Aristophanes, plays (J. H. Frere (Tr.), Everyman's Library, N.Y., 1929; B. B. Rogers (Tr.), Loeb Classical Library, N.Y., 1924–1927). Aristotle, On the Athenian Constitution (E. Poste (Tr.), 2d ed., N.Y., 1892); works (Loeb Classical Library, N.Y.). Euripides, plays (Everyman's Library, N.Y., 1916; A. S. Way (Tr.), Loeb Classical Library, N. Y., 1925–1929). Herodotus (A. D. Godley (Tr.), Loeb Classical Library, N.Y., 1924–1928; G. Rawlinson (Tr.), Everyman's Library, N.Y., 1930). Hesiod (A. W. Mair (Tr.), Oxford, 1908; J. Davies (Tr.), Philadelphia, 1873). Homer, Iliad (Edward, Earl of Derby (Tr.), Everyman's Library, N.Y., 1912; A. Lang, W. Leaf, and E. Myers (Trs.), London, 1929); Odyssey (W. Cowper (Tr.), Everyman's Library, N.Y., 1913; S. H. Butcher and A. Lang (Trs.), London, 1925). Nepos, Cornelius, Epaminondas (J. C. Rolfe (Tr.), Loeb Classical Library, N.Y., 1929; J. S. Watson

(Tr.), London, 1910). PAUSANIAS, *Tour of Greece* (W. H. S. Jones and H. A. Ormerod (Trs.), Loeb Classical Library, N.Y., 1918–). PINDAR, odes (E. Myers (Tr.), N.Y., 1899; Sir J. Sandys (Tr.), Loeb Classical Library, N.Y., 1915). PLATO, Apology (H. N. Fowler (Tr.), Loeb Classical Library, N.Y., 1933; B. Jowett (Tr.), Vol. II, N.Y., 1892). PLUTARCH, Lives (the "Dryden Plutarch," rev. by A. H. Clough, Everyman's Library, N.Y., n.d.). THEOGNIS (J. Davies (Tr.), Philadelphia, 1873; E. Harrison, *Studies in Theognis*, Cambridge University Press, 1902). THUCYDIDES, History of the Peloponnesian War (C. Forster-Smith (Tr.), Loeb Classical Library, N.Y., 1919–1923; R. Crawley (Tr.), Everyman's Library, N.Y., 1929). XENOPHON, works (Loeb Classical Library, N.Y., 1918– ; H. G. Dakyns (Tr.), N.Y., 1890–1897).

Supplementary pamphlets and booklets may be obtained from the Service Bureau for Classical Teachers, 51 W. 4th St., Washington Sq. E., New York.

CHAPTERS XIX–XXI

A. **General works.** ADAMS, C. D., *Demosthenes and his Influence* (N.Y., 1927). ALLCROFT, A. H., *The Decline of Hellas: a History of Greece, 362–323 B.C.* (London, 1894). BEVAN, E. R., *History of Egypt under the Ptolemaic Dynasty* (London, 1927); *House of Seleucus* (2 vols.; London, 1902). BURY, J. B., BARBER, E. A., BEVAN, E., and TARN, W. W., *The Hellenistic Age* (2d ed., Cambridge University Press, 1925). *Cambridge Ancient History*, Vols. VI, VII (1928), *passim*. *Cambridge History of India* (N.Y., 1922), Vol. I, chap. XV. CARY, M., *The Legacy of Alexander* (N.Y., 1932). CURTEIS, A. M., *Rise of the Macedonian Empire* (N.Y., 1916). DICKINS, G., *Hellenistic Sculpture* (Oxford, 1920). DODGE, T. A., *Alexander* (2 vols.; Boston, 1918). EHRENBERG, V., *Alexander und Ägypten* (Leipzig, 1926). FERGUSON, W. S., *Hellenistic Athens* (London, 1911). HEIBERG, J. L., *Mathematics and Physical Science in Classical Antiquity* (Oxford University Press, 1922). HOGARTH, D. G., *Philip and Alexander of Macedon* (N.Y., 1897). JOUGUET, P., *Macedonian Imperialism and the Hellenization of the East* (N.Y., 1928). MACURDY, G. H., *Hellenistic Queens* (Johns Hopkins Press, 1932). MAHAFFY, SIR J. P., *Alexander's Empire* (N.Y., 1902); *Greek Life and Thought from the Death of Alexander to the Roman Conquest* (2d ed., N.Y., 1896); *Progress of Hellenism in Alexander's Empire* (University of Chicago Press, 1905); *The Silver Age of the Greek World* (University of Chicago Press, 1906). MORE, P. E., *Hellenistic Philosophies* (Princeton University Press, 1923). POWELL, J. U., and BARBER, E. A. (Eds.), *New Chapters in the History of Greek Literature* (1st and 2d series, Oxford, 1921, 1929). RADET, G. A., *Alexandre le Grand* (Paris, 1931). ROBINSON, C. A., *The Ephemerides of Alexander's Expedition* (Brown University, 1932). ROGERS, R. W., *History of Ancient Persia*, pp. 261–376. ROSTOVTZEFF, M. I., *Out of the Past of Greece and Rome* (Yale University Press, 1932), pp. 93 ff. STIER, H. E., *Aus der Welt des Pergamonaltars* (Berlin, 1932). SUHR, E. G., *Sculptured Portraits of Greek Statesmen* (Johns Hopkins Press, 1931). SYKES, SIR P. M., *History of Persia*, Vol. I, chaps. xx–xxvi. TARN, W. W., *Antigonos Gonatas* (Oxford, 1913); *Hellenistic Civilization* (2d ed., London, 1930). TILLYARD, H. J. W., *Agathocles* (Cambridge University Press, 1908). WHEELER, B. I., *Alexander the Great* (N.Y., 1909). WILCKEN, U., *Alexander der Grosse* (Leipzig, 1931).

B. **Ancient authors in translation.** ARRIAN, Anabasis of Alexander (E. I. Robson (Tr.), Loeb Classical Library, N.Y., 1929–). CALLIMACHUS (A. W. Mair (Tr.), Loeb Classical Library, N.Y., 1921). DEMOSTHENES, *Oration on the Crown* and *Third Philippic* (A. W. Pickard-Cambridge (Tr.), *The Public Orations of Demosthenes*, Vol. II, Oxford, 1912). ISOCRATES (G. Norlin (Tr.), Loeb Classical Library, N.Y., 1928). JUSTIN, Abr., History of the World (J. S. Watson (Tr.),

London, 1910), Bks. IX, XI–XIII. PLUTARCH, lives of *Demosthenes, Phocion, Alexander, Aratus, Demetrius, Pyrrhus, Agis, Cleomenes,* and *Eumenes.* POLYBIUS, histories (W. R. Paton (Tr.), Loeb Classical Library, 6 vols., N.Y., 1922–1927).

See also the general bibliography for Greek history, chaps. ix–xviii.

CHAPTERS XXII–XXVIII

A. **General and political histories.** BEVAN, E. R., *The World of Greece and Rome* (London, 1928). BOAK, A. E. R., *History of Rome to A.D. 565* (rev. ed., N.Y., 1929). BONUS, A. R., *Where Hannibal Passed* (London, 1925). BRYANT, E. E., *The Reign of Antoninus Pius* (Cambridge University Press, 1895). BURY, J. B., *Student's Roman Empire* (N.Y., 190–). *Cambridge Ancient History,* Vols. IV, VII, and VIII (1930), *passim.* DURUY, V., *History of Rome* (8 vols. in 16; Boston, 1890). FELL, R. A. L., *Etruria and Rome* (Cambridge University Press, 1924). FERRERO, G., *Greatness and Decline of Rome* (5 vols.; N.Y., 1909). FERRERO, G., and BARBAGALLO, C., *Short History of Rome* (2 vols.; N.Y., 1918–1919). FOWLER, W. W., *Rome* (N.Y., 1912). FRANK, T., *History of Rome* (N.Y., 1923). FREEMAN, E. A., *Story of Sicily: Phœnician, Greek, and Roman* (2d ed., N.Y., 1894). GREENIDGE, A. H. J., *History of Rome* (N.Y., 1905). GRUNDY, G. B., *History of the Greek and Roman World.* HAVELL, H. L., *Republican Rome* (London, 1923). HEITLAND, W. E., *Short History of the Roman Republic* (Cambridge University Press, 1916). HOLMES, T. R. E., *Cæsar's Conquest of Gaul* (2d ed., Oxford, 1911); *The Roman Republic* (3 vols.; Oxford, 1923). HOW, W. W., and LEIGH, H. D., *History of Rome to the Death of Cæsar* (N.Y., 1917). IHNE, W., *History of Rome* (5 vols.; London, 1871–1882). JOLLIFFE, R. O., *Phases of Corruption in Roman Administration in the Last Half-century of the Roman Republic* (Menasha, Wis., 1919). LONG, G., *Decline of the Roman Republic* (5 vols.; London, 1864–1874). MCCARTNEY, E. S., *Warfare by Land and Sea.* MAGOFFIN, R. V. D., and DUNCALF, F., *Ancient and Medieval History* (N.Y., 1934). MASON, W. F., *Decline of the Oligarchy: a History of Rome, 133–78 B.C.* (London, 1895). MERIVALE, C., *History of the Romans under the Empire* (8 vols.; London, 1904). MOMMSEN, T., *History of Rome* (4 vols.; N.Y., 1911). MYRES, J. L., *Dawn of History.* NILSSON, M. P., *Imperial Rome* (N.Y., 1926). PELHAM, H. F., *Outlines of Roman History* (4th ed., N.Y., 1907). RANDALL-MACIVER, D., *The Etruscans* (Oxford, 1927); *Italy before the Romans* (Oxford, 1928). ROSTOVTZEFF, M. I., *History of the Ancient World* (Oxford, 1928), Vol. II. SMITH, R. B., *Carthage and the Carthaginians* (N.Y., 1902). TORR, C., *Hannibal Crosses the Alps* (2d ed., Cambridge University Press, 1925). WESTERMANN, W. L., *Story of Ancient Nations.*

B. **Constitutional and institutional histories.** ABBOTT, F. F., *History and Description of Roman Political Institutions* (3d ed., Boston, 1911); *Roman Politics* (Boston, 1923). ABBOTT, F. F., and JOHNSON, A. C., *Municipal Administration in the Roman Empire* (Princeton University Press, 1926). ARNOLD, W. T., *Roman System of Provincial Administration* (3d ed., rev. by E. S. Bouchier, Oxford, 1914). BOTSFORD, G. W., *Roman Assemblies* (N.Y., 1909). BUCKLAND, W. W., *Manual of Roman Private Law* (Cambridge University Press, 1928). FRANK, T., *Roman Imperialism* (N.Y., 1921). GREENIDGE, A. H. J., *The Legal Procedure of Cicero's Time* (Oxford University Press, 1901); *Roman Public Life* (London, 1922). HADLEY, H. S., *Rome and the World Today* (2d ed., rev., N.Y., 1923). HADLEY, J., *Introduction to Roman Law* (Yale University Press, 1931). HUNTER, W. A., *Introduction to Roman Law* (new ed., revised and enlarged by A. F. Murison, London, 1921). MATTINGLY, H., *Imperial Civil Service of Rome* (Cambridge University Press, 1910). REYNOLDS, P. K. B., *The Vigiles of Imperial Rome* (Oxford University Press, 1926). TAYLOR, T. M., *Constitutional and Political History of Rome* (4th ed., London, 1915).

C. **Economic and social life.** ABBOTT, F. F., *Common People of Ancient Rome* (N.Y., 1917); *Society and Politics in Ancient Rome* (N.Y., 1916). BAILEY, C. (Ed.), *The Legacy of Rome* (Oxford University Press, 1924). BECKER, W. A., *Gallus; or, Roman Scenes of the Time of Augustus* (new ed., London, 1898). BRITISH MUSEUM, *A Guide to the Exhibition illustrating Greek and Roman Life.* BUCKLAND, W. W., *Roman Law of Slavery* (Cambridge University Press, 1908). CHARLESWORTH, M. P., *Trade-routes and Commerce of the Roman Empire* (2d ed., rev., Cambridge University Press, 1926). DAVIS, W. S., *A Day in Old Rome* (Boston, 1925); *Influence of Wealth in Imperial Rome* (N.Y., 1933). DILL, SIR S., *Roman Society from Nero to Marcus Aurelius* (London, 1925). FOWLER, W. W., *Social Life at Rome in the Age of Cicero* (N.Y., 1926). FRANK, T., *Economic History of Rome* (2d ed., Johns Hopkins Press, 1927); *Economic Survey of Ancient Rome* (Johns Hopkins Press, 1933), Vol. I. FRIEDLANDER, L., *Roman Life and Manners under the Early Empire* (tr. of 7th ed., rev.; 4 vols.; Vol. I, 2d ed., N.Y., 1909–1928). GWYNN, A. O., *Roman Education from Cicero to Quintilian* (Oxford, 1926). HARRISON, F. (Ed.), *Roman Farm Management; the Treatises of Cato and Varro* (tr., with notes of modern instances, by a Virginia farmer, N.Y., 1913). HEITLAND, W. E., *Agricola, a Study in Agriculture and Rustic Life in the Greco-Roman World* (Cambridge University Press, 1921). JOHNSTON, H. W., *Private Life of the Romans* (Chicago, 1932). LOUIS, P., *Ancient Rome at Work* (London, 1927). McDANIEL, W. B., *Roman Private Life and its Survivals* (N.Y., 1929). PELLISSON, M., *Roman Life in Pliny's Time* (Philadelphia, 1901). PRESTON, H. W., and DODGE, L., *Private Life of the Romans* (Chicago, 1900). ROSTOVTZEFF, M. I., *Out of the Past of Greece and Rome*; *The Social and Economic History of the Roman Empire* (Oxford, 1926). SANDYS, SIR J. E., *A Companion to Latin Studies* (3d ed., Cambridge University Press, 1921). SHOWERMAN, G., *Rome and the Romans* (N.Y., 1931). SOTTAS, J., "The Ship of St. Paul's Last Voyage," in the *Mariner's Mirror*, Vol. VII (1921), pp. 258–266. TOUTAIN, J., *The Economic Life of the Ancient World* (N.Y., 1930). TREBLE, H. A., and KING, K. M., *Everyday Life in Rome* (Oxford, 1930). TUCKER, T. G., *Life in the Roman World of Nero and St. Paul* (N.Y., 1929).

D. **Mythology and religion.** *Cambridge Ancient History*, Vol. VIII, chap. xiv. CARTER, J. B., *Religion of Numa* (N.Y., 1906); *Religious Life of Ancient Rome* (Boston, 1922). CUMONT, F., *Mysteries of Mithra* (2d ed., Chicago, 1910); *Oriental Religions in Roman Paganism* (Chicago, 1911). FOWLER, W. W., *Religious Experience of the Roman People* (London, 1922). GLOVER, T. R., *Conflict of Religions in the Early Roman Empire* (11th ed., London, 1927). HALLIDAY, W. R., *Lectures on the History of Roman Religion from Numa to Augustus* (Boston, 1923). PAIS, E., *Ancient Legends of Roman History* (N.Y., 1905).

See also section *E* in the general bibliography for Greek history, chaps. ix–xviii.

E. **Art and archæology.** BARKER, E. R., *Buried Herculaneum* (London, 1908). EHRENBERG, V., "Karthago," in *Morgenland*, Heft 14 (1927). ENGELMANN, W., *New Guide to Pompeii* (2d ed., rev., Leipzig, 1929). FERRERO, F. L., "That Amphora and the Death of Pliny the Elder," in *Art and Archæology*, Vol. XXIX (1930), pp. 51–55 and 75. HUELSEN, C. C. F., *The Forum and the Palatine* (N.Y., 1928). HUSSEY, M. I., "The Pompeii of Palestine," in *Art and Archæology*, Vol. XXXV (1934), pp. 3–17. JOHNSTONE, M. A., *Etruria Past and Present* (London, 1930). *Journal of Roman Studies* (London), 1911– . LANCIANI, R. A., *Ancient and Modern Rome* (Boston, 1925); *Ruins and Excavations of Ancient Rome* (Boston, 1897). LUGLI, G., *The Classical Monuments of Rome and its Vicinity* (Rome, 1929), Vol. I; *Horace's Sabine Farm* (Rome, 1930). MAGOFFIN, R. V. D., *The Lure and Lore of Archæology* (Baltimore, 1930). MAU, A., *Pompeii, its Life and Art* (N.Y., 1902). ORECCHIA, J., "*May I Show you Rome?*" (Rome, 1930). PLATNER, S. B., *Topographical Dictionary of Ancient Rome* (completed and revised by T. Ashby; Oxford, 1929); *Topography and Monuments of*

Ancient Rome (2d ed., Boston, 1911). POULSEN, F., *Etruscan Tomb Paintings* (Oxford, 1922). RAMSAY, W., *Manual of Roman Antiquities* (18th ed., rev. by R. A. Lanciani; London, 1909). RIVOIRA, G. T., *Roman Architecture* (Oxford, 1925). ROSE, H. J., *Primitive Culture in Italy* (N.Y., 1926). SHOWERMAN, G., *Eternal Rome* (Yale University Press, 1924). STRONG, E., *Art in Ancient Rome* (Ars Una : Species Mille ; 2 vols. ; N.Y., 1928). WALTERS, H. B., *The Art of the Romans* (2d ed., London, 1928). WARSHER, T., *Pompeii in Three Hours* (Rome, 1930).

***F.* Literature, philosophy, and science.** ARNOLD, E. V., *Roman Stoicism* (Cambridge University Press, 1911). BOISSIER, G., *Cicero and his Friends* (N.Y., 1925). *Cambridge Ancient History,* Vol. VIII, chap. xiii. CONWAY, R. S., *New Studies of a Great Inheritance* (London, 1921). DUFF, J. W., *Literary History of Rome, from the Origins to the Close of the Golden Age* (7th ed., London, 1927) ; *Literary History of Rome in the Silver Age* (N.Y., 1927). FOWLER, H. N., *History of Roman Literature* (N.Y., 1928). FRANK, T., *Life and Literature in the Roman Republic* (University of California Press, 1930). GUMMERE, R. M., *Seneca the Philosopher and his Modern Message* (Boston, 1922). HAMILTON, E., *The Roman Way* (N.Y., 1932). MACKAIL, J. W., *Latin Literature* (N.Y., 1925). NORWOOD, C., and DUFF, J. W., *Writers of Greece and Rome.* ROLFE, J. C., *Cicero and his Influence* (Boston, 1923). SELLAR, W. Y., *Roman Poets of the Augustan Age: Horace, and the Elegiac Poets* (2d ed., Oxford, 1899) ; *Roman Poets of the Augustan Age: Virgil* (3d ed., Oxford, 1897) ; *Roman Poets of the Republic* (3d ed., Oxford, 1905). SIKES, E. E., *Roman Poetry* (London, 1923). SUMMERS, W. C., *Silver Age of Latin Literature from Tiberius to Trajan* (London, 1920). TEUFFEL, W. S., *History of Roman Literature* (2 vols. ; rev. by L. Schwabe, London, 1900).

***G.* Source selections.** BAILEY, C. (Ed.), *The Mind of Rome* (Oxford, 1926). BLAKENEY, E. H., *Pages from Latin Authors* (N.Y., 1924). BOTSFORD, G. W. and L. S., *Source Book of Ancient History.* DAVIS, W. S., *Readings in Ancient History* (N.Y., 1913), Vol. II. GREENOUGH, J. B., KITTREDGE, G. L., and JENKINS, J., *Virgil and Other Latin Poets* (Boston, 1930). HOWE, G., and HARRER, G. A., *Roman Literature in Translation* (N.Y., 1924). LAING, G. J., *Masterpieces of Latin Literature* (Boston, 1903). MUNRO, D. C., *Source Book of Roman History* (Boston, 1911).

***H.* Authors in translation.** AMMIANUS MARCELLINUS, Roman history (C. D. Yonge (Tr.), London, 1887). APPIAN, Roman history (H. White (Tr.), 2 vols., N.Y., 1899). AUGUSTUS, *Monumentum Ancyranum* (W. Fairley (Tr.), *Pennsylvania Translations and Reprints,* Vol. V, No. 1 ; E. G. Hardy (Tr.), *Monumentum Ancyranum,* 1924 ; D. Robinson (Tr.), *The Deeds of Augustus as Recorded on the Monumentum Antiochenum,* 1926). AURELIUS ANTONINUS, MARCUS, Meditations (C. R. Haines (Tr.), Loeb Classical Library, London, 1924 ; M. Casaubon (Tr.), Everyman's Library, N.Y., 1919). CÆSAR, JULIUS, *Gallic War* (H. J. Edwards (Tr.), Loeb Classical Library, N.Y., 1917). CASSIODORUS, letters (T. Hodgkin (Tr.), London, 1886). CICERO, letters (E. S. Shuckburgh (Tr.), 4 vols., London, 1915–1920 ; W. G. Williams (Tr.), Loeb Classical Library, 3 vols., N.Y., 1927–1929) ; speeches (N. H. Watts (Tr.), Loeb Classical Library, N.Y., 1931). DIO CASSIUS, Roman history (E. Cary (Tr.), Loeb Classical Library, 9 vols., N.Y., 1914–1927). DIODORUS SICULUS, Historical Library (London, 1814). FLORUS, LUCIUS ANNÆUS, Epitome of Roman History (E. S. Forster (Tr.), Loeb Classical Library, N.Y., 1929 ; J. S. Watson (Tr.), London, 1889). HORACE (E. C. Wickham (Tr.), *Horace for English Readers,* in prose, Oxford University Press, 1930 ; H. Macnaghten (Tr.), in verse, Cambridge University Press, 1926). JOSEPHUS, works (W. Whiston (Tr.), 5 vols., London, 1900 ; H. St. J. Thackeray (Tr.), Loeb Classical Library, N.Y., 1926–). JUVENAL, Satires (G. G. Ramsay (Tr.), Loeb Classical Library, N.Y., 1928 ; J. H. Bolton (Tr.), London, 1930). LIVY, history of Rome (B. O. Foster (Tr.), Loeb Classical Library, N.Y., 1919– ; D. Spillan and C. R. Edmonds (Trs.), 2 vols., N.Y., 1895). LUCRETIUS, *On the*

Nature of Things (W. H. D. Rouse (Tr.), Loeb Classical Library, N.Y., 1924; C. Bailey (Tr.), Oxford, 1929). OVID, works (H. T. Riley (Tr.), 3 vols., London, 1869; Loeb Classical Library: translations of various works). PLINY THE ELDER, *Natural History* (J. Bostock and H. T. Riley (Trs.), Bohn, 6 vols., London, 1855–1857). PLINY THE YOUNGER, letters (W. M. L. Hutchinson (Tr.), Loeb Classical Library, 2 vols., N.Y., 1915). PLUTARCH, Lives. POLYBIUS, histories (W. R. Paton (Tr.), Loeb Classical Library, 6 vols., N.Y., 1922–1927). PROPERTIUS, elegies (C. R. Moore (Tr.), in verse, London, 1870; H. E. Butler (Tr.), Loeb Classical Library, N.Y., 1916). SALLUST, *Jugurthine War* (J. S. Watson (Tr.), Bohn, London, 1889). STRABO, Geography (H. L. Jones (Tr.), Loeb Classical Library, 8 vols., N.Y., 1917–1932). SUETONIUS, *Lives of the Cæsars* (J. C. Rolfe (Tr.), Loeb Classical Library, 2 vols., N.Y., 1914). TACITUS, *Annals* (A. J. Church and W. J. Brodribb (Trs.), London, 1921). VIRGIL (H. R. Fairclough (Tr.), Loeb Classical Library, 2 vols., N.Y., 1916–1918; J. Rhoades (Tr.), World's Classics, N.Y., 1926).

I. **Biographies.** BAKER, G. P., *Hannibal* (London, 1930); *Sulla the Fortunate* (London, 1927). BUCHAN, J., *Julius Cæsar* (Edinburgh, 1932). CUTTS, E. L., *Constantine the Great* (N.Y., 1881). DODGE, T. A., *Hannibal* (2 vols.; 3d ed., Boston, 1896). DOVE, C. C., *Marcus Aurelius Antoninus* (London, 1930). FIRTH, J. B., *Augustus Cæsar and the Organization of the Empire of Rome* (N.Y., 1923). FOWLER, W. W., *Julius Cæsar and the Foundations of the Roman Imperial System* (N.Y., 1925). FRANK, T., *Vergil, a Biography* (N.Y., 1922). GREGOROVIUS, F., *The Emperor Hadrian* (N.Y., 1898). HENDERSON, B. W., *Five Roman Emperors* (Cambridge University Press, 1927); *The Life and Principate of the Emperor Hadrian* (N.Y., 1923); *The Life and Principate of the Emperor Nero* (London, 1903). HOLMES, T. R. E., *The Architect of the Roman Empire* (Oxford, 1928); *The Architect of the Roman Empire, 27 B.C.–A.D. 14* (Oxford, 1931). HOPKINS, R. V. N., *Life of Alexander Severus* (Cambridge University Press, 1907). LIDDELL HART, B. H., *A Greater than Napoleon: Scipio Africanus* (Edinburgh, 1927). LONGFORD, C., *Vespasian* (Dublin, 1928). MORRIS, W. O., *Hannibal* (new ed., N.Y., 1897). OMAN, C. W. C., *Seven Roman Statesmen of the Later Republic* (N.Y., 1902). PETERSSON, T., *Cicero, a Biography* (University of California Press, 1920). PLATNAUER, M., *The Life and Reign of the Emperor Lucius Septimius Severus* (Oxford University Press, 1918). ROSTOVTZEFF, M. I., "Augustus" (in *University of Wisconsin Studies in Language and Literature*, No. 15; Madison, Wis., 1922). SHUCKBURGH, E. S., *Augustus* (London, 1908). SIHLER, E. G., *Annals of Cæsar, a Critical Biography* (N.Y., 1911). SIMPSON, W. D., *Julian the Apostate* (Aberdeen, 1930). STRACHAN-DAVIDSON, J. L., *Cicero* (N.Y., 1903). TARVER, J. C., *Tiberius the Tyrant* (N.Y., 1902).

J. **History and culture of the provinces.** BOISSIER, G., *Roman Africa* (N.Y., 1899). BOUCHIER, E. S., *Life and Letters in Roman Africa* (Oxford, 1913); *Spain under the Roman Empire* (Oxford, 1914); *Syria as a Roman Province* (Oxford, 1916). HARRER, G. A., *Studies in the History of the Roman Province of Syria* (Princeton University Press, 1915). HAVERFIELD, F. J., *The Roman Occupation of Britain* (Oxford University Press, 1924). MOMMSEN, T., *The Provinces of the Roman Empire* (London, 1909). QUENNELL, M. and C. H. B., *Everyday Life in Roman Britain* (London, 1924). RAMSAY, W. M., *Studies in the History and Art of the Eastern Provinces of the Roman Empire* (Aberdeen, 1906).

CHAPTERS XXIX–XXX

A. **General works.** BAKER, G. P., *Constantine the Great and the Christian Revolution* (N.Y., 1930). BAYNES, N. H., *The Byzantine Empire* (London, 1925). BURY, J. B., *History of the Later Roman Empire from the Death of Theodosius I to the*

Death of Justinian (2 vols.; London, 1923); *Invasion of Europe by the Barbarians* (London, 1928). COTTERILL, H. B., *Medieval Italy* (N.Y., 1915). CUTTS, E. L., *Saint Jerome* (N.Y., 1878). DAVIS, H. W. C., *Medieval Europe* (N.Y., 1911). DILL, S., *Roman Society in the Last Century of the Western Empire* (London, 1921). EAKIN, F., *Revaluing Scripture*, chap. xvii. EMERTON, E., *An Introduction to the Study of the Middle Ages* (Boston, 1916). FERRERO, G., *Ruin of the Ancient Civilization and the Triumph of Christianity* (N.Y., 1921). FIRTH, J. B., *Constantine the Great* (N.Y., 1923). FISHER, G. P., *The Beginnings of Christianity* (N.Y., 1906). GIBBON, E., *History of the Decline and Fall of the Roman Empire* (7 vols., ed. by J. B. Bury; London, 1930). GROUSSET, R., *The Civilizations of the East*, pp. 133–162. HAARHOF, T. J., *Schools of Gaul* (Oxford, 1920). HATCH, E., *Organization of the Early Christian Churches* (N.Y., 1901). HAY, J. S., *The Amazing Emperor Heliogabalus* (London, 1911). HEITLAND, W. E., *The Roman Fate* (Cambridge University Press, 1922); *Iterum* (Cambridge University Press, 1925). HODGKIN, T., *Dynasty of Theodosius* (Oxford, 1889). HUTTON, W. H., *The Church and the Barbarians* (N.Y., 1906). IORGA, N., *The Byzantine Empire* (London, 1907). KIDD, B. J., *A History of the Church to A.D. 461* (3 vols.; Oxford, 1922). MUNRO, D. C., *The Middle Ages, 395–1500* (rev. ed., N.Y., 1928). OMAN, SIR C. W. C., *The Byzantine Empire* (London, 1922). STEVENS, C. E., *Sidonius Apollinaris and his Age* (Oxford, 1933). WRIGHT, W., *An Account of Palmyra and Zenobia* (N.Y., 1895).

B. **Sources and source selections.** BONIFACE, SAINT, *English Correspondence* (E. J. Kylie (Tr.), King's Classics, London, 1911). BROOKE, D. (Ed.), *Private Letters, Pagan and Christian* (London, 1929). EUGIPPIUS, *Life of St. Severinus* (G. W. Robinson (Tr.), Harvard University Press, 1914). JORDANES, *The Origin and Deeds of the Goths* (C. C. Mierow (Tr.), Princeton University Press, 1908). *Notitia Dignitatum* (Department of History of the University of Pennsylvania, 1899). ROBINSON, J. H., *Readings in European History* (Boston, 1904), Vol. I, pp. 14–27, and chaps. iii–vi. TACITUS, *Agricola*; *Germania* (M. Hutton (Tr.), Loeb Classical Library, N.Y., 1914).

See also the general bibliography for Roman history, chaps. xxii–xxviii.

Atlases and miscellaneous reference books. AMERICAN COUNCIL OF EDUCATION, COMMITTEE ON MATERIALS OF INSTRUCTION, Achievements of Civilization Series (5835 Kimbark Avenue, Chicago, Illinois). BREASTED, J. H., HUTH, C. F., and HARDING, S. B., *Ancient and European History Atlas* (Denoyer-Geppert Co., Chicago, 1920); *Ancient-Medieval-Modern History Maps* (2d ed., Denoyer-Geppert Co., Chicago, 1918). GRUNDY, G. B. (Ed.), *Murray's Small Classical Atlas* (2d ed., London, 1917). KIEPERT, H., *Manual of Ancient Geography* (London, 1881). LOGASA, HANNAH (compiler), *Historical Fiction and Other Reading References for History Classes in Junior and Senior High Schools* (Philadelphia, 1930). NEUBERGER, A., *The Technical Arts and Sciences of the Ancients* (London, 1930). PUTZGER, F. W., *Historischer Schulatlas zur alten, mittleren und neueren Geschichte* (44. verm. und verb. Aufl., Leipzig, 1923). SHEPHERD, W. R., *Historical Atlas* (7th ed., N.Y., 1929). SIEGLIN, W., *Schulatlas zur Geschichte des Altertums* (5 Aufl., Gotha, 192–). SMITH, G. A., and BARTHOLOMEW, J. G., *Atlas of the Historical Geography of the Holy Land* (London, 1915). SMITH, W., *A Classical Dictionary of Greek and Roman Biography, Mythology, and Geography* (London, 1925); *A Smaller Classical Dictionary* (rev. by E. H. Blakeney; Everyman's Library, N.Y., 1927). SWINDLER, M. H., *Ancient Painting from the Earliest Times to the Period of Christian Art* (Yale University Press, 1929).

INDEX

KEY. ă *as in* at; ā *as in* ate; ȧ *as in* senate; ä *as in* arm; à *as in* ask; â *as in* care; ạ *as in* sofa; ĕ *as in* met; ē *as in* be; ê *as in* enough; ẽ *as in* her; ẹ *as in* novel; ĭ *as in* it; ī *as in* ice; ŏ *as in* not; ō *as in* note; ȯ *as in* obey; ô *as in* horse; ọ *as in* anchor; ŭ *as in* us; ū *as in* use; û *as in* unite; û *as in* fur; ụ *as in* stirrup; ü *as in German* grün; ŏŏ *as in* foot; ōō *as in* food; ṉ *like* ng *in* song; th *as in* then; zh *like* z *in* azure; K *like* ch *in German* ich *or* ach; N *like* n *in French* bon

Ancyra (ăn sī'ra̤) monument, 696
Andronicus (ăn drō nī'ku̧s), 635 f.
Angles, 772
Animals, domestication of, 2, 10, 26 ff., 30, 35; prehistoric, 6 f., 10
Antigonus (ăn tĭg'ō nu̧s), 514
Antigonus II, 514, 518
Antioch (ăn'tĭ ŏk), 513, 517, 519, 674, 723
Antiochus (ăn tī'ō ku̧s) I, 517, 518
Antiochus (III) the Great, 625 f.
Antoninus Pius (ăn tō nī'nu̧s pī'u̧s), 713, 740
Antony (ăn'tō nĭ), Mark, 672 ff.
Apelles (a̤ pĕl'ēz), 536
Aphrodite (ăf rō dī'tē), 175, 339, 576
Apollo (a̤ pŏl'ō), 338, 370, 378, 686
Apollodorus (a̤ pŏl ō dō'ru̧s), 472 ff.
Aqueducts, 192, 196, 203, 699, 710, 723
Arabia, 136
Arabs, 136, 786 ff.
Aramaic (ăr a̤ mā'ĭk), 186 ff., 205, 207, 228, 234, 265, 738
Arameans (ăr a̤ mē'a̤nz), 185 ff., 205, 331
Ararat (ăr'a̤ răt), *see* Urartu
Arbela (är bē'la̤), 499
Arcadius (är kā'dĭ u̧s), 770 f.
Archæology, 9
Archimedes (är kĭ mē'dēz), 538 f., 617
Architecture, Egyptian, 69, 71 ff., 89 ff., 108 ff.; of Western Asia, 149, 176, 191, 200, 208 ff., 252, 274 f.; of Ægean World, 292 f., 296, 299, 300; Greek, 356, 371 f., 423 ff., 468 f., 521, 525 ff., 596, 597, 635; Roman, 631 ff., 686 ff., 725 ff.; church, 782 ff.
Areopagus (ăr ē ŏp'a̤ gu̧s), 400, 427
Arginusæ (är jĭ nū'sē), 452
Argos, 343
Ariana (ă rĭ ā'na̤), 256
Aristarchus (ăr ĭs tär'ku̧s), 540, 733
Aristides (ăr ĭs tī'dēz), 398 f.
Aristogiton (a̤ rĭs tō jī'to̤n), 367, 374
Aristophanes (ăr ĭs tŏf'a̤ nēz), 445, 478 f., 481
Aristotle (ăr'ĭs tŏt'l), 493, 504, 548 f.
Armageddon (är ma̤ gĕd'o̤n), *see* Megiddo
Armenia (är mē'nĭ a̤), 244, 661, 708
Armenians (är mē'nĭ a̤nz), 246, 312
Arrian (ăr'ĭ a̤n), 731
Art, Stone Age, 19 ff.; Egyptian, 78 ff., 85 ff., 110 ff., 117, 121; of Western Asia, 155 ff., 160 f., 176, 200 f., 252, 328 f.; Cretan, 285, 291, 292 ff., 301; Greek, 325, 372 ff., 422, 429 f., 470 ff., 533 ff., 635; Roman, 691, 729
Artemis (är'tē mĭs), 339
Artemisium (är tē mĭsh'ĭ u̧m), 389
Aryans (är'ya̤nz), 254 ff.
Asia Minor, connections with Europe, 36, 288; connections with Fertile Crescent, 159, 181, 194, 218; history of, 244 ff., 262, 304 f., 312, 348, 495, 517, 626, 658 f.
Assur (ä so͝or), city of, 179 ff.
Assur (god), 191, 229
Assurbanipal (ä so͝or bä'nē päl), 193, 200, 203 f.
Assyria (a̤ sĭr'ĭ a̤), 179 ff., 228 ff., 249
Astrology, 175, 211 f., 551, 733
Astronomy, 212 ff., 272, 376, 418, 482, 539 f.
Athena (a̤ thē'na̤), 324, 338, 425, 430, 455, 458
Athenæum (ăth ē nē'u̧m), 721
Athenian (a̤ thē'nĭ a̤n) Empire, 398 ff.
Athens (ăth'e̤nz), 409 ff., 548 ff., 721, 730, 780; history of, 344, 359, 385 ff., 395, 396 ff., 441 ff., 460, 462 f., 491, 494, 658 f.; government of, 364 ff., 400 f., 457 f., 520; art and literature of, 370 f., 372, 422 ff., 468 ff.
Athletic games, 350 f., 368, 414 f., 596

PRINTED IN THE UNITED STATES OF AMERICA